Policing Beyond Coercion

A NEW IDEA FOR A TWENTY-FIRST CENTURY MANDATE

EDITORIAL ADVISORS

Policing Beyond Coercion

A NEW IDEA FOR A TWENTY-FIRST CENTURY MANDATE

Robert J. Kane, PhD

Drexel University

ASPEN
PUBLISHING

Cover image: iStock.com/kali9

To contact Customer Service, e-mail customer.service@aspenpublishing.com, call 1-800-950-5259, or mail correspondence to:

Aspen Publishing
Attn: Order Department
PO Box 990
Frederick, MD 21705

Printed in the United States of America.

1 2 3 4 5 6 7 8 9 0

ISBN 978-1-5438-3284-6

Library of Congress Cataloging-in-Publication Data

Names: Kane, Robert J., author.
Title: Policing beyond coercion: a new idea for a twenty-first century
  mandate / Robert J. Kane, PhD, Drexel University.
Description: Frederick, MD: Aspen Publishing, [2023] | Includes
  bibliographical references and index. | Summary: "This book examines,
  describes, and explains the current state of American policing. It
  proposes a new paradigm that emphasizes the protection of life as the
  primary mandate, moving away from mere coercion and social control"—
  Provided by publisher.
Identifiers: LCCN 2022026439 | ISBN 9781543832846 (paperback) | ISBN
  9781543832853 (ebook)
Subjects: LCSH: Community policing—United States—History—21st century. |
  Police—United States—Social conditions. | Police—United
  States—History—21st century.
Classification: LCC HV7936.C83 K364 2023 | DDC
  363.2/30973—dc23/eng/20220610
LC record available at https://lccn.loc.gov/2022026439

About Aspen Publishing

Aspen Publishing is a leading provider of educational content and digital learning solutions to law schools in the U.S. and around the world. Aspen provides best-in-class solutions for legal education through authoritative textbooks, written by renowned authors, and breakthrough products such as Connected eBooks, Connected Quizzing, and PracticePerfect.

The Aspen Casebook Series (famously known among law faculty and students as the "red and black" casebooks) encompasses hundreds of highly regarded textbooks in more than eighty disciplines, from large enrollment courses, such as Torts and Contracts to emerging electives such as Sustainability and the Law of Policing. Study aids such as the *Examples & Explanations* and the *Emanuel Law Outlines* series, both highly popular collections, help law students master complex subject matter.

Major products, programs, and initiatives include:

- **Connected eBooks** are enhanced digital textbooks and study aids that come with a suite of online content and learning tools designed to maximize student success. Designed in collaboration with hundreds of faculty and students, the Connected eBook is a significant leap forward in the legal education learning tools available to students.

- **Connected Quizzing** is an easy-to-use formative assessment tool that tests law students' understanding and provides timely feedback to improve learning outcomes. Delivered through CasebookConnect.com, the learning platform already used by students to access their Aspen casebooks, Connected Quizzing is simple to implement and integrates seamlessly with law school course curricula.

- **PracticePerfect** is a visually engaging, interactive study aid to explain commonly encountered legal doctrines through easy-to-understand animated videos, illustrative examples, and numerous practice questions. Developed by a team of experts, PracticePerfect is the ideal study companion for today's law students.

- The **Aspen Learning Library** enables law schools to provide their students with access to the most popular study aids on the market across all of their courses. Available through an annual subscription, the online library consists of study aids in e-book, audio, and video formats with full text search, note-taking, and highlighting capabilities.

- Aspen's **Digital Bookshelf** is an institutional-level online education bookshelf, consolidating everything students and professors need to ensure success. This program ensures that every student has access to affordable course materials from day one.

- **Leading Edge** is a community centered on thinking differently about legal education and putting those thoughts into actionable strategies. At the core of the program is the Leading Edge Conference, an annual gathering of legal education thought leaders looking to pool ideas and identify promising directions of exploration.

This book is dedicated to the memory of
William "Bill" Kane — A good cop

SUMMARY OF CONTENTS

CONTENTS

This preface is the only part of the forthcoming book that I will write in the first person. I do this because I want the opportunity from the outset to connect with my readers in ways that the traditional academic conventions of third person make difficult. The preface allows me to explain myself, to provide some backstory to this project that will not be found in the substantive chapters. For me, backstory is important because it offers insights into my rationale for writing a book like this in the first place. It might be considered ironic, but as a police scholar who has spent a career conducting original research and publishing the results of that work in peer-reviewed journals, I never considered writing a textbook. It seemed that writing such a book would require me to deep-dive into many policing topics that were typically outside my usual areas of inquiry, and I was not convinced that I could add anything new to the textbook literature. But after the summer of 2020, my outlook on textbook writing changed. I could see that policing was entering a dark period. Despite the legitimate criticisms of policing made by the media and social commentators, as well as the calls to defund the police, I felt I needed to contribute something to the public dialogue that might offer some hope as to how policing might move forward. I continue to believe in policing as a crucial public institution, but it is an institution in drastic need of change. Not just reform, but actual, structural change. I wanted to create a forum to speak to as many future police officers as possible. I hope this book becomes that forum.

The first thing a reader should know about me is that I am a geek for the police. I always have been. Since that warm California summer day in 1971 when my mother snapped a photo of then-four-year-old me and my one-year-old sister perched beside my dad's marked patrol car, I have been hooked on the police. In that particular photo, my dad was a new officer sitting in the driver's seat, window down and almost totally obscured by my sister, who was sitting on the door frame of the open window. My dad's arm is visible, as he wrapped it around my sister's legs for support. The door of the patrol car is emblazoned with the city's seal that had been created as part of a city planning campaign in the 1960s. It read: "City of Santa Rosa, California: *The City designed for living!*" The car was green and had a painted white top on which was mounted a red "gumball" emergency light. Even then, at that age, I remember being a little disappointed because in my mind, police cars were supposed to be black and white, like they were in the television series, *Adam-12*. Still, at the moment that photograph was taken, I felt that my dad was just about the most important person in town.

I grew up wanting to be a police officer. I was enamored with the gear that police officers wore on their utility belts, the heft of the police cars, the Unity spotlight that could be controlled from the driver's seat, the Motorola radio mounted just under the dashboard, and the switches that controlled the lights and siren. To me, the patrol cars, and everything contained within them, embodied the very essence of scientific policing and professional crime fighting. For most of my early and teen years, I was largely oblivious to the heavy-handed policing—much of it racially charged—that was, and had been, taking place in the more urbanized jurisdictions just down the road from our small town in places like Berkeley, Oakland, Richmond, San Francisco, South San Francisco, East Palo Alto, and San Jose. To my mind, police officers did not enforce the color line or bring their night sticks to bear on college students and others who demonstrated against police brutality or structural racism in housing, education, and employment. The police were there to do good, and it did not occur to me during those years that different groups of people would have vastly different interpretations of the police.

Even in college as a criminal justice major, my impressions of the police remained untested and unchanged. Perhaps I wasn't paying attention in class (I wasn't the best student), or perhaps I wasn't exposed to the research and writings that were critical of the police, but throughout most of my undergraduate years, I did not question. I accepted that the police were there to do good, especially in the areas of crime fighting, gang interdiction, and crime prevention. Until one night in Sacramento when I was on a ride-along with officers from the Sacramento Police Department. An interaction between three downtown officers and two suspected drug dealers challenged for the first time my impressions of who the police were, and it made me question my intention to join the police department after graduation. Readers can listen to a full account of that night in the first podcast episode (linked in Chapter 1), "One Night in Sacramento." In the meantime, I will note that the officers during that interaction on a downtown Sacramento street corner treated two Black men as if they were nothing more than a violation of the criminal code. The officers had every chance to do good by those men, but they instead defaulted to the use of coercion, seemingly for the sake of coercion itself. And that moment changed me.

Fast-forward to graduate school at Temple University when I began working with (the now late) James J. Fyfe, perhaps the most celebrated scholar of police authority accountability in the country at that time. Fyfe was the real deal because, in a previous career, he had worked his way up the ranks to become a lieutenant in the New York City Police Department before earning his PhD in criminal justice from SUNY Albany. He retired from police work shortly thereafter and joined the faculty in the Department of Criminal Justice at Temple. Fyfe had an insider's view on policing even when criticizing the police, which allowed him to critique police practices while not vilifying the police institution. His perspective was important to me, because I needed to see firsthand that as policing scholars we could study things like police violence, police corruption, and other troubling aspects of street-level policing, all with an eye toward helping improve the police institution. I have spent my professional career as a scholar and social scientist trying to balance many of the inequities I see in policing against the good I know the institution is capable of achieving.

As readers will come to learn, the origins of this book reside in Carl Klockars's 1985 book, *The Idea of Police*. In that relatively brief volume (160 pages total), Klockars deciphered the highly theoretical writings of the classic sociologist Egon Bittner for a mostly undergraduate readership in ways that not only made Bittner accessible, but also revolutionized the way many readers thought about the police at such a formative moment in our academic development. I was one of those readers, having first read *The Idea of Police* in my undergraduate policing class in 1987. From that point forward, Klockars became an intellectual hero to me.

Just after I graduated with my PhD in 2001, Jim Fyfe introduced me to Carl Klockars for the first time at the American Society of Criminology meetings. During our conversation, Carl told me of the many kind emails and letters he'd received over the years from readers of *The Idea of Police*, many of whom had read it in college and gone on to become police officers. To that end, Klockars believed his book had made a real impact on the most important audience of all: the next generation of cops. Not shy, he also told me that *The Idea of Police* was the all-time best-selling book that his publisher had ever published. I have been unable to confirm his assertion, though not for a lack of trying. When I asked why he had never published an updated edition, he said it was because most undergraduate readers no longer knew *Hill Street Blues*, the television show—and specifically, several of its primary police characters—on which he relied to illustrate several personality types of police officers in his book. The fact that fewer and fewer undergraduate students knew anything about *Hill Street Blues*, he argued, made his appeal to the show and its characters dated. He also said there had never been another police drama produced on television since *Hill Street Blues* with the authenticity and diversity of characters needed to successfully update *The Idea of Police*.

My appeal to *Hill Street Blues* in Chapter 1 of this book is partly an homage to the now-late Carl Klockars (he died in 2003), and also a chance to demonstrate the transition that has occurred in the U.S. police mentality since *Hill Street Blues* was on the air. Although I have never seen a rigorous historical analysis of how policing has changed over time with respect to the increased use of coercion to solve the problems that police officers and departments face on a daily basis, I can say that I have noticed the police institution ramp up its coercive capacities since *Hill Street Blues* concluded in 1987. That is also the year that crack cocaine began ravaging U.S. cities, resulting in the War on Drugs that dominated policing for at least two generations.

It wasn't until policing scholar Peter Kraska published his 1997 study detailing the rise of police paramilitarism that our academic field learned just how much U.S. policing was beginning to resemble the U.S. military, in terms of both hardware and deployments. Police officers in cities were increasingly carrying automatic weapons, dressing in battle dress uniforms (BDUs), and deploying in platoon-sized groups as police paramilitary units (PPUs). When the Ferguson protests occurred in the wake of the shooting death of Michael Brown by a Ferguson, Missouri, police officer, the world beyond our discipline saw firsthand what had been happening in U.S. policing, largely under the nose of the public: We saw the Ferguson and St. Louis County Police Departments quickly deploy armored personnel carriers, mine-resistant ambush protected vehicles (MRAPs), rifles based on the military M4 Carbine, tear gas, and long-range acoustic devices (LRADs) designed to not just disperse crowds (which generally enjoy First Amendment protections to assemble) but also to inflict severe pain through their 149-decibel sound emissions.[1] It was while watching the protests, and particularly the police responses to them, that I realized policing in America had gone off the rails. It was also during those fall months of 2014 that I began to formulate the idea for this book. I continued to believe that policing could become a crucial public institution, but to get there was going to require a mental reset to reduce the harm that officers and departments were bringing into American — mostly *African* American — communities.

Admittedly, my research and work as an academic department head caused my progress on the original iteration of this book to stall, but after watching Derek Chauvin kill George Floyd using a neck restraint while at least three other officers stood by and let it happen, I became once again invigorated to write a book about the dangers and consequences of what I viewed was a coercion-for-the-sake-of-coercion policing paradigm. Instead of speaking primarily to scholars (as most academic and university press books do), I decided I could achieve a greater impact by writing for an audience I understood well: college students who hoped to someday become police officers. I was once one of those very college students, and I continue to owe Carl Klockars a debt of gratitude for writing *The Idea of Police* just as I

---

[1] Taub, "What Was THAT? A Guide to the Military Gear Being Used Against Civilians in Ferguson."

was entering university. I believe it is now time for an updated idea of police, or what I refer to in this book as a new idea of police—one that advocates moving beyond coercion as the primary means and ends of policing to a protection of life mandate that might ultimately reduce harm in the most vulnerable communities while also increasing the life chances of those who live there.

In his memoir, *Chief: My Life in the LAPD*, Daryl Gates (LAPD chief 1978–1992) wrote about a time when he was asked his opinion on the (then) nascent community policing movement. Responding to the question of whether he valued the concept and practice of community policing, Gates said something to the effect that the police can't be all things to all people, meaning that community policing was beyond the mission of police and not something he was keen to implement in the LAPD. As this book will argue, though, the police do not have to be all things to all people. They just need to be cool and reasonable: cool in the coercion they bring into the communities they police and reasonable with the intrusions they make into the lives of the people they encounter. Cool and reasonable is nothing more than a mentality—much the same as the protection of life mandate proposed in this book—that has the capacity to translate into practices that can produce enormous good from a police institution that is in desperate need of producing something good.

Robert J. Kane
Fairfax, Virginia

August 2022

ACKNOWLEDGMENTS

The author of any book is simply the public face of the published work. But inside the pages of that book reside the efforts, support, and technical assistance of many people who generally do not get credit for the finished product. This book is, of course, no exception. Without the expertise, creativity, insights, and encouragement of many people, this book never would have been written, let alone published.

First, I thank Stacie Goosman, Managing/Acquisitions Editor at Aspen. When Stacie first emailed me almost exactly two years ago to the day (as of this writing), asking if I was interested in putting together a proposal for a policing textbook, I was initially skeptical. I had never written a textbook; they seemed like a lot of work; and I was currently writing a policing book with an eye toward getting a contract from a university press. After several conversations with Stacie, though, I became convinced that my work would have greater impact as a textbook, giving me access to as many undergraduate policing students as possible, than as a university press book written for an audience of other scholars. Moreover, Stacie gave me the freedom to write an Intro to Policing textbook that presented a particular perspective. Yes, it would cover most topics that are important to introductory textbooks, but it would also offer critiques and an idea about an alternative mandate for the police—something that might help policing remain a valued public institution in a post-George Floyd world. I offer Stacie many thanks and much gratitude for sharing—and *backing*—my vision of what a policing textbook can look like. And of course, her flexibility with due dates was key!

Then there's Nick Lasoff, the developmental editor who kept my feet on the ground and the keyboard clicking during the entire writing process. Nick was a great champion of this book, but he never soft-pedaled his critiques. He let me know when my ideas were not clear, when the maps and tables I created made little sense, and when my writing became so conversational that it would likely shock the average academic reader. More than that, though, Nick offered many great substantive ideas about how to incorporate case studies, review questions, and exercises at the end of each chapter. He also helped create several of the original graphics in the book designed to visually convey different ideas and themes. He word-smithed countless sentences so that they actually made sense. In short, Nick played a pivotal role in one simple area: He made this book much better than it otherwise could have been. And along the way, he turned me on to a great bourbon I'd previously never heard of. For all those things, I thank Nick very much.

Also at Aspen, I thank the publisher, Joe Terry, who hosted the launch meeting and gave me the green light to write the book that I wanted to write. I thank the many other folks who worked behind the scenes at Aspen to copyedit, design graphics, and format the interior so that this book will look like a book worth reading.

Closer to home, I owe a great debt of gratitude to my wife and best friend, Dr. Anne-Marie O'Brien. Anne-Marie—a health care provider, research scientist, and university professor—is the true scholar of the family, and it's been through conversations with her (usually over wine and cheese) that I have come to think of the police more in terms of a public health institution than as one whose primary goals are merely crime fighting and social control. Without Anne-Marie with whom to share ideas about policing, nursing, and health care, I never would have evolved my thinking on a new police mandate. As we once wrote in a paper we authored together, policing is a social determinant of health. I thank Anne-Marie for helping me realize that. On a more day-to-day level, during most of the time that I was writing this book, Anne-Marie was writing her own book about building antiracist clinical health care practices that promote inclusion and cultural humility. Although it wasn't exactly a competition about who could finish their book first, I must admit that watching her spend time researching and writing helped keep me on track. And although she ultimately finished her book before I finished mine, I came in a close second.

I also need to thank Maryann Mingrino, a recent graduate of Drexel University's Department of Criminology and Justice Studies (my home department). Maryann spent much of her summer in 2020 working remotely for me to help find royalty-free music and other sound effects for the *Policing Beyond Coercion* podcast series. She provided great feedback on the first podcast episode, which helped guide the ways in which I produced the subsequent episodes.

Finally, I thank Dr. Matthew Teti. He is the former undergraduate student whose story begins Chapter 12 about police recruitment. Matt is the person who interviewed for a crime analyst position, and after not getting it, came back to the university to declare, "Doc! They just want to hire themselves!" That single observation became the basis for much of Chapter 12 and much of my thinking on the importance of cognitive diversity in workgroups and organizations. I thank Matt very much for his insight. The crime analyst profession's loss, however, is criminology's gain: After not securing that crime analyst job, which would have sent him down the policing career path, Matt decided to attend Northeastern University for graduate school, where he recently completed his PhD in criminology and criminal justice. He is now back at Drexel working as my postdoctoral fellow on a large research project in conjunction with the transit police in Philadelphia. Who says you can't go home again?

Robert J. Kane, PhD, is Professor and Department Head of Criminology and Justice Studies at Drexel University in Philadelphia. His primary research interests include police authority and accountability; communities, crime, and health; and technology and justice. In the late 1990s and early 2000s, Kane (with his academic mentor, James J. Fyfe) completed a study of police misconduct in the New York City Police Department—to date, the largest study of misconduct ever conducted in a U.S. police agency. Since then, Kane has published numerous peer-reviewed articles on police misconduct, legitimacy, and accountability in the NYPD, culminating in his 2014 book, *Jammed Up: Bad Cops, Police Misconduct, and the New York City Police Department* (NYU Press, coauthored with Michael D. White).

In 2011, Kane and his colleagues were awarded a grant from the National Institute of Justice to examine the effects of Taser exposure on cognitive functioning (Michael D. White served as Principal Investigator; Kane and Justin Ready served as Co-Principal Investigators). The project concluded in 2013 and remains the only randomized controlled trial of the Taser conducted outside the purview of Axon Enterprises (the company that owns Taser). Results from his Taser research informs public policy in the area of police interrogations, specifically addressing the length of time police departments should wait before interviewing suspects who have been "Tazed" (and who tend to suffer substantial declines in cognitive functioning) by police officers.

In January 2022, Kane was funded to conduct a randomized controlled trial of Project SCOPE in conjunction with the Southeastern Pennsylvania Transit Authority Police Department (Dr. Jordan Hyatt is the Co-Principal Investigator). Project SCOPE is a modified police "co-responder" model that deploys social workers to subway stations in Philadelphia characterized by large numbers of vulnerable population members (e.g., people experiencing homelessness, addiction, and mental health crises). As part of SCOPE, social workers engage with vulnerable population members independent of the police (but while having access to officers in the subway stations as needed) in ways that (1) might help reduce disruptive (and illegal) behaviors in the subway system, and (2) link vulnerable individuals to much-needed city services. The primary goals of SCOPE are to reduce arrests, reduce conflict between police and members of vulnerable groups, and increase access to social services for those in need.

Kane is also an advocate for international educational opportunities for students. He regularly takes students to Germany and the Czech Republic to teach about the rise of the Nazi police state (and authoritarian policing more generally); he has taken students to London to study the police and the British criminal justice system; and just before the pandemic, he developed a transnational policing class in conjunction with colleagues at the Israeli National Police Academy. Although the pandemic has thus far prevented him from taking students to Israel to take the class, he remains hopeful that 2023 will be the year!

CHAPTER 1

Introduction

So Long, *Hill Street Blues*

The room hummed in muffled chaos. Like a middle school classroom in which the adolescent students fidgeted with disinterest, carrying on minor conversations with each other, issuing random quips—some biting, others provocative—occasionally being dragged back to the item at hand with a strategically raised voice or a punctuated rap on the podium. But they weren't middle school students, they were cops. They worked a dangerous job in a dangerous precinct of an aging postindustrial city. He gave them their space and respected their intractability because he knew they respected him. After all, he'd been one of them. He came from their ranks. And although he wore the stripes of a squad sergeant, in the end, he functioned more like a teacher. A guide, really. And as he concluded his briefing—just at the moment when he knew he was losing them—while they gathered up their hats, their ticket books, and their batons, and just as that muffled chaos was devolving into cacophony, he stole back their attention for one last bit of advice. And for this, they all stopped. They became quiet because they knew what was coming, just as the audience did. Every Thursday night for three-and-a-half seasons (1981–1984) Sgt. Phil Esterhaus[1] never dismissed his squad without telling them how much he cared for them, how much he valued their lives. And he did it in just five words. Five earnest words that became his officers' nightly lesson: "Let's be careful out there."

His sign-off was so powerful and so unique to Phil Esterhaus that when Michael

Podcast Episode: "One Night in Sacramento"

Scan the QR code or enter the short URL shown below into a browser window to listen to this chapter's podcast. https://bit.ly/3s8SlmN

---

[1] "Michael Conrad - IMDb."

See for Yourself . . .

Scan the QR code to watch the *Hill Street Blues* roll call from Episode 1.

Conrad—the actor who played him—died partway through Season 3, he took those words with him, never again to be uttered in that roll call room. Indeed, "Let's be careful out there" so endures as a piece of U.S. television history that IMDB ranks it fifth out of 26 "Iconic TV Series Catchphrases."[2]

Hill Street Blues[3] (1981–1987) was more than just a cop show. It transcended its genre tags dubbing it a crime, drama, and mystery series. It was certainly more than car chases, hostage scenarios, shootings, and SWAT deployments. *Hill Street Blues* was a study in U.S. policing at a moment in time when the emphasis was still on the people of policing rather than the gadgets and the data of policing. If art mimics life, then the art of *Hill Street Blues* resided in its complex characterizations of the officers of Hill Street Station, particularly its two main characters.

There was Bobby Hill,[4] the compassionate African American patrol officer who had the ability to see the world through the eyes and lived experiences of those he policed. He knew when to listen, he knew when to speak, and when he used force, he did so with circumspection and restraint. His partner, Andrew Renko,[5] was somewhat less than that. He was a White officer with a southern affect who had earned the nickname "Cowboy." Renko was rougher than Bobby, less interested in talking and listening, and quicker to use force. He was generally ethical, usually making the right choice at just the right moment, but he was also highly judgmental, often referring to the residents of Hill Street precinct—most of whom were Black or Brown—as "those people." It seemed Bobby Hill's burden in life was to somehow instill in Renko the capacity for empathy.

Hill Street Blues was so rich with policing archetypes that in 1985 when Carl Klockars published his now-classic book, *The Idea of Police*, he used the characters of *Hill Street Blues* to illustrate William Muir's iconic typology of police officers he described in *his* book, *Police: Streetcorner Politicians*. In that book, published in 1977, Muir argued that when it came to using physical force as part of their job, police officers could be classified into one of four distinct types: Avoider, Reciprocator, Enforcer, and Professional. In *The Idea of Police*, Klockars matched each of the four main characters of *Hill Street Blues* to one of Muir's types to help his readers understand through dramatization how Muir's typology could play out in street-level policing.[6] He was able to do this, partly because in 1985 *Hill Street Blues* enjoyed wide popularity among television viewers, having been nominated for 11 Emmy

---

[2] "Iconic TV Series Catchphrases - IMDb."
[3] Created by Stephen Bochco and Michael Kozoll. https://www.imdb.com/title/tt0081873/?ref_=nv_sr_srsg_0.
[4] "Michael Warren - IMDb."
[5] "Charles Haid - IMDb."
[6] Klockars, *The Idea of Police*, 136–145.

Awards in that year alone,[7] and partly because the creators of the show made painstaking efforts to ensure the authenticity of both the show's characterizations and its "gritty" policing settings.[8]

As *Hill Street Blues* moved through its final seasons, though, something began to happen in U.S. cities that would ultimately change the balance between policing and its working environment. Just one year after Klockars published *The Idea of Police* (1985), crack invaded New York City.[9] According to the Drug Enforcement Administration, "Crack distribution and abuse exploded in 1986, and by year-end was available in 28 states and the District of Columbia."[10] Its use and consequences spread so quickly and rampantly through urban neighborhoods around the country that it would almost instantly become labeled an epidemic.[11]

Crack is highly addictive, produces an intense high, and leads to an acute "drive for more drugs."[12] Through the 1990s and into the 2000s, widespread crack use and addiction, primarily in vulnerable communities of color, led to the creation of sex-for-money drug markets, increased rates of sexually transmitted infections, produced an overflow of emergency room visits, and led to high mortality rates, both in the United States[13] and the United Kingdom.[14] A secondary consequence of the crack epidemic in many urban communities was the toll it took on the health of grandmothers who filled the role of raising their grandchildren when the mothers of those children were incarcerated, killed, or otherwise rendered unable to care for their children due to crack use.[15] This was an epidemic with multigenerational consequences.

And with crack came the violence. In 1984, the national homicide rate was 7.9 per 100,000 population and was enjoying a steep decline after a peak in 1980.[16] By 1992, however—and at its new height—the national homicide rate reached 9.3 homicides per 100,000 population.[17] That trendline fails to provide the full context of U.S. homicides through the first half of the 1990s, though. By 1995, for example, most homicides were urban and gun-related, and more than 90 percent of those were due to gangs or drugs.[18] Eighty percent of both the victims and offenders of those homicides were under 20 years old.[19] Indeed, by the mid-1990s, crack cocaine and the violence it created was destabilizing U.S. cities, particularly those with populations of at least 100,000, which accounted for more than half of all U.S. homicides (more than 16,000 homicides in 1995).[20]

---

7 "Hill Street Blues - Emmy Awards, Nominations and Wins | Television Academy."
8 Manly, "Being Careful out There? Hardly."
9 Kerr, "Opium Dens for the Crack Era."
10 Drug Enforcement Administration, "Hist. 1985–1990."
11 Kerr, "Opium Dens for the Crack Era."
12 Watkins and Fullilove, "The Crack Epidemic and the Failure of Epidemic Response."
13 Watkins and Fullilove.
14 Schifano and Corkery, "Cocaine/Crack Cocaine Consumption, Treatment Demand, Seizures, Related Offences, Prices, Average Purity Levels and Deaths in the UK (1990–2004)."
15 Roe et al., "Health of Grandmothers Raising Children of the Crack Cocaine Epidemic."
16 Cooper and Smith, "Homicide Trends in the United States, 1980–2008," Fig. 1, p. 2
17 Cooper and Smith, Fig. 1, p. 2.
18 Cooper and Smith, Figs. 40 & 41, p. 26.
19 Cooper and Smith, Fig. 43, p. 27.
20 Cooper and Smith, Fig. 45, p. 29.

How did we respond to this epidemic? In 1986, then Attorney General of the United States Edwin Meese pledged federal resources to "fight" and "combat" the national crack epidemic.[21] Yet, the National Public Health Service, the Centers for Disease Control, and the National Institutes of Health—the leading organizations designated to "fight" epidemics—were largely absent from discussions of mobilization.[22] By using the language of war to describe our response to crack, Meese legitimized the widespread use of police to fight what began as a public health crisis. By 1987, most cities around the country had "unleashed" the police, primarily in urban communities of color, in a next-generation war on drugs.[23] During this war, the police responded with gusto, initiating raids on crack houses, conducting aggressive corner sweeps, and deploying officers wearing battle dress uniforms (BDUs) and carrying automatic weapons into drug-plagued neighborhoods.[24]

As police departments waged their collective war on drugs through the 1990s, they systematically increased their capacities to bring coercion and violence into urban neighborhoods by purchasing and deploying decommissioned surplus military equipment—such as automatic weapons, armored personnel carriers, and night-vision goggles—at low prices through the federal government's 1033 Program.[25] By the late 1990s, many police departments around the country, large and small, had developed police paramilitary units (PPUs) and were deploying them to conduct neighborhood drug raids and execute high-risk "no-knock" search and arrest warrants.[26] The problem is, the development and regular deployment of PPUs soon could not be justified by rates of violent crime,[27] and as PPUs became "normalized"[28] in U.S. policing, they began to respond to increasingly nonviolent incidents, such as vehicle stops and the execution of routine search warrants.[29] Along the way—and because their deployments always carry a high risk for violence—the misuse of PPUs led to hundreds of deaths nationally of bystanders and innocent people who were mistakenly targeted by these special units.[30,31] Think Breonna Taylor in the spring of 2020.[32]

---

[21] Shenon, "24 Task Forces Sought by Meese to Fight Crack."

[22] Watkins and Fullilove, "The Crack Epidemic and the Failure of Epidemic Response."

[23] Walker, *Sense and Nonsense about Crime and Drugs: A Policy Guide*, 100.

[24] Kraska and Kappeler, "Militarizing American Police: The Rise and Normalization of Paramilitary Units"; Walker, *Sense and Nonsense about Crime and Drugs: A Policy Guide*.

[25] Radil, Dezzani, and McAden, "Geographies of U.S. Police Militarization and the Role of the 1033 Program."

[26] Balko, "Overkill: The Rise of Paramilitary Police Raids in America."

[27] Kappeler and Kraska, "Normalising Police Militarisation, Living in Denial."

[28] Kraska and Kappeler, "Militarizing American Police: The Rise and Normalization of Paramilitary Units."

[29] Kraska, "Militarization and Policing—Its Relevance to 21st Century Police."

[30] Delehanty et al., "Militarization and Police Violence: The Case of the 1033 Program"; Balko, "Overkill: The Rise of Paramilitary Police Raids in America."

[31] This is not to be taken as a generalized indictment of police paramilitary units, per se, but rather a commentary on how they have been used in U.S. policing. Elsewhere in this volume the author acknowledges the value of Special Weapons and Tactics (SWAT) teams, which allow police departments to quickly mobilize against mass shootings, hostage and barricaded persons events, and other exigent incidents that might require a specialized police response.

[32] Oppel, Taylor, and Bogel-Burroughs, "Breonna Taylor's Case and Death: What We Know."

Hill Street Blues did not prepare its viewing audiences for what was coming in U.S. policing. It did not showcase many of the crime-fighting tactics we take for granted today, such as hot-spot policing or stop-question-and-frisk, because the strategies that underlie those deployments had not yet been conceptualized. We did not see police using big data to predict which neighborhoods would experience spikes in violent crime over a short period of time. We never heard of police departments deploying mine-resistant ambush protected (MRAP) vehicles on city streets, as the nation saw during the Ferguson, Missouri, protests of 2014.[33] Indeed, in *Hill Street Blues*, the SWAT team leader—Lt. Howard Hunter—was often viewed with suspicion and seen as an eccentric. He was treated as someone who needed to be reined in, not trotted out at the first sign of public disorder. Views on this have dramatically changed in the past 35 years, as PPUs have come to be regarded as "elite," and are highly sought assignments among contemporary police officers.[34]

Then the George Floyd tragedy occurred in Minneapolis. This event did not put police militarism or highly aggressive police tactics in the spotlight, as the shooting of Michael Brown and the rapid dominance-like response[35] of police in Ferguson had.[36] Rather, the George Floyd killing highlighted the extent to which a White police officer in public view, and surrounded by other police officers who did nothing to stop him, could slowly and methodically use the carotid neck restraint[37] to take the life of an African American man who, for the entire eight minutes and 46 seconds of the ordeal, begged the officer to release him so he could breathe.[38]

The homicide of George Floyd showed the public a different problem in U.S. policing that also might be a consequence of the military mentality that developed during the wars on drugs and terrorism. It showed that some police officers in some communities believed they could use force and deadly force with impunity against the people who resided in or traveled through those neighborhoods. It showed the problems of groupthink that characterizes much of what is known about the police subculture—a subculture that is unkind to police officers who try to intervene when their peers use excessive force or otherwise make mistakes during street-level encounters.[39] It also highlighted the need at that moment in time to initiate a national—if not global—conversation about police reform and how to remake the police into an institution that serves the entire public rather than treading on a segment of it, and having this conversation must start with an examination of the very idea of police.

---

[33] Taub, "What Was THAT? A Guide to the Military Gear Being Used against Civilians in Ferguson - Vox."

[34] Kraska, "Militarization and Policing—Its Relevance to 21st Century Police"; Kraska and Kappeler, "Militarizing American Police: The Rise and Normalization of Paramilitary Units."

[35] Ullman, Wade, and Edney, *Shock and Awe: Achieving Rapid Dominance.*

[36] Curry and Martinez, "Ferguson Police's Show of Force Highlights Militarization of America's Cops."

[37] Commission on Peace Officer Standards and Training, "Basic Course Unit Guide: Weaponless Defense."

[38] Hill et al., "How George Floyd Was Killed in Police Custody."

[39] Crank, *Understanding Police Culture.*

Deconstructing the Idea of Police

This book argues that coercion is why we have the police: because at certain moments in our lives many of us experience immediate threats to our well-being, and in some cases, our very existence. We might be confronted by a robber at gunpoint, a burglar in our home, or a driver with road rage as we try to navigate the highway. And in the writings of the classic police sociologist Egon Bittner,[40] when "something ought not to be happening, about which something ought to be done . . . NOW!!,"[41] we mobilize the police to respond immediately to events we define as exigent. Indeed, the need for expedience explains why police training is so tightly organized around field tactics, because of the "deal" the U.S. public has made with state authorities: We, the people, have given up our general right to use coercive force, and have centralized that authority with a full-time, paid police institution.

The "something" that Bittner wrote about did not have to be criminal, however—even though the police are typically thought of as "crime fighters"—and it did not even have to be dangerous. It just had to be something we believed required an immediate response and for which there was no one else to call. This is what makes policing such a complex proposition in any society: Some people call the police on the worst day of their lives, whereas others call because their power is out and they think the police should deliver them a pizza.[42] This fact is what prompted Klockars to write *The Idea of Police* in the first place: to help readers understand why we have the police and how we have created so many different role expectations for them.

In the opening pages of *The Idea of Police*, Klockars—writing in the first person—takes the reader through the same pedagogical process he used with his undergraduate policing students at the University of Delaware to create a definition of the police that applied to all police, all the time. In that initial chapter he argues that when people define the police, they typically do so in terms of what they expect of them, rather than who the police actually are, leading to "norm derivative"[43] descriptions that say more about the people giving the definition than about the police.

Klockars's exercise was so illustrative that it is useful to replicate a portion of it here. Take a few moments to think about how you would define the police to someone who has no concept of policing. "What are the police?" the person asks. A reasonable answer might be, "The police are an occupational group who wear uniforms, drive around in marked cars, and respond to emergencies." Although that description might be true of some police, it is also true of firefighters, or paramedics working for private ambulance companies. Any definition of the police must distinguish policing from all other occupational groups all the time. We can perhaps modify the above description

---

[40] *See* https://en.wikipedia.org/wiki/Egon_Bittner.
[41] Bittner, *The Functions of Police in Modern Society.*
[42] Kane, "Policing in Public Housing: Using Calls for Service to Examine Incident-Based Workload in the Philadelphia Housing Authority"; Greene and Klockars, "What Police Do."
[43] Klockars, *The Idea of Police,* 8–9.

to read: "The police are an occupational group who wear uniforms, drive around in marked cars, and respond to crimes." Just like with the previous definition, although this one does describe some police, it also describes private security guards. Moreover, not all police officers wear uniforms, drive marked police cars, and respond to calls for service. Some police officers wear plain clothes and do not make radio runs. So, although our definition of police must distinguish policing from all other occupational groups, it also has to apply to all police officers all the time.

Based on those criteria, our definition needs work. It requires us to insert an element that distinguishes the police from all other occupational groups while applying to all police all the time. This is what made *The Idea of Police* such an elegant statement of who police are and why we have them. As Klockars—and Bittner[44] before him—noted, the occupational element that applies to all police and distinguishes the police from all other occupational groups is the general right to use coercive force.[45] Not just the right to use coercive force, because plenty of people and occupational groups have the right to use coercive force. These include hospital staff when having to manage a combative patient, a football player on the field, and even a parent under limited circumstances. And that is the point: limited circumstances. Although many occupational groups (and parents) maintain a limited right to use coercive force to accomplish their roles and mandates, they are to use force only in specified contexts and only to control a limited subset of persons. Football players are not allowed to body-block or tackle people when walking down a sidewalk, as such behavior would likely result in assault and battery charges being filed against them.

The police maintain the general right to use coercive force within the boundaries of the state—which distinguishes them from firefighters, ambulance drivers, football players, hospital health care teams, and parents. And the general right to use coercive force applies to all police all the time, whether they are wearing a uniform and driving a patrol car or sitting at a desk and answering the phone. Indeed, the general right to use coercive force is what makes the police both "intrinsically good" and intrinsically "dangerous"[46] (more on this in Chapter 4).

In the end, Klockars posited that, because the general right to use coercive force represents the only constant distinction between the police and the public, both groups have been able to create and re-create the police mandate largely in the images of what suited them at any given time.[47] For Klockars, this was both the idea of police and its dilemma: a simple means-based definition that leads to an almost endless list of role expectations, always deriving from the general right to use coercive force. This is why "calling the cops" is such a profound expression in society, because calling the

---

[44] Bittner, "Florence Nightingale in Pursuit of Willie Sutton: A Theory of the Police."
[45] Klockars, *The Idea of Police*, 12.
[46] Banton, *The Policeman in the Community*.
[47] *See also* Manning, "The Police: Mandate, Strategies, and Appearances."

cops means mobilizing the authority of the state to send an armed institution to our immediate location in response to something we have defined as an emergency. When police arrive, we expect them to bring the tool we have given them—the general right to use coercive force—to solve our problem. This is the idea of police.

Although coercion has been frequently called the tool that enables police to fulfill their role in society, it also seems that over the past 30-plus years—at least since Sgt. Phil Esterhaus last told his officers to "be careful out there"—the tactics of policing have become tangled up with the strategies of policing. As this book argues, we have come to a point where coercion has become both the tool and the mandate, much to the detriment of the public and the police institution, itself. Stop-and-frisk is a clear example of this tangling.

In 1994, the New York City Police Department (NYPD) adopted stop-and-frisk as a strategy to reduce "disorder" on the streets of New York, invoking the "broken windows" theory that urban disorder leads to serious crime.[48] Thus, by stopping and potentially frisking anyone who looked as if they might be contributing to neighborhood social disorder, the NYPD argued that they could reduce serious crime.[49] Stop-and-frisk was never intended to be a crime control strategy, though. It was a field tactic designed to keep officers safe. When the U.S. Supreme Court affirmed the use of stop-and-frisk in the case of *Terry v. Ohio* (1968), it did so out of concern for officer and public safety. As the Court noted in *Terry*:[50]

> Where a reasonably prudent officer is warranted in the circumstances of a given case in believing that his [sic] safety or that of others is endangered, he [sic] may make a reasonable search for weapons of the person believed by him [sic] to be armed and dangerous.

That is, the Court in *Terry* intended stop-and-frisk to be applied as a "one-off" tactic when officers were suspicious that a person with whom they were dealing might pose a serious physical risk to officers and public safety.[51] It was not intended as a crime control strategy to be conducted based on a general sense of reasonable suspicion; in fact, the Court in *Terry* noted that anything more than a pat-down of the suspect's outer clothing for weapons was tantamount to a search and would normally require a warrant under the provisions of the Fourth Amendment.[52] Yet, for a full generation of policing, the NYPD used stop-and-frisk as part of an overall crime control strategy, stopping several hundred thousand individuals—mostly African American

---

[48] Fagan and Davies, "Street Stops and Broken Windows: Terry, Race and Disorder in New York City"; Harcourt, "Reflecting on the Subject: A Critique of the Social Influence Conception of Deterrence, the Broken Windows Theory, and Order-Maintenance Policing New York Style."

[49] Greene, "Zero Tolerance: A Case Study of Police Policies and Practices in New York City."

[50] Terry v. Ohio, 392 U.S. 1, 3 (1968).

[51] Meares, "The Law and Social Science of Stop and Frisk," 340.

[52] Terry v. Ohio, 392 U.S. 1, 20 (1968).

and Latino men—until in 2014 a federal district court intervened, deeming the NYPD's stop-and-frisk program unconstitutional under both the Fourth and Fourteenth Amendments.[53]

But New York City itself was not a one-off. Since 2009, the Civil Rights Division of the U.S. Department of Justice has initiated investigations of at least 25 local police departments, 19 of which resulted in some degree of federal oversight due to unlawful use of force, as well as stop-and-frisk practices.[54] Big-city police departments subjected to consent decrees[55] in recent years include Seattle,[56] Chicago,[57] New Orleans,[58] Los Angeles,[59] and Philadelphia.[60] It is this tangling of the definition of police with the role of police that has led to our current situation, where police have integrated the tactics with the strategies of policing, leading to what we might call a coercion for the sake of coercion paradigm.

On the Limits of the Idea of Police

Let us refer back to Klockars's original proposition in *The Idea of Police*, where he asserted that the best way to define all police all the time was by the tool society has given them. Recall Klockars's argument that a means-based definition (i.e., defining the police based on the general right to use coercive force) is superior to an ends-based definition because the latter simply represents the expectations that different societal groups have placed on the police. To some, the police are an institution that fights crime. To others, the police are an institution that maintains social order. To still others, the police are an institution that puts young Black men against the wall every time they step off their front porch. Those are ends-based definitions of the police, which derive from the experiences and expectations of those who offer them.

This is precisely why Klockars argued that a means-based definition of the police was so important: It applied to all police all the time, independent of the expectations of the police and the public. In defining the "new" idea of police, though, this book argues that a means-based definition of the police is no longer sufficient because the police are too good at using those means; that is, they are too good at using coercion to accomplish their ends. The police have become too creative at adapting their technologies—even those

---

[53] Floyd v. City of New York, 959 F. Supp. 2d 668 - Dist. Court, SD New York (2013).
[54] U.S. Department of Justice, "Justice Department Releases Report on Civil Rights Division's Pattern and Practice Police Reform Work."
[55] A legal settlement between a police department and the Department of Justice—usually resulting from a lawsuit—that defines actions the departments must take to eliminate unfair patterns or practices, usually in the areas of stop-and-frisk, use of force, deadly force, or generally failing to protect certain groups of people. *See also* https://legaldictionary.net/consent-decree/.
[56] "Seattle Police Department—Settlement Agreement History."
[57] Madhani, "Federal Judge Approves Consent Decree for Chicago Police Department."
[58] City of New Orleans, "NOPD - Consent Decree - City of New Orleans."
[59] U.S. Department of Justice, "U.S. v. City of Los Angeles - Consent Decree - Introduction."
[60] ACLU Pennsylvania, "After Seven Years, Report Shows Philadelphia Police Continue to Illegally Stop and Frisk Pedestrians."

initially designed to increase police accountability—for coercive purposes.[61] If there is blame to be had for this, it is not precisely with the police. They have been simply operating at expectations. The blame for allowing the perversion of the idea of police resides largely with the public, with our elected officials, and with public policymakers who have failed to adequately define the role of police.

In its subtitle, "So Long, *Hill Street Blues*," this introduction acknowledges the transition from one era of U.S. policing to the next: the one that existed before the 1980s war on drugs—and well before the war on terror—and the one that exists now, which, as this book argues, emphasizes coercion and control over community protection and the protection of life.

To the extent that the shooting of Michael Brown by a Ferguson, Missouri police officer in 2014, or the killing of Eric Garner at the hands of New York City police officers—also in 2014—might have represented a watershed moment leading society to reexamine police tactics and strategies, particularly in the most vulnerable communities of color, it also seemed that that moment passed with little actual reform until finally fading from public consciousness. Indeed, despite then President Barack Obama's creation of the President's Taskforce on 21st Century Policing, that group's final report—submitted in July 2015 and making many recommendations to build community "trust and legitimacy"[62]—seemed to have little actual impact on policing practices around the country. So, when Derek Chauvin, a Minneapolis police officer, killed George Floyd during the summer of 2020 in a horrific display of police dominance, that event so shocked the collective U.S. conscience that it led many (including this author)[63] to publicly wonder how the police could possibly move past that.

That is what this book is about: moving forward and reimagining the police as the crucial institution for public safety that it can become. We have left the definition of the police too vague for too long, which has left policing to its own devices. As recent events demonstrate, it is important to include something of their essence in their definition if for no other reason than to give policing the conscience it so desperately needs.

This book is intended as both an introduction to police in the United States and an examination of police and society. It will describe, explain, and critique the police, as well as the public that created it, but it will not vilify the police institution. Quite the opposite: This book will argue that policing remains a crucial public good in U.S. society. Paradoxically, it is in the very communities in which police experience the greatest difficulties (and most conflict) that they might one day achieve the greatest positive impact. No policing textbook, though, can ignore what has happened in U.S. policing

---

[61] Ferguson, *Rise of Big Data Policing: Surveillance, Race, and the Future of Law Enforcement.*

[62] President's Task Force on 21st Century Policing, "Final Report of the President's Task Force on 21st Century Policing," 1.

[63] Kane, "Abolish Police? No, But Change Recruitment"; Kane, "What Current Police Reform Efforts Lack: A Call to Federalize."

over the past several years. Michael Brown, Eric Garner, Breonna Taylor, and George Floyd—even Daunte Wright, who was accidentally and fatally shot by a police officer in Minnesota who mistook her gun for a Taser—deserve more than that. So does the U.S. public, and so do the people who don a uniform every day and take to the streets in marked patrol cars. In acknowledging the consequences of a coercion-based paradigm, *Policing Beyond Coercion* will provide a conceptual nudge that can hopefully help the institution of the police realize its full potential as an integral component of neighborhoods—particularly the most vulnerable neighborhoods of color—with both the means and the mission to protect life and help communities achieve and maintain healthy living conditions.

Organization of the Book

Policing Beyond Coercion is divided into three sections, each of which includes several chapters that encapsulate a common theme. Part I, "Foundations," consists of chapters that provide some historical context for the present analysis, an examination of the typical police organizational structure, and the current recruitment and socialization processes at work in U.S. policing, which help perpetuate the current paradigm. Part I concludes with a full chapter (Chapter 4) devoted to explaining the "new" idea of police—that is, the protection of life mandate. This chapter argues that the development and role of police has been largely informed by German political scientist Max Weber's conceptualization of the "state" as an institution that exists strictly on the basis of the general right to use coercive force to maintain itself. Chapter 4 then describes an alternate conceptualization of the state, grounded in the philosophy of French sociologist Emile Durkheim, that could help us reimagine the police institution as something larger than its current definition. The chapter also includes a case study showing how a subtle change in police mentalities could profoundly alter—for the common good—some of the interactions officers have with members of the public. In essence, this appeal to Durkheim helps set the tone for the remainder of the book.

Part II, "Pathways and Remedies to a Coercion Paradigm," includes chapters that examine the police subculture as it currently exists, as well as an alternative—and positive—conceptualization of the metaphorical "thin blue line" of police. Part II also includes chapters that examine police discretion, the use of force and deadly force, and stop-and-frisk as both an important officer safety tactic and a larger crime control strategy. In addition, Part II includes chapters describing police accountability structures, as well as the big data revolution in policing and its logical expansion into predictive policing. Part II also includes Chapter 6, "The Rise and 'Stall' of Community Policing," arguing that community policing can be viewed as a parable of U.S. policing: It was conceived as a philosophy to encourage police to move away from a strictly coercive deployment structure to one based more on problem-solving, decentralized decision-making, community partnerships,[64] and the "co-production of safety" between the police and the public.[65] But over time in many places, community policing became the basis for order maintenance policing,[66] which ultimately evolved into the Stop, Question, and Frisk strategic paradigm.[67] Although community policing still exists in U.S. police departments, it does so largely as a "unit" within agencies, rather than as a guiding organizational philosophy—as it was originally intended.[68] As the chapter explains, though, community policing can still provide an important basis for the protection of life mandate.

The chapters in Part III tell the story of how policing can evolve beyond its coercion mandate to one that emphasizes the protection of life. Titled, "Creating the New Idea of Police," Part III translates the new idea into practice by arguing that this evolution must begin with society and the police officer recruitment paradigm. The final chapter of Part III examines what the protection of life mandate would look like if integrated throughout the police institution.

Supplemental Materials

To complement the text, the opening of most chapters will link to a podcast in which the author describes the rationale for the chapter, conducts an interview with a police professional or scholar, or conducts a roundtable discussion on a topic of interest to that chapter. Selected parts of the chapters will also link to a dedicated author's blog to which students can subscribe and be notified when new posts are made, again giving students and the author opportunities to engage with one another beyond the pages of the book. The blog will also give students a forum to interact with other policing students around the country over contemporary issues in both U.S. and international policing.

Finally, the last pages of Chapter 2 will include links to three online "operations dashboards" that show mapping visualizations for the cities of Philadelphia, San Francisco, and Washington, DC. The operations dashboards are interactive mapping applications maintained by the author in Esri's ArcGIS Online platform. They show the spatial distributions of different aspects of policing and crime, Emergency Medical Services (EMS) calls for service, different types of land use (e.g., schools, parks, and other features of the built environment), and sociodemographic compositions of communities. Each dashboard includes somewhat different mapping layers based on the data that the cities make publicly available. The operations dashboards give users opportunities to interact with live policing and crime data across different cities in ways that hopefully

---

[64] Kelling, "Police and Communities: The Quiet Revolution"; Brown, "Community Policing: A Partnership with Promise"; Goldstein, "Toward Community-Oriented Policing: Potential, Basic Requirements, and Threshold Questions."

[65] Skogan, *Disorder and Decline: Crime and the Spiral of Decay in American Neighborhoods.*

[66] Greene, "Zero Tolerance: A Case Study of Police Policies and Practices in New York City."

[67] Fagan and Davies, "Street Stops and Broken Windows: Terry, Race and Disorder in New York City."

[68] For example, Greene, "Zero Tolerance"; Trojanowicz and Carter, "Philosophy and Role of Community Policing."

encourage data-driven understandings of policing activities and how, for example, public health issues intersect with crime and policing.

Final Introductory Thoughts

Policing Beyond Coercion largely refers to street-level municipal policing in metropolitan areas because this is where most of the policing in this country is conducted: Over half of all police officers employed in the United States work for municipal police departments in cities with populations of at least 40,000 residents.[69] This percentage likely underrepresents the true number of police officers employed in metropolitan areas because it does not include smaller suburbs that reside just outside cities, transit and housing police departments with jurisdictions within cities and their immediate suburbs, or sheriff's departments with patrol functions in the unincorporated parts of metropolitan areas. For example, the Los Angeles Sheriff's Department, the nation's largest—whose deputies are not included in the 40 percent figure—serves as the primary police agency for 42 contracted cities in Los Angeles County,[70] which is, of course, a highly metropolitan county. Thus, most of what happens in U.S. policing happens in metro areas.

This focus on metropolitan policing does not mean to minimize the contributions or importance of policing in smaller communities, however. Indeed, of the 17,398 police agencies that report data to the FBI's Uniform Crime Reports, 12,028 (69.13 percent) serve jurisdictional populations of fewer than 10,000 residents.[71] That is, whereas more than half of all U.S. police officers are employed in metropolitan areas, over two-thirds of all U.S. police agencies serve relatively small populations. Officers employed in smaller jurisdictions experience many of the same events and see many of the same issues as their colleagues employed by metropolitan agencies. It is just a matter of scale: They might not see those issues or events quite as frequently. This book contends that whether conducted in metro versus rural America, policing across the country is confronted every day by difficult social issues related to race, poverty, conflict, substance abuse, mental health crises, and other structural features of communities that require a police intervention. This book hopes to speak to all of them.

In the end, *Policing Beyond Coercion*, and everything it encompasses—the chapters, the podcasts, the blog, and the data dashboards—is organized around four basic tenets: description, analysis, criticism, and hope. There is enough description to suffice as the sole text for Introduction to

---

[69] As no single source reports the number of local police officers employed in cities and their suburbs, the 40 percent reported here is derived from a combination of two sources: Banks et al., "National Sources of Law Enforcement Employment Data"; and United States Department of Justice, Office of Justice Programs, Bureau of Justice Statistics, "Law Enforcement Management and Administrative Statistics (LEMAS), 2016. ICPSR37323-V1."

[70] Los Angeles County Sheriff's Department, "About Us."

[71] Banks et al., "National Sources of Law Enforcement Employment Data," 3.

Policing and Police & Society courses. There is analysis of how and why policing functions as it does. There is criticism of how the police—particularly over the past 35 years—have come to rely so heavily on coercion and control as both their means and their mission. There is hope that a new generation of police officers can take something from this book that inspires them to reimagine the police institution into a public good that brings value to people they contact and the places they work.

To recall our discussion of *Hill Street Blues* at the start of this chapter, this author imagines a near future in which all police officers have moved beyond Andrew Renko to become Bobby Hill. When that future arrives, and we call the police, we can rest assured that they will bring more than their definition to us when they come. They will be more than their definition, and showing them how to imagine that future is the point of this book.

Questions for Review and Reflection

Question 1. Policing a Public Health Emergency

When crack cocaine made its way into U.S. cities in the mid-1980s, government officials appropriately branded it an "epidemic." Its use led to increased addiction, sexually transmitted infections (STIs), the spread of HIV, the rise of open-air sex-for-drugs markets, child abandonment, and neighborhood violence. Containing such an epidemic would normally require a massive public health mobilization, presumably led and coordinated by the U.S. Public Health Service. But this did not happen. Instead, cities sent in their police forces to fight the epidemic, and U.S. government officials framed the widespread crack use as a criminal justice problem rather than a public health crisis.

- Why did the police become the primary responders to the crack epidemic of the 1980s?
- What is the legacy of sending the police in to fight a public health problem, almost to the exclusion of public health agencies?
- What should be the role of police during public health emergencies, such as a drug epidemic or a global pandemic?

Question 2. Costs and Benefits of a Police Institution

The classic police sociologist Egon Bittner once wrote that we have the police so they can respond to situations where "something ought not to be happening about which something ought to be done, now!!" To stop that "something" from "happening," we mobilize the police on our own behalf.

- Why is "calling the cops" such a profound right in U.S. society?
- Who wins and who loses when the cops get called?
- Does the "something ought not to be happening about which something ought to be done now" phenomenon justify society's support for the police, despite the social costs we often pay for having them? If so, why? If not, what are some legitimate alternatives to a police institution?

Exercises

Exercise 1. Defining the Police

Ask five to seven peers (friends, classmates, teammates) to write down their definition of who the police are. Once you collect their written responses, go through them to pick out the similarities and differences among them.

- In what ways are the written definitions similar to one another?
- In what ways are the written definitions different from one another?
- Are the definitions generally means-based or ends-based (or both)?
- What do the definitions say about the people who wrote them?

Exercise 2. Policing a "Drug Deal"

Revisit the *Policing Beyond Coercion* podcast page on Soundcloud (use the QR code or URL at the beginning of the chapter) and listen to Log 1: One Night in Sacramento. After listening to the episode, write an alternate ending for the encounter in which no one gets arrested and goes to jail.

- In what ways would you have to change the personalities of the police officers to support an alternate ending where no one gets arrested?
- How does your alternate ending become an example of police officers moving beyond the coercion paradigm to solve a problem?

Bibliography

ACLU Pennsylvania. "After Seven Years, Report Shows Philadelphia Police Continue to Illegally Stop and Frisk Pedestrians." 2018. https://www.aclupa.org/en/press-releases/after-seven-years-report-shows-philadelphia-police-continue-illegally-stop-and-frisk.

Balko, Radley. "Overkill: The Rise of Paramilitary Police Raids in America." Washington, DC, 2006. http://www.ncjrs.gov/App/publications/abstract.aspx?ID=238405.

Banks, Duren, Joshua Hendrix, Matthew Hickman, and Tracey Kyckelhahn. "National Sources of Law Enforcement Employment Data." Washington, DC, 2016.

Banton, Michael. *The Policeman in the Community*. New York: Basic Books, 1964. https://books.google.com/books/about/The_Policeman_in_the_Community.html?id=F0NMwQEACAAJ.

Bittner, Egon. "Florence Nightingale in Pursuit of Willie Sutton: A Theory of the Police." In *The Potential for Reform of Criminal Justice*, edited by Herbert Jacob, 352. London: Sage, 1974.

Bittner, Egon. *The Functions of Police in Modern Society*. Chevy Chase, MD: National Institute of Mental Health, 1970. https://www.google.com/books/edition/The_Functions_of_the_Police_in_Modern_So/rQcXAAAAIAAJ?hl=en&gbpv=1&printsec=frontcover.

Brown, L. P. "Community Policing: A Partnership with Promise." *The Police Chief* 59 (1992): 45–47.

"Charles Haid - IMDb." Accessed July 22, 2020. https://www.imdb.com/name/nm0354024/?ref_=ttfc_fc_cl_t9.

City of New Orleans. "NOPD - Consent Decree - City of New Orleans." 2019. https://nola.gov/nopd/nopd-consent-decree/.

Commission on Peace Officer Standards and Training. "Basic Course Unit Guide: Weaponless Defense." Sacramento, CA, 1990. https://www.ncjrs.gov/pdffiles1/Digitization/133229NCJRS.pdf.

Cooper, Alexia, and Erica Smith. "Homicide Trends in the United States, 1980–2008." *Patterns & Trends*. Vol. 17. Washington, DC, 2011. https://doi.org/10.2307/2061058.

Crank, John P. *Understanding Police Culture*. 2nd ed. New York: Routledge, 2015. https://books.google.com/books?hl=en&lr=&id=wRugBAAAQBAJ&oi=fnd&pg=PP1&dq=police+culture&ots=qScQCOmu2N&sig=sHK8RZ_xKg1TOO235D7i9D3S73k#v=onepage&q=police culture&f=false.

Curry, Colleen, and Luis Martinez. "Ferguson Police's Show of Force Highlights Militarization of America's Cops." ABC News, 2014. https://abcnews.go.com/US/ferguson-police-small-army-thousands-police-departments/story?id=24977299.

Delehanty, Casey, Jack Mewhirter, Ryan Welch, and Jason Wilks. "Militarization and Police Violence: The Case of the 1033 Program." *Research and Politics* 4, no. 2 (2017): 1–7. https://doi.org/10.1177/2053168017712885.

Drug Enforcement Administration. "History: 1985–1990," n.d. https://www.dea.gov/sites/default/files/2018-07/1985-1990 p 58-67custom2.pdf.

Fagan, Jeffrey, and Garth Davies. "Street Stops and Broken Windows: Terry, Race and Disorder in New York City." *Fordham Urban Law Journal* 28 (2000): 457–504. https://doi.org/10.2139/ssrn.257813.

Ferguson, Andrew G. *Rise of Big Data Policing: Surveillance, Race, and the Future of Law Enforcement*. New York: NYU Press, 2017.

Floyd v. City of New York, 959 F. Supp. 2d 668 - Dist. Court, SD New York (2013).

Goldstein, Herman. "Toward Community-Oriented Policing: Potential, Basic Requirements, and Threshold Questions." *Crime & Delinquency* 33, no. 1 (1987): 6–30. https://doi.org/10.1177/0011128787033001002.

Greene, Jack R. "Community Policing in America: Changing the Nature, Structure, and Function of the Police." In *Policies, Processes, and Decisions of the Criminal Justice System*, edited by Julie Horney, John Martin, Doris L. MacKenzie, Ruth Peterson, and Dennis Rosenbaum, Crim Just 2000: V.3., 299–370. Washington, DC: National Institute of Justice, 2000. https://books.google.com/books?id=npJYG7kS-3AC&printsec=frontcover#v=onepage&q&f=false.

Greene, Jack R., and Carl B. Klockars. "What Police Do." In *Thinking About Police: Contemporary Readings*, edited by Carl B. Klockars and Stephen D. Mastrofski, 2nd ed. New York: McGraw-Hill, 1991.

Greene, Judith A. "Zero Tolerance: A Case Study of Police Policies and Practices in New York City." *Crime and Delinquency* 42 (1999): 171–187. https://doi.org/10.1177/0011128799045002001.

Harcourt, Bernard E. "Reflecting on the Subject: A Critique of the Social Influence Conception of Deterrence, the Broken Windows Theory, and Order-Maintenance Policing New York Style." *Michigan Law Review* 97, no. 2 (1998): 291–389. https://doi.org/10.2307/1290289.

Hill, Evan, Ainara Tiefenthaler, Christiaan Triebert, Drew Jordan, Haley Willis, and Robin Stein. "How George Floyd Was Killed in Police Custody." *The New York Times*, May 31, 2020. https://www.nytimes.com/2020/05/31/us/george-floyd-investigation.html.

"Hill Street Blues - Emmy Awards, Nominations and Wins | Television Academy." Accessed August 3, 2020. https://www.emmys.com/shows/hill-street-blues.

"Iconic TV Series Catchphrases - IMDb." Accessed June 16, 2020. https://www.imdb.com/list/ls094232413/?ref_=nm_rls_1.

Kane, Robert J. "Abolish Police? No, but Change Recruitment." *Philadelphia Inquirer*, June 8, 2020. https://www.inquirer.com/opinion/commentary/abolish-police-reform-recruitment-george-floyd-20200608.html.

Kane, Robert J. "Policing in Public Housing: Using Calls for Service to Examine Incident-Based Workload in the Philadelphia Housing Authority." *Policing* 21, no. 4 (1998): 618–631. https://doi.org/10.1108/13639519810241656.

Kane, Robert J. "What Current Police Reform Efforts Lack: A Call to Federalize." *The Hill*, July 17, 2020. https://thehill.com/opinion/criminal-justice/507847-what-current-police-reform-efforts-lack-a-call-to-federalize.

Kappeler, Victor E., and Peter B. Kraska. "Normalising Police Militarisation, Living in Denial." *Policing and Society* 25, no. 3 (2015): 268–275. https://doi.org/10.1080/10439463.2013.864655.

Kelling, George L. "Police and Communities: The Quiet Revolution." *Perspectives on Policing*. Washington, DC: National Institute of Justice, 1988.

Kerr, Peter. "Opium Dens for the Crack Era." *New York Times*, May 18, 1986.

Klockars, Carl B. *The Idea of Police*. Thousand Oaks, CA: Sage, 1985.

Kraska, Peter B. "Militarization and Policing—Its Relevance to 21st Century Police." *Policing* 1, no. 4 (2007): 501–513. https://doi.org/10.1093/police/pam065.

Kraska, Peter B., and Victor E. Kappeler. "Militarizing American Police: The Rise and Normalization of Paramilitary Units." *Social Problems* 44, no. 1 (1997): 1–18. https://doi.org/10.2307/3096870.

Los Angeles County Sheriff's Department. "About Us." Accessed December 29, 2021. https://www.lasd.org/about_us.html.

Madhani, Aamer. "Federal Judge Approves Consent Decree for Chicago Police Department." *USA Today*, January 21, 2019. https://www.usatoday.com/story/news/nation/2019/01/31/chicago-police-department-consent-decree-reforms-attorney-general-lisa-madigan/2734415002/.

Manly, Laura. "Being Careful out There? Hardly." *The New York Times*, May 1, 2014. https://www.emmys.com/shows/hill-street-blues.

Manning, Peter K. "The Police: Mandate, Strategies, and Appearances." In *Policing: A View from the Street*, edited by Peter K Manning and John Van Maanen. Santa Monica, CA: Goodyear, 1978.

Meares, Tracey L. "Programming Errors: Understanding the Constitutionality of Stop-and-Frisk as a Program, Not an Incident." *University of Chicago Law Review* 82, no. 1 (2015): 159–179. https://doi.org/10.2139/ssrn.2524930.

"Michael Conrad - IMDb." Accessed June 16, 2020. https://www.imdb.com/name/nm0175700/.

"Michael Warren - IMDb." Accessed July 22, 2020. https://www.imdb.com/name/nm0912966/?ref_=tt_ov_st_sm.

Oppel, Richard A., Derrick Bryson Taylor, and Nicholas Bogel-Burroughs. "Breonna Taylor's Case and Death: What We Know." *The New York Times*, October 2, 2020. https://www.nytimes.com/article/breonna-taylor-police.html.

President's Task Force on 21st Century Policing. "Final Report of the President's Task Force on 21st Century Policing." Washington, DC, 2015.

Radil, Steven M., Raymond J. Dezzani, and Lanny D. McAden. "Geographies of U.S. Police Militarization and the Role of the 1033 Program." *The Professional Geographer* 69, no. 2 (2017): 203–213. https://doi.org/10.1080/00330124.2016.1212666.

Roe, Kathleen M., Meredith Minkler, Frances Saunders, and Gregg E. Thomson. "Health of Grandmothers Raising Children of the Crack Cocaine Epidemic." *Medical Care* 34, no. 11 (1996): 1072–1084.

Schifano, Fabrizio, and John Corkery. "Cocaine/Crack Cocaine Consumption, Treatment Demand, Seizures, Related Offences, Prices, Average Purity Levels and Deaths in the UK (1990–2004)." *Journal of Psychopharmacology* 22, no. 1 (2008): 1–10.

"Seattle Police Department - Settlement Agreement History." Accessed July 8, 2020. https://www.seattle.gov/police/about-us/professional-standards-bureau/settlement-agreement-history.

Shenon, Philip. "24 Task Forces Sought by Meese to Fight Crack." *New York Times*, October 3, 1986.

Skogan, Wesley G. *Disorder and Decline: Crime and the Spiral of Decay in American Neighborhoods*. Berkeley: University of California Press, 1992.

Taub, Amanda. "What Was THAT? A Guide to the Military Gear Being Used against Civilians in Ferguson - Vox." Vox, 2014. https://www.vox.com/2014/8/18/6003377/ferguson-military-gear.

Terry v. Ohio, 392 U.S. 1 (1968).

Trojanowicz, Robert, and Davide Carter. "Philosophy and Role of Community Policing." Washington, DC, 1988.

Ullman, Harlan, James P. Wade, and L. A. Edney. *Shock and Awe: Achieving Rapid Dominance*. Washington, DC: Center for Advanced Concepts and Technology, National Defense University, 1996. https://www.google.com/books/edition/_/bNfTAQAACAAJ?hl=en&sa=X&ved=2ahUKEwjMjqfYrffqAhXsknIEHS4qB3cQre8FMBF6BAgOEAc.

U.S. Department of Justice. "Justice Department Releases Report on Civil Rights Division's Pattern and Practice Police Reform Work," 2017. https://www.justice.gov/opa/pr/justice-department-releases-report-civil-rights-division-s-pattern-and-practice-police-reform.

U.S. Department of Justice. "U.S. v. City of Los Angeles - Consent Decree - Introduction," 2015. https://www.justice.gov/crt/us-v-city-los-angeles-consent-decree-introduction.

U.S. Department of Justice, Office of Justice Programs, Bureau of Justice Statistics. "Law Enforcement Management and Administrative Statistics (LEMAS), 2016. ICPSR37323-V1." Ann Arbor, MI: Inter-university Consortium for Political and Social Research [producer and distributor], 2020.

Walker, Samuel. *Sense and Nonsense About Crime and Drugs: A Policy Guide*. 8th ed. Stamford, CT: Cengage Learning, 2015.

Watkins, Beverly Xaviera, and Mindy Thompson Fullilove. "The Crack Epidemic and the Failure of Epidemic Response." *Temple Political & Civil Rights Law Review* 10 (2001): 371–386.

PART I

Foundations

CHAPTER 2

The Modern American Police Department

The police are everywhere.

Or so they'd have us think. To be sure, they patrol our streets, walk our sidewalks, stroll our parks, and increasingly deploy as a regular presence in our public schools. They eat in our restaurants, stand side-by-side with us at large sporting events and public gatherings, and Segway among us at shopping malls. When we call them, they come. Even when we don't, they frequently show up anyway, occasionally with ticket book in hand. Employing just over 750,000 sworn[1] members nationally,[2] spread across almost 14,000 local departments,[3] the police are integrated into our daily public lives like no other single public-sector protective service institution.[4]

---

[1] This figure includes patrol officers from municipal police and sheriff's departments (excluding jailers and correctional officers), detectives, and sworn supervisors of patrol officers and detectives. It excludes state police officers. *See* U.S. Department of Justice, Office of Justice Programs, Bureau of Justice Statistics, "Law Enforcement Management and Administrative Statistics (LEMAS), 2016. ICPSR37323-V1."

[2] "May 2018 National Occupational Employment and Wage Estimates."

[3] Federal Bureau of Investigation, "2018 Crime in the United States—Police Employee Data."

[4] According to the Bureau of Labor Statistics, as of 2018 there were 415,000 correctional officers, 387,490 line and supervisory firefighters, and 257,210 emergency medical technicians and paramedics. The nearly 4.2 million preschool, elementary, middle, and secondary school teachers are not included in this comparison because they are not classified as protective service employees. *See generally* https://www.bls.gov/oes/current/oes_nat.htm#33-0000.

Podcast Episode: "Guardians of the Underground: How the Pandemic has changed Transit Policing"

Scan the QR code or enter the short URL shown below into a browser window to listen to this chapter's podcast. https://bit.ly/3s8SlmN

And they are watching.

With body cams, dash cams, license plate readers, closed circuit TV, facial recognition, and even the geocoding of pedestrian stops, vehicle stops, and arrests, the police can "see" us almost wherever we travel through public space, and certainly, wherever they go. Some of this comes in the form of direct surveillance, where our images are captured on video, frequently through police contact (e.g., police-worn body cameras and patrol car dashboard cameras). Some of it comes from tracking us though geotagged contacts, such as field interrogations and vehicle stops, reducing our whereabouts to points on a digital map. Historically, the surveillance and tracking capacities of the police were limited to direct police–citizen interaction, but increasingly, we can be seen, heard, and tracked without a physical police officer ever sharing the same space at the same time with us.

But how did we get here? What are the origins of formal policing in the United States? How did police departments develop into a quasi-military bureaucracy despite the fact that (unlike the military) police officers working the street maintain a great deal of discretion to solve problems? Why are some police departments highly complex organizations with many rank structures and special units, whereas others are more modest in how they divide up their work? These are some of the questions this chapter addresses.

By the end of this chapter, readers should be able to answer the following questions:

1. What factors led to the development of formal policing in the United States?
2. How did the concept of "dangerous classes" influence the historical development of the police?
3. In what ways do police departments become vertically and functionally differentiated?
4. How does the quasi-military bureaucratic model of most police organizations reconcile with police officers themselves working as "street-level bureaucrats"?
5. How do police departments use "territoriality" to manage geographic space?
6. In what ways might the different social, economic, and crime conditions in different police beats affect the ways in which police manage space and people in those areas?

American Police Departments: Two Agencies in One

The modern American police department is, organizationally speaking, two agencies. One is physical, residing as a tangible feature of the built environment. This is the one the public sees, and it is made up of the physical assets we normally associate with policing: marked police cars, the police officers themselves, buildings, motorcycles, horses, cops on foot patrol, cops on scooters, and so on. The physical police organization is the one that practices "territoriality," or the processes of "making" and "marking" space.[5] They manage that space largely through the patrol function. That is, police departments attempt to maintain and establish social control mostly through the deployment of marked patrol cars and within discrete units of geography, such as police beats.

See for Yourself . . .

Scan the QR code to watch this *Digital Trends* video on surveillance tech in policing.

There is another police organization that most of us never see, although it sees us. This is the virtual police department, whose hub exists in the form of a records management system (RMS)—the virtual container that receives and holds all information that police departments collect.[6] Historically, RMSs were comprised of all the individual pieces of paper a police department produced and then stored in filing cabinets.[7] Some of the larger police agencies, in particular, the New York City Police Department at least into the early 2000s, were so bureaucratically complex that they produced "personnel orders" at least once but often several times per day just to keep track of who was hired, who was fired, who was placed on suspension, who was promoted, and so on.[8] Personnel orders are a method police departments used to "talk" to themselves so that commanders across divisions had common knowledge of organizational activities. Over time, and as technology evolved and became more accessible, police departments began to convert those paper files into electronic records in the form of electronic records management systems.[9] In contemporary policing, the RMS is fed by multiple databases, such as the computer-aided dispatch (CAD) system, police report-writing software, incident reports, citations, investigations reports, field contacts, and traffic accident reports.[10]

---

[5] Herbert, "The Normative Ordering of Police Territoriality: Making and Marking Space with the Los Angeles Police Department."
[6] Santos, *Crime Analysis with Crime Mapping.*
[7] Penn, Pennix, and Coulson, *Records Management Handbook.*
[8] Kane and White, *Jammed Up: Bad Cops, Police Misconduct, and the New York City Police Department.*
[9] Penn, Pennix, and Coulson, *Records Management Handbook.*
[10] Santos, *Crime Analysis with Crime Mapping.*

In the applied sense, RMS is the domain of crime and intelligence analysts, usually "non-sworn"[11] members of the organization who tap into the police department's databases to create actionable reports and visualizations, often in the form of hot-spot maps and crime-trend plots. To a great extent, today's police officers are a kind of field lens who collect data wherever they go and send it back to the organization along wireless highways in the form of 4.9-GHz transmissions and mesh-enabled networks.[12] Increasingly, the modern U.S. police department exists in cyberspace, and its digital footprint and infrastructure are growing (more on this in Chapter 11).

The Tangled Roots of U.S. Policing

It is commonly argued that the "seeds" of U.S. policing were sown in England.[13] The passage of the Metropolitan Police Act of 1829[14] in England, establishing the London Metropolitan Police, provided a template for the creation and practice of policing in the United States.[15] Although this might be true for New York City and other police departments in the industrial North, it appears less accurate for other regions of the United States that did not contain large cities for which London could be used as a model.[16] For example, in the Southern states that practiced slavery before the Civil War (e.g., Alabama, Arkansas, Delaware, Florida, Georgia, Kentucky, Louisiana, Maryland, Mississippi, Missouri, North Carolina, South Carolina, Tennessee, Texas, and Virginia), policing was mostly organized around controlling the enslaved populations.[17] This meant preventing and responding to slave "revolts," monitoring the activities of enslaved people in public settings, and hunting down "runaways" when they escaped their bondage.[18] Indeed, as Dulaney argues, "The slave patrol was the first distinctly American police system"[19] that would set the tone for how African Americans would experience the police from the slave patrol paradigm forward.

On the Western frontier the development of policing coincided with the settlement of people migrating from the Eastern United States.[20] These were lands—such as the Territories of Arizona, New Mexico, and Utah, as well as the Great Plains—already populated by indigenous peoples, and where

---

[11] Employees of a police organization who are not licensed police officers. Non-sworn members of police departments are often erroneously referred to as "civilians," when in fact, the sworn members of virtually all police organizations (except for military police officers) are also civilians; hence, the distinction between military and civilian law enforcement. *See generally* Dunlap, "The Police-Ization of the Military."

[12] "How Municipal WiFi Works | HowStuffWorks."

[13] Lane, "Urban Police and Crime in Nineteenth-Century America."

[14] "Metropolitan Police - UK Parliament."

[15] Miller, *Cops and Bobbies: Police Authority in New York and London, 1830–1870.*

[16] Brown, "Policing in American History."

[17] Walker, *Popular Justice.*

[18] Reichel, "Southern Slave Patrols as a Transitional Police Type."

[19] Dulaney, *Black Police in America,* 2.

[20] Brown, "Policing in American History."

there was little to no formal (i.e., U.S.) law and no formal property rights per se.[21] As a result, frontier policing was organized around controlling lands that settlers did not own, removing indigenous people from those lands while responding to the backlash effects and resistance efforts through vigilantism, and using the "posse" to round up "wanted" individuals who violated the new social order.[22] Because Western expansion preceded formal U.S. law, early frontier policing was inherently informal and frequently uneven in its application.[23] By 1873, however, informal vigilante policing along the frontier had largely given way to formal mounted constabularies, such as the Texas Rangers, constituting the first official police forces in the Southwest territories, the Great Plains, and even into Canada with the formation of the Royal Canadian Mounted Police.[24]

Thus, from the most reliable and thorough historical writings, it appears that the strands of early U.S. policing originated in at least three different regions—Northern industrial cities, the South, and the frontiers of the West and Great Plains—each with its unique territorial style largely based on specific geographic, social, and political contexts.[25] Still, despite different roles and tactics, nineteenth-century regionalized policing systems were characterized by a few common attributes, leading them to converge into a single system as they transitioned to modern policing.

First, all three regional policing systems seemed to emphasize the need to control so-called dangerous classes. In Northern industrial cities, the dangerous classes were primarily made up of newly arrived immigrants, particularly the Irish, who were seen as a threat to the upper classes and the moral order of the city more generally.[26] The dangerous classes—or more specifically, those who needed active controlling—in the Southern slave states were African Americans, and the dangerous classes along the frontier mostly comprised indigenous peoples or Native Americans. In the early generations of regionalized formal U.S. policing, police forces focused their control efforts mostly on groups of people rather than on specified areas (i.e., beats or zones)—a strategy that would shift during the mid-twentieth century.

Next, at least in the industrial North and in the South, early regional policing systems were used to respond to—and attempt to put down—revolts. In the urban North, for example, the informal (unpaid) constable-watch police force in Cincinnati tried unsuccessfully to quell an urban race riot in 1842, which led to the deployment of military troops and the subsequent

---

[21] Langworthy and Travis, *Policing in America: A Balance in Forces.*
[22] Reichel, "Southern Slave Patrols as a Transitional Police Type."
[23] Langworthy and Travis, *Policing in America: A Balance in Forces.*
[24] Graybill, *Policing the Great Plains: Rangers, Mounties, and the North American Frontier, 1875–1910.*
[24] Graybill, *Policing the Great Plains: Rangers, Mounties, and the North American Frontier, 1875–1910.*
[25] Miller, *Cops and Bobbies: Police Authority in New York and London, 1830-1870*; Palmer, *Police and Protest in England and Ireland: 1780–1850*; Dulaney, *Black Police in America*; Langworthy and Travis, *Policing in America: A Balance in Forces*; Graybill, *Policing the Great Plains: Rangers, Mounties, and the North American Frontier, 1875–1910*; Monkkonen, "History of Urban Police"; Brown, "Policing in American History"; Lane, "Urban Police and Crime in Nineteenth-Century America."
[26] Miller, *Cops and Bobbies: Police Authority in New York and London, 1830–1870.*

creation of the Police Guard[27]—a precursor to the Cincinnati Police Department. In Philadelphia, the Nativist Riots, which occurred in May through July 1844, were so destructive (particularly in the Kensington neighborhood) that they led to the creation of both a paid Philadelphia Police Department and a dedicated riot division (linked to the Pennsylvania militia) that was the first to wear formal and recognizable police uniforms.[28] The Draft Riots of 1862 in New York City are another example of urban policing attempting to control—unsuccessful though they were—a massive riot.[29]

In the Southern states that practiced slavery before the Civil War, the "free" populations lived in regular fear of "slave revolts" and "conspiracies,"[30] legitimizing (in their minds) the use of slave patrols to both respond to revolts (the Southern analogue to riots) and uncover attempts to organize them. The perceived need to prevent slave revolts was particularly strong in Southern states where the enslaved populations "approached, or were in fact, the numeric majority,"[31] such as in South Carolina and Virginia,[32] two states that experienced some of the deadliest revolts. Indeed, the Stono Rebellion of 1739—so named because it originated along the banks of the Stono River, just 20 miles outside Charleston[33]—was the largest slave revolt during the Colonial era and was responsible for the establishment of the slave patrol system in South Carolina.[34] In 1831, the Nat Turner Rebellion, which originated in Southampton County, Virginia, was among the most consequential slave revolts because of the number of White people it killed (between 57 and 60), and how close it came to breaching the armory in Jerusalem, Virginia.[35]

In addition to their roles of controlling the dangerous classes and responding to riots and revolts (at least in the North and South), early regionalized policing systems often relied on the military for help in reestablishing and maintaining social order during times of unrest; and all three regional systems used the military as an organizational model as they developed formalized systems of policing. Along the frontier it was the U.S. Calvary;[36] in the South it was a combination of the U.S. Army and state militias;[37] and in the industrial North it was a combination of state militias and the British Army[38]—insomuch as the British Army served as the organizational model

---

[27] Monkkonen, *Police in Urban America: 1860–1920.*
[28] Montgomery, "The Shuttle and the Cross: Weavers and Artisans in the Kensington Riots of 1844."
[29] Monkkonen, *Police in Urban America: 1860–1920.*
[30] Reichel, "Southern Slave Patrols as a Transitional Police Type," 55.
[31] Reichel, 57.
[32] Greene and Harrington, *American Population Before the Federal Census of 1790.*
[33] "Today in History—September 9."
[34] Reichel, "Southern Slave Patrols as a Transitional Police Type."
[35] Greenberg, *Nat Turner: A Slave Rebellion in History and Memory.*
[36] Little and Sheffield, "Frontiers and Criminal Justice: English Private Prosecution Societies and American Vigilantism in the Eighteenth and Nineteenth Centuries"; Graybill, *Policing the Great Plains: Rangers, Mounties, and the North American Frontier, 1875–1910.*
[37] Reichel, "Southern Slave Patrols as a Transitional Police Type"; Greenberg, *Nat Turner: A Slave Rebellion in History and Memory.*
[38] Monkkonen, *Police in Urban America: 1860–1920*; Miller, *Cops and Bobbies: Police Authority in New York and London, 1830–1870.*

for the London Metropolitan Police Department, which served as the model of the New York City Police Department.[39] Through the close of the nineteenth century and into the twentieth Century, the threads of regionalized policing began to merge into a type of policing recognizable by contemporary standards. As Brown[40] aptly observed:

> It is important to understand how policing developed in the early stages, in the early history and traditions of these regions, because over time policing in America became a blend of these traditions and practices. Changes in technology, laws, the development and implementation of professional standards, and changes in societal norms have surely improved many aspects of American policing. (190)

Although the assertion of improved policing maybe an arguable point, the convergence of regional policing systems into a U.S. policing paradigm, at least in terms of a crime-fighting goal and exertion of social control through the exercise of geographic territoriality (i.e., the patrol function), seems apparent.

Models of U.S. Police Organizations: A Study in Contradictions

The modern American police department represents some combination of "street-level bureaucracy" and quasi-military organization. Within that collective organizational model, police agencies also own a monopoly on the general right to use coercive force. As such, police agencies tend to emphasize authority, control, chain of command, safety, and discipline, which they draw from military bureaucracy. They are also rather "messy" organizations, however, sharing much in common with other public agencies that "process people,"[41] such as welfare offices, public schools, public health offices, and municipal courts. Line officers are supposedly given very little authority to exercise discretion when carrying out their occupational duties, as dictated by the quasi-military aspects of their organizations; and yet, because most street-level officers (unlike military foot soldiers) conduct their work generally beyond the eyes of their immediate supervisors, they exercise discretion with virtually every step they take.

Michael Lipsky coined the term "street-level bureaucracy" to describe government organizations that provide social and public services. Lipsky noted that police and other social service agencies are made up of employees who "interact with and have wide discretion over the dispensation of benefits or the allocation of public sanctions."[42] Indeed, Lipsky identified several

---

[39] Miller, *Cops and Bobbies: Police Authority in New York and London, 1830–1870.*
[40] Brown, "Policing in American History."
[41] Kappeler, Sluder, and Alpert, "Breeding Deviant Conformity: The Ideology and Culture of Police," 192.
[42] Lipsky, *Street-Level Bureaucracy: Dilemmas of the Individuals in Public Services,* xi.

occupational elements associated with the jobs of "street-level bureaucrats," such as discretionary decision-making, working in uncertain environments, and allocating resources in ways that sometimes conflict with law and policy. It was as if Lipsky was specifically writing about the world of street-level policing! Importantly, Lipsky went on to argue that, given the autonomy that street-level bureaucrats (e.g., line-level police officers) enjoy, in conjunction with the stressful environments in which they often work, they become accountable not just to the hierarchies of their organizations, but also to each other in their workgroups through the process of creating informal norms of occupational conduct.

To a great extent, Lipsky's identification and discussion of street-level bureaucracies—and linking them specifically to police and policing (among other organizations)—has great implications for the examination of police discretion and policing subcultures. Although police subcultures and police discretion are more fully discussed in Chapters 5 and 7, respectively, they are important to identify here as the by-products of street-level bureaucracies because they exist in opposition to the quasi-military model of policing.

What is that model? When Sir Robert Peel established the London Metropolitan Police Department in 1829, he modeled its organizational structure after the British Army, largely because the army was among the most successful bureaucracies known at that time, and it was viewed as having great legitimacy.[43] When New York City created its police force in 1844, it used the London Met as a loose template, adopting military ranks for police supervisors, using morning roll calls as an analogue to military reveille, requiring military-style uniforms, and even training police officers to conduct parade drills.[44] In one major departure from the British model, the new NYPD almost immediately issued its officers firearms as part of their duty equipment.[45] Even at that time, however, use of firearms by police was not particularly controversial, given the Second Amendment and the "gun culture" that seemed to develop during the American Colonial era.[46]

Thus, the modern U.S. police department to some extent exists at odds with itself in terms of its daily operations and overall organizational philosophy. On one hand, it emphasizes hierarchical structures and chain of command, where everyone in the organization has a supervisor, and every supervisor is supposed to maintain direct control over their subordinates. Police officers are expected to exercise limited discretion and are required to document virtually every official field contact and decision they make. The realities of the job make this chain-of-command structure virtually impossible to fully adhere to because so much of street-level policing occurs beyond the reach of supervisors and involves situations or conflicts best resolved without formal—or even enforcement—interventions. In short, the

---

[43] Miller, *Cops and Bobbies: Police Authority in New York and London, 1830–1870.*
[44] Lane, "Urban Police and Crime in Nineteenth-Century America."
[45] Lane.
[46] Anderson and Kennett, *The Gun in America: The Origins of a National Dilemma.*

job of processing people does not always conform to the inflexible nature of a quasi-military organizational structure. In fact, the military model might hinder good decision-making among police officers who are forced by the rank structure and military mindset to make decisions based on norms of enforcement, authority, and control rather than on what a member of the public might actually need at any given moment (more on this in Chapter 7 and Part III more generally).

The Structure of U.S. Police Departments

For the most part, police departments are bureaucracies. Although bureaucracies are often maligned as inefficient, ineffective, inflexible, and cumbersome, the fact is that bureaucracies help organizations accomplish two goals: (1) divide up the work of the organization, and (2) coordinate the workload of the organization.[47] So, if the goals of most police departments are to respond to emergencies, fight crime, and reduce victimizations (among others) while maintaining quasi-military lines of control and communication, then a bureaucracy provides the infrastructure to help them accomplish those goals.

Between the late 1960s and the mid-1980s, a large body of research developed that examined the nature of organizations, contributing to a comprehensive understanding of the behaviors of individuals who make up organizations, the behaviors of the organizations themselves, and the relationships organizations maintained with their external environments.[48] More recently, in his large study of police organizations, Maguire synthesized much of that early work, noting that when it comes to trying to understand the organizational structure of police departments, it is useful to think about "structure" in terms of two dimensions: structural "complexity" and structural "control."[49]

Structural complexity, Maguire notes, describes the degree of organizational differentiation that police departments maintain, such as how hierarchical their rank and chain-of-command structures are (i.e., vertical differentiation), how many divisions and units exist within the organization (i.e., functional differentiation), and how much territory or space they have to control (i.e., spatial differentiation). The more vertical and hierarchical the rank structure, the more administrative units that exist, and the more physical territory there is to cover, the greater the complexity within a police organization.

Structural control describes how the police department is set up to coordinate the work of the organization and can be understood in terms of

---

[47] Scott, *Organizations: Rational, Natural, and Open Systems.*
[48] A small, but representative sample, of this collective work: Robbins, *Organization Theory: Structure, Design, and Applications*; Hall, Johnson, and Haas, "Organizational Size, Complexity, and Formalization"; Pugh et al., "Dimensions of Organizational Commitment"; Kasarda, "The Structural Implications of Social System Size: A Three-Level Analysis."
[49] Maguire, *Organizational Structure in American Police Agencies: Context, Complexity, and Control*, 13.

administration, formalization, and centralization.[50] According to Maguire, administration refers to density of the administrative infrastructure designed to maintain the organization itself (e.g., budgeting, managing contracts, alarm permits, facilities, etc.). Formalization describes the complexity of the written rules and how the organization governs itself and its employees. The more formalized a police organization is, for example, the more it governs the behaviors of its employees by policies, procedures, and general orders. Finally, centralization represents how much "the decision-making capacity within an organization is concentrated in a single individual or small, select groups." Perhaps the best way to illustrate structural complexity and structural control is through the organizational chart of an actual police department.

Figure 2.1 represents the organizational chart for the Metropolitan Police Department of the District of Columbia (MPD). This is the municipal department that polices Washington, DC, employing just under 3,800 full-time sworn officers and covering a geographic area of 68 square miles. It has primary jurisdiction over the 700,000-plus residents of Washington, DC.[51]

The MPD ranks as the sixth largest municipal police department in the United States[52] and is made up of eight distinct bureaus. As Figure 2.1 shows, the Office of the Chief of Police is represented by a red bubble, the bureaus are represented by blue bubbles, and the units within the bureaus are represented by yellow bubbles. Figure 2.1 also shows that the MPD maintains a high degree of functional differentiation, as the bureaus range from Patrol, to Homeland Security, to Internal Affairs, to Information Technology, and so on. In terms of MPD's functional differentiation, two observations are worth making. First, note that Patrol Services are split into two bureaus, indicating the complexity of managing the city's territory. DC is a fairly compact city, bounded by the Potomac River on its western border, but it is subjected to a great deal of pedestrian and vehicular traffic, large daytime fluctuations in its population due to commuters, many year-round tourists, and numerous public events due to sports, government, and entertainment—all of which make it difficult to effectively patrol.

Next, both Internal Affairs and Information Technology (IT) are organized into their own bureaus, demonstrating the importance the department places on both those aspects of the organization. The Internal Affairs Bureau (IAB) in any police department is the unit that receives and investigates complaints against police officers, which can originate from members of the public, other police officers, or police supervisors. Historically, the IAB might be a unit under a larger bureau, making it difficult for the commander of the IAB to report findings to the chief, given the chain-of-command structure. Or the IAB might not exist at all. Contemporary police organizations with any degree of complexity normally maintain an IAB, and for such bureaus to be effective and independent, they must have a direct line to the chief of

---

[50] Maguire, 16–18.
[51] "Metropolitan Police Department, District of Columbia."
[52] "The Largest Police Departments in the US - WorldAtlas."

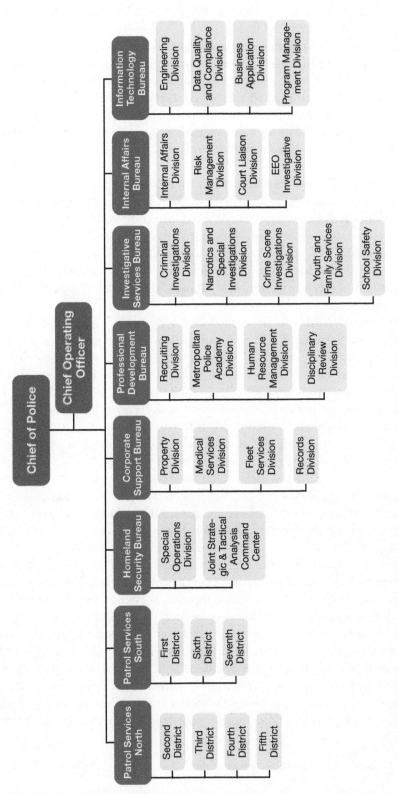

▲ **Figure 2.1** Organizational Chart of the Metropolitan Police Department, Washington, DC.

police. As Figure 2.1 shows, commander of the IAB (blue bubble) indeed reports directly to the chief of police.

The Information Technology Bureau also has a direct line to the Chief of Police and maintains units related to software management, data quality, business applications, and program management. This is the bureau that houses and maintains the RMS described earlier in this chapter. Over the generations, IT has become an increasingly important division in midsize to large police departments as data collection, quality, storage, and analysis have become central to policing operations.

Figure 2.1 also suggests something about the MPD's structural control capacities. The administration density is high, with two of the department's eight bureaus—Corporate and Support, and Professional Development—existing to maintain the organization. Within Corporate and Support, for example, are the divisions responsible for maintaining records, the department's facilities, and fleets of vehicles. Professional Development contains human resources and recruiting divisions. Figure 2.1 also demonstrates that the MPD relies on highly centralized decision-making, as all the bureau chiefs report directly to the chief of police.

Finally, there is little to no cross-bureau reporting, indicating a mostly vertical chain-of-command and communication structure. A sergeant in the Fifth Patrol District, for example, who wanted to report something to a colleague in the First Patrol District would have to send the communication up through the chain of command to the chief of Patrol Services North, who might then send the communication over to the Patrol Services South bureau chief, who might then send it down to the colleague in the First Patrol District. Of course, the formal chain of command excludes (on paper) the informal communication channels that develop in agencies where people move from one assignment to the next. That same sergeant in the Fifth Patrol District could just as easily pick up the phone and call the colleague in the First Patrol District and relay whatever information there was to give. Such circumventing is often effective, but then the organization has no record of the communication, which would violate the chain of command.

According to Maguire in his comprehensive study of police organizations, the complexity and structure of police agencies are largely determined by four primary factors:[53] age of the organization, size, access to and use of technology, and the environment in which it is located. In general, as police departments age, they tend to add new organizational or administrative structures to previously existing ones, increasing their structural complexity.[54] As they grow in size, their workload and workforce tend to increase, requiring more structural differentiation and structural control; and as they invest in new technologies (e.g., RMS, police-worn body cameras, license plate readers, and new types of patrol vehicles), they must increase both their operational

[53] Maguire, *Organizational Structure in American Police Agencies: Context, Complexity, and Control*, 19–34.

[54] Kriesburg, "Centralization and Differentiation in International Non-Governmental Organizations."

and administrative support structures to integrate the technologies into the organization and maintain them. Finally, as a police department's environment becomes more complex and more uncertain, as the population over which it has jurisdiction grows in size and diversity, and as more people "call the cops," the agency increases its structural diversity and control.

That is the subject of the remainder of this chapter: the environment in which police departments reside. As noted in Chapter 1, "calling the cops" is why we have police in the first place. Since at least the 1950s, police departments have been set up to get to those callers as soon as possible.[55]

Police Patrol and the Management of Space

Police scholars will often assert that police patrols have been around since thirteenth-century England.[56] This might have been true during the nightwatch era of informal policing and throughout the history of formalized policing in the United States, but the concept of preventive patrol—that is, police officers deployed mostly in cars to designated beat areas so they could quickly respond to calls for service—was not translated into a "police science" until the 1930s by O. W. Wilson. As the chief of three different police departments during a career that spanned from 1925 to 1967, Wilson worked to create a "professional" police service that would require a college education for officers, rigorous accountability standards, adherence to a quasi-military organizational structure, and the sweeping use of patrol cars (equipped with two-way radios) to give an impression of police "omnipresence" in a city.[57] As Wilson noted in his classic textbook on police administration, "Patrol is an indispensable service that plays a leading role in the accomplishment of the police purpose. It is the only form of police service that directly attempts to eliminate opportunity for (criminal) misconduct."[58]

To Wilson, patrol was the backbone of U.S. policing. It was how police departments managed crime and service demands in the city. More fundamentally, patrol is the mechanism police departments use to enforce the social order and maintain social control.[59] All political jurisdictions are bounded by geographic borders, and the authorities distribute their social control within those borders. Recall, for example, our definition of the police from Chapter 1: an institution whose members possess the general right to use coercive force within the boundaries of the state. For the most part, the way the police distribute that coercive force is through the exercise of territoriality, or the police patrol function, within designated police service areas, or beats.

---

[55] Kansas City Police Department, "Police Response Time Analysis, 1975."
[56] Kelling et al., "The Kansas City Preventive Patrol Experiment: A Summary Report."
[57] Bopp, "OW Wilson and the Search for a Police Profession."
[58] Wilson, *Police Administration*.
[59] Herbert, "The Normative Ordering of Police Territoriality: Making and Marking Space with the Los Angeles Police Department."

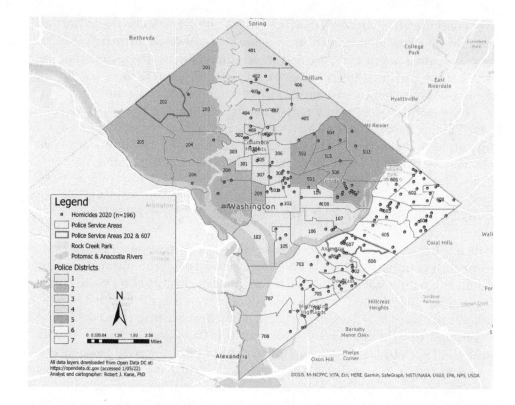

Let us return to Washington, DC, for an illustrative example. Recall from Figure 2.1 that the MPD maintains two patrol bureaus: North and South. Within those bureaus are contained seven police districts. The districts are then subdivided into 57 police service areas, which represent the geographic beats that officers patrol. Figure 2.2 visually represents those districts and beat areas, along with the known homicide counts for the year 2020.

Figure 2.2 shows the police districts delineated by unique colors with the outlines and numeric designations of the police service areas (PSAs) contained within them. Note that from a taxonomy standpoint, the first number of each PSA derives from the district in which it resides. For example, all PSAs in the 7th District begin with the number 7, and so on. This is important because most police officers are assigned to a district, with stations that function almost as autonomous police departments. During any given shift, two to three uniformed patrol units will be assigned to each PSA; frequently (particularly in larger cities, such as Washington, DC), each shift also maintains a division-wide tactical unit that focuses on a specific problem affecting one or more PSAs in the district. These tactical units can be staffed by either plainclothes officers in unmarked vehicles or uniformed officers in marked patrol vehicles, depending on their specific missions. They are generally free to travel throughout the district. (Chapter 10 provides an example of how tactical units are sometimes deployed for "predictive policing" purposes.)

Figure 2.2 also shows how DC used the natural topography of the city to inform the drawing of the district boundaries. Using natural land breaks, geologic features, and even large roads to bound police districts is common practice in most cities and helps to create "natural" divisions between district or beat areas (depending on the size of the jurisdiction). In DC, for example, Rock Creek Park (pictured in Figure 2.2) generally runs north–south, dividing the 2nd and 4th districts; it also serves as the boundary between Northwest and Northeast DC. The National Mall (not shown), along with the major federal government buildings, are encapsulated primarily by the 1st District. The Anacostia River, which runs south by southeast through the city until draining into the Potomac River, divides the 6th and 7th Districts from the 1st and 5th Districts.

As Figure 2.2 also shows, the same topographic features of DC that create district boundaries also appear to constrain violent crime—as they do in many cities[60]—at least in terms of homicides. Note, for example, that most of the homicides reported in 2020 were clustered in the 6th and 7th Districts, which reside below (or southeast of) the Anacostia River. The remaining homicides tended to cluster in the 3rd, 4th, and 5th Districts. Interestingly, homicides in the 1st District tended to occur along the boundaries of the 3rd, 5th, and 6th Districts. Perhaps the most noteworthy visual element in Figure 2.2 is the contrast in homicide patterns between the 2nd District (particularly west of Rock Creek Park) and the 6th and 7th Districts: Districts 6 and 7, which collectively cover 19.64 square miles, experienced 114 homicides, representing 58 percent of the citywide total; District 2, which covers 18.9 square miles, contained just six homicides, representing just .03 percent of the citywide total. How was it that areas of the city almost equal in size experienced such disparate patterns of homicide in 2020? Moving to an even lower unit of geography in those districts, Figure 2.2 shows that PSA 202 experienced no homicides in 2020, whereas PSA 607 experienced eight homicides. Again, what accounts for these differences, and how might such differential exposure to community violence influence how the police department operates in those PSAs? Table 2.1 summarizes the demographic features of PSAs 202 and 607.

A review of Table 2.1 shows several stark differences in the social and economic conditions of PSAs 202 and 607. The median household income in PSA 202 is $189,915 and the median disposable income is $126,956. The median household income in PSA 607 is $43,121 and the median disposable income is just $36,253. Of particular note is the difference in median net worth: In PSA 202, the median net worth is just over $1 million, whereas in PSA 607 it is just under $16,000. Moreover, in PSA 202 only 1 percent of the adult population does not have a high school diploma, and 88 percent of the adult population has at least a bachelor's degree. In PSA 607, 11 percent of the adult population does not have a high school diploma, and only 24 percent of the adult population has at least a bachelor's degree. The social and economic conditions, coupled with the relatively large number of homicides in PSA 607,

---

[60] Farrell, "Crime Concentration Theory."

Table 2.1 Demographic Comparison of PSA 202 and PSA 607

	PSA 202	PSA 607
Key facts		
Population	13,017	10,600
Households	4,840	4,737
Median age	41.2	41.9
Median household income	$126,956	$36,253
Education		
No high school diploma	1%	11%
High school graduate	3%	33%
Some college	8%	32%
Bachelor's/graduate/ professional degree	88%	24%
Employment		
White collar	94%	68%
Blue collar	2%	16%
Services	4%	17%
Unemployed	2.1%	14.6%
Income		
Median household income	$189,915	$43,121
Per-capita income	$97,428	$29,165
Median net worth	$1,045,950	$15,992

Source: U.S. Census Bureau (2022). *2016–2020 American Community Survey 5-Year Estimates, Washington, DC.* Retrieved from https://data.census.gov/cedsci/profile?g=1600000US1150000 (accessed March 31, 2022).

suggest a very challenging environment for those who reside there, particularly when contrasted with the same indicators in PSA 202.

Such different social, economic, and risk conditions in these PSAs affects both the crime control strategies of the MPD and the tactics of officers. Indeed, the local conditions of different PSAs have profound consequences for how officers interact with residents of those beats, how those beats might shape officers' worldviews, and how those worldviews might shape the enforcement behaviors of officers.[61] Thus, officers assigned to one beat area in

---

[61] Klinger, "Negotiating Order in Patrol Work: An Ecological Theory of Police Response To Deviance"; Herbert, *Policing Space: Territoriality and the Los Angeles Police Department*; Kane, "The Social Ecology of Police Misconduct."

one part of a city will have different police–public interactions than officers assigned to another beat area in a different part of the city. These interactions help to shape workgroup norms, which ultimately leads to the formation of different police subcultures, often within the same city.[62] (Chapter 5 explores policing subcultures in great detail.)

The initial pages of this chapter noted that the modern U.S. police department is, organizationally speaking, two agencies. One is physical, the other is digital, and the functions of both can influence the other. While police officers patrol their beats or service areas and contact people for a variety of reasons, they are also collecting information and feeding it back to the police department's RMS. Every time officers run a driver's license or license plate check, conduct a stop-and-frisk or a vehicle stop, write a summons, or make an arrest, they are sending information to the RMS. When the crime analysts run their hot-spot analyses and create "risk profiles" of certain communities, they send that information back to the officers, creating and reinforcing ideas about where the "problem places" are in a given jurisdiction.

Thus, through the patrol function of police departments, police officers travel through geographic and social space, painting a composite picture of the city in the form of points on a map. As the points become aggregated into PSAs or districts to tell a "story" about crime, drug deals, drug use, and weapons, they allow the department and individual officers to make inferences about those places—and ultimately, about the people who live there. Such inferences can affect the ways in which police officers approach people in their working environments. As Part II will show, these inferences can often explain stop-and-frisk patterns, use of force, and the use of deadly force.

Some Concluding Observations

In its earliest forms in the United States, policing adopted the quasi-military organizational model that emphasized chain of command, authority, discipline, and adherence to specified lines of communication. Although it is probably true that certain police deployments (e.g., SWAT or PPUs) and certain exigencies that departments face, such as barricaded persons and hostage situations, active shooter events, or mass incidents of civil unrest, require military-like coordination, communication, and execution of tactics—loosely justifying the quasi-military model—most policing is done between people. That is, most policing involves cops trying to figure out how best to manage disagreements between store owners and alleged shoplifters, find kids who wander off the playground, decide whether to issue a summons or make an arrest for the possession of marijuana, and convince people who get into fender benders in shopping mall parking lots that those are civil rather than criminal matters. In other words, and for the most part, although policing is organized around the quasi-military model—governed by policies, procedures, and general

---

[62] Herbert, "Police Subculture Reconsidered."

orders—it is mostly a street-level bureaucracy, particularly as one moves down the chain of command from police headquarters to the street.

Still, for all its limitations, the quasi-military model presents great opportunities for police departments to make positive impacts in some of the most vulnerable communities. As noted at the start of this chapter, the police are everywhere. They are the only full-time public agency deployed in virtually every part of the city (or other jurisdictions that maintain a police department) to drive around and mingle with members of the public in nonemergency situations. The structural features of police bureaucracies make police departments efficient at coordinating work from the chief of police down to a single officer working a specified sector. If police agencies reduced some of their military rhetoric and recognized that that their role isn't just law enforcement and social control, they could increase the quality of their contacts with members of the public in ways that ultimately reduce crime through a protection of life mindset. The chapters in Part III explore these issues in greater detail.

A Case Study to Introduce the Operations Dashboards

As noted in Chapter 1, *Policing Beyond Coercion* makes use of three operations dashboards maintained by the author to help readers visually understand how social and economic demographics, land use, crime, health, and policing data intersect in ways that might inform police resource deployments and explain community crime and health problems. Although all three dashboards include crime and policing data, they each also contain unique data elements that allow users to explore different aspects of crime and policing in different cities. Operations dashboards typically bring in a combination of live data feeds and static data sources (e.g., locations of police stations, fire departments, schools, hospitals, parks, etc.) to visualize on a map, which is often surrounded by charts and other graphical data summaries. Dashboards typically allow users to activate different data layers, change features (e.g., crimes) to be visualized on the map, change the geographic focus, manipulate time, and change the mapping canvas (called a basemap) to see different details of local land use.

Because the maps are interactive—for example, users can visualize attributes such as crime by type, pedestrian and vehicle stops, police shootings, and arrests within different geographies—and because several sources of police data are based on live feeds, the dashboards are suitable for projects where students might explore relationships between different geographic elements, such as shootings located near schools, police arrests within different neighborhood contexts, or police "workload" across districts within the same city. Moreover, because many of the attributes include date and time fields, readers could examine, for example, how residential burglaries might have changed during the coronavirus quarantines, and how they changed as the

City	Summary of Data Elements	QR Code
Philadelphia	Live feeds for serious crimes, shooting victimizations, and police pedestrian stops. Users can select police districts, manipulate dates, and select times of day for display.	https://arcg.is/1v4CiX
San Francisco	Serious crimes, police arrests, EMS calls for service, community demographics. Users can select police districts and manipulate visualizations by date and time.	https://arcg.is/0SbK550
Washington, DC	Serious crimes, juvenile and adult arrests, shootings, community health and demographics, recent crime hot spots, pedestrian stops, layers suitable to conduct workload demand analysis.	https://arcg.is/1Sj8Hq

Table 2.2 Summary of Operations Dashboards to Be Used with This Book

cities began their phased reopenings. Table 2.2 summarizes the three operations dashboards and provides QR codes that can serve as weblinks to the dashboards.

The operations dashboards are optimized for larger screens, such as those on laptop and desktop computers. The best way to use the QR codes in Table 2.2 is to aim a phone or tablet camera at them to bring them up in the mobile browser. Once the dashboards are loaded, readers can save the URL as a shared bookmark (accessible across your devices), and then access the dashboards on a computer via the shared bookmark. Readers who do not use shared bookmarks can simply tap the URL in the mobile browser to copy it, and then paste it into an email to send to themselves.

As an introduction to the dashboards and how to navigate them, the following exercise is designed to show readers the fundamental elements of an operations dashboard while also providing a demonstration of how they can be used. For the best experience, it is recommended that readers follow along with the case study below by opening the Philadelphia operations dashboard and taking the steps as directed in the case study. Because all three operations dashboards described in Table 2.2 share similar user interfaces, the use of the Philadelphia dashboard for this case study will also help readers quickly learn to navigate the dashboards for Washington, DC, and San Francisco.

Exercise in Patrol Deployments Using the Philadelphia Operations Dashboard

Thinking about police "territoriality," or the process that patrol officers use to make and mark space—as discussed earlier in the chapter—might lead us to wonder how a police department uses crime data to inform its deployment of officers, especially to target a specific crime. Imagine you are the new inspector in charge of the 39th Police District in Philadelphia. You are interested in trying to make a quick impact on a specific crime problem, so you work with your crime analysts to figure out the best ways to identify the most reasonable crime to target. You plan to use information you gather about specific crimes to direct your patrol resources to the places and times of most need. At the moment, however, you do not know which crime(s) to focus on, and you do not know where or when to send the extra patrol teams you have at your disposal. To acquire this information, you will refer to your operations dashboard.

As noted above, it will be instructive for readers to follow along with this exercise. To do so, using a desktop or laptop computer, navigate to the Philadelphia operations dashboard using the QR code contained in Table 2.2. Once you open the dashboard, spend a few minutes taking in the visualizations to understand the information that the data feeds, charts, and map are conveying. Feel free to click around the dashboard, selecting different tables to change feeds, charts, and time graphics. Examine the crime summaries and become familiar with the data elements contained in the dashboard. It is important to keep in mind that the Philadelphia dashboard includes just serious crimes (in addition to police pedestrian stops and shooting victimizations): aggravated assault (with and without a firearm), burglary (residential and commercial), criminal homicide, robbery (with and without a firearm), and rape.

For this exercise, you will assume the hypothetical role of the 39th District's inspector, which means you will want to select that district and focus on the crimes contained within it. Also, given that recent crimes are often the best predictors of near-future crime (we discuss this more in Chapter 11), you will want to focus on serious crimes that have occurred in just the past three months. Given these parameters, you will need to make some selections in the dashboard. Note that the crime, shootings, and pedestrian stop data feeds are live, and they automatically update daily, which means their patterns and distributions will change over time. To try to ensure that the data you see in the dashboard are mostly consistent with the data as of this writing (and thus described in this exercise), you will need to "freeze" the time period in the operations dashboard. To do so, locate the banner across the top of the dashboard that reads, "Show Crimes & Pedestrian Stops that occurred during past" and select the "For Chapter 2 Tutorial" option in the dropdown menu. This will allow you to restore crime, shooting, and pedestrian stop patterns to the point in time of this writing. Still, given the ways in which crimes can become recoded after being initially recorded, the patterns you see in the dashboard may not fully match the descriptions in this exercise.

Next, use the drop-down menu to select Police District 39. Once selected, the map should pan to the 39th District and highlight its boundaries for approximately five seconds. Depending on Internet speed and the amount of traffic on the Esri and Philadelphia servers, it might take the elements (map, charts, time feed, etc.) a minute or two to refresh. Once the visualizations update, use the layer selector button to select Serious Crime Incidents by checking the box next to the layer name. Doing so will simplify the visualization if pedestrian stops and shooting victimizations are not selected (i.e., leaving their layer boxes unchecked). You should also make sure the subway stations are selected, given that Philadelphia's Broad Street Line runs north–south along the eastern edge of the 39th District. Once you make your selections, zoom into the 39th District so that your map is almost exclusively focused on it. At this zoom level, the Police Service Areas layer (outlined and labeled in turquoise) should become visible so you can see the police beats within the 39th District. This will be important for directing patrol deployments.

Next, click the Crimes by the Hour tab under the map and examine the bar chart along with the Crimes by Type doughnut chart to the left. You should notice that beginning at 8:00 a.m., crimes per hour increase throughout the day, peaking during the 19:00 (7:00 p.m.) hour. Referring to the crime doughnut chart, notice that a few different crimes make up large sections of the graphic. Hovering your mouse over the doughnut pieces will bring up summaries of the numbers and percentages of crimes that make up each crime category shown in the doughnut chart. Remember that because you have selected the 39th District to visualize, the crime distributions shown in the doughnut chart refer to only this district.

At the time of this writing, aggravated assault with a firearm (bright green segment) was the most common serious crime in the 39th District for the prior three months, accounting for 25.39 percent ($n = 82$) of all crimes during the period. As important as that crime is, you (as inspector) also know it is difficult to prevent aggravated assaults through police patrols because they tend to be committed during "heat of the moment" arguments, and often indoors.[63] As such, you would rather focus your efforts on "serial" crimes (i.e., those typically committed for money and often in a sequence). Referring back to the doughnut chart – again, as of this writing—robbery with a firearm (i.e., a serial crime) has accounted for 17.34 percent of the crimes, representing a large proportion of all serious crimes. You decide to focus on robberies with a firearm for this operation because of its seriousness and the fact that it is often considered a "suppressible" crime.[64]

In the dashboard, click the Robbery with a Firearm doughnut piece to filter out all other crimes. Again, it might take a minute or so for the crimes to filter. Next, click the Crimes by Hour tab at the bottom of the map display to bring up the bar chart showing the numbers of crimes committed during each hour of the day. Then observe during which hour of the day robberies with a firearm have been most common. Select the most common hour of the day and observe how that changes the doughnut chart.

As of this writing, the 19:00 (7:00 p.m.) hour was the most common for robberies with a firearm. Select the 19:00 bar by clicking on it and notice that robbery with a firearm now becomes the most common serious crime in the 39th District, accounting for 30 percent ($n = 8$) of all serious crimes in the district. That is, while aggravated assaults with a firearm represent the most common serious crime in the 39th District over the prior three months, during the 7:00 p.m. hour, robbery with a firearm has been the most common.

In the dashboard, click the Map tab to redisplay the map. You should still be focused on the 39th District and should see the nine robberies visualized as yellow points. At this point, it is useful to make the map as large as possible so you can zoom down to a low elevation to view the district. To accomplish this, click the window expander symbol in the upper-right corner of the map, just above and to the right of the action menu.

Once you have expanded the map to its full extent, zoom into the 39th District again to view all the robberies that occurred in the past three months during the 7:00 p.m. hour. The first thing to notice is that eight of the nine robberies occurred in PSAs 392 and 393, which represent the southeast section of the district. At least four of the robberies were committed very close to subway stations (visualized on the map and in the figure as orange diamonds), suggesting that offenders might have (1) robbed their victims just after coming up from the stations, or (2) used the subway as a quick getaway after committing the robberies. It is important to point out that although the map shows just seven robberies in PSAs 392 and 393, it obscures the fact that two robberies were committed in the same location on different dates. Close inspection of the robbery committed near the subway station at North Broad and West Allegheny shows that the symbol is somewhat larger and brighter than the others plotted on the map. This means that more than one

---

[63] Kane, "On the Limits of Social Control: Structural Deterrence and the Policing of 'Suppressible' Crimes."

[64] Kane.

robbery was geocoded to that location. Clicking the robbery will open a pop-up window that describes each layer visualized on the map. It will show, for example, the PSA and district layers, as well as the robberies.

Clicking the left or right arrows along the header of the pop-up window allows the user to scroll through the selected mapped elements. The fourth and fifth elements are the two robberies geocoded at the same location. Notice that when the pop-up window shows the details of the robberies, the robbery symbol on the map becomes selected, indicated by the blue square that delineates it.

Click out of the pop-up window and scroll south and west until centered on PSA 393. Visual inspection shows that three robberies occurred in somewhat close proximity to one another over the prior three months during the 7:00 p.m. hour. To get a better sense of why these robberies might have concentrated in that location, change the basemap from Dark Grey Canvas to Open Street Map to see the local land usage. To make the switch, click the basemap symbol on the right side of the action menu in the top-right corner of the map. Scroll down and select the Open Streets basemap, as this map is excellent for showing local land use features. After changing the basemap, visually relocate the three robberies, which will be more difficult to spot on the lighter canvas.

As the map shows, the robberies seem to be constrained by the rail lines heading northwest, Fox Street heading south by southeast, West Indiana Avenue that generally runs east–west, and North 20th Street that generally runs north–south. That rough catchment area contains mostly residential housing, a considerable number of churches, and a large playground in the approximate center (the Vincent G. Panati Playground). As a police inspector, it would be your job to try to make sense of these results. Crime pattern theory generally tells you that certain features of the built environment, such as subway stations, often attract certain types of crimes, such as robbery, because they facilitate a quick mode of escape.[65] Thus, referring back to the dashboard suggests that the robberies in PSA 392 were likely committed by different offenders who might have used the subway stations to facilitate their crimes. This might lead you to create a police operation involving plainclothes officers deployed during the 7:00 p.m. hour to conduct surveillance at the subway stations and quickly intervene if they see a crime in progress. You might also increase patrol presence around the three subway stations during the 7:00 p.m. hour to discourage further robberies from being committed. The advantage of examining specific crimes at a certain time is that it allows police commanders to deploy additional resources at targeted locations and times. This is where "preventive" patrol becomes "directed" patrol (more on this in Chapter 11).

The robberies that occurred in PSA 393 seem to have different origins than those near the subway stops in PSA 392. The so-called "near repeat"

---

[65] Weisburd and Amram, "The Law of Concentrations of Crime at Place: The Case of Tel Aviv-Jaffa."

crime perspective generally predicts that serial crimes (e.g., burglary and robbery) committed in the same general location at roughly the same time of day likely have the same offender in common.[66] Thus, the three robberies committed over the past three months in that relatively small catchment area in PSA 393 might have been committed by the same offender, perhaps someone who lives or periodically stays in that area. As police inspector of the 39th District, you might take any combination of the following actions to catch the offender and prevent future robberies:

- Talk with local church leaders to find out if anyone new has moved into the community who might pose a risk to the residents.
- Check the RMS to learn if anyone has been released on parole into the community over the prior three months.
- Increase patrol presence in that relatively small area of PSA 393 during the 7:00 p.m. hour.
- Deploy plainclothes officers as decoys during the 7:00 p.m. hour in an effort to draw out the robbery offender.

This exercise represents an introduction to the operations dashboards while also showing readers how police organizations can use crime and other sources of data to deploy officers in ways that might address a crime problem. A primary point of this exercise was to demonstrate that without an analysis of local crimes over the prior three months, the police commander might not have even known to target the two areas contained in PSAs 392 and 393. Thus, use of the dashboards can lead to data-driven policing, which becomes the basic foundation of evidence-based policing (again, more on this in Chapter 11).

Readers who work through the dashboard-related exercises in this book might wish to consult a standard framework that helps evaluate the crime or public safety issues and inform the responses they develop. As the hypothetical inspector of the 39th District in Philadelphia, readers were presented with a crime problem and were then taken through a series of steps to address it. In subsequent exercises that use a similar pedagogy, readers can appeal to the SARA model of problem-oriented policing[67] to help guide their assessments and responses—particularly if they are assigned to create a written report for the exercises. The SARA model and its origins are described more thoroughly in Chapter 6, but its definition here can help readers navigate the dashboard exercises in a systematic way. The following is a summary of the SARA model and how it is often used in policing.

- **Scanning:** In the real world, officers, crime analysts, and even community members—sometimes together, sometimes independently—scan a local

---

[66] Glasner and Leitner, "Evaluating the Impact the Weekday Has on Near-Repeat Victimization: A Spatio-Temporal Analysis of Street Robberies in the City of Vienna, Austria."
[67] "The SARA Model | ASU Center for Problem-Oriented Policing."

area to identify emerging or persistent problems in the community that affect the safety of residents. In the exercise above, the scanning phase led the inspector to identify robberies with firearms as the problem of interest. The scanning process is not always data-driven; it is often based on personal observations, reports from community members, and discussions with officers working the street. Readers who work through the subsequent exercises will discover that much of the scanning has been done for them because the case studies often identify the problems of interest. But readers might also wish to supplement some of the scanning by conducting a bit of independent research that could include use of the dashboards and other sources of public data.

- **Analysis:** This phase identifies and clarifies the nature of the problem, often through the use of data, and often through discussions with relevant stakeholders. Analyzing the problem allows teams of police officers and commanders to learn of the problem's origins, how it persists, and how current police deployments might or might not be currently managing the problem. Readers working through the exercises can use the dashboards to examine the crime or public safety issues in local areas; they can change the basemaps to try to learn something about local land use; and they can conduct research outside the dashboards on the nature of certain crimes and how they often cluster in the physical environment. Readers might also use Google Street View to get a sense of what the physical land use looks like in the areas under analysis.

- **Response:** This is when officers and analysts (and readers) identify a range of possible solutions to the problem, often by relying on the kinds of materials contained in this book, as well as supplemental reading materials. Using this information, readers then create an action plan that they can implement in the hopes of solving the problem. Of course, it is understood that the dashboards show what is currently happening (or what has happened in the past); they do not allow users to create interventions or responses to the problems. This is where readers participating in the exercises will be asked to create responses informed by the academic and other materials they have read.

- **Assessment:** This is the evaluation phase where officers in the real world determine (1) whether the response they developed was actually implemented as planned, and (2) the extent to which the response solved the problem. Such an evaluation usually means that officers will continue to collect data—for example, calls for service information—to monitor the progress of the response. Readers participating in the exercises can write hypothetical assessments that identify where the responses were correct, or where the responses might have had no or deleterious outcomes.

Questions for Review and Reflection

Question 1. The "Tangled Roots" of U.S. Policing

As noted in the chapter, the origins of formalized policing in the American Colonies and ultimately the United States varied by the presumed "needs" of different regions: Northern cities used police to reduce crime and disorder; areas in the West and the Great Plains used police to support westward expansion; and Southern states adopted policing largely to maintain the plantation system, which relied on the enslavement of African American people.

■ Although the local circumstances of the three regions might have created different reasons for adopting formalized policing, there are likely some common themes among them. Identify some of those common themes. That is, what were police in the North, the South, and the West and Great Plains ultimately directed to accomplish in those regions?

■ Who were the "dangerous" classes and how were they generally treated by police?

■ In what ways did the police in each of those three regions look to the military for their organizational models?

Question 2. Police Organizations as "Self-Contradictions"

Policing across the United States has widely adopted the military model of organizational bureaucracy. It tends to rely on a military rank structure and maintains vertical lines of organizational communication to ensure the control of information. Yet, at the street level, police officers themselves have been called "street-level bureaucrats" who must operate outside the military organizational model to do their jobs effectively.

■ In what ways is the military model of U.S. policing an obstacle to police officers on the street who must help community members solve complicated, but often not crime-related, problems?

■ In what ways might the military model ensure that policing functions with efficiency and effectiveness from the office of the chief down to individual officers working the street?

■ How might police organizations alter their "vertical" and "functional" differentiations in ways that can accommodate the military bureaucratic structure while still allowing officers on the street to use their autonomous judgment for solving community problems?

Question 3. Policing on Patrol

Many scholars and police professionals have argued that patrol is the backbone of U.S. policing. That is, deploying officers to local beat areas and having them cover those areas for crime responses and prevention is the primary way police departments practice "territoriality" across their jurisdictions. Such a deployment paradigm, though, also means that some police officers will be differentially exposed to high-crime, highly disadvantaged communities for extended periods of time, which could affect the ways in which they respond to local residents.

■ Given the above, in what ways might the paradigm of deploying officers to specific beat areas—often for long periods of time—lead to the reinforcement of racial stereotypes in high-crime, highly disadvantaged communities of color?

- In what ways can police departments maintain their beat structures while ensuring that officers do not become burned out and develop negative views and behaviors toward people living in high-crime, highly disadvantaged communities?

- Are there better ways to deploy officers that do not rely on police beats? If so, what might be some examples of how police departments can ensure coverage while not deploying officers to specific geographic locations?

Exercises

Exercise 1. Police Paramilitary Structure in Your Own Backyard

Visit the website of your local police department and click through the pages it includes. Notice the pictures they post and the language they use. Keep in mind that police department websites are designed to convey information to the public.

- What messages is your police department conveying to members of your community?
- In what ways does your police department use military ranks in its description of officers? Does the website, for example, draw distinctions between "sworn" officers and "civilians?"
- Locate, if possible, the organizational chart of your police department and notice how it is drawn. Can you determine the extent to which the department is vertically and horizontally differentiated?
- Overall, to what extent does your local police department rely on a paramilitary organizational structure?
- What conclusions do you draw about your local police department from completing this exercise?

Exercise 2. Organizational Complexities of U.S. Police Departments

Conduct some research to identify three U.S. police departments located in differently sized jurisdictions. Find one that serves a population of up to 10,000 residents, one that serves a population between 40,000 and 60,000 residents, and a third department that serves a population of at least 250,000 residents. Locate the departments' organizational charts (similar to Figure 2.1) on their websites. Not all police departments (particularly smaller agencies) post their organizational charts on their websites, so keep searching for departments in the designated size ranges that do. Once you locate your three departments, review their organizational charts, and then answer the following questions.

- Describe the degrees to which each department is both vertically and functionally differentiated. How many different ranks can you identify on the organizational charts, and how many different divisions, units, and special units can you identify on the charts?
- What factors do you think account for the differences in the vertical and functional differentiations across the departments? Is it sheer population size? Population density (i.e., number of residents per square mile)? Crime levels of the jurisdiction?
- What are the major similarities in the organizational charts across the three departments? That is, what do the organizational charts have in common with one another, despite the differences in department sizes?
- What do the organizational charts convey about how the work of the police departments is divided up or segmented? Which

officers in which agencies have more opportunities to do different kinds of work within their police organizations?

■ In what ways might officers in the smaller agencies get more opportunities to perform different kinds of work in the organization?

Bibliography

Anderson, James, and Lee Kennett. *The Gun in America: The Origins of a National Dilemma*. Reprint. Westport, CT: Preager, 1975.

Bopp, W.J. "OW Wilson and the Search for a Police Profession." Washington, DC, 1977. https://www.ncjrs.gov/App/Publications/abstract.aspx?ID=47846.

Brown, Robert A. "Policing in American History." *Du Bois Review* 16, no. 1 (2019): 189–95. https://doi.org/10.1017/S1742058X19000171.

Dulaney, Marvin W. *Black Police in America*. Bloomington, IN: Indiana University Press, 1996.

Dunlap Jr., C. J. "The Police-Ization of the Military." *Journal of Political & Military Sociology* 27, no. 2 (1999): 217.

Farrell, Graham. "Crime Concentration Theory." *Crime Prevention and Community Safety* 17, no. 4 (2015): 233–48. https://doi.org/10.1057/cpcs.2015.17.

Federal Bureau of Investigation. "2018 Crime in the United States - Police Employee Data." Accessed August 4, 2020. https://ucr.fbi.gov/crime-in-the-u.s/2018/crime-in-the-u.s.-2018/topic-pages/police-employee-data.

Glasner, Philip, and Michael Leitner. "Evaluating the Impact the Weekday Has on Near-Repeat Victimization: A Spatio-Temporal Analysis of Street Robberies in the City of Vienna, Austria." *ISPRS International Journal of Geo-Information* 6, no. 1 (2016): 3. https://doi.org/10.3390/ijgi6010003.

Graybill, Andrew R. *Policing the Great Plains: Rangers, Mounties, and the North American Frontier, 1875-1910*. Lincoln, NE: University of Nebraska Press, 2007.

Greenberg, Kenneth S., ed. *Nat Turner: A Slave Rebellion in History and Memory*. New York: Oxford University Press, 2003. https://books.google.com/books?hl=en&lr=&id=FoAeDQAAQBAJ&oi=fnd&pg=PR7&dq=nat+turner+rebellion&ots=T0TIjIen-N5&sig=5a0QSQPYWCa54hv1a72GU8hgXYU#v=onepage&q=nat turner rebellion&f=false.

Greene, Evarts B., and Virginia D. Harrington. *American Population Before the Federal Census of 1790*. Baltimore: Genealogical Publishing Co., Inc., 1997. https://www.amazon.com/American-Population-Before-Federal-Census/dp/0806313773.

Hall, Richard H., Norman J. Johnson, and J. Eugene Haas. "Organizational Size, Complexity, and Formalization." *American Sociological Review1* 32, no. 6 (1967): 903–12.

———. "The Normative Ordering of Police Territoriality: Making and Marking Space with the Los Angeles Police Department." *Annals of the Association of American Geographers*, 1996. https://doi.org/10.1111/j.1467-8306.1996.tb01767.x.

Herbert, Steve. "Police Subculture Reconsidered." *Criminology* 36, no. 2 (1998): 343–70. https://doi.org/10.1111/j.1745-9125.1998.tb01251.x.

———. *Policing Space: Territoriality and the Los Angeles Police Department*. Minneapolis, MN: University of Minnesota Press, 1996. https://www.upress.umn.edu/book-division/books/policing-space.

"How Municipal WiFi Works | HowStuffWorks." Accessed August 7, 2020. https://computer.howstuffworks.com/municipal-wifi.htm.

Kane, Robert J. "On the Limits of Social Control: Structural Deterrence and the Policing of 'Suppressible' Crimes." *Justice Quarterly* 23, no. 2 (2006): 186–213. https://doi.org/10.1080/07418820600688768.

———. "The Social Ecology of Police Misconduct." *Criminology* 40, no. 4 (2002): 867–96. https://doi.org/10.1111/j.1745-9125.2002.tb00976.x.

Kane, Robert J., and Michael D. White. *Jammed Up: Bad Cops, Police Misconduct, and the New York City Police Department*. New York: NYU Press, 2013. https://nyupress.org/9780814748411/jammed-up/.

Kansas City Police Department, Missouri. "Police Response Time Analysis, 1975." Kansas City, MO: 2006. https://doi.org/10.3886/ICPSR07760.v1.

Kappeler, Victor E., Richard D. Sluder, and Geoffrey P. Alpert. "Breeding Deviant Conformity: The Ideology and Culture of Police." In *Critical Issues in Policing: Contemporary Readings*, edited by Roger G. Dunham, Geoffrey P. Alpert, and Kyle D. McLean, 8th ed., 187–213. Long Grove, IL: Waveland Press, 2020.

Kasarda, John D. "The Structural Implications of Social System Size: A Three-Level Analysis." *American Sociological Review* 39, no. 1 (1974): 19–28.

Kelling, George L., Tony Pate, Duane Dieckman, and Charles E. Brown. "The Kansas City Preventive Patrol Experment: A Summary Report." Washington, DC, 1974.

Klinger, David A. "Negotiating Order in Patrol Work: An Ecological Theory of Police Response To Deviance." *Criminology* 35, no. 2 (1997): 277–306. https://doi.org/10.1111/j.1745-9125.1997.tb00877.x.

Kriesburg, L. "Centralization and Differentiation in International Non-Governmental Organizations." *Sociology and Social Research* 61, no. 1 (1976): 1–23.

Lane, Roger. "Urban Police and Crime in Nineteenth-Century America." *Crime and Justice* 15 (1992): 1–50. https://doi.org/10.1086/449192.

Langworthy, Robert H., and Lawrence F. Travis. *Policing in America: A Balance in Forces*. Upper Saddle River, NJ: Prentice Hall Publishing, 1999.

"The Largest Police Departments in the US - WorldAtlas." Accessed August 28, 2020. https://www.worldatlas.com/articles/the-largest-police-departments-in-the-us.html.

Lipsky, M. *Street-Level Bureaucracy: Dilemmas of the Individuals in Public Services*. New York: Russell Sage Foundation, 1980.

Little, Craig B., and Christopher P. Sheffield. "Frontiers and Criminal Justice: English Private Prosecution Societies and American Vigilantism in the Eighteenth and Nineteenth Centuries." *American Sociological Review* 48, no. 6 (1983): 796. https://doi.org/10.2307/2095326.

Maguire, Edward. *Organizational Structure in American Police Agencies: Context, Complexity, and Control*. Albany: State University of New York, 2003.

"May 2018 National Occupational Employment and Wage Estimates." U.S. Bureau of Labor Statistics, Occupational Employment Statistics, 2018. https://www.bls.gov/oes/current/oes_nat.htm#33-0000.

"Metropolitan Police - UK Parliament." Accessed August 25, 2020. https://www.parliament.uk/about/living-heritage/transformingsociety/laworder/policeprisons/overview/metropolitanpolice/.

"Metropolitan Police Department, District of Columbia." The Officer Down Memorial Page. Accessed August 28, 2020. https://www.odmp.org/agency/2463-metropolitan-police-department-district-of-columbia.

Miller, Wilbur R. *Cops and Bobbies: Police Authority in New York and London, 1830-1870*. Chicago: University of Chicago Press, 1976.

Monkkonen, Eric H. "History of Urban Police." *Crime and Justice* 15 (1992): 547–80. https://doi.org/10.20595/jjbf.19.0_3.

———. *Police in Urban America: 1860-1920*. New York: Cambridge University Press, 1981.

Montgomery, David. "The Shuttle and the Cross: Weavers and Artisans in the Kensington Riots of 1844." *Journal of Social History* 5, no. 4 (1972): 411–46. https://doi.org/10.1353/jsh/5.4.411.

Palmer, Stanley H. *Police and Protest in England and Ireland: 1780-1850*. New York: Cambridge University Press, 1988.

Penn, Ira A., Gail B. Pennix, and Jim Coulson. *Records Management Handbook*. New York: Routledge, 2016.

Pugh, D.S., D.J. Hickson, C.R. Hinings, and C. Turner. "Dimensions of Organizational Commitment." *Administrative Science Quarterly* 13, no. 1 (1968): 65–105.

Reichel, Philip L. "Southern Slave Patrols as a Transitional Police Type." *American Journal of Police* 7, no. 2 (1988): 51–77.

Robbins, S.P. *Organization Theory: Structure, Design, and Applicationa*. 2nd ed. Englewood Cliffs, NJ: Prentice Hall Publishing, 1987.

Santos, Rachel Boba. *Crime Analysis with Crime Mapping*. 4th ed. Thousand Oaks, CA: Sage, 2017.

"The SARA Model | ASU Center for Problem-Oriented Policing." Accessed March 8, 2021. https://popcenter.asu.edu/content/sara-model-0.

Scott, Richard W. *Organizations: Rational, Natural, and Open Systems*. 5th ed. Upper Saddle River, NJ: Prentice Hall, 2002. https://www.amazon.com/W-Richard-Scott-dp-013016559X/dp/013016559X/ref=mt_other?_encoding=UTF8&me=&qid=.

"Today in History - September 9." *Library of Congress, Washington, D.C. 20540 USA*. Accessed August 25, 2020. https://www.loc.gov/item/today-in-history/september-09/.

United States Department of Justice. Office of Justice Programs. Bureau of Justice Statistics. "Law Enforcement Management and Administrative Statistics (LEMAS), 2016. ICPSR37323-V1." Ann Arbo, MI: Inter-university Consortium for Political and Social Research, 2020.

Walker, Sam. *Popular Justice*. New York: Oxford University Press, 1980.

Weisburd, David, and Shai Amram. "The Law of Concentrations of Crime at Place: The Case of Tel Aviv-Jaffa." *Police Practice and Research: An International Journal* 15, no. 2 (2014): 101–14.

Wilson, O.W. *Police Administration*. 2nd ed. New York: McGraw-Hill Publishing Company, 1963.

CHAPTER 3

The Funnel of U.S. Policing:

Recruitment, Mandate, and Working the Street

Everyone is nested. We are individuals, but we are also family members. Our families participate in, and identify with, local organizations such as clubs, schools, athletic teams, and places of worship.

Those local organizations help form a basis for our communities. Our communities provide the space and opportunities we need to develop and grow during our formative years. They also give us the perspective we require to see the world beyond our local regions. Some of us grow up in one place, connecting with our local institutions early and permanently. Some of us move around, frequently forging new relationships with new peer groups, new schools, and new neighborhoods. And always, the experiences we accumulate become our story, determining who we are and who we were born to become. In short, we are individuals, but we cannot be fully understood or articulated without considering the nested nature of our lived experience—or what researchers call our social ecological contexts.[1]

The same is true for policing. It has been written that Sir Robert Peel—the primary founder of the London Metropolitan Police Department—famously said, "The police are the public, and the public are the police."[2] Although it is nearly impossible to pinpoint the precise source of that quote, the statement itself could not be truer. Police officers grow up in the same communities as the rest of us. They are socialized by the same institutions that socialize us. They watch the same television, go to the same movies, eat in the same

---

[1] Bronfenbrenner, *The Ecology of Human Development: Experiments by Nature and Design.*
[2] Lentz and Chaires, "The Invention of Peel's Principles: A Study of Policing 'Textbook' History."

restaurants, enjoy the same sporting events, and experience the same ups and downs we all experience. Contrary to popular assertions about the police, there is no "them" and there is no "us." There is just us. All of us. The police are the public, and the public are the police.

Until they join the police department. Because when they join the police department, virtually everything changes. This chapter examines the processes of how police departments draw recruits from society and how they socialize those recruits into police officers. It also examines how the police mandate affects — and is affected by — the "funnel" of policing from the top of the organization down to the officers working the street.

By the end of this chapter, readers should be able to answer the following questions:

1. In what ways are the police and the public one and the same?
2. What is the funnel of U.S. policing as it is described in this chapter?
3. What is the police mandate, and how has it been created and perpetuated?
4. What is the impossible mandate, and why do police departments accept it?
5. What is the "negotiated order" perspective of policing?
6. Why are police work groups so important in policing?
7. Why are arrests so difficult to predict in any policing environment?

From Society Come the Police

The moment members of society join the police department as recruits, they become initiated and socialized into the policing occupation. During that initiation they become "set apart" from the rest of society.[3] Police recruits are taught to think like police officers and act like police officers. Like the rest of us, they are nested. That is, by the time they leave the academy and get through training, they are individual officers, but they are also part of a workgroup — a squad of officers assigned a specific beat area and shift during a specific time over specific days or nights of the week.[4] The behaviors of their workgroup — who they stop, who they search, who they arrest, who they send on their way — are influenced by the types and characteristics of the people and events their workgroup experiences in their local areas.[5]

Those workgroups are also connected to the organization, a police agency with a history of its own, a legacy from prior chiefs of police, its own folklore, its own heroes, and its own villains. As described in Chapter 2, although police departments tend to be organized as quasi-military bureaucracies with

---

[3] Banton, *The Policeman in the Community*, 237.
[4] Klinger, "Negotiating Order in Patrol Work: An Ecological Theory of Police Response to Deviance."
[5] Herbert, "The Normative Ordering of Police Territoriality: Making and Marking Space with the Los Angeles Police Department."

lots of rules, procedures, and general orders, they also resemble street-level bureaucracies that "process" people, often in very informal ways. Thus, at the top of the hierarchy, particularly within headquarters, police organizations tend to be highly formalized. As we travel down the chain of command, though, coming closer to the people individual officers actually contact on the street, the strict application of rules begins to compete with the norms of the workgroup (more on this when we discuss police subcultures in Chapter 5). Consider Figure 3.1, which illustrates the nested nature of policing.

As Figure 3.1 suggests, the public "universe" envelops policing and the police organization. From that universe, some number of people select—and are selected—into the police occupation. The selection process, however, is not random, either on the part of those seeking the job or the organizations evaluating their candidacy: People are motivated to enter policing for a variety reasons, such as the desire to help people, the power and authority given to police officers, and the job security typically associated with the occupation.[6] Of those motivated to choose policing, however, a much smaller number is actually accepted, usually after a rigorous process of screening out "undesirable" applicants[7] (this selection bias is more thoroughly discussed in Chapter 12 when examining recruitment). Once the successful candidates make it into the police organization, they are sent to an academy where they are socialized into the occupation through a kind of ritualistic process that trains them on the rules, procedures, norms, and mission of policing.[8]

---

[6] Morrow et al., "Examining a Ferguson Effect on College Students' Motivation to Become Police Officers," 589.
[7] Metchik, "An Analysis of the 'Screening out' Model of Police Officer Selection."
[8] Conti, "A Visigoth System: Shame, Honor, and Police Socialization."

After they pass through the training and organizational filter, officers are funneled into various assignments or (in larger departments) districts where they spend the following years working various assignments with different workgroups.[9] These different levels—district, assignment, and workgroup—influence how officers respond to different events in their work settings. The shape of the illustration in Figure 3.1 (i.e., a cone or funnel) is purposeful, illustrating that workgroups are contained within larger units, and that those units are often nested in districts, which fall within the larger organization. Every level of the funnel influences the behaviors of individual police officers. Thus, when asking why a group of police officers acted a certain way toward a suspect on a street corner, we must first ask what brought those officers to that street corner in the first place. To answer that question, we need to understand the police mandate.

Is Policing a Profession?

The Oxford English Dictionary (online) defines a profession as:

> *An occupation in which a professed knowledge of some subject, field, or science is applied; a vocation or career, especially one that involves prolonged training and a formal qualification.*

Certainly, policing requires knowledge of law, tactics, and strategies, and it is increasingly becoming grounded in some aspects of applied science (e.g., forensics, evidence-based practice, etc.). But does it require "prolonged training" and "formal qualification"? Most police training academies run between four and six months long, which is formal but not exactly prolonged. The vast majority of U.S. police departments do not require a baccalaureate college degree as an entry requirement into the occupation.

Chapter 12 addresses the issue of a police profession and why it is important.

Setting the Police Mandate

It is useful to think of an occupational mandate as a set of expectations that both the occupation itself and its customers, clients, or the public at large have agreed is both reasonable and achievable. To a great extent, the creation of the initial mandate is likely an organic process owing to the creation of the occupation and the niche it will presume to fill. For example, societies are not likely to develop a police institution unless they have some a priori sense of what they want that institution to do: fight crime, keep the public safe, and so on. The mandate then becomes refined by different stakeholders in ways meant to distinguish the occupation or profession from others and to gain recognition of its need in some sector of the economy and society. In addition to centering around "skills and expertise" to convey an occupation's unique qualification to accomplish whatever it aims to accomplish, the mandate also conveys the value system of the occupation or profession.[10]

Most professions that require licensure claim authority over defining their role, or mandate, in society. They set the education and training standards for those wishing to practice the profession, and they define the outcomes to demonstrate success in the profession. This is true for medicine, nursing,

---

[9] Klinger, "Negotiating Order in Patrol Work: An Ecological Theory of Police Response to Deviance"; Herbert, "The Normative Ordering of Police Territoriality: Making and Marking Space with the Los Angeles Police Department"; Rubinstein, *City Police*.

[10] Fayard, Stigliani, and Bechky, "How Nascent Occupations Construct a Mandate: The Case of Service Designers' Ethos."

law, engineering, architecture, and accountancy, among others. It remains a point of discussion as to whether policing is a full profession, per se, but it is certainly the case that policing is at the very least a highly skilled vocation, requiring licensure among those who practice it.[11] Unlike many other professions or highly skilled vocations, though, policing is generally supported through local taxes and can therefore be regarded as a public good; that is, a public enterprise whose services are to be distributed across society based on need. But what are those needs, and what are the services?

Chapter 2 noted that the "services" provided by the early policing systems in the United States (and even the American colonies) came in the form of controlling the so-called dangerous classes. As those regionalized policing systems began to converge, however, they took on the more general responsibilities of enforcing the law, developing standards and training for police officers, as well as adopting new forms of technology, for the purposes of providing their law enforcement services. Although it might appear obvious that law enforcement has become the police mandate, it is nevertheless useful to examine how the police mandate has evolved, how it has been maintained, and the value system it fosters.

Recall our previous examination of means- versus ends-based definitions of the police, and Klockars's assertions that it is best to define the police based on the tool society gives them, the general right to use coercive force.[12] With that in mind, it is time to give more attention to the ends-based definitions, those descriptions of the police that might say more about the people giving them than about the police themselves. As Klockars pointed out,[13] ends-based, or norm-derivative, "definitions" of the police tend to reflect the experiences of those who give them, but they also reflect the expectations people develop of the police, partly through direct contact with police officers, partly through indirect contact (e.g., stories we hear from friends and family members about their experiences with the police), and certainly through images portrayed in the media.[14] These expectations provide a foundation for society on which to develop a collective idea of what the police mandate should be.

In 1978, Peter Manning published an essay that would become one of the most important examinations of the police role of all time: "The Police: Mandate, Strategies, and Appearances."[15] Essentially, Manning argued that, unlike with many other professions (such as those listed above), society takes primacy in defining the role of the police. In the modern United States, society has decided that policing should mostly center around law enforcement, maintaining public order, and protecting individual rights.[16] The problem

---

[11] "Police Officer License and Certifications."

[12] Klockars, *The Idea of Police*.

[13] Klockars, 8–9.

[14] Donovan and Klahm, "The Role of Entertainment Media in Perceptions of Police Use of Force"; Rosenbaum et al., "Attitudes Toward the Police: The Effects of Direct and Vicarious Experience."

[15] Manning, "The Police: Mandate, Strategies, and Appearances."

[16] President's Commission on Law Enforcement and the Administration of Justice, "The Challenge of Crime in a Free Society."

is—as Manning points out—crime fighting (i.e., the primary role) represents a relatively small proportion of all police activities. Even in the most challenging settings, police–public contacts are mostly associated with giving advice, managing disputes (many of which are not criminal), and providing other categories of "service."[17] Police organizations themselves—despite their primary public persona of a crime-fighting institution—are responsible for responding to medical emergencies, maintaining traffic safety programs, and managing vulnerable populations, such as emotionally disturbed persons and people experiencing homelessness.[18]

Police therefore find themselves in the unenviable position of having to justify their value to society based on about a third of what they actually do. Moreover, that third (i.e., managing crime) proves incredibly difficult for police departments to control. Although the police can be excellent at responding to crime, their capacity to reduce crime, especially across large municipal geographies and over the long term, remains tenuous at best.[19]

Still, and although the difficulty of meeting public expectations around crime reduction leads to what Manning calls the "impossible mandate," Manning also points out that the "police in modern societies are in agreement with their audiences."[20] As noted, the police are the public, and the public are the police. When society develops its idea of what the police should accomplish (i.e., their mandate), that idea filters into police organizations through the recruitment process because, after all, police departments recruit from the public "universe" as illustrated in Figure 3.1. Moreover, although policing itself recognizes the difficulty of the mandate it has been given, Manning reminds us that:

> In an effort to gain the public's confidence in their ability, and to insure thereby the solidity of their mandate, the police have encouraged the public to continue thinking of them and their work in idealized terms . . . which grossly exaggerate the actual work done by police.[21]

In other words, Manning argues that despite the otherwise "impossible" mandate of crime control, the police institution encourages the public to continue to regard them as crime fighters because crime fighting and maintaining order are dangerous, heroic, and hard to achieve. Fulfilling those obligations to society requires a specialized institution that carries the general right to use coercive force and that wields a budget large enough to buy equipment, maintain buildings and training academies, purchase computer systems, and hire a large workforce. That is, the impossible mandate

---

[17] Greene and Klockars, "What Police Do"; Kane, "Policing in Public Housing: Using Calls for Service to Examine Incident-Based Workload in the Philadelphia Housing Authority"; Cumming, Cumming, and Edell, "Policeman as Philosopher, Guide and Friend."

[18] Lum and Nagin, "Reinventing American Policing," 342.

[19] Telep and Weisburd, "What Is Known About the Effectiveness of Police Practices in Reducing Crime and Disorder?"

[20] Manning, "The Police: Mandate, Strategies, and Appearances," 196.

[21] Manning, 196.

requires society to maintain a paid and well-funded police institution, or so the logic goes.

As previously noted, though, an occupational mandate does more than simply describe the unique qualifications of those who practice the vocation, and it goes beyond distinguishing an occupation or profession for all others in society. A mandate also conveys the value system of the occupational or professional institution.[22] Thus, if law enforcement, maintaining public order, and preserving individual rights—as Manning and others have argued[23]—represent the collective police mandate, then what is the value system that drives that mandate? This book argues that the value system inherent to the police mandate is coercion. That is, law enforcement, maintaining public order, and even protecting individual rights represent occupational goals inherent to a coercion-based value system of policing. As discussed in Chapter 1, coercion is why we "call the cops." We want law enforcement, we want the restoration of public order, and we want the protection of our individual rights. We want state-sanctioned coercion, or at the very least, the threat of state-sanctioned coercion. And if society wants it, then police organizations strive to deliver it.

How Police Organizations Foster the Police Mandate

Considering again Figure 3.1, when society (the public in Figure 3.1) tells the police that their role is law enforcement and order maintenance, then the rational responses of police organizations are to (1) create policies that encourage enforcement-related activities, and (2) develop metrics that assess officers' enforcement "productivity" on an annual basis through performance evaluations. Such is the process by which public sentiment makes its way into the funnel of policing as illustrated in Figure 3.1. In adopting public demands, police organizations create incentives that help filter down through the chain of command to the individual officers working the streets. Although many police performance evaluation systems are designed to primarily encourage officers to follow internal police department policies,[24] they still widely hold officers accountable to expectations regarding enforcement output, for example, arrests (particularly for felonies), citations, and even stop-and-frisk contacts.[25]

That is, police departments encourage the use of coercion by setting "average . . . minimum number(s) of enforcement actions and citations each

---

[22] Fayard, Stigliani, and Bechky, "How Nascent Occupations Construct a Mandate: The Case of Service Designers' Ethos," 270.

[23] Manning, "The Police: Mandate, Strategies, and Appearances"; President's Commission on Law Enforcement and the Administration of Justice, "The Challenge of Crime in a Free Society"; de Lint, Virta, and Deukmedjian, "The Simulation of Crime Control."

[24] Lilley and Hinduja, "Organizational Values and Police Officer Evaluation: A Content Comparison Between Traditional and Community Policing Agencies."

[25] Iannone, Iannone, and Bernstein, *Supervision of Police Personnel*; Lum and Nagin, "Reinventing American Policing."

day,"[26] and then penalizing officers on annual performance reviews for not achieving those averages. Thus, police officers can effectively advance through their career pathways, getting promoted and assigned to highly valued assignments, by following departmental rules and procedures and by meeting their enforcement goals on an annual basis, both of which become enshrined in their performance evaluation scores.

Apart from creating formal incentive systems designed to encourage minimum numbers of enforcement contacts, police departments also maintain informal reward systems that run parallel to the formal incentive structure. As alluded to at the start of this chapter, police agencies have their own histories, develop their own folklore, venerate their heroes, and scorn their villains. For so-called management cops—those who hold administrative ranks and work the bureaucracy of the organization—the "heroes," or at the very least the assets to the organization, tend to be officers who follow the rules and meet their numbers without embarrassing the department by engaging in scandalous behavior.[27] For the "street cops," though, the heroes are officers who effectively use coercion in ways that earn and maintain respect for police authority on the street and accomplish the enforcement goals of police officer workgroups.[28] For those street cops, when the heroes leave the organization, they become part of the folklore that helps perpetuate the enforcement culture.

Recall the proposition made at the start of this chapter: When asking why a group of police officers acted a certain way toward a suspect on a street corner, it is first important to ask what brought them to that corner in the first place. By now, the answer should be clear: Coercion brought police to that street corner because coercion is what society expects them to bring, and coercion is what police departments demand of their officers. This is not to suggest that society or police organizations demand the excessive or unnecessary use of force. Coercion and force are not always the same thing: Physical force is a form of police coercion, but not all police coercion involves physical force (more on this in Chapter 8). Police departments can send troubling mixed signals to officers by allowing them to remain on the job despite accumulating a record of complaints for the use of excessive force. This was the case for Derek Chauvin, the Minneapolis police officer who killed George Floyd in the summer of 2020. According to reports, by the time Chauvin had arrived on-scene where he contacted George Floyd, he had already accumulated 18 citizen complaints during his career, only two of which had resulted in some form of minor discipline.[29]

By allowing Chauvin to remain on the street, despite his record of citizen complaints, the Minneapolis Police Department conveyed to him and other

---

[26] *See, e.g.,* Gravitte v. North Carolina DMV, U.S. App.
[27] Reuss-Ianni, *Two Cultures of Policing: Street Cops and Management Cops.*
[28] Reuss-Ianni; Herbert, *Policing Space: Territoriality and the Los Angeles Police Department*; Van Maanen, "The Asshole."
[29] Andres, "Derek Chauvin: What We Know about the Former Officer Charged in George Floyd's Death."

officers in the organization that it was acceptable to engage in overly aggressive tactics even if it meant triggering citizen complaints. This is an example of when the formal organizational incentive system becomes conflated with the informal reward structure; it can occur when "management cops" forget that their primary responsibility is to protect the organization and the lives of the people within the jurisdiction of the police organization.

Working the Street: Arrests and the Police Mandate

The arrest. Next to deadly force, it is the most consequential outcome in all of policing. When police officers collect enough evidence to believe a crime has been committed, and when they believe the person they have contacted likely committed that crime, they are allowed to arrest them.[30] Police have the authority to take alleged offenders into physical custody and transport them to jail, where they must wait for some undetermined amount of time to be processed and eventually released. In most if not all U.S. states, officers must personally witness the commission of misdemeanor crimes—those punishable by up to one year in jail[31]—before they are allowed to arrest. For felony crimes, those punishable by at least one year in prison, up to and including death,[32] officers may arrest when they have strong suspicion that the person committed the crime, despite not having seen it occur.

The arrest is not to be taken lightly, even for misdemeanor crimes, because the direct and collateral consequences of arrest are vast. As a practical matter, adults who get arrested might be the primary wage earners in their families (whether the income is legal or illegal), which means while they reside in custody they cannot work and bring in the economic resources needed to support their households. This places their families at risk of experiencing food insecurity and the inability to make their rent or mortgage payments. Moreover, being arrested leaves some adults susceptible to losing their jobs, partly because of the absences they might accumulate while awaiting release, and partly because some employers would rather distance themselves and their businesses from employees with records of police or criminal justice contacts. Indeed, research shows that even if arrests do not lead to conviction, the arrests themselves represent a barrier to future employment opportunities. This finding has shown to hold for both prior felony and misdemeanor arrests.[33]

For juveniles, getting arrested can produce even more severe and longer term consequences. Arrests could trigger suspension from school, which can lead to juveniles being involuntarily transferred to so-called alternative

---

[30] Lum, "The Influence of Places on Police Decision Pathways: From Call for Service to Arrest."
[31] "Misdemeanor | Wex | US Law | LII / Legal Information Institute."
[32] "Felony | Wex | US Law | LII / Legal Information Institute."
[33] Grogger, "The Effect of Arrests on the Employment and Earnings of Young Men"; Uggen et al., "The Edge of Stigma: An Experimental Audit of the Effects of Low-Level Criminal Records on Employment."

schools—often outside their communities and beyond the reach of their peer support networks.[34] Assuming they return to school, they might be labeled as "deviant" by teachers, former friends, and parents, which can isolate them and make it difficult to reintegrate into the mainstream school environment. This potential labeling might lead the returning students to seek out deviant peer groups, ultimately drop out of school, and embark on a longer career in delinquency,[35] which could lead to adult criminal offending.

If the police mandate centers around law enforcement, though, and if police organizations structure their incentive systems to encourage coercion as a means to fulfilling their law enforcement function, then a reasonable person outside policing might expect that every time police officers take to the streets they will cite and arrest every person for every infraction or crime they encounter. Yet, this does not happen. In fact, arrests are relatively rare events, even when police officers have probable cause to make them,[36] and even when there are administrative policies that demand them—such as in cases of intimate partner violence.[37] So how is it, then, that police officers confronted by people who have likely committed a crime often pass on the opportunity to arrest them? To a great extent, the answer resides in a blunt statement made by anthropologist Michael Banton in his 1964 book that reported on his social scientific study of police, the first of its kind: "In different neighborhoods the police provide different services."[38] For many at the time, this statement was an epiphany.[39]

In the ecology of policing, neighborhoods matter. Some have high levels of crime and risk, whereas others are "safe" and quiet. Some communities are characterized by racial residential segregation, economic resource deprivation, and many police calls for service. Others are high-income, racially homogenous areas that generally have little need for police. Such differences in neighborhood contexts can set the tone for how police workgroups organize their time and respond to criminal and noncriminal events alike. In some neighborhoods, police officers are exposed to so much public deviance and so many demands for their services that they have to triage the less serious incidents, reserving their time for events that are particularly exigent and require more resources.[40] In other communities, police have time—and they are expected by local residents—to respond to events that would be classified as service rather than law enforcement.

[34] St. George, "Ousted from School."

[35] Kirk and Sampson, "Juvenile Arrest and Collateral Educational Damage in the Transition to Adulthood."

[36] Engel et al., *Power to Arrest*; Gottfredson and Gottfredson, *Decision Making in Criminal Justice: Toward the Rational Exercise of Discretion.*

[37] Kane, "Responding to Restraining Orders in Domestic Violence Incidents: Identifying the Custody-Threshold Thesis"; Walker, *Taming the System: The Control of Discretion in Criminal Justice, 1950–1990.*

[38] Banton, *The Policeman in the Community,* 136.

[39] Reiner, "Revisiting the Classics: Three Seminal Founders of the Study of Policing: Michael Banton, Jerome Skolnick and Egon Bittner," 312–316.

[40] Herbert, *Policing Space: Territoriality and the Los Angeles Police Department.*

When considering the neighborhood ecology of policing, it is important to define our terms. For policing, neighborhoods are beats: administratively defined areas within which police officers patrol in marked cars, respond to calls for service, and generally keep an eye out for signs of crime and disorder (recall the police districts and service areas of Washington, DC shown in Figure 2.2 in Chapter 2). Beat areas are often organized under larger sectors or districts, particularly in larger cities. Beats are permeable in that officers are usually allowed to cross from one beat to another, particularly to cover for other officers who may be working calls for service. Officers are usually not allowed to cross district boundaries without permission, however. There are a few reasons for this. In midsized and larger cities, police districts function as mini-police departments to which officers are assigned.[41] At a basic level, patrol officers are workload units assigned to a district. Commanders, colleagues, and dispatchers count on them to be prepared to respond to an event in that district. Officers who cross district lines without permission are no longer able to provide services in their home district.

In terms of what it means to work the street as a patrol officer, perhaps no one has summarized it more clearly (despite the dated and gendered language) than did Jonathan Rubinstein in his 1973 book on policing in Philadelphia:

> Before a policeman can do any work easily, he must know where he is. The framework of a patrolman's geographical knowledge is established by the extent of his territorial jurisdiction. . . . He has no need to know about places beyond the district's limits. The first thing he learns about his district, after the station house, is its boundaries. His knowledge of what lies beyond them is limited and his curiosity restricted. If he is assigned a border sector, he may get to know several of the . . . (officers) who work opposite him; he may even share lunch with them occasionally. Otherwise contacts across district lines are limited to chance encounters at local hospitals and occasional exchanges when the . . . (officers) come to each other's aid on assists.[42]

"Knowing where they are" usually requires knowledge of their local areas, which officers develop after spending time on their beats, and in their districts more generally. Although they may patrol alone or in pairs, police officers rarely respond alone to crimes—they almost always work calls for service or other incidents with other local officers, which is why workgroups are so important to shaping the behaviors—particularly, arrest behaviors—of officers.[43] So, when do police officers make arrests?

---

[41] Klinger, "Negotiating Order in Patrol Work: An Ecological Theory of Police Response to Deviance"; Herbert, *Policing Space: Territoriality and the Los Angeles Police Department*; Kane, "The Social Ecology of Police Misconduct."

[42] Rubinstein, *City Police*, 129.

[43] Klinger, "Negotiating Order in Patrol Work: An Ecological Theory of Police Response to Deviance"; Herbert, *Policing Space: Territoriality and the Los Angeles Police Department*; Lum, "The Influence of Places on Police Decision Pathways: From Call for Service to Arrest."

Scholar David Klinger drew on prior police research, as well as research conducted in hospital emergency rooms, to apply the "negotiated order" perspective to policing in an effort to explain when officers make arrests. As Klinger noted, police workgroups—that is, officers working overlapping and contiguous beat areas during the same shift—are faced with many demands that can take officers out of service or otherwise occupy their time, such as making arrests. Indeed, making an arrest can take officers off the street for several hours of a shift, making them unavailable to their colleagues should situations arise that require multiple officers to respond. Police workgroups therefore establish agreements about the norms of their working behaviors and how they will respond to certain people and events in their beats. The norms become informal rules of conduct for officers, establishing a sense of order over their work and what they can expect of each other. Thus, negotiated order is the process of creating norms around the management of workload and productivity—particularly arrests—and then sticking with those norms in their local areas.

Under the negotiated order framework, Klinger argued that arrests are often a function of four factors related to officers' local beat areas: (1) how much crime there is, (2) how many calls for service they respond to, (3) whether victims are "deserving" of police intervention, and (4) how cynical officers are about their jobs and life in their beat areas.[44] Klinger observed that the more crime a beat contains, the more "normal" certain crimes become, which tends to decrease the likelihood of arrest for those crimes. For example, in beats containing open-air drug markets, only offenders who violate the "norms" of drug offending usually risk getting arrested.

In addition, when officers work in beats that require them to run from call to call, they experience more pressure to move quickly from one event to the next, making sure they remain available to assist other officers who might require help at some point during the shift. Because arrests take a great deal of time for officers to process, the more workload (i.e., calls for service) officers experience in their beats, the less likely arrests become because they take officers off the street for so long.[45] Moreover, when police officers encounter victims who seem deserving of police attention (i.e., they did not "bring" the victimization on themselves through risky lifestyle behaviors), they are more likely to take their situations seriously and make arrests. Finally, when police officers become cynical about their jobs, their roles in society, and their ability to change local beat conditions for the better, they develop cynicism—a type of fatalism in policing that scholars have been researching for generations.[46]

---

[44] Klinger, "Negotiating Order in Patrol Work: An Ecological Theory of Police Response to Deviance," 298.
[45] Klinger, 292.
[46] Osborne, "Observations on Police Cynicism: Some Preliminary Findings"; Mastrofski and Willis, "Police Organization Continuity and Change: Into the Twenty-First Century"; Lum, "The Influence of Places on Police Decision Pathways: From Call for Service to Arrest."

Despite the influences of beat ecology, it is nevertheless important to point out that the decision to arrest is more complicated than simply representing a function of localized working conditions. Individual officers and workgroups bring their own ideas of arrest-worthiness to an incident, which include considerations of the incentive system that the organization has created. Scholars have found that when officers are confronted by alleged offenders accused of committing serious crimes, regardless of local beat conditions, they almost always make arrests.[47] This "custody threshold thesis," identified by previous research, finds that police officers will almost always make arrests when at least one of the following four conditions is met: (1) to prevent a dangerous offender from committing future crimes, (2) to demonstrate to the offender the seriousness of their crimes, (3) to achieve an investigative or administrative purpose (e.g., a lineup, police crackdown, or complying with protective orders), or (4) to facilitate medical treatment.[48]

The dynamics of these processes—the negotiated order perspective and the custody threshold thesis—can be illustrated by the map of San Francisco shown in Figure 3.2. This map shows elements of police workload (represented by calls for service geographic densities), "normal" deviance (in the form of drugs and narcotics possession criminal incidents), and police drug arrests. Specifically, the purple-to-yellow areas of the map show the geographic densities[49] of calls for service (CFS) to the San Francisco Police Department (SFPD) in 2021. The purple areas show medium CFS density and the brighter and yellow areas (somewhat obscured by overlapping drug crime and arrest concentrations) show high CFS densities. The gray points represent aggregated drug and narcotics crime incidents with larger points including more crimes covering larger geographic areas than smaller points. The blue points represent drug possession arrests, again with larger points representing more arrests across a wider geography than smaller points. The map showcases drug and narcotics possession crime incidents (as opposed to possession with intent to distribute) because such crimes are among the most discretionary for police officers to handle.[50]

Finally, the map in Figure 3.2 shows the neighborhoods (shaded green) of San Francisco that were above the city mean of households receiving public assistance in 2018.[51] Such a measure of economic resource depri-

---

[47] Gottfredson and Gottfredson, *Decision Making in Criminal Justice: Toward the Rational Exercise of Discretion*; Kane, "Patterns of Arrest in Domestic Violence Encounters: Identifying a Police Decision-Making Model"; Engel et al., *Power to Arrest*.

[48] Kane, "Responding to Restraining Orders in Domestic Violence Incidents: Identifying the Custody-Threshold Thesis," 565.

[49] In 2021 SFPD received more than 700,000 calls for service. Rather than show every call as a point on the map, which would have overwhelmed the visualization, we instead created a density surface that shows areas of medium-to-high call densities, providing a more accurate sense of where calls for service mostly concentrate in the city.

[50] Kane, Gustafson, and Bruell, "Racial Encroachment and the Formal Control of Space: Minority Group-Threat and Misdemeanor Arrests in Urban Communities."

[51] American Community Survey, 5-year average, 2014–2018.

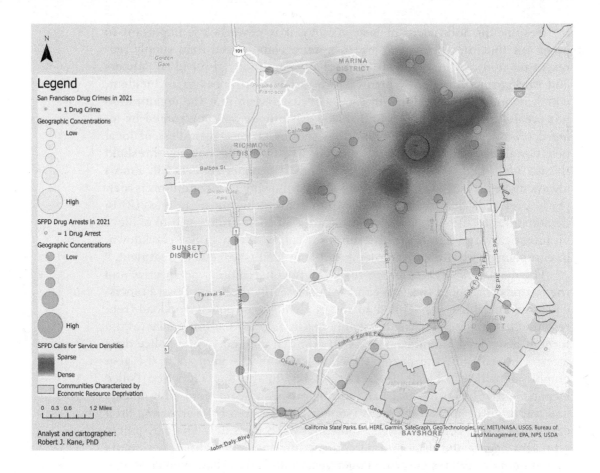

▲ **Figure 3.2**

The Ecology of Police Workload, Drug Crimes, and Arrests in Disadvantaged Communities

vation can indicate high levels of "legal cynicism" because residents often believe their neighborhoods are broadly mistreated—in terms of receiving inadequate services—by city authorities.[52] Legal cynicism has been shown to translate into daily tensions between local residents and police officers,[53] which can be associated with high levels of police cynicism.[54] Thus, the map in Figure 3.2 attempts to illustrate most elements of Klinger's negotiated order perspective.

As Figure 3.2 shows, communities characterized by economic resource deprivation tended to contain some of the highest densities of calls for service (i.e., police workload demands), although the overlap is not perfect. They also tended to contain the most drug crimes and drug arrests. Following

---

[52] Sampson and Bartusch, "Legal Cynicism and (Subcultural?) Tolerance of Deviance: The Neighborhood Context of Racial Differences."

[53] Carr, Napolitano, and Keating, "We Never Call the Cops and Here Is Why: A Qualitative Examination of Legal Cynicism in Three Philadelphia Neighborhoods"; Kane, "Compromised Police Legitimacy as a Predictor of Violent Crime in Structurally Disadvantaged Communities."

[54] Osborne, "Observations on Police Cynicism: Some Preliminary Findings"; Corsaro, Frank, and Ozer, "Perceptions of Police Practice, Cynicism of Police Performance, and Persistent Neighborhood Violence: An Intersecting Relationship."

the negotiated order logic, we would expect that areas of high call volume and drug crimes (our indicator of "normal" deviance) would experience disproportionately lower levels of drug arrests, particularly in the green-shaded communities. In general, we observe the opposite: The single area of the map showing the highest call volume and the largest areas of drug crime incidents (shown on the map as the largest gray point) also contains the highest level of drug arrests. This finding runs counter to what the negotiated order perspective would predict. It may be that officers have been directed to focus their arrest efforts in that single area of high drug crime, high call volume, and a community characterized by economic resource deprivation. Interestingly, there are many areas of the map that experienced low density calls for service (again, representing police workload) and where drug arrests and crimes overlapped; and there are many areas where drug crime and arrests are disparately located. Appealing again to the negotiated order perspective, some of the differences in patterns observed in Figure 3.2 also could be due to unknown differences (and workgroup norms), different custody thresholds among individual officers, and distinct norms of arrest "worthiness" across districts.

The visualization in Figure 3.2 suggests that when police find themselves in environments where drug incidents are high, they did not make arrests in every situation in which they could have done so. Is it workload? Is it "normalized" crime? Is it conflict between local residents and police? The map cannot answer those questions, but it does show the "messy" nature of street-level policing. Crimes, service demands, and arrests tend to concentrate in the most economically challenged communities, which indicates the complexity of serving as police officers in those locations, particularly when the only formal tools society gives police are rooted in coercion. Although the police mandate and its associated organizational incentives encourage police to use their arrest powers whenever they have the opportunity to do so, by the time our funnel (i.e., Figure 3.1) moves from the police organization down to a focus on street-level cops who must "process people," we observe that arrests are not always a predictable outcome. Because society gives the police so few options to formally process people—that is, police are allowed to stop, frisk, cite, arrest, or do nothing—it could be that we lose a great deal of information about how they informally process people they encounter across such different neighborhood contexts. As we discuss in Chapter 7, if police officers were offered a larger set of formal dispositions that were not exclusively tied to coercion, they might invoke different outcomes, which could change the look of our "ecology of police workload" map.

Some Concluding Observations

Policing from top to bottom is organized around coercion, from a mandate that perpetuates law enforcement and crime control as the primary collective function of police, to police organizations that design their formal incentive structures to encourage coercive interventions (e.g., field stops, citations, arrests), and finally to the development of informal reward systems that often lionize "aggressive" policing, especially among officers who work the street. To a great extent, the police mandate is the mediator, that thing that stands between society and the police. Perhaps more directly, the mandate is the filter through which society's conceptions of policing become translated to police organizations. This makes sense: Society should have a great deal to say about the shape and size of the police mandate. After all, policing is a public good; it was created and continues to be supported by public taxes. In creating the police, society gave up its general right to use coercive force in favor of centralizing that authority with a paid, well-trained, and presumably impartial institution in the police. Thus, from the public good standpoint, policing represents a great democratic institution: It is the recognition that enforcing society's laws is such an important responsibility that it should be entrusted only to those trained in the fundamentals of applying coercion in ways that fulfill their mandate, but also in ways that recognize the importance of restraint, at least, in theory.[55]

But what of that mandate to enforce the law? As Peter Manning argued,[56] police departments do not simply accept and execute the mandate as delivered by society; they also perpetuate the mandate as a way of conveying their importance to society. They have developed great capacities to capture data and present them in ways that demonstrate crime problems so as to further solidify their role as the leading, and necessary, crime-fighting institution.[57] (Recall the discussion of RMSs in Chapter 2.) There is nothing wrong with this, because all organizations and institutions engage in survival behaviors. Recall the previous discussion about mandates, though: They not only serve to distinguish occupations from each other, they also communicate the value systems of those occupations. If the police mandate is mostly about crime control and law enforcement, then the value system of that mandate is rooted in coercion. As a result, much police academy training, officer socialization, and street-level tactics promote coercion and control, perhaps to the exclusion of other values.

Despite the emphasis on coercion and control, we saw from the San Francisco map in Figure 3.2 that police officers do not necessarily make arrests everywhere they go, even when they likely have the opportunity to do so. Arrests are difficult to predict precisely because the environments in which police work can be difficult to predict. Emphasizing arrest as a primary outcome in policing serves the coercion mandate, but how does it serve society's investment in the police as a public good? It appears from the map in Figure 3.2 that there are a lot of missed opportunities for police to use

---

[55] de Lint, "Autonomy, Regulation and the Police Beat."
[56] Manning, "The Police: Mandate, Strategies, and Appearances."
[57] Manning, *The Technology of Policing: Crime Mapping, Information Technology, and the Rationality of Crime Control*; Ferguson, *Rise of Big Data Policing: Surveillance, Race, and the Future of Law Enforcement*.

other interventions to more effectively respond to drug incidents. Expecting the police to arrest our way out of public drug markets and addiction did not work during the war on drugs of the 1980s, and there is little reason to believe it will work now. It might be time to show the police that they can engage in another kind of intervention that is not necessarily grounded in coercion. Yes, the police will always maintain the general right to use coercive force, but perhaps we should recognize that not every encounter between the police and the public must be characterized by a coercive intervention or outcome.

That's where this book comes in, to advance a revised paradigm of policing and the police role, which will hopefully become a new mandate that is fed by the public and integrated into policing in the same way the current mandate travels down the funnel of policing. To accomplish that, we're going to need a new idea.

Questions for Review and Reflection

Question 1. The Police, the Public, and the Police Mandate

Police organizations are "fed" by members of society who apply for, and ultimately obtain, jobs as police officers. New recruits are then socialized into the police occupation until they become "set apart" from the rest of society, take on the police mandate, and become crime fighters and law enforcers.

- Is policing the only occupation that is "set apart" from the rest of society? Are there other occupations or careers that socialize their practitioners to think of themselves as different from other members of the public?
- In what ways do the police and the public work together to create and perpetuate the police mandate?
- If the police mandate is to ever change, who would be the catalyst of that change? Would a change in the police mandate come from within the police institution, or would it come from members of the public?
- What does it take for a society to want to change the police mandate?

Question 2. The Value System of Policing

Scholars have noted that occupational mandates do three things: (1) distinguish the occupation from others by creating a set of unique professional skills, (2) create a niche in the economy or society where the occupation appears to be needed, and (3) convey the value system of the occupation. Chapter 1 has already described the unique tool (i.e., coercive force) that defines the police and distinguishes it from other occupational groups, but coercion has also likely created a value system in policing that is unique.

- What value system does the police mandate convey to both its occupational members and society as a whole?
- How does the general right to use coercive force become part of the value system of policing?
- Does the value system of policing need to change? If so, in what ways? If not, why?

Question 3. Policing and Arrests

Research has shown that police workgroups create "norms" about when to arrest potential offenders and when to let them go. They do this partly to manage the workloads in their local areas, and partly as a function of how much "normal" crime exists there.

- In what ways was it surprising to learn that police officers do not always arrest people they encounter as potential criminal suspects?
- If a police workgroup decides it will not arrest drug dealers or users in a particular area as long as the dealers or users do not violate the "norms" of that place, how does this decision fit with the police mandate of law enforcement? Shouldn't the police arrest every suspected offender they encounter? If not, why?
- What are the social benefits of police officers not arresting every suspected criminal offender they encounter? What are the social costs? In what ways might the "negotiated order" policing dynamic perpetuate or protect against racial biases in policing?

Exercises

Exercise 1. Interpreting the Value System of Policing

Conduct a web search of "U.S. Regions," and then examine the map images that result from that search. You will likely see many maps of the United States delineated by large regions, such as West, Northwest, Southwest, Midwest, Southeast, Mid-Atlantic, and Northeast (or some combination thereof). Select two U.S. regions and locate four police departments in each of those regions (a total of eight police departments). Visit the websites of those eight police departments and download, view, or screen capture their mission statements. (If you find you have identified one or more agencies that do not publish their mission statements, keep searching for departments that do.)

- In what ways do the mission statements across all eight departments convey the mandates and value systems of the organizations?
- What are the common mandate and value system propositions across all eight mission statements?

- Does one or more department mission statement contain language about its mandate and value system that stands out as unique among the others? If so, describe that uniqueness.
- When examining the two groups of mission statements separately from each other, do one group's collective statements and language about its mandates and value system seem different than the other group's statements? If so, how?
- Create a word cloud of the "action" words in the mission statements drawn from all eight departments (a variety of free websites can help you create a word cloud; try this one: https://tinyurl.com/y9vt96as). How does the word cloud help illustrate the mandate and value system of the eight police departments? What conclusions do you draw?

Exercise 2. In Their Own Words

Conduct some research to identify three U.S. police departments located in differently sized jurisdictions. Find one that serves a population of up to 10,000 residents, one that serves a population between 40,000 and 60,000 residents, and a third department that serves a population of at least 250,000 residents. Locate the departments' organizational charts (similar to Figure 2.1) on their websites. Not all police departments (particularly smaller agencies) post their organizational charts on their websites, so keep searching for departments in the designated size ranges that do. Once you locate your three departments, review their organizational charts, and answer the following questions.

■ Describe the degrees to which each department is both vertically and functionally differentiated. That is, how many different ranks can you identify on the organizational charts and how many different divisions, units, and special units can you identify on the charts?

■ What factors do you think account for the differences in the vertical and functional differentiations across the departments? Is it sheer population size? Population density (i.e., number of residents per square mile)? Crime levels of the jurisdiction?

■ What are the major similarities in the organizational charts across the three departments? That is, what do the organizational charts have in common with one another, despite the differences in department sizes?

■ What do the organizational charts convey about how the work of the police department is divided up or segmented? Which officers in which agencies have more opportunities to do different kinds of work within their police organizations?

■ In what ways might officers in the smaller agencies get more opportunities to perform different kinds of work in the organization?

Exercise 3. **See for Yourself**

Sometimes, the best way to learn about something is to experience it yourself. In that spirit, consider conducting a ride-along with a police officer in your area. During the ride, ask the officer the following questions.

■ What is your definition of the police?
■ What is the primary police mandate?
■ Who are heroes of the organization (not by name, but rather by actions and attributes)?
■ Who are villains of the organization (again, not by name, but by actions and attributes)?

In addition to asking the above questions, observe how the officer interacts with other officers and members of the public, including suspects, victims, and people who might stop the officer to ask questions.

After the ride-along, write a brief report that summarizes your experiences, and note the answers to the questions you asked. Also, describe how the officer's interactions with colleagues and members of the public conformed with, or perhaps contradicted, the answers the officer gave to the questions above.

Bibliography

Andres, Scottie. "Derek Chauvin: What We Know about the Former Officer Charged in George Floyd's Death." CNN, June 1, 2020. https://www.cnn.com/2020/06/01/us/derek-chauvin-what-we-know-trnd/index.html.

Banton, Michael. *The Policeman in the Community*. New York: Basic Books, 1964. https://books.google.com/books/about/The_Policeman_in_the_Community.html?id=F0NMwQEACAAJ.

Bronfenbrenner, Urie. *The Ecology of Human Development: Experiments by Nature and Design*. Cambridge, MA: Harvard University Press, 1979.

Carr, Patrick J., Laura Napolitano, and Jessica Keating. "We Never Call the Cops and Here Is Why: A Qualitative Examination of Legal Cynicism in Three Philadelphia Neighborhoods." *Criminology* 45, no. 2 (2007): 1–36. http://users.soc.umn.edu/~uggen/Carr_CRIM_07.pdf.

Conti, Norman. "A Visigoth System: Shame, Honor, and Police Socialization." *Journal of Contemporary Ethnography* 38, no. 3 (2009): 409–432. https://doi.org/10.1177/0891241608330092.

Corsaro, Nicholas, James Frank, and Murat Ozer. "Perceptions of Police Practice, Cynicism of Police Performance, and Persistent Neighborhood Violence: An Intersecting Relationship." *Journal of Criminal Justice* 43, no. 1 (2015): 1–11. https://doi.org/10.1016/j.jcrimjus.2014.10.003.

Cumming, Elaine, Ian Cumming, and Laura Edell. "Policeman as Philosopher, Guide and Friend." *Social Problems* 12 (1965): 276–286.

de Lint, Willem. "Autonomy, Regulation and the Police Beat." *Social and Legal Studies* 9, no. 1 (2000): 55–83. https://doi.org/10.1177/096466390000900104.

de Lint, Willem, Sirpa Virta, and John Edward Deukmedjian. "The Simulation of Crime Control." *American Behavioral Scientist* 50, no. 12 (2007): 1631–1647. https://doi.org/10.1177/0002764207302472.

Donovan, Kathleen M., and Charles F. Klahm. "The Role of Entertainment Media in Perceptions of Police Use of Force." *Criminal Justice and Behavior* 42, no. 12 (2015): 1261–1281. https://doi.org/10.1177/0093854815604180.

Engel, Robin S., Robert E. Worden, Nicholas Corsaro, Hannah D. McManus, Danielle Reynolds, Hannah Cochran, Gabrielle T. Isaza, and Jennifer Calnon Cherkauskas. *The Power to Arrest*. New York: Springer International, 2019. https://doi.org/10.1007/978-3-030-17054-7.

Fayard, Anne-Laure, Ileana Stigliani, and Beth A. Bechky. "How Nascent Occupations Construct a Mandate: The Case of Service Designers' Ethos." *Administrative Science Quarterly* 62, no. 2 (2017): 270–303. https://doi.org/10.1177/0001839216665805.

"Felony | Wex | US Law | LII / Legal Information Institute." Accessed October 1, 2020. https://www.law.cornell.edu/wex/felony.

Ferguson, Andrew G. *Rise of Big Data Policing: Surveillance, Race, and the Future of Law Enforcement*. New York: NYU Press, 2017.

Gottfredson, Michael R., and Don M. Gottfredson. *Decision Making in Criminal Justice: Toward the Rational Exercise of Discretion*. New York: Springer, 1988. https://doi.org/10.1007/978-1-4757-9954-5_1.

Gravitte v. North Carolina DMV (2002).

Greene, Jack R., and Carl B. Klockars. "What Police Do." In *Thinking About Police: Contemporary Readings*, 2nd ed., edited by Carl B. Klockars and Stephen D. Mastrofski, New York: McGraw-Hill, 1991.

Grogger, Jeffrey. "The Effect of Arrests on the Employment and Earnings of Young Men." *Quarterly Journal of Economics* 110, no. 1 (1995): 51–71. https://doi.org/10.2307/2118510.

Herbert, Steve. "The Normative Ordering of Police Territoriality: Making and Marking Space with the Los Angeles Police Department." *Annals of the Association of American Geographers* 68, no. 3 (1996): 567–582. https://doi.org/10.1111/j.1467-8306.1996.tb01767.x.

Herbert, Steve. *Policing Space: Territoriality and the Los Angeles Police Department*. Minneapolis: University of Minnesota Press, 1996. https://www.upress.umn.edu/book-division/books/policing-space.

Iannone, Nathan, Marvin D. Iannone, and Jeff Bernstein. *Supervision of Police Personnel*. 9th ed. New York: Pearson, 2019.

Kane, Robert J. "Compromised Police Legitimacy as a Predictor of Violent Crime in Structurally Disadvantaged Communities." *Criminology* 43, no. 2 (2005): 469–497. https://doi.org/10.1111/j.0011-1348.2005.00014.x.

Kane, Robert J. "Patterns of Arrest in Domestic Violence Encounters: Identifying a Police Decision-Making Model." *Journal of Criminal Justice* 27, no. 1 (1999): 65–79. https://doi.org/10.1016/S0047-2352(98)00037-3.

Kane, Robert J. "Policing in Public Housing: Using Calls for Service to Examine Incident-Based Workload in the Philadelphia Housing Authority." *Policing* 21, no. 4 (1998): 618–631. https://doi.org/10.1108/13639519810241656.

Kane, Robert J. "Responding to Restraining Orders in Domestic Violence Incidents: Identifying the Custody-Threshold Thesis." *Criminal Justice and Behavior* 27, no. 3 (2000): 561–580.

Kane, Robert J. "The Social Ecology of Police Misconduct." *Criminology* 40, no. 4 (2002): 867–896. https://doi.org/10.1111/j.1745-9125.2002.tb00976.x.

Kane, Robert J., Joseph L. Gustafson, and Christopher Bruell. "Racial Encroachment and the Formal Control of Space: Minority Group-Threat and Misdemeanor Arrests in Urban Communities." *Justice Quarterly* 30, no. 6 (2013): 957–982. https://doi.org/10.1080/07418825.2011.636376.

Kirk, David S., and Robert J. Sampson. "Juvenile Arrest and Collateral Educational Damage in the Transition to Adulthood." *Sociology of Education* 86, no. 1 (2013): 36–62. https://doi.org/10.1177/0038040712448862.

Klinger, David A. "Negotiating Order in Patrol Work: An Ecological Theory of Police Response to Deviance." *Criminology* 35, no. 2 (1997): 277–306. https://doi.org/10.1111/j.1745-9125.1997.tb00877.x.

Klockars, Carl B. *The Idea of Police*. Thousand Oaks, CA: Sage, 1985.

Lentz, Susan A., and Robert H. Chaires. "The Invention of Peel's Principles: A Study of Policing

'Textbook' History." *Journal of Criminal Justice* 35, no. 1 (2007): 69–79. https://doi.org/10.1016/j.jcrimjus.2006.11.016.

Lilley, David, and Sameer Hinduja. "Organizational Values and Police Officer Evaluation: A Content Comparison Between Traditional and Community Policing Agencies." *Police Quarterly* 9, no. 4 (2006): 486–513. https://doi.org/10.1177/1098611105281628.

Lum, Cynthia. "The Influence of Places on Police Decision Pathways: From Call for Service to Arrest." *Justice Quarterly* 28, no. 4 (2011): 631–665. https://doi.org/10.1080/07418825.2010.526130.

Lum, Cynthia, and Daniel S. Nagin. "Reinventing American Policing." *Crime and Justice* 46, no. 1 (2017): 339–393. https://doi.org/10.1086/688462.

Maanen, John Van. "The Asshole." In *Policing: A View from the Street*, edited by Peter K. Manning and John Van Maanen, 1st ed., 221–238. Santa Monica, CA: Goodyear, 1978.

Manning, Peter K. "The Police: Mandate, Strategies, and Appearances." In *Policing: A View from the Street*, edited by Peter K. Manning and John Van Maanen. Santa Monica, CA: Goodyear, 1978.

Manning, Peter K. "The Police: Mandates, Strategies, and Appearances." In *Policing: Key Readings*, edited by Tim Newburn, 191–214. New York: Routledge, 2005.

Manning, Peter K. *The Technology of Policing: Crime Mapping, Information Technology, and the Rationality of Crime Control*. New York: NYU Press, 2008. https://nyupress.org/9780814761366/the-technology-of-policing/.

Mastrofski, Stephen D., and James J. Willis. "Police Organization Continuity and Change: Into the Twenty-First Century." *Crime and Justice* 39, no. 1 (2010): 55–144. https://doi.org/10.1086/653046.

Metchik, Eric. "An Analysis of the 'Screening out' Model of Police Officer Selection." *Police Quarterly* 2, no. 1 (1999): 79–95. https://doi.org/10.1177/109861119900200104.

"Misdemeanor | Wex | US Law | LII / Legal Information Institute." Accessed October 1, 2020. https://www.law.cornell.edu/wex/misdemeanor.

Morrow, Weston J., Samuel G. Vickovic, Lisa M. Dario, and John A. Shjarback. "Examining a Ferguson Effect on College Students' Motivation to Become Police Officers." *Journal of Criminal Justice Education* 30, no. 4 (2019): 585–605. https://doi.org/10.1080/10511253.2019.1619793.

Osborne, Randall. "Observations on Police Cynicism: Some Preliminary Findings." *North American Journal of Psychology* 16, no. 3 (2014): 607.

"Police Officer License and Certifications." Accessed September 10, 2020. https://www.policeofficer.education/police-officer-license-certifications/.

President's Commission on Law Enforcement and the Administration of Justice. "The Challenge of Crime in a Free Society." Washington, DC, 1967. https://doi.org/10.3138/cjcor.9.4.347.

Reiner, Robert. "Revisiting the Classics: Three Seminal Founders of the Study of Policing: Michael Banton, Jerome Skolnick and Egon Bittner." *Policing and Society* 25, no. 3 (2015): 308–327. https://doi.org/10.1080/10439463.2015.1013753.

Reuss-Ianni, Elizabeth. *Two Cultures of Policing: Street Cops and Management Cops*. New Brunswick, NJ: Transaction, 1983.

Rosenbaum, Dennis P., Amie M. Schuck, Sandra K. Costello, Darnell F. Hawkins, and Marianne K. Ring. "Attitudes Toward the Police: The Effects of Direct and Vicarious Experience." *Police Quarterly* 8, no. 3 (2005): 343–365. https://doi.org/10.1177/1098611104271085.

Rubinstein, Jonathan. *City Police*. New York: Farrar, Straus and Giroux, 1973.

Sampson, Robert J., and Dawn Jeglum Bartusch. "Legal Cynicism and (Subcultural?) Tolerance of Deviance: The Neighborhood Context of Racial Differences." *Law & Society Review* 32, no. 4 (1998): 777–804. https://doi.org/10.2307/827739.

St. George, Donna. "Ousted from School." *The Washington Post*, May 8, 2011. https://www.washingtonpost.com/local/education/ousted-from-school/2011/05/31/AGElfXMH_story.html.

Telep, Cody W., and David Weisburd. "What Is Known About the Effectiveness of Police Practices in Reducing Crime and Disorder?" *Police Quarterly* 15, no. 4 (2012): 331–357. https://doi.org/10.1177/1098611112447611.

Uggen, Christopher, Mike Vuolo, Sarah Lageson, Ebony Ruhland, and K. Hilary Whitham. "The Edge of Stigma: An Experimental Audit of the Effects of Low-Level Criminal Records on Employment." *Criminology* 52, no. 4 (2014): 627–654. https://doi.org/10.1111/1745-9125.12051.

Walker, Samuel. *Taming the System: The Control of Discretion in Criminal Justice, 1950–1990*. New York: Oxford University Press, 2011. https://doi.org/10.1093/acprof:oso/9780195078206.001.0001.

CHAPTER 4

Protection of Life as the New Idea of Police

It's time to take a step back.

It's time to take a moment to summarize what we have studied thus far in U.S. policing and then to examine why this book proposes a new idea of police. The first three chapters covered substantial conceptual ground in policing, examining the following:

1. Evolution of policing strategies and tactics through the 1980s and into the present era.
2. Origins of policing in the United States.
3. Collective structure and functions of the modern U.S. police department.
4. Tension that often exists between the highly formalized quasi-military bureaucracy of policing and the highly informal processing of people that characterizes policing at the street level.
5. Sources of the police mandate.
6. Adherence to the police mandate through the development of formal organizational incentive structures and informal reward systems.
7. Translation of the mandate to police arrests.

We have explored enough of U.S. policing to conclude that the nature of the institution is rooted in coercion. This is not a value statement or a judgment. It is not even a particularly insightful observation. It is a conclusion based on three chapters of describing who the police are, why society has them, and how they have organized themselves to both fulfill the mission society has given them and perpetuate their own existence. As this book argues, though, the current policing paradigm, as it now exists, seems to have run its course. If society intends to maintain a police institution that represents the people and maintains any degree of legitimacy among large segments of the U.S. population, then society needs to reconsider the value proposition of policing in the United States. Indeed, this book argues for a transition to a version of policing that moves beyond coercion as its primary means and its primary ends.

This chapter examines the theory on which policing in the United States has been based since its creation as a formal institution. It then argues that reimagining the police on the basis of a new theory might help produce a new idea of police—one that moves beyond coercion as its primary means and ends. By the end of this chapter, readers should be able to answer these questions:

- How has Max Weber's conceptualization of the state appeared to influence the definition and role of the police in the United States since its development as a formal institution?
- How might Emile Durkheim's writings on state morality and how society should treat its criminal offenders help us move from an "ends-based" definition of police to a "means-based" definition?
- What is the new idea of police as proposed in this chapter?
- How might the new idea of police be practiced in ways that might limit conflict between police and the public? (Think about the case study of Jazmine Headley at the end of the chapter.)

To begin to answer these questions requires an examination of some of the foundational political and sociological theory that has described the role—and the very idea—of the Western state. The material covered in this chapter helps demonstrate where we currently reside with the police and where we might advance to, theoretically, by adopting a new perspective on the police. This chapter thus begins by visiting the perspectives of two foundational social theorists who did most of their writing during the first decades of the twentieth century, one in Germany and the other in France. Taken together, their work will inform us about how we might reimagine the police in the United States in ways that minimize their dangerousness while maximizing the good they can accomplish.

Max Weber and the Definition of State

The origins of this book reside in Carl Klockars's 1985 book, *The Idea of Police*. In that relatively brief volume (160 pages), Klockars deciphered the highly theoretical writings of the classic sociologist Egon Bittner for a mostly undergraduate readership in ways that not only made Bittner accessible, but also revolutionized the way many readers thought about the police at such a formative moment in their academic development. It was Bittner, after all—and quoted by Klockars—who wrote that the reason we have police in the first place is to respond to situations where "something ought not to be happening, about which something ought to be done . . . now!!"[1] As Klockars noted, Bittner rooted his theory of police in the assumption that the police possess a relatively open-ended right to use coercive force to accomplish their mandate, unlike the citizenry, whose rights to use force exist only under strictly defined circumstances. As such, when we call the police, we expect them to bring sweeping coercive authority—even violence when needed—to solve our problem.

While Klockars was translating Bittner in *The Idea of Police*, Bittner in his 1970 book, *The Functions of Police in Modern Society*, seemed to channel the German political theorist and sociologist, Max Weber.[2] In his 1919 essay, "Politics as a Vocation," Weber argued that the state could be defined as an institution that owned "a monopoly of the legitimate use of physical force" within its defined territory.[3] Indeed, this was the full extent of Weber's definition of the state, which was echoed by Bittner's arguments that "the police are nothing else than a mechanism for the distribution of situationally justified force in society."[4] Although Bittner's theory of police is not a precise generalization of Weber's conceptualization of the state, the two perspectives share a crucial common element: coercion. Indeed, in "Politics as a Vocation," which Weber originally delivered as a lecture in Munich, Germany, he asserted:

> Sociologically, the state cannot be defined in terms of its ends. There is scarcely any task that some political association has not taken in hand, and there is no task that one could say has always been exclusive and peculiar to . . . the modern state. . . . Ultimately, one can define the modern state sociologically only in terms of the specific *means* peculiar to it, as to every political association, namely, the use of physical force.[5]

In other words, according to Weber, to properly define the state (i.e., a country or some reasonable analogue), society must create a means-based definition that distinguishes the state from all other institutions because the function or role (i.e., the ends) of the state will vary depending on who is running it and who can influence its mandate. The state can be many things to many people, which makes defining it based on a "peculiar" function inadequate because any definition must apply to all states and all times. Weber concludes that we can only define the state based on its unique means: the capacity to use violence.

---

[1] Bittner, *The Functions of Police in Modern Society*.
[2] Bittner maintained that Weber did not influence his theory of police, although his perspectives on the police are similar enough to Weber's writings on the state that it is difficult to overlook what appears to be the application of Weber to Bittner's work. See Brodeur, "An Encounter with Egon Bittner," for a fuller elaboration.
[3] Weber, *From Max Weber: Essays in Sociology*, 78.
[4] Bittner, *The Functions of Police in Modern Society*, 39.
[5] Weber, *From Max Weber: Essays in Sociology*, 78–79.

Weber's concept of the state should sound familiar. It is the very definition Klockars gave of the police in his book, *The Idea of Police*. Although the police are not precisely the state, per se, they are the enforcement branch of state government. Indeed, in the United States, federal police (e.g., FBI, U.S. Marshal Service, Customs and Border Protection) fall under the executive branch of government, and even at the local levels of government—where most policing is located—the police are authorized by the various state legislatures with enforcement powers falling under the governors' offices (state-level versions of the federal executive branch). Thus, whereas Weber in 1919 was not specifically writing about, or defining, the police, he did advance a definition of the state that later scholars, such as Bittner and Klockars, could apply to the police as a very natural generalization. And so they did.

Something else happened along the policing timeline, though. Before Bittner presented his theory of police in his 1970 book, *The Functions of Police in Modern Society*, and certainly well before Klockars interpreted that theory and applied it to various aspects of the police occupation in his book, *The Idea of Police*, anthropologist Michael Banton conducted the first social scientific study of the police and published the results in his 1964 book, *The Policeman in the Community*. In that book Banton wrote that the police "are treated as both intrinsically good and dangerous."[6] Although Banton was referring to the British police, his statement is every bit as true for any police institution in a liberal democracy, including the United States. In fact, Banton's statement is so profound that it bears repeating: As an institution, the police are both intrinsically good and intrinsically dangerous. This statement is well captured by any definition of the police rooted in Weberian political theory because the general right to use coercive force can be harnessed for the public good, but it can also be wielded in very dangerous ways that cause great harm.

Is this as far as society can go with its definition—or idea—of police? Is society limited to a Weberian perspective that antiseptically conceives of the police solely in terms of the primary tool given to them? If the answer is "yes," then the next generation of policing seems destined to look remarkably similar to the previous generations of policing, even though it feels like, after the summer of 2020, policing has come to a crossroads. Society can continue down the conceptual pathway of defining policing by its general right to use coercive force and all that it brings—law enforcement, crime fighting, and order maintenance—or it can make a turn, divert from that pathway, and try something new. For the sake of an exercise, let's do that. Let us examine an alternate conceptualization of the state, which might help us create a new idea of the police.

---

[6] Banton, *The Policeman in the Community*, 237.

Emile Durkheim's Morality and the State

It has been argued that Weber's conceptualization of the state was a negative one, given its emphasis on violence as the state's primary means and definition.[7] Perhaps it was because Weber was born in the aftermath of the Prussian Revolution and then experienced life through the uncertainties of burgeoning statehood that culminated in the unification of Germany in 1871. He then lived to see his young country wage the Great War from 1914 through 1919, no doubt feeling the national humiliation that occurred at the Paris Peace Conference, which led his country's leaders to sign the Treaty of Versailles.[8] Recall that Weber wrote "Politics as a Vocation" in 1919, just as World War I was concluding, and just at the tail end of Germany's revolution that brought the Weimar Republic into existence.[9] Thus, Weber in his relatively short lifetime, experienced several different iterations of the meaning of national statehood, much of which was defined by war and state-sanctioned violence.

Another political theorist writing at the same time as Weber—Emile Durkheim (1858–1917), the *original* sociologist—brought an alternate perspective to the conceptualization of the state. Durkheim was born into the France of Victor Hugo,[10] who by 1858 was already writing about politics, justice, and a new French Republic. Indeed, Durkheim came of age during France's Third Republic (1870–1940), an era that coincided with the beginning of the French Industrial Revolution.[11] It was during the Third Republic that France made public schooling free, compulsory, and secular (i.e., non-religious), hoping to achieve through public education a French citizenry that could transcend class distinctions and find "solidarity" and "cooperation" in the fulfillment of France's political agenda of republicanism.[12] Unlike the empires and monarchies of the past, the liberal state of France's Third Republic hoped to become a positive force in the lives of French citizens.[13]

As Durkheim would observe in *The Division of Labor in Society* (1893)—his first major theoretical work and based on his doctoral dissertation—the economic organization of the modern state (during France's Third Republic) made it difficult for people to maintain their social and kinship ties to each other when the emerging paradigm of industrialization and factory production de-

---

[7] Terpstra, "Two Theories on the Police—The Relevance of Max Weber and Emile Durkheim to the Study of the Police," 6.

[8] Harkavy, "National Humiliation in International Politics."

[9] Evans, *Rethinking German History: Nineteenth-Century Germany and the Origins of the Third Reich.*

[10] Lived 1802–1885. Hugo was the author of *The Hunchback of Notre-Dame* (1831) and *Les Misérables* (1862). He lived his formative years during France's First Empire (1804–1815), created by Napoleon Bonaparte, just five years after the conclusion of the French Revolution. Hugo wrote about politics, justice, and social oppression and was a strong advocate of republicanism. *See generally* Graham Robb, *Victor Hugo: A Biography.* It is my position that *Les Misérables* would be the perfect companion to this book insofar as sparking discussion about the role of the state—and by extension, the police—in managing citizens who get labeled as "deviant."

[11] Lehning, *To Be a Citizen: The Political Culture of the Early French Third Republic.*

[12] Maynes, *Taking the Hard Road: Life Course in French and German Workers' Autobiographies in the Era of Industrialization.*

[13] Lehning, *To Be a Citizen: The Political Culture of the Early French Third Republic.*

manded loyalty to employers and focused on the divisions of labor in society.[14] Instead, the modern state, as Durkheim argued, seemed to create a more individualistic and "autonomous" citizen, while also leading those citizens to increasingly depend on the state for their social bonds and solidarity.[15] Durkheim wrote that "without these social links (to the state), individuals would be independent and develop separately (from one another), but instead they pool their efforts."[16] By "pooling their efforts," Durkheim meant that citizens relied on the state to maintain their social connections with each other.

Durkheim devoted most of his career to thinking and writing about social bonds, ethics, and the role of the state in "cementing" citizens to each other through its own moral actions.[17] He argued that in promoting social solidarity, the state had a "fundamental duty to persevere in calling an individual to a moral way of life."[18] That is, in Durkheim's view, the state should become a source of moral grounding for citizens, which would help maintain the social bonds of society. This is a very optimistic view of the state that generally runs counter to that of Weber. Recall that in his writings, Weber defined the state as an institution that maintained a monopoly on violence. He did not ascribe a role to the state, because in his view, the state can mean different things to different people (in much the same way that Klockars defined the police). Whereas Weber focuses on the "means" of the state in creating his definition, Durkheim focuses on the "ends," the promotion of public morality among the state's citizens.

By creating policies guided by strong moral reasoning, the state—as Durkheim maintained—would encourage citizens to bond with their government, which would then link them to each other through a new type of social solidarity. In other words, in Durkheimian sociology, the state should provide the moral grounding and public ethics needed to reduce the anomie[19]—or social chaos—that develops in modern societies resulting from industrialization and complex divisions of labor that tend to fragment people, rather than bring them together. A state that promotes public morality, according to Durkheim, would help create a "common" or "collective conscience," leading to a belief system that would bind all members of society around a common good.[20] Again, where Weber focused on the means of the state, Durkheim focused on the ends.

Although Durkheim—like Weber—wrote little on the police, he did write extensively about crime and deviance. His work in this area can further guide this chapter's application of Durkheimian sociology to policing, to help move toward a new idea of police.

---

[14] Durkheim, *Durkheim: The Division of Labour in Society*, 37.
[15] Durkheim, 37.
[16] Durkheim, 61.
[17] Varga, "Social Morals, the Sacred and State Regulation in Durkheim's Sociology."
[18] Durkheim, *Durkheim: The Division of Labour in Society*, 69.
[19] A sociological state of social "normlessness" first identified by Durkheim in his book, *Suicide* (initially published in 1897). For a compact, but useful, description of anomie, see https://sociologydictionary.org/anomie/
[20] Durkheim, 79–80. *See also* Morrison, *Marx, Durkheim, Weber: Formations of Modern Social Thought*, 131.

Durkheim argued that part of the state's morality was to recognize the fluidity of deviance, noting that all societies will have deviance (and crime) because deviance is a socially defined concept. Crime should be considered "normal," even crucial in "all healthy societies,"[21] because it helps societies define the boundaries of their own moral behaviors. Therefore, a state should respond to (or sanction) deviance and crime, but it should do only as much as is required, without treating offenders as if they are somehow morally defective. Indeed, if a state responds too aggressively to crime, or if crime control is viewed as overly oppressive, then such responses can undermine the very social solidarity that Durkheim argued the state should promote.[22]

Weber, Durkheim, and a New Idea of Police

Let us start from the very basic position that we do not need the police. Despite that many among us popularly refer to the police as "law enforcement" officers—and indeed, the undergraduate class in which many readers find themselves right now might be titled Introduction to Law Enforcement—we do not actually need the police to enforce the law. In fact, in the most formal sense, the police do not enforce the law because at the point of police contact with a criminal suspect—even throughout an investigation—no law has been broken.[23] There is only probable cause that a law has been broken. The police work with the district attorney to gather the evidence required for prosecution, but it is the latter who represents the people in presenting the case in court that a law has been broken and that the person on trial has broken it. In the end, it is the court that decides guilt or innocence, applies the sanction to convicted offenders, and enforces the law.

So why do we have the police? In large part, we have the police because at 3:00 a.m. on a Tuesday, when we are confronted by someone we believe might harm or kill us, we need someone to call. The police, in those situations, are frequently the only institution that will take our call. That's why we have the police: because of their relatively open-ended authority to use coercion to respond to our problem. To reinvoke Michael Banton, this makes the police an "intrinsically good" institution.[24] It is important not to forget Banton's assertion because much of the "new" idea of police assumes that the police possess the capacity to do good.

There is much about the police that is also dangerous, though. When we give them the general right to use coercive force with few legal strings attached (more on this in Chapter 8) and with no real moral philosophy to guide their application of coercion, then over time, coercion becomes both

---

[21] Durkheim, *Rules of Sociological Method*, 70.
[22] Terpstra, "Two Theories on the Police—The Relevance of Max Weber and Emile Durkheim to the Study of the Police," 7.
[23] Remember that in the U.S. system of justice, the accused enjoy the presumption of innocence throughout the criminal process.
[24] Banton, *The Policeman in the Community*, 237.

their means and their ends. Even if we remove the law enforcement assumptions of policing, we are still left with crime control and the maintenance of order as their primary mandate (recall our discussion of the police mandate in Chapter 3). But crime control and order maintenance are themselves coercive. Thus, coercion for the sake of crime control becomes coercion for the sake of coercion. We got here because society initially conceived of the police as an institution designated to control the "dangerous" classes. Society did not do enough at the beginning of policing's evolution to provide the moral guidance necessary to capitalize on the good that policing might accomplish, while reducing their potential for dangerousness.

Simply put, society has been saddled with a Weberian perspective on the police for more than 250 years if we rightly assume that slave patrols were the first formalized system of policing in what would become the United States,[25] which has placed an inherent limitation on how much policing as an institution can move forward. Every policing strategy, every reform, and every piece of technology purchased by police departments—indeed, much of the research produced by policing scholars—is in some way rooted in the presumption that coercion is the primary role of police. Although coercion will always represent the threat behind the badge, the badge must come to symbolize something bigger than the threat of coercion. For that to happen, society needs to expand its definition of policing to include both a means and an end. It's time to bring in Durkheim.

We can balance the collective Weberian and Bittner perspective on the police with a value system drawn from Durkheim's writings on state morality. This is not to suggest that the U.S. citizenry will begin to pull its moral grounding from the police, or that the police are to become the country's moral role model. Rather, the Durkheimian perspective on state morality, and how a state should treat those it has labeled deviant, suggests the creation of a value system in policing based on the (1) moral treatment of all people, and (2) withholding of judgment or moral contempt for the people police officers encounter. If the historic idea of police was one that defined policing simply as an institution to which society has given the general right to use coercive force, then a new idea of police can be one that defines police as an institution to which society has given the general right to use coercive force to achieve a moral end. This book argues that that moral end is the protection of life. Indeed, there is no more moral calling for a public institution than to strive to protect life.

Protection of Life as the New Idea of Police

As the strands of regionalized policing fused to create the system of modern policing we know today in the United States, they reinforced and perpetuated

---

[25] Reichel, "Southern Slave Patrols as a Transitional Police Type."

the notion that coercion and control were the dominant elements of the police occupation. This likely happened partly because (1) the origins of regionalized policing are found in the control of the so-called dangerous classes, and (2) at a basic level, the regionalized policing systems drew their institutional legitimacy from the uniformed military services. Policing has a checkered past, however, when it comes to the distribution of law and coercive authority across population groups.[26] In just the past 30 years, the United States has witnessed (due to video recordings) the police beating of Rodney King, and the police killings of Eric Garner, Freddie Gray, and Michael Brown. As previously noted, during the summer of 2020 when Minneapolis police officer Derek Chauvin killed George Floyd, something felt different. The collective conscious of the country seemed to be genuinely shocked.[27] At the very least, the killing of George Floyd and the protests that followed demonstrated that it is no longer enough to think of the police simply as an institution that claims the general right to use coercive force. The stakes are too high. Indeed, policing's history shows the need to include something of the essence of what society expects of them in their definition.

The new idea of police is not a call for police reform, per se, nor is it a call to return to a "better" era in U.S. policing. The new idea of police is a redefinition of the police identity. It is a mentality as much as anything else—a change of mandate—that can hopefully encourage the creation of a next-generation police institution that views itself as more than just enforcers—that views itself an institution to which society has given the general right to use coercive force for the purposes of protecting life.

But wait, don't the police already protect life? This is where society's relationship with the police becomes complicated. Protecting life is often an indirect outcome of their primary mission of enforcing the law and maintaining order. When the police arrive at our house at 3:00 a.m., they want to secure the scene by eliminating any threats. They want to establish control. Then they want to decide who is the victim and who is the offender, because such a judgment determines who bears the brunt of their coercive authority. Another way of putting it is this: After they have secured the scene and established control, they want to deduce who their client is. It was the client, after all—the "reporting party"—who mobilized the police. The other person (whether still on the scene or gone on police arrival) will be the object of control. It must also be emphasized that at any given moment during such an encounter the client and the offender can change places, depending on how the interactions unfold.

What does the protection of life mean at the street level? It means, among other things, that the police should not force confrontations just for the sake of exercising coercion and control. It means they should view both parties—the alleged victim and the alleged offender—as their clients because

---

[26] Cashmore and McLaughlin, *Out of Order? Policing Black People.*
[27] King, Lee, and Kaleem, "George Floyd's Death and the National Conversation: Pain, Anger and Hope."

both have value as human beings. It means, in David Klinger's vernacular (recall Chapter 3), that all victims are "deserving victims,"[28] worthy of police consideration, regardless of their lifestyles, the neighborhoods they were born into, and the race, gender, and ethnicity with which they identify. The protection of life means that when the police enter any given neighborhood, their presence, at the very least, should not decrease the life chances of the people who live there.

Perhaps at this moment the best way to offer a glimpse of what could be possible under a protection of life mandate, and how a subtle change in mentality might make big impacts on policing outcomes, is through a counter-example of policing that occurred a few years ago and appeared to be solely the product of the coercion and control paradigm. It was not a deadly force incident; it was something far more ordinary, and therefore, likely far more common. Officers did not have to decide whether or not to pull a trigger; all they really needed to do was get a young mother a chair.

A Case in Point: The Story of Jazmine Headley

In early December 2018, 23-year-old Jazmine Headley entered the Supplemental Nutrition Assistance Program (SNAP) office in Brooklyn, New York. She was carrying her one-year-old son, hoping to renew her SNAP benefits.[29] The waiting area was full with other clients, and there were no chairs available for Ms. Headley. Rather than leave, she took a seat on the floor to wait for her name to be called. Two hours into her wait, she was approached by a security guard and told to move or leave because she was "blocking a fire zone."[30] She refused to move, pointing out that there were no available chairs and she needed to renew her benefits. Both she and the security guard persisted in their protestations, leading a few more security guards to join their colleague.

As the disagreement grew louder, someone in the office called the police, prompting the arrival of four NYPD officers—one female sergeant, two female officers, and one male officer. According to reports, the officers initially ordered Ms. Headley to leave because they claimed she was causing a disturbance. When she refused, again arguing that she needed SNAP benefits for her son, the officers surrounded her and demanded that she give them her child, an order she also refused. It is not clear why the police ordered her to give them her son. The more they demanded it, the more she refused, leading one officer to draw a Taser and aim it toward the crowd of clients in the SNAP office, who were apparently voicing their "outrage" at the behavior of police.[31]

---

[28] Klinger, "Negotiating Order in Patrol Work: An Ecological Theory of Police Response to Deviance," 294.
[29] Southall, "'Appalling' Video Shows the Police Yanking 1-Year-Old from His Mother's Arms."
[30] Stewart, "Jazmine Headley, Whose Child Was Torn From Her Arms at a City Office, Gets a Public Apology."
[31] Southall, "'Appalling' Video Shows the Police Yanking 1-Year-Old From His Mother's Arms."

At that point, one of the officers reached for Ms. Headley's son and "repeatedly yanks [sic] the child in an apparent attempt to separate him from his mother."[32] When that effort failed, the officer tackled Ms. Headley to the floor (while she continued to clutch her son) and tried again to force her to release the child. Several people in the SNAP office pulled out their cell phones and began recording the incident, with at least one of the videos landing on Facebook.[33] The video begins with Ms. Headley lying on the floor clutching her son, and with at least three officers bent over her, trying in vain to separate her from her child. Ms. Headley can be heard yelling, "They're hurting my son! They're hurting my son! They're hurting my son!" Sixteen seconds into the video, one of the female NYPD officers establishes a firm grip on the child and begins repeatedly yanking to wrench him from his mother's arms. After viewing the video, it is difficult to describe this officer's action as anything other than violent. This action lasts for at least 10 seconds while the other officers provide cover, and while several people in the crowd repeatedly shout, "Oh, my God! Oh, my God!" in disapproval at the officers' overresponse.

Eventually, the officers succeeded in prying Ms. Headley's son from her arms, and they arrested her for "acting in a manner injurious to a child, obstructing governmental administration, criminal trespass and resisting arrest,"[34] all of which, it should be noted, are misdemeanor crimes. Within five days of the incident and arrest, the New York District Attorney's Office dropped all charges. Although the dismissal occurred on a Tuesday morning, Ms. Headley was not released from Riker's Island jail until late that evening.[35] Ms. Headley has since won a $625,000 settlement from New York City as the result of a federal lawsuit she filed that alleged, among other charges, police brutality.[36]

After reviewing newspaper accounts of the incident and watching the video, one might ask this question: When the officers arrived at the SNAP office, why did they not simply find Ms. Headley a chair?

It is easy to imagine a possible narrative of the 911 call into the NYPD communications center (whether true or not): A woman with her baby screaming at people in the social service center; she might be high; she's yelling at everyone and seems dangerous. Automatically, the responding officers might be thinking that they are walking into a potentially violent encounter and perhaps a child endangerment situation. This would be a fair enough assumption, at least initially, because the officers should be prepared to face conflict when they enter the SNAP office. Indeed, when they arrive at the scene, the sergeant and officers are likely in "threat" mode, ready to

---

[32] Southall.

[33] The video has since been removed from Facebook.

[34] Mettler and Noori Farzen, "Jazmine Headley Case: Charges Dropped Against Mother Whose Baby Was Torn Away by NYPD in Viral Video."

[35] Mettler and Noori Farzen.

[36] Stewart, "$625,000 Settlement for Woman Whose Child Was Torn From Her Arms."

take action against any possible confrontation they might encounter at the moment they walk through the doors.

The problem is, they appeared to remain in "threat" mode throughout the incident. They approached Ms. Headley as if she were the offender—that is, the object of their control—rather than as someone who might be a victim and deserving of their consideration. They seem never to have taken the time to (1) consider the new information they were taking in as the situation unfolded, or (2) redefine the incident as something other than a potentially violent encounter, given that Ms. Headley was not armed with a weapon, and she was not swinging a tire iron or anything else at officers or bystanders. In fact, she was clutching her son to her chest, which fully occupied her arms and rendered her a threat to nobody. The officers should have taken the time to realize that Ms. Headley was every bit as much a client as the security guards who worked at the SNAP office. Instead, in an effort control Ms. Headley, they used their coercive authority to force a confrontation with her that ultimately could have injured her and her infant son. And they arrested her for creating a disturbance.

Join the Discussion . . .

Scan the QR code to visit the author's blog and read a summary of the Jazmine Headley incident. Offer your thoughts and perspective on the event and engage with other readers on the meaning of the protection of life mandate of police.

In "handling" Ms. Headley, the NYPD officers were not acting as the moral conscience of the state, they were acting as enforcers—that is, the bearers of coercion. They approached the situation under the full embrace of the Weberian perspective without an ounce of Durkheim. Therein lies the problem: Although it is true (and as noted in Chapter 1) that the general right to use coercive force is a defining characteristic of the police institution, coercion does not have to define every encounter between the police and the public. Coercion might get them through the door—because after all, that is why we call them—but coercion does not have to determine their actions throughout the event. The four NYPD officers who showed up to the social services office failed to look beyond the coercion and control paradigm, which led them to deploy a highly aggressive use of force response against a parent who was too afraid to give them her child. If they had simply found Ms. Headley a chair, engaged her in conversation, and slowed down the event, they might have remembered that her life was worth protecting, too, and they could have worked with her and the SNAP office staff to find a solution that ensured Ms. Headley's son got the SNAP benefits he deserved while avoiding her arrest in the process.

Some Concluding Observations

To those outside of policing—or this incident, specifically—the alternate course the NYPD officers could have taken that would have avoided conflict with Ms. Headley and her arrest almost appears obvious. As the materials in the first three chapters of this book should demonstrate, however, policing is designed from top to bottom—or perhaps more precisely, from society down to the individual officer—to not just encourage coercive responses, but to value them. The police mandate, which is firmly rooted in Weber's conception of the state and Bittner's subsequent theory of police, tells the police they are law enforcers, crime fighters, and restorers of public order. Police departments operationalize the mandate by evaluating officers on the quantity of coercive outcomes they produce: field stops, citations, and arrests. They create informal reward systems that incentivize such outcomes through accolades and adoration.

The moment Ms. Headley failed to leave the SNAP office when ordered by officers, she became a problem to them. And how did they presume to solve that problem? By turning up the volume of coercion they initially deployed and ordering her to give them her child. When she refused to follow that order, at least one officer switched from verbal to physical coercion by trying to snatch the infant from Ms. Headley's arms. When that did not work, they tackled her. The coercion paradigm guided the entire encounter between officers and Ms. Headley, and it does not allow for "resistance" on any level because it cannot comprehend resistance as anything other than a response that requires more coercion. So, when the above description of the protection of life mandate argues that police officers should not force confrontations with people simply to accomplish a coercive end, it refers directly to Ms. Headley's situation. Had officers simply gotten her a chair and engaged her in conversation, they would have sent the encounter down a different pathway.

Did the officers' actions decrease the life chances of Jazmine Headley and her son? We cannot know how the trauma of forced separation, arrest, and four days spent in jail while her child might have been in emergency foster care might affect the long-term health of her and her child. We can speculate that this event will become part of the child's life "story" in ways that could engender distrust of the police and other public institutions as he grows up. An equally important question is this: How did the police officers balance the "intrinsic" good that coercion can achieve with the intrinsic dangerousness it risks? This book argues that the NYPD officers used their coercion in dangerous ways that harmed two of their clients: Ms. Headley and her son. Had the officers taken a conceptual step back from the immediate incident, they might have realized that they could have used their coercion as a form of moral authority to help realize a positive end for Ms. Headley and her son.

Finally, although the protection of life mandate recognizes the occasional necessity of placing people into handcuffs, arresting them, using physical force, and sometimes even using deadly force—an ironic and tragic way of "protecting" life—such a mandate always means treating people with dignity and as if they matter; it means police officers trying to put themselves into other people's life circumstance while also trying to achieve compliance. Again, it is a change in mentality that makes coercion secondary to achieving a moral end.

Questions for Review and Reflection

Question 1. Parsing Out the "Means" of Policing

A primary theoretical premise of this chapter is that policing, since its beginnings, has been largely rooted in Max Weber's conceptualization of the state; that is, that the state can be defined based on its legitimate monopoly on violence.

- In what ways is Weber's idea of the state similar to Carl Klockars's idea of the police?
- Given that the state is a political entity and the police are the enforcement branch of a political entity, is it reasonable to argue that Weber's idea of the state can be perfectly applied to the police? Why or why not?
- Most police officers and members of the public are likely unaware that the policing occupation seems grounded in a means-based definition. How might we explain the means-based definition of policing to them in ways that make sense? What examples could we use that demonstrate a means-based, or coercion-driven, paradigm of police?

Question 2. The Proposition of an Ends-Based Definition of Police

Emile Durkheim's philosophy about the role of the state in the lives of citizens suggests that the state can become an entity that promotes public morality. In Durkheim's time, people were increasingly having to shift their loyalties (or connectedness) from their traditional kinship groups to their employers due to the rapid industrialization occurring in Europe; Durkheim argued that the government could help keep people connected to each other through its own moral actions.

- As the United States becomes increasingly diverse, in what ways might the police institution set the example for how government can act in a moral way that binds citizens to one another?
- Relatedly, how might a protection of life mandate infuse morality into policing in ways that set an example for the entire citizenry?
- What would it take for society and police to move from a Weberian to a Durkheimian mentality that might help reimagine the role of the police institution?

Question 3. Police Coercion and the Protection of Life Mandate

The new idea of police argues that policing should move beyond the coercion paradigm to one that mandates the protection of life as the primary role of police.

- Can the police still adequately enforce the law while practicing a protection of life mandate? If so, how? If not, why?
- How does the use of deadly force by a police officer reconcile with a protection of life mandate? In other words, can police still use deadly force when necessary while practicing a protection of life mandate?

Exercises

Exercise 1. Discovering the Social Contexts of the Coercion Paradigm

As noted earlier in the chapter, Egon Bittner, the scholar who originally argued that policing is best defined in terms of its general right to use coercive force, once stated that his definition of police was not based on Max Weber's conceptualization of the state. That is, despite that Weber defined the state based on its monopoly on violence to protect its borders, Bittner noted that his definition of police did not flow from Weber's idea of the state. This exercise seeks to explain how two scholars writing at two different times could develop remarkably similar conceptualizations of the state and the police.

- Review the discussion of Weber in this chapter and then conduct outside research on Weber to get a better sense of how the historical circumstances of his time might have influenced how he came to define the state based on its capacity to use violence.
- Conduct outside research on Egon Bittner to learn where and when he grew up and came of age. You will find that Bittner was born in 1921 in what was then Czechoslovakia—just two years after Max Weber defined the state in his essay, "Economy & Society."
- What was happening in Czechoslovakia around the time Bittner was born? Specifically, what happened to Czechoslovakia in 1918, 1938, and then from 1945 to 1989?
- How might the social and political history of Czechoslovakia have influenced Bittner's later ideas of what and who the police are (or were)? Specifically, what features of Bittner's personal history might have led him to define the police as no more than an institu-

tion that maintains the general right to use coercive force?
- Why might it be important to examine the social and political contexts of scholars and philosophers who come to define the meaning of our social institutions?

Exercise 2. Writing Alternate Endings

Conduct some research to identify a controversial incident in policing that involved the use of force, the use of a Taser, or the use of deadly force. The incident could be something shocking and highly public such as the killing of George Floyd, or it can be something that happened in a small police department that did not generate massive media coverage. Whatever the incident you identify, it should represent an example of policing driven by the coercion paradigm. To that end, it should be a controversial use of force or deadly force application, or a situation where the police might have forced a conflict with a suspect that left someone dead or injured. To complete this exercise, do the following:

- Write a summary of the incident that provides a step-by-step description of how the interaction between police and suspect(s) became increasingly heated.
- Describe the final outcome of the event as it actually occurred.
- Write an alternate ending to the incident in which the police deescalated the event in ways that avoided the use of force or deadly force.
- How does your alternative ending suggest a possible transition from the coercion paradigm to the protection of life paradigm?

Operations Dashboard Exercise

Load the San Francisco operations dashboard via QR code on the left, or enter the following URL into a browser window:

https://arcg.is/0SbK550

This exercise is designed to help readers better understand how police actions in communities can be driven more by a protection of life mandate than the coercion paradigm.

To participate in this exercise, readers should visit the San Francisco operations dashboard, being sure to load it on a laptop or desktop computer, rather than on a mobile device. Once the dashboard is up and running, click the Bookmark button and then select the City Extent option to view the entire city of San Francisco.

The map of San Francisco falls in the center of the screen. On the right side, there are three interactive widgets: crime and arrests doughnut charts, and a census tract selector. Users can scroll through these widgets using the tabs along the bottom right. On the left side of the screen, there are four census tract display sliders. Moving the sliders left and right changes which census tracts are displayed on the map.

Setting up the dashboard for this exercise requires the reader (who has just become the user) to activate certain data layers and inactivate others. To do that, click the Layer button on the ribbon along the top right of the map. The Layer button is two from the right of the Bookmark button. For now, make sure the heat maps of arrests and crimes are visible (i.e., checked), as well as the census tract layer.

After selecting the layers, close the layers window and zoom into the map to get a better visual of crime and arrest heat maps. The multicolored heat areas indicate locations where crimes and arrests are most densely concentrated, and they are delineated by color bands (similar to heat ranges on a weather map). Generally, the center of the heat maps shows the highest density crime and arrest areas, with densities decreasing outward in successive bands. Users can decipher density areas by clicking the legend (located on the map ribbon between the Layer and Bookmark buttons) and examining the density values and ranges.

Click the Layer button to show the data layers, making sure to keep the heat map areas still visible (drag the map if necessary so that the heat areas do not fall under the open Layers window). Click the Heat Maps of Arrest layer a few times to turn it off and on, noticing how arrest densities and crime densities greatly overlap. Such an overlap should make sense: Police tend to go where the crime is, and they tend to make arrests there. Once done, scroll out again to see most of the city in the map window.

Question

How much of San Francisco is covered by arrest and crime heat maps? Would you say crime and arrest densities cover most of the city, or are they concentrated in just a few areas? Before going any further with the exercise, take a moment to think about why the crimes and arrests might concentrate where they do on the map.

Take a moment to scroll through the arrests and crimes doughnut charts. What do you notice about the breakdowns for crimes and arrests? Which crimes account for the largest percentages? What arrests account for the largest percentages? Do you notice any apparent incongruencies between crimes and arrests? Next, select the Neighborhoods tab to see a list of all the census tracts in San Francisco. Note that for this and all San Francisco exercises, census tracts are regarded as neighborhoods or local communities. Click a census tract in the list and see what happens to the map. The dashboard is designed to pan and zoom to selected census tracts and to filter out crimes and arrests so that the user will see just the totals in the selected tract(s). For example, with a census tract selected, scroll back to the arrest and crime doughnut charts to see how they have changed. The data have been filtered to show just the crimes and arrests in the tract (or tracts) you selected. To deselect the tract, click on it again so that it is no longer highlighted in blue in the list. Scroll out again until you can see most of the crime and arrest heat areas but can still also see a large portion of the city not covered by heat areas.

For this exercise, we will identify census tracts that are mostly populated by members of vulnerable populations, and we will examine the crime and arrest patterns in those communities. By default, the map shows all census tracts. It is time to begin to eliminate tracts, or communities, based on their vulnerabilities. Locate the Census Tract data display left of the map and hover over the % Households in Poverty slider. With the left mouse button, click and drag the slider until it shows 30. Release the slider at that point. You will now see just the communities in San Francisco in which at least 30 percent of the residents live in poverty. Also, notice that the list of census tracts on the right shrinks to show just the tracts visible on the map.

When 30 percent of a community lives in poverty, that creates a social and economic situation that is problematic for all residents: Not only do the impoverished residents have difficulties surviving on a weekly basis, but such a high rate of poverty also discourages businesses from investing in the community. Such communities become "deserts of disadvantage," offering few job opportunities, a challenged education system, and few fresh food opportunities.[37]

---

[37] Johnson and Kane, "Deserts of Disadvantage: The Diffuse Effects of Structural Disadvantage on Violence in Urban Communities."

At this point, it might be a good idea to turn off the heat maps so the user can see the remaining tracts. Next, grab and drag the % Non-White Residents slider to the right until the number reads 65. This action will show the census tracts that are at least 65 percent non-White, and it will cause the nonvisible tracts to disappear in the list of census tracts on the right. You are now viewing a map that shows only census tracts in which at least 30 percent of the residents live in poverty and at least 65 percent of residents are non-White.

Now is a good time to activate the Households with Disabilities layer. To do this, click the Layer button on the map ribbon and select the check box next to the Disabilities layer. Once selected, close the layer window. You will now see a representation on the map showing the percentage of households in every census tract (or neighborhood) with at least one disabled member. To get a sense of the range, click the Legend button to view the ranges that are based on proportionally sized dots. Now grab and drag the % Households with at Least 1 Disabled Member slider to the right until the indicator reads 20. Notice a number of tracts disappear from the map and list, leaving visible just the census tracts in which at least 20 percent of the households have at least one disabled person.

Finally, to add some economic context to the exercise, it is useful to examine the Housing Affordability Index (HAI), which also appears as a slider on the left side of the dashboard. In general, the HAI shows the extent to which the "average" family residing in a community has the economic resources to purchase a median-priced home. A score of 100 indicates that the average family in a tract is able to afford a median-priced home. Scores higher than 100 show that the average family can more than afford a median-priced home in the community, and scores lower than 100 show when the average family is unable to afford a median-priced home. Grab the HAI and slowly side it to the right until the remaining census tracts begin to disappear. At the point at which the tracts disappear, take note of the HAI score on the slider. Do any of the remaining tracts come close to 100?

Question

What are we left with? Our map now shows five census tracts—or residential communities—in San Francisco in which at least 35 percent of the residents reside in poverty, 65 percent are non-White, and at least 20 percent of the households contain at least one member who has a disability. These are unhealthy communities characterized by racially concentrated economic disadvantage. Just to add context, we note that in none of these communities does the average family have the financial ability to purchase a median-priced home. Now that we have identified these communities, what initial conclusions can we draw about the lived experiences of those who reside there?

From the census tract list, click tracts 125.01 and 125.02. Once they are selected, the map should pan and zoom to those two contiguous tracts. Click to activate the crime and arrest heat maps in those tracts. Do these tracts generally reside in the center of the heat maps (i.e., the densest areas), or at the edges? Visual inspection should lead you to conclude that these tracts reside in the center of the crime and arrest densities, suggesting that not only are these very unhealthy communities characterized by racially concentrated structural disadvantages, but they are also highly criminalized.

Click through the tabs on the right to visualize the crime doughnut chart. Notice that the most typical crime in those two selected tracts is assault. Drug crimes run second at almost 20 percent of all crimes, and robbery accounts for 15.36 percent of all crimes. Notably, disorderly conduct accounts for 7.29 percent of the crimes. This composition of crimes is important because communities that experience significant drug crimes also tend to experience robbery and burglary at high rates (as these tracts do) so that people who use drugs can obtain the money to purchase them. Assault is typically part of the composite, as well, as buyers and users often have disagreements over cost, turf, and other issues.

Now visualize the arrest doughnut chart and notice the percentages. Assaults and robbery account for the large majority of arrests, whereas drug offenses amount to under 2 percent. This is an interesting finding because it does suggest that the police are reserving arrests for the more serious crimes and not emphasizing drug arrests. Interestingly, though, almost 15 percent of all arrests are for disorderly conduct, even though disorderly conduct accounts for just over 7 percent of the reported crimes. These two census tracts in particular, but all five tracts more generally, are clearly difficult places to police. They are characterized by severe population vulnerabilities, high crime, and high arrest rates. Indeed, the intersectionality of health, crime, economic disadvantage, and racial concentrations cannot be ignored. Despite the fact that the police tend to arrest people for drug offenses at very low rates, these highlighted communities still experience some of the highest arrest rates in the entire city.

In many ways, the communities highlighted in this exercise are stigmatized at several intersections: They contain large numbers of disabled people, have high rates of poverty, and are mostly populated by people of color. In addition, they experience some of the highest crime and arrest concentrations in the city. In the Durkheimian sense, these communities are isolated by their stigmas and operate essentially as autonomous units within the larger city. How, then, might the police function in these communities in ways that connect the local residents to social resources and increase their links to one another? In other words, and again using Durkheim's terminology, how do the police fulfill their "fundamental duty to persevere in calling an individual to a moral way of life"?[38]

---

[38] Durkheim, *Durkheim: The Division of Labour in Society.*

This is not a literal question, as this book does not argue that the police can become the moral conscience of a society. As a figurative question, though, it does ask how the police can reduce the coercion they bring into highly vulnerable communities in ways that help reduce some of the pressures on the people who live there. Clearly, in these highlighted communities, the police have lots of time to do their work. After all, arrests can take officers off the street for hours, and the police in these communities make lots of arrests. The primary purpose of this exercise is to encourage readers to think beyond the traditional boundaries of the police role and reimagine an institution that tries to improve the life chances of people who live in communities characterized by the most challenging, social, economic, crime, and health conditions, while still having to enforce the law and trying to maintain some degree of order.

Bibliography

Banton, Michael. *The Policeman in the Community*. New York: Basic Books, 1964. https://books.google.com/books/about/The_Policeman_in_the_Community.html?id=F0NMwQEACAAJ.

Bittner, Egon. *The Functions of Police in Modern Society*. Chevy Chase, MD: National Institute of Mental Health, 1970. https://www.google.com/books/edition/The_Functions_of_the_Police_in_Modern_So/rQcXAAAAIAAJ?hl=en&gbpv=1&printsec=frontcover.

Brodeur, Jean Paul. "An Encounter with Egon Bittner." *Crime, Law and Social Change* 48, no. 3–5 (2007): 105–132. https://doi.org/10.1007/s10611-007-9084-2.

Cashmore, E., and E. McLaughlin, eds. *Out of Order? Policing Black People*. London: Routledge/Taylor & Francis, 1991.

Durkheim, Emile. *Durkheim: The Division of Labour in Society*, edited by Steven Lukes. 2nd ed. London: Palgrave Macmillan, n.d.

Durkheim, Emile. *Rules of Sociological Method*, edited by Steven Lukes. New York: Free Press, n.d.

Evans, Richard J. *Rethinking German History: Nineteenth-Century Germany and the Origins of the Third Reich*. London: Routledge, 1987. https://www.amazon.com/Rethinking-German-History-Routledge-Revivals-dp-1138842842/dp/1138842842/ref=mt_other?_encoding=UTF8&me=&qid=1602348156.

Harkavy, Robert E. "National Humiliation in International Politics." *International Politics* 37 (2000): 345–368.

Johnson, Lallen T., and Robert J. Kane. "Deserts of Disadvantage: The Diffuse Effects of Structural Disadvantage on Violence in Urban Communities." *Crime and Delinquency* 64, no. 2 (2018): 143–165. https://doi.org/10.1177/0011128716682228.

King, Laura, Kurtis Lee, and Jaweed Kaleem. "George Floyd's Death and the National Conversation: Pain, Anger and Hope." *Los Angeles Times*, June 5, 2020. https://www.latimes.com/world-nation/story/2020-06-05/george-floyds-death-sparks-voices-on-americas-deep-pain-and-searing-rage.

Klinger, David A. "Negotiating Order in Patrol Work: An Ecological Theory of Police Response to Deviance." *Criminology* 35, no. 2 (1997): 277–306. https://doi.org/10.1111/j.1745-9125.1997.tb00877.x.

Lehning, James, R. *To Be a Citizen: The Political Culture of the Early French Third Republic*. Ithaca, NY: Cornell University Press, 2001.

Maynes, Mary Jo. *Taking the Hard Road: Life Course in French and German Workers' Autobiographies in the Era of Industrialization*. Chapel Hill: University of North Carolina Press, 1995.

Mettler, Katie, and Antonia Noori Farzen. "Jazmine Headley Case: Charges Dropped Against Mother Whose Baby Was Torn Away by NYPD in Viral Video." *The Washington Post*, December 12, 2018. https://www.washingtonpost.com/nation/2018/12/11/prosecutors-drop-charges-against-new-york-mother-whose-baby-was-yanked-away-by-police/.

Morrison, Ken. *Marx, Durkheim, Weber: Formations of Modern Social Thought*. Thousand Oaks, CA: Sage, 1995.

Reichel, Philip L. "Southern Slave Patrols as a Transitional Police Type." *American Journal of Police* 7, no. 2 (1988): 51–77.

Robb, Graham. *Victor Hugo: A Biography*. New York: W.W. Norton, 1997.

Southall, Ashley. "'Appalling' Video Shows the Police Yanking 1-Year-Old from His Mother's Arms." *The New*

York Times, December 9, 2018. https://www.nytimes .com/2018/12/09/nyregion/nypd-jazmine-headley -baby-video.html.

Stewart, Nikita. "$625,000 Settlement for Woman Whose Child Was Torn from Her Arms." *The New York Times*, December 13, 2019. https://www.nytimes .com/2019/12/13/nyregion/jazmine-headley-video -settlement.html.

Stewart, Nikita. "Jazmine Headley, Whose Child Was Torn From Her Arms at a City Office, Gets a Public Apology." *The New York Times*, February 4, 2019. https:// www.nytimes.com/2019/02/04/nyregion/jazmine -headley-nypd-arrest.html.

Terpstra, Jan. "Two Theories on the Police—The Relevance of Max Weber and Emile Durkheim to the Study of the Police." *International Journal of Law, Crime and Justice* 39, no. 1 (2011): 1–11. https://doi .org/10.1016/j.ijlcj.2011.01.009.

Varga, Ivan. "Social Morals, the Sacred and State Regulation in Durkheim's Sociology." *Social Compass* 53, no. 4 (2006). https://doi.org/10.1177/0037768606070408.

Weber, Max. *From Max Weber: Essays in Sociology*, edited by H. H. Gerth and C. Wright Mills. London: Routledge, 1991. https://www.amazon.com/Max-Weber-Essays -Sociology-dp-0343212765/dp/0343212765/ref =mt_other?_encoding=UTF8&me=&qid=.

PART II

Pathways and Remedies to a Coercion Paradigm

CHAPTER 5

The Police Subculture

Reimagining the Thin Blue Line

Recall Jazmine Headley's encounter with the NYPD from the previous chapter. She was the young mother who entered the Supplemental Nutrition Assistance Program (SNAP) office in Brooklyn, New York, with her one-year-old son, hoping to renew her SNAP benefits. Unable to find a chair in the waiting area, she took a seat on the floor to wait for her turn to be called.

Soon thereafter, a security guard approached and asked her to leave because she was (he claimed) causing a disturbance by sitting on the floor. When she refused to leave, arguing that she needed to renew her benefits so her child could eat, the security guard called the police. Four NYPD officers arrived, asked her first to leave, and then—when she attempted to explain her situation—ordered her to surrender her son to them.[1] Frightened, Ms. Headley refused to give over her son, at which point the officers surrounded her, threatened her with a Taser, attempted to yank her son from her arms, and ultimately tackled her and forcefully pried her son from her clenched hands. Although she was arrested for trespassing and endangering a child, she was almost immediately released with all charges dropped and has since won a settlement against the NYPD for a claim of excessive force.

Podcast Episode: "Cop's Kid: Growing Up in a Police Family"

Scan the QR code or enter the short URL shown below into a browser window to listen to this chapter's podcast.

https://bit.ly/3s8SlmN

---

[1] Southall, "'Appalling' Video Shows the Police Yanking 1-Year-Old From His Mother's Arms."

The experience of Ms. Headley was predictable. It was emblematic of any number of situations where police officers may have forced confrontations and then arrested someone because they effectively—and metaphorically—backed themselves into a corner. Under the coercion paradigm, when a person fails to submit readily to police authority, even just verbally, that person likely will be subject to *more* coercion because that is how police are trained and socialized to respond to perceived or real noncompliance.[2] Viewing this encounter through a social interactionist lens might help explain the dynamic. Social interactionism is a sociological perspective that assumes that all social processes, such as cooperation and conflict, are the product of interactions between human beings. Thus, even at the societal level, social processes are still the result of small groups of human individuals interacting with each other.[3]

Thus, during a police–citizen encounter, an escalation of coercion can be expected when the subject of the encounter—in this case, Ms. Headley—violates police norms that govern what Alpert and Dunham have called the "authority maintenance ritual,"[4] an assumption about who is in charge during a police–citizen encounter. From the police standpoint, when they enter into an interaction with one or more members of the public, they (the police) are in charge of the incident. They give the instructions; they ask the questions; they take control. For the most part, members of the public also understand this arrangement, and they normally defer to police authority in such interactions.[5]

But not always, and for a variety of reasons. When police arrive on scene to a "disturbance" call, for example, they might be confronted by the person allegedly causing the disturbance, who is eager to explain that they are the victim, not the offender. This presents a tricky situation for police because they might view this person as having a different understanding of who is in charge of the interaction. Officers might assume that the person is rejecting the socially understood norms of the authority maintenance ritual. In the case of Ms. Headley, in trying to convince the police that she was the victim rather than the offender—and thus resisting their commands to comply and turn over her child to them—she was viewed as trying to redefine the situation in a way that gave *her* the balance of authority. Under such circumstances, however, many police officers will escalate force as a way of maintaining or regaining control of the encounter.[6] As Albert and Dunham noted in their volume on the police use of force:

---

[2] Hine et al., "Too Much or Too Little? Individual and Situational Predictors of Police Force Relative to Suspect Resistance"; Klinger, "Demeanor or Crime? Why 'Hostile' Citizens Are More Likely to Be Arrested"; Van Maanen, "The Asshole."

[3] Shalin, "Pragmatism and Social Interactionism."

[4] Alpert and Dunham, *Understanding Police Use of Force: Officers, Suspects, Reciprocity,* 172.

[5] Alpert and Dunham; Goffman, *The Presentation of Self in Everyday Life.*

[6] Hine et al., "Too Much or Too Little? Individual and Situational Predictors of Police Force Relative to Suspect Resistance"; Terrill, "Police Use of Force: A Transactional Approach"; Van Maanen, "The Asshole"; Kane and Cronin, "Maintaining Order under the Rule of Law: Occupational Templates and the Police Use of Force."

"Authority maintenance" is used to characterize the exaggerated role that authority plays in police–citizen interactions, and also acknowledges the overriding concern of officers with maintaining their authoritative edge in interactions with citizens.[7]

The authority maintenance ritual can be viewed as a feature of the policing subculture. Although authority rituals are not unique to policing, per se—indeed, physicians also have been shown to want to maintain control over their patients[8]—they are distinct in policing because of the general right to use coercive force. No other occupation gives its practitioners the general right to physically assert their authority over others, a fact that gets to the point of this chapter: to develop an understanding of how authority—among other important concepts—helps shape the "worldview"[9] of police in ways that explain the development and expressions of the police subculture.

Specifically, this chapter identifies the processes that have led to the development of a distinct subculture of police, which is characterized largely by the elements of danger, authority, and isolation. It will then illustrate how the subculture of police leads to and perpetuates what sociologist Jerome Skolnick has called the "working personality" of police officers,[10] which has become a manifestation of the policing subculture. The chapter then discusses the thin blue line of policing as a symbolic concept designed to secure the role of police as the primary protective institution in society. Finally, the chapter argues that there is another way to conceptualize the thin blue line that can make the policing subculture more consistent with a protection of life mandate.

By the end of this chapter, readers should have the knowledge to discuss and answer the following questions:

1. In what ways have the occupational elements of danger, authority, and isolation led to the development of the policing subculture?
2. What is the "working personality" of police, and how does it lead police to look out for the "symbolic assailant"?
3. What are the primary themes of the policing subculture, and how are morality and "righteousness" woven into them?
4. What is the thin blue line of policing, and how might it be reconceptualized to better "fit" the protection of life mandate?

Developing the Policing Subculture

The first thing to understand is that policing is dirty work.[11] Yes, policing is generally regarded by most Americans as a relatively prestigious

---

[7] Alpert and Dunham, *Understanding Police Use of Force: Officers, Suspects, and Reciprocity*, 171.
[8] Heritage, "Revisiting Authority in Patient-Physician Interaction."
[9] Kappeler, Sluder, and Alpert, "Breeding Deviant Conformity: The Ideology and Culture of Police," 191.
[10] Skolnick, *Justice Without Trial: Law Enforcement in Democratic Society*, 1966.
[11] Hughes, "Work and the Self," 391.

occupation,[12] garnering historically high levels of support;[13] but that collective high regard for policing derives from the "sacred" aspects of the occupation—the heroic parts of the job where violence is used as both a sword and a shield to save lives and protect the vulnerable. It is the "profane"[14] elements of the work that make policing dirty—the parts of the job that place police officers in sometimes "physically disgusting," dangerous, and risky settings; the parts of the job that bring them into routine contact with persons who are homeless, addicted, and mentally unwell. In having to manage members of the public who have "spoiled"[15] or "tainted"[16] social identities, police officers themselves become, to an extent, stigmatized.[17] As philosophy professor Joseph Beltz put it, "[A police officer] has one foot planted in decent society and one in the criminal underworld."[18] Moreover, the "dirty work" aspects of the job are further amplified by the common perception that the practitioners of policing sometimes "employ methods that are deceptive, intrusive, confrontational, or that otherwise defy norms of civility."[19]

Because policing is dirty work, it is isolating. Most members of the public are simply unable to fathom the profane aspects of the police occupation—the dangers, the risks, the almost daily need to use some form of coercion to fulfill their mandate. As a result, the public has tended to ascribe a symbolic meaning to the police institution in ways that minimalize the individuality of police officers themselves. As the sociologist Victor Strecher wrote in his classic essay, "People Who Don't Even Know You,"

> Transactions involving uniformed police officers and citizens occur primarily between social roles rather than between individual human beings. . . . [W]hile on duty a police officer is rarely able to function solely as a person. An officer's role easily overwhelms his or her personal characteristics and identity as an individual human being.[20]

The first sentence of Strecher's paragraph is particularly powerful and helps explain in just a few words how a policing subculture has developed. Yes, police officers tend to isolate themselves from the public for reasons we discuss below, but the public also isolates itself from the police, and the police *know* this. They know the public often distrusts them and views them with

---

[12] Pollack, "Doctors, Military Officers, Firefighters, and Scientists Seen as Among America's Most Prestigious Occupations."

[13] Ekins, "Policing in America: Understanding Public Attitudes Toward the Police. Results from a National Survey."

[14] Banton, *The Policeman in the Community*.

[15] Goffman, *Stigma: Notes on the Management of Spoiled Identity*, 5.

[16] Hughes, "Work and the Self."

[17] Goffman, *Stigma: Notes on the Management of Spoiled Identity*, 5.

[18] Betz, "Police Violence," 183.

[19] Ashforth and Kreiner, "'How Can You Do It?' Dirty Work and the Challenge of Constructing a Positive Identity," 415.

[20] Strecher, "People Who Don't Even Know You," 241.

animosity.[21] They are aware that even relatively minor enforcement interactions, such as vehicle stops, can engender resentment toward the police by the public.[22] In response, the police solidify their own cultural norms, which increases their within-group solidarity.[23] Thus, to understand the policing subculture—and how the elements of police work lead to the development of a policing worldview—it is equally important to acknowledge the role of the public in helping to frame the dynamics of that subculture through its own isolating beliefs and behaviors.

By observing that police officers and citizens generally interact with each other more as "social roles" than as "individual human beings," Strecher was describing the *expectations* that each brings to the encounter toward the other. According to the logic, when people contact a police officer—particularly one they do not know—they tend to invoke a "social shorthand" that helps them quickly identify (1) the function of the officer, and (2) the intentions of the officer during the encounter.[24] For example, a person stopped by a police officer for an apparent traffic violation might see the officer approaching on foot in the rearview mirror. The person notices that the officer is a White male with a stocky build, dark sunglasses, and a shaved head. The driver of the stopped vehicle might automatically assume the officer will be a "militant jerk," who "gets off" on writing tickets to people, despite knowing absolutely nothing about him. The driver's assumptions about the officer become the social shorthand that could influence the way the driver acts toward the officer, at least during the initial phases of the encounter.

It might be useful to think of this social shorthand as similar to Carl Klockars's discussion of "norm derivative" definitions of the police that we described in Chapter 1. The source of this social shorthand, and of norm derivative definitions, might be direct prior experiences with other police officers. More often than not, though, they are the result of stories people hear about others' experiences with the police through outlets such as YouTube or other media or family and friends. Those vicarious experiences can lead to the development of both norm derivative definitions of police and a social shorthand that could influence the way a person treats an officer during an encounter.

This shorthand works both ways, however: Because police officers, by definition, routinely work in risky settings and with people who themselves could be characterized as "risky," they also invoke a social shorthand that tries to predict the motivations or intentions of those with whom they are dealing at any given moment. The "dirty work" aspects of policing create a constant risk of danger to police officers; the stigma of the occupation and resulting attitudes and beliefs that people might bring to their encounters

---

[21] Marier and Moule, "Feeling Blue: Officer Perceptions of Public Antipathy Predict Police Occupational Norms."

[22] Skolnick, *Justice Without Trial: Law Enforcement in Democratic Society*, 2011.

[23] Marier and Moule, "Feeling Blue: Officer Perceptions of Public Antipathy Predict Police Occupational Norms."

[24] Strecher, "People Who Don't Even Know You," 241.

with officers creates uncertainty with respect to the authority maintenance ritual; and both concepts—danger and authority—create a degree of social isolation in policing that leads officers to largely stand apart from members of broader society. The result is a policing worldview that leads police officers to distrust members of the public, to be suspicious of people and situations they encounter, and to view every interaction or incident as potentially harmful to them.[25]

This worldview can be off-putting to members of the public outside the police occupation, which can further isolate police officers from the general public. Where some people, for example, regard a party as an opportunity to socialize with others and meet new friends, police officers might view parties as settings where illicit drug use or dating violence occurs, and places where at any given moment they might have to switch from socializing to enforcing the law. This reality leads officers not only to view members of the public (specifically, those who are not police officers) with suspicion and distrust, but to develop great solidarity with other officers, creating a strong subcultural norm of within-policing loyalty.[26]

But the danger and authority aspects of the police occupation, as well as the distrust and suspicion they engender, do more than socially isolate the police from other occupations and groups. They contribute to a worldview that also becomes part of their personality. When they are in uniform and policing the streets, this personality becomes their "working" personality, and it, too, has become part of the policing subculture.

The Working Personality of Police

In the summer of 1962, Sociologist Jerome Skolnick began conducting observational research with the police.[27] He was interested in understanding the roles and behaviors of police officers in a democratic, rule-of-law, society. He participated in ride-alongs with police officers primarily in "Westville," a pseudonym that is widely understood by people who know the work to represent the city of Oakland, California. He supplemented those observations with ride-alongs conducted in "Eastville," a New Jersey city in the New York City metropolitan area. Skolnick's research culminated in the publication of his 1966 masterpiece, *Justice Without Trial*.

In addition to its substantive material, a few historical elements make Skolnick's book a fascinating examination of police. First, Skolnick conducted the research just one year after the U.S. Supreme Court decided *Mapp v. Ohio*, the case that applied the Exclusionary Rule to local policing, rendering evidence obtained illegally excluded from any subsequent court

---

[25] Kappeler, Sluder, and Alpert, "Breeding Deviant Conformity: The Ideology and Culture of Police," 191.

[26] Kappeler, Sluder, and Alpert.

[27] Skolnick, *Justice Without Trial: Law Enforcement in Democratic Society*, 1966, 30.

proceedings.[28] So, during the summer of 1962, most U.S. police departments still would have been working to normalize the "legal" collection of evidence into their daily routines through the implementation of policies that restricted searches without warrants. In addition—and perhaps more important—at the time Skolnick conducted his observations, *Miranda v. Arizona* had not been decided, so the words "You have a right to remain silent"[29] had not yet become embedded in U.S. culture. Finally, the summer of 1962 was well before the Supreme Court had decided the landmark case of *Tennessee v. Garner* in 1985, which eliminated the so-called fleeing felon rule,[30] prohibiting police officers from shooting at unarmed and apparently nondangerous suspected felons simply because they were fleeing from officers (Chapter 11 discusses these cases in greater detail). Thus, in the summer of 1962 when Jerome Skolnick conducted his research on policing, the rule of law as he knew it was much less constraining than the rule of law known today.

Skolnick was among the first to identify how the danger and authority associated with policing led to social isolation and created a policing worldview (i.e., a subcultural outlook) that made police officers suspicious of virtually all members of the public. This included both members of the public with whom they socially identified (e.g., "middle-class" people with whom officers mostly identified), and members of the public they viewed as "symbolically dangerous"[31] (more on this group below). In addition to the danger and authority that characterized much of uniformed policing, though, Skolnick observed that patrol officers also operated under the "constant pressure to appear efficient" to their supervisors.[32] That is, because uniformed policing is primarily call-driven, and because police officers are usually evaluated based on numbers of stops, frisks, and arrests they make, they strive to become efficient in identifying the most likely criminal suspects, or in Skolnick's taxonomy, the "symbolic assailants." The process by which the working personality of police develops can be summarized in Figure 5.1.

As Figure 5.1 suggests, two primary aspects of police work act on the police officer to ultimately lead to the development of the working personality: (1) the patrol officer's working environment, and (2) the organizational demands of the police department itself. The working environment leads to the danger and authority we have already identified, which lead to suspicion and social isolation. Importantly, however, danger and authority are not merely distinct elements of the patrol officer's work setting; they interact in ways that reinforce each other (hence the double-headed arrow between danger and authority noted in Figure 5.1). For example, there are times when a dangerous encounter requires officers to amplify their authority to assure as much as possible that the situation does not escalate out of control. There

---

[28] Mapp v. Ohio, 367 U.S. 643 (1961).
[29] Miranda v. Arizona, 384 U.S. 436 (1966), 437.
[30] Tennessee v. Garner, 471 U.S. 1 (1985), 7–22.
[31] Skolnick, "A Sketch of the Policeman's Working Personality," 16.
[32] Skolnick, 17.

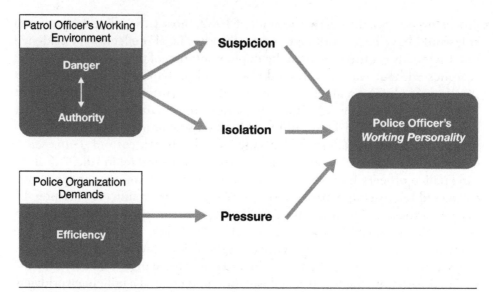

Note: Illustration adapted from Skolnick's discussion of the development of the working personality as described in Chapter 3 of *Justice Without Trial.*

are also times, though, when the danger is low enough that members of the public feel little need to comply with police authority.

For example, officers working crowd control at an outdoor crime scene or the scene of an accident have great interest in making sure the affected area remains secure and free from external interference. Members of a crowd who might have gathered to try to catch a glimpse of the scene likely do not understand the importance of crime or accident scene security (in terms of preserving possible evidence for court and investigating the scene free of external contamination). They simply want to try to get a look at the aftermath of the event. In such cases, the officers likely realize that members of the crowd pose little danger to them, and the crowd likely knows the scene itself poses little to no danger to anyone. As such, the crowd might test the boundaries, which requires officers to turn up the volume of authority to accomplish their goals of protecting the crime or accident scene from contamination.

Moreover, as Figure 5.1 shows, the dangers of the police work environment lead to both suspicion and isolation because danger—or the perceived risk of personal harm—causes officers to be suspicious of most people they encounter, while also leading them to trust other police officers almost exclusively. As a result, danger leads to isolation because many police officers effectively cut themselves off from those who aren't police officers due to a lack of trust. Finally, as Figure 5.1 shows, organizational demands for efficiency lead to occupational pressure, which has an independent impact on the development of the working personality.

What is the working personality of police? It is the mindset police develop that leads them to want to identify, seek out, and control "symbolic assailants"—or those who would do harm to police officers. As Skolnick wrote:

[Police officers] . . . develop a perceptual shorthand to identify certain kinds of people as symbolic assailants, that is, persons who use gesture, language, and attire that the policeman [sic] has come to recognize as a prelude to violence.[33]

Skolnick emphasized that (1) a person need not have ever committed violence against a police officer to be labeled a symbolic assailant, and (2) people labeled symbolic assailants might have no intention of committing violence against officers; they simply fit the "profile." In this way, labeling people symbolic assailants can be an efficient way for officers to cope with the potential violence the job might bring, but given that many or most symbolic assailants never actually attempt to commit violence against police officers, such labeling might not be effective. Indeed, the concept of the symbolic assailant might lead officers to develop and invoke stereotypes based on the static characteristics (i.e., race and ethnicity) of people, which could lead to racial profiling, particularly in high-crime communities. This issue is more thoroughly discussed in Chapter 9 when we examine stop-and-frisk.

For present purposes, it is important to note that most, if not all, U.S. police officers are socialized into the policing subculture; that is, the police worldview that emphasizes danger, authority, and isolation, as well as the development of a working personality. This is because in the United States, virtually all police officers must begin their careers working uniformed patrol. The socialization into the police subculture begins as early as the police academy, where officers are immediately and routinely reminded of the dangers of police work.[34] Once out of the training academy, new officers don their uniforms and become the "social role," as described earlier, which furthers their socialization into the subculture of policing. Although not every officer fully adopts the policing subculture, virtually every officer is exposed to it.[35]

Themes and Consequences of the Policing Subculture

Identifying the features and characteristics of the policing subculture is helpful because such recognition leads researchers, students, and others to begin to understand how and why the subculture develops. Now that this chapter has identified the nature of the subculture, the next logical question is this: What are the themes and behavioral consequences of the subculture? To answer that question, it is instructive to appeal to the framework that policing scholar John Crank created that identifies several themes of

---

[33] Skolnick, *Justice Without Trial: Law Enforcement in Democratic Society*, 1966, 45.
[34] Twersky-Glasner, "Police Personality: What Is It and Why Are They Like That?"; Kappeler, Sluder, and Alpert, "Breeding Deviant Conformity: The Ideology and Culture of Police."
[35] Skolnick, *Justice Without Trial: Law Enforcement in Democratic Society*, 1966; Muir, *Police: Street-corner Politicians*.

the policing subculture that can help explain subcultural behaviors. Crank identified three categories of police subcultural themes:[36]

- **Themes of the unknown:** characterized by danger, suspicion, authority, and anticipation of violence.
- **Themes of coercive territorial control:** characterized by supremacy, force, militarization, and guns.
- **Themes of solidarity:** characterized by police morality, solidarity, masculinity, and racism.

Crank's "themes of the unknown," again, characterized by danger, suspicion, authority, and situational uncertainty, can help explain the encounter between NYPD officers and Jazmine Headley as discussed in the previous chapter and at the beginning of this chapter. When Ms. Headley failed to submit immediately to police authority, and then refused to surrender her son to officers, her noncompliance might have contributed to the danger and uncertainty mindset that officers likely brought into the encounter from the beginning. Her lack of submission conflicted with police presumptions of who was in charge during the encounter. As described earlier, police officers are trained and socialized to overemphasize the role of authority during their encounters with members of the public.[37] So, at least one behavioral consequence of the policing subculture, and informed by the themes of the unknown, is the propensity of police officers to escalate or force confrontations with people who appear to challenge their authority, primarily as a means of preserving their authoritative edge.

Themes of coercive territorial control[38] help describe the subcultural norms of police officers' desires to create and maintain order in their patrol environments. As previously discussed, the patrol function is the most visible and prevalent form of policing, and it tends to rely on the assumptions that (1) police can be anywhere and everywhere, and (2) highly visible and assertive policing prevents or discourages crime. Indeed, police territoriality—or the processes of making, marking, and in some cases, controlling, space—represents an important collective aspect of policing. Most policing is conducted in neighborhoods, commercial districts, and public spaces—spaces that belong to "everyone" and "no one,"[39] such as parks, open lots, and fields. In these usual patrol settings, police territoriality is practiced in a diffuse way that still emphasizes control, but brings with it a sense of morality; that is, police officers' beliefs that that they have a moral responsibility to control and protect *their* territory. As John Crank noted:

---

[36] Crank, *Understanding Police Culture*, 77–268.
[37] Alpert and Dunham, *Understanding Police Use of Force: Officers, Suspects, and Reciprocity*, 171.
[38] Crank, *Understanding Police Culture*, 77–140.
[39] Groff and McCord, "The Role of Neighborhood Parks as Crime Generators," 16.

Territory is, for cops, more than a geographical assignment. It is their prize for being morally righteous. . . . [Territory is] placed in their care so that they can deal with the assholes and bad guys of the world. A cop's territory is theirs. . . . And cops take it very seriously.[40]

Crank went on to describe the control of territory as police officers exerting "dominion" over a designated geography. As he noted, "Officers do not simply patrol areas, they control them."[41] Thus, *dominion* over space represents a subcultural attribute of police territoriality and can explain, for example, Skolnick's notion of the working personality of police. The desire to control territory—as wrapped up in morality and dominion—leads officers to seek out potential offenders while remaining suspicious of symbolic assailants. Because of the moral imperative to control space, many police officers also demand respect for police authority and the maintenance of that authority during field encounters. Suspects who challenge officers' belief that they (the police) hold dominion over their territory are often labeled "assholes,"[42] and then subjected to violence as punishment for violating police officers' subcultural belief that they own the spaces they patrol.[43]

Apart from the potential for violence as a product of dominion, the subcultural themes of territoriality also help explain, among others, stop-and-frisk behaviors. Police might regard certain people on their beats as "assholes,"[44] symbolic assailants, or both. Moreover, as part of their military rhetoric, police do not simply patrol an area, they "deploy," further legitimizing the war symbolism,[45] which is also a subcultural theme falling under territoriality.[46] Therefore, when police patrol their beats—particularly in places they might regard as "deviant"[47] or hostile—they might view certain "types" of people as deserving of police intervention through stop, question, and frisk. Frequently, these "types" are young Black males residing in communities characterized by racially concentrated disadvantage.

Crank's third category of themes falls under the collective concept of solidarity and is characterized by police morality, masculinity, and even, at times, racism.[48] Themes of solidarity help explain how officers develop the so-called us vs. them mentality because of the moral judgments officers often make, which help reinforce the "us" part, while drawing a clear distinction from "them." And who is "them?" The assholes, people of color, or those who are judged as lacking any kind of moral standing. "Angels" (i.e., the legitimate

---

[40] Crank, *Understanding Police Culture*, 82.

[41] Crank, 82.

[42] Kane and Cronin, "Maintaining Order Under the Rule of Law: Occupational Templates and the Police Use of Force"; Van Maanen, "The Asshole."

[43] Silver et al., "Traditional Police Culture, Use of Force, and Procedural Justice: Investigating Individual, Organizational, and Contextual Factors"; Herbert, "Police Subculture Reconsidered."

[44] Van Maanen, "The Asshole."

[45] Walker, *Sense and Nonsense About Crime and Drugs: A Policy Guide*.

[46] Crank, *Understanding Police Culture*, 113–126.

[47] Klinger, "Negotiating Order in Patrol Work: An Ecological Theory of Police Response to Deviance."

[48] Crank, *Understanding Police Culture*, 197–254.

victims) garner sympathy and "assholes" draw the rebuke. Moreover, just the process of deciding who should be labeled "angels" and "assholes" helps create and foster police solidarity. As Crank noted, "Each theme (of solidarity) in its own way celebrates a shared sense of purpose, and together they help to understand the way in which the 'brotherhood' looks inward for cultural identity."[49]

In looking inward, officers often believe that they are practicing their own form of morality, applying their judgments to the people they encounter. The themes of solidarity do not develop in a vacuum, though. Indeed, the themes of territoriality—also partly characterized by police morality—influence the labeling processes because of the different social, economic, and crime conditions inherent to different police beats. Depending on the local territorial conditions, police officers' workgroups often emphasize different subcultural priorities: In "dangerous" beats, for example, officers become preoccupied by the subcultural norms of "safety" and masculinity to ensure that they maintain authority and control; in less dangerous, but perhaps more publicly traversed beats, officers tend to emphasize the subcultural norms of law and professional competence as a way of staying out of trouble and ensuring the proper flows of traffic.[50] In the end, however, territoriality and solidarity still emphasize the "brotherhood" and morality, which fosters their cultural identity.

It is important to point out that not all aspects of the police culture produce troubling mentalities or behaviors. Indeed, themes of the unknown, coercive territorial control, and solidarity give officers common job-related experiences that are distinct from all other occupations. These shared occupational experiences allow officers to cope as a group with the stresses and uncertainties of the job. Policing is, after all, *dirty work*: It is dangerous, it is often stigmatized, and it is often viewed as a less than moral occupation. For all the cynicism, prejudice, judgment, suspicion, authoritarianism, and bias that might be associated with "traditional police culture,"[51] that same culture also fosters group loyalty, teamwork, caring, support, camaraderie, and sacrifice.[52] The shared sense of identity and group experience helps police officers cope with some of the more atrocious and harrowing encounters they have when policing the streets.

Still, the elements of danger and authority lead police to develop a distinct worldview, causing many officers to both isolate themselves from broader society and try to identify, up front, members of the public who might wish to do them harm. This overall policing subculture creates an us vs. them mentality that is amplified by the presumption that the police are the only

---

[49] Crank, 199.
[50] Herbert, "The Normative Ordering of Police Territoriality: Making and Marking Space With the Los Angeles Police Department."
[51] Silver et al., "Traditional Police Culture, Use of Force, and Procedural Justice: Investigating Individual, Organizational, and Contextual Factors."
[52] McCartney and Parent, *Ethics in Law Enforcement*.

professionally qualified crime fighters in society. This leads to the next elaboration of the policing subculture, commonly referred to as the "thin blue line" of policing.

Policing as the Thin Blue Line

In his 1971 book, *The Police and the Public*, Albert Reiss made the point succinctly: "Given their small numbers relative to the magnitude of their task, the police regard themselves as the 'thin blue line,' maintaining law and order in the community."[53] Reiss wrote those words at a particular historic moment for the police—just three years after the President's Commission on Law Enforcement and the Administration of Justice (created in 1965 by then-President Lyndon B. Johnson) published its report, "The Challenge of Crime in a Free Society."[54] President Johnson's commission was the first presidential commission to conduct a comprehensive examination of crime and the administration of justice since the Wickersham Commission published its report in 1931.[55] Whereas the latter was largely convened to study the failures of policing and criminal justice during the Prohibition era, the former was convened to examine crime and criminal justice in the midst of Civil Rights–era urban race riots, Vietnam War protests, accelerating crime rates, and increasing fear of crime across the country.[56] "The Challenge of Crime in a Free Society" was to set the tone for the federal government's approach to crime control through the end of the 1960s and beyond, which would increasingly emphasize law enforcement. If we can look past the dated, gendered language of the time, we can see that the authors of the 1967 report very clearly made their point:

> In society's day-to-day efforts to protect its citizens from the suffering, fear, and property loss produced by crime and the threat of crime, the policeman occupies the front line. It is he who directly confronts criminal situations, and it is to him that the public looks for personal safety. The freedom of Americans to walk their streets and be secure in their homes . . . depends to a great extent on their policemen.[57]

Although it is not at all clear that the President's Commission, or the 1967 report it published, made a significant impact on crime or fear of crime, it did solidify the position of the police as the nation's leading edge in the

---

[53] Reiss, *The Police and the Public*, 1.
[54] President's Commission on Law Enforcement and the Administration of Justice, "The Challenge of Crime in a Free Society."
[55] Wickersham, "National Commission on Law Observance and Enforcement: Report."
[56] King and Conley, "The 1967 President's Crime Commission Report: Its Impact 25 Years Later."
[57] President's Commission on Law Enforcement and the Administration of Justice, "The Challenge of Crime in a Free Society," 92.

fight against crime.[58] In effect, the President's Commission legitimized, and perhaps even launched, the very idea of police as the thin blue line. Thus, when Reiss wrote, "the police regard themselves as the 'thin blue line,'" he was telling only part of the story. The federal government via the President's Commission had already established policing as the thin blue line responsible for making it safe for all Americans to "walk their streets."

And pop culture responded. The mid- to late 1960s became the era of *Adam-12* and *Dragnet*, two primetime television shows that were as much techno-fiction as they were entertainment. Both were police procedural dramas, and both were essentially propaganda TV designed to showcase the efficiency and effectiveness of the Los Angeles Police Department (LAPD).[59] *Adam-12*,[60] a show that debuted in 1968 and featured two patrol officers—one a rookie, the other a veteran—demonstrated that the LAPD could be anywhere and everywhere at any time, and that marked patrol cars, crisp blue uniforms, a police radio, and the .38-caliber Police Special represented not just the thin blue line, but a moral barrier between good and evil. *Dragnet*,[61] on the other hand, demonstrated how the LAPD responded to crimes after they had been committed. Debuting for its second run[62] on television in 1967, *Dragnet* was a detective show featuring the iconic Sgt. Joe Friday, showcasing the use of "police science" as the ultimate systematic methodology for catching "criminals." And Joe Friday always caught the criminal.

Both *Adam-12* and *Dragnet* were widely popular in the late 1960s and through the mid-1970s; both were seemingly designed to reassure an increasingly fearful U.S. middle class that, despite what they might have been watching in newscasts about race riots in Detroit[63] (and other cities) and Vietnam protesters marching on the Pentagon,[64] against the backdrop of a national heroin epidemic,[65] the police were on the job to protect them and their families from lawbreakers. There was a great deal of morality woven into the subtexts of *Adam-12* and *Dragnet*, in much the same way that morality permeates the themes of the police subculture, as previously described.

As the United States emerged from the turbulent, and often violent, decade of the 1960s, its police forces continued their collective march toward paramilitarism, heeding the calls of the President's Commission to "occupy"

---

[58] It has also been argued that in emphasizing the crime-fighting function of the police, the 1967 report likely set into motion the race toward the mass incarceration of Black Americans that accelerated through the 1980s and 1990s. *See generally* Fernandes and Crutchfield, "Race, Crime, and Criminal Justice: Fifty Years Since The Challenge of Crime in a Free Society."

[59] Dowler, "Police Dramas on Television."

[60] "Adam-12 (TV Series 1968–1975) - IMDb."

[61] "Dragnet 1967 (TV Series 1967–1970) - IMDb."

[62] The series began as an NBC radio show, running from 1949 to 1957. NBC moved it to television in 1951, running it until 1959. After a lengthy hiatus, it "debuted" again (with the same characters and actors) as *Dragnet* in 1967.

[63] "Six Days in July—Coverage of the 1967 Detroit Riots - YouTube."

[64] "This Week in Universal News: The March on the Pentagon, 1967 – The Unwritten Record."

[65] Agar and Reisinger, "A Heroin Epidemic at the Intersection of Histories: The 1960s Epidemic Among African Americans in Baltimore."

the "front line" as the country's primary defense against crime. The thin blue line became increasingly durable as a metaphor defining the police subculture. The language of war used to describe the police role during the crack epidemic (and the violence it wrought) of the 1980s, emphasized the subcultural elements of danger and authority, and heroized police as "protectors of society."[66] Equally important, the war symbolism and the increasingly common analogy of "cops as soldiers"[67] led the police (and likely the public) to view criminal offenders as "foreign enemies," undeserving of due process rights.[68] As a subcultural symbol of policing, the thin blue line "unites officers in militaristic identity,"[69] which strengthens their group loyalty. Thus, the thin blue line becomes a shorthand for defining the police subculture, as the line itself represents all three of the primary elements of policing that contribute to the maintenance of the subculture: danger, authority, and ultimately, isolation.

Some Concluding Observations

This chapter opened with a discussion about Ms. Jazmine Headley, attempting to explain why a group of NYPD officers forced a confrontation with her, throwing her to the floor when she refused to give up her infant son to them or otherwise submit to their authority. As we have learned, authority plays two roles in the policing subculture. To some extent, authority is an element of the policing occupation that allows the subculture to develop, along with danger and isolation; but to another extent, authority represents a subcultural norm among police. Indeed, authority holds so much value for the police that they have developed a ritual, the authority maintenance ritual, around its preservation.[70] When suspects violate the norms of this ritual, they are usually met with increased levels of authority that can be expressed in the form of coercive force. Thus, authority holds a special place in the subculture of police because of the two meanings it embodies.

Danger is also an element of policing that helps foster the policing subculture. Indeed, the occupational characteristic of danger is one of the primary reasons policing has been regarded as "dirty work."[71] Like authority, danger takes on two meanings to the police. The job can be dangerous for a variety of reasons—partly the settings in which the work is accomplished and partly the potentially violent situations into which officers enter. Thus, there are known dangers of policing. There are also the unknown dangers of the job, however, which also contribute to the subculture. The unknown

---

[66] Crank, *Understanding Police Culture*, 118.
[67] Skolnick and Fyfe, *Above the Law: Police and the Excessive Use of Force*, 113–133.
[68] Walker, *Sense and Nonsense About Crime and Drugs: A Policy Guide*, 20.
[69] Crank, *Understanding Police Culture*, 119.
[70] Alpert and Dunham, *Understanding Police Use of Force: Officers, Suspects, and Reciprocity*.
[71] Ashforth and Kreiner, "'How Can You Do It?' Dirty Work and the Challenge of Constructing a Positive Identity."

dangers lead police to develop a worldview that embodies suspicion, distrust, territorial control, and the need to try to determine quickly the motivations of people they contact. Are they dealing with an "asshole" or an "angel"? Danger is perhaps the most important occupational element that leads to the development of the working personality and the labeling of certain people as "symbolic assailants."

Finally, policing is isolating. It is isolating in part because of the elements of danger and authority, and the fact that virtually no occupational groups outside policing can truly understand how the risks of the job and the need to use, or at least threaten the use, of coercion as part of an occupational mandate lead police officers to stand apart from other members of society. Isolation is an element of policing—like danger and authority—that helps explain the development of the police subculture, but isolation is also partly the result of danger and authority. That isolation works two ways: Police officers have been known to isolate themselves from broader society because the conditions of their job make it virtually impossible for those who aren't police to understand them; but society also isolates itself from the police, particularly because of distrust and antipathy toward people—in some cases, *friends*—who at any moment can turn a social encounter into a law enforcement encounter.

The thin blue line of policing has become a symbolic culmination of the danger, authority, and isolation that characterize the job. It is the reason society "calls the cops" in the first place: because police officers have the authority to meet danger head-on and stop a situation that needs to be stopped now. That the idea of the thin blue line was enshrined in perhaps the most important federal government study of crime and criminal justice (i.e., "The Challenge of Crime in a Free Society") in the past 50-plus years has made it an enduring part of the police role that glorifies the elements of danger and authority. The notion of the thin blue line—that the police are that *thing* that stands between order and anarchy—is all by itself unfairly isolating to the police. This isolation contributes to the durability of the policing subculture.

Is this what we want of our police, though: domestic soldiers who divide human groups into two categories of good ones and bad ones? Because that is precisely what the thin blue line has been designed to do—by the public, by government policymakers, and to an extent by the police themselves. It does not have to be that way. As Ristroph recently observed, "A line can separate, or it can connect."[72] Although society has promoted the thin blue line as something that separates, it is the case that police actually do more "connecting" than they do dividing.[73] Police officers on the street routinely interact with social service providers and members of the public, with some of this work done officially, but much of it done informally. In cases of family violence, for example, many police

---

[72] Ristroph, "The Thin Blue Line From Crime to Punishment," 305.
[73] Ristroph, 305.

departments require officers to refer victims to victim service agencies so they can get emotional, social, or even financial support as needed. More informally, police officers frequently provide information to inquiring members of the public about how to handle fix-it tickets, how to get a speed bump placed on their street, or how to visit a relative in a local jail who had been recently arrested. These are all examples of the connecting that police accomplish every day in U.S. communities. At least two studies that examined police workload through calls for service noted that large proportions of police officers' time were devoted to "service" calls, such as giving advice or information.[74]

Such research findings are important because, although the thin blue line of policing can exist, it is capable of accomplishing far more than simply dividing people. It can connect people to each other, to service providers, and to other institutions. Indeed, the thin blue line as a metaphor used to describe the role of police is not necessarily a problematic concept. It has just been wrongly applied. The thin blue line grew out of an era dominated by the coercion paradigm of policing. If allowed to evolve, though—much like the police institution itself might do—then it can become a far more useful vessel of the policing subculture. Thinking of the thin blue line as a metaphor designed to connect rather than divide would allow the police to move beyond coercion as their primary role and move toward practicing a protection of life mandate. To do so, though, would require the police to deemphasize the importance of authority in accomplishing their mandate—as Alpert and Dunham[75] have suggested—and decrease the subcultural element of isolation. Some research, for example, has suggested that members of the public will make informal service requests of the police only if they trust police officers and view them as an integrated part of the communities they serve.[76]

Community policing, as conceptualized in the 1980s, hoped to accomplish just that: helping police work with local communities to solve local problems in ways that did not necessarily involve law enforcement (but would hopefully reduce crime in the long run). To practice community policing, however, police departments would have to begin to share authority with residents, something the coercion paradigm—and the mindset it created—made difficult for them to do. As we will see in the next chapter, community policing as practiced has found it difficult to live up to the philosophies of its original architects, perhaps in part due to traditional police culture and the perpetuation of the thin blue line as something that divides rather than connects.

---

[74] Greene and Klockars, "What Police Do"; Kane, "Policing in Public Housing: Using Calls for Service to Examine Incident-Based Workload in the Philadelphia Housing Authority."

[75] Alpert and Dunham, *Understanding Police Use of Force: Officers, Suspects, and Reciprocity.*

[76] Bennett, "Calling for Service: Mobilization of the Police Across Sociocultural Environments."

Questions for Review and Reflection

Question 1. Policing as Dirty Work

While policing can be regarded as a prestigious, and even heroic, occupation, it has also been referred to as "dirty" work because of the "profane" aspects of the job. Indeed, the profane aspects of policing have stigmatized the occupation, contributing to the social isolation that police officers often experience as part of their subculture.

- What are some of the ways in which policing can be regarded as dirty work?
- What are the profane elements of policing that can both stigmatize and isolate police officers from broader society?
- Can society and police departments themselves do anything to reduce the "dirty work" aspects of policing, or is policing destined to remain stigmatized as a "spoiled" occupation?

Question 2. Elements of the Police Subculture

As noted in the chapter, danger, authority, and isolation make up the primary elements of the policing subculture. Virtually all U.S. police officers are exposed to these elements of the subculture by virtue of attending academies and being socialized into the occupation.

- What are some of the ways in which danger and authority likely lead to social isolation among police officers?
- How do danger and authority interact with one another in ways that amplify social isolation among officers?

- How might society and police departments themselves reduce danger or authority (or both) to decrease the social isolation of police officers?
- How do members of society contribute to the social isolation of police officers?
- Although virtually all police officers are exposed to the elements of the police subculture, not all officers adopt them. What can police officers do to avoid adopting danger, authority, and isolation as their own subculture norms?

Question 3. Policing and the Thin Blue Line

The metaphor of police acting as a thin blue line that separates members of "civil" society from criminal offenders was championed by the 1968 presidential report, "The Challenge of Crime in a Free Society." This document helped create both the tone and federal policies that would guide policing for generations to come.

- What is the "thin blue line" of policing? Is this a term that still resonates with people outside policing? That is, do people still buy into the concept of the thin blue line?
- In what ways might the concept of the thin blue line contribute to the social isolation of police officers?
- How might the thin blue line help to create group loyalty among police officers in ways that can perpetuate the us vs. them mentality (with society representing "them")?

Exercises

Exercise 1. Testing the Durability of Traditional Police Subculture

The occupational elements of danger, authority, and isolation have characterized the traditional police subculture for generations. It is, however, unclear whether the traditional police subculture continues to define the social relationships of police officers. If police officers of today still take on the police subculture, we expect them to maintain relatively few social relationships outside policing. This exercise is designed to examine whether the traditional police subculture continues to "separate" police officers from broader society.

- Identify a police officer to interview for this exercise. The officer need not necessarily be a stranger, as it might be difficult for them to trust you well enough to complete the exercise. Tell the officer you plan to create a social network map that will illustrate their social relationships.
- Once you are sitting with the officer, take out a piece of paper and write the officer's name in the center of that paper. Draw a circle around the officer's name.
- Ask the officer to name the people they normally interact with socially and professionally on a monthly basis. These might be their immediate work colleagues, other friends, family members, coaches, members of sports teams, neighbors, chiropractors, and so on. It would be useful for you to encourage the officer to identify at least 10 people, and even more than 20, to put on the page. You can arrange the people in a large circle with the officer remaining in the center of the page.
- Draw lines from the officer to each of the people identified and ask the officer to indicate (1) the type of relationship they have

with each person listed, (2) the strength of that relationship, and (3) how often they see each person on a monthly basis. You can circle the names of each person and write the information (type, strength, frequency) inside the circles. Here, you are trying to determine the diversity of relationships the officer has with people, as well as the quality of those relationships.

- Ask the officer to indicate the occupations of all the people they identified on the paper. You should write the occupations in the circles of each person.
- Ask the officer to draw arrows between the people arranged on the page to illustrate how they might be socially related (if at all) to each other. This part of the exercise aims to illustrate how connected the people on the page are to each other. Then ask the officer to indicate the nature of relationships people on the page have with each other; for example, some might be friends with other people on the page, they might be family members with each other, and so on.
- Once you have completed the diagram, review it with the officer. What conclusions do you draw about the officer's "connectedness" to people both inside and outside policing? In general, is the officer connected to people who are connected to each other? What network of people is the officer most connected to?
- At the conclusion of this exercise, you should offer to leave the diagram with the officer so that it stays just with him or her.

Exercise 2. Symbolizing Traditional Police Subculture

Research has indicated that traditional police culture can be defined largely in terms of danger and authority and the social isolation those two elements promote. There are different ways to convey danger, authority, and isolation. One way is by observing how police officers act toward members of the public and toward each other. Another way is to try to identify the symbols of danger, authority, and isolation based on how police officers and departments present themselves to the public. Symbolism is an implicit language that sends messages to an external audience—in this case, the public outside the police occupation. For this exercise, you will try to identify symbols of policing that convey the subculture elements of danger, authority, and isolation.

- Take time to observe one or more uniformed police officers at work in your local area.
- Can you identify aspects of their uniforms that symbolize the subcultural elements of danger, authority, and isolation?
- In answering the above, it will be important for you to consider all features of the police uniform (and the items the officers carry) as symbols that may communicate danger and authority, as well as isolation.
- Consider also how the vehicles the police in your local area use might convey the subcultural elements of danger, authority, and isolation.
- If necessary, supplement your personal observations of the officers and vehicles with research conducted on the police department website. You should be able to see the types of vehicles they use; and you should be able to get close-up looks at their badges, uniforms, and patches.
- Once you complete your observations, write a report that describes how the elements of police uniforms and vehicles might represent symbols of danger, authority, and isolation.

Exercise 3. How the Police Subculture Affects Police Families

Listen to Episode 4 of the *Policing Beyond Coercion* Podcast, "Cop's Kid: Growing Up in a Police Family" (use the QR code or URL contained in the text box at the start of this chapter to access the podcast). While listening, try to pick out language, phrases, and other verbal descriptions that might suggest how the aspects of traditional police culture might have diffused into the lives of the immediate members of the police family. To complete the exercise, write a report that answers the following questions:

- How did the cops' kids interviewed for the podcast describe life in their families as they were growing up? Specifically, did they get a sense that their families were somehow different from nonpolice families?
- To what extent did the cops' kids interviewed in the podcast indicate that their families tended to socialize mostly (or mostly not) with other police families?
- Did the cops' kids interviewed for the podcast indicate that they knew their police parent(s) worked a dangerous job? If so, how did that sense of danger affect life for everyone in the family?
- Did the cops' kids feel that the authority their policing parent(s) had somehow separated them (the cops' kids) from their own friends?
- How did growing up as a cop's kid influence the social relationships they developed with people outside their own families?
- What conclusions can you draw about how traditional police culture might influence both the individual officers who work the job and their immediate families?

Bibliography

"Adam-12 (TV Series 1968–1975) - IMDb." Accessed February 18, 2021. https://www.imdb.com/title/tt0062539/?ref_=fn_al_tt_1.

Agar, Michael, and Heather Schacht Reisinger. "A Heroin Epidemic at the Intersection of Histories: The 1960s Epidemic Among African Americans in Baltimore." *Medical Anthropology* 21, no. 2 (2002): 115–156. https://doi.org/10.1080/01459740212904.

Alpert, Geoffrey P., and Roger G. Dunham. *Understanding Police Use of Force: Officers, Suspects, and Reciprocity*. Cambridge, UK: Cambridge University Press, 2004.

Ashforth, Blake E., and Glen E. Kreiner. "'How Can You Do It?' Dirty Work and the Challenge of Constructing a Positive Identity." *The Academy of Management Review* 24, no. 3 (1999): 413–434.

Banton, Michael. *The Policeman in the Community*. New York: Basic Books, 1964. https://books.google.com/books/about/The_Policeman_in_the_Community.html?id=F0NMwQEACAAJ.

Bennett, Richard R. "Calling for Service: Mobilization of the Police Across Sociocultural Environments." *Police Practice and Research* 5, no. 1 (2004): 25–41. https://doi.org/10.1080/1561426042000191314.

Betz, Joseph. "Police Violence." In *Moral Issues in Police Work*, edited by F. A. Elliston and M. Feldberg, 177–196. Totowa, NJ: Rowman and Allanheld, 1988.

Crank, John P. *Understanding Police Culture*. 2nd ed. New York: Routledge, 2015. https://books.google.com/books?hl=en&lr=&id=wRugBAAAQBAJ&oi=fnd&pg=PP1&dq=police+culture&ots=qScQCOmu2N&sig=sHK8RZ_xKg1TOO235D-7i9D3S73k#v=onepage&q=police culture&f=false.

Dowler, K. "Police Dramas on Television." *Oxford Research Encyclopedia of Criminology*, 2016. https://oxfordre.com/criminology/view/10.1093/acrefore/9780190264079.001.0001/acrefore-9780190264079-e-175.

"Dragnet 1967 (TV Series 1967–1970) - IMDb." Accessed February 18, 2021. https://www.imdb.com/title/tt0061248/?ref_=fn_al_tt_2.

Ekins, Emily. "Policing in America: Understanding Public Attitudes Toward the Police. Results from a National Survey." December 7, 2016. https://www.cato.org/survey-reports/policing-america.

Fernandes, April D., and Robert D. Crutchfield. "Race, Crime, and Criminal Justice: Fifty Years Since The Challenge of Crime in a Free Society." *Criminology and Public Policy* 17, no. 2 (2018): 397–417. https://doi.org/10.1111/1745-9133.12361.

Goffman, Erving. *The Presentation of Self in Everyday Life*. New York: Doubleday, 1956.

Goffman, Erving. *Stigma: Notes on the Management of Spoiled Identity*. New York: Simon & Schuster, 1963.

Greene, Jack R., and Carl B. Klockars. "What Police Do." In *Thinking About Police: Contemporary Readings*, 2nd ed., edited by Carl B. Klockars and Stephen D. Mastrofski. New York: McGraw-Hill, 1991.

Groff, Elizabeth, and Eric S. McCord. "The Role of Neighborhood Parks as Crime Generators." *Security Journal* 25, no. 1 (2012): 1–24. https://doi.org/10.1057/sj.2011.1.

Herbert, Steve. "The Normative Ordering of Police Territoriality: Making and Marking Space With the Los Angeles Police Department." *Annals of the Association of American Geographers*, (1996). https://doi.org/10.1111/j.1467-8306.1996.tb01767.x.

Herbert, Steve. "Police Subculture Reconsidered." *Criminology*, 1998. https://doi.org/10.1111/j.1745-9125.1998.tb01251.x.

Heritage, John. "Revisiting Authority in Patient–Physician Interaction." In *Diagnosis as Cultural Practice*, edited by Monica Heller and Richard J. Watts, 83–102. New York: Mouton de Gruyter, 2005.

Hine, Kelly A., Louise E. Porter, Nina J. Westera, and Geoffrey P. Alpert. "Too Much or Too Little? Individual and Situational Predictors of Police Force Relative to Suspect Resistance." *Policing and Society* 28, no. 5 (2018): 587–604. https://doi.org/10.1080/10439463.2016.1232257.

Hughes, E. C. "Work and the Self." In *Social Psychology at the Crossroads*, edited by J. H. Rohrer and M. Sherif, 313–323. New York: Harper and Brothers, 1951.

Kane, Robert J. "Policing in Public Housing: Using Calls for Service to Examine Incident-Based Workload in the Philadelphia Housing Authority." *Policing* 21, no. 4 (1998): 618–631. https://doi.org/10.1108/13639519810241656.

Kane, Robert J., and Shea W. Cronin. "Maintaining Order Under the Rule of Law: Occupational Templates and the Police Use of Force." *Journal of Crime and Justice* 34, no. 3 (2011): 163–177. https://doi.org/10.1080/0735648X.2011.609732.

Kappeler, Victor E., Richard D. Sluder, and Geoffrey P. Alpert. "Breeding Deviant Conformity: The Ideology and Culture of Police." In *Critical Issues in Policing: Contemporary Readings*, 8th ed., edited by Roger G. Dunham, Geoffrey P. Alpert, and Kyle D. McLean, 187–213. Long Grove, IL: Waveland Press, 2020.

King, Daniel, and John A. Conley. "The 1967 President's Crime Commission Report: Its Impact 25 Years Later." *The Police Journal: Theory, Practice and Principles* 67, no. 3 (1994): 269–274.

Klinger, David A. "Demeanor or Crime? Why 'Hostile' Citizens Are More Likely to Be Arrested." *Criminology* 32, no. 3 (1994): 475–493.

Klinger, David A. "Negotiating Order in Patrol Work: An Ecological Theory of Police Response to Deviance." *Criminology* 35, no. 2 (1997): 277–306. https://doi.org/10.1111/j.1745-9125.1997.tb00877.x.

Mapp v. Ohio, 367 U.S. 643 (1961).

Marier, Christopher J., and Richard K. Moule. "Feeling Blue: Officer Perceptions of Public Antipathy Predict Police Occupational Norms." *American Journal of Criminal Justice* 44, no. 5 (2019): 836–857. https://doi.org/10.1007/s12103-018-9459-1.

McCartney, Steve, and Rick Parent. *Ethics in Law Enforcement*. Victoria, BC, Canada: BCcampus, 2015.

Miranda v. Arizona, 384 U.S. 436 (1966).

Muir, William Ker. *Police: Streetcorner Politicians*. Chicago: University of Chicago Press, 1977.

Pollack, Hannah. "Doctors, Military Officers, Firefighters, and Scientists Seen as Among America's Most Prestigious Occupations," September 10, 2014. https://theharrispoll.com/when-shown-a-list-of-occupations-and-asked-how-much-prestige-each-job-possesses-doctors-top-the-harris-polls-list-with-88-of-u-s-adults-considering-it-to-have-either-a-great-deal-of-prestige-45-2/.

President's Commission on Law Enforcement and the Administration of Justice. "The Challenge of Crime in a Free Society." Washington, DC, 1967. https://doi.org/10.3138/cjcor.9.4.347.

Reiss, Albert J. *The Police and the Public*. New Haven, CT: Yale University Press, 1971. https://books.google.com/books?hl=en&lr=&id=2ErEylE6PUgC&oi=fnd&pg=PP12&dq=thin+blue+line+in+policing&ots=tHzLJnkdw1&sig=Ammri4L13o3NuhL4cEFKueSM-MGA#v=snippet&q=blue line&f=false.

Ristroph, Alice. "The Thin Blue Line From Crime to Punishment." *Journal of Criminal Law and Criminology* 108, no. 2 (2018): 305–334.

Shalin, Dmitri. "Pragmatism and Social Interactionism." *American Sociological Review* 51, no. 1 (1986): 9–29.

Silver, Jasmine R., Sean Patrick Roche, Thomas J. Bilach, and Stephanie Bontrager Ryon. "Traditional Police Culture, Use of Force, and Procedural Justice: Investigating Individual, Organizational, and Contextual Factors." *Justice Quarterly* 34, no. 7 (2017): 1272–1309. https://doi.org/10.1080/07418825.2017.1381756.

"Six Days in July—Coverage of the 1967 Detroit Riots - YouTube." Accessed February 18, 2021. https://www.youtube.com/watch?v=xH-x7uGSDZM.

Skolnick, Jerome. *Justice Without Trial: Law Enforcement in Democratic Society*. New York: Wiley, 1966. https://doi.org/10.2307/2574920.

Skolnick, Jerome. *Justice Without Trial: Law Enforcement in Democratic Society*. 4th ed. New Orleans, LA: Quid Pro Books, 2011.

Skolnick, Jerome. "A Sketch of the Policeman's Working Personality." In *Race, Ethnicity, and Policing: New and Essential Readings*, edited by Stephen Rice and Michael White, 15–31. New York: NYU Press, 2010.

Skolnick, Jerome, and James J. Fyfe. *Above the Law: Police and the Excessive Use of Force*. New York: Free Press, 1993.

Southall, Ashley. "'Appalling' Video Shows the Police Yanking 1-Year-Old From His Mother's Arms." *The New York Times*, December 9, 2018. https://www.nytimes.com/2018/12/09/nyregion/nypd-jazmine-headley-baby-video.html.

Strecher, Victor. "People Who Don't Even Know You." In *The Police and Society: Touchtone Readings*, 4th ed., edited by Victor Kappeler and Brian P. Schaefer, 241–257. Long Grove, IL: Waveland Press, 2019.

Tennessee v. Garner, 471 U.S. 1 (1985).

Terrill, William. "Police Use of Force: A Transactional Approach." *Justice Quarterly* 22, no. 1 (2005): 107–138. https://doi.org/10.1080/0741882042000333663.

"This Week in Universal News: The March on the Pentagon, 1967—The Unwritten Record." Accessed February 18, 2021. https://unwritten-record.blogs.archives.gov/2014/10/20/this-week-in-universal-news-the-march-on-the-pentagon-1967/.

Twersky-Glasner, Aviva. "Police Personality: What Is It and Why Are They Like That?" *Journal of Police and Criminal Psychology* 20, no. 1 (2005): 56–67. https://doi.org/10.1007/BF02806707.

Van Maanen, John. "The Asshole." In *Policing: A View From the Street*, edited by Peter K. Manning and John Van Maanen, 221–238. Santa Monica, CA: Goodyear, 1978.

Walker, Samuel. *Sense and Nonsense About Crime and Drugs: A Policy Guide*. 8th ed. Stamford, CT: Cengage Learning, 2015.

Wickersham, George W. "National Commission on Law Observance and Enforcement: Report." Washington, DC, 1931.

CHAPTER 6

The Rise and "Stall" of Community Policing: A Parable

In the fall of 1997, a researcher[1] made his way on foot through the grounds of a north Philadelphia public housing complex. The neighborhood was tough, characterized by high crime, battered infrastructure, and concentrated economic disadvantage. From looking at census data, the researcher knew that most people in the community were unemployed or underemployed, that many of them lived on wages below the poverty line, and that there were few jobs or neighborhood amenities to be had within a mile or so of the community. The census and crime data summarized its statistical "toughness," but the neighborhood itself exhaled a sense of desolation to those who walked through it. It contained few businesses, several vacant lots littered with trash, crumbling sidewalks with scattered

Podcast Episode: "Is Community Policing Dead? A Conversation With Two Experts"

Scan the QR code or enter the short URL shown below into a browser window to listen to this chapter's podcast.

https://bit.ly/3s8SlmN

---

[1] The researcher was the author of this book. I was a PhD student at Temple University and had just joined a research team (as part of my doctoral studies) to help design, implement, and evaluate a community policing program in five public housing developments in Philadelphia.

fragments of broken glass, and needles and syringes laying where they were dropped in the gutters. None of the basketball hoops had nets, and the courts themselves were just neglected asphalt with large cracks running across the surface. A person living in that community could no more play a safe game of basketball, due to the condition of the decrepit courts, than they could get a pizza delivered to their door by any national chain.

Heading to the housing complex's community center—his destination on that day—the researcher spied up the block the one market that served the neighborhood. It sat a few blocks from the subway station, sported bars on the windows, and had graffiti covering much of the exterior walls. The closer he came to the market, the more the researcher realized that what he initially thought was graffiti was actually a mural, visualizing the story of the bonds that tied children and their mothers together. Poking his head inside the market, the researcher saw no displays of fresh fruits or vegetables, just dry carbohydrates on the shelves and frozen dinners in the freezer section. For what the place lacked in fresh foods, it made up for in security measures: The cash register counter was fully encased in what appeared to be a bullet-resistant transaction window, complete with a pass-through drawer for exchanges of currency. There were closed-circuit cameras mounted in every corner of the ceiling, and a television screen behind the register that broadcast the live black-and-white video feeds from all four cameras.

The researcher moved on until he found the community center. Once inside, he took a seat in the back of the room and waited for the meeting to start. He was there to observe and take notes. Looking around, he saw that the room was a good size, a comfortable meet-up place for local residents. He noticed a foosball table that sat next to a compact metal shelving unit that held children's books. His eye followed a countertop with a sink that ran along one of the short walls. Chairs and a few tables occupied the middle of the room.

By the time the meeting started there were eight residents from the neighborhood sitting in chairs loosely arranged so they all generally faced the same direction. Seven were African American women around 40 years of age, and one was an African American man in at least his mid-60s. At the front of the room, behind a rectangular folding table, sat a police officer wearing the uniform of the Philadelphia Public Housing Authority Police Department (PHA Police). He was one of the 20 or so officers assigned to work the newly created community policing unit deployed across five public housing developments in what is known as Philadelphia's 11th Street Corridor. He and the researcher were known to each other because the latter was part of the university team that had designed the community policing program and was evaluating its effectiveness.

The officer was in the community center that afternoon to participate in a meeting designed to be a dialogue with local neighbors who came to share their concerns about problems they had identified on their street blocks.

They were hoping the PHA police could use their authority and knowledge of city government to help residents implement solutions that might solve those problems. For example, several residents said that young kids frequently stayed outside too late after dark—well after 11:00 p.m.—and made trouble in the playground across from their apartments. They thought a locking gate at the playground's entrance, or maybe some bright overhead lighting, might discourage kids from congregating there at night. They were also concerned that too many young men in the neighborhood were driving their cars too fast up and down the streets, endangering the young kids playing outside and the mothers pushing their babies in strollers. The residents were hoping to convince the city to place a speed bump on 11th Street. An older man did not care for the beer drinking on front stoops of the apartments. More to the point, he didn't so much mind the beer drinking as he did the loud music with all the curse words that seemed to result from the beer drinking late into the evenings.

This was community policing: Officers and local residents jointly identifying community problems and then working together to solve those problems, thereby "co-producing" public safety for everyone in the neighborhood. The idea was to address these "nuisances," usually through nonenforcement police actions, as a way of alleviating some of the community "disorder"—both physical and social—that came to characterize public life for many neighborhood residents. Community policing was partly based on the "broken windows" model of policing (discussed in detail below), which presumed that by solving quality-of-life problems, such as broken windows, police and residents could discourage more serious crime from occurring. It was also based on routine activities theory and the so-called crime triangle (also discussed below).

As the eight residents in the community center finished ticking off the problems they hoped the PHA officer—and the new community policing team—would help them address, the officer nodded while remaining focused on his notepad as he finished writing some notes. After a moment, he set down his pen, looked around the room, and smiled at everyone while gathering his thoughts. Finally, he declared, "You know what you really need? You need drug enforcement! You have a major drug problem in this development, so we need to put some officers near doorways and behind bushes for jump-outs. That way, they can arrest the dealers and get them off the street for you." In other words, this officer hadn't heard a word the residents had said, and they knew it. He was not interested in gates, lighting, or speed bumps. He did not want to facilitate the co-production of safety; and perhaps more than anything, he did not want to share authority. He wanted surveillance, pedestrian stops, and arrests. He wanted business as usual, the same business-as-usual policing that had characterized that public housing development for two generations.

This chapter examines the rise of community policing in U.S. police departments, focusing on both its rationale and practice from about the late 1970s to the present. As we shall see, community policing initially developed in response to the emerging evidence that (1) police tactics and strategies in the 1960s and 1970s were having little impact on overall crime rates, (2) the "professional" model of policing, based on paramilitary hierarchy, was ill-equipped to handle the new demands being made on police, and (3) most police officers—despite the emphasis placed on crime control and law enforcement—spent more of their time handling "nuisance" or disorder situations than they did serious crimes.[2] By the mid-1980s, some commentators and researchers were arguing that the time was right to try a new way of policing that deemphasized the call-driven paradigm in favor of working collaboratively with local residents to solve so-called small problems so they would not escalate into big problems.[3]

It wasn't easy, though. The hierarchical nature of policing, as expressed through the paramilitary organizational structure, made it difficult for many agencies to adapt to a new model that encouraged police officers to work independently with local residents to address community problems. Moreover, traditional police culture, as described in Chapter 5, made it particularly difficult for both line officers and many command staff police administrators to embrace the idea that police–community partnerships might be more important as a long-term crime control strategy than driving around in marked cars looking for crime.[4] By the late 1990s, some police organizations (i.e., the NYPD) found it so difficult to adopt the tenets of community policing that they used broken windows theory—one of the initial perspectives that guided the development of community policing—as a justification to shift from community partnerships to zero tolerance, a strategy that emphasized stopping and frisking people suspected of committing quality-of-life crimes.[5]

Still, community policing remains a component of most U.S. police departments, particularly those in cities with more than 50,000 residents. According to the Bureau of Justice Statistics, as of 2016 (the most recent year for which data are available), almost two-thirds of all local police departments serving populations of at least 50,000 reportedly maintained written community policing plans, and that percentage significantly increased as city populations increased.[6] The experience with community policing in many U.S. police departments remains a cautionary tale, however, hence the title of this chapter. Zero tolerance, stop-and-frisk, and the paramilitary nature of police organizations continue to relegate much of community policing to the sidelines of police organizations; yet, community policing is arguably the closest reform to date that encourages the police to break free from the coercive paradigm to try something new. For that reason, the story of community policing in the United States becomes a parable.

---

[2] Goldstein, "Toward Community-Oriented Policing: Potential, Basic Requirements, and Threshold Questions."

[3] Kelling, "Police and Communities: The Quiet Revolution."

[4] *See generally* Mastrofski, Willis, and Kochel, "The Challenges of Implementing Community Policing in the United States."

[5] Greene, "Zero Tolerance: A Case Study of Police Policies and Practices in New York City."

[6] U.S. Department of Justice, "Local Police Departments: Policies and Procedures, 2016," 2.

By the end of this chapter, readers should have the knowledge to discuss and answer the following questions:

1. What were initial philosophical principles of community policing?
2. What is the "means-over-ends" syndrome, and how did it lead to the development of community and problem-oriented policing?
3. What is problem-oriented policing—and the SARA model—and how does it relate to community policing?
4. How does the so-called crime triangle of routine activities theory help guide problem-oriented policing strategies?
5. How would adopting community policing require police departments to rethink their adherence to the quasi-military bureaucratic model of police organizations?
6. What is the status of community policing today?

The Idea of Community Policing

It started as a philosophy, with the recognition in some police departments and among some policing scholars that policing—contrary to the symbolism of the thin blue line—was not a "community's professional defense" against crime, but rather that "community institutions" represented the first line of defense.[7] This change in mentality challenged the traditional belief structure of the policing subculture and became a powerful emerging movement in the early 1980s in some of the nation's more progressive police departments: Madison, Wisconsin; Baltimore County, Maryland; Newport News, Virginia; and San Diego, California.[8] The recognition that community institutions, and community members themselves, could become crucial partners in the fight against crime and disorder had big implications for police departments willing to adopt the philosophy. It meant taking some officers out of police cars (i.e., out of reactive patrol) and deploying them on foot, on horses, or on bicycles so they could meet with community members and become more than just "flashing faces" in police cars driving with windows up through neighborhoods.[9]

There was more, too. The new community policing philosophy also aimed to decentralize police officer decision-making, allowing officers on the street to work with community groups to help identify and solve problems that were compromising the quality of life for community residents. The mere fact that police departments were willing to focus on minor, or "disorder," crimes—particularly during the formative years of the war on drugs—represented a significant departure from previous generations of policing that emphasized the response to, and reduction of, just the major index

[7] Kelling, "Police and Communities: The Quiet Revolution," 2.
[8] Kelling, 3.
[9] Reiss, "Policing a City's Central District, The Oakland Story," 9.

crimes.[10] This meant that police departments would reduce their reliance on the call-driven model while adopting a more proactive role that empowered line officers to investigate and implement proposed solutions to community problems. It also meant that police officers could become more than a line that separates: They could become a line that connects.

Aside from affecting deployment structures (i.e., moving some officers out of patrol cars and into walking beats), community policing also presented implications for the organizational structure of police departments. As discussed in previous chapters, most U.S. police departments are configured as organizational hierarchies emphasizing chain-of-command communications and control, emulating a quasi-military bureaucratic model. Recall from Chapter 2, for example, that the "distance" between the top of the organizational chart (i.e., the chief or commissioner of police) and the bottom (i.e., the line officer) can be thought of as "vertical differentiation," describing the rank and chain-of-command hierarchy.[11] Most midsize and large U.S. police departments are highly vertically differentiated, maintaining many command layers between the police administration and line officers. Such hierarchies traditionally reduce the decision-making authority given to line—or patrol—officers on the street, often requiring them to seek approval for nonroutine actions (or prohibiting them altogether). Indeed, in police departments that are both highly vertically and functionally differentiated, patrol officers would normally turn over a case that resulted from a call for service to detectives and get "back on the air"—meaning they would vacate the scene and make themselves available again for patrolling and taking radio calls. Community policing challenged such tightly construed organizational control because its practice requires officers to "work" their cases by developing local solutions to local problems. Such solutions are rarely routine.

Ironically, police officers on the street take "nonroutine" action every day, practicing outside the confines of the chain of command. As a street-level bureaucracy, policing's primary function at the street level is to "process people,"[12] which means police officers regularly make on-the-fly discretionary decisions to solve problems in ways that satisfy the public and keep them (the officers) in service and available to take the next call. Thus, by adopting community policing and flattening the organizational hierarchies, participating police departments could formally acknowledge the realities of policing: Line officers worked in uncertain environments and had to make quick decisions that often meant implementing creative solutions to problems they encountered without waiting for approval to do so. The need to flatten the organization to accommodate a new model of policing that empowered line officers would prove difficult for many—and insurmountable to some—police organizations, however. Traditional police culture and the command-and-control mindset of police

---

[10] These include murder, rape, robbery, aggravated assault, burglary, larceny, motor vehicle theft, and arson.

[11] Maguire, *Organizational Structure in American Police Agencies: Context, Complexity, and Control,* 16–18.

[12] Lipsky, *Street-Level Bureaucracy: Dilemmas of the Individuals in Public Services,* xi.

administrators meant that many organizations would not adopt community policing as a philosophy so much as a special unit that fit within the existing bureaucratic structure.[13] More on this is presented later in the chapter.

Community policing as originally conceptualized was to become a policing paradigm that would reduce crime and thus fulfill the police mandate. Theoretically, community policing was initially grounded in the broken windows model of criminology—that focusing on not-so-serious quality-of-life problems in neighborhoods, such as fixing real and metaphorical broken windows, reducing social disorder, and fixing up the physically dilapidated infrastructure, would send the message to would-be offenders that serious crime would not be tolerated on a particular street block because that block was well cared for and well surveilled.[14] Along the way, police officers got to work with community residents in ways that helped them to better integrate into the communities they served, which could hopefully improve (and in some cases repair) police–community relationships.[15] Historically, police officers had no formal role in working with community members to improve quality of life on the street block, but once such measures became linked to the prospects of reducing serious crimes, some police departments began to adopt the community policing model.

Strategically, community policing is most frequently operationalized as problem-oriented policing, wherein police officers work within a prescribed framework to help community members identify and assess local problems and then implement and evaluate local solutions. Problem-oriented policing has its roots in a 1979 article published by Herman Goldstein in which he argued that through the 1970s many U.S. police departments suffered from what he called the "means over ends syndrome."[16] That is, police departments were investing too much effort toward improving their bureaucracies—enhancing communications, developing special units, shuffling patrol deployments across their jurisdictions—as a method for reducing crime (and controlling officers in the organization). These were the "means" of policing. Goldstein argued that departments should move away from emphasizing the means by focusing on the "ends," such as crime reductions through solving local community problems. Shifting from organizational efficiencies to community-based problem-solving as a lead focus, Goldstein concluded, would lead to the crime reductions policing strove to achieve.[17]

The Move Toward Problem-Oriented Policing

In the mid-1980s, Goldstein's concept of problem-oriented policing was translated into action through a partnership between the police department in Newport News, Virginia, and scholars working for the Police Executive

---

[13] Mastrofski, "Community Policing: A Skeptical View."
[14] Kelling, "Police and Communities: The Quiet Revolution."
[15] Skogan and Hartnett, "Community Policing in Chicago."
[16] Goldstein, "Improving Policing: A Problem-Oriented Approach," 236.
[17] Goldstein.

Research Forum in Washington, DC.[18] Together, they developed a program of policing designed to reduce certain types of crime through the problem-solving approach. To accomplish this, the authors[19] created the SARA model, which has since become the leading framework—almost the archetype—of problem-oriented policing. The SARA approach involves four phases of implementation: scanning, analysis, response, and assessment.[20] Through this process, police officers and community members gather information on the extent of a community problem, create and implement a response to that problem, and then evaluate the results of the implementation. Importantly, the problem is frequently (but not always) related to a quality-of-life issue, and the response is often not a criminal justice intervention. Appealing to Eck and Spelman and others,[21] the following is a summary of the SARA approach to problem-oriented policing:

- **Scanning:** Officers and community members—sometimes together, sometimes independently—identify persistent problems in the community that affect the quality of life for residents. The problem might be crime-related, or it might be more related to "disorder," which is not always illegal, per se, but could be part of a larger crime issue.

- **Analysis:** Identify the context of the problem, for example, its origins, how it persists, the degree to which it affects life on the street or block, and how residents and police are currently managing the problem. In this stage, officers will also search for any data that might help them better understand the dynamics of the problem. For example, if the problem is younger kids playing loud music on their porch late into the evening, the officer might examine call dispatch data to learn whether residents have been calling the police for disturbances, and what responding officers have done in the past to address the issues. Did they issue citations? Did they simply advise the kids to go inside? Did they talk to parents? As part of the analysis phase, officers typically develop a working hypothesis about how to effectively solve the problem.

- **Response:** Officers work with residents to identify a range of possible solutions to the problem, and they also try to learn what other communities might have done to effectively solve the problem. The officers then create an action plan that they can implement in the hopes of solving the problem.

---

[18] Eck and Spelman, *Problem-Solving: Problem-Oriented Policing in Newport News.*

[19] As Eck and Spelman, themselves, noted in their final report, they consulted with Herman Goldstein (the original problem-oriented policing scholar) and other researchers at the start of the Newport News project to gain insights into developing a problem-solving approach. The result of that consultation was the SARA model.

[20] Eck and Spelman, *Problem-Solving: Problem-Oriented Policing in Newport News,* 42.

[21] Eck and Spelman; Mastrofski, "Community Policing: A Skeptical View"; "The SARA Model | ASU Center for Problem-Oriented Policing."

■ **Assessment:** This is the evaluation phase where officers determine (1) whether the response they developed in conjunction with the community was actually implemented as planned, and (2) the extent to which the response solved the problem. Such an evaluation usually means that officers will continue to collect data—for example, calls for service information—to monitor the progress of the response.

Two elements of the SARA model are important to highlight. First, although problem-oriented policing aims to ultimately reduce crime, it is also designed as a method for helping police reduce repeat calls for service to the same locations.[22] By solving, or at least addressing, quality-of-life problems with local residents, police departments could reduce the number of repeat calls for service, which frees up policing resources that might be used for more serious types of crimes. Second, problem-oriented policing is often designed to find solutions outside the criminal justice system,[23] both as a way of conserving justice system resources, and (perhaps more important) to keep quality-of-life offenders from getting arrested and processed through the formal criminal justice system.

The SARA Model at Work: A Case Study in Problem-Oriented Policing, British Style

In the mid-2000s a U.S. policing scholar[24] traveled to England to learn about a new policing initiative being piloted in the United Kingdom that was designed to reduce persistent social disorder. As a proposed method of problem-oriented policing, the approach there was to implement a new type of civil intervention called an antisocial behavior order (ASBO) to legally compel people labeled "antisocial" to cease their problematic behaviors.[25] The U.S. researcher was there mostly to observe how the police in Essex County, just northeast of London, were applying the new ASBOs, primarily to juveniles engaged in unruly behaviors when out of school.

One night, a couple of weeks into his stay, the researcher was participating in a ride-along with a pair of uniformed constables (i.e., police officers) in a marked patrol car. At approximately 2:20 a.m., the constables received a priority call for service directing them to respond with lights and siren to a large fight that had just broken out on a public street in the middle of one of the nearby towns. When the researcher and officers arrived, they found multiple uniformed

---

[22] Hinkle et al., "Problem-Oriented Policing for Reducing Crime and Disorder: An Updated Systematic Review and Meta-Analysis."

[23] Cordner and Biebel, "Problem-Oriented Policing in Practice."

[24] The policing scholar was the author of this book. In 2006, I was awarded a grant to spend much of my summer between the United Kingdom and the Netherlands studying two different types of policing. In the United Kingdom, I spent much time riding along with uniformed constables to learn how they policed the towns around London.

[25] *See* Hodgkinson and Tilley, "Policing Anti-Social Behaviour: Constraints, Dilemmas and Opportunities."

constables already in the street trying to stop the altercation that seemed to involve at least 20 men, most of whom appeared to be intoxicated. The two constables removed and handed their watches and rings to the researcher before jumping from the vehicle to join the brawl. Within about 20 minutes the fight was brought under control, but only after several of the participants, including a few constables, had been bloodied or otherwise injured. It took an ambulance, a transport wagon, and multiple police cars to clear the scene.

The following morning, while attending a debrief meeting about the fight, the researcher learned that such violent outbreaks on that street had become increasingly common over the prior few weeks, as patrons from two pubs that sat kitty-corner to one another funneled out onto the street at 2:00 a.m. when the bars closed. The "regulars" at one of the pubs were staunch supporters of West Ham United FC, a local Premier League football (soccer) club that played in East London. Recently, however, the other pub had become increasingly frequented by fans of Millwall FC—also an East London football club, and importantly, the greatest rival of West Ham. On Friday or Saturday nights (and sometimes both), when the patrons of both pubs met in the street just after closing time, they tended to argue and then get into fights. The problem for the police was that it took many officers and a wagon to restore order on the one or two nights per week the fights were happening. More than that, it was seen as a tremendous waste of criminal justice and health care resources to arrest, process, jail, and release—sometimes with hospital treatment—more than 20 intoxicated soccer fans every weekend. The Chief Constable asked the researcher to collaborate with him and his officers on a problem-oriented policing intervention to reduce the potential for fights when the pubs let out at 2:00 a.m.

After several visits and discussions with the pub owners—both of whom shared an interest in stopping the fights—the problem-oriented policing team (and the researcher) developed a plan whereby at 2:00 a.m. on the weekends (the most typical fight nights), one pub owner would direct his patrons to exit the bar through the front doors as usual, and the other pub owner would direct his patrons to exit through a back door, which fed out onto another street block. As it was illegal for customers of a pub to be in the establishments' kitchen, the pub owner—with the help of the constables—worked to get special permission from the town council to allow the patrons to walk through the kitchen when the bar closed to reach the back door. For the first weekend of the intervention, police would be on standby just at the perimeter to respond if any violence should break out.

The next weekend, with the new exit protocols in place, the pub owners funneled their patrons out the different doors, keeping the rival soccer fans from coming into contact with one another. From that point forward, no fights occurred on the street in front of the two pubs. There were no more repeat calls for service, no more ambulances and police transport wagons, and no more injuries.

This discrete example of how problem-oriented policing can be applied to reduce situational crime demonstrates the potential benefits of implementing a non-law-enforcement police approach to solve a crime and disorder problem. Police constables worked with community stakeholders (i.e., the pub owners) and town officials to create a solution to a serious problem that had begun to routinely disrupt the center of a small town, tie up criminal justice and health care resources, and result in injuries to both police constables and members of the public.

The case study also shows how problem-oriented policing had begun to appeal to theories outside the traditional broken windows perspective for its operational functioning. In this case, the constables and researchers applied the routine activities theory of crime to problem-oriented policing in hope of "breaking" the so-called crime triangle. Routine activities theory predicts that a crime (or victimization) will occur when a motivated offender and a suitable target converge in time and space, and in the absence of capable guardianship.[26] This theory is illustrated in Figure 6.1.

Initially, routine activities theory was specified to explain just crime and victimization, predicting that, when motivated offenders came into contact with targets they deemed suitable (the targets could be people, homes, businesses, etc.)—and in the absence of anyone or anything to stop them—then they would commit the crime.[27] As applied to problem-oriented policing, the theory can be expanded to include disorder or other local problems of interest. If just one element from the triangle in Figure 6.1 is eliminated, the crime, victimization, or problem will not occur. In the case of the Essex football fan brawlers, the constables and researcher presumed that once the pub customers went outside, they would represent both the motivated offenders and the suitable targets (especially to one another). The problem-oriented policing team therefore directed their intervention toward the other leg of the triangle: keeping the presumed victims and offenders from meeting each other in the same time and space. In making a relatively simple change to the flow of foot traffic into the street at 2:00 a.m., the police department, in

◀ Figure 6.1

Routine Activities Model as Translated to Problem-Oriented Policing

---

[26] Cohen and Felson, "Social Change and Crime Rate Trends: A Routine Activity Approach."
[27] *See* Cohen and Felson; Roundtree and Land, "Burglary Victimization, Perceptions of Crime Risk, and Routine Activities: A Multilevel Analysis Across Seattle Neighborhoods and Census Tracts."

conjunction with community and local government parties, prevented future brawls from occurring without using their primary tool: the general right to use coercive force.

The Practice of Community Policing in the United States

In 1994, Congress passed into law the Violent Crime Control and Law Enforcement Act, which, in addition to funding the hiring of 100,000 new local police officers and deputy sheriffs, created the Office of Community Oriented Policing Services (COPS Office).[28] Situated in the U.S. Department of Justice, the COPS Office was the first federal government agency specifically designed to encourage community policing through technical assistance grants, national workshops, and funded research partnerships between police agencies and universities.[29] As a result, the 1990s saw a wave of multisite research projects across the country intended to implement and test the results of various community policing programs in both local (e.g., municipal) and specialized (e.g., public housing, transit, and college) police agencies.[30] Since that time, and perhaps as a result of the COPS Office, community policing has become widely acknowledged by many police agencies as an important part of their operational structure. Figure 6.2 visualizes the extent of police department stated support for community policing across the contiguous United States.

As the data in Figure 6.2 show, police departments with published mission statements offering explicit support for some component(s) of community policing are ubiquitous across the contiguous United States. Among the 2,784 local police departments that provided data for the 2016 Law Enforcement Management and Administrative Statistics (LEMAS) survey (the most comprehensive national survey of police agencies), almost 82 percent of them reported that their mission statements contained language supporting some elements of community policing. To the extent that a mission statement conveys an operational philosophy—or perhaps even a value system—it is noteworthy that such a large sample of local police agencies have incorporated some language about the importance of community policing into their mission statements.

Translating mission statements into action can be challenging, though, as it requires a commitment within the organization to operationalize that mission statement at the street level. In police departments, such translation usually occurs in the form of training—for example, training some combination of police officer recruits (i.e., those in the police academy) and

---

[28] "COPS Office."

[29] COPS Office, "Advancing Public Safety Through Community Policing: The First 25 Years of the COPS Office."

[30] Collins et al., *Implementing Community Policing in Public Housing: Philadelphia's 11th Street Corridor Program*; Mazerolle et al., *Problem-Oriented Policing in Public Housing: Final Report of the Jersey City Project*; Skogan and Hartnett, *Community Policing, Chicago Style*.

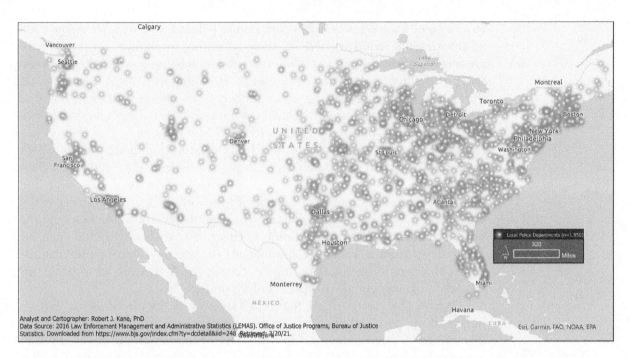

Analyst and Cartographer: Robert J. Kane, PhD
Data Source: 2016 Law Enforcement Management and Administrative Statistics (LEMAS). Office of Justice Programs, Bureau of Justice
Statistics. Downloaded from https://www.bjs.gov/index.cfm?ty=dcdetail&iid=248 (Retrieved: 3/20/21.

▲ **Figure 6.2**

Community Policing
Across the United
States

existing police officers in some aspects of community policing practice. As
the LEMAS data in Table 6.1 show, local police departments nationally experience a great deal of variability in their community policing training requirements.

As the data in Table 6.1 show, 41.8 percent of all local agencies reporting
in the 2016 LEMAS survey required all their police officer recruits to receive
at least eight hours of community policing training. An additional 12.8 percent
required some of their recruits to receive at least eight hours of community policing training. Still, more than 24 percent of all local agencies that participated in LEMAS reported that they required none of their police officer recruits

Table 6.1. Community Policing Training in Local Police Agencies Across the United States			
Local Police Agencies That . . .	**All**	**Some**	**None**
Require a proportion of police recruits to receive at least 8 hours of community policing training	1,142 (41.8 %)	349 (12.8%)	667 (24.4%)[1]
Require a proportion of police personnel to receive at least 8 hours of community policing training via in-service	583 (21.3%)	1,071 (39.2%)	1,029 (37.6%)[2]

Note: Data from 2016 Law Enforcement Management and Administrative Statistics. Retrieved March 20, 2021, from
https://www.bjs.gov/index.cfm?ty=dcdetail&iid=248.
[1] Row percentages do not equal 100 because 22 (0.8%) local agencies did not report data, and 555 (20.3%) agencies reportedly hired no new police recruits at time of survey.
[2] Row percentages do not equal 100 because 52 (1.9%) local agencies did not report data.

to receive at least eight hours of community policing training. The proportion of departments requiring none of their personnel to receive this training increases to almost 38 percent when referring to existing sworn police officers. Only 21.3 percent of all local agencies participating in LEMAS reported that they required all their existing police officers to receive at least eight hours of community policing training. That is, whereas almost three-quarters of police departments that participate in LEMAS require some or all their police recruits to receive at least eight hours of community policing training, that proportion drops to just under two-thirds for existing police officers. When training that is required in the police academy does not fully carry over into the police organization itself, it is unclear how well the existing officers in the organization can help support the training recruits receive in the academy.

Moreover, moving from training to practice can also be a challenge for police departments. Table 6.2 summarizes the extent of local police departments that encouraged patrol officers to use the SARA model of problem-oriented policing as part of their regular duties.

Perhaps the most striking figure in Table 6.2 is the one showing that almost half (48 percent) of all local police departments that participated in the 2016 LEMAS survey reported that they encouraged none of their full-time patrol officers to use the SARA model as part of their regular patrol duties. This finding stands in contrast to the virtually 82 percent of local police agencies (referring to Figure 6.2) reporting that they included at least some language supporting community policing in their mission statements. Such a gap, again, suggests something of a disconnect between what some scholars have called the rhetoric of community policing, as embodied by mission statements, and the reality of community policing, as translated into practice by police organizations.[31]

What is particularly interesting about the data shown in Table 6.2 is the almost dichotomous nature of the figures presented. Although almost

Table 6.2. Police Departments That "Encourage" Full-Time Patrol Officers to Use the SARA Model During Their Regular Duties

Among Local Police Departments, This Percentage of Them . . .	Encouraged This percentage of Their Full-Time Patrol Officers to Use the SARA Model During Their Daily Work
48.0%	0.0%
18.0%	up to 4.3%
17.0%	up to 62.5%
17.0%	up to 100.0%

Note: Data from 2016 Law Enforcement Management and Administrative Statistics. Retrieved March 20, 2021, from https://www.bjs.gov/index.cfm?ty=dcdetail&iid=248.

---

[31] For an example of an initial volume questioning the efficacy of community policing, *see* Greene and Mastrofski, *Community Policing: Rhetoric or Reality*.

half of all reporting local police departments encourage zero full-time patrol officers to practice the SARA model of problem-oriented policing (which is, again, the primary strategy of the community policing philosophy), nearly 34 percent encouraged at least 62.5 percent of their full-time patrol officers to practice SARA. Indeed, half of that 34 percent encouraged up to of 100 percent of their full-time patrol officers to practice SARA. The encouragement to use SARA varies greatly by size of the police organization, however: The larger the jurisdiction (based on residential population size), the more that police departments encouraged patrol officers to use the SARA model as part of their regular duties. It could be the case that community and problem-oriented policing are primarily a metropolitan policing strategy.

Finally, if community policing is primarily about police working with the community to facilitate the co-production of safety, then it would be important for police departments that claim to practice community policing to establish partnerships with different community groups. The ability of police to implement nontraditional approaches to help solve community problems—which would hopefully increase the quality of life and decrease crime—would seem to hinge on the partnerships police develop with a variety of community stakeholders. Fortunately, the LEMAS survey asks a battery of questions about police-community partnerships, and the response data are presented in Table 6.3.

Table 6.3. Community Policing Partnerships or Written Agreements Across Local Police Agencies

Agency Has a Partnership or Written Agreement With	Number and Percentages of Agencies Reporting "Yes"	
	Agencies With Community-Oriented Policing in Their Mission Statements (*n* = 1,930)	Agencies With No Community-Oriented Policing in Their Mission Statements (*n* = 2,735)
Advocacy groups	936 (48.5%)	1,145 (41.9%)
Business groups	698 (36.2%)	804 (29.4%)
Neighborhood associations	857 (44.4%)	1,004 (36.7%)
University or research group	453 (23.5%)	500 (18.3%)
Other law enforcement agencies	1,413 (73.2%)	1,833 (67.0%)

Note: Universe includes local police and sheriff's departments with primary patrol functions that participated in the 2016 LEMAS survey. Data from 2016 Law Enforcement Management and Administrative Statistics. Retrieved March 20, 2021, from https://www.bjs.gov/index.cfm?ty=dcdetail&iid=248.

Table 6.3 shows the extent of community policing partnerships among police agencies whose mission statements include language supporting community policing, as well as agencies whose mission statements do not include any support for community policing. For the purposes of this discussion, we refer to the former agencies as COP police departments, and the latter as non-COP police departments.

As the data in Table 6.3 show, 48.5 percent of COP police agencies reportedly maintained partnerships with advocacy groups, compared to 41.9 percent of non-COP agencies. A total of 36.2 percent of COP agencies maintained partnerships with business groups, whereas 29.4 percent of non-COP agencies maintained such partnerships. Although these differences between COP and non-COP agencies are clear, they are not stark. Indeed, the point differences are less than 7 percent for both items. In general, maintaining partnerships with advocacy and business groups is not necessarily limited to community policing, as both types of groups represent clear stakeholders in local jurisdictions. The differences, however, between COP and non-COP police agencies increase when focusing on community groups. A total of 44.4 percent of COP police agencies reportedly maintained partnerships or written agreements with neighborhood associations, compared to 36.7 percent of non-COP agencies. Although the differences between the two "types" of police agencies are pronounced, it is particularly interesting that less than half of all police agencies whose mission statements include language about community policing maintained partnerships or written agreements with neighborhood associations, arguably the most important local stakeholder for co-producing community safety.

Among COP agencies, 23.5 percent reportedly maintained partnerships or written agreements with university or research groups, whereas 18.3 percent of non-COP agencies did. The implication of this finding is subtle, but important: Among COP agencies, less than one-quarter of them maintained partnerships with universities or other research groups, which means that if they were practicing community or problem-oriented policing at all, they were likely doing so without research partners who could assist in developing, implementing, and—importantly—evaluating the effects of community and problem-oriented policing strategies. More on this finding is presented below.

Finally, as the summary in Table 6.3 indicates, 73.2 percent of COP police agencies reportedly maintained partnerships or written agreements with other law enforcement agencies; even 67.0 percent of non-COP agencies did so as well. In total, almost three-quarters of COP agencies reportedly maintained partnerships or written agreements with other police agencies. Although some of these partnerships might well have been created to facilitate cross-jurisdiction community- or problem-oriented policing strategies, almost two-thirds of non-COP agencies also maintained such partnerships. This finding suggests that regardless of whether the mission statements include support for some component(s) of community policing, all police departments are still more comfortable interfacing with each other than with other groups outside policing.

Overall, the findings shown in Table 6.3 suggest that police departments with COP language in their mission statements tend to establish partnerships with groups outside policing at higher rates than police departments whose mission statements do not include language about COP. Still, as the data in Table 6.3 also indicate, although the differences between COP and non-COP agencies were consistent, they were not vast. It could be the case that including language supporting community policing in departmental mission statements does not fully distinguish agencies from those that do not include language about community policing in their mission statements. These findings might also indicate that most police departments have learned that they cannot rightly fulfill their missions without engaging local groups outside policing. Perhaps many of these agencies are already using the thin blue line as a connector rather than a divider, as described in Chapter 5.

Some Concluding Observations

As a policing philosophy, community policing is the closest organizational model we have seen that promotes something beyond the traditional confines of the coercion paradigm. It is a community-focused, problem-based framework that encourages police departments to try something other than coercion—or coercive force—to improve the quality of life and potentially reduce crime. When problem-oriented policing is implemented well, it does seem to reduce crime. In the most recent large-scale meta-analysis to date, one team of scholars examined 39 studies of problem-oriented policing (also referred to as POP in the literature) that were published between 2006 and 2018, finding that on average, POP programs that were driven by the SARA model led to a reduction of nearly 35 percent in crime and disorder.[32] Given all the structural causes of crime (e.g., neighborhood disadvantage, racial segregation, and household risk factors), it is noteworthy that targeted POP interventions can reduce crime in communities by over one-third.

The problem is, however, that this observed average 35 percent crime reduction came from a small number of studies, all of which used highly rigorous research designs,[33] meaning that these were police agencies that partnered with universities to develop, implement, and evaluate the POP programs. As we saw in Table 6.3, though, only 23.5 percent of all COP police departments maintained partnerships with universities or other research groups, and only 18.3 percent of non-COP agencies did so. This means that most problem-oriented policing programs across the United States are being implemented without outside social scientific expertise; equally important, it means the collective academic discipline of criminal justice and criminology does not know anything about their effectiveness. It is thus unclear how well

---

[32] Hinkle et al., "Problem-Oriented Policing for Reducing Crime and Disorder: An Updated Systematic Review and Meta-Analysis."
[33] Hinkle et al., 2.

the police agencies without a university partner adhere to the prescriptive elements of the SARA model. Indeed, as the author of one large-scale review of problem-oriented policing programs noted, many police departments practicing POP failed to conduct reliable assessments of the problems or the response, rendering the effectiveness of the POP strategy unknowable.[34]

The San Diego Police Department (SDPD) offers a useful example. During the 1990s the SDPD invested heavily (from an organizational standpoint) in community policing and tried to create a more community-oriented culture across the entire agency. Like many police departments, it operationalized community policing as problem-oriented policing, adopting the SARA model to help identify, implement, and evaluate interventions designed to improve quality of life and reduce crime in communities.[35] In 1998, the SDPD was among the first local police agencies in the country to incorporate community policing into all facets of academy recruit training, and it was among the very few police agencies to incorporate community policing into its annual performance reviews of police officers.[36] As one study reports, through the late 1990s and into the 2000s, the SDPD "had a national and international reputation for supporting problem-oriented policing and for producing exemplary POP projects."[37] Indeed, the SDPD moved their community policing program from a special unit within the department to an agency-wide expectation for all police officers to engage in problem-oriented policing.[38] This is something many police departments have been unwilling or unable to do, given their commitment to the quasi-military bureaucratic structure that requires fidelity to chain-of-command operations.

Still, despite the organizational push toward community policing and problem-solving, as well as the structural changes made to support POP, that same report in 1998 showed that few police officers—a level as low as 10 percent—in San Diego actually practiced problem-oriented policing.[39] Moreover, 10 years into POP, an audit of the SDPD showed that only "3 of the documented 32 POP cases" had received any problem-oriented solutions, and that "(e)nforcement responses were used" for 84 percent of the POP interventions.[40] Most telling was that, among surveyed officers, the vast majority still believed that they could effectively police the city without using any form of problem-oriented policing, and about half of those surveyed reported that they believed it was their choice whether to use community and problem-oriented policing strategies on the job.

This is not an indictment of the SDPD. Indeed, the SDPD seems to have done everything it could have done to support community and problem-oriented

---

[34] Scott, *Problem-Oriented Policing: Reflections on the First 20 Years*, 141.
[35] San Diego Police Department, "Evaluating the Analysis and Response Components of Problem Solving in Community Policing."
[36] San Diego Police Department.
[37] Cordner and Biebel, "Problem-Oriented Policing in Practice," 163.
[38] Cordner and Biebel, 163.
[39] Cordner and Biebel, 162.
[40] Cordner and Biebel, 162.

policing. Rather, the experience in San Diego shows an internal disconnect between the philosophy of community policing and the practice of its primary strategy—problem-oriented policing. It shows how difficult it can be for some police departments—even one considered to be among the most progressive in the country—to move beyond coercion as a primary police response to quality-of-life issues, disorder, and crime. It also highlights the struggles a police department faces when trying to break down traditional police culture among officers who seem to want business-as-usual policing (recall the case study presented in the opening pages of this chapter).

If community policing was born out of a police reform movement, then there is a cautionary tale to be told about the potential success for such movements. Thinking back to Chapters 2 and 5 might remind us that traditional police culture that emphasizes danger, authority, and isolation—fostered by police bureaucracies rooted in paramilitary command structures—likely has made it improbable for community policing to permeate the whole of the institution. Indeed, what seems to have happened since the mid-1980s when some police departments began experimenting with community policing is that the philosophy became a strategy, and the strategy was bent to fit into the quasi-military model of policing. The statistics presented in this chapter suggest the difficulty for police departments to translate a mission statement supportive of community policing principles into action through training and the development of partnerships outside policing.

As this book has argued thus far, though, the protection of life mandate is not a reform: It is a reshaping of the very idea of police. It can be as subtle as a change in mindset by which officers are recruited, trained, and socialized to value life over law enforcement. It must be coarse enough, though, to force change from outside the police institution. Community policing was largely an internal movement led by many progressive police chiefs of the late 1970s. They heard the demands for reform due to Civil Rights–era failures of policing, proposing community takeovers of the police as a way of reducing police violence, and even redistributing many police duties to other government offices as a way of diluting police authority.[41] Indeed, calls for post-Civil Rights–era police reforms in the 1970s foreshadowed recent demands for change and the "defund the police" movement in the wake of the 2020 killing of George Floyd.

This book, however, argues that, although the community policing philosophy embodies much of the value system promoted by a protection of life mandate, the moment community policing became a strategy, it lost its revolutionary potential. Changing the idea of police from coercion to the protection of life as a primary mandate will require a movement from outside the police institution. It will mean changing society's expectations of the police, which hopefully can start with readers of this book. Some—perhaps most—readers will never enter the police occupation

---

[41] Mastrofski, "Community Policing: A Skeptical View," 45.

but will instead become that part of society that insists on change. Others will take the new idea with them as they take on the job to become next-generation police officers.

Questions for Review and Reflection

Question 1. The Philosophy of Community Policing

As noted in the chapter, community policing began as a philosophy that hoped to move the police beyond call-driven law enforcement as their primary role to one that valued community partnerships as a way of improving quality of life and ultimately reducing crime in neighborhoods.

- Describe the philosophy of community policing and how it differs from the traditional paradigm of law enforcement. What were some of the catalysts of the early community policing movement?
- Why is it important to know the history of policing when trying to understand why community policing has or hasn't been fully adopted by all local police agencies in the United States?
- Describe the types of partnerships police departments should develop to fully implement the community policing philosophy. For example, should police departments engage with churches and local businesses? Should they regularly meet with community activist groups?
- How does the community policing philosophy reconcile with the crime control and law enforcement paradigm of policing? Can a police department that fully adopts community policing still hope to reduce crime?
- How might the full adoption of the community policing philosophy by police departments help redefine the thin blue line of

policing as something that connects rather than divides?

Question 2. Integrating Problem-Oriented Policing Into Police Departments

Problem-oriented policing mostly developed along the same timeline as community policing. Whereas the latter appears as more of a philosophy, the former appears to be more of a strategy. In other words, where community policing seems to set an overall tone for a police organization's approach to fulfilling its role, problem-oriented policing represents the "nuts and bolts" strategy that helps implement community policing.

- What is problem-oriented policing, and how did the so-called means over ends syndrome help lead to its development?
- In what ways does problem-oriented policing hope to decrease calls for service to repeat locations? Why would the reduction of repeat calls be useful to police organizations?
- Is it possible for a police department to have problem-oriented policing without community policing? What might that look like?
- In what ways does a department-wide community policing philosophy help decide the strategies for problem-oriented policing?

Question 3. Applications of Problem-Oriented Policing

Many crime prevention efforts adopted by police departments are rooted in the routine activities perspective; that is, trying to "break" the so-called crime triangle. Moreover, many police departments use the SARA model as the primary framework that drives their problem-oriented policing approaches. As noted, problem-oriented policing hopes to address chronic crime and other problems that tax policing resources. The link, however, between routine activities and the SARA model is not always explicit, which can make identifying problems, developing interventions to solve them, and then creating evaluations to assess those interventions difficult when the roots of the problems have not been adequately identified.

- Please describe the elements of the routine activities theory of crime.

- How does the element of time help inform both the routine activities theory and the development of any strategies designed to break the crime triangle?
- What is the SARA model of problem-oriented policing? How can the use of the SARA model guide police departments' problem-solving strategies?
- How would a police department use the SARA model to identify a problem that needs addressing, use the routine activities theory to help determine which aspect of the crime triangle to attack, and then go back to the SARA model to develop the intervention and evaluate its results?

Exercise

Exercise Integrating the Philosophy of Community Policing

For this exercise you will use information taken from the website of a municipal police department to develop a plan that infuses the community policing philosophy throughout the entire police organization.

- Visit the website of a municipal police department. This can be the department in your local area, or it can be any department that interests you. At the very least, however, the department's website should offer detailed information about the mission, values, and organization of the department.
- Explore the police department's website and familiarize yourself with (1) its mission and value statement, (2) its organizational structure, (3) the kinds of outreach it might (or might not) do, (4) the partnerships it might

(or might not) have with local groups, (5) the degree to which it might emphasize crime fighting and law enforcement, and (6) the imagery it uses (e.g., photos and other graphics) to convey its mission and values.

- Write a report about how to explicitly integrate community policing throughout the police organization that includes the following:
  - Rewrite the police department's mission statement, values statement, or both to reflect a full commitment to the community policing philosophy.
  - Rearrange the organizational chart in a way that integrates both community policing and problem-oriented policing into the fabric of the department.
  - Identify areas of the website where you could include information about community partnerships and problem-oriented policing activities.

- Indicate in your report the degree to which the police department you selected has already integrated community policing philosophy into its mission, values, and organizational structure.
- When writing up your report, feel free to include screenshots of the department's website to better illustrate your points and arguments, a graphical illustration of any changes to the organizational chart you might recommend, and other graphics that help "create" a department steeped in community policing.

Bibliography

Cohen, Lawrence E., and Marcus Felson. "Social Change and Crime Rate Trends: A Routine Activity Approach." *American Sociological Review* 44, no. 4 (1979): 588–608.

Collins, Patricia, Jack R. Greene, Robert J. Kane, Robert Stokes, and Alexis Piquero. *Implementing Community Policing in Public Housing: Philadelphia's 11th Street Corridor Program*. Washington, DC: U.S. Department of Justice, 1999.

"COPS Office." Accessed March 11, 2021. https://cops.usdoj.gov/.

COPS Office. "Advancing Public Safety Through Community Policing: The First 25 Years of the COPS Office." Washington, DC, 2021.

Cordner, Gary, and Elizabeth Perkins Biebel. "Problem-Oriented Policing in Practice." *Criminology and Public Policy* 4, no. 2 (2005): 155–180. https://doi.org/10.1111/j.1745-9133.2005.00013.x.

Eck, John E., and William Spelman. *Problem-Solving: Problem-Oriented Policing in Newport News*. Washington, DC: Police Executive Research Forum, 1987.

Goldstein, Herman. "Improving Policing: A Problem-Oriented Approach." *Crime & Delinquency* 25, no. 2 (1979): 236–258. https://doi.org/10.1177/001112877902500207.

Goldstein, Herman. "Toward Community-Oriented Policing: Potential, Basic Requirements, and Threshold Questions." *Crime & Delinquency* 33, no. 1 (1987): 6–30. https://doi.org/10.1177/0011128787033001002.

Greene, Jack R., and Stephen D. Mastrofski. *Community Policing: Rhetoric or Reality*. Santa Barbara, CA: Praeger, 1988. https://www.google.com/books/edition/Community_Policing/7ZraAAAAMAAJ?hl=en.

Greene, Judith A. "Zero Tolerance: A Case Study of Police Policies and Practices in New York City." *Crime and Delinquency* 45, no. 2 (1999): 171–187. https://doi.org/10.1177/0011128799045002001.

Hinkle, Joshua C., David Weisburd, Cody W. Telep, and Kevin Petersen. "Problem-Oriented Policing for Reducing Crime and Disorder: An Updated Systematic Review and Meta-Analysis." *Campbell Systematic Reviews* 16, no. 2 (2020). https://doi.org/10.1002/cl2.1089.

Hodgkinson, Sarah, and Nick Tilley. "Policing Anti-Social Behaviour: Constraints, Dilemmas and Opportunities." *Howard Journal of Criminal Justice* 46, no. 4 (2007): 385–400. https://doi.org/10.1111/j.1468-2311.2007.00484.x.

Kelling, George L. "Police and Communities: The Quiet Revolution." *Perspectives on Policing*, no. 1. Washington, DC: National Institute of Justice, 1988.

Lipsky, M. *Street-Level Bureaucracy: Dilemmas of the Individuals in Public Services*. New York: Russell Sage Foundation, 1980.

Maguire, Edward. *Organizational Structure in American Police Agencies: Context, Complexity, and Control*. Albany: State University of New York, 2003.

Mastrofski, Stephen D. "Community Policing: A Skeptical View." In *Police Innovations: Contrasting Perspectives*, 2nd ed., edited by David L. Weisburd and Anthony A. Braga, 45–68. New York: Cambridge University Press, 2019. https://www.google.com/books/edition/Police_Innovation/Z7OQDwAAQBAJ?hl=en&gbpv=1&dq=community+policing:+a+skeptical+view&pg=PA45&printsec=frontcover.

Mastrofski, S. D., J. J. Willis, and T. R. Kochel. "The Challenges of Implementing Community Policing in the United States." *Policing* 1, no. 2 (2007): 223–234. https://doi.org/10.1093/police/pam026.

Mazerolle, Lorraine G., Justin Ready, Bill Terrill, and Frank Gajewski. *Problem-Oriented Policing in Public Housing: Final Report of the Jersey City Project*. Washington, DC: U.S. Department of Justice, 1999.

Reiss, Albert J. "Policing a City's Central District: The Oakland Story." Washington, DC, 1985. https://play.google.com/books/reader?id=kpHaAAAAMAAJ&hl=en&pg=GBS.PP1.

Roundtree, Pamela Wilcox, and Kenneth C. Land. "Burglary Victimization, Perceptions of Crime Risk, and Routine Activities: A Multilevel Analysis Across Seattle Neighborhoods and Census Tracts." *Journal of Research in Crime and Delinquency* 33, no. 2 (1996): 147–180. https://doi.org/10.1177/0022427896033002001.

San Diego Police Department. "Evaluating the Analysis and Response Components of Problem Solving in Community Policing." San Diego, CA, 1998.

"The SARA Model | ASU Center for Problem-Oriented Policing." Accessed March 8, 2021. https://popcenter.asu.edu/content/sara-model-0.

Scott, Michael. *Problem-Oriented Policing: Reflections on the First 20 Years*. Washington, DC: U.S. Department of Justice, Office of Community Oriented Policing Services, 2000.

Skogan, Wes, and Susan Hartnett. "Community Policing in Chicago." In *Policing: Key Readings*, edited by Tim Newburn, 428–441. New York: Routledge, 2005.

Skogan, Wesley G., and Susan M. Hartnett. *Community Policing, Chicago Style*. New York: Oxford University Press, 1997.

U.S. Department of Justice. "Local Police Departments: Policies and Procedures, 2016." Bureau of Justice Statistics, Washington, DC, 2020. http://www.ojp.usdoj.gov.

CHAPTER 7

Every Moment a Decision

What is a moment? The *Oxford English Dictionary* (OED) defines a moment as "a small quantity of something, *esp.* a very short period of time."[1] This definition seems consistent with the way typical human beings likely conceive of a moment: a moment in time, as in, "Let's take a moment," "I'll be there in a moment," or "Give me a moment." In a secondary definition, the OED also defines moment as "a very short period or extent of time, *esp.* one too brief for its duration to be significant." But this might be where dictionary definitions can diverge from lived experience, because when thought of as a crossroads (i.e., a decision point at which a person can choose one action over another) moments can be highly significant. Indeed, as "short periods of time," moments punctuate our human timelines like notches along the shaft of an arrow, giving us the opportunity to pause while we consider decisions that could have a great impact on our pathways forward. We are presented with moments on such a routine and frequent basis that we often fail to even recognize them—fail to realize all the decisions we make on a moment-to-moment basis. Ultimately, our lives become the sum of all those moments, and all those decision points.

Policing is also about moments. Officers are routinely presented with situations, or moments in time, that require them to make a

Podcast Episode: "A Good 'Pinch': The Art and Science of Police Discretion"

Scan the QR code or enter the short URL shown below into a browser window to listen to this chapter's podcast.

https://bit.ly/3s8SlmN

---

[1] *Oxford English Dictionary*.

choice: the decision to write a ticket, the decision to arrest, or the decision to shoot. Each of these moments represents a crossroads; depending on which decision the officer makes while standing at that crossroads, a new pathway is created for them and the people they encounter. In policing, more than most other occupations, those decisions can represent the difference between life and death.

Imagine a police officer on patrol. It's late into the evening hours, dark, and just after a rain, and he's working alone. His patrol area is somewhere out of the center of town, so the roads are long and not heavily traveled. He passes a vehicle that's traveling in the opposite direction. He had a hard time seeing the vehicle on approach because it was traveling without its head-lamps on. Besides being unsafe, no headlights at night, particularly in the rain, is a violation of the vehicle code. The officer is in a moment in time. He has to make a decision. Does he turn his patrol car around to track down the other vehicle for a traffic stop? Or does he let it slide, thinking the person will at some point figure out they're driving with no headlights? What factors might the officer consider before deciding on a course of action (because not pulling over the offending driver is also a course of action)? Type of car? Speed of the vehicle? The intrinsic nature of the violation? Could he make out the race of the driver? The gender? The age? Does the law offer any guidance, or is his decision purely discretionary?

In that moment, the officer makes a U-turn and sets himself down a new pathway. He switches on the light bar and punches the accelerator, and within 25 seconds he's overtaking the suspect vehicle. For about 15 seconds the driver of the suspect car gives no indication of awareness that a police cruiser is following. The car is not traveling at a particularly high rate of speed, but there is no immediate deceleration, no quick flashes of brake lights to let the officer know the car is pulling over. The officer issues three or four siren squawks, which finally leads the driver to begin slowing the vehicle. After about 30 seconds, both cars are pulled to the side of the road. The officer rotates his Unity spotlight to the upright position, turns it on, and aims it at the suspect vehicle. The officer hopes that, in addition to lighting up the night, the beam catches the suspect's rearview mirror, reflecting light into the driver's eyes, and rendering it nearly impossible to see the officer's approach.

There's a bit of history surrounding this stretch of road. A generation back, a police officer was killed during a vehicle stop similar to this one. Although nothing like that had ever happened before or since, local police officers have made sure the memory of that killing remains a part of the surrounding departments' collective institutional memory.

The officer steps from his vehicle and decides on a passenger-side approach. Because he prefers to never put himself between his own car and a suspect's vehicle on a traffic stop, he strides around the back of his patrol car before turning to make his approach to the suspect's car. He walks briskly. Given the darkness and the fact that he's alone, he pulls his sidearm from its holster, carrying it aimed at a low angle toward the ground. The gun is in his right hand. He holds a flashlight in his left. When he reaches the back corner of the vehicle—an American-made late-model sedan—he can see the driver illuminated through the rear window. It appears the driver has no idea the officer is there, which means the Unity spotlight and passenger-side approach have done the trick. He slows his walk and takes a few seconds to scan the interior of the vehicle. One driver and no visible passengers. Appears to be female. Youngish. African American. He cannot see her hands.

With the tail cap of his long metal flashlight, he raps lightly on the passenger-side window, startling the driver, causing her to jerk in her seat. She seems nervous, which makes him nervous. He makes sure to keep his gun hidden but nimble in his hand. She puts down the window just enough for him to speak to her. He asks for her license, registration, and proof of insurance. She's ready with the first two but says she doesn't have a current printed card showing her insurance, although she does have insurance, she assures him. He asks if she knows why he pulled her over, and she says that she doesn't. He explains that when they passed each other on the road, she was driving without her headlights on. She seems flustered and looks at her dashboard. "But all my gauges are lit up," she finally says. "You might just have your parking lights on," he replies. "I noticed when I was walking up here your taillights were on." With her left hand she flips a switch on the dashboard, and the headlights turn on. She looks at him and gives a weak smile with a combination of apology and anxiety on her face. He asks her to sit tight while he checks her information and walks back to his cruiser.

Sitting in his patrol car, he's able to confirm that she's the registered owner of the vehicle and that she does indeed have insurance. But she also has a bench warrant for failure to appear (FTA). This probably means that she had received a traffic ticket at some point in the past and failed to appear in court to either contest the ticket or pay the fine. Now it becomes a question of what to do. He could issue her a citation for the headlight violation; he could arrest her on the bench warrant and make sure she gets in front of a judge; he could do both of those things; or he could release her with a warning and stern admonishment to take care of the bench warrant.

He steps from his cruiser and follows his original routine to get back to her vehicle, only this time, he keeps his firearm holstered. He makes contact again and passes her license and registration back through the partially opened window. When she takes them from him, he notices her hand has a slight but visible tremble. It's then that he grasps the meaning: She's not nervous about getting into trouble, she's afraid of him. He realizes that, for all the stories passed down through generations of police about the dangerousness of traffic stops, she must have her own stories involving Black women being stopped by White male cops at night on a stretch of deserted road.

He asks her if she knows she has an FTA on her license. He explains that FTAs lead to bench warrants being issued, which means any police officer who stops her could take her into immediate custody. She explains that she knew she was supposed to go to court on a previous traffic citation, but that she's the primary caregiver for her mother, who's suffering from Alzheimer's disease. This is why she's out driving so late: The group home where her mother lives called to say that her mother was having a hard night, prompting her to have to drive there to settle her mother. She continues that, between her own kids, her job, and her mother, she finds it difficult to do anything outside her normal daily routine, including going to court on a minor traffic violation. He decides then and there that he's not going to cite her for the headlight violation, although he advises her to be more mindful when operating a motor vehicle. He also decides not to arrest her on the bench warrant. Instead, he digs a card out of his pocket and gives her a phone number for the court. He tells her if she calls that number, she should be able to schedule a virtual court appearance. She thanks him, and they go their separate ways, timelines interrupted, but otherwise unchanged.

How many decisions did the officer make during that encounter? How many alternate decisions might have sent the encounter down different pathways? To be clear, the two "official" decisions that faced the officer involved whether to (1) issue a citation for the headlight violation, and (2) arrest the suspect driver on the bench warrant. In the end, the officer took neither of these actions, instead allowing the suspect to drive off with no official sanction. But why did he make those decisions—two examples of police discretion exercised? Did he feel sympathy for the driver's personal struggle of having to care for an aging mother with health issues? Is that an adequate reason for not issuing a legally founded citation, or not taking someone to jail on a bench warrant? Did he let her go because he became self-conscious about being a White officer pulling over a Black woman alone on a deserted stretch of roadway, seeing the fear in her eyes and the tremble of her hand? Was there something about the gender and race dyads that made him uncomfortable? Is it ever reasonable for a police officer to use race as a factor when deciding whether to take official action—even if race seems to work to the benefit of a suspect?

Imagine a different timeline where the driver sees the officer's gun in his hand. She's already terrified of him—or at least the concept of him. She remembers George Floyd, Breonna Taylor, and Michael Brown, and she has no intention of being shot for no good reason by a White cop in the middle of the night. She struggles with her seatbelt, hoping to jump from her vehicle—an action that she believes is self-preservation—but the officer thinks she's trying to reach for a gun. He steps back, raises his firearm, and screams at her to stop moving and show him her hands. The officer's actions scare her even more, causing her to redouble her efforts to break from the seatbelt and her car. Because of the sudden adrenaline surges, neither of them sees or hears the large truck speeding up the roadway toward them. When she finally gets her door open and springs from her car, she's immediately struck and killed by the truck, as the driver never had a chance to swerve and miss her. All because the officer decided to remove his gun from its holster as he approached the suspect's vehicle.

That is what this chapter is about: the moment-to-moment decisions police officers make that add up to a field of academic and professional inquiry known as *police discretion*. Most Introduction to Policing and Police and Society courses cover police discretion because it is such an important and controversial part of the policing occupation. It is important because without the ability to exercise discretion, police and the public could not possibly function together. As scholar Kenneth Culp Davis argued in his now-classic 1969 book, *Discretionary Justice*, "police officer discretion not to arrest represents the triumph of common sense over the . . . 'unwisdom' of legislators."[2] Police discretion is also controversial, though, because of the frequently identified misuses of discretion that more than 70 years of research on the police has identified.[3] This chapter examines the concept and practice of police discretion, focusing on its history, its use, its misuse, and its implications for the protection of life mandate.

By the end of this chapter, readers should be able to answer the following questions:

1. What is police discretion, and why is it an important concept to study in policing?
2. What are the primary decision points in policing that have been susceptible to misuses of discretion?
3. Why were courts and policymakers seemingly more successful at controlling the deadly force decision than the decisions to stop and frisk and arrest alleged domestic violence offenders?
4. How might the practice of "structured discretion" improve police officer decision-making and contribute to the protection of life mandate?

The Concept of Police Discretion

The very idea of police discretion was unknown to policymakers, social researchers, and others outside policing through the first half of the twentieth century. Research on policing, and even the criminal justice system at large, prior to the mid-1950s usually examined the "technical" or "managerial" aspects of how the system functioned[4] (e.g., the bureaucratic structures of the organizations) with an eye toward making them more efficient.[5] But as a watershed American Bar Foundation (ABF) study, published in 1958, found, the criminal justice "system" was not much of a system at all. It existed more as a collection of discretionary decisions made by people working as police officers, prosecutors, judges, correctional officers, and prison administrators.[6] These justice officials decided when to arrest, when to charge, when to allow bail, and when to grant parole. To be sure, the decisions they

---

[2] Cited by Walker, *Taming the System: The Control of Discretion in Criminal Justice, 1950–1990*, 4.

[3] Davis, *Discretionary Justice: A Preliminary Inquiry*, 1969; American Bar Foundation, *The Administration of Criminal Justice in the United States: Pilot Project Report*; Fyfe, "Administrative Interventions on Police Shooting Discretion: An Empirical Examination"; Gottfredson and Gottfredson, *Decision Making in Criminal Justice: Toward the Rational Exercise of Discretion*, 1988; Beckett, "The Uses and Abuses of Police Discretion: Toward Harm Reduction Policing."

[4] Nickels, "A Note on the Status of Discretion in Police Research," 570.

[5] *See, e.g.*, Wilson, *Police Administration*.

[6] American Bar Foundation, *The Administration of Criminal Justice in the United States: Pilot Project Report*.

made were partly rooted in law, but they were also based on professional determinations of what was best for the state and for the individuals involved as arrestees, defendants, and inmates. As scholar Ernest Nickels noted, the discovery of discretion "was perhaps the single most important event in the history of criminal justice studies," because it initiated a new paradigm of research examining the day-to-day operations of criminal justice practitioners.[7]

What is *discretion*? Drawing again from Kenneth Culp Davis's landmark 1969 book, *Discretionary Justice*, "A public officer has discretion whenever the effective limits on his [sic] power leave him [sic] free to make a choice among possible courses of action or inaction."[8] In other words, according to Davis, "Where the law ends, discretion begins."[9] This is not a universal belief, however. Indeed, in 1682 when British philosopher John Locke published his essay, "On Tyranny," he argued, "Where-ever law ends, tyranny begins."[10] That is, when criminal justice officials (or in Locke's words, "magistrates") made decisions that fell outside the authority of law, they were guilty of tyranny—oppressive or arbitrary government rule. By Locke's logic, the police officer from the case study that began this chapter would be guilty of tyranny because he failed to cite or arrest the driver of the car he pulled over. Although the officer's actions were not oppressive, they could be considered arbitrary, and arbitrary decisions on the part of state officers can be regarded as violations of the rule of law, and therefore, tyrannical.

One could argue, however, that the officer's decision not to cite or arrest the driver of the car represented the opposite of tyranny—it represented beneficence. The officer made the determination that it would better serve the state and the driver to release her with a warning and advice about how to contact the court to settle her FTA charge. In that sense, and with all due respect to Locke, it could be argued that the officer in the case study administered justice with the proper "mixtures of law and discretion."[11]

It should also be noted that discretion in policing is not going away. Indeed, the Supreme Court ruled in 1987 that discretion represented a "fundamental" element of the criminal justice system that provided "substantial benefits" to both the state and to defendants.[12] Although the case was not a policing case, its implications for the entire criminal justice process make clear that, substantively speaking, police discretion is, at the very least, legal. It is true that certain state laws and some police administrative policies have reduced the authority of police officers to make discretionary decisions on procedural grounds (more on this below), but discretionary decision-making as a general practice constitutes an essential feature of U.S. policing.

---

[7] Nickels, "A Note on the Status of Discretion in Police Research," 570.
[8] Davis, *Discretionary Justice: A Preliminary Inquiry*, 2.
[9] Davis, 2.
[10] "John Locke on the Idea That 'Wherever Law Ends, Tyranny Begins' (1689) | Online Library of Liberty."
[11] Davis, *Discretionary Justice: A Preliminary Inquiry*, 2.
[12] McCleskey v. Kemp, 481 U.S. 279 (1987).

The Trouble with Police Discretion

As several scholars have recognized, police discretion is not the problem. Police abuse or *misuse* of discretion is the problem,[13] particularly when police officers and police departments appear to base their discretionary decisions on personal characteristics such as race and gender or on other nonlegal factors. Indeed, a body of research—some of which is reviewed below—has identified certain decision points in policing that have been particularly susceptible to race and gender bias, including vehicle and pedestrian stops, misdemeanor (including domestic violence) arrests, and deadly force. That same research has often found that controlling police discretion at those decision points is not easy.

Stop-and-frisk represents perhaps the quintessential example of a problematic application of police discretion. Although stop-and-frisk gets its own chapter in this book, it is important to note here that the practice of stop-and-frisk as a police discretionary decision has been fraught with racial bias.[14] Initially, and as described in previous chapters, the practice of stopping and patting down a person the police thought to be dangerous was formally recognized as a legal police field tactic by the Supreme Court in the 1961 case *Mapp v. Ohio*.[15] As New York City in the 1990s pushed stop-and-frisk from a police tactic to a crime control strategy, however, it gave street-level officers much more discretion—beyond the "reasonable suspicion" they needed under *Mapp*—to detain and frisk individuals.[16] The justification for initiating stop-and-frisk as a crime control strategy was that by focusing on people who appeared to be committing disorder offenses, police officers would reduce overall crime by taking prostitutes, drug dealers and users, potential robbers, and maybe even guns off the street.[17]

In the early 2000s, even as many police departments around the country began following the NYPD's lead in using stop-and-frisk as a crime control strategy,[18] research began to show that the NYPD's so-called zero tolerance program led to African American and Latino pedestrians being stopped by police at far higher rates than White pedestrians[19] with very modest, at best, homicide and robbery crime reductions as the payoff.[20] Indeed, despite this

---

[13] Walker, *Taming the System: The Control of Discretion in Criminal Justice, 1950–1990*; Beckett, "The Uses and Abuses of Police Discretion: Toward Harm Reduction Policing"; Gottfredson and Gottfredson, *Decision Making in Criminal Justice: Toward the Rational Exercise of Discretion*, 1988.

[14] White and Fradella, *Stop and Frisk: The Use and Abuse of a Controversial Policing Tactic*; Meares, "Programming Errors: Understanding the Constitutionality of Stop-and-Frisk as a Program, Not an Incident."

[15] Mapp v. Ohio, 367 U.S. 643 (1961).

[16] Meares, "Programming Errors: Understanding the Constitutionality of Stop-and-Frisk as a Program, Not an Incident."

[17] Taylor, "The Incivilities Thesis: Theory, Measurement, and Policy"; Fagan and Davies, "Street Stops and Broken Windows: Terry, Race and Disorder in New York City"; Greene, "Zero Tolerance: A Case Study of Police Policies and Practices in New York City."

[18] Fagan et al., "Stops and Stares: Street Stops, Surveillance, and Race in the New Policing."

[19] Gelman, Fagan, and Kiss, "An Analysis of the New York City Police Department's 'Stop-and-Frisk' Policy in the Context of Claims of Racial Bias."

[20] Rosenfeld, Fornango, and Rengifo, "The Impact of Order-Maintenance Policing on New York City Homicide and Robbery Rates: 1988–2001."

emerging paradigm of "new policing," which relied on aggressive stop-and-frisk and arrests for misdemeanor crimes,[21] investigations of the NYPD's stop-and-frisk program showed that officers actually made few arrests as a result of detaining and searching pedestrians, but because those stops disproportionately involved African American and Latino individuals, legitimacy of the police among those groups was steadily declining.[22] Then in 2014, a federal circuit court decided that the NYPD program of stop-and-frisk was racially biased and therefore unconstitutional as practiced.[23] Although the NYPD has been forced by a federal court order to change its stop-and-frisk practices in ways that reduce racial disparities,[24] many police departments nationally continue to use stop-and-frisk as part of their crime control strategy.[25] Indeed, several of these departments have now come under federal monitoring due to their unconstitutional stop-and-frisk practices.[26] Stop-and-frisk, and the discretion it gives officers to engage pedestrians in street stops, is a strategy that will "not go gentle into that good night."[27]

Similar findings of racial bias have been made in police traffic stops, although the research on this topic is less consistent than for stop-and-frisk. Ironically, the Supreme Court might have inadvertently encouraged racial biases in police vehicle stops with its 1996 decision in *Whren v. United States*. In very straightforward language, the Court simply ruled that "any traffic offense committed by a driver was a legitimate legal basis for a stop."[28] Although this decision sounds reasonable—grounded, even, in common sense—it allowed police officers to make so-called pretextual traffic stops, or as scholar David A. Harris noted, it allowed the police to apply a "could have" standard when deciding who to stop: "[A]ny time the police could have stopped the defendant for a traffic infraction, it does not matter that the police actually stopped him to investigate a crime for which the police had little or no evidence."[29] In effect, the *Whren* decision allowed police officers to target drivers based on certain characteristics (i.e., race) when they wanted to make a stop for a reason for which they lacked probable cause. They could then wait for those drivers to commit a traffic infraction—no matter how minor—so they could legally pull them over. This is what is meant by a "pretextual" traffic stop: using a traffic violation to stop a vehicle because the officer might believe the driver is a drug trafficker, has an outstanding

---

[21] Fagan et al., "Stops and Stares: Street Stops, Surveillance, and Race in the New Policing," 541–542.

[22] Howell, "Broken Lives from Broken Windows: The Hidden Costs of Aggressive Order-Maintenance Policing."

[23] Floyd v. City of New York, 959 F. Supp. 2d 668 - Dist. Court, SD New York (2013).

[24] "Overview | NYPD Monitor."

[25] Harris, "Across the Hudson: Taking the Stop and Frisk Debate Beyond New York City."

[26] U.S. Department of Justice, "Justice Department Releases Report on Civil Rights Division's Pattern and Practice Police Reform Work."

[27] This quote is an homage to the Dylan Thomas poem, "Do Not Go Gentle into That Good Night," first published in 1951. For the full verse, *see* https://poets.org/poem/do-not-go-gentle-good-night.

[28] Whren v. United States, 517 U.S. 806 (1996).

[29] Harris, "'Driving While Black' and All Other Traffic Offenses: The Supreme Court and Pretextual Traffic Stops," 544.

warrant, or is guilty of some other offense. They use the traffic violation as a pretext for stopping the vehicle.

Research in the early 2000s showed that African American drivers reported being pulled over by police at much higher rates than White drivers, and further reported that the reasons for the stops lacked legal legitimacy.[30] Subsequent research showed that African American drivers were more likely to be stopped when they were viewed by police as "out of place," or driving through majority-White areas.[31] Collectively, this research appeared to support the emerging "driving while Black" hypothesis, the idea that African American drivers had to be careful where they traveled on roadways and through communities, lest their presence arouse police suspicion and result in a pretextual traffic stop.[32] More recent research, however, has made the same finding for White drivers, showing that they (White drivers) tended to be stopped at high rates when they were seen driving through communities of color.[33] Regardless of whether it is referred to as driving while Black, or simply out-of-place driving, research has demonstrated that race represents a significant factor in the police decision to initiate a vehicle stop.

Race is not the only personal characteristic that has driven police discretionary decision-making, however. Research in the second half of the twentieth century showed that police officers tended not to make arrests when responding to domestic violence calls, and in fact questioned the utility of arresting intimate partner violence (IPV) suspects, at all.[34] Traditionally, IPV and family violence were viewed by the police institution as private matters that should not receive an official law enforcement response.[35] Police officers who participated in surveys mostly reported that domestic violence calls were a "nuisance" and that arresting alleged domestic violence offenders was not "real police work."[36] This was despite the National Family Violence Survey of 1986 showing that over one-third of all male assaults on female spouses were serious and involved punching, kicking, biting, beating, and attacks with guns and knives;[37] other research showed that homicide was among the leading causes of death for married women.[38]

As part of an awaking to the seriousness of IPV, a wave of court cases and legislative changes across the country throughout the 1980s and into

[30] Lundman and Kaufman, "Driving While Black: Effects of Race, Ethnicity, and Gender on Citizen Self-Reports of Traffic Stops and Police Actions."

[31] Meehan and Ponder, "Race and Place: The Ecology of Racial Profiling African American Motorists."

[32] Harris, *Profiles in Injustice: Why Police Profiling Cannot Work.*

[33] Novak and Chamlin, "Racial Threat, Suspicion, and Police Behavior: The Impact of Race and Place in Traffic Enforcement."

[34] President's Commission on Law Enforcement and the Administration of Justice, "The Challenge of Crime in a Free Society," 92, 104.

[35] Rubinstein, *City Police*; Sherman and Berk, "The Specific Deterrent Effects of Arrest for Domestic Assault"; Kane, "Patterns of Arrest in Domestic Violence Encounters: Identifying a Police Decision-Making Model."

[36] Oppenlander, "Coping or Copping Out: Police Service Delivery in Domestic Disputes," 449.

[37] Straus and Gelles, "Societal Change and Change in Family Violence from 1975 to 1985 as Revealed by Two National Surveys," 471.

[38] Websdale, *Understanding Domestic Homicide.*

the 1990s began to strongly encourage—and in some cases require—police officers to arrest alleged domestic violence offenders, even those accused of misdemeanor assault.[39] Yet a 1997 study showed that police officers rarely arrested suspects of "spousal"[40] assault and were much more likely to arrest suspects of stranger assault.[41] This finding led to the creation of the so-called leniency thesis—a hypothesis gaining empirical support[42] that police officers continued to place greater law enforcement value on stranger assaults over domestic assaults.

As Kane (the author of this book) found in two studies, though, the relationship between IPV and arrest was nuanced. In the first study, Kane examined pathways to arrest among IPV offenders in Boston, Massachusetts, finding that when "fists," "feet," and "guns" were used as part of the assaults, Boston police officers made arrests in just over 70 percent of the incidents (compared to an overall arrest rate of 43 percent).[43] When no weapons were used, however—and as the event seemed to decline in seriousness—officers not only made many fewer arrests, but they tended to rely on nonlegal factors when deciding whether to arrest. These factors included whether the victim and offender were living together, the number of prior incidents between the couple, employment status of the victim, and whether children were present.[44]

In the second study, also conducted with Boston Police Department data, Kane examined the effects of restraining orders on arrests in domestic violence encounters, which were an increasingly common legal mechanism to encourage police officers to make arrests during IPV calls. Findings from that study showed that victim injuries were the strongest predictor of arrests, regardless of the presence of restraining orders. Indeed, offenders who injured their victims were more than three times more likely to be arrested for IPV than offenders who did not injure their victims.[45] In fact, restraining orders only predicted arrests when there were no other serious risk factors associated with the event. Interestingly, the more times the police had been called to an address, the less likely they were to make an arrest, regardless of whether a restraining order was in effect.[46] Recalling David Klinger's discussion of "deserving victims"[47] in Chapter 3, it could be that police officers

---

[39] Sherman and Berk, "The Specific Deterrent Effects of Arrest for Domestic Assault"; Kane, "Patterns of Arrest in Domestic Violence Encounters: Identifying a Police Decision-Making Model"; Sherman, "Policing Domestic Violence 1967–2017."

[40] Although the term *spousal assault* is dated by contemporary standards, it was the preferred terminology in 1997 when the study was published. In fact, the researchers studied assaults among married couples.

[41] Fyfe, Klinger, and Flavin, "Male-on-Female Spousal Violence."

[42] *E.g.*, Avakame and Fyfe, "Differential Police Treatment of Male-on-Female Spousal Violence: Additional Evidence on the Leniency Thesis."

[43] Kane, "Patterns of Arrest in Domestic Violence Encounters: Identifying a Police Decision-Making Model."

[44] Kane, 71.

[45] Kane, "Responding to Restraining Orders in Domestic Violence Incidents: Identifying the Custody-Threshold Thesis," 573.

[46] Kane.

[47] Klinger, "Negotiating Order in Patrol Work: An Ecological Theory of Police Response to Deviance."

regarded women who called the police multiple times (but who obviously stayed with their partners) as less than deserving victims who therefore did not meet Kane's identified "threshold"[48] for arrest. It is important to note that at that time, and for the duration of both studies, the Boston Police Department operated under a Massachusetts state law requiring police officers to arrest suspected domestic violence offenders, even those suspected of misdemeanor assaults.[49]

Recall that we are still discussing police discretion, and in particular, the observed misuses of discretion at certain decision points. Police discretion is, again, that moment when police officers are presented with the option of either taking action or taking no action. For stop-and-frisk and vehicle stops, the actions are the stops themselves, and then the decision to pat down the suspect's outer clothing, search the vehicle, or both. Police officers are not required by law, or usually even administrative policy, to stop pedestrians for questioning or to stop drivers for suspected vehicle code violations. Those are choices based partly on professional judgment, organizational incentives, and perhaps even personal biases. Yet the research has shown that for pedestrian and vehicle stops, police often take action based on race.

For situations involving IPV, research has demonstrated the relative opposite: Despite evidence of assaults—and in some places, despite mandatory arrest policies and laws—police have historically declined to take law enforcement action when confronted with a domestic violence situation. Whereas stop-and-frisk and vehicle stops have led to disproportionate numbers of African Americans becoming justice-involved, the historic lack of action in domestic violence incidents has likely left some victims of IPV (mostly women) at risk for further violence.

Why has it been so difficult to control police discretion in the areas of stop-and-frisk, vehicle stops, and arrests in IPV situations? Before we can answer that, it is instructive to examine another decision point in policing—perhaps the most important decision point—where discretion has been effectively controlled. Once we learn about a successful effort to reduce the misuse of discretion, we will be in a stronger position to develop discussion around why some discretionary decisions are harder than others to control.

Deadly Force: A Study in the Control of Police Discretion

Let us be clear: The police do not punish. That is not their role. They try to stop crime, they can attempt to apprehend alleged offenders, and along the way they are authorized to use many different types and levels of coercion, up to and including deadly force. Although it might look like the police are

[48] Kane, "Responding to Restraining Orders in Domestic Violence Incidents: Identifying the Custody-Threshold Thesis," 565.
[49] Mignon and Holmes, "Police Response to Mandatory Arrest Laws."

sometimes delivering a punishment through the application of force, they are not. The reason? Because the people with whom the police typically deal are not adjudicated criminal offenders; that is, people who have been fully processed through the courts with a criminal conviction. They are people presumed innocent until proven guilty. Only the courts can punish. When it comes to crime fighting, the role of the police is to get criminal defendants in front of a judge, sometimes at all reasonable costs.

Therefore, when the U.S. Supreme Court in 1972, with its decision in *Furman v. Georgia*, halted the use of the death penalty as a criminal sanction on procedural grounds, its ruling would have ripple effects into policing—despite the fact that the police do not punish. In the *Furman* decision, the Court observed that racial disparities in the application of capital punishment made it an "arbitrary"—and therefore unconstitutional—criminal sanction.[50] The *Furman* decision led several states to revise their capital punishment statutes in ways that attempted to reduce racial disparities in the death penalty. In recognizing those efforts, the Supreme Court reinstated the use of capital punishment (for states that wanted to employ it) in 1976 with its decision in *Gregg v. Georgia*.[51]

Although racial disparities persist in the application of capital punishment across the United States,[52] two things are noteworthy about the *Furman* and *Gregg* decisions. First, the Court imposed a moratorium on the most consequential criminal sanction in U.S. jurisprudence due to findings showing it was applied differentially across racial groups: African American defendants were far more likely to receive the death penalty than White defendants. The Court, then, halted the use of the death penalty and required states to develop new statutes designed to reduce racial disparities in capital punishment before allowing them to reinstate it. In effect, the Court saw a misuse of judicial discretion that produced negative consequences for defendants of color, then tried to rectify that misuse by requiring states to create procedures that would control that discretion and ultimately reduce racial disparities.

Now for the ripple effect into policing. During that same *Furman-Gregg* era, policing was largely exempt from serious legal regulations governing the use of deadly force. The historic custom and practice (until 1985) for judging deadly force in policing was the so-called *fleeing felon rule*, derived from English common law,[53] which allowed police officers to shoot alleged felony suspects who were trying to evade them. This historic British custom was carried over into the American colonies and then continued in the newly established United States of America, flourishing through the nineteenth and most of the twentieth centuries.[54] The rationale was that, because "felonies

---

[50] Furman v. Georgia, 408 U.S. 238 (1972).
[51] Gregg v. Georgia, 428 U.S. 153 (1976).
[52] Kovera, "Racial Disparities in the Criminal Justice System: Prevalence, Causes, and a Search for Solutions."
[53] Simon, "The Fleeing Felon Rule," 1263, fn. 27, 28.
[54] Simon, 1264.

were viewed as extremely dangerous offenses, society's interest in the apprehension of a suspected felon was sufficient to warrant the use of deadly force."[55] The suspects did not have to be dangerous; they just needed to be presumed felony offenders actively avoiding police apprehension. Again, although deadly force is not a criminal sanction, it does share two characteristics with capital punishment: It is a form of state-sanctioned violence, and it is final.

In 1976, when scholar John Goldkamp published a study of the police use of deadly force, he likened the police decision to shoot to a trial court's decision to impose the death penalty on a criminal suspect. As Goldkamp noted, though, whereas the Supreme Court in both *Furman* and *Gregg* established legal standards to limit judicial discretion in ways that sought to reduce racial disparities in the application of the death penalty, the Court had never heard a case that might have led it to create similar standards to control police shooting discretion. As such, and as Goldkamp's study showed, African American suspects were much more likely than White suspects to be shot by police,[56] owing to the enormous discretion police officers had when deciding whether or not to shoot. Thus, the era of trying to understand and control the police deadly force discretion was initiated.

Just after Goldkamp published his 1976 paper, police scholar James J. Fyfe—a university professor and retired NYPD lieutenant—began conducting a study of the NYPD's newly implemented deadly force policy to learn how it might have affected patterns of police shootings. The NYPD had changed its deadly force policy in 1972 to make it administratively impermissible for officers to shoot at suspects who did not pose an immediate threat to life.[57] In other words, the NYPD eliminated the fleeing felon rule in the department and replaced it with a policy that allowed officers to shoot only in defense-of-life situations. This was a highly controversial policy change within the department. Many NYPD officers argued that reducing their discretion to use deadly force—discretion police had enjoyed in the United States since the colonial era—would expose them to higher rates of injury and death because they would now have to "think twice" about pulling the trigger.[58] This delay, they argued, would be dangerous to them.

In 1979, Fyfe published the results of his study in a landmark paper demonstrating that the restrictive NYPD deadly force policy not only significantly (and substantially) reduced the non-defense-of-life shootings (i.e., fleeing felon shootings), but it also did so without leading to any increases in the numbers of officers killed or injured.[59] Indeed, Fyfe showed that before the NYPD's implementation of the restrictive deadly force policy, non-defense-of-life shootings accounted for 13.9 percent of all police shootings

---

[55] Simon, 1264.

[56] Goldkamp, "Minorities as Victims of Police Shootings: Interpretations of Racial Disproportionality and Police Use of Deadly Force."

[57] Fyfe, "Administrative Interventions on Police Shooting Discretion: An Empirical Examination," 311.

[58] Fyfe, personal communication.

[59] Fyfe, "Administrative Interventions on Police Shooting Discretion: An Empirical Examination," 318–319.

in New York City. Within three years after the policy was implemented, non-defense-of-life shootings accounted for just 4.3 percent of all police shootings. Moreover, the rate of police officer injuries was virtually cut in half as a result of the restrictive deadly force policy.[60]

In that 1979 paper, Fyfe made the point that reducing non-defense-of-life shootings was important because most people shot and killed by police in such situations would be guilty of crimes that would carry relatively light sentences were they to be convicted. Like Goldkamp in 1976, Fyfe argued that the police use of deadly force was tantamount to state-sanctioned violence—not unlike capital punishment—and therefore should be treated with the same degree of circumspection.[61] Thus, reducing the overall number of police shootings (as the NYPD policy did), with a specific impact on non-defense-of-life shootings, was more aligned with a preservation of life mandate that, according to Fyfe, the NYPD was striving to foster.[62] Still, this was only one police department in the United States that created a defense-of-life deadly force policy that applied only to its own officers. While deadly force discretion came under control in the NYPD, most other departments around the country still practiced the fleeing felon rule. But not for long.

In 1982 Fyfe followed up his NYPD study with research that examined police discretion in deadly force encounters with a specific focus on racial disparities. Fyfe conducted this research in Memphis, Tennessee, where the police department still operated under the fleeing felon rule. Officers in Memphis were allowed to shoot alleged fleeing felony offenders, even if they were unarmed and posed no imminent threat to life.[63] Based on the shooting data he collected, Fyfe divided Memphis police shootings into two categories:

- *Elective* shootings, in which the alleged fleeing felon posed no danger to life, therefore giving the officers the legitimate choice not to fire at them.
- *Nonelective* shootings, in which the offender posed an imminent threat to life, which meant if officer(s) did not fire at them, someone else's life would be immediately endangered.

Under Fyfe's taxonomy, elective shootings were those most commonly associated with the fleeing felon rule that would be most influenced by police discretion.[64]

Fyfe found no racial disparities in the nonelective shootings. When presented with defense-of-life situations, Memphis police officers appeared to consider only the dangerousness of the situation when deciding whether to shoot. In such cases, the race of the suspects did not matter—only the judgment by officers that not using deadly force would place other lives in danger.

---

[60] Fyfe, 319.
[61] Fyfe, 309–311.
[62] Fyfe, personal communication.
[63] Fyfe, "Blind Justice: Police Shootings in Memphis."
[64] Fyfe, 710.

For the elective shootings, though, those that presented no immediate threat to life and thus gave officers the option of not shooting, Fyfe found that police officers used deadly force against African American alleged fleeing felons significantly more often than against White alleged fleeing felons. When it came to examining deadly force under the fleeing felon rule, Fyfe's finding appeared to confirm Goldkamp's 1976 argument that "police have one trigger finger for whites, and one trigger finger for blacks."[65] Fyfe's findings in Memphis demonstrated that too much unregulated discretion in deadly force policy cost lives, and specifically the lives of African Americans.

The results of Fyfe's 1982 study were so important to the field of police scholarship that they were used by the U.S. Supreme Court as empirical evidence in *Tennessee v. Garner*, a landmark case that would redefine the boundaries of the police use of deadly force across the United States.

On October 3, 1974, Edward Garner was a 15-year-old boy who had allegedly broken into and entered a house located in a residential area of Memphis. Police were called by a neighbor, and when they arrived on scene they saw Garner running across the backyard of the house, apparently trying to evade police. The officers themselves would later testify that Garner did not appear to be armed and that he was not carrying anything in his arms or hands. When Garner reached the back fence and prepared to jump it, one of the officers shot him. Garner died in an ambulance on the way to the hospital.[66] Garner's family filed suit against the Memphis Police Department, arguing that the shooting of their unarmed son was a violation of his constitutional rights. After a protracted journey through the court system, the case was presented to the U.S. Supreme Court in October 1984. The Court subsequently ruled that under the Fourth Amendment to the U.S. Constitution (which regulates search and seizure), the use of deadly force by police was tantamount to a seizure of the person, and that shooting someone who did not pose an immediate threat to life was an unlawful seizure.[67] Thus, the Supreme Court in 1985 eliminated the fleeing felon rule, establishing a defense-of-life deadly force standard for all police agencies across the United States.

Like capital punishment, racial disparities still exist in pattens of deadly force, particularly among unarmed victims.[68] Still, as recent research has found, the relationship between race and police shootings is complicated by neighborhood factors, such as levels of economic disadvantage and local violent crime rates, which to some extent might help explain some of the persistent racial disparities observed in police shootings.[69] Deadly force research is hampered by the fact that there are no national

---

[65] Goldkamp, "Minorities as Victims of Police Shootings: Interpretations of Racial Disproportionality and Police Use of Deadly Force," 170. Goldkamp was actually quoting Finch's 1976 comment in *Harvard Civil Rights–Civil Liberties Law Review*, "Deadly Force to Arrest - Triggering Constitutional Review."

[66] Tennessee v. Garner, 471 U.S. 1 (1985), 4–6.

[67] Tennessee v. Garner, 471 U.S. 1 (1985), 20–22.

[68] Ross, Winterhalder, and McElreath, "Racial Disparities in Police Use of Deadly Force Against Unarmed Individuals Persist After Appropriately Benchmarking Shooting Data on Violent Crime Rates."

[69] Klinger et al., "Race, Crime, and the Micro-Ecology of Deadly Force."

data collection requirements on the police use of deadly force,[70] or even in policing more generally.[71] This means that, although the Supreme Court eliminated the fleeing felon rule with its decision in *Garner*, the field of police scholarship still does not know the full impact of *Garner* because research on policing is very much a department-to-department endeavor.

Nevertheless, *Garner* was a watershed decision in U.S. policing because it created a national standard—that is, a *minimum* national standard—that has required every police department across the United States to adopt it. In that sense, reducing the misuse of discretion in deadly force has followed a reasonably rational pathway: Research identified problems with the abuse of deadly force discretion; the Supreme Court intervened and created a national rule (guided by the Fourth Amendment to the Constitution) that limited the scope of discretion in the application of deadly force; and racial disparities and the shooting of unarmed individuals seem to have been reduced. The same conclusions cannot necessarily be drawn for police discretionary decisions that do not carry the same degree of finality as deadly force decisions; that is, those involving stops and arrests. In the next section, we attempt to make sense of these differences.

Reconciling Police Discretion

If deadly force can be considered something of a success story with respect to controlling police discretion, why has it been so difficult to control discretion in stop-and-frisks, vehicle stops, and arrests? The answer can be framed partly in terms of culture and partly in terms of circumstances.

Often, incidents of domestic or interpersonal violence take place in the homes of the victims, who reside with the perpetrators. These are private settings outside the immediate view of neighbors, other bystanders, and police supervisors. As such, police officers often have the autonomy to decide how to settle the cases as long as the incidents did not create any physical evidence of abuse, such as bruises or other injuries. As previously noted, historically, police were reluctant to intervene formally in cases of interpersonal violence because they often considered it a family matter to be handled privately. Thus, the combination of private setting and a police cultural orientation that discouraged arrest likely explain the historic difficulty controlling police discretion in domestic violence encounters.

Vehicle and pedestrian street stops share some of the same attributes as domestic violence incidents. Although vehicle and pedestrian stops usually occur in public (rather than private) settings, they are still highly discretionary, produce virtually no physical evidence, and typically occur outside the

---

[70] White, "Transactional Encounters, Crisis-Driven Reform, and the Potential for a National Police Deadly Force Database."

[71] Kane, "Collect and Release Data on Coercive Police Actions."

view of police supervisors. Moreover, and like domestic violence incidents, stop-and-frisk practices have a cultural element associated with their use: Many police departments in the United States implemented stop, question, and frisk as a crime control strategy—that is, a method designed to achieve one of their primary goals—and as such, it remains a very difficult discretionary habit for them to break.

By contrast, the deadly force decision typically takes place in a public setting, produces a great deal of physical evidence, and has not been subjected to any particular cultural pressure within policing. Indeed, the decisions to initiate stop-and-frisk and make arrests are important, but they are not nearly as consequential as the decision to use force that kills or is likely to kill. Again, because there is no identified cultural orientation that encourages police officers to use deadly force, it stands to reason that this decision has been the most controllable.

Some Concluding Observations

As described at the outset of this chapter, police officers are routinely faced with moments that require them to make a choice. Sometimes it can be the difference between action or inaction, and other times it can be a range of options designed to fit the nuances of specific situations. Discretionary decision-making plays a key role during those moments. It requires officers to use their professional judgment to determine the best pathway to resolve a particular situation. Sometimes making an arrest represents the proper response to a problem, whereas at other times, avoiding the arrest better serves the interests of justice (recall the case study that began this chapter). As previously described, police discretion is not a problem, per se, so much as the misuse of discretion—particularly when officers appear to use the static characteristics (i.e., race, gender) of people as criteria for making their discretionary decisions.

Historically, police researchers and policymakers have examined, and sometimes critiqued, police discretion at the occupation's primary decision points: stops, arrests, and deadly force. Attempts to control police discretion have come from many sources, including police departments' disciplinary practices, legal statutes, new ways of recruiting and training police recruits, and implementing long-term beat assignments so officers might better integrate into communities.[72] For the most part, however, such efforts to control discretion in ways designed to limit racial or gender biases during coercive interventions place the focus on reducing bad policing rather than encouraging good policing. That is, police officers should be recruited, trained, and socialized to work in ways that avoid racial biases in stop-and-frisk and deadly force incidents because allowing race and ethnicity to guide decision-making

---

[72] Mastrofski, "Controlling Street-Level Police Discretion," 102.

during such encounters is bad policing. The same would be true for any other coercive action that might be susceptible to race, ethnic, or gender bias.

What about embracing police discretion for the purposes of achieving good policing? Because controlling discretion to discourage bad policing does not necessarily encourage good policing (we dig into this topic more thoroughly in the final chapter of the book), what would it look like if policing created a system of discretion designed to produce positive community outcomes beyond the traditional coercive decision points? One way of doing this might be to create a system of structured discretion that uses a mix of rules designed to control discretion while also encouraging good decision-making. In his classic book, *Discretionary Justice*, Kenneth Culp Davis described the rationale as follows: "The problem is not merely to choose between rule and discretion but to find the optimum point on the rule-to-discretion scale."[73] This would mean viewing police discretion beyond policing's law enforcement decision points, and it would mean encouraging police officers to blend rules with discretion to improve the life chances of people they encounter.

To a great extent, community policing was supposed to exemplify Davis's "rule-to-discretion" scale, where ordinary line officers assigned to community policing worked within a rule structure that gave them the autonomy to make discretionary decisions about how to solve community problems. The decisions were to be based on their professional judgment and consultations with community members. Community policing promoted discretionary decision-making beyond the traditional law enforcement decision points in an effort to make life in neighborhoods better for local residents. As argued in Chapter 6, though, community policing in many U.S. police departments has been subsumed by law enforcement and crime control mandates, often relegating community policing to a strategy rather than the philosophy it was supposed to become, thus limiting the ability of officers to practice discretionary decision-making.

If policing is to move beyond the coercion paradigm toward a model of policing that emphasizes the protection of life, it will have to continue to embrace discretionary decision-making for the purposes of promoting good policing, rather than just limiting bad policing. This will require substantial changes to policing organizations and mindsets. Again, we discuss police discretion as a component of the protection of life mandate in the final chapter of this book.

---

[73] Davis, *Discretionary Justice: A Preliminary Inquiry*, 169.

Questions for Review and Reflection

Question 1. Police Discretion and Democracy

In its narrowest conception, policing is about comparing human behaviors to legal standards and then determining when an intervention is legally justified; for example, a stop-and-frisk, citation, arrest, or even the use of deadly force. As research has shown, though, police officers are asked to negotiate many types of situations that do not neatly fit within a legal framework. So, on the one hand, we ask our police to use the law as their guide when deciding how to handle field encounters with one or more citizens, but on the other hand, we ask them to use their professional judgment when making decisions about who to arrest, who to cite, and who to let go with a warning. Explain your answers.

- As noted in the chapter, Kenneth Culp Davis wrote, "Where the law ends, (police) discretion begins," and philosopher John Locke wrote in 1682, "Where-ever law ends, tyranny begins." Is it possible to reconcile these two diametrically opposed beliefs?
- Is it ever justified for police officers to forego arresting offenders who probably committed a crime?
- When does the police use of discretion become a misuse of discretion?
- How might a system of structured discretion protect against tyranny?

Question 2. Controlling Police Discretion

Historically, police discretion has been difficult to control, although policymakers had more success with deadly force than arrest in domestic violence incidents. Explain your answers.

- Why was the deadly force decision so much easier to control than the decision to arrest suspects of domestic violence? What is it about

deadly force that makes it different from arresting offenders of domestic violence?
- Is law an effective mechanism for controlling police discretion? How about police policies? Are there better ways to control police discretion?
- Given the difficulty policymakers had with getting police to arrest domestic violence offenders, how difficult will it be to better control the stop-and-frisk decision?
- Is it ever justified for officers to use the personal characteristics of people (e.g., race, ethnicity, gender, age) as factors that help them decide whether to make an arrest or write a citation? If so, when?

Question 3. Race and the Future of Police Discretion

As noted in the chapter, the Supreme Court's decision in *Whren v. United States* held that police officers were allowed to initiate a traffic stop on any driver who had committed a traffic offense. Although this decision sounds reasonable, it became the basis for pretextual traffic stops: Officers could now get behind a driver they wanted to pull over for anything other than a traffic offense, and then wait for them to commit any infraction to justify the stop.

- Was the decision in *Whren* the right decision? Should the Supreme Court have imposed some limits on how and when the police decide to pull someone over for a minor infraction?
- Are pretextual traffic stops—which are legal under the *Whren* ruling—even a problem? If so, why? If not, why not?
- How might the current Supreme Court decide a case like *Whren*? What if the current Court were to hear another case involving police discretion and race? How might it decide that case?

Exercise

Exercise Implementing a System of Structured Discretion

Imagine you are the new police chief of a department that employs 250 officers in a city with a residential population of about 200,000 residents. Recently, the city council voted to decriminalize possession of marijuana and to deemphasize the enforcement of possession for most other illegal drugs. At the same time, the council also authorized additional funding for drug treatment and education programs for drug-addicted persons. The city council has left it up to the police department to determine when officers are authorized to make arrests for drug possession (particularly, the more serious drugs). You, as police chief, can already envision the trouble this new nonenforcement orientation can bring to your department: Marijuana remains a Schedule I substance under the Controlled Substances Act, which means police officers are allowed to arrest people who possess it, regardless of what the city council might decree. Second, other drugs, such as cocaine, crack, and heroin are dangerous, and officers will be reluctant to ignore their possession and use among members of the public. It is your job to create a policy that balances the intent of the city council's nonenforcement

statement with policing's traditional values of arresting drug possessors and users.

- Create a drug enforcement policy based on a system of structured discretion that gives police officers the professional latitude to determine when to arrest people for possession or use of marijuana and other illegal drugs.

- In creating the arrest guidelines under the structured discretion framework, identify the factors officers should consider when deciding whether to arrest someone for drug possession or use. Are the factors different for marijuana than for other more serious drugs?

- Describe in your report how you, as police chief, would work with the local prosecutor to make sure that drug arrests made under your structured discretion policy are prosecuted. Remember that because the city council asked the police department to deemphasize the importance of drug enforcement, it also pressured the district attorney's office not to prosecute any drug cases brought to them by police. How does your system of structured discretion encourage the DA to prosecute people against whom your officers have brought drug charges?

Bibliography

American Bar Foundation. *The Administration of Criminal Justice in the United States: Pilot Project Report.* Vol. 5. Chicago: American Bar Foundation, 1958. https://www.google.com/books/edition/The_Administration_of_Criminal_Justice_i/_cQ_AAAAIAAJ?hl=en.

Avakame, Edem F., and James J. Fyfe. "Differential Police Treatment of Male-on-Female Spousal Violence: Additional Evidence on the Leniency Thesis." *Violence Against Women* 7, no. 1 (2001): 22–45. https://doi.org/10.1177/10778010122182280.

Beckett, Katherine. "The Uses and Abuses of Police Discretion: Toward Harm Reduction Policing." *Harvard Law and Policy Review* 10 (2016): 77.

Davis, Kenneth Culp. *Discretionary Justice: A Preliminary Inquiry.* Baton Rouge: Louisiana State University Press, 1969. https://www.amazon.com/Discretionary-Justice-Kenneth-Culp-Davis/dp/0313225036.

Fagan, Jeffrey, Anthony Braga, Rod Brunson, and April Pattavina. "Stops and Stares: Street Stops, Surveillance, and Race in the New Policing." *Fordham Urban Law Journal* 43, no. 3 (2016): 539.

Fagan, Jeffrey, and Garth Davies. "Street Stops and Broken Windows: Terry, Race and Disorder in New York City." *Fordham Urban Law Journal* 28 (2000): 457–504. https://doi.org/10.2139/ssrn.257813.

Floyd v. City of New York, 959 F. Supp. 2d 668 - Dist. Court, SD New York (2013).

Furman v. Georgia, 408 U.S. 238 (1972).

Fyfe, James J. "Administrative Interventions on Police Shooting Discretion: An Empirical Examination." *Journal of Criminal Justice* 7, no. 4 (1979): 303–323. https://www.sciencedirect.com/science/article/pii/0047235279900655.

Fyfe, James J. "Blind Justice: Police Shootings in Memphis." *The Journal of Criminal Law and Criminology* 73, no. 2 (1982): 707–722. https://doi.org/10.2307/1143112.

Fyfe, James J., David A Klinger, and Jeanne M Flavin. "Male-on-Female Spousal Violence." *Criminology* 35, no. 3 (1997): 455–473.

Gelman, Andrew, Jeffrey Fagan, and Alex Kiss. "An Analysis of the New York City Police Department's 'Stop-and-Frisk' Policy in the Context of Claims of Racial Bias." *Journal of the American Statistical Association* 102, no. 479 (2007): 813–823. https://doi.org/10.1198/016214506000001040.

Goldkamp, John. "Minorities as Victims of Police Shootings: Interpretations of Racial Disproportionality and Police Use of Deadly Force." *Justice System Journal* 2, no. 2 (1976): 169–183.

Gottfredson, Michael R., and Don M. Gottfredson. *Decision Making in Criminal Justice: Toward the Rational Exercise of Discretion*. New York: Springer, 1988. https://doi.org/10.1007/978-1-4757-9954-5_1.

Greene, Judith A. "Zero Tolerance: A Case Study of Police Policies and Practices in New York City." *Crime and Delinquency* 45, no. 2 (1999): 171–187. https://doi.org/10.1177/0011128799045002001.

Gregg v. Georgia, 428 U.S. 153 (1976).

Harris, David A. "Across the Hudson: Taking the Stop and Frisk Debate Beyond New York City." *New York University Journal of Legislation and Public Policy* 16, no. 853 (2013): 1–24.

Harris, David A. "'Driving While Black' and All Other Traffic Offenses: The Supreme Court and Pretextual Traffic Stops." *Journal of Criminal Law & Criminology* 87, no. 2 (1997): 544–582. http://www.autolife.umd.umich.edu/Race/R_Casestudy/R_Casestudy1.htm.

Harris, David A. *Profiles in Injustice: Why Police Profiling Cannot Work*. New York: The New Press, 2002.

Howell, K. Babe. "Broken Lives from Broken Windows: The Hidden Costs of Aggressive Order-Maintenance Policing." *NYU Review of Law & Social Change* 33 (2009): 271–329.

"John Locke on the Idea That 'Wherever Law Ends, Tyranny Begins' (1689) | Online Library of Liberty." Accessed March 19, 2021. https://oll.libertyfund.org/quote/john-locke-on-the-idea-that-wherever-law-ends-tyranny-begins-1689.

Kane, Robert J. "Collect and Release Data on Coercive Police Actions." *Criminology & Public Policy* 6, no. 4 (2007): 773–780. https://doi.org/10.1111/j.17459133.2007.00485.x.

Kane, Robert J. "Patterns of Arrest in Domestic Violence Encounters: Identifying a Police Decision-Making Model." *Journal of Criminal Justice* 27, no. 1 (1999): 65–79. https://doi.org/10.1016/S00472352(98)00037-3.

Kane, Robert J. "Responding to Restraining Orders in Domestic Violence Incidents: Identifying the Custody-Threshold Thesis." *Criminal Justice and Behavior* 27, no. 3 (2000): 561–580.

Klinger, David A. "Negotiating Order in Patrol Work: An Ecological Theory of Police Response to Deviance." *Criminology* 35, no. 2 (1997): 277–306. https://doi.org/10.1111/j.1745-9125.1997.tb00877.x.

Klinger, David, Richard Rosenfeld, Daniel Isom, and Michael Deckard. "Race, Crime, and the Micro-Ecology of Deadly Force." *Criminology and Public Policy* 15, no. 1 (2016): 193–222. https://doi.org/10.1111/17459133.12174.

Kovera, Margaret Bull. "Racial Disparities in the Criminal Justice System: Prevalence, Causes, and a Search for Solutions." *Journal of Social Issues* 75, no. 4 (2019): 1139–1164. https://doi.org/10.1111/josi.12355.

Lundman, Richard J., and Robert L. Kaufman. "Driving While Black: Effects of Race, Ethnicity, and Gender on Citizen Self-Reports of Traffic Stops and Police Actions." *Criminology* 41, no. 1 (2003): 195–220. https://doi.org/10.1111/j.1745-9125.2003.tb00986.x.

Mapp v. Ohio, 367 U.S. 643 (1961).

Mastrofski, Stephen D. "Controlling Street-Level Police Discretion." *Annals of the American Academy of Political and Social Science* 593 (2004): 100–118. https://doi.org/10.1177/0002716203262584.

McCleskey v. Kemp, 481 U.S. 279 (1987).

Meares, Tracey L. "Programming Errors: Understanding the Constitutionality of Stop-and-Frisk as a Program, Not an Incident." *University of Chicago Law Review* 82, no. 1 (2015): 159–179. https://doi.org/10.2139/ssrn.2524930.

Meehan, Albert J., and Michael C. Ponder. "Race and Place: The Ecology of Racial Profiling African American Motorists." *Justice Quarterly* 19, no. 3 (2002): 399–430.

Mignon, Sylvia I., and William M. Holmes. "Police Response to Mandatory Arrest Laws." *Crime & Delinquency* 41, no. 4 (1995): 430–442. https://doi.org/10.1177/0011128795041004004.

Nickels, Ernest L. "A Note on the Status of Discretion in Police Research." 2007. https://doi.org/10.1016/j.jcrimjus.2007.07.009.

Novak, Kenneth J., and Mitchell B. Chamlin. "Racial Threat, Suspicion, and Police Behavior: The Impact of Race and Place in Traffic Enforcement." *Crime and Delinquency* 58, no. 2 (2012): 275–300. https://doi.org/10.1177/0011128708322943.

Oppenlander, Nan. "Coping or Copping Out: Police Service Delivery in Domestic Disputes." *Criminology* 20, no. 3/4 (1982): 449–465. http://10.0.4.87/j.1745-9125.1982.tb00471.x%0Ahttps://libproxy.wlu.ca/login?url=http://search.ebscohost.com/login.aspx?direct=true&AuthType=ip,cookie,url,uid&db=i3h&AN=16731779&site=ehost-live.

"Overview | NYPD Monitor." Accessed April 2, 2021. http://nypdmonitor.org/overview/.

Oxford English Dictionary. Oxford, UK: Oxford University Press, 2000.

President's Commission on Law Enforcement and the Administration of Justice. "The Challenge of Crime in a Free Society." Washington, DC, 1967. https://doi.org/10.3138/cjcor.9.4.347.

Rosenfeld, Richard, Robert Fornango, and Andres F. Rengifo. "The Impact of Order-Maintenance Policing on New York City Homicide and Robbery Rates: 1988–2001." *Criminology* 45, no. 2 (2007): 355–384. https://doi.org/10.1111/j.1745-9125.2007.00081.x.

Ross, Cody T., Bruce Winterhalder, and Richard McElreath. "Racial Disparities in Police Use of Deadly Force Against Unarmed Individuals Persist After Appropriately Benchmarking Shooting Data on Violent Crime Rates." *Social Psychological and Personality Science* 12, no. 3 (2020): 323–332. https://doi.org/10.1177/1948550620916071.

Rubinstein, Jonathan. *City Police*. New York: Farrar, Straus and Giroux, 1973.

Sherman, Lawrence W. "Policing Domestic Violence 1967–2017." *Criminology and Public Policy* 17, no. 2 (2018): 453–465. https://doi.org/10.1111/1745-9133.12365.

Sherman, Lawrence W., and Richard A. Berk. "The Specific Deterrent Effects of Arrest for Domestic Assault." *American Sociological Review* 49, no. 2 (1984): 261–272. https://doi.org/10.2307/2095575.

Simon, John. "The Fleeing Felon Rule." *Saint Louis University Law Journal* 30, no. 4 (1986): 1259–1278.

Straus, Murray A., and Richard J. Gelles. "Societal Change and Change in Family Violence from 1975 to 1985 as Revealed by Two National Surveys." *Journal of Marriage and Family* 48, no. 3 (1986): 113–132. https://doi.org/10.4324/9781315126401.

Taylor, Ralph B. "The Incivilities Thesis: Theory, Measurement, and Policy." In *Measuring What Matters: Proceedings from the Policing Research Institute Meetings*, edited by Robert H. Langley, 65–88. Washington, DC: National Institute of Justice, 1999.

Tennessee v. Garner, 471 U.S. 1 (1985).

U.S. Department of Justice. "Justice Department Releases Report on Civil Rights Division's Pattern and Practice Police Reform Work." Washington, DC, 2017. https://www.justice.gov/opa/pr/justice-department-releases-report-civil-rights-division-s-pattern-and-practice-police-reform.

Walker, Samuel. *Taming the System: The Control of Discretion in Criminal Justice, 1950–1990*. New York: Oxford University Press, 1993. https://doi.org/10.1093/acprof:oso/9780195078206.001.0001.

Websdale, Neil. *Understanding Domestic Homicide*. Boston: Northeastern University Press, 1999.

White, Michael D. "Transactional Encounters, Crisis-Driven Reform, and the Potential for a National Police Deadly Force Database." *Criminology and Public Policy* 15, no. 1 (2016): 223–235. https://doi.org/10.1111/1745-9133.12180.

White, Michael D., and Henry F. Fradella. *Stop and Frisk: The Use and Abuse of a Controversial Policing Tactic*. New York: NYU Press, 2019. https://nyupress.org/books/9781479857814/.

Whren v. United States, 517 U.S. 806 (1996).

Wilson, O. W. *Police Administration*. 2nd ed. New York: McGraw-Hill, 1963.

CHAPTER 8

Policing and the Use of Force

It can start with something as subtle as mere presence: a police officer pulling into a parking lot, stepping out of her vehicle to make sure the teenagers see her. Realizing she's there to stay, the teenagers, who earlier had been blocking the entrance and making a commotion in the parking lot, grab their boards and skate off. The owner of the convenience store gives the officer a thumbs-up through the window as she slides back into the driver's seat of her cruiser. She never had to approach, never had to say a word. She merely had to be there. That's not always the way it goes, though. Sometimes the encounter ends with something as final as the pull of a trigger. That same officer might confront a robbery suspect in the parking lot of that same convenience store. As the suspect emerges from inside, the officer takes cover behind her open car door. With weapon drawn, she orders him to stop, show his hands, and get on the ground. He reaches for something inside his jacket, and she fires two times. The man drops where he stood, lifeless on the ground, hand loosely clutching the gun he had been attempting to draw. Between those two anchor points of merely being there and using deadly force resides a full continuum of use of force options for police officers.

Podcast Episode: "Training to Avoid Unnecessary Force"

Scan the QR code or enter the short URL shown below into a browser window to listen to this chapter's podcast.

https://bit.ly/3s8SlmN

To a great extent, coercion is the tool that gives policing its legitimacy as an institution. Coercion is the reason we call the police; it is the reason they have the authority to respond. It is that thing that makes them all at once intrinsically good and intrinsically dangerous.[1] Use of force is the threat that underlies coercive authority, always residing just below the surface until it is needed. When used properly, coercive force can achieve a moral end. When used improperly, it leaves tragedy in its wake. Although use of force represents an expression of policing's coercive authority, it is not inherently driven by the coercion paradigm. Even a protection of life mandate—the "new" idea on which much of this book is based—would require policing to maintain its general right to use coercive force. Until members of society cease to use force on each other as a means to achieve an illegal end, policing will need to retain its general right to use force to protect society from itself.

That is what this chapter is all about: how the use—or threatened use—of force permeates the occupation of policing. The chapter examines some of the conceptual aspects of the police use of force as well as the transactional mechanics that invoke its need and often its escalation. It identifies the different levels of force and some of the goals officers might hope to achieve by applying them. As the chapter explains, sometimes the use of force is about gaining compliance, and other times it is about establishing control.

There are times, though, when a legitimate application of force goes too far, to the point of becoming excessive. There are other times when any force at all should have been avoided. When Derek Chauvin placed George Floyd in a neck restraint, using his knee to keep pressure on Mr. Floyd's neck for more than nine minutes, was that excessive force? Was it unnecessary force? The distinction is subtle but crucial for a full understanding of the use of force as a social construct.

By the end of this chapter, readers should be able to answer the following questions:

1. What are the different forms of police use of force?
2. What is the use-of-force matrix?
3. In what ways is the police use of force a transaction?
4. When does use of force become excessive force?
5. What is unnecessary force, and why is it a problem?
6. How does the police use of force reconcile with a protection of life mandate?

The Phases of Force

Historically, the police use of force has been described as a continuum with different force applications and tools or weapons rank-ordered in ways that "fit" an escalation of force process.[2] The traditional continuum begins with the mere presence of a police officer under the assumption that in some

---

[1] Banton, *The Policeman in the Community*, 237.
[2] Skolnick and Fyfe, *Above the Law: Police and the Excessive Use of Force*; Alpert and Dunham, *Understanding Police Use of Force: Officers, Suspects, and Reciprocity*; "The Use-of-Force Continuum | National Institute of Justice."

cases, simply being there is enough to maintain or establish compliance and control. Imagine a motorist traveling at 75 miles per hour along a divided highway on which the speed limit is 65 miles per hour. The driver sees a highway patrol cruiser parked in the median and immediately takes his foot off the gas pedal and checks the speedometer, not replacing his foot until the vehicle has slowed to the legal speed limit. This is an example of how mere presence can result in traffic control. Referring back to the example at the opening of this chapter, the officer who pulled into the parking lot of the convenience store never had to make contact with the teenagers loitering near the entrance. Simply arriving and stepping out of her cruiser was enough to get the teenagers to skate off, allowing her to establish control of the setting.

Is the mere presence of a police officer really an application of force? Or is it something more analogous to the threatened, or implied, use of force? In answering those questions, we might consider the goals of police when using or threatening force. What are police officers hoping to accomplish during encounters characterized by the potential use of force? Arguably, the two primary outcomes are compliance and control. To be sure, the goals of self-defense, the defense of others, the restoration of public order, and in some cases the maintenance of respect for officers' authority often count as reasons for the police use of force.[3] Those are immediate justifications, though. The *goals* of the use of force—that is, what police officers ultimately hope to accomplish—are more rooted in gaining compliance (which helps reestablish order) and exerting control (which reduces threats to public and officer safety). To the extent that the mere presence of a police officer changes the behaviors of individuals, then mere presence can be considered the entry-level use of force. Indeed, police officers are trained to use their bodies—in terms of gesture, position, and bearing—in ways to convey authority that will help them establish control and gain compliance, often without ever saying a word.[4]

But what happens when mere presence does not work to achieve compliance and control? At that point, police officers might advance from mere presence to verbal commands. When an officer contacts a driver during a traffic stop, she might ask, "May I see your license and registration, please?" This is an example of a verbal command issued in the form of a question that is designed to establish control and achieve compliance. Suppose, though, that the driver of the vehicle fails to understand that the question was not really a question at all, but really a command. Instead of handing the officer the license and registration, the driver says, "Why are you pulling me over? Don't you have anything better to do?" At that point, the officer is likely to restate the question in the form of a command by replying, "I asked you for your license and registration. Hand them over, please."

---

[3] *See generally* Kane and Cronin, "Maintaining Order Under the Rule of Law: Occupational Templates and the Police Use of Force"; Alpert and Dunham, *Understanding Police Use of Force: Officers, Suspects, Reciprocity*.
[4] Skolnick and Fyfe, *Above the Law: Police and the Excessive Use of Force*.

The point of police verbalization is that it represents a nonphysical application of force that is nevertheless active and authoritative.[5] Through verbalization, police officers might ask questions of drivers or other subjects that direct them to do something or take some action, such as handing over a driver's license, stepping out of a vehicle, or moving away from traffic. Officers use a calm voice and typically do not raise the volume unless the person fails to comply, or the situation appears to carry more danger or risk than a "typical" encounter. In such cases, when the risk to personal or public safety becomes elevated, officers often issue short commands using a forceful tone: "Stop!" "Don't move!" "Show hands!" Such commands are designed to be quick and readily understandable so that the person being directed has the opportunity to comply immediately. Verbalization is the last stop on the use-of-force continuum that does not involve physical coercion.

When verbal commands fail to achieve compliance or control, officers often move to "empty-hand control" tactics, which are typically categorized as either soft or hard techniques.[6] *Soft techniques* usually involve officers placing subjects in various holds, such as finger grips, joint locks, or arm bar holds (the latter is often used for take-downs, as well). Soft techniques can also be classified as "pain compliance" tactics because they are often used to achieve compliance by inflicting pain without also causing residual injury.[7] Indeed, once the officer releases the hold, grip, or lock, the pain should quickly subside, and it should leave no injury. *Hard techniques* typically involve punching or kicking as a way of establishing control and gaining compliance; they might cause residual injury.

When empty-hand control techniques fail to achieve the outcomes of compliance and control—or if the situation is such that empty-hand techniques were never going to be successful (more on this below)—police officers will often employ *less-than-lethal* technologies to gain compliance and establish control. These technologies, or tools, are often categorized into three types:[8]

1. Blunt impact: Batons (including those with a handle, and those that expand and retract) and projectiles (e.g., beanbags).
2. Chemical: Oleoresin capsicum (OC or pepper spray) or other chemicals embedded within projectiles. Chemical sprays are typically used for crowd or riot control.
3. Conductive energy weapons (CEW): Devices designed to deliver a high-voltage, but low-amperage "shock" to temporarily incapacitate a resisting or otherwise noncompliant subject. The most common CEW used in U.S. police departments is the Taser.[9]

---

[5] "The Use-of-Force Continuum | National Institute of Justice."
[6] "The Use-of-Force Continuum | National Institute of Justice."
[7] Skolnick and Fyfe, *Above the Law: Police and the Excessive Use of Force.*
[8] "The Use-of-Force Continuum | National Institute of Justice."
[9] White et al., "Examining Cognitive Functioning Following TASER Exposure: A Randomized Controlled Trial."

It is important to note that less-than-lethal technologies are designed to counter intermediate suspect resistance or noncompliance (discussed in detail below) and that their use could cause residual injury. In this way, less-than-lethal technologies typically reside higher on the use-of-force continuum than pain compliance techniques because of the potential for injury and the potential need for immediate transport to the hospital on their deployment.

The highest level of force on the use-of-force continuum is deadly force, which is typically defined as "force that kills or is likely to kill." It normally, but not always, involves a firearm.[10] Deadly force does not have to lead to the death of a suspect: Whenever a police officer invokes a firearm, or uses a type of hold that occludes blood flow or an airway, that officer has used deadly force, whether the subject of that force dies or not. As noted in Chapter 7, during our discussions of police discretion and its control, the use of deadly force—and in particular, the firearm—is largely governed by federal case law. The Supreme Court in its 1985 *Tennessee v. Garner* decision held that police officers were allowed to use deadly force only to defend life.[11]

The phases of force, or the traditional use-of-force continuum, are important for helping the police and society distinguish among the types and severity of use of force tools and applications, but they do little to define the circumstances that might invoke their uses. For that, we should examine the use-of-force matrix, which matches use of force levels to suspect resistance.

The Force Factor: Suspect Resistance and Police Coercion

How does an officer know when to move from mere presence to verbal commands? What kinds of behaviors by a suspect justify the application of "hard" open-hand techniques vs. pain compliance tactics? Is a police officer required to start with the entry-level use of force before escalating to higher levels, regardless of suspect resistance or combative behavior when the officer makes first contact? To help answer these questions, it is instructive to turn to the Commission on the Accreditation of Law Enforcement Agencies (CALEA).

Established in 1979, CALEA is a nonprofit organization that works with the major police executive organizations (e.g., International Association of Chiefs of Police, National Sheriffs' Association, Police Executive Research Forum) to create and maintain a set of standards that law enforcement agencies should adopt to become nationally accredited.[12] To this end, CALEA has created model policies, general orders, and procedures designed to guide public safety agencies (e.g., police departments) through a process of meeting

---

[10] Fyfe, "Administrative Interventions on Police Shooting Discretion: An Empirical Examination."
[11] Tennessee v. Garner, 471 U.S. 1 (1985).
[12] "About Us | CALEA® | The Commission on Accreditation for Law Enforcement Agencies, Inc."

"best practice" standards across their organizations. Police departments that adopt the CALEA standards and fulfill other requirements can apply for, and receive, accreditation. Once accredited, agencies become part of the CALEA membership.

Among the model policies CALEA has created is a model use-of-force policy, which describes proper use-of-force procedures, establishes definitions of different use-of-force tools and tactics, and provides a use-of-force matrix that guides officers on the use of force as a response to suspect resistance.

Figure 8.1 is a representation of a typical use-of-force matrix as informed by the CALEA model use-of-force policy. The first thing to note about use-of-force encounters, and the use-of-force matrix in particular, is that suspects set the tone for the interactions with police, or at least that is the way it is supposed to work. The left column of Figure 8.1 shows the levels, rising from 1 to 6, of suspect behavior and resistance *as perceived* by the officer. The right-side column shows the levels and types of force officers are allowed to use to overcome perceived suspect resistance at each level. For example, at Level 1 of the matrix, the mere presence of a suspect should be met with nothing more than the mere presence of police officers, much like in the scenario that opened this chapter. If, however, officers query a suspect (e.g., "Are you here for a reason?" "Do you know how fast you were going?" "Can

Figure 8.1 ▶
CALEA-Informed
Use-of-Force Matrix

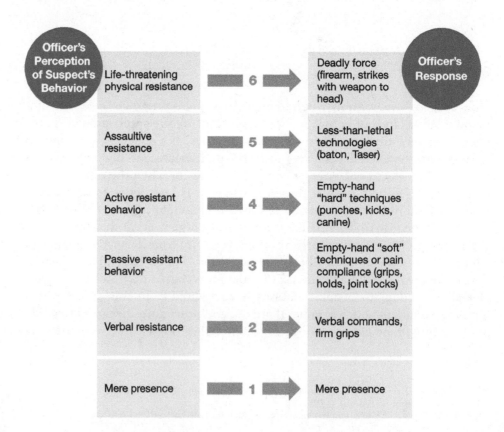

Officer's Perception of Suspect's Behavior		Officer's Response
Life-threatening physical resistance	6	Deadly force (firearm, strikes with weapon to head)
Assaultive resistance	5	Less-than-lethal technologies (baton, Taser)
Active resistant behavior	4	Empty-hand "hard" techniques (punches, kicks, canine)
Passive resistant behavior	3	Empty-hand "soft" techniques or pain compliance (grips, holds, joint locks)
Verbal resistance	2	Verbal commands, firm grips
Mere presence	1	Mere presence

you please step onto the sidewalk?") and they feel their query has been met with verbal resistance (e.g., "None of your business." "Yeah, I know how fast I was going, do you?" "I'll stay right where I am, thank you!"), then officers might escalate to issuing commands or even a finger grip to physically direct someone (particularly to bring them off the shoulder of the road and away from traffic). As the subsequent levels indicate, perceived suspect passive resistance can be met with empty-hand pain compliance techniques, and active resistance behaviors can be met with hard techniques. Again, police use of force should not exceed the levels of perceived suspect resistance.

The second thing to note about any use-of-force matrix is that suspect behaviors are not necessarily objective: They are perceived by officers. Thus, the person(s) who define suspect behaviors and the nature of resistance are the officers participating in and witnessing the encounter. Indeed, there is case law that solidifies this issue. In *Graham v. Connor* (1989), the Supreme Court held, "The 'reasonableness' of a particular use of force must be judged from the perspective of a reasonable officer on the scene, and its calculus must embody an allowance for the fact that police officers are often forced to make split-second decisions about the amount of force necessary in a particular situation."[13]

In applying an "objective reasonableness" standard to police use of force, the Court made it clear that "reasonable" police officers at the scene are the people who determine the proper (or improper) application of force, and that people evaluating the use of force after the fact must still do so from the perspective of a reasonable officer at the scene. To some extent, this standard favors police officers, making it difficult to prove excessive use of force in lawsuits or administrative complaint actions. But it also protects police officers from having their use-of-force decisions judged for "surgical" precision in the relative safety and quiet of a courtroom by people who were not on the scene and could not possibly understand the "feeling" of threat officers might have perceived in that moment.[14]

The final thing to note about any use-of-force matrix is that officers are not required to progress through each level of force in a linear fashion. As noted, perceived suspect resistance sets the tone for encounters with police officers. If officers perceive that a suspect escalates, for example, from mere presence to assaultive resistance—directly from Level 1 to Level 5 in the use-of-force matrix—then officers are allowed to jump to Level 5 without moving through Levels 1 to 4.

Although the use-of-force matrix might appear to represent an empirical standard that seamlessly guides police officers through use-of-force encounters, it is far from that. Potentially violent encounters between the police and the public are rarely predictable, and if they do turn violent, they usually turn ugly. Indeed, any time a democratic government is compelled to use force

---

[13] *Graham v. Connor*, 490 US 386 (1989), 2.
[14] Wolf et al., "Police Use of Force and the Cumulative Force Factor."

against one of its citizens, it likely represents a failure of some institution along the way that that might have helped prevent the police-citizen encounter in the first place. Still, as a CALEA model framework, the use-of-force matrix helps create a professional standard among accredited police agencies designed to apply at least minimal expectations for how officers should respond to different types of perceived suspect resistance. This is particularly important when considering that there are few laws that actually govern the police use of force.

How Much Police Use of Force Is There?

How many times, and to what degree, do police officers use force during any given year? The simplest answer is that no one really knows. That's right: The American public has little idea how much force police officers use and how often they use it over any given period of time. As described elsewhere in this book, the U.S. police system is highly decentralized, meaning that most police agencies are situated at the municipal or county levels. Of the estimated 15,471 full-authority police and law enforcement agencies in the United States,[15] 12,326 (79.67 percent) are local police departments, and 3,012 (19.46 percent) are county sheriff's departments. This means that 15,338 (99.14 percent) of all full-authority police agencies in the United States are authorized at the municipal or county levels; and none of them is required to report their use of force data to any federal authority. As a result, it remains virtually impossible to determine how often and to what extent police agencies in the United States use force.

The Federal Bureau of Investigation is trying to remedy that situation. In 2015 the FBI created the National Use-of-Force Data Collection program for which local police and law enforcement agencies voluntarily report their use of force statistics, including brief summaries of the circumstances under which the force was used.[16] Although the program was chartered in 2015, it did not begin receiving data until January 1, 2019. As of this writing, and according to the FBI's Crime Data Explorer website,[17] 5,030 of all local, state, federal, and tribal police and law enforcement agencies report their data to the National Use-of-Force Data Collection program. Although this represents a relatively small percentage of police agencies across the United States, the FBI notes that these agencies employ 42 percent of all police and

---

[15] This figure represents the sum of municipal, county, state, and federal police and law enforcement agencies from the following two reports: Brooks, "Federal Law Enforcement Officers, 2016 — Statistical Tables"; and Reaves, "Local Police Departments, 2013: Personnel, Policies, and Practices." The 15,471 figure excludes tribal police and other specialized (e.g., housing, transit, school) agencies that maintain police powers.
[16] Federal Bureau of Investigation, "National Use-of-Force Data Collection."
[17] "Federal Bureau of Investigation Crime Data Explorer — Use-of-Force."

federal law enforcement officials in the country. Before it releases any use of force data, however, the FBI notes on its website that the program must meet two additional milestones:

> When 60% of the total officer population is represented, ratios and percentages, as well as the most frequently reported responses to questions (in list format without actual counts) may be published. When 80% of officers are represented by submitted data, aggregate use-of-force data may be presented. If at any time the data from agencies represents less than 40% of the total officer population, the FBI will not disseminate use-of-force data.[18]

Because only 42 percent of all police officers and law enforcement agents are represented in the use-of-force database, the FBI will not release more use-of-force data until that number almost doubles in size. It is not clear when the FBI hopes to achieve that goal. Currently many states are in the process of developing plans that describe how they will begin collecting and sending use-of-force data to from their local agencies to the FBI's National Use-of-Force Data Collection program. Until such time as the FBI releases use-of-force data on local police agencies, the best we can do is estimate how often and to what extent police officers use force during their encounters with the public.

In 2018, a group of university researchers published the results of a study that intended to do just that. Joel Garner, Matthew Hickman, and their colleagues compiled use-of-force data from two national sources: (1) the Police–Public Contact Survey, which is a supplemental survey tacked onto the nationally representative National Crime Victimization Survey (NCVS); and (2) several national surveys of police and law enforcement agencies' reported use of force.[19] Together, these data sources represent information collected from both members of the public who reported use of force against them by the police on the NCVS, as well as use-of-force data reported by police departments across several waves of voluntary national policing surveys. To create use-of-force estimates, the researchers found where the NCVS and police department surveys had the greatest overlap and pinpointed 2012 as the most reliable year. They thus went about creating estimates of how often and to what extent police departments used force on members of the public for that year, defining use of force as any application of force on the use-of-force continuum from open-hand techniques upward. They did not include, for example, handcuffing, because handcuffs are a restraint device, not a use-of-force tool. Table 8.1 summarizes the primary findings reported by Garner et al.

---

[18] "FBI Releases 2019 Participation Data for the National Use-of-Force Data Collection."

[19] Garner et al., "Progress Toward National Estimates of Police Use of Force," 24.

Table 8.1. Use of Force Estimates for Local, County, and State Police Forces for the Year 2012

	Number of Agencies	Use of Force Estimates	Use of Force Rate per Agency Type
Local police departments	12,326	253,361	20.56
County sheriff's departments	3,012	76,295	25.33
Primary state police agencies	50	7,938	158.76
All agency types	15,388	337,594	21.94

Note: Adapted from Table 6 of Garner et al.[20]

As the data in Table 8.1 show, police officers used force an estimated 337,594 times in 2012, with state police departments showing the highest use of force rates per agency. Although it appears from Table 8.1 that local police agencies had the lowest use of force rates per agency, those rates might be underestimated by data not shown in the table: Garner et al. were quick to point out that agencies with 100 officers or more reported the highest use-of-force rates.[21] Such agencies, of course, represent the most urbanized settings with greater opportunities (or risks) for the use of force. Garner et al. noted that among local police departments, about 19 percent of all arrests included some use of force by officers. For sheriff's departments, about 25 percent of all arrests involved the use of force among deputies. At primary state police agencies, almost 15 percent of all arrests involved some use of force. In the aggregate—when combining data from all types of police agencies—about 20 percent of all arrests involved some degree of force used by officers.[22]

Is 20 percent too high? Without more context about how the force was used and the degree to which force was applied, there is no systematic way of determining the "proper" rate of use of force among police officers. When officers make an arrest, they are effectively extracting someone from society, if even for a short time, often against the person's will. Thus, the fact that police officers and deputy sheriffs appear to use some degree of force (beyond mere presence or verbal commands) in about one in five arrests seems plausible. These estimates indicate nothing, though, about the reasonableness of the force that was used, or the goals officers hoped to achieve by using it. They do not indicate, for example, the degrees to which officers might have improperly jumped levels on a use-of-force matrix, essentially engaging in excessive force.

---

[20] Garner et al., 15.
[21] Garner et al., 15.
[22] Garner et al., 16.

They do not indicate whether officers had to resort to a Taser because they placed themselves in harm's way, forcing a conflict that might otherwise have been avoided. Assessing reasonableness in the absence of data is speculative at best. We can, however, appeal to the proposed protection of life mandate to create some expectations about how force might be applied.

The Fluidity of Use of Force Encounters

When does the use of force become excessive use of force? When does any force become unnecessary? These are often difficult questions to answer because, again, coercive force is a tool society has given the police to help them accomplish their mandate. When the police use more force than necessary during encounters with the public, they can often be seen as simply "overusing" their tool. This is what makes judging the police use of force so difficult during so many contacts with the public: At some point during an encounter, the use of force might have been appropriate and necessary, but then, after some tipping point, any additional force might have become unjustified, perhaps even illegal. Although it is true that the Supreme Court in *Graham v. Connor* established a standard for helping identify excessive use of force, *Graham* does not create empirical criteria for the evaluation of police use of force, per se.

Consider this scenario: Two police officers respond to a disturbance call at a local bank, where it has been reported that a bank teller's irate husband has shown up and been verbally abusing his wife (while she is trying to work), continuing an unfinished argument that occurred earlier that morning. The officers arrive on scene, make contact with the person who called them, and then approach the husband. At that point, a third officer arrives and joins the two colleagues. The officers separate the husband and wife, with two officers moving the husband off to the side of the bank's interior. The husband is barely cooperative and continues to bad-mouth his wife, prompting one of the officers to tell him, "Dude, cut it out." The officer talking with the wife quickly flashes a hand signal to his two colleagues across the room, which they know to mean that the husband must be arrested, and that it is most likely for domestic assault.

The two officers dealing with the husband tell him he is under arrest and that he needs to turn around so they can handcuff him. Rather than follow their commands, the husband tells the officers, "Fuck off!" and shoves his hands into his pockets and locks his arms. This posture of going stiff-armed with his wrists buried in his pockets makes it impossible for the officers to cuff him while he is standing up. After a moment of trying to pull the man's hands from his pockets, the officer who had originally told him to "cut it out" sweeps the husband's feet out from under him and takes him face-down onto the floor. The husband hits the floor with both a loud thud and pained groan. The officer then jumps on the man's back and punches him two or three times in the back of the head while yelling, "Let my partner pull your hands from your pockets! You're going to jail!" At that point, the officer's colleague is able to remove the man's hands from his pockets and handcuff him. Despite the cuffs, the officer who initially knocked the husband to the floor punches him two more times in the back of the head then kicks him once in the ribs when he stands up. The other officer brings the husband to his feet and walks him through the bank out to the police vehicle.

This scenario illustrates the "fluidity" of encounters where force is employed because it involves an appropriate example of force, a gray-area application of force, and a clear example of excessive force. When the husband went stiff-armed and refused to allow the officers to handcuff him, the officer was justified in sweeping the husband's feet out from under him to get him to the ground and into a prone position for handcuffing. When the officer jumped onto the man's back to give his partner a chance to pull the husband's hands from his pocket, his strikes to the back of the husband's head represent a gray-area application of force. Although it might be true that the officer struck the husband out of anger and frustration more than as a result of good police tactics, the "objective reasonableness" standard established by the Supreme Court in *Graham*[23] would require a court to ask, "What would a reasonable officer at the scene have done to help get the husband properly restrained in handcuffs?" The answer is not clear because one "reasonable" officer at the scene could argue that striking the man on the back of the head was a reasonable tactic to provoke the man to take his hands from his pockets in an effort to defend his head, thus allowing the other officer to grab and cuff him. Another "reasonable" officer might argue that the officer's punches to the back of the head were committed clearly out of anger, and that he should have used one or more types of pain compliance techniques to gain control, thereby avoiding striking a defenseless person in such a vulnerable area of the body.

Once the husband was handcuffed, any further use of force would be simply impermissible. Punches to the back of the man's head once he was in handcuffs was a clear violation of any reasonable use-of-force matrix; kicking him in the ribs could result in criminal charges filed against the officer for assault and battery—perhaps even prosecution under the federal civil rights statute, as summarized below by the U.S. Department of Justice:

> Section 242 of Title 18 (of the US Code) makes it a crime for a person acting under color of any law to willfully deprive a person of a right or privilege protected by the Constitution or laws of the United States. . . . Persons acting under color of law within the meaning of this statute include police officers, prisons [sic] guards and other law enforcement officials, as well as judges, care providers in public health facilities, and others who are acting as public officials. . . . The offense is punishable by a range of imprisonment up to a life term, or the death penalty, depending upon the circumstances of the crime, and the resulting injury, if any.[24]

---

[23] Graham v. Connor, 490 U.S. 386 (1989).

[24] "Deprivation of Rights Under Color of Law."

Recall from Chapter 7 that the Supreme Court in *Tennessee v. Garner* held that the police use of deadly force was tantamount to a seizure of the person and therefore subject to Fourth Amendment scrutiny. With its decision in *Graham v. Connor*, the Court reaffirmed its decision in *Garner* and made it clear that all police use of force—including excessive force—was tantamount to a seizure of the person under the Fourth Amendment, which meant that officers could be charged under the federal civil rights statute (i.e., Title 18 USC, Section 242) for excessive force.[25] Still, the "What would a reasonable officer at the scene have done?" standard for evaluating the police use of force heavily favors police officers and continues to offer them what Carl Klockars called the relatively "open-ended" authority to use force.[26]

Excessive Force vs. Unnecessary Force: A Subtle but Crucial Distinction

Despite the fact that excessive force by police is the type that attracts much scrutiny, the unnecessary use of force, by comparison, is likely more common and likely kills or injures more people in any given year.[27] The term *likely* is used because there is no way to estimate its prevalence, largely due to the fact that unnecessary force disguises itself as appropriate force when initially scrutinized.

In a 1980 article, scholars Arnold Binder and Peter Scharf argued that investigations of the police use of deadly force typically focused on what they called the "final frame" of a police-citizen encounter, the moment the officer pulled the trigger or otherwise exerted the deadly force.[28] Focusing on the final frame of the event, they argued, ignored the previous decisions the officer made to reach that final moment, such as failing to find cover or forcing the initial confrontation that led to the use of deadly force. Applying Binder and Scharf's logic to all use-of-force encounters, scholar James J. Fyfe elaborated that unnecessary force is force that is reasonable at the time of commission, but that could have been avoided had the officer practiced a more competent form of policing.[29] Fyfe further asserted that many use-of-force and deadly force encounters could be avoided if police officers worked harder to avoid conflict and putting themselves in harm's way. By way of illustration, consider the following scenario.

A state trooper stops a vehicle along a long stretch of deserted highway at night. There are no streetlamps illuminating the highway, and the trooper's nearest backup is at least 10 minutes out (assuming lights and siren).

---

[25] Karsch, "Excessive Force and the Fourth Amendment: When Does Seizure End?"
[26] Klockars, *The Idea of Police*.
[27] Binder and Scharf, "The Violent Police-Citizen Encounter"; Fyfe, "Training to Reduce Police–Civilian Violence"; Skolnick and Fyfe, *Above the Law: Police and the Excessive Use of Force*.
[28] Binder and Scharf, "The Violent Police-Citizen Encounter," 118.
[29] Fyfe, "Training to Reduce Police–Civilian Violence."

The trooper contacts the driver at the driver-side window and asks to see his license and registration. The driver, who is clearly seat-belted by both a lap and shoulder strap, asserts that he is a "sovereign citizen" and therefore not subject to the laws of the United States or any state within the United States.[30] It is his position that he need not show any identification to the state trooper, because the officer has no authority over him. The trooper at that point uses his shoulder-mounted radio receiver to call for backup. In the meantime, the trooper again orders the driver to produce his driver's license and vehicle registration, reminding him that in their state, all drivers must be licensed. Again, the driver refuses, asserting his status as a sovereign citizen.

The trooper orders the driver to turn off the engine, remove the keys from the ignition, and drop them onto the shoulder of the road. The driver refuses. The trooper quickly reaches through the window opening and tries to grab the keys to the vehicle, but the driver successfully thwarts the effort. The trooper then reaches in and tries to unbuckle the driver's seatbelt and attempts to pull him physically from the vehicle, leading to a lengthy and intense struggle. When the trooper's efforts fail (and by this time, he is winded from the exertion), he takes a short step back from the vehicle, draws his Taser, and orders the driver out of the vehicle under threat of being "Tased." The driver again refuses, and the trooper fires the Taser. The problem, however, is that the trooper is too close to the driver, which fails to allow the Taser probes to reach the full "spread" required to effectively deliver the jolt of electricity. Moreover, one probe fails to penetrate the driver's skin, preventing the Taser from completing its circuit. As a result, the Taser exposure fails. Nevertheless, the pain from one probe sticking into his chest angers the driver, who opens the door and rushes the trooper, tackling him to the ground.

The trooper and driver are now rolling around on the shoulder of the road with the driver punching the trooper repeatedly in the face while trying to rip his gun from its holster. At length, and after taking many hard blows to the head, the trooper is able to force some separation between himself and the driver. The trooper rolls onto his back, sits up, draws his firearm and commands to driver to stop what he's doing and get face-down on the ground. The driver instead jumps to his feet and lunges at the trooper, who in turn fires four shots, stopping the driver dead in his tracks. Six minutes later (yes, that entire encounter took just four minutes to unfold from start to finish) the trooper's backup arrives.

It would be difficult for any reasonable officer at the scene to classify the trooper's use of deadly force as anything other than appropriate and necessary, given the aggression of the driver once he attacked the trooper. Indeed, it is likely that any reasonable officer at the scene would have felt his or her life was in danger and therefore would have pulled the trigger when the driver made his final lunge toward the trooper. The driver had already delivered

---

[30] An excellent description of the sovereign citizens movement can be found at "Sovereign Citizens Movement | Southern Poverty Law Center."

multiple blows to the trooper's head, had tried to take the trooper's firearm from its holster, and then tried to attack the trooper one last time before the trooper was able to fire. Thus, this example of deadly force was likely not excessive. But was it necessary?

Again, examining just the final frame of the event would likely lead a reasonable officer at the scene to conclude that the use of deadly force was justified, but what about the events leading up to the driver springing from the vehicle and attacking the trooper? Suppose the trooper had made a tactical and controlled retreat from the driver's vehicle when he (the driver) had initially refused to produce a driver's license, asserting sovereign citizen status? It should be noted that police officers since at least 2015 have been aware of the sovereign citizen movement and so-called sovereign citizens' potential for violence against the police.[31] When the driver mentioned his self-proclaimed sovereign citizen status, the trooper was correct to have immediately called for backup, but why not fall back to the rear of his vehicle to wait for his colleagues to arrive? Positioning himself at the rear of his vehicle places two cars between him and the driver while keeping at least one high-powered spotlight trained on the driver's vehicle. Once the backup officers arrived, they could have conducted a felony traffic stop from a safe distance to remove the driver from the vehicle.

A felony traffic stop occurs when officers believe they have encountered a high-risk individual or group of individuals driving in a vehicle. Rather than approach the suspect vehicle, they wait for backup officers to arrive. One officer then issues step-by-step commands to remove the driver and any passengers from the vehicle and get them into handcuffs. At any point during the encounter, if the driver or passengers make any furtive movements, or if they appear to draw weapons, the officers generally have time to respond, given that they already have weapons drawn and are positioned at a safe distance behind large parts of their patrol vehicles. The point is, although felony traffic stops might result in deadly force being used against combative subjects, they are likely the best method for reducing the risk of deadly force during high-risk traffic stops.[32]

In the traffic stop scenario above, once the driver asserted sovereign citizen status, this would have signaled to the trooper that he was now dealing with a high-risk traffic stop. Had he fallen back to the rear of his vehicle and waited for his backup to arrive, he likely would have avoided the initial failed attempts to rip the car keys from the ignition and pull

See for Yourself . . .

Scan the QR code to watch the YouTube video showing an actual, and tactically excellent, felony traffic stop in action.

---

[31] "5 Responses to a Sovereign Citizen at a Traffic Stop"; "Sovereign Citizens Movement | Southern Poverty Law Center."

[32] For a useful discussion of this topic, *see* Pinizzotto et al., "Law Enforcement Restraint in the Use of Deadly Force Within the Context of 'the Deadly Mix.'"

the driver from the vehicle. He also would have avoided the ineffective deployment of the Taser, which is what led to the driver springing from his vehicle to attack the trooper. In the end, a tactical retreat to wait for backup so they could conduct a felony traffic stop might have avoided the use of deadly force altogether. Although it might be difficult to garner sympathy for a person who attacks a police officer with a seemingly clear attempt to do him serious bodily harm, we must also remember that the police do not punish. The police are obligated to work in ways that minimize the use of force and deadly force so that accused offenders can be brought into open court for scrutiny—and potentially, judgment—by the public criminal justice system.

Use of Force and the Protection of Life

The new idea of police, and its proposed protection of life role, recognizes the necessity of the use of force in policing. As stated elsewhere, the general right to use coercive force is the reason society maintains a police institution, because at any given time, someone might need a coercive intervention to prevent from being harmed. We can recognize the need for policing to maintain its general right to use coercive force, yet we can also work to ensure that policing uses force in ways guided by a philosophy to protect life. Recall from Chapter 4 the discussion of Max Weber and Emile Durkheim and their different conceptualizations of the state. Weber argued the state could be defined as an institution that owned "a monopoly of the legitimate use of physical force" within its defined territory.[33] And it foreshadowed Bittner's conceptualization of the police as "a mechanism for the distribution of situationally justified force in society."[34] Such definitions of the state and the police almost promote forced confrontations between the police and members of the public who do not immediately comply with commands to submit to their authority.

A conceptualization of the police as nothing more than a centralized instrument of state-sanctioned coercive force means that the police institution will focus much of its efforts on developing tactics and strategies designed to gain compliance and control, not allowing for any form of resistance. Recall, for example, Jazmine Headley from Chapter 4, the frightened mother of an infant son who was tackled by four NYPD officers because she first refused to leave a social services agency and then refused to give officers her child. The coercion paradigm, largely grounded in Bittner's and Weber's ideas of police and government, generally cannot fathom resistance as anything other than a reason to amplify the use of coercion.

Recall also Emile Durkheim's approach to defining the state. Durkheim argued that advanced societies, whose members became increasingly fragmented

---

[33] Weber, *From Max Weber: Essays in Sociology*, 78.
[34] Bittner, *The Functions of Police in Modern Society*, 39.

by occupational demands, should find solidarity in the moral actions of their government.[35] For Durkheim, the state was not simply an entity that owned a monopoly on coercive authority; it was to be an institution that promoted the morality of "autonomous" citizens, largely by the way it treated those it labeled deviant.[36] If police officers were trained and socialized to believe that even "deviant" people were their clients, they might approach potentially violent encounters with the mindset that they possessed the moral authority to use, or choose not to use, coercive force during such encounters. Sometimes such moral authority means allowing for some degree of noncompliance without immediately forcing confrontations. If police officers believed that their primary role was to protect life, then they might evolve from the coercion paradigm into one that does more to promote the public good for all subgroups in society. It might also keep police officers from forcing confrontations with people they view as high-risk individuals, which could decrease the use of deadly force.

Some Concluding Observations

The general right to use coercive force is what makes the police "intrinsically good" or "intrinsically dangerous."[37] It is a virtual paradox to argue that by using force, even deadly force under certain circumstances, police officers can protect life. Again, though, it is their coercive authority that gives policing its legitimacy in society. If we are to maintain an armed institution whose primary tool is coercion, then we have an obligation to ensure that it is driven by a value system that emphasizes the minimal use of that coercion. Although Supreme Court cases have identified some of the outer boundaries of the police use of force, they certainly have not provided a standard for which to strive. For that, policing needs a new mandate that moves beyond coercion for the sake of compliance and control. It should emphasize the good the institution can do while minimizing the dangerousness it might otherwise cause. It needs a mandate that drives all encounters between the police and the public—particularly segments of the public that have been historically viewed as "classes" to be controlled by police.

A protection of life mandate is a mindset that can ensure that most police officers do not escalate confrontations to the point where deadly force is necessary, that tactical retreats are sometimes the best alternative to coercion, and that everyone police officers encounter is a client. A protection of life mandate minimizes the emphasis on coercion and coercive force while promoting the intrinsic good the occupation can achieve, even if that "good" comes as the result of the use of force.

---

[35] Durkheim, *Durkheim: The Division of Labour in Society*, 37.
[36] Durkheim, *Rules of Sociological Method*, 70.
[37] Banton, *The Policeman in the Community*.

Questions for Review and Reflection

Question 1. Police Use-of-Force Policies and Matrixes

Despite the case law and statutes that attempt to control the police use of force, police departments should maintain policies that guide officers on when it is appropriate to use force, how much they are allowed to use, and the use-of-force techniques authorized based on suspect resistance.

- In what ways does it matter (or not) where on the use-of-force continuum a police department places a certain use-of-force technique or weapon? For example, is it reasonable for a police department to designate conductive energy weapons (e.g., Tasers) as a pain compliance technique (which are often listed at the empty-hand level) vs. a less-than-lethal technology?
- Considering the typical use-of-force matrix, if suspects set the tone for the potential use-of-force encounter, how can police departments ensure that police officers are correctly, or reasonably, perceiving the degree of resistance the suspect is using?
- Under typical use-of-force policies, when does an officer's use of force become excessive?
- As noted in the chapter, police departments—as a collective armed institution—have an obligation to foster a philosophy on use of force that is guided by a value system emphasizing the minimal applications of force during police–citizen interactions. Why is such a value system important for police departments to nurture? How might such a value system be integrated as a value statement into police departments' use of force policies? What, if anything, does it say about a police department that fails to include a value statement in its use-of-force policy?

Question 2. Objective Reasonableness and the Evaluation of Police Use of Force

As noted in the chapter, in the case *Graham v. Connor*, the Supreme Court held that evaluations of the use of force by police officers had to be conducted from the standpoint of "reasonable" police officers at the scene. The Court was clear that when officials tried to determine the proper or improper use of force by police officers, they were required to do so from the standpoint of any "reasonable" officer at the scene during the event.

- In what ways might the "objective reasonableness" standard favor police officers when others are attempting to determine whether they (the officers) used force properly or improperly?
- Is the objective reasonableness standard simply asking police officers to determine the proper use of force by other police officers? If so, is this the proper standard by which to evaluate the use of force by police? Explain your answers.
- If the objective reasonableness standard too heavily favors police officers, what might be a more neutral standard? Should community members (i.e., people explicitly outside policing) be allowed to help determine the reasonableness of the use of force by a police officer?

Question 3. Unnecessary Use of Force by Police

Unlike excessive force—which can be defined as force disproportionate to a suspect's resistance—unnecessary force is force that was reasonable at the moment of its use, but that could have been avoided had the officer practiced more competent policing.

- Is the concept of unnecessary force important for society to address in policing? Or should society be content with simply classifying force as either justified or excessive? Explain your answer.
- If unnecessary force is important to address and control, how would police use-of-force policies do that? Can police department policies, which rely heavily on a use-of-force matrix to help police officers determine appropriate levels of force, also attempt to control against unnecessary applications of force? Discuss.
- How might a protection of life mandate help reduce unnecessary use of force by police officers?

Exercise

Exercise Comparing Police Department Use of Force Policies

As noted in the chapter, police departments commonly maintain use-of-force policies that help guide officers on the proper use of force under different circumstances. But use-of-force policies can vary greatly in terms of where they place certain techniques or weapons on the use-of-force continuum, what weapons or techniques are allowed, and whether the policies outline a value system that informs the use-of-force policy. For this exercise, you will search the Internet to find and download the use-of-force policies of between 5 and 10 local police departments and then conduct an analysis of the policies to determine their similarities and differences. You will write and submit a report that responds to and incorporates the following items:

- How many of the policies contain a written value statement that guides the use of force? What are some of the common words used in those value statements?
- For the police departments whose policies contain written value statements, create a word cloud that shows the most common words used in those value statements. (A variety of free websites can help you create a word cloud; try the one at https://tinyurl.com/y9vt96as.)

- How many of the policies contain a use-of-force matrix? Among those that include the matrix, in what ways are the matrixes different from or similar to one another?
- How are the use-of-force policies similar to or different from each other in terms of where they place certain weapons or techniques on the use-of-force continuum? For example, do some police departments allow Taser use for mild active resistance, where others allow Taser use only as an alternative to deadly force?
- Do certain police department policies ban certain weapons or techniques where others do not? For example, how many police department use-of-force policies ban the use of carotid restraints, knee to the neck (the technique that killed George Floyd), choke holds, or bar arm restraints?
- How many use-of-force policies mention the de-escalation of force as a specific goal of the agency?
- What do the differences and similarities among the use-of-force policies lead you to conclude about policing and the use of force?
- In what ways might some of the policies discourage the unnecessary use of force as defined in the chapter?

Operations Dashboard Exercise

Load the Philadelphia operations dashboard via QR code on the left, or enter the following URL into a browser window:

https://arcg.is/1v4CiX

For this exercise, you will examine police-involved shootings in Philadelphia as an example of police use of deadly force. Your goals will be to learn about (1) how often police officers in one big city use their firearms, (2) the "types" of communities in which police shootings occur most often, and (3) the extent to which police shootings occur in locations characterized by high crime—especially violent crimes with a firearm. After working with the dashboard and collecting your information, you will write a report that addresses the three points above and that also draws some conclusions about the police use of deadly force in communities and how it might be reduced (at least in terms of police-involved shootings).

To get started, please open the Philadelphia operations dashboard using either the QR code appearing in the box above or by typing the link into a web browser. Once the dashboard loads, take a few minutes to navigate and become familiar with the various data feeds and selection features. By default, the dashboard displays serious crime on the map over the past 30 days. A serial chart is situated below the map, showing the monthly breakdown of crime types over the past year. The right side of the map shows the serious crime feed with the most recent crimes at the top; and on top of the serious crime feed the year-to-date homicide gauge is displayed. The far left side of the map shows serious crimes by category, as well as the year-to-date changes in crime levels by type. Recall that selecting any crime categories, bars in the serial chart, or the date selector across the top panel will change the crime feed and points displayed on the map.

To complete this exercise, you will work with the shootings layer, selecting police-involved shootings, as well as a few additional mapping layers. At the top right of the map, click the Layers button to show the available mapping layers. Point and click to deselect the Serious Crime Incidents (causing the yellow points to disappear from the map) and select the Shooting Victimizations layer, which will begin to populate the map with many red points. Allow the map several seconds to refresh the view. Next, select the Shooting Feed by clicking its tab at the bottom right of the dashboard. Your map should now show shootings as red points, and the data feed along the right panel should show shooting victimizations with the most recent appearing on top. Note that for each shooting victimization, the feed shows the date of the incident; the victim's race, gender, and age; type of wound; whether the shooting was fatal; and whether it was a police shooting.

Move your mouse to the left side of the screen and click either the left or right arrow along the tab on the bottom left to display Shootings data. You will see all shooting victimizations in the feed (roughly 9,500) along with a doughnut chart showing fatal vs. nonfatal shootings. As the data indicate (at the time of this writing), 19.48 percent of all shooting victimizations in Philadelphia were fatal. Clicking the Fatal category in the doughnut chart will filter out all nonfatal shootings on the map and in the shooting feed to the far right. Clicking it again shows all shootings on the map and in the feed. It is now time to refine our shooting selections based on year and officer involvement. To do so, at the far left of the screen (midway down), click the small left arrow that points to the right to open the slide over panel.

Here, under Officer Involved Shooting? select the Yes box. From the Select Shootings by Year drop-down menu, select Shootings in all Years. This will result in a map that shows all police shootings in Philadelphia since the start of 2017. Close the left panel by clicking the arrow and notice that the Shooting Victimization Counts reads (at the time of this writing) 42. As the Philadelphia dashboard updates the crime, shooting, and pedestrian stop feeds in real time, the number of police shootings might be higher than 42.

Now direct your attention to the Shooting Victimization Feed along the far-right panel of the dashboard. You should notice that the feed now only includes police shootings. Scrolling through the feed, you should notice that the police department does not include age, race, and gender of the victim (or "suspect" in police taxonomy) for officer-involved shootings, but the police department does show whether the suspect was injured or killed. Scroll through the feed to get a sense of how many suspects shot by police were killed. Is the percentage of those killed by police higher or lower than for nonpolice shootings? Or is it about the same?

Let us now focus exclusively on the map. To do that, click the map expander button at the very top right corner of the map (above and to the right of the ribbon containing the five map navigation buttons). With the map now displayed in full-screen mode, feel free to recenter it so that Philadelphia is the central view. At this point, you might wish to simplify the map by deactivating the police districts. To do so, click the layer selector button at the top right of the map to deselect the Police Districts layer. You should be left with a view of streets, police shootings, and three major universities in Philadelphia: Temple University (symbolized in red), the University of Pennsylvania (symbolized in blue), and Drexel University (symbolized in yellow).

Notice the distribution of police shootings. In what ways do they cluster? In what ways are they isolated? It is important to point out that in a given year, there are few police shootings in Philadelphia, which is why we must examine almost six years of data just to see 42 (as of this writing) police shootings. Over the past several years, the demographic profiles of the communities in which the shootings mostly took place have not changed much, which means shootings that happened in 2017 were likely driven by similar neighborhood characteristics that exist in 2022.

Now it is time to try to provide some explanation or context for these deadly force events. First, activate the Highly Structurally Disadvantaged Communities map layer. These are the Philadelphia communities characterized by high rates of poverty, unemployment, households receiving public assistance, female-headed households with children, and low rates of high school graduation among the adult population. Taken together, these community factors create an index known as structural disadvantage; that is, communities that are not only poor, but where local residents have few options to achieve upward mobility. Structural disadvantage in an urban context usually predicts poor neighborhood health outcomes,[38] crime and violence,[39] police use of force and deadly force,[40] and even police misconduct.[41]

With the highly structurally disadvantaged communities displayed on the map, notice the extent to which police shootings are (or are not) contained within them. What initial conclusions do you draw about where police shootings have occurred in Philadelphia? Do you see a difference between shootings that appear to be clustered versus those that are more isolated from the others? Does one group of shootings (i.e., clustered, or isolated) tend to fall more inside or outside the structurally disadvantaged communities?

Next, to further refine the social context of police shootings in Philadelphia, activate the Communities at least 51% Black or Brown mapping layer. Once visualized, you will see the extent of Philadelphia's mostly Black and Brown communities. Does visualizing this new layer add clarity to police shootings in Philadelphia? If so, how? What proportion of police shootings fall outside structurally disadvantaged communities and communities of color? Do shootings tend to cluster where structurally disadvantaged and Black and Brown communities intersect with one another? Researchers often refer

---

[38] Kane, "The Ecology of Unhealthy Places: Violence, Birthweight, and the Importance of Territoriality in Structurally Disadvantaged Communities"; Turney and Harknett, "Neighborhood Disadvantage, Residential Stability, and Perceptions of Instrumental Support Among New Mothers"; Cohen, Farley, and Mason, "Why Is Poverty Unhealthy? Social and Physical Mediators"; Do et al., "Does Place Explain Racial Health Disparities? Quantifying the Contribution of Residential Context to the Black/White Health Gap in the United States"; Weisburd and White, "Hot Spots of Crime Are Not Just Hot Spots of Crime: Examining Health Outcomes at Street Segments"; Schempf, Strobino, and O'Campo, "Neighborhood Effects on Birthweight: An Exploration of Psychosocial and Behavioral Pathways in Baltimore, 1995–1996."

[39] Drawve, Thomas, and Walker, "Bringing the Physical Environment Back Into Neighborhood Research: The Utility of RTM for Developing an Aggregate Neighborhood Risk of Crime Measure"; Kurbin and Weitzer, "Retaliatory Homicide: Concentrated Disadvantage and Neighbourhood Culture"; Johnson and Kane, "Deserts of Disadvantage: The Diffuse Effects of Structural Disadvantage on Violence in Urban Communities"; Peterson, Krivo, and Harris, "Disadvantage and Neighborhood Violent Crime: Do Local Institutions Matter?"; Stretesky, Schuckt, and Hogan, "Space Matters: An Analysis of Poverty, Poverty Clustering, and Violent Crime"; Kane, "Compromised Police Legitimacy as a Predictor of Violent Crime in Structurally Disadvantaged Communities"; Sampson, Raudenbush, and Earls, "Neighborhoods and Violent Crime: A Multilevel Study of Collective Efficacy"; Stucky and Ottensmann, "Land Use and Violent Crime"; Thompson and Gartner, *The Spatial Distribution and Social Context of Homicide in Toronto's Neighborhoods*; Vélez, "The Role of Public Social Control in Urban Neighborhoods: A Multilevel Analysis of Victimization Risk."

[40] Renauer, "Neighborhood Variation in Police Stops and Searches: A Test of Consensus and Conflict Perspectives"; Terrill and Reisig, "Neighborhood Context and Police Use of Force"; La Vigne, Fontaine, and Dwivedi, "How Do People in High-Crime, Low-Income Communities View the Police?"; Klinger et al., "Race, Crime, and the Micro-Ecology of Deadly Force."

[41] Kane, "The Social Ecology of Police Misconduct."

to such communities as those characterized by racially concentrated structural disadvantage.[42]

Now activate the Serious Crimes Incidents layer, but let's look at only the crimes that have occurred in the past three months (to help simplify the map display). To do so, select the appropriate date category at the top of the dashboard. Moreover, because police shootings may reflect the overall distribution of violent crime that exists in cities, we should filter out all nonviolent crimes from our map view. To do this, exit the full-screen map view by clicking the small circle in the top-right corner of the map. Next, on the lower left side of the dashboard, click arrows along the tab to see the Crimes by Type doughnut chart. On the chart, select homicide, aggravated assault with firearm, and robbery with firearm. At this point, you might want to reenter the full-screen map view. To what extent does adding the most serious violent crimes to the map help explain the locations of police shootings? There might be areas on the map that have experienced high clustering of violent crime. Where that happens, do you also see police shootings located there?

Based on the visualizations you have made in this exercise, would you conclude that the police use of deadly force is randomly distributed across the city, or do factors such as neighborhood characteristics and the locations of violent crime help explain the locations of police shootings? Do police shootings tend to cluster more in certain police districts than in others? If so, what do you think explains such clustering? What additional information would you need to draw conclusions about (1) why shootings cluster as they do within the city, and (2) the extent to which the police use of deadly force as visualized in Philadelphia is appropriate? Finally, if you noticed that police shootings tend to cluster in certain locations, what do you think that clustering suggests about the relationship—or potential conflict that exists—between the police and local community residents? Can the spatial distribution of the police use of deadly force tell us something about the state of affairs between the police and certain communities? If so, what? And how might a police department repair its relationship with certain communities to reduce deadly force?

---

[42] Johnson and Kane, "Deserts of Disadvantage: The Diffuse Effects of Structural Disadvantage on Violence in Urban Communities."

Bibliography

"5 Responses to a Sovereign Citizen at a Traffic Stop." Accessed July 13, 2021. https://www.police1.com/patrol-issues/articles/5-responses-to-a-sovereign-citizen-at-a-traffic-stop-FZ4ruThuMxTHVgEO/.

"About Us | CALEA® | The Commission on Accreditation for Law Enforcement Agencies, Inc." Accessed June 4, 2021. https://www.calea.org/about-us.

Alpert, Geoffrey P., and Roger G. Dunham. *Understanding Police Use of Force: Officers, Suspects, and Reciprocity.* Cambridge, UK: Cambridge University Press, 2004.

Banton, Michael. *The Policeman in the Community.* New York: Basic Books, 1964. https://books.google.com/books/about/The_Policeman_in_the_Community.html?id=F0NMwQEACAAJ.

Binder, Arnold, and Peter Scharf. "The Violent Police–Citizen Encounter." *The Annals of the American Academy of Political and Social Science* 452 (1980): 111–121.

Bittner, Egon. *The Functions of Police in Modern Society.* Chevy Chase, MD: National Institute of Mental Health, 1970. https://www.google.com/books/edition/The_Functions_of_the_Police_in_Modern_So/rQcXAAAAIAAJ?hl=en&gbpv=1&printsec=frontcover.

Brooks, Connor. "Federal Law Enforcement Officers, 2016—Statistical Tables." Washington, DC, 2019. https://www.bjs.gov/content/pub/pdf/fleo16st.pdf.

Cohen, Deborah A., Thomas A. Farley, and Karen Mason. "Why Is Poverty Unhealthy? Social and Physical Mediators." *Social Science and Medicine* 57, no. 9 (2003): 1631–1641. https://doi.org/10.1016/S0277-9536(03)00015-7.

"Deprivation of Rights Under Color of Law." Accessed July 8, 2021. https://www.justice.gov/crt/deprivation-rights-under-color-law.

Do, D. Phuong, Brian Karl Finch, Ricardo Basurto-Davila, Chloe Bird, Jose Escarce, and Nicole Lurie. "Does Place Explain Racial Health Disparities? Quantifying the Contribution of Residential Context to the Black/White Health Gap in the United States." *Social Science and Medicine* 67, no. 8 (2008): 1258–1268. https://doi.org/10.1016/j.socscimed.2008.06.018.

Drawve, Grant, Shaun A. Thomas, and Jeffery T. Walker. "Bringing the Physical Environment Back into Neighborhood Research: The Utility of RTM for Developing an Aggregate Neighborhood Risk of Crime Measure." *Journal of Criminal Justice* 44 (2016): 21–29. https://doi.org/10.1016/j.jcrimjus.2015.12.002.

Durkheim, Emile. *Durkheim: The Division of Labour in Society.* Edited by Steven Lukes, 2nd ed. London: Palgrave Macmillan, n.d.

Durkheim, Emile. *Rules of Sociological Method.* Edited by Steven Lukes. New York: Free Press, n.d.

"FBI Releases 2019 Participation Data for the National Use-of-Force Data Collection." 2020. https://www.fbi.gov/news/pressrel/press-releases/fbi-releases-2019-participation-data-for-the-national-use-of-force-data-collection.

Federal Bureau of Investigation. "National Use-of-Force Data Collection." Accessed June 11, 2021. https://www.fbi.gov/services/cjis/ucr/use-of-force.

"Federal Bureau of Investigation Crime Data Explorer—Use-of-Force." Accessed June 11, 2021. https://crime-data-explorer.app.cloud.gov/pages/le/uof.

Fyfe, James J. "Administrative Interventions on Police Shooting Discretion: An Empirical Examination." *Journal of Criminal Justice* 7, no. 4 (1979): 303–323. https://www.sciencedirect.com/science/article/pii/0047235279900655.

Fyfe, James, J. "Training to Reduce Police–Civilian Violence." In *Police Violence: Understanding and Controlling the Police Abuse of Force*, edited by William Geller and Hans Toch, 165–179. New Haven, CT: Yale University Press, 1996.

Garner, Joel H., Matthew J. Hickman, Ronald W. Malega, and Christopher D. Maxwell. "Progress Toward National Estimates of Police Use of Force." *PLOS ONE* 13, no. 2 (2018): e0192932. https://doi.org/10.1371/journal.pone.0192932.

Graham v. Connor, 490 U.S. 386 (1989).

Johnson, Lallen T., and Robert J. Kane. "Deserts of Disadvantage: The Diffuse Effects of Structural Disadvantage on Violence in Urban Communities." *Crime and Delinquency* 64, no. 2 (2018): 143–165. https://doi.org/10.1177/0011128716682228.

Kane, Robert J. "Compromised Police Legitimacy as a Predictor of Violent Crime in Structurally Disadvantaged Communities." *Criminology* 43, no. 2 (2005): 469–497. https://doi.org/10.1111/j.0011-1348.2005.00014.x.

Kane, Robert J. "The Ecology of Unhealthy Places: Violence, Birthweight, and the Importance of Territoriality in Structurally Disadvantaged Communities." *Social Science and Medicine* 73, no. 11 (2011): 1585–1592. https://doi.org/10.1016/j.socscimed.2011.08.035.

Kane, Robert J. "The Social Ecology of Police Misconduct." *Criminology* 40, no. 4 (2002): 867–896. https://doi.org/10.1111/j.1745-9125.2002.tb00976.x.

Kane, Robert J., and Shea W. Cronin. "Maintaining Order Under the Rule of Law: Occupational Templates and the Police Use of Force." *Journal of Crime and Justice* 34, no. 3 (2011): 163–177. https://doi.org/10.1080/0735648X.2011.609732.

Karsch, Mitchell W. "Excessive Force and the Fourth Amendment: When Does Seizure End?" *Fordham Law*

Review 58, no. 4 (1990): 823–841. https://ir.lawnet.fordham.edu/flr/vol58/iss4/10.

Klinger, David, Richard Rosenfeld, Daniel Isom, and Michael Deckard. "Race, Crime, and the Micro-Ecology of Deadly Force." *Criminology and Public Policy* 15, no. 1 (2016): 193–222. https://doi.org/10.1111/1745-9133.12174.

Klockars, Carl B. *The Idea of Police*. Thousand Oaks, CA: Sage, 1985.

Kurbin, C. E., and R. Weitzer. "Retaliatory Homicide: Concentrated Disadvantage and Neighbourhood Culture." *Social Problems* 50, no. 2 (2003): 157–180. https://doi.org/10.1525/sp.2003.50.2.157.

La Vigne, Nancy, Jocelyn Fontaine, and Anamika Dwivedi. "How Do People in High-Crime, Low-Income Communities View the Police?" Washington, DC, 2017.

Peterson, Ruth, Lauren Krivo, and Mark Harris. "Disadvantage and Neighborhood Violent Crime: Do Local Institutions Matter?" *Journal of Research in Crime and Delinquency* 37, no. 1 (2000): 31–63. https://doi.org/10.1177/0022427800037001002.

Pinizzotto, A. J., E. F. Davis, S. B. Bohrer, and B. J. Infanti. "Law Enforcement Restraint in the Use of Deadly Force Within the Context of 'the Deadly Mix.'" *International Journal of Police Science & Management* 14, no. 4 (2012): 285–298. https://doi.org/10.1350/ijps.2012.14.4.289.

Reaves, Brian. "Local Police Departments, 2013: Personnel, Policies, and Practices." Bureau of Justice Statistics, Washington, DC, 2015.

Renauer, Brian C. "Neighborhood Variation in Police Stops and Searches: A Test of Consensus and Conflict Perspectives." *Police Quarterly* 15, no. 3 (2012): 219–240. https://doi.org/10.1177/1098611112447746.

Sampson, R. J., S. W. Raudenbush, and F. Earls. "Neighborhoods and Violent Crime: A Multilevel Study of Collective Efficacy." *Science* 277, no. 5328 (1997): 918. https://doi.org/10.1126/science.277.5328.918.

Schempf, Ashley, Donna Strobino, and Patricia O'Campo. "Neighborhood Effects on Birthweight: An Exploration of Psychosocial and Behavioral Pathways in Baltimore, 1995–1996." *Social Science and Medicine* 68, no. 1 (2009): 100–110. https://doi.org/10.1016/j.socscimed.2008.10.006.

Skolnick, Jerome, and James J. Fyfe. *Above the Law: Police and the Excessive Use of Force*. New York: Free Press, 1993.

"Sovereign Citizens Movement | Southern Poverty Law Center." Accessed July 9, 2021. https://www.splcenter.org/fighting-hate/extremist-files/ideology/sovereign-citizens-movement.

Stretesky, Paul B., Amie M. Schuckt, and Michael J. Hogan. "Space Matters: An Analysis of Poverty, Poverty Clustering, and Violent Crime." *Justice Quarterly* 21, no. 4 (2004): 817–841. https://doi.org/10.1080/07418820400096001.

Stucky, Thomas D., and John R. Ottensmann. "Land Use and Violent Crime." *Criminology* 47, no. 4 (2009): 1223–1264. https://doi.org/10.1111/j.1745-9125.2009.00174.x.

Tennessee v. Garner, 471 U.S. 1 (1985).

Terrill, William, and Michael D. Reisig. "Neighborhood Context and Police Use of Force." *Journal of Research in Crime and Delinquency* 40, no. 3 (2003): 291–321. https://doi.org/10.1177/0022427803253800.

Thompson, Sara K., and Rosemary Gartner. "The Spatial Distribution and Social Context of Homicide in Toronto's Neighborhoods." *Journal of Research in Crime and Delinquency* 51, no. 1 (2014): 88–118. https://doi.org/10.1177/0022427813487352.

Turney, K., and K. Harknett. "Neighborhood Disadvantage, Residential Stability, and Perceptions of Instrumental Support Among New Mothers." *Journal of Family Issues* 31, no. 4 (2010): 499–524. https://doi.org/10.1177/0192513X09347992.

"The Use-of-Force Continuum | National Institute of Justice." Accessed May 18, 2021. https://nij.ojp.gov/topics/articles/use-force-continuum#citation--0.

Vélez, María B. "The Role of Public Social Control in Urban Neighborhoods: A Multilevel Analysis of Victimization Risk." *Criminology* 39 (2001): 837–864. https://doi.org/10.1111/j.1745-9125.2001.tb00942.x.

Weber, Max. *From Max Weber: Essays in Sociology*. Edited by H. H. Gerth and C. Wright Mills. London: Routledge, 1991. https://www.amazon.com/Max-Weber-Essays-Sociology-dp-0343212765/dp/0343212765/ref=mt_other?_encoding=UTF8&me=&qid=.

Weisburd, David, and Clair White. "Hot Spots of Crime Are Not Just Hot Spots of Crime: Examining Health Outcomes at Street Segments." *Journal of Contemporary Criminal Justice* 35, no. 2 (2019): 142–160. https://doi.org/10.1177/1043986219832132.

White, Michael D., Justin T. Ready, Robert J. Kane, Carl T. Yamashiro, Sharon Goldsworthy, and Darya Bonds Mcclain. "Examining Cognitive Functioning Following TASER Exposure: A Randomized Controlled Trial." *Applied Cognitive Psychology* 29, no. 4 (2015): 600–607. https://doi.org/10.1002/acp.3128.

Wolf, Ross, Charlie Mesloh, Mark Henych, and L. Frank Thompson. "Police Use of Force and the Cumulative Force Factor." *Policing* 32, no. 4 (2009): 739–757. https://doi.org/10.1108/13639510911000795.

CHAPTER 9

Stop, Question, and Frisk

The Pinnacle in Police Coercion

At 2:30 in the afternoon on a Wednesday in Cleveland, two men stood on the corner of Huron Road and Euclid Avenue discussing something that was unknown to the passersby around them. Periodically, each man would walk alone up Huron Road, past a row of stores, to peer into a particular storefront. Then he would walk back to the corner and once again engage in conversation with the other. This taking turns walking up Huron Road and then returning to the corner to hold a brief discussion happened about 12 times, arousing the suspicion of Cleveland Police Detective Martin McFadden, who had been surreptitiously observing the two men from an adjacent street corner. At one point, a third man joined the other two men on the corner of Huron and Euclid, conferred with them for a few moments, and then retraced his steps back up Euclid Avenue until he was out of sight. Detective McFadden would later testify that the men on the corner of Euclid and Huron "didn't look right to me at the time."[1]

After the third man disappeared up Euclid Avenue, the two original men on the corner of Euclid and Huron resumed taking turns walking up the street to look through the windows of a particular store, then returning to the corner. After doing this a few more times, the two men moved off the corner to walk up Euclid Avenue in the same direction as the third man who had briefly joined them and then left. Detective McFadden suspected that the two men were "casing a job" for "a stick-up" and felt it was his responsibility as a police officer to follow them.[2]

---

[1] Terry v. Ohio, 392 U.S. 1 (1968), 5.
[2] Terry v. Ohio, 392 U.S. 1 (1968), 6.

Trailing behind them, McFadden saw the three men regroup a few blocks up the street, at which point he contacted them. He asked for their names but received a "mumbled" response;[3] from their gestures and general demeanor, McFadden believed one or more of the men might have been armed with a pistol. He spun one of the men around and attempted to pat down his outer clothing for a weapon. Although he felt what seemed to be a pistol in the suspect's overcoat pocket, McFadden was unable to remove it. He shoved all three men inside a store, yanked the overcoat from the suspect's body, and retrieved the gun. He then patted down the other two men and found another pistol on one of them. McFadden placed two men under arrest for carrying concealed weapons and booked them both into jail.[4]

See for Yourself . . .

Scan the QR code to see a 3D Google Map image of the intersection of Huron Road and Euclid Avenue in Cleveland.

The year was 1963. The two suspects were Richard Chilton and John W. Terry. At that moment in U.S. history, it was unclear whether police officers were allowed to conduct so-called pat-down searches of a suspect's outer clothing for weapons without a search warrant. Indeed, just six years earlier, the U.S. Supreme Court had decided *Mapp v. Ohio*. That case affirmed the need for police officers to obtain warrants in most enforcement situations before conducting a search, and even applied the Exclusionary Rule to evidence obtained through police searches deemed unlawful.[5] Thus, it was no surprise that, once Chilton and Terry were convicted of their firearms crimes (their attorney's motion to suppress the guns as illegally obtained evidence was rejected by the trial court), they both appealed the ruling, arguing that Detective McFadden's pat-down search of their outer clothing was illegal because he did not have a search warrant.[6] In December 1967, the Supreme Court heard the case.[7]

As evidenced by the case syllabus, the justices were immediately skeptical of the State of Ohio's defense arguments in which the attorneys suggested that a "stop and frisk" did not constitute a search or seizure under the Fourth Amendment to the Constitution (this was done in an attempt to argue that the provisions in *Mapp* did not apply to Terry's case). In the majority opinion, Chief Justice Earl Warren wrote:

> We emphatically reject this notion. . . . And it is nothing less than sheer torture of the English language to suggest that a careful exploration of the outer surfaces of a person's clothing all over his or her body in an attempt to find weapons is not a "search."[8]

---

[3] Terry v. Ohio, 392 U.S. 1 (1968), 7.
[4] Terry v. Ohio, 392 U.S. 1 (1968), 7.
[5] Mapp v. Ohio, 367 U.S. 643 (1961).
[6] Terry v. Ohio, 392 U.S. 1 (1968), n. 2.
[7] By the time the Court granted certiorari, Richard Chilton had died, leaving John Terry as the sole petitioner. *See* Terry v. Ohio, 392 U.S. 1 (1968), n. 2.
[8] Terry v. Ohio, 392 U.S. 1 (1968), 16.

Warren went on to chastise the State's position by noting:

> [I]t is simply fantastic to urge that such a procedure (stop and frisk) performed in public by a policeman [sic] while the citizen stands helpless, perhaps facing a wall with his hands raised, is a "petty indignity." It is a serious intrusion upon the sanctity of the person, which may inflict great indignity and arouse strong resentment, and it is not to be undertaken lightly.[9]

Nevertheless, in June 1968, and despite its own reticence to do so, the Supreme Court ruled in favor of the State of Ohio, affirming the right of police officers to (1) conduct an "investigatory" stop of a suspect when suspicious of criminal activity, and (2) pat down (or "frisk") the suspect's outer clothing for weapons the officers might believe the suspect is carrying.

Warren's majority opinion was fraught with ideological tension concerning the Constitution, taking pains to emphasize that a "frisk" and a "search" were substantively the same thing—and hence were both regulated by the Fourth Amendment and the Exclusionary Rule as applied to local police in its *Mapp v. Ohio* decision. He also noted, though, that in the context of street-level policing, where officers frequently contacted suspicious individuals who might be armed, it was not always feasible to expect officers to wait to obtain enough probable cause to make an arrest or to secure a warrant before conducting a pat-down search of the outer clothing to ensure their own safety and that of the public.[10] Writing in the gendered language customary of the era, Warren concluded:

> Where a reasonably prudent officer is warranted in the circumstances of a given case in believing that his safety or that of others is endangered, he may make a reasonable search for weapons of the person believed by him to be armed and dangerous regardless of whether he has probable cause to arrest that individual for crime or the absolute certainty that the individual is armed.[11]

Two points in Warren's affirming statement deserve further attention: First, under the *Terry* decision, police officers were now expressly allowed to conduct a pat-down search of a suspect's outer clothing without a search warrant even when the officers did not have enough probable cause to first make an arrest. This means that during an "investigatory" stop, and when evaluating the perceived dangerousness of a suspect, officers were allowed to use a lower evidentiary threshold (i.e., "reasonable suspicion") than they would otherwise need to use for an arrest (i.e., "probable cause"). This is important because when police officers make an arrest, they are allowed to conduct a search of the suspect, as well as the area under the suspect's "immediate control" without a search warrant.[12] Known as a "search incident to

---

[9] Terry v. Ohio, 392 U.S. 1 (1968), 16–17.
[10] Terry v. Ohio, 392 U.S. 1 (1968), 20–27.
[11] Terry v. Ohio, 392 U.S. 1 (1968), 2–3.
[12] Logan, "An Exception Swallows a Rule: Police Authority to Search Incident to Arrest," 391.

arrest," this exception to the warrant requirement of the Fourth Amendment has been affirmed by the Supreme Court across multiple decisions.[13] Thus, allowing police officers to base their stop-and-frisks on reasonable suspicion means that any weapons or other contraband the officers might find during legal pat-down searches can be used to establish probable cause for an arrest. Once the arrest is made, officers are then allowed to conduct a full search incident to that arrest—all of which will be accomplished outside the warrant requirement of the Fourth Amendment, initially triggered by the relatively low evidentiary threshold of reasonable suspicion.

Next, and relatedly, as Warren's opinion in *Terry* made clear, officers did not have to be absolutely certain that the suspects they were stopping and frisking were actually armed and dangerous. The officers just needed to articulate their reasonable suspicion based on the "totality of the circumstances"[14] that the suspects *might* be armed and dangerous. Again, using the "reasonable suspicion" evidentiary threshold gives police officers broad authority to seize a person they believe might be involved in criminal activity and then search their outer clothing if they feel the suspect might be armed or otherwise dangerous. Even if the officers do not recover any weapons during the frisk—as long as the frisk was legal—they can seize any contraband found during the pat-down of the suspect's outer clothing. Officers can then use that contraband (e.g., weapons, drugs, etc.) as probable cause to make an arrest and then conduct a full search of the suspect without a warrant.

The logic of the Court's decision in *Terry* thus begs the question: What factors make a frisk illegal, and what are the consequences of an illegal frisk? To reiterate, the Court in *Terry* imposed a "reasonableness" standard on police officers who wished to conduct an investigatory stop and potential frisk of a suspect. This means that officers were allowed to use their own experiences, as well as the local setting, to help establish reasonable suspicion that "some interrogation should be made" of the suspect(s). But, as the Court also ruled in *Terry*, the reasonableness of the stop must be evaluated separately from the reasonableness of the frisk. As the Court noted, the government's interest in controlling crime is what allows police officers to conduct the investigatory stop, again, as long as the officer has reasonable suspicion of criminal activity. Once the investigatory stop is initiated, the interest transfers from the state to the officer: It is the interest of personal safety that allows officers to conduct a pat-down search for weapons. As Chief Justice Warren noted in his majority opinion, given the number of guns and armed offenders on U.S. streets, as well as the physical "close range" between officers and the suspects they are investigating, it is reasonable to allow officers to conduct a pat-down search if they reasonably feel their safety is threatened.[15] The *Terry*

---

[13] Weeks v. United States, 232 U.S. 383 (1914); Chimel v. California, 395 U.S. 752 (1969); Terry v. Ohio, 392 U.S. 1 (1968).

[14] del Carmen, "Terry v. Ohio," 70.

[15] Terry v. Ohio, 392 U.S. 1 (1968), 25.

decision, therefore, made it relatively easy for police officers to articulate reasonable suspicion to conduct both a stop and a frisk.

A subsequent ruling, however, did define some limits to the lawfulness of pat-down searches. In 1993, the Supreme Court decided the case *Minnesota v. Dickerson,* ruling that a pat-down search that went beyond a search for weapons was not legally justified, rendering any contraband seized as the result of the illegal pat-down inadmissible in court.[16] In *Dickerson*, a police officer conducted an investigatory stop of a person suspected of possessing illegal drugs. During the frisk, which was less about personal safety and more about discovering evidence of a crime, the officer felt something "soft" in the pocket of the suspect. The officer then "squeezed, slid, and otherwise manipulated" the soft item in the pocket, ultimately determining that it was a small bag of crack cocaine.[17] The officer seized the drugs and arrested the person for possession. The officer did not find any weapons and stated in court that he knew the soft object in the suspect's pocket was not a weapon. The Court in *Dickerson* therefore held that the frisk was illegal because searching for something other than weapons during a pat-down search went beyond the original intention of *Terry*, which allowed frisks only out of concern for officer and public safety.[18] Thus, whereas the initial investigatory stop might have been legal, the frisk was not.

Still, and despite *Dickerson's* affirmation of the Court's attempt in *Terry* to limit frisks to searches for weapons, the Court in *Dickerson* did not change anything about the reasonable suspicion evidentiary threshold for frisks. Officers were still allowed fairly broad latitude in forming reasonable suspicion for both an investigatory stop and a frisk. To an extent, and among officers who might wish to abuse the system, a stop-and-frisk conducted under reasonable suspicion can become a kind of "back-door" method for generating probable cause to make an arrest and then conducting a subsequent full search without a warrant.

It is not difficult, therefore, to understand why the Court's majority opinion in *Terry* was so determined to make clear that frisks and searches were guided by the same Fourth Amendment doctrine. Again, writing for the majority, Chief Justice Warren noted:

> The distinctions of classical "stop-and-frisk" theory thus serve to divert attention from the central inquiry under the Fourth Amendment—the reasonableness in all the circumstances of the particular governmental invasion of a citizen's personal security. "Search" and "seizure" are not talismans. We therefore reject the notions that the Fourth Amendment does not come into play at all as a limitation upon police conduct if the officers stop short of something called a "technical arrest" or a "full-blown search."[19]

---

[16] Minnesota v. Dickerson, 508 U.S. 366 (1993).
[17] Minnesota v. Dickerson, 508 U.S. 366 (1993), 337.
[18] Minnesota v. Dickerson, 508 U.S. 366 (1993), 339.
[19] Terry v. Ohio, 392 U.S. 1 (1968), 19.

In plainer language, Warren was putting future attorneys and police officers on notice, making it clear that anyone who would attempt to diminish the intrusiveness and seriousness of a stop-and-frisk by arguing that it does not amount to a "full-blown search" would be making an assumption that is both incorrect and incongruent with Fourth Amendment doctrine. Just because officers may choose, in the end, not to arrest the detainee and conduct a full search incident to that arrest does not mean the initial investigatory stop was *not* subject to the rules of the Fourth Amendment. It was.

Although Earl Warren wrote an unambiguous defense of Fourth Amendment doctrine, he balanced his constitutional perspective against the state's compelling interest to "prevent" and "detect" crime.[20] To that end he noted that, although police officers were typically required to secure a search warrant before conducting a seizure of the person and a subsequent search, there were moments in policing that required officers to take "swift action based upon on-the-spot observations" to make sure the person with whom they were dealing was not armed and dangerous.[21] He acknowledged that street-level policing sometimes required officers to make their best judgments about who was safe, who was a potential threat, and who needed to be detained and potentially searched—all without a warrant. Indeed, Warren's language was so clear in telling police officers that stop-and-frisk was, in limited circumstances, a permissible and sometimes necessary field tactic, that no court since the Warren Court has seriously reconsidered the *Terry* decision for its constitutionality[22]—which is why stop-and-frisk was poised to evolve from a simple officer safety tactic to a full-blown crime control strategy soon after *Terry* was decided. It started just 10 years later.

Stop-and-Frisk: From "One-Off" to Crime Control Strategy

In 1978, scholars James Q. Wilson and Barbara Boland published a law review article in which they argued that policing should move away from "passive" patrol deployments that had been so thoroughly championed by famed police administrator O. W. Wilson[23] throughout the 1950s and 1960s because random patrols were simply ineffective against crime.[24] Instead, Wilson and Boland proposed that "aggressive" patrols, where officers were directed to target certain high-crime communities, would be more likely to reduce crime because police would focus their patrol resources on the most troubled places.[25] Wilson and Boland were quick to note that by

---

[20] Terry v. Ohio, 392 U.S. 1 (1968), 22.
[21] Terry v. Ohio, 392 U.S. 1 (1968), 20.
[22] del Carmen, "Terry v. Ohio," 62.
[23] Wilson, *Police Administration*. Recall, also, the discussion of preventive patrol in Chapter 2.
[24] Wilson and Boland, "The Effect of the Police on Crime," 370.
[25] Wilson and Boland, 370.

"aggressive," they did not mean "hostile." Rather, they argued that an aggressive style of policing would direct officers to make many field contacts with people in high-crime communities in an effort to detect and prevent illegal behaviors. Citing data from a previous San Diego study, Wilson and Boland noted that "field interrogations—or 'street stops'"—had led to significant crime reductions in that city.[26] The era of stop-and-frisk as a crime control strategy had begun.

In 1995, roughly three years after the NYPD implemented its now-infamous "Stop-Question-Frisk" enforcement program, scholars Lawrence Sherman and Dennis Rogan published a study based on an experiment they conducted in Kansas City that seemed to confirm Wilson and Boland's previous arguments about the effectiveness of "aggressive" patrol. In their study, Sherman and Rogan produced evidence that when police focused their enforcement efforts on removing guns from the streets in locations deemed gun-crime "hot spots," gun-related violence was reduced by almost 50 percent during the study period. A centerpiece of the hot-spot patrols was officers conducting "safety frisks" based on *Terry v. Ohio*.[27]

As noted in Chapter 7, since the mid-1990s, many U.S. police departments have implemented crime control strategies based on maximizing the number of field contacts officers make with people residing in, or traversing, certain communities. Those contacts frequently take place in the form of a stop, question, and frisk.[28] Before discussing why a stop-and-frisk program might be problematic—both from a constitutional and from an efficiency perspective—let us first discuss what is meant by a stop-and-frisk program. To a great extent, stop-and-frisk as a crime control strategy is premised on the argument that when police identify high-crime areas of their city, they send officers into those areas to contact as many people as possible who they believe could be engaged in some form of criminal behavior. The theories of *deterrence*, which presumes to reduce crime by creating sanctions (e.g., arrests and sentences) strong enough to discourage would be offenders,[29] and *incapacitation*, which presumes to reduce crime by taking offenders off the street via arrest and incarceration,[30] tend to drive the justifications for a stop-and-frisk approach to crime control.

From a deterrence standpoint, police departments can argue that when their officers enter high-crime communities and engage in aggressive stop-and-frisk practices, they send the message that people carrying guns will

---

[26] Wilson and Boland, 370.
[27] Sherman and Rogan, "Effects of Gun Seizures on Gun Violence: 'Hot Spots' Patrol in Kansas City," 680.
[28] Fagan et al., "Stops and Stares: Street Stops, Surveillance, and Race in the New Policing"; Floyd v. City of New York, 959 F. Supp. 2d 668 - Dist. Court, SD New York (2013); ACLU Pennsylvania, "After Seven Years, Report Shows Philadelphia Police Continue to Illegally Stop and Frisk Pedestrians"; Harris, "Across the Hudson: Taking the Stop and Frisk Debate Beyond New York City"; Meares, "The Law and Social Science of Stop and Frisk"; White and Fradella, *Stop and Frisk: The Use and Abuse of a Controversial Policing Tactic*.
[29] Kennedy, *Deterrence and Crime Prevention: Reconsidering the Prospect of Sanction*; Kane, "On the Limits of Social Control: Structural Deterrence and the Policing of 'Suppressible' Crimes."
[30] Piquero and Blumstein, "Does Incapacitation Reduce Crime?"

likely be caught doing so because they have a high risk of being stopped and frisked. The high levels of perceived risk should discourage would-be offenders from carrying guns or other weapons in public. Fewer guns on the street at any given time can translate into fewer gun crimes in high-crime communities.[31] The incapacitation perspective assumes that when officers enter high-crime neighborhoods and engage in aggressive stop-and-frisk tactics, they will seize guns and arrest the offenders carrying them. These arrests take active offenders off the streets, thereby reducing crime. Whereas the deterrence perspective relies on *discouragement* to reduce crime, incapacitation relies more on the actual removing of offenders from neighborhoods, making it physically impossible for them to commit crimes (at least while they are incarcerated). Deterrence and incapacitation are often viewed as complementary perspectives when considering how best to reduce and prevent place-based crimes.[32]

This is where translating stop-and-frisk from a single event that requires case-by-case justification into an overall crime control strategy becomes legally tricky, however, and this is also where the *Terry* decision becomes relevant again. Recall that the Court in *Terry* set the legal threshold for stop-and-frisk to reasonable suspicion, noting that police officers were allowed to conduct investigatory stops when they observed "unusual conduct" on the street that led them to "conclude in light of . . . (their) . . . experience that criminal activity may be afoot."[33] The Court in *Terry* also noted, though, that police officers must have more than just an "unparticularized suspicion or 'hunch'"[34] that someone might be engaged in criminal activity. They needed something *more* that they could articulate. Thus, if a police officer sees a person standing on a street corner in a high-crime neighborhood, the mere presence of that person does not give the officer enough reasonable suspicion to conduct an investigatory stop—even if the officer assumes that the person is up to no good. Recall that a mere "hunch" that a person might be engaged in criminal activity is not enough to meet the reasonable suspicion threshold for an investigatory stop.

But what if, upon making eye contact with the officer, the person immediately turns away and crosses the street? Does an apparent measure to avoid contact with a police officer constitute "unusual activity" of the sort that can give an officer reasonable suspicion to stop the person? According to the Supreme Court, the answer is a qualified *yes*. This, after all, is almost exactly what happened in Chicago in 1995. Sam Wardlow, holding an opaque bag in one of his hands, was standing on a street corner that was known to police as a heavy narcotics trafficking area. When Mr. Wardlow saw several police vehicles converge on the corner, he immediately ran from the corner

---

[31] Sherman and Rogan, "Effects of Gun Seizures on Gun Violence: 'Hot Spots' Patrol in Kansas City."
[32] For an expanded discussion on deterrence vs. incapacitation, *see* Kane, "On the Limits of Social Control: Structural Deterrence and the Policing of 'Suppressible' Crimes."
[33] Terry v. Ohio, 392 U.S. 1 (1968), 30.
[34] Terry v. Ohio, 392 U.S. 1 (1968), 27.

in an attempt to avoid contact with the officers. Two Chicago police officers chased him in their patrol car and caught up with him in an alley. When they contacted him, one of the officers "conducted a protective patdown [sic] search for weapons because in his experience it was common for there to be weapons in the near vicinity of narcotics transactions."[35] The officers recovered a .38-caliber handgun from the bag and arrested Wardlow on a weapons charge.

Wardlow appealed his subsequent conviction, arguing that the officers did not have enough reasonable suspicion to conduct the investigatory stop in the first place. After all, his attorneys argued, the Court had previously held that people in public places were allowed to "go on one's way" without arousing suspicions of the police.[36] But Chief Justice William Rehnquist, writing for the majority in *Wardlow* disagreed:

> Unprovoked flight is the exact opposite of "going about one's business." While flight is not necessarily indicative of ongoing criminal activity, *Terry* recognized that officers can detain individuals to resolve ambiguities in their conduct.[37]

Wardlow represents a key decision in stop-and-frisk doctrine because in it the Court reaffirmed that police officers could use their knowledge and experience of "high-crime" places as factors that might arouse their suspicion for the purposes of conducting investigatory stops. It also allowed police officers to use "unprovoked flight" in high-crime areas to provide reasonable suspicion for stops. In the end, the combination of *Wardlow*, the vagueness of the language in *Terry v. Ohio* itself, and the Court's 1972 decision in *Adams v. Williams*[38] that allowed police officers to use information obtained from informants to establish reasonable suspicion to conduct an investigatory stop, has given police officers broad authority to articulate the reasonable suspicion needed to conduct investigatory stops.

It is important to keep in mind that the investigatory *stop* and the *frisk* are two different police interventions, both of which are regulated by the Fourth Amendment. For both interventions, however, it is relatively easy for police to articulate enough reasonable suspicion to (1) make the stop, and then (2) conduct the frisk. In both cases, officers are allowed to use their experiences, their knowledge of high-crime and high-drug-trafficking communities, and certain "unusual" behaviors of presumed suspects to conduct stops and frisks. Again, as Rehnquist noted in his majority opinion in *Wardlow*: "*Terry* recognized that officers can detain individuals to resolve ambiguities in their conduct."[39] It is those "ambiguities" that go toward establishing the reasonable suspicion necessary for police to conduct the stop and the frisk. It is the

---

[35] Illinois v. Wardlow, 528 U.S. 119 (2000), 121.
[36] *E.g.*, Florida v. Royer, 460 U.S. 491 (1983).
[37] Illinois v. Wardlow, 528 U.S. 119 (2000), 120.
[38] Adams v. Williams, 407 U.S. 143 (1972).
[39] Illinois v. Wardlow, 528 U.S. 119 (2000), 120.

combination of "ambiguities," police experience, and the otherwise articulated "totality of circumstances" that have allowed stop-and-frisk to evolve from a limited investigation and officer safety tactic into an omnibus crime control paradigm.

What have been the consequences of that paradigm? Throughout the 2000s, multiple studies have demonstrated that stop-and-frisk has had a greatly disproportionate impact on both communities and individuals of color.[40] In communities of color, Black and Brown men have been almost exclusively subjected to stop-and-frisk. In White communities, Black and Brown men have been disproportionately stopped and frisked as being "out of place."[41] Racial disparities have become so apparent across some U.S. cities that civil rights groups have filed federal lawsuits alleging that police departments have violated the Equal Protection Clause of the Fourteenth Amendment by creating patterns and practices that disproportionately place individuals of color at risk of being stopped and frisked.[42] Several of these lawsuits have led to federal oversight of local police departments, with judges requiring the cities to effectively eliminate the racial disparities in their police departments' stop-and-frisk practices. Still, and importantly, no identified court has ruled the stop-and-frisk crime control strategy illegal, per se. But they have ruled that the strategy must be practiced in a more race-neutral manner.

Stop-and-frisk lawsuits alleging violations of the Fourteenth Amendment go beyond some of the Fourth Amendment objections to investigatory stops and frisks. Fourteenth Amendment lawsuits, and the empirical research that supports them, argue that some police departments have taken stop-and-frisk to such an extreme as to create and perpetuate crime control strategies that systematically target and harm young Black and Brown men, both in their home communities and beyond. Legal and empirical findings of clear racial bias in many stop-and-frisk policies have led scholar Tracy Meares to describe such stop-and-frisk practices in terms of "programming errors."[43] Meares argued that today's stop-and-frisk programs go beyond what the Supreme Court

---

40 Jones, "Terry v. Ohio: Its Failure, Immoral Progeny, and Racial Profiling"; Tyler, Jackson, and Mentovich, "The Consequences of Being an Object of Suspicion: Potential Pitfalls of Proactive Police Contact"; Fagan et al., "Stops and Stares: Street Stops, Surveillance, and Race in the New Policing"; Vito, Higgins, and Vito, "Police Stop and Frisk and the Impact of Race: A Focal Concerns Theory Approach"; Fagan and Davies, "Street Stops and Broken Windows: Terry, Race and Disorder in New York City"; Gelman, Fagan, and Kiss, "An Analysis of the New York City Police Department's 'Stop-and-Frisk' Policy in the Context of Claims of Racial Bias"; ACLU Pennsylvania, "After Seven Years, Report Shows Philadelphia Police Continue to Illegally Stop and Frisk Pedestrians"; Harris, "Across the Hudson: Taking the Stop and Frisk Debate Beyond New York City."

41 Meehan and Ponder, "Race and Place: The Ecology of Racial Profiling African American Motorists"; Lundman and Kaufman, "Driving While Black: Effects of Race, Ethnicity, and Gender on Citizen Self-Reports of Traffic Stops and Police Actions"; Renauer, "Neighborhood Variation in Police Stops and Searches: A Test of Consensus and Conflict Perspectives"; Carroll and Gonzalez, "Out of Place: Racial Stereotypes and the Ecology of Frisks and Searches Following Traffic Stops."

42 Floyd v. City of New York, 959 F. Supp. 2d 668 - Dist. Court, SD New York (2013); Collins v. City of Milwaukee, Case No. 17-CV-234-JPS (E.D. Wis. Jun. 14, 2017); Bailey v. City of Philadelphia, Court of Appeals, 3rd Circuit (2010).

43 Meares, "Programming Errors: Understanding the Constitutionality of Stop-and-Frisk as a Program, Not an Incident."

might have envisioned in 1968 when it decided *Terry v. Ohio*. Indeed, Meares argued that when stop-and-frisk moves from a "one-off" event to a crime control program, the assumptions of who gets stopped and frisked change:

> In the program context, police on patrol looking to prevent crime do not seek out particular crimes in progress. Instead, they engage in assessments of suspicious characteristics. . . . Less ideally, the officer will act simply on the basis of suspicious characteristics, making an assumption that anyone who looks a certain way is someone who *could* be a person about to engage in crime.[44]

For Meares, that is where stop-and-frisk as a program begins to push the threshold of what stop-and-frisk was initially intended to accomplish. After all, in *Terry v. Ohio*, Detective McFadden spotted Terry and his two companions engaging in suspicious behaviors that led him to believe they were involved in ongoing criminal behavior. He watched the three men for some time before conducting his investigatory stop, and because he was already suspicious that they were engaged in criminal activity, he conducted his frisk. This is what Meares would call a "one-off" stop-and-frisk, and it was the basis for the Court's decision in *Terry v. Ohio*.

As a crime control strategy, though, stop-and-frisk sends police officers into high-crime and high-drug-trafficking areas to make as many investigatory stops as possible while using factors such as prior police experiences in those areas, local crime conditions, and whether would-be suspects made haste to leave the area when police arrived—all of which can legally arouse suspicion and justify an investigatory stop. The obvious question, of course, is whether police officers can use race as a factor when deciding whether to conduct an investigatory stop. By itself, it seems unlikely because targeting people based strictly on race would seem to directly conflict with the Equal Protection Clause of the Fourteenth Amendment. As legal scholar Rolando del Carmen has written, though, "The more difficult question . . . is whether race can be taken as one factor in the 'totality of circumstances' when determining reasonable suspicion for the purposes of a stop."[45] To date, the courts have yet to resolve this question.

In the end, perhaps no one conveyed it better than Chief Justice Earl Warren in his majority opinion in *Terry v. Ohio*. On one side, Warren and the majority Court sought to preserve constitutional protections by making it clear that stops and frisks were highly intrusive police contacts that potentially tread on the dignity of those being stopped; as such, they needed to be regulated by strict Fourth Amendment doctrine. On the other side, though, Warren made it equally clear that street-level policing was unpredictable, that police officers routinely contacted potentially dangerous characters, that they did not always have time to secure search warrants if they wanted to frisk someone for weapons, and that the state (through

---

[44] Meares, 169.
[45] *See also* del Carmen, "Terry v. Ohio," 70.

the police) maintained a strong and compelling interest in controlling and preventing crime. It is that interest that has perpetuated stop-and-frisk as an important crime control strategy despite the legal challenges to how it is often practiced. This is the dilemma that currently faces many U.S. police organizations.

Identifying the Complexities of the Stop-and-Frisk Paradigm: The Philadelphia Story

Like many U.S. police departments, the Philadelphia Police Department (PPD) implemented a new stop-and-frisk policy in 2007 designed to reduce violent crime in high-violence communities by conducting investigatory stops and safety frisks of individuals suspected of criminal activity. Referring to the situation in Philadelphia as a "crime emergency,"[46] then-mayoral candidate Michael Nutter promised a new stop-and-frisk policy that would be effective against gun violence and homicides, while respecting constitutional constraints.[47] Once Nutter was elected mayor, he directed the police department, under the leadership of his commissioner Charles Ramsey, to implement a stop-and-frisk crime control policy. The effect on police behavior was almost immediate: The PPD went from conducting 136,711 investigatory stops in 2007 to 253,276 stops in 2009[48]—a 60 percent increase in the number of police stops in just two years. These figures include both vehicle and pedestrian stops. Indeed, Commissioner Ramsey was a public proponent of stop-and-frisk, noting to the *New York Times* in 2012 that between 2007 and 2009 when the PPD increased its use of stop-and-frisk to take guns off the street, homicides declined by 20 percent, and "shootings went down."[49]

One problem, though, is that the number of stops does not perfectly reflect the number of individuals being stopped. Numerous court filings and media reports have shown that young Black and Brown men tend to be stopped multiple times in their neighborhoods and beyond.[50] As the data in Philadelphia showed, the vast majority of those stops did not end in an arrest. As a result, the vast numbers of stops and frisks have been concentrated on a somewhat smaller universe of people, which, in the words of Earl Warren in *Terry*, means that mostly young men of color were subjected

---

[46] Goode, "Philadelphia Defends Policy on Frisking, With Limits."
[47] "ACLU-PA and Civil Rights Firm File Class Action Lawsuit Against Philadelphia Police Department for Racial Profiling | ACLU Pennsylvania."
[48] Goode, "Philadelphia Defends Policy on Frisking, With Limits."
[49] Goode.
[50] White and Fradella, *Stop and Frisk: The Use and Abuse of a Controversial Policing Tactic*; ACLU Pennsylvania, "After Seven Years, Report Shows Philadelphia Police Continue to Illegally Stop and Frisk Pedestrians"; Goode, "Philadelphia Defends Policy on Frisking, With Limits"; Huq, "The Consequences of Disparate Policing: Evaluating Stop and Frisk as a Modality of Urban Policing"; Floyd v. City of New York, 959 F. Supp. 2d 668 - Dist. Court, SD New York (2013); Bailey v. City of Philadelphia, Court of Appeals, 3rd Circuit (2010).

to serious indignities and intrusions on their persons at the hands of police, perhaps over and over again.

Moreover, if stop-and-frisk contributed to the reduction in violence, it came at a high social cost for many residents of the city: In 2009, 72.2 percent of stop-and-frisk detainees were African American in a city whose residential population was 44.0 percent African American.[51] Moreover, of the more than 253,000 stop-and-frisks conducted by the PPD in 2009, only 8.4 percent of them led to an arrest.[52] In fact, these disparities led to a federal lawsuit being filed against the City of Philadelphia in 2010, alleging that the PPD violated the Equal Protection Clause of the Fourteenth Amendment by creating a pattern and practice that disproportionately subjected people of color to very high rates of stop-and-frisk. The case, *Bailey v. The City of Philadelphia*,[53] made virtually the same allegations against the PPD as *Floyd v. City of New York*[54] did against the NYPD (recall Chapter 7) in its stop-and-frisk lawsuit.

Ultimately, the *Bailey* case in Philadelphia led to a settlement agreement and federal consent decree that required the police department to reduce its overall numbers of stop-and-frisk activities and to eliminate the racial disparities of stop-and-frisk.[55] Although the city has created strategies designed to comply with the consent decree, it has done so while continuing to rely on stop-and-frisk as an important crime control—and particularly, a gun violence reduction—strategy. Thus, as in many U.S. cities, stop-and-frisk is alive and well in Philadelphia, although with a few caveats about how it is practiced. One of those caveats is that, as part of the monitoring program, the city was required to make much of its stop-and-frisk data publicly available.

An examination of those data for the 2021 calendar year showed that the combined numbers of pedestrian and vehicle stops made by the PPD was 143,976, which is still higher than the baseline level of 2007, but much lower than the numbers of stops when the stop-and-frisk policy ran unabated. It would appear the federal monitoring that took effect as part of the consent decree in *Bailey* has had some success in bringing down the total number of vehicle and pedestrian stops. The arrest rate for calendar year 2021, however, was 7.29 percent, which is a bit lower than the arrest rate during the program's early years. So, although the sheer number of stops has declined over the years, which means fewer intrusions into the lives of mostly African American and Latino young men, the arrest rates, as an indicator of crime control effectiveness, have not moved much.

Investigatory stops and their associated arrest rates tell only part of the story with stop-and-frisk policies, though. The dynamics of sending police

---

[51] "ACLU-PA and Civil Rights Firm File Class Action Lawsuit Against Philadelphia Police Department for Racial Profiling | ACLU Pennsylvania."
[52] "ACLU-PA and Civil Rights Firm File Class Action Lawsuit Against Philadelphia Police Department for Racial Profiling | ACLU Pennsylvania."
[53] Bailey v. City of Philadelphia, Court of Appeals, 3rd Circuit (2010).
[54] Floyd v. City of New York, 959 F. Supp. 2d 668 - Dist. Court, SD New York (2013).
[55] Consent Decree, Bailey v. City of Philadelphia et al. (C.A. No. 10-5952, E.D. Penn, June 21, 2011). Available as Document No. 16, Case 2:10-Cv-05952-SD at https://Aclupa.Org/Sites/Default/Files/Field _documents/Bailey_consent_decree_6-21-11_.pdf.

into neighborhoods, which are usually majority-minority, are multilayered because those also tend to be the high-crime neighborhoods whose residents experience considerable health challenges. To better understand how stop-and-frisk plays out in Philadelphia, which will help us make some inferences about stop-and-frisk as a crime control strategy across many U.S. cities, it is instructive to examine Philadelphia's police and community data, which are presented in the following maps and table. Note that the following analyses include data on just pedestrian stops (meaning they exclude vehicle stops) because pedestrian stops are typically more intrusive and controversial than vehicle stops. Focusing on just pedestrian stops reduces the full stop data set from 143,976 (the figure reported above that includes all stops in 2121) to 13,349 pedestrian stops.

Figure 9.1 is a map showing the spatial distribution of pedestrian stops conducted by the PPD from January 1 to December 31, 2021 (most current year as of this writing). Although it is somewhat difficult to fully appreciate the clustering, given the sheer number of points on the map (n = 13,349 stops), the point distribution indicates that most stops were conducted near the center of the city and somewhat south, as well as in the southwest section of the city. The map also shows that most stops were of Black or African American individuals, followed in numbers by White and then Latino individuals, respectively.

Figure 9.1 ▶

Map of Pedestrian Stops Made by the Philadelphia Police Department During 2021

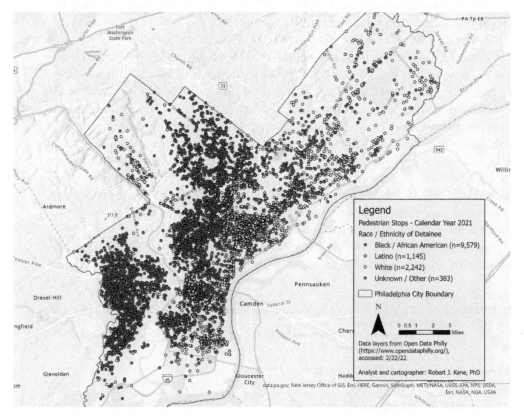

In addition to showing the number and racial and ethnic composition of investigatory pedestrian stops and their spatial distribution throughout the city, it is also important to highlight racial differences at different decision points in the pedestrian stops. Table 9.1 shows the progression of stop events by racial and ethnic groups, beginning with counts of stops by group, then showing the percentages of those frisked, how often contraband (illegal substances, devices, and weapons) was found, and finally, the percentages of stops that resulted in arrests by group.

The data in Table 9.1 show that in terms of the racial or ethnic composition of stops, Black or African American "detainees" represented 71.76 percent of all pedestrian stops in Philadelphia. This is despite the fact that African Americans make up 44.10 percent of the residential population, demonstrating an almost 28 percent racial mismatch between stops and African American representation in the population. Latino detainees represented 8.58 percent of all pedestrian stops while making up 13.60 percent of the overall city population; White detainees made up 16.80% of the total while representing 35.80% of the city's population. White and Latino detainees were statistically underrepresented in terms of pedestrian stops, whereas Black detainees were substantially overrepresented. This disparity persists despite 10 years of federal monitoring as part of the federal lawsuit.

Setting aside the disparities in who gets stopped (which we will examine more fully below), it is instructive to examine the logical next steps in the stop-and-frisk progression: Who gets frisked, who is identified as possessing contraband, and who gets arrested? As the data in Table 9.1 show, Black detainees were frisked 25.41 percent of the time they were stopped. This means that police officers not only had to articulate reasonable suspicion for the investigatory stop, but also had to justify conducting a pat-down search for weapons in about a quarter of all stops of Black detainees. For Latino

Table 9.1. Stop, Frisk, and Arrest by Racial and Ethnic Groups in Philadelphia for 2021

Race or Ethnicity of Detainee	Total Number of Stops by Group	Percentage of Detainees Frisked	Percentage of Stops When Contraband Was Found	Percentages of Detainees Arrested
Black or African American	9,579 (71.76%)	25.41%	12.67%	34.92%
White	2,242 (16.80%)	19.40%	12.28%	34.57%
Latino	1,145 (8.58%)	29.34%	15.81%	40.52%
Unknown or other	383 (2.87%)	24.01%	12.01%	38.38%

Note: Data from https://www.opendataphilly.org/ (Vehicle & Pedestrians data file).

detainees, that number was higher, with a 29.34 percent frisk rate. At 19.40 percent, White detainees had the lowest frisk rates. What explains these frisk rates? Is it that police officers believed they were dealing with dangerous persons more frequently when they stopped persons identified as Latino, as compared to those identified as African American or White? Recall the case law around stop-and-frisk, which allows officers to use their experience and knowledge of local crime rates to justify not just the stops, but also the frisks. But are officers also using race and ethnicity to help guide their decisions? The current data cannot answer that question.

Despite the high frisk rates for African American and Latino detainees, police found contraband—that is, illegal substances, devices, and weapons—in just 12.67 percent and 15.81 percent of stops of Black and Latino detainees, respectively. It is tempting to use "frisks" as the denominator when examining how often contraband was found as the result of a frisk. The problem is that many individuals were both frisked and searched, leaving no way to determine whether contraband was found as a result of a frisk or a search. Also, because contraband includes weapons, there was no way to determine how often frisks led to the recovery of guns or other weapons. As such, the denominator remains "stops" throughout the analysis.

For White detainees, the contraband "hit rate" was just 12.28 percent. That is, of all people stopped and ultimately frisked, police on average found contraband in 1 out of every 12 stops.

Finally, Table 9.1 shows the percentage of stops that resulted in arrest. At 40.52 percent, Latino detainees were arrested at higher rates than Black or White detainees. Indeed, Black and White detainees were arrested at nearly identical rates: 34.92 and 34.57 percent, respectively. These arrests rates might seem high, and perhaps even incongruent with the contraband "hit" rates per group, but it is important to point out that not all pedestrian stops are conducted based on chance encounters between police officers and suspects. In any policing context, some number of pedestrian stops are the result of officers recognizing individuals who have warrants out for their arrest.

Let us now synthesize the information we have examined. First, by inspecting the map in Figure 9.1, it is apparent that investigatory stops are not normally (or randomly) distributed throughout the city. They tend to concentrate in certain areas, and that concentration—as we shall see below—is driven by a few different factors, such as racial composition of communities and violent crime rates. Moving on from the stops themselves, though, we see that only about a quarter of Black detainees were frisked, and well under a third of Latino detainees were frisked. This can indicate that, for the vast majority of stops, the person(s) with whom the police were dealing could verbally "resolve ambiguities in their conduct"[56]—in the words of Chief Justice William Rehnquist in his *Wardlow* opinion—satisfactorily enough that officers did not feel compelled to pat them (the detainees) down for weapons.

---

[56] Illinois v. Wardlow, 528 U.S. 119 (2000), 120.

Such a finding raises questions about the importance of conducting so many stops in the first place.

Moreover, does the fact that, on average, the police found illegal substances, materials, and weapons in only 12.91 percent of all pedestrian stops suggest that the deterrence argument that justifies stop-and-frisk is correct? That is, do all the stops that police conduct—finding contraband in just 12.91 percent of them—mean that police have sent the signal that when walking through public space in certain places, people can expect to be stopped and potentially frisked, which might discourage them from carrying illegal items, such as weapons? If so, to the extent that stop-and-frisk is effective, is it efficient? It would seem that having to conduct 100 investigatory stops just to find contraband in 12 to 13 of those stops raises questions about the use of police resources and the sustainability of creating high-risk environments for would-be offenders.

Moving on to arrests that result from investigatory stops, we see a somewhat higher hit rate. Recall that the arrest rate for all stops—vehicle and pedestrian—in Philadelphia over 2021 was 7.29 percent. In this exercise, however, we only examined the arrest rates for pedestrian stops. Overall, 35.44 percent of all pedestrian stops in Philadelphia resulted in an arrest. For Black detainees, the rate was 34.92 percent; for Latino detainees, the rate was 40.52 percent; and for White detainees, the rate was 34.57 percent. The arrest rates can be highly misleading, though, because, despite that stop-and-frisks are often viewed as discretionary police enforcement activities (recall Chapter 7), they are also driven in part by arrest warrants. It is much easier for officers to recognize people wanted on warrants when they are walking on a sidewalk as opposed to riding in a vehicle. So, although many investigatory stops are the result of "sight"—that is, officers eyeing someone they view as suspicious and then stopping them—a significant proportion of investigatory stops are directed by arrest warrants that officers bring from the roll call room into neighborhoods. To some extent, many of the stops and arrests are predetermined by orders to arrest certain people who might be traversing public space. Unfortunately, Philadelphia's public data do not distinguish between "mere encounter" (i.e., discretionary) and "directed" (i.e., based on warrants) investigatory stops, which means the arrest rates as a result of those pedestrian stops is inflated. So, although Philadelphia's stop-and-frisk strategy takes about a third of all detainees off the street via arrest, some proportion of those arrests are nondiscretionary on the part of the officer.

We now turn toward trying to understand the spatial distribution of investigatory stops in Philadelphia. Whereas the previous analysis examined who was stopped, the next analysis examines where the majority of pedestrian stops were conducted in 2021.

Figure 9.2 shows the results of a density analysis of pedestrian stops in Philadelphia. Density map surfaces are useful when an analyst is working with many points (e.g., pedestrian stops) on a two-dimensional mapping surface. Points on a map show spatial distribution, but they do not show density—or when the points overlap with each other. In Figure 9.1,

Figure 9.2 ▶

Pedestrian Stop
Densities in
Majority Non-
White Commu-
nities for 2021

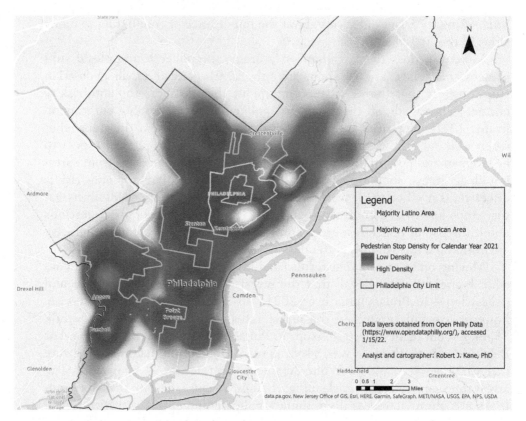

for example, although the map shows the spatial arrangement of pedestrian stops across Philadelphia, it does not show the extent to which points may be piled on top of each other due to multiple stops occurring at the same location at different times. Conducting a density analysis[57] solves this issue by creating an invisible grid over the geography (in this case, the city of Philadelphia), then adding the points to the cells of the grid. The more points (or pedestrian stops) a cell gets, the denser it becomes. The densities are displayed in terms of color bands on the map (similar to weather maps commonly seen in news broadcasts).

The density surface shown in Figure 9.2 generally aligns with the thick distribution of points shown in Figure 9.1. The bright yellow and red bands show the boundaries of high and medium pedestrian stop densities and then gradually move outward in a concentric pattern with the bands becoming shades of purple and blue. The question is this: What explains those densities?

Figure 9.2 also shows the blue outline of majority African American communities (i.e., those containing at least 51 percent African American residents) in Philadelphia overlaying the pedestrian stop density surface. As the

---

[57] Specifically, the maps in Figure 9.2 show the results of a kernel density function, completed in Esri ArcGIS Pro, v. 2.8.

map shows, communities made up of majority African American residents overlap with large swaths of medium- to high-density areas of pedestrian stops. The fact that the blue bands do not reach the edges of all African American communities does not mean that there were no pedestrian stops conducted there. It just means those areas were not dense enough in the number of stops to fall within the outer bands. Still, it is important to note that 8,780, or 52.05 percent, of all pedestrian stops occurred within the confines of those majority African American communities. Put another way, Philadelphia covers an area of 141 square miles, and the majority African American communities cover 46.05 square miles. Thus, 32.66 percent of Philadelphia's land mass accounted for 52.05 percent of all pedestrian stops. This does not mean that everyone stopped in majority African American communities was Black or African American. It means that the PPD focused much of its stop-and-frisk efforts in that concentrated location. Still, taken in combination, Figures 9.1 and 9.2 suggest that the PPD's stop-and-frisk program has been heavily focused on majority African American communities, which helps explain why almost 72 percent of all pedestrian stop detainees were African American.

Figure 9.2 also includes the outline of majority Latino communities (i.e., those that are at least 51 percent Latino) overlayed on the density surface. Note that, despite its relatively small geographic area, the majority Latino communities overlap almost perfectly with the area that contains the highest density of pedestrian stops. During 2021, the PPD made 2,464 pedestrian stops in the majority Latino communities, accounting for 14.61 percent of all stops made in the city. Placing these stops into geographic context, the majority Latino communities cover 6.53 square miles, which means that 4.6 percent of Philadelphia's land mass accounted for 14.61 percent of all pedestrian stops. Again, this does not mean that every person stopped in the majority Latino area was Latino. It means that the PPD made a disproportionate number of pedestrian stops in communities that were at least 51 percent Latino.

Figures 9.1 and 9.2 show two different ways of examining the racial and ethnic dynamics of pedestrian stops in Philadelphia. The data in Figure 9.1 show who was stopped and where they were stopped, irrespective of neighborhood racial composition. It represents an individual-level examination of stop-and-frisk by the race and ethnicity of those who were stopped. Figure 9.2 shows the densities of pedestrian stops made in majority African American and majority Latino communities. Figure 9.2 shows that the highest density of pedestrian stops occurred in majority Latino communities, and to a somewhat lesser extent in majority African American communities. Regardless of how we examine the dynamics of pedestrian stops in Philadelphia, the data clearly suggest that both individuals of color and communities of color have been the major focus of the PPD stop-and-frisk program.

Based on the preceding discussion, it might seem easy to conclude that stop-and-frisk in Philadelphia is a racist crime control strategy designed to intrude primarily into Black and Brown communities. Like in many cities, though, the issue of race and pedestrian stops in Philadelphia is complicated by other social-ecological factors, such as violent crime and the overall health of the communities. For this reason, it is useful to consider additional analyses, such as those below.

Figure 9.3 is a map visualization that shows pedestrian stop densities in Philadelphia (as in Figure 9.2) overlayed with shooting victimizations during the same time period. During 2021, Philadelphia experienced 2,290 shooting victimizations. These are more than just firearms discharges or shooting incidents where the bullet failed to strike a human target. They are all shootings that found human victims, and they carried a fatality rate of 21 percent. There is perhaps no more serious indicator of community-level violence than shooting victimizations because they represent one of the most lethal forms of violence in U.S. society: violence at the barrel of a firearm. As noted, 21 percent of these shootings would ultimately become homicides, and many others—although nonfatal—would have multiple victims and in some cases, multiple wounds per victim.

As the data in Figure 9.3 show, shooting victimizations overlay almost perfectly with pedestrian stop densities. It is clear that the vast majority of the shootings occur within the mid- to high-density bands of the pedestrian stops. Thus, by extension, and referring to Figure 9.2, the shooting victimizations also align very closely with the boundaries of communities that

Figure 9.3 ▶

Pedestrian Stop Densities and Shooting Victimizations in Philadelphia for 2021

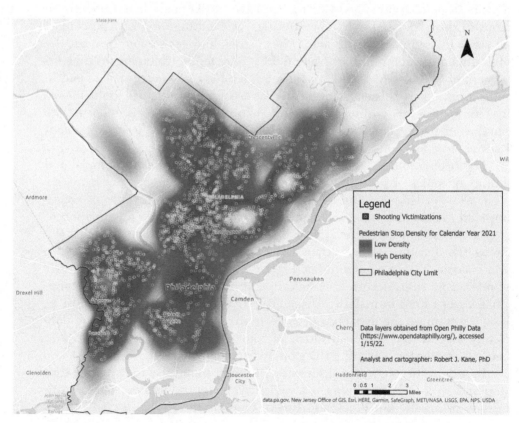

are majority non-White. Thus, although the Philadelphia Police Department tends to focus its stop-and-frisk activities on majority non-White communities, these are the same communities that experience the highest levels of community violence—that is, the very places where a crime-fighting institution would expect to focus its enforcement resources. The story of stop-and-frisk in Philadelphia is even more nuanced than that, however, as the visualization in Figure 9.4 shows.

Figure 9.4 includes the same information as Figure 9.3, but with the addition of data on early childhood risk communities. In 2012 (and updated in 2017), the City of Philadelphia, in partnership with the University of Pennsylvania, conducted a records search to count the number children between birth and five years old who had experienced early childhood risk factors. The risks were compiled to the neighborhood level, allowing researchers and analysts to examine communities in which children during their earliest formative period experienced any of the following, either in utero or after birth: low birthweight or preterm birth, inadequate prenatal care, teen mother, low maternal education level, homelessness, high blood lead levels, and child maltreatment. For the map in Figure 9.4, only the neighborhoods in which at least 25 percent of the resident children from birth to five years old experienced at least three risk factors are displayed. These would be considered among the most health-compromised, at-risk communities in the entire city.

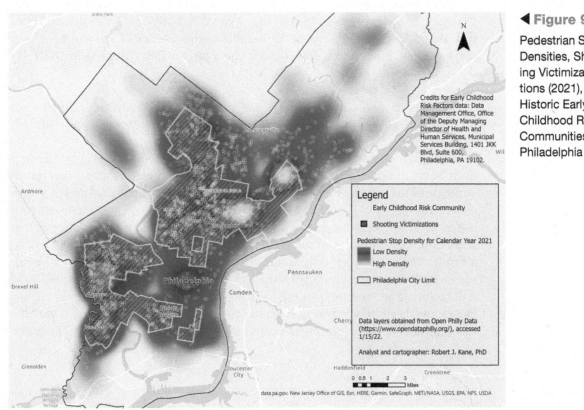

◀ **Figure 9.4**

Pedestrian Stop Densities, Shooting Victimizations (2021), and Historic Early Childhood Risk Communities in Philadelphia

As the data in Figure 9.4 show, the early childhood risk communities almost perfectly encompass all geographic areas containing shooting victimizations in Philadelphia. They also substantially overlap with stop-and-frisk activities; by extension, their borders align almost perfectly with the communities that are at least 51 percent African American and Latino (i.e., Figure 9.2). In short, the most health-compromised and physically dangerous communities in the city, which also contain most of the communities that are at least 51 percent non-White, are where the PPD focuses its stop-and-frisk crime control efforts. Again, there are significant racial disparities in stop-and-frisk, but there are equally significant racial disparities in terms of exposure to violence and compromised health. All of this makes stop-and-frisk in any urban police department in the United States both a challenge and an opportunity.

Some Concluding Observations

As the title of this chapter suggests, stop-and-frisk represents the pinnacle of police coercion for a variety of reasons. First, it is pervasive and deceptively intrusive. Stop-and-frisk activities tend to be concentrated in communities marginalized by racial segregation and high crime, which are essentially hidden away from most members of society. As a mostly discretionary police practice, stops and frisks can seem to an outsider an innocuous crime control measure—an "easy" way to get guns off the street. Stop-and-frisk is more than just an enforcement strategy, however; it is a policy of formal social control aimed largely at the most vulnerable communities of color. Pedestrian stops are not innocuous. To reiterate the words of Earl Warren in the *Terry* decision, stop-and-frisk

> is a serious intrusion upon the sanctity of the person, which may inflict great indignity and arouse strong resentment, and it is not to be undertaken lightly.[58]

Although stop-and-frisk has been shown to produce modest crime reductions in small-scale locations,[59] it is nevertheless inefficient as a crime control strategy, as the data in Figure 9.1 demonstrate. Any crime reductions it brings come at a high social cost. Moreover, given that violent crime often concentrates in urban communities of color (as the Philadelphia data showed), it seems difficult to believe that if the police continue to use stop-and-frisk as a crime control strategy that racial disparities will ever go away. So, why not reconceptualize the meaning of stop-and-frisk? Given that violence, childhood risk factors, and race tend to concentrate in the same communities, it seems like an overly simplistic proposition to expect the police to fight crime in those neighborhoods while ignoring the other social factors that likely drive the crime

---

[58] Terry v. Ohio, 392 U.S. 1 (1968), 16–17.
[59] Weisburd et al., "Do Stop, Question, and Frisk Practices Deter Crime? Evidence at Microunits of Space and Time."

rate in the first place. In that way, a reimagined version of stop-and-frisk, more than anything else, seems like an opportunity for the police to make a positive impact on highly vulnerable communities.

As evidenced by the map in Figure 9.1, it is clear that the Philadelphia Police Department (like others around the country) have the time and resources to devote to stop-and-frisk, given the more than 16,000 pedestrian stops the PPD made in 2021. Although the police represent society's primary crime control institution, not every contact between a police officer and member of the public needs to be a crime-related event. As the title of this book might suggest, stop-and-frisk can evolve from a crime control-centric strategy to one that makes the protection of life its primary goal. For example, rather than refer to them as pedestrian or investigatory stops, perhaps we might refer to them instead as SAFE stops, which would deemphasize coercion and control in favor of a SAFE mentality:

- **Service:** Recognizing that the primary goals of a police officer are to provide service to communities and to approach everyone as if they are a client.

- **Assessment:** Bringing more than just a law enforcement mentality into communities by assessing the needs of everyone who lives there. Through assessment, police can decide how best to use their coercive authority to improve life for the residents of vulnerable communities.

- **Foster:** Interacting with members of the public in ways that demonstrate respect for communities and the people who live there, including the people involved in criminal activity. Fostering respect means that community members will trust officers and cooperate with them when needed.

- **Enforcement:** Using their authority when necessary to respond to crime, make arrests, and even use force when the circumstances demand it.

The idea of SAFE stops is not to bring a new program into policing so much as to help police officers reorder the importance they place on the goals of contacting people in neighborhoods. A SAFE stop mentality is a recognition that, yes, police might be entering a high-crime or high-violence community, but they do so as visitors, and they should recognize that crime is generated by something other than the compromised morality of the people who live there. The only way a reimagining of stop-and-frisk into something like a SAFE stop mentality would work, though, is if police departments changed their recruiting practices to attract people with an up-front belief that the police can be more than just crime fighters. Then police academies would have to train recruits to regard police–citizen contacts as more than just opportunities to find guns and drugs, and to actually provide public service to all residents of the community. Finally, for a SAFE stop mentality to be integrated into the operations of policing, new police officers would have to be socialized by veteran officers to believe in the values of service, assessment, fostering, and enforcement.

As a police tactic, stop-and-frisk will not go away, nor should it. Police and the public rely on stop-and-frisk as a way of allowing police to detain people for the purposes of conducting cursory investigations of potential criminal behavior and to conduct pat-down searches when they feel the person might be dangerous. As a strategy (which is very different from a tactic), though, stop-and-frisk can be revised in ways that continue to leverage police resources to contact people in vulnerable communities, but to do so with a broad range of goals in mind, all of which could be driven by a protection of life mandate.

There were 13,349 pedestrian stops in Philadelphia in 2021. Just 13 percent of those stops produced contraband, including weapons. As a crime control strategy, stop-and-frisk is inefficient, but it presents a great opportunity for a new way of thinking about police-public contacts in high-crime, high-vulnerability communities. We return to stop-and-frisk and the concept of SAFE stops in the final chapter of this book when discussing how a protection of life mandate might be applied to policing places and policing people.

Questions for Review and Reflection

Question 1. The Warren Court's Reticence

The Supreme Court under Chief Justice Earl Warren (1953–1969) has been popularly credited (or criticized, depending on one's point of view) with advancing the so-called due process revolution through the 1960s. It was during the 1960s that the Warren Court decided several landmark cases, such as *Mapp v. Ohio* (1961), *Gideon v. Wainwright* (1962), *Miranda v. Arizona* (1966), and *Loving v. Virginia* (1967), all of which dealt with criminal procedure, applying rights to counsel, and due process protections to all state-level defendants. *Terry v. Ohio* (1968) can be viewed as a kind of exception to the due process body of law the Warren Court created because it favored the state by recognizing the state's interest in reducing and detecting crime and the safety of

police officers who routinely contacted potentially dangerous suspects.

- From the materials presented in this chapter, and particularly Earl Warren's quotes taken from his majority opinion in the *Terry* case, would you conclude that Chief Justice Warren was reluctant to decide the *Terry* case in favor of the State of Ohio? Whether you conclude yes or no, explain your reasoning.
- In what ways did Earl Warren view stop-and-frisk as an "intrusion" into the lives of people living in communities? How did his belief in the intrusiveness of stop-and-frisk appear to influence his rationale in deciding *Terry v. Ohio*?
- What was Warren's rationale for rejecting the argument that an investigatory stop and safety frisk were not subject to the Fourth Amendment's warrant requirements?

Question 2. A Possible "Back Door" to Illegal Searches

As noted in the chapter, the evidentiary standard for stop-and-frisk is reasonable suspicion, which is recognized as a lower standard than that necessary for arrest—that is, probable cause. Police officers who have reasonable suspicion that a person (or persons) is involved with criminal activity can conduct a brief investigatory stop to resolve "ambiguities" in their suspicious behaviors. If, during the course of the investigatory stop, officers have reasonable cause to believe the person (or persons) is armed with a weapon, they may conduct a pat-down search.

- What is the difference in extent between a pat-down search (i.e., a frisk) and a search incident to an arrest?
- How might police officers use an investigatory stop and safety frisk as a way of ultimately skirting the probable cause requirement for arrests and searches incident to arrest?

Question 3. From "One-Offs" to a Crime Control Strategy: The Presumed Value of Stop-and-Frisk

The history of stop-and-frisk shows that within 10 years of the *Terry v. Ohio* decision, police departments began adopting stop-and-frisk as a crime control strategy. Although a federal court of appeals in 2013 found that the NYPD's stop-and-frisk policy violated the constitutional rights of racial minorities, stop-and-frisk remains an important crime control strategy for many U.S. police departments.

- How has the U.S. Supreme Court helped police officers use locations to help establish reasonable cause for an investigatory stop?
- Is stop-and-frisk an effective crime control strategy? What do the data from the Philadelphia case study show?
- Is stop-and-frisk efficient? Why or why not?
- In what ways might stop-and-frisk as a crime control strategy represent a missed opportunity for police officers in communities?
- What must change in policing before police departments will adopt a SAFE stop mentality?

Exercises

Exercises for this chapter can be found in the instructor's manual that accompanies this textbook (see AspenPublishing.com/Kane-Policing).

Bibliography

"ACLU-PA and Civil Rights Firm File Class Action Lawsuit Against Philadelphia Police Department for Racial Profiling | ACLU Pennsylvania." 2010. https://live-aclu-pennsylvania.pantheonsite.io/en/press-releases/aclu-pa-and-civil-rights-firm-file-class-action-lawsuit-against-philadelphia-police.

ACLU Pennsylvania. "After Seven Years, Report Shows Philadelphia Police Continue to Illegally Stop and Frisk Pedestrians." 2018. https://www.aclupa.org/en/press-releases/after-seven-years-report-shows-philadelphia-police-continue-illegally-stop-and-frisk.

Adams v. Williams, 407 U.S. 143 (1972).

Ariel, Barak, Lawrence W. Sherman, and Mark Newton. "Testing Hot-Spots Police Patrols Against No-Treatment Controls: Temporal and Spatial Deterrence Effects in the London Underground Experiment." *Criminology*, August (2019): 101–128. https://doi.org/10.1111/1745-9125.12231.

Bailey v. City of Philadelphia, Court of Appeals, 3rd Circuit (2010).

Braga, Anthony A., Andrew V. Papachristos, and David M. Hureau. "The Effects of Hot Spots Policing on Crime: An Updated Systematic Review and Meta-Analysis." *Justice Quarterly* 31, no. 4 (2014): 633–663. https://doi.org/10.1080/07418825.2012.673632.

Carroll, Leo, and M. Lilliana Gonzalez. "Out of Place: Racial Stereotypes and the Ecology of Frisks and Searches Following Traffic Stops." *Journal of Research in Crime and Delinquency* 51, no. 5 (2014): 559–584. https://doi.org/10.1177/0022427814523788.

Chimel v. California, 395 U.S. 752 (1969).

Collins v. City of Milwaukee, Case No. 17-CV-234-JPS (E.D. Wis. Jun. 14, 2017).

Consent Decree, Bailey v. City of Philadelphia et al. (C.A. No. 10-5952, E.D. Penn, June 21, 2011). Available as Document No. 16, Case 2:10-Cv-05952-SD at https://Aclupa.Org/Sites/Default/Files/Field_documents/Bailey_consent_decree_6-21-11_.pdf.

del Carmen, Rolando V. "Terry v. Ohio." In *Criminal Procedure and the Supreme Court: A Guide to the Major Decisions on Search and Seizure, Privacy, and Individual Rights*, edited by Rolando V. del Carmen and Craig Hemmens, 57–74. Lanham, MD: Rowman and Littlefield, 2010.

Fagan, Jeffrey, Anthony Braga, Rod Brunson, and April Pattavina. "Stops and Stares: Street Stops, Surveillance, and Race in the New Policing." *Fordham Urban Law Journal* 43, no. 3 (2016): 539.

Fagan, Jeffrey, and Garth Davies. "Street Stops and Broken Windows: Terry, Race and Disorder in New York City." *Fordham Urban Law Journal* 28 (2000): 457–504. https://doi.org/10.2139/ssrn.257813.

Florida v. Royer, 460 U.S. 491 (1983).

Floyd v. City of New York, 959 F. Supp. 2d 668 - Dist. Court, SD New York (2013).

Gelman, Andrew, Jeffrey Fagan, and Alex Kiss. "An Analysis of the New York City Police Department's 'Stop-and- Frisk' Policy in the Context of Claims of Racial Bias." *Journal of the American Statistical Association* 102, no. 479 (2007): 813–823. https://doi.org/10.1198/016214506000001040.

Goode, Erica. "Philadelphia Defends Policy on Frisking, With Limits." *The New York Times*, July 12, 2012. https://www.nytimes.com/2012/07/12/us/stop-and-frisk-controls-praised-in-philadelphia.html.

Hallak, Maram, Kathryn Quina, and Charles Collyer. "Preventing Violence in Schools." In *Violence in Schools: Cross-National and Cross-Cultural Perspectives*, edited by Florence Denmark, Herbert H. Krauss, Robert W. Wesner, Elizabeth Midlarsky, and Uwe P. Gielen, 275–292. New York: Springer, 2005. https://doi.org/10.1007/0-387-28811-2_14.

Harris, David A. "Across the Hudson: Taking the Stop and Frisk Debate Beyond New York City." *New York University Journal of Legislation and Public Policy* 16, no. 853 (2013): 1–24.

Huq, Aziz Z. "The Consequences of Disparate Policing: Evaluating Stop and Frisk as a Modality of Urban Policing." *Minnesota Law Review* 101, no. 6 (2017): 2397–2480.

Illinois v. Wardlow, 528 U.S. 119 (2000).

Jones, Russell L. "Terry v. Ohio: Its Failure, Immoral Progeny, and Racial Profiling." *Idaho Law Review* 54, no. 2 (2018): 511–542.

Kane, Robert J. "On the Limits of Social Control: Structural Deterrence and the Policing of 'Suppressible' Crimes." *Justice Quarterly* 23, no. 2 (2006): 186–213. https://doi.org/10.1080/07418820600688768.

Kennedy, David M. *Deterrence and Crime Prevention: Reconsidering the Prospect of Sanction*. New York: Routledge, 2012.

Logan, Wayne A. "An Exception Swallows a Rule: Police Authority to Search Incident to Arrest." *Yale Law & Policy Review* 19, no. 2 (2001): 381–441.

Lundman, Richard J., and Robert L. Kaufman. "Driving While Black: Effects of Race, Ethnicity, and Gender on Citizen Self-Reports of Traffic Stops and Police Actions." *Criminology* 41, no. 1 (2003): 195–220. https://doi.org/10.1111/j.1745-9125.2003.tb00986.x.

Mapp v. Ohio, 367 U.S. 643 (1961).

Meares, Tracey L. "The Law and Social Science of Stop and Frisk." *Annual Review of Law and Social Science* 10, no. 1 (2014): 335–352. https://doi.org/10.1146/annurev-lawsocsci-102612-134043.

Meares, Tracey L. "Programming Errors: Understanding the Constitutionality of Stop-and-Frisk as a Program, Not an Incident." *University of Chicago Law Review* 82, no. 1 (2015): 159–179. https://doi.org/10.2139/ssrn.2524930.

Meehan, Albert J., and Michael C. Ponder. "Race and Place: The Ecology of Racial Profiling African American Motorists." *Justice Quarterly* 19, no. 3 (2002): 399–430. https://doi.org/10.1080/07418820200095291.

Minnesota v. Dickerson, 508 U.S. 366 (1993).

Piquero, Alex, and Alfred Blumstein. "Does Incapacitation Reduce Crime?" *Journal of Quantitative Criminology* 23 (2007): 267–85.

Renauer, Brian C. "Neighborhood Variation in Police Stops and Searches: A Test of Consensus and Conflict Perspectives." *Police Quarterly* 15, no. 3 (2012): 219–240. https://doi.org/10.1177/1098611112447746.

Sherman, Lawrence W., and Dennis P. Rogan. "Effects of Gun Seizures on Gun Violence: 'Hot Spots' Patrol in Kansas City." *Justice Quarterly* 12, no. 4 (1995): 673–693. https://doi.org/10.1080/07418829500096241.

Terry v. Ohio, 392 U.S. 1 (1968).

Tyler, Tom R., Jonathan Jackson, and Avital Mentovich. "The Consequences of Being an Object of Suspicion: Potential Pitfalls of Proactive Police Contact." *Journal of Empirical Legal Studies* 12, no. 4 (2015): 602–636. https://doi.org/10.1111/jels.12086.

Vito, Anthony, George Higgins, and Gennaro Vito. "Police Stop and Frisk and the Impact of Race: A Focal Concerns Theory Approach." *Social Sciences* 10, no. 6 (2021): 230. https://doi.org/10.3390/socsci10060230.

Weeks v. United States, 232 U.S. 383 (1914).

Weisburd, David, Alese Wooditch, Sarit Weisburd, and Sue Ming Yang. "Do Stop, Question, and Frisk Practices Deter Crime? Evidence at Microunits of Space and Time." *Criminology and Public Policy* 15, no. 1 (2016): 31–56. https://doi.org/10.1111/1745-9133.12172.

White, Michael D., and Henry F. Fradella. *STOP AND FRISK: The Use and Abuse of a Controversial Policing Tactic.* New York: NYU Press, 2019. https://nyupress.org/books/9781479857814/.

Wilson, James Q., and Barbara Boland. "The Effect of the Police on Crime." *Law & Society Review* 12, no. 3 (1978): 367–390.

Wilson, O. W. *Police Administration.* New York: McGraw-Hill, 1950. https://www.amazon.com/Police-Administration-W-Wilson/dp/0070707243.

CHAPTER 10

Holding the Police Accountable

It is an axiom of any liberal democracy that *consent* represents a foundational philosophical tenet of government. The people consent to be governed; the people consent to be policed. Indeed, from a functional standpoint, and in terms of the latter, in the United States the people have given up their general right to use coercive force in matters of policing and law enforcement and have centralized that right with the state. In doing this, the people made a deal with the state that goes something like this: We, the people, give the state the general right to use coercion to intervene on our behalf for the purposes of law enforcement, crime responses, traffic enforcement, and other exigencies that might require a coercive intervention. In exchange for giving up their general right to use coercive force, the people expect to have a voice in how policing is conducted. This is why police legitimacy is so important: The people will consent to be policed only when they regard the police as a legitimate institution of government.[1]

When the police lack or lose their legitimacy, the people tend to engage in certain forms of resistance, such as refusing to

Podcast Episode: "Are Lawsuits Still the Best Remedy for Police Accountability?"

Scan the QR code or enter the short URL shown below into a browser window to listen to this chapter's podcast.

https://bit.ly/3s8SlmN

---

[1] Sabel and Simon, "The Duty of Responsible Administration and the Problem of Police Accountability"; Walker, "'Not Dead Yet': The National Police Crisis, a New Conversation About Policing, and the Prospects for Accountability-Related Police Reform"; Trinkner, Jackson, and Tyler, "Bounded Authority: Expanding 'Appropriate' Police Behavior Beyond Procedural Justice"; Kane, "Compromised Police Legitimacy as a Predictor of Violent Crime in Structurally Disadvantaged Communities."

cooperate and share information with police, protesting (and in some cases, rioting against) real or perceived police injustices, and starting media campaigns to "defund" the police.[2] Citizen noncompliance and society's active call to abolish the police make it difficult for police officers to do their jobs without applying elevated levels of coercion to gain compliance for otherwise routine police-public interactions, such as traffic stops. When the police lose legitimacy, the people take back their consent to be policed, which brings us full circle: Legitimacy leads to consent only to the extent that the police remain legitimate; and legitimacy is often a function of adequate measures of police accountability. Although we often think of police accountability as a system designed to prevent and respond to misconduct, it might be time to think of accountability in broader terms: as a system designed, not just to limit the worst of policing behaviors, but to bring out the best in our police.

This chapter describes the traditional tools and remedies of police accountability, from administrative policies to Supreme Court decisions to the federal statutes that allow people to sue the police and the prosecutors to try them in criminal court. Ultimately, the chapter describes how a system of accountability that relies on police departments, the law, and citizen oversight is the best protection against police misconduct and other misbehaviors society finds objectionable. The chapter also argues that developing a system of accountability designed to limit bad policing is not the same as developing an accountability system designed to encourage good policing. The chapter concludes with a brief discussion of how striving for "constitutional policing," as the Final Report of the President's Task Force on 21st Century Policing[3] suggests, stops short of encouraging the new idea of police: policing for the protection of life.

By the end of this chapter readers should be able to answer the following questions:

1. What are the differences between "tools" and "remedies" of police accountability?
2. How can police department policies be written in ways to ensure effective police accountability?
3. What are some of the areas of policing in which departments should implement policies to promote police accountability?
4. What are some of the primary Supreme Court cases that serve as tools of police accountability?
5. What are the primary remedies of police accountability?

---

[2] Kane, "Compromised Police Legitimacy as a Predictor of Violent Crime in Structurally Disadvantaged Communities"; Tyler, Fagan, and Geller, "Street Stops and Police Legitimacy: Teachable Moments in Young Urban Men's Legal Socialization"; Mazerolle et al., "Shaping Citizen Perceptions of Police Legitimacy: A Randomized Field Trial of Procedural Justice"; Reisig and Lloyd, "Procedural Justice, Police Legitimacy, and Helping the Police Fight Crime"; Eaglin, "To 'Defund' the Police."
[3] President's Task Force on 21st Century Policing, "Final Report of the President's Task Force on 21st Century Policing," 2015.

6. How might a "system" of police accountability ensure that police departments create an infrastructure that ensures accountability across all facets of the organization?

7. Why might an accountability system designed to limit "bad" policing fail to create a system of "good" policing within a police department?

Traditional Mechanisms of Police Accountability

Historically, society has relied on three different—yet, not always mutually exclusive—mechanisms of police accountability designed to both prevent and respond to behaviors by police officers and departments deemed problematic, such as those that violate policies or laws. The mechanisms are:

- **Administrative policies:** These policies are written and implemented to establish the parameters of acceptable behaviors, as well as to direct officers toward remaining compliant with organizational rules of conduct. Like most highly structured bureaucratic organizations, police departments maintain policy and procedure manuals that prescribe and prohibit behaviors and duties ranging from when officers are required to wear name tags to when they are allowed to use deadly force.

- **Law:** These include state and federal statutes—both criminal and civil—as well as case law, created to define the legal limits of police conduct and authority. Law, or legal mechanisms, can range from state laws governing certain aspects of police officer training to federal civil rights statutes, to U.S. Supreme Court cases establishing legal requirements for the use of deadly force.

- **Public sources:** These entities are usually external to police organizations and the law that attempt to exert accountability pressures on police organizations or policing in general. Public sources include news media outlets reporting on incidents of known police misconduct or potential misuses of police authority, private citizens who record police behaviors and post to social media sites, and citizen review boards that examine allegations of police misconduct or consider the appropriateness of certain police department policies. Although citizen review boards are considered public mechanisms of police accountability, they are usually authorized and funded by the cities or counties in which police departments reside. For example, the Civilian Complaint Review Board in New York City investigates allegations of police misconduct against the NYPD; although it is an "independent" entity, it is funded by the City of New York.[4]

In what follows, we examine the three traditional dimensions of police accountability in greater detail: administrative, legal, and public.

---

[4] "About — Civilian Complaint Review Board (CCRB)."

Administrative Tools and Remedies

Police policies, standard operating procedures (SOP), and general orders are designed to control virtually all aspects of police behaviors across the spectrum of their duties. These administrative "tools" have become their own type of "rule of law" in police departments; they are designed to direct officer behavior in certain situations and limit police discretion in other situations.[5] To this end, many police policies and general orders are designed so that police departments (or more specifically, police commanders) have the ability to hold individual officers accountable to the rules of the organization through departmental disciplinary processes. In this sense, the policies and procedures represent the *tools* of administrative accountability, and the disciplinary system represents the *remedies* that police commanders can use to punish or otherwise correct officer behaviors that violate the rules. Although many police department policies have little relevance to police-public encounters, others do. For example, although the typical member of the public might have no opinion about which uniforms officers wear during a given season, many police rule books direct officers about wearing the proper "uniform of the day."[6] This type of administrative rule is typically implemented so that police departments can maintain control over most aspects of a police officer's work life.[7]

A range of policies, however, do directly affect police officer accountability to the public, such as those that govern the use of force and deadly force, high-speed pursuits, body-worn cameras, and stop-and-frisk. Policies are crucial to an organization because in addition to outlining the rules of conduct for employees (in this case, police personnel), they also communicate the organization's value system to employees and the public and what it expects from its personnel. Thus, the types of policies police departments maintain can suggest something about the importance the organization places on certain types of conduct. Similarly, the types of policies that police departments do not have in place can also convey something about the agency's value system.

For example, in the wake of Michael Brown's police-involved shooting death in Ferguson, Missouri, many police departments across the country (including the Ferguson PD) began to require officers to use body-worn cameras, and they implemented policies to govern how the body-worn cameras should be used.[8] Since 2015, body cameras have become ubiquitous in U.S. police departments, to the point that at least seven states have mandated their use in all their local police departments.[9] Currently, any midsize U.S.

---

[5] Ericson, "Rules in Policing: Five Perspectives."

[6] To see just how ubiquitous "uniform of the day" policies are in U.S. policing, the interested reader can follow this Google search: https://tinyurl.com/yzhe55xn.

[7] Maguire, *Organizational Structure in American Police Agencies: Context, Complexity, and Control.*

[8] Fallik, Deuchar, and Crichlow, "Body-Worn Cameras in the Post-Ferguson Era: An Exploration of Law Enforcement Perspectives."

[9] "Body-Worn Camera Laws Database."

police department that does not maintain a policy governing the use of police body-worn cameras might be tacitly communicating that it does not value police accountability in the area of police-citizen interactions. Similarly, given the recent reporting among media outlets on racial bias in policing,[10] any midsize police department that does not maintain a policy against biased policing might be sending the message to its people and communities of color that it is not interested in protecting against biased policing.

The following is a short list of policies that most, if not all, police departments in the United States should implement because they directly relate to holding officers and departments accountable to the public for potentially coercive interactions. Several of the policy choices might seem obvious to the average reader, such as use of force and deadly force, because they attempt to regulate the most intrusive and dangerous aspects of policing the public. Other policies, such as drone or communicable disease policies, are less obvious, but they have become increasingly important due to advances in technology and the country's recent experience with the COVID-19 pandemic. The number of topics here is in no way exhaustive; it draws from a variety of industry, academic, and professional sources[11] and is meant to highlight the complexities associated with developing and implementing police policies for accountability.

Police Drones

Unmanned aerial vehicles (UAVs) have been used in military operations, particularly in Iraq and Afghanistan, since at least the George W. Bush administration.[12] In the past 25 years, UAVs have been used by U.S. Customs and Border Protection (CBP), primarily to surveil the U.S.–Mexico border,[13] representing the adoption of military assets by a federal police force. By 2014, drones had made it into U.S. municipal policing with the Los Angeles Police Department's purchase and deployment of two UAVs.[14]

For several scholars, the transfer of military assets, such as drones, into civilian policing represents a significant police accountability issue, particularly related to the tension between privacy rights and public surveillance.[15] At least one political theorist has argued that the evolution from unarmed drones used for surveillance to armed drones used for enforcement and

---

[10] "ACLU Seeks Federal Probe of Taylor Police for Use of Force, Bias"; "Police Face a 'Crisis of Trust' With Black Motorists. One State's Surprising Policy May Help"; "Probe Spurred by Elijah McClain's Death Finds Aurora Police 'Racially Biased' | TheHill."
[11] "12 Crucial Law Enforcement Policies"; Fan, "Body Cameras, Big Data, and Police Accountability"; Commission on Accreditation for Law Enforcement Agencies, "CALEA Law Enforcement Manual"; Sisti, Rickards, and Caplan, "Cops Must Roll up Their Sleeves to Protect Themselves and the Public."
[12] Tahir, "Louder Than Bombs."
[13] Wall, "Unmanning the Police Manhunt: Vertical Security as Pacification."
[14] Anderson, "Game of Drones: How LAPD Quietly Acquired the Spy Birds Shunned by Seattle."
[15] Kaplan and Miller, "Drones as 'Atmospheric Policing': From US Border Enforcement to the LAPD"; Tahir, "Louder Than Bombs"; Wall, "Unmanning the Police Manhunt: Vertical Security as Pacification"; Balko, *Rise of the Warrior Cop: The Militarization of America's Police Forces*; Salter, "Toys for the Boys? Drones, Pleasure and Popular Culture in the Militarisation of Policing."

crowd control represents the next logical step in the continued militarization of U.S. civilian police.[16] Thus, as UAVs continue to proliferate U.S. policing, local police agencies should adopt policies that outline the parameters and limits of drone usage. For example, should drones be used as part of the patrol function of police departments with UAVs proactively photographing public space to essentially "place" people at specific locations at specific times of day? Should UAVs be used strictly during public demonstrations to surveil crowds for possible weapons and make announcements over their public address systems? Are there circumstances where police departments might use armed drones to provide air cover during major crime or terrorism events? How long should drone video and photographic footage be retained? These are all questions that police departments should address in any policies related to drone usage.

It is important to note that police departments using drones must abide by state and federal laws when deploying their UAVs, particularly the relatively recent "Operations Over People" rule that specifies when UAVs are allowed to fly over inhabited areas.[17] Thus, police UAV policies would need to be consistent with Federal Aviation Administration regulations and state and federal laws.

Social Media

Increasingly, police departments are using social media to engage with their local jurisdictions. Some agencies use Twitter and Facebook to communicate crime prevention information, some use social media platforms to report about recent crimes, and others use social media to post information about upcoming large public events.[18] While police departments have been increasing their social media presence, so have individual police officers. What, then, should (or can) a police department do when it discovers that a group of its officers are found to have posted anti-Islamic, homophobic, and pro-violence messages on Facebook? This is exactly what happened recently in the Philadelphia Police Department,[19] and it raises concerns about how to balance First Amendment protections for officers with the need for police departments to protect against officers whose private behaviors might compromise the legitimacy of the department. In this case, the PPD ended up firing 13 police officers for making the inappropriate posts,[20] although it remains unclear how many police departments have implemented policies limiting the social media behaviors of police officers.

Social media policies in policing should address both the official department use and its use by police officers in their private time. For example, a

---

[16] Davis, "Theorizing the Advent of Weaponized Drones as Techniques of Domestic Paramilitary Policing."
[17] "Operations Over People General Overview."
[18] Dai et al., "Working With Communities on Social Media Varieties in the Use of Facebook and Twitter by Local Police."
[19] Palmer et al., "Group Catalogs Racist, Intolerant Facebook Posts by Hundreds of Philly Police Officers."
[20] Palmer, "Philadelphia Police Department to Fire 13 Officers Over Offensive Facebook Posts."

police department should decide whether it will post mug shots of arrested persons, as well as the extent to which such postings might disproportionately identify people of color as criminal defendants. A police department should also decide if it will allow police officers to post photographs they might have taken at crime or accident scenes while they were on duty and in uniform. Departments should also make clear the parameters of prohibited speech for officers, even when they are posting as private citizens.

Police Body-Worn Cameras

As previously noted, since 2015, police body-worn cameras (PBWCs) have become increasingly omnipresent in U.S. policing; at least seven states have mandated their use in all of their local police departments.[21] The reason why PBWCs have become so popular among community members is the perceived transparency—and thus, elevated or restored legitimacy—they bring during police officer interactions with members of the public.[22] Although PBWCs have not been universally welcomed into policing by the officers who actually have to wear them, evidence suggests that over time, officers can come to tolerate (if not appreciate) their usage.[23]

PBWCs can serve several functions in policing. First, as a recording device, they can keep an audio-visual record of interactions between the police and the public, which helps to not only document any potential abuse or misconduct committed by police officers, but also to exonerate officers who have been wrongfully accused of using excessive force or committing some other form(s) of misconduct. Moreover, the footage from PBWCs can often be used as evidence in court cases either to prosecute cases of police misconduct or to defend officers against unfounded allegations of excessive force or other forms of misconduct. PBWCs come with some inherent limitations, however, such as the fact that they only capture the parts of a scene on which the cameras are focused. As such, even when body camera footage is released by a police department, and even if there are multiple cameras recording an incident, the footage only shows what the cameras "saw" at any given moment. Sometimes the difficulty of piecing together an incident from footage recorded by multiple PBWCs creates more confusion than resolution, which can be a problem in any administrative hearing or court case.[24]

As an administrative accountability tool, PBWCs have enormous potential, particularly when coupled with other sources of evidence. However, as scholars Geoff Alpert and Kyle McLean have recently noted, before police departments implement PBWC policies, they should know the objectives

---

[21] "Body-Worn Camera Laws Database."
[22] Fallik, Deuchar, and Crichlow, "Body-Worn Cameras in the Post-Ferguson Era: An Exploration of Law Enforcement Perspectives."
[23] White, Todak, and Gaub, "Examining Body-Worn Camera Integration and Acceptance Among Police Officers, Citizens, and External Stakeholders"; Wooditch et al., "Perceptions of Body-Worn Cameras: Findings From a Panel Survey of Two LAPD Divisions"; Alpert and McLean, "Where Is the Goal Line? A Critical Look at Police Body-Worn Camera Programs."
[24] Alpert and McLean, "Where Is the Goal Line? A Critical Look at Police Body-Worn Camera Programs."

they hope to achieve by using body-worn cameras in the first place, lest their adoption of cameras create more problems than it solves. As Alpert and McLean noted:

> Without a clear goal for the BWC program, there is little direction for exter-nal stakeholders to assess the department's success. In turn, the incentive for line-level officers to activate their cameras is to avoid disciplinary infractions, not necessarily to capture evidence.[25]

Thus, whereas several policing strategies, such as hot-spot policing, have crime reduction as their goals, the adoption of PBWCs often lacks the same clarity in what police agencies hope to accomplish: Are PBWCs being used to hold officers accountable? Hold the public accountable? Create an audio-visual transcript of every police-citizen encounter?

To be effective, PBWC policies should consider the following elements:

- When should officers activate them, and should they record the entire encounter with members of the public? Once activated, PBWCs record all conversations that an officer has with anyone standing in close range, even alleged victims. Thus, recording such interactions poses significant privacy concerns for potential victims and the officers themselves.[26]
- Should officers be given the discretion to decide when to activate their PWBCs, or should they be required to activate them during every en-counter they have with the public? It is true that giving police officers the discretion to activate and deactivate their cameras can protect against privacy concerns, but it can also mean that officers do not record events that contain questionable police tactics or behaviors.
- How long will the organization store footage recorded by PBWCs? Some police agencies contract to third-party entities (e.g., Axon, Unisys, and Amazon Web Services) to store PBWC footage on a cloud server, whereas other police departments have purchased their own servers to store their own data. Either way, storage of PBWC footage is very expensive because of the size of the audio-video files. There is no clear answer to the ques-tion of how long police departments should retain PBWC footage, but all agencies should at least consult with their local prosecutor's office to determine a "best practice" for data storage and retention.[27]

Use of Force and Deadly Force

Given our focus on the police use of force in Chapter 8, it almost goes without discussion that police departments should implement policies that

---

[25] Alpert and McLean, 680.

[26] Fan, "Body Cameras, Big Data, and Police Accountability."

[27] Bureau of Justice Assistance, "Body Worn Camera Toolkit: Body-Worn Camera Frequently Asked Ques-tions."

govern the use of force and deadly force. Considering that much of what we covered in Chapter 8 was grounded in case law—*Graham v. Connor*[28] and *Tennessee v. Garner*[29]—a natural question might be this: How can policies on the use of force and deadly force add to the legal restrictions already imposed by case law? Recall that in *Graham* the Court held that examinations of the use of force must be conducted from the standpoint of a "reasonable" officer at the scene, thus making the judgment of excessive force based on what other reasonable officers might have done in those circumstances. In *Garner* the Court established a defense-of-life standard for the use of deadly force, ruling that officers were allowed to use deadly force only when they believed their lives or the lives of others were in immediate danger. Do these two Supreme Court cases negate the need for policies in the areas of use of force and use of deadly force?

No, and here is why: Recall that coercion, and by extension, the use of force, is the tool society gives police to accomplish their mandate. Although the Supreme Court created frameworks for how to evaluate the boundaries of the legal use of force and deadly force, it did not provide guidance on how to integrate those forms of coercion into the daily lives of police officers. For that, police departments need policies. For example, and at a minimum, a use-of-force policy should specify when a police officer can escalate from pain compliance (e.g., arm-bar hold) to an impact (e.g., baton) weapon. It should indicate where on the use-of-force continuum the police department places conductive energy weapons (e.g., the Taser). For example, should officers be allowed to use the Taser when meeting passive resistance? Or should they have to wait until a suspect is engaged in serious physical resistance before being authorized to deploy the Taser? These are questions of policy.

With respect to deadly force, should police departments allow officers to fire warning shots? Should they allow officers to fire their guns at moving vehicles? What types of ammunition should police officers be allowed to use in their firearms? Should officers, for example, be authorized to use hollow-point bullets, even though the military has banned them for most firearms?[30] These are questions the Supreme Court did not address in its *Garner* ruling, but that must be incorporated into police department deadly force policies.

In creating use-of-force and deadly force policies, police departments should start with a value statement that provides officers with some degree of moral guidance on the application of force and deadly force.[31] Beyond that, and at the very least, police departments should define levels of force, create a use-of-force matrix (recall Figure 8.1 in Chapter 8), describe where certain weapons should be placed on the use-of-force continuum, identify any de-escalation tactics that might be used to reduce physical conflict and therefore

---

[28] Graham v. Connor, 490 U.S. 386 (1989).
[29] Tennessee v. Garner, 471 U.S. 1 (1985).
[30] Berry, "The DOD Law of War Manual Returns Hollow Point Bullets to Armed Conflict."
[31] Wasserman and Moore, "Values in Policing."

avoid force, and generally describe the types of force that are appropriate and the types that are not (e.g., carotid chokehold or the neck restraint).

Racial Profiling and Biased Policing

By now, most readers are familiar with at least some of the issues concerning racial profiling and bias in policing. Recall our examination of police discretion in Chapter 7 and the broad discussion of racial profiling in the areas of stop-and-frisk and vehicle stops. As we noted then, when driven by a crime control paradigm and given a great deal of discretion, police officers have often used race as a factor that produces coercive outcomes, including stops, use of force, and use of deadly force. We also know that using race as a factor to determine when to stop someone, when to use force, and when to use deadly force generally violates the Warrant Clause of the Fourth Amendment and the Equal Protection Clause of the Fourteenth Amendment.[32] Thus, even though racial profiling and biased policing have been deemed illegal by the Supreme Court and other district courts, police departments should implement anti-biased policing policies if for no other reason than to communicate, both to its officers and to its community, their commitment to protect all members of the neighborhoods they serve.

An effective anti-biased policing policy should state in unequivocal language that the police department will not tolerate the use of race, ethnicity, gender, national origin, or other personal characteristics as bases to contact any individuals for potential crimes or other reasons. Moreover, and perhaps equally important, police officers should be trained on the anti-biased policing policy and be given the opportunity to participate in simulated encounters where race or other static characteristics could be a factor in stopping or otherwise contacting someone. Even though racial profiling and biased policing are generally considered illegal, police departments should still make clear policy statements about their prohibition and they should train officers effectively on the policies.

Communicable Diseases

The national COVID-19 lockdown and stay-at-home orders of 2020 made it clear that police have a role in helping manage a pandemic while also remaining a functioning public safety institution. Like other first-responder organizations with 24-hour public safety responsibilities, police departments during a pandemic, or other public health emergencies[33] (PHEs), must develop protocols to protect themselves (i.e., their employees) from the disease to provide uninterrupted service. They must also develop strategies to help mitigate community transmission of the disease. Both types of communicable disease protocols—protecting themselves and developing strategies to

---

[32] Floyd v. City of New York, 959 F. Supp. 2d 668 - Dist. Court, SD New York (2013); Collins v. City of Milwaukee, Case No. 17-CV-234-JPS (E.D. Wis. Jun. 14, 2017); Tennessee v. Garner, 471 U.S. 1 (1985).
[33] Laufs and Waseem, "Policing in Pandemics: A Systematic Review and Best Practices for Police Response to COVID-19."

mitigate possible community spread—are police accountability issues be-cause the former ensures (as much as possible) that policing resources will remain available during the crisis, and the latter could involve the enforce-ment of stay-at-home orders, lockdowns, and quarantine requirements.

To protect the organization against the possible internal spread of a com-municable disease, police administrators should develop policies that create emergency shift rotations to allow teams of officers to work and then quaran-tine as part of a regular cycle. For example, during a pandemic, and knowing that the incubation period for infection might range from 4 to 14 days, a police department might deploy three teams of patrol officers as follows:

- **Team 1:** Works 14 days on, then 14 days off. While off, officers quarantine or self-isolate for the entire 14 days to ensure they are disease-free before returning to work.

- **Team 2:** Works 14 days on, then 14 days off. This team works while Team 1 undergoes quarantine, thus ensuring that one team is always active while another team is self-isolating.

- **Team 3:** Made up of officers held in reserve. Team 3 officers work only when officers assigned to Teams 1 or 2 contract the disease and leave work to go into recovery. At such time, officers on Team 3 are assigned to either Team 1 or Team 2 to ensure that those teams can provide continuous ro-tating coverage.

Police agencies that use a pandemic-informed shift structure could peri-odically reshuffle the teams so that officers initially assigned to Teams 1 and 2 could later be assigned to Team 3 for respite and work only on an as-needed basis. Such a reshuffling plan would help ensure equity among the teams of officers and help preserve not just their physical health, but also their mental well-being.[34] Moreover, a communicable disease shift policy would probably require most police departments to reassign detectives and other special unit officers to uniformed patrol during the PHE to ensure sufficient numbers of officers could be assigned to the three teams. Finally, the rotation sched-ules of Teams 1 and 2 would, of course, be altered to account for different incubation periods and the development of therapies (e.g., vaccines) to fight infections.

In conjunction with including an emer-gency shift structure, a communicable dis-ease policy should also specify the types of enforcement protocols to be used during a pandemic. A big piece of such protocols

See for Yourself . . .

Scan the QR code to see how one California police department successfully implemented a pandemic staffing plan during the height of the COVID-19 pandemic.

---

[34] Brooks and Lopez, "Policing in a Time of Pandemic: Recommendations for Law Enforcement."

Join the Discussion . . .

Scan the QR code to visit the author's blog and read about how the agents of the U.S. Customs and Border Patrol managed social distancing procedures at Liberty International Airport at the start of the COVID-19 pandemic.

should be to specify how police officers will enforce local stay-at-home orders and social distancing measures. History has shown that during natural disasters, when police have vigorously enforced stay-at-home or evacuation orders, some affected local residents—who are already experiencing a great deal of anxiety—have forced violent confrontations with police officers, particularly when they have viewed the police as elevating their militaristic posture.[35] Thus, during the heightened stress of any PHE (including a pandemic), police departments should implement policies that allow officers to enforce local pandemic-related laws or ordinances while also giving them the discretion to forgo enforcement in favor of preserving the peace between the police and the community.[36]

Moreover, any communicable disease policy should also call for the suspension of law enforcement practices that typically bring police officers into close contact with members of the public and that also bring members of the public into close contact with each other.[37] For example, during a pandemic, police should refrain from conducting raids or corner sweeps of drug or prostitution markets, particularly when there is high probability that the people caught up in those sweeps will be infected with the disease. Indeed, rather than focusing on custodial arrests during a pandemic (unless otherwise necessary for the safety of officers and the community), police during a pandemic should work closely with public health officials to both contain drug and prostitution markets while also bringing health resources to the people participating in those markets.

Like most police policies related to accountability, a communicable disease policy should include language acknowledging that policing is a social determinant of health, meaning that, when police enforce laws, they can have both a positive effect on community health as well as a negative effect.[38] This is especially true in vulnerable communities. Thus, a sound communicable disease policy should direct the department and its officers to forgo many traditional law enforcement activities during the crisis.

Duty to Intervene

It is likely that prior to summer 2020 most U.S. residents had never considered, nor heard of, "active bystandership," "duty to intervene," or "peer

---

[35] Chirambwi, "Militarizing Police in Complex Public Emergencies"; Faull, "State Abuses Could Match the Threat of COVID-19 Itself."

[36] Laufs and Waseem, "Policing in Pandemics: A Systematic Review and Best Practices for Police Response to COVID-19."

[37] Brooks and Lopez, "Policing in a Time of Pandemic: Recommendations for Law Enforcement," 4.

[38] O'Brien and Kane, "Policing as a Social Determinant of Health: The Impact of Drug Enforcement on Prenatal Care Utilization in Urban Communities."

intervention" as they related to policing field practices. But when media broadcasts of Derek Chauvin killing George Floyd in Minneapolis were seen, quite literally, around the world,[39] many people also saw at least three uniformed police officers at the scene do nothing to stop Chauvin from slowly killing Floyd.[40] This failure to intervene raised immediate questions about active bystandership and the duty of police officers to stop their colleagues from using excessive or unnecessary force on a suspect during field encounters. Indeed, after much public outrage and a full investigation by the U.S. Department of Justice, in May 2021 a federal grand jury in Minneapolis indicted the three officers who failed to intervene to stop Chauvin's use of a neck restraint against Floyd.[41] Specifically, the indictment charged the three officers for violating Title 18, United States Code, Section 242 for willfully failing to act against Chauvin.

The indictment itself represents a *legal* tool of police accountability (which we describe in the next section of this chapter), and the fact that the Justice Department filed it—charging the officers under the federal civil rights *criminal* statute—should suggest the importance of police departments creating and implementing a "duty to intervene" or "police peer intervention" policy, which should also include the training to support that policy. Indeed, on this latter point, it should be noted that at the time Derek Chauvin killed George Floyd, the Minneapolis Police Department maintained a "duty to intervene" policy, which would have required other Minneapolis police officers on the scene to step in and stop Chauvin from using "unreasonable force," such as the neck restraint.[42]

Police department duty-to-intervene policies should follow the philosophy of the airline industry, which relies on a framework of *crew resource management* to ensure that cockpit crew members step in to stop other members from engaging in misbehavior or making mistakes.[43] Policing workgroups are in some ways similar to airline cockpit crews in that officers frequently work in small groups to cover the same geography, particularly during serious or critical field encounters.[44] They should be trained to help each other in these groups to create a culture of safety that minimizes the use of force, the use of unnecessary or excessive force, as well as mistakes—which might be more common than acts of misconduct. For example, an officer who believes her partner is beginning to escalate a potential use-of-force encounter might use a previously agreed-on code word to remind her partner that he should cool

---

[39] "Protests Around the World as George Floyd Death Draws International Sympathy and Scorn Today"; Cheung, "George Floyd Death: Why US Protests Are so Powerful This Time"; "International Reaction to George Floyd Killing | Black Lives Matter News."

[40] Pereira, "3 Former Officers Charged in George Floyd's Death Make 1st Court Appearance."

[41] "Four Former Minneapolis Police Officers Indicted on Federal Civil Rights Charges for Death of George Floyd; Derek Chauvin Also Charged in Separate Indictment for Violating Civil Rights of a Juvenile."

[42] "Minneapolis Police Department Policy and Procedure Manual, Volume Five—Code of Conduct and Use of Force," 7.

[43] Helmreich and Merritt, "Safety and Error Management: The Role of Crew Resource Management."

[44] Herbert, "The Normative Ordering of Police Territoriality: Making and Marking Space With the Los Angeles Police Department."

down. The officer might use a different code word to let her partner know that he has not taken proper cover when confronting a hostile suspect. In this case, the officer's partner is not committing misconduct, so much as a tactical error. Finally, officers should be trained on their departments' peer intervention policies and allowed to use the subtle gestures they created during simulated field encounters to let their colleagues know that they are taking over the event.

As previously noted, police department policies (such as those described above) represent administrative tools of accountability, but they are not the remedies. For policies to encourage conformity to organizational rules, police departments must create disciplinary systems that provide the sanctions they can use to hold officers accountable for not complying with the policies. To that end, many larger police departments, such as the NYPD, maintain highly formalized and sophisticated disciplinary systems that allow the department to impose a variety of penalties for violating departmental policies and procedures.[45] Depending on the seriousness of the violation, sanctions can range from a few days' suspension to some period of probation, up to dismissal from the department. Smaller agencies might be less formalized but still tend to maintain systems of accountability where the organizational policies represent the rules, and the disciplinary process includes the sanctions.

Many police policies are implemented to conform to legal requirements that govern certain aspects of policing. For example, when the Supreme Court decided *Tennessee v. Garner* in 1985, creating the "defense of life" standard for evaluating the use of deadly force, many police departments responded by creating restrictive deadly force policies that not only conformed to the minimum requirements of *Garner*, but also defined situations in which police officers were administratively allowed to discharge their firearms (e.g., whether they were allowed to shoot at moving vehicles).[46] The next section moves beyond administrative mechanisms and describes the primary legal tools and remedies of police accountability.

Legal Tools and Remedies

When students, policymakers, and scholars think about the "legal" mechanisms of police accountability, they likely do so mostly in terms of Supreme Court decisions. Indeed, the U.S. Supreme Court has decided many cases that have in different ways affected the authority of the police in areas such as search and seizure, the use of force, the use of deadly force, and the authority to use professional discretion outside the law. The Supreme Court even had to tell the police in a 1936 decision that officers were not allowed to use physical violence to obtain confessions from defendants during custodial interrogations.[47] Most Supreme Court cases serve as a tool of accountability

---

[45] Kane and White, *Jammed Up: Bad Cops, Police Misconduct, and the New York City Police Department.*
[46] Fyfe, "Police Use of Deadly Force: Research and Reform."
[47] Brown v. Mississippi, 297 U.S. 278 (1936).

with some cases creating the remedy. In fewer instances, a single case can become both the tool and the remedy, such as the 1914 case *Weeks v. United States*.

In *Weeks*, the Court held that federal officers were prohibited from seizing without a warrant, and then retaining for use in court, personal documents from a defendant's home.[48] To allow the government to retain personal documents in violation of the rules of search and seizure, the majority in *Weeks* argued, would render the Fourth Amendment functionally meaningless.[49] With its decision in *Weeks*, the Court, for the first time in history, excluded evidence from a federal court proceeding that had been illegally seized, creating what would come to be called the Exclusionary Rule.[50] Thus, *Weeks* became both a tool and a remedy of police accountability, at least at the federal level. Again, this is not the norm. In fact, there are many more cases that serve as tools rather than as remedies of police accountability; perhaps the best known example is a case that originated in Arizona in 1963.

When many adults hear the words, "You have the right to remain silent," they might immediately think of their favorite police procedural drama, such as *Hill Street Blues*, *NYPD Blue*, the entire *Law & Order* and *NCIS* franchises, or *Blue Bloods*. Although most Americans probably cannot name the Supreme Court case that institutionalized those words, they can probably recite some version of the remaining script: ". . . Anything you say can and will be used against you in a court of law. You have the right to speak with an attorney and to have one present with you during questioning. If you cannot afford an attorney, one will be appointed to you by the court." *Miranda v. Arizona*,[51] the case that created that "script" in 1966, represents such a fundamental feature of U.S. policing that when it faced its last serious challenge more than 20 years ago in the case *Dickerson v. United States*, Chief Justice William Rehnquist wrote in his majority opinion: "We do not think there is such justification for overruling *Miranda*. *Miranda* has become embedded in routine police practice to the point where the warnings have become part of our national culture."[52]

Arguably the most famous Supreme Court case ever decided in the policing arena, *Miranda v. Arizona* describes the legal requirements governing police custodial interrogations. Beyond the warnings themselves (i.e., "You have the right to remain silent . . ."), *Miranda* tells police officers that before conducting a custodial interrogation of a suspect, they must advise the suspect of their Fifth Amendment rights protecting them against self-incrimination. As a legal rule of police accountability, *Miranda* represents one of the most directive Supreme Court decisions ever made. Unlike most cases, *Miranda* tells police officers exactly what they must do to ensure that they

---

[48] Weeks v. United States, 232 U.S. 383 (1914).
[49] Weeks v. United States, 232 U.S. 383 (1914), 393.
[50] "Weeks v. United States."
[51] Miranda v. Arizona, 384 U.S. 436 (1966).
[52] Dickerson v. United States, 530 U.S. 428, 120 S. Ct. 2326, 147 L. Ed. 2d 405 (2000), 444.

conduct legal custodial interrogations. Subsequent cases have even helped police determine when "custody" attaches to the interrogation, which triggers the need to issue the so-called *Miranda* warnings.[53]

The *Miranda* ruling is not a remedy of police accountability, however; it is a tool. *Miranda* provides the legal framework within which officers must work to conduct lawful custodial interrogations. The Exclusionary Rule is the remedy that makes *Miranda* meaningful. If officers violate the rules of *Miranda*, thereby obtaining confessions or other incriminating statements illegally, it is the Exclusionary Rule that makes such confessions or statements inadmissible in court. Thus, just as with police policies and departmental disciplinary processes, the "legal" mechanisms of police accountability include both tools and remedies. Although there are far too many tools (or cases) to list here, there are a handful of basic legal remedies, identified below, that allow the law—both in the form of case law and statutes—to serve as an effective mechanism of police accountability. Borrowing from legal scholar Rachel Harmon's[54] excellent taxonomy of the legal remedies of police accountability, the following discussion represents a compilation of those remedies.

Exclusionary Rule

As previously noted, the Exclusionary Rule was created by the decision in *Weeks v. United States* and initially applied only to *federal* law enforcement agencies and cases. The rule excludes evidence deemed to have been gathered or obtained in violation of the Fourth Amendment's protection against illegal search and seizure from criminal court proceedings.[55] It was the decision in *Mapp v. Ohio*[56] that applied the Exclusionary Rule to local and state police agencies, making it a powerful remedy of police accountability. Indeed, most Supreme Court cases regulating police authority, and functioning as tools of accountability, rely on the Exclusionary Rule as their remedy. This goes for both Fourth Amendment cases regulating search and seizure and Fifth Amendment cases regulating the right to counsel during police custodial interrogations and protection against self-incrimination. For example, although *Miranda* represents a Fifth Amendment case, protecting criminal suspects against self-incrimination, its remedy is the Exclusionary Rule as applied under the Fourth Amendment's Search and Seizure Clause.[57]

Federal Civil Rights Statute: A Civil Remedy

The 1871 Civil Rights Act empowered Congress to pass Title 42, Section 1983 of the U.S. Code,[58] creating the federal civil rights statute that allowed

---

[53] *E.g.*, Oregon v. Mathiason, 429 U.S. 492 (1977).
[54] Harmon, "Legal Remedies for Police Misconduct," 30–44.
[55] Harmon, 30.
[56] Mapp v. Ohio, 367 U.S. 643 (1961).
[57] Brown v. Illinois, 422 U.S. 590 (1975), 2258–2259.
[58] 42 U.S.C. §1983.

citizens to sue the police for violations of their constitutional rights. Lawsuits filed under 42 U.S.C. §1983 are often referred to as "patterns and practices" lawsuits because they typically allege that police departments have engaged in formal or informal practices that have systematically violated the rights of suspects. For example, lawsuits filed against police departments for alleged illegal stop-and-frisk practices generally argue that such practices illegally targeted people of color, a violation of the Fourteenth Amendment's Equal Protection Clause.[59] People can also sue the police under U.S.C. §1983 for specific actions (e.g., wrongful death) when they can demonstrate that the police officers, under "color of authority," violated an individual's constitutional rights.

A watershed Supreme Court decision in 1978, which had nothing to do with policing, held that local governments could be treated as individuals for the purposes of lawsuits,[60] which began allowing individuals to sue government entities—including police departments—for damages. According to legal and policing scholar Candice McCoy, this 1978 Supreme Court ruling made civil lawsuits an effective remedy of police accountability because prevailing plaintiffs were often awarded damages in the form of large sums of money from the government that employed the police force.[61] To date, civil liability under U.S.C. §1983 represents perhaps the most powerful tool and remedy of police accountability because it targets the large budgets of cities, counties, states, and the federal government during civil lawsuits.

Federal Civil Rights Statute: A Criminal Remedy

Title 18, Section 242 of the U.S. Code[62] allows police officers to be criminally prosecuted for willfully depriving anyone of their constitutional rights under color of authority. Police officers convicted under 18 U.S. Code §242 can face a range of penalties from a fine to imprisonment to even the death penalty.[63] Successful prosecution under the federal civil rights criminal statute is far more difficult than successfully suing officers and their agency under the federal civil rights civil statute for three primary reasons. First, as with all criminal trials, prosecutors must prove their case beyond a reasonable doubt, which is a higher legal threshold than the preponderance of evidence required in civil cases. Next, prosecutors must prove that, not only did officers violate the Constitution in their treatment of the alleged victim, but that they also did so "willfully,"[64] which raises the level of legal intent from "general" to "specific"—again, a difficult legal threshold to prove. Finally,

---

[59] Floyd v. City of New York, 959 F. Supp. 2d 668 - Dist. Court, SD New York (2013); Bailey v. City of Philadelphia, Court of Appeals, 3rd Circuit (2010).
[60] Monell et al. v. Department of Social Services of the City of New York et al., 436 U.S. 658 (1978).
[61] McCoy, "How Civil Rights Lawsuits Improve American Policing."
[62] 18 U.S. Code §242.
[63] "18 U.S. Code § 242—Deprivation of Rights Under Color of Law | U.S. Code | US Law | LII / Legal Information Institute."
[64] Screws v. United States, 325 U.S. 91 (1945), 102; "18 U.S. Code § 242—Deprivation of Rights Under Color of Law | U.S. Code | US Law | LII / Legal Information Institute."

the U.S. Attorney's Manual allows federal prosecutors to bring charges under 18 U.S. Code §242 only when they believe "the government will likely prevail at trial."[65] This rule almost acts as a deterrent against filing criminal charges against police officers, in part, a recognition that most juries historically have been reluctant to convict police officers of crimes.[66]

As with the federal civil rights civil statute, the criminal statute is authorized largely by the Fourth and Fourteenth Amendments. Specifically, and as noted, officers can be tried criminally by the federal government for civil rights violations when they are alleged to have violated (1) the Equal Protection Clause of the Fourteenth Amendment, or (2) the provisions of the Exclusionary Rule (Fourth Amendment) where there is no evidence to exclude. For example, recall from Chapter 7 that the Supreme Court decision in *Tennessee v. Garner* held that the police use of deadly force is tantamount to a seizure of the person and therefore subject to Fourth Amendment exclusions. Four years later, the Court held that any use of force is considered a seizure under the Fourth Amendment[67] and therefore subject to exclusions. Although excessive force does not produce any tangible evidence that could be excluded from trial, it does involve an illegal seizure of the human body for which police officers can be criminally prosecuted or sued in civil court for federal civil rights violations.

State Criminal Statutes

In addition to federal remedies, most states have civil rights statutes, or designated criminal statutes, that allow local police officers to be sued in civil court or prosecuted in criminal court for alleged misconduct committed under color of authority.[68] Especially in terms of the criminal statutes, states vary considerably on the types of legal intent required to prove excessive force or criminal homicide, which makes the likelihood of successful prosecution also highly variable from state to state. For example, whereas the State of New York allows police officers to be tried criminally for negligent homicide[69] (which carries only a general intent requirement), the State of Washington allows for the prosecution of police only when the court can demonstrate the officer intended to commit the crime with "malice and without a good faith belief."[70] This difference in legal thresholds means the likelihood of successfully prosecuting police officers in Washington is much lower than in New York. It is noteworthy that former Minneapolis police officer Derek Chauvin was not tried under the federal civil rights statute; he was instead tried and convicted of second-degree murder while committing a felony in a Minnesota state court.[71]

---

[65] Harmon, "Legal Remedies for Police Misconduct."
[66] Cheh, "Are Lawsuits an Answer to Police Brutality?"
[67] Graham v. Connor, 490 U.S. 386 (1989).
[68] Harmon, "Legal Remedies for Police Misconduct."
[69] N.Y. Penal Law §§125.10, 35.30.
[70] Wash. Rev. Code §9A.16.040.
[71] State of Minnesota v. Derek M. Chauvin, 27 CR 20 (4th Dist. Minn 2021).

State Decertification

Every state maintains a process for licensing police officers to legally work in that state. State-level governing bodies of police are typically called Peace Officer Standards and Training (POST) agencies. All POST agencies must certify police officers before the officers are allowed to work in their given state, and they can also decertify police officers for various reasons, such as misconduct. In essence, decertification is the process of revoking a police officer's license to work as a sworn officer in that state. Although policing is highly decentralized, and largely authorized at the state level, many POST agencies report their decertifications to the National Decertification Index, which is maintained by the International Association of Directors of Law Enforcement Standards and Training.[72] The goal of the National Decertification Index is to ensure as much as possible that police officers decertified in one state are unable to become licensed police officers in another state.

Public Sources of Police Accountability

Legal tools and remedies represent crucial and sometimes effective mechanisms of police accountability, but it is important to look beyond the courts and statutes—and even the police administration—as the primary instruments holding police to account.

Media

In a seminal article published in 1984, describing how the media can serve as a mechanism of police accountability, scholars Jerome Skolnick and Candice McCoy introduced the idea of public sources of police accountability—that is, news organizations vigorously reporting on apparent acts of police misconduct, such as the excessive use of force—as a way of compelling police departments to (1) hold offending officers responsible, and (2) change their policies, if not their cultures.[73] At the time of their writing, Skolnick and McCoy had no idea how platforms such as YouTube, Facebook, and Instagram would eventually transform the concept and practice of "public" accountability.

The first "viral" video of police violence, foreshadowing the video revolution, was recorded on March 3, 1991. On that date, George Holliday was testing his brand-new camcorder (a bulkier version of today's video cameras) and happened to capture the car stop that preceded the beating of motorist Rodney King by at least three Los Angeles police officers. The most compelling portion of the video occurred in the first 89 seconds, during which officers struck a writhing King no less than 56 times with their batons. After that, one of the officers could be seen stomping on King's back (as he lay on

---

[72] Atherley and Hickman, "Officer Decertification and the National Decertification Index," 421.
[73] Skolnick and McCoy, "Police Accountability and the Media."

the ground) as officers moved in to finally handcuff him.[74] Holliday sold the video to KTLA, a local news station, which broadcast it repeatedly until it was picked up by CNN and shown around the world.[75]

George Holliday was among the first in what would become a long line of "citizen journalists" recording the conduct and misconduct of police officers during field encounters. One recent study demonstrated that such videos have become "profoundly integrated into the consciousness of most rank-and-file officers," and that police organizations have often responded to such videos by changing their policies and practices.[76] In short, videos recorded by private citizens can represent a powerful tool of police accountability, especially when used as evidence in court, as was the case with Holliday's video of the King beating.[77]

Citizen Review Boards

Another important source of public accountability is the police citizen review board. Such boards can take a few different forms and serve a few different functions, but they are generally designed to serve as an independent investigator and auditor of alleged police misconduct and police department policies.[78] Some police citizen review boards serve as just an agency that takes and investigates complaints against police officers; some boards serve just as an independent reviewer of police department policies and practices. The majority of police citizen review boards, however, serve both functions: They take complaints of misconduct against officers and investigate them independently from the police department, and they also periodically review police policies and practices.[79] Citizen review boards are almost always created and maintained by the local government authority that employs the police department. When they investigate complaints of alleged police misconduct, they often do so while the department conducts its own internal investigation.

Police citizen review boards are limited in a couple of key ways. First, as an independent investigator of alleged misconduct—usually, use of force or abuse—they tend to "sustain" complaints (i.e., find in favor of the citizen making the complaint) at about the same rate as police department internal affairs units do (nationally, just under 20 percent), which often leads to criticism of such boards.[80] The relatively low sustain rates for use-of-force and abuse complaints likely has much to do with the difficulty of proving that police officers used more force than was necessary during a police-citizen encounter, particularly when considering the "objective reasonableness" standard

[74] Skolnick and Fyfe, *Above the Law: Police and the Excessive Use of Force.*
[75] History.com Editors, "LAPD Officers Beat Rodney King on Camera."
[76] Brown, "The Blue Line on Thin Ice: Police Use of Force Modifications in the Era of Cameraphones and YouTube," 293.
[77] History.com Editors, "LAPD Officers Beat Rodney King on Camera."
[78] Perez, *Common Sense About Police Review.*
[79] Walker, *Police Accountability: The Role of Citizen Oversight.*
[80] Walker.

established by *Graham v. Connor* (recall Chapter 8). A second limitation is that no known police citizen review board can claim disciplinary authority over police officers with sustained complaints. The review boards generally send their findings and recommendations to the chief or commissioner of police, but they are just that: recommendations. In every known U.S. police department, the authority to discipline officers resides exclusively with the police chief or commissioner.

Still, and despite some of the limitations, police citizen review boards represent an important tool of police accountability because they give the public an avenue for filing complaints outside the police organization against which they are complaining. Moreover, in many cities with long-standing police citizen review boards—such as New York City—the boards themselves often form a working relationship with both the police department and the office general counsel (i.e., the city's or county's legal department) that allow them to serve in a kind of consulting capacity to the local government and police department. Thus, although police citizen review boards are often created in the wake of a police scandal—and therefore initially distrusted by the police department—they can often become an integral part of the overall police accountability infrastructure, representing the interests of the public while working with the police department itself to strive for greater transparency and accountability.

Although it is important to define and learn the different tools and remedies of police accountability, such as administrative policies, civil and criminal statutes, and Supreme Court decisions, it is perhaps more important to realize that these mechanisms work best when they are part of a thoughtful system of police accountability. As alluded to above, for example, when laws around police interrogations or the use of force change, police department policies should also change to incorporate the new legal requirements. Thus, for best results, we should regard the collective tools and remedies of police accountability as a system that is greater than the sum of its parts.

Creating a System of Police Accountability

As historians Samuel Walker and Carol Archbold have written, the concept of police accountability applies to police organizations themselves and the individual officers who work for them.[81] At the department level, as Walker and Archbold noted, police departments should have in place a set of standard operating procedures (SOP) that include (1) effective and up-to-date policies, (2) the processes in place to properly train its officers on those policies, (3)

---

[81] Walker and Archbold, *The New World of Police Accountability*, 13.

a review and feedback process that allows the department to revise policies as needed and retrain officers on those new policies, and (4) a value system that emphasizes de-escalation of force and public service that permeates the organization through its policies and training.[82] In this way, the SOP manual provides a methodology for accountability that helps a police department communicate its value system to itself across all organizational dimensions.

This means that officers on the street should follow the policies and procedures implemented by the department, and they should carry out the value system conveyed in the SOP. If they violate policy or law, they should be held accountable by the police organization—perhaps as the result of an internal investigation or an investigation conducted by a citizen review board. In this way, police accountability becomes a system where the department provides the infrastructure for creating a values-based organization with officers who are recruited, trained, and socialized to fulfill their role within the parameters of the department's SOP. For officers who fail to work within the rule structure of the department, the department should have a system of remedies that properly respond.

What happens, though, when the department itself begins engaging in some form of misconduct at the systemic level? For example, what if the department fails to properly train officers on a new use-of-force policy, which ultimately leads to officers on the street inadvertently violating the law? Or perhaps when a law regulating search and seizures changes, a department fails to incorporate the changes into its search and seizure policies and procedures, again, leading officers on the street to conduct illegal searches and seizures? Under such circumstances, police officers on the street might believe they are operating within legal or administrative boundaries, when in fact, they are not. It is only when police departments study themselves, perhaps through their own internal auditing systems or in conjunction with the local police citizen review board, that they can identify when their own patterns and practices might be contributing to organizational misbehavior and the violation of citizens' constitutional rights.

Consider the following scenario, which is based in part on an actual case.[83] A large U.S. police department maintained a K-9 unit made up of a lieutenant, who was in charge of policies and overall deployments, several K-9 sergeants who managed the different K-9 shifts, a single K-9 training officer, and 10 police officers who worked as K-9 handlers for the 10 police dogs. Over a period of three years, on-duty K-9 supervisors ordered police dogs deployed in 400 instances, usually to locate suspects who fled an active crime scene. The policy

---

[82] Walker and Archbold, 15.

[83] The concept for this case study comes from a study that examined police dog deployments and dog bites in the Los Angeles Police Department in the early 1990s. The dog deployments and dog bite rates became the subject of a lawsuit filed against the LAPD for violations of the Equal Protection Clause of the Fourteenth Amendment. The interested reader can review the full case account in Campbell, Berk, and Fyfe, "Deployment of Violence: The Los Angeles Police Department's Use of Dogs."

governing K-9 deployments gave K-9 supervisors much discretion as to when they could deploy the dogs and their handlers. Crimes that typically resulted in deployments include robberies, burglaries, assaults and batteries, motor vehicle theft, and vehicle break-ins. The common attribute of all deployments was that the suspect fled the scene. K-9 units were successful in helping locate suspects in 296 (74 percent) of the 400 deployments. At some point during those encounters, police dogs bit 130 (44 percent) of the 296 suspects they helped locate, in many cases inflicting wounds serious enough so that the suspects required immediate transport to a hospital.

After a series of high-profile dog deployments occurred in which African American men were bitten and seriously injured by police dogs, the local office of the American Civil Liberties Union (ACLU) filed a Freedom of Information Act request, demanding all K-9 deployment data from the police department covering the past three years. ACLU analysts found that African American suspects were bitten in 45 percent of their encounters with police dogs, while White and Latinx suspects were bitten in 48 percent and 50 percent of their encounters with police dogs, respectively. On its face, it appears that African American suspects were the least likely racial or ethnic group to be bitten during encounters with police dogs. These figures failed to tell the full story of K-9 deployments and dog bites, though. The ACLU analysts further found that as the percentage of African American residents increased in neighborhoods, the police department increased its deployment of K-9s by several factors. For example, in neighborhoods that were at least 40 percent African American, the police department deployed K-9 units five times more often than it did in majority White neighborhoods—independent of the type of crime and reported "dangerousness" of the suspect. These findings led the ACLU to file a "patterns and practice" lawsuit against the police department, alleging that the department was using the racial composition of neighborhoods to help determine when to deploy dogs, placing African American residents at higher risk than others of being bitten by police dogs.

Referring back to our tools and remedies of police accountability, let us reconstruct how this lawsuit could be filed under federal law. Recall that the Equal Protection Clause of the Fourteenth Amendment makes it clear that state governments (including police departments) are not allowed to violate the constitutional rights of their citizens, and that states must apply all laws equally across groups of people. The first several sentences of the Fourteenth Amendment make it clear:

> No State shall make or enforce any law which shall abridge the privileges or immunities of citizens of the United States; nor shall any State deprive any person of life, liberty, or property, without due process of law; nor deny to any person within its jurisdiction the equal protection of the laws.

It is the "equal protection of the laws" part that gave the ACLU its standing to file the federal lawsuit. But the Fourteenth Amendment is just the tool of accountability; it is not the remedy. To operationalize the Fourteenth Amendment, the ACLU filed the lawsuit under Title 18, Section 242 of the U.S. Code—the federal civil rights statute (previously described) that draws its legal authority from the Equal Protection Clause of the Fourteenth Amendment. In essence, the ACLU alleged in its civil rights lawsuit that the police department, under color of authority (i.e., in its official capacity), violated the constitutional rights of African American residents because it deployed the K-9 units partly on the basis of the racial composition of communities. Using race as a factor for determining a police deployment denied African American residents of the city equal protection of the law.

This case study is both interesting and complicated because it did not actually allege excessive use of force by individual police officers. Indeed, the case recognized that on the ground, the individual dog handlers were working well within legal use-of-force parameters: Their dogs actually bit African American suspects in a somewhat smaller percentage of deployments than White or Latinx suspects; yet, because of the way the department deployed the K-9 units, far more African American suspects were bitten because the department was more likely to send the dogs into African American communities than others—again, regardless of the types of crimes being committed. Once the case was finally adjudicated (and the police department lost), we are left with reconciling the findings of the lawsuit with our "system" of police accountability.

It would be easy to simply conclude, "The law has spoken." The Fourteenth Amendment makes it illegal for a police department to use force (even in the case of dog bites) differentially on people based on race. Under 42 U.S.C. §1983, the ACLU was able to win a monetary settlement against the city on behalf of several African American plaintiffs. How does the responsible police department move forward from this kind of lawsuit? How might the findings from this case feed back to the police department to ensure that the "patterns and practices" of K-9 deployments do not continue to violate the rights of some citizens going forward? Based on the lawsuit, the police department could attempt to prevent further systemic abuses of the K-9 units by informing its system of accountability in the following ways:

■ Rewrite the K-9 deployment policy in a way that conveys the value system of the police organization. A new policy should formally recognize that K-9 deployments are a serious intrusion into communities that can pose physical risk to those who encounter a police dog. Such a value statement would set the tone for any deployments, leading reasonable police administrators to practice caution when deciding whether to deploy K-9s.

■ The revised policy should also more clearly delineate the types of crimes or other public safety events that would trigger a K-9 deployment, and it might even list a set of factors that K-9 supervisors could consider when deciding whether to deploy the dogs. Factors might include type of crime, whether the suspect was armed, whether a victim or officer had been injured, and so on. The more comprehensive the list of objective factors, the less likely that neighborhood racial composition could influence the decision.

■ Train all K-9 handlers on the new policy using simulated field situations rather than lectures and PowerPoint slides. The training should convey to K-9 handlers that they have a shared responsibility for determining the appropriateness of a deployment. Part of their simulation training might be a role-play where they are put into a position to have to refuse to deploy when they believe their sergeant is violating policy, law, or both.

■ Reevaluate the command structure of the K-9 unit. Perhaps having a single lieutenant running the unit places too much responsibility with a single person. It might be more effective to create a committee of command personnel with the authority to revise policies around training and deployments.

■ Share K-9 deployment data, perhaps on a quarterly or semiannual basis, with the local police citizen review board so that members of the board can audit the patterns of dog deployments in communities. After completing their periodic analysis, the review board can share the findings with the police department, which might confirm the department's overall usage of K-9s or suggest areas of improvement with respect to deployment patterns and dog bites.

For any system of accountability to work, a police department must value the process of self-evaluation and must operate as a learning organization. Being compelled to "do the right thing" simply on the basis of lawsuits means remaining stuck in the traditional ways of doing business. Police departments that embrace a full system of accountability that voluntarily seeks input from external and independent organizations can help create a collective culture of accountability and transparency, and it can help solve any legitimacy crises that might be hindering a police organization's ability to connect with its local populations.

Some Concluding Observations

Police departments that treat accountability as a robust system of checks and balances are poised to move beyond the coercion paradigm into an era where the protection of life becomes the new mandate. For the most part, though, systems of police accountability are still largely designed to limit "bad" policing—for example, profit-motivated corruption, excessive use of force and deadly force, illegal search and seizure practices, and so on. Such systems even reach back to recruitment, where departments apply a series of exclusionary criteria that prevent so-called undesirable candidates from becoming police officers, with the hope that such exclusions will limit the number of police recruits who might become "problem officers" at some later point. Although reducing opportunities and instances of police misconduct remains an important part of any effective police accountability system, eliminating "bad" policing does not necessarily promote "good" policing. Indeed, as this book argues, "good" policing and "bad" policing do not even reside on the same continuum. That is, it might seem like common sense to argue that by eliminating bad policing, a police department will promote good policing, but that is simply not the case.

After all, what does eliminating "bad" policing really mean? It means creating a police culture that does not tolerate, or at least tries to protect against, excessive force, corruption, or other illegal police officer activities. To this end, it is noteworthy that the Final Report of the President's Task Force on 21st Century Policing,[84] which in many ways has become a kind of handbook for the future of policing in the United States, uses the word "constitutional" no less than 13 times. Its use spans the police use of technology (e.g., drones, surveillance equipment, etc.), the use of force, the use of alternatives to deadly force, and the overall concept of "Constitutional policing."[85] Policing to constitutional standards, however, simply means, "Don't violate the law." Another way of expressing it is this: Policing to constitutional standards promotes legal minimalism, which translates to, "At the very least, don't violate the law."

Is that the best we can do with our policing? Foster an institution to whom society has given the general right to use coercive force, and all we ask of them in terms of accountability is, "Don't get in trouble"? Let us recall the moments in this book when we have discussed the early police ethnographer Michael Banton. Recall that it was Banton who, in 1964, wrote that the police are "intrinsically" good, but they are also "intrinsically" dangerous.[86] Although it makes sense to encourage the police to create a system of accountability that, at the very least, reduces their inherent dangerousness, we should also strive to encourage police to maximize the inherent good they can do. This means promoting a protection of life standard that moves beyond crime control and law enforcement as the primary mission. In an era where one hears calls to "defund the police," this book argues that instead of defunding, we should actually expand their mission. This expansion must include a system of police accountability designed to not just minimize the harm police can do, but to maximize the good they can accomplish in communities. We discuss this in greater detail in Chapter 13.

---

[84] President's Task Force on 21st Century Policing, "Final Report of the President's Task Force on 21st Century Policing."
[85] President's Task Force on 21st Century Policing, *e.g.,* at 45.
[86] Banton, *The Policeman in the Community,* 237.

Questions for Review and Reflection

Question 1. Tools and Remedies of Police Accountability.

The chapter makes a distinction between "tools" of police accountability and "remedies" of police accountability, noting that most Supreme Court cases represent the former, but not often the latter.

- What are the differences between tools and remedies of police accountability? Why is the distinction between the two important?
- Identify and describe the Supreme Court case(s) discussed in the chapter that represent both a tool and a remedy of police accountability.
- Was *Miranda v. Arizona* a tool and a remedy of police accountability? If so, how? If not, why?
- Describe how the federal civil rights statutes described in this chapter represent the remedies of police accountability as allowed by certain Supreme Court decisions.
- Can "unofficial" sources of police accountability, such as the media, represent remedies of accountability? If so, why? If not, why not?

Question 2. Policing and the Duty to Act

We often hear of cases in which police officers' actions were found to be examples of police misconduct, such as incidents of excessive force, unjustified deadly force, or when they have violated the rules of *Miranda*. Recently, police officer failure to act has become an accountability issue, particularly in light of the officers who did not take action to stop the death of George Floyd. This raises questions about the duty of the police to intervene.

- To what extent is doing nothing on the part of police worse than doing something? Give examples.
- It seems clear that the officers who did not intervene to stop Derek Chauvin from killing George Floyd have been (and continue to be) held accountable for their failure to take action. Describe other situations in which police should act and be held accountable if they do not.
- In policing, there is the authority to act and the duty to act. Describe the differences between them. When are authority and duty two separate things? Can you think of situations where a police officer has the duty to act despite not having the authority to act? What should the officer do in these situations and why? What should happen to police officers who fail to take the right action even if they do not have the authority to do so?

Question 3. Creating a System of Police Accountability

As noted in the chapter, a system of police accountability creates a cycle of accountability that is self-reinforcing.

- What does "self-reinforcing" mean in this context? How does a system of police accountability come to reinforce itself?
- Is it important for police departments to infuse a set of guiding principles into their policies and procedures? If so, why? If not, why not?
- What does it say to both officers and members of the public when a police department fails to include value statements in their policies, particularly their use of force policy?
- Should the public "defund" police departments that do not include value statements in their policies, particularly their use of force, deadly force, drone, and stop-and-frisk policies? How would such defunding be accomplished?
- Does police accountability always have to be adversarial toward policing? Is there anything positive that police agencies can take away from forcing accountability on themselves?

Exercise

Exercise Examining a Local Citizen Review Board

Conduct web research to identify the closest local jurisdiction (e.g., city, town, county) to where you live that maintains a police citizen review board. Note that citizen review boards are often called a police advisory commission, citizen oversight board, police oversight commission, civilian review board, or civilian oversight board. Once you locate a citizen review board near you, visit its webpage to familiarize yourself with its functions. For this exercise, you will analyze the mission, responsibilities, and make-up of your local citizen review board and write a short report that describes the following:

- What is the stated mission of the citizen review board? What words does the mission statement contain (if any) that convey the value system of the board?
- What is the role of the citizen review board? Does it take complaints against the police from residents? Does it analyze or review police department policies and procedures? Does it hold public meetings about police matters?
- Does the citizen review board also acknowledge local police officers, or the department itself, for doing something "right"? For example, does the board highlight officers or actions that saved lives, helped a vulnerable person, brought an offender into custody, or otherwise contributed to the well-being of the community? If so, please provide details. If not, please discuss the implications of a review board that only reports on problematic behaviors to the exclusion of exemplary behaviors of officers.
- Does your citizen review board post annual reports or reports on its website that address specific topics—for example, local police misconduct or use-of-force issues, how the police might have treated protesters during

recent demonstrations, and so on? If you locate reports on the board's website, please examine the most recent one and describe the following: What local policing topics did the report address? Did the report make any police department policy recommendations? Did the report identify its sustain rate for complaints against the police? Recall that a sustain rate is the number of sustained complaints over the total number of complaints made against the police.

- What is the history of your citizen review board? Was it created in the wake of a police scandal or at a particular moment in history when local, state, or national leaders were publicly discussing the importance of citizen review boards? Answering this question might require you to conduct some Internet research to pull up news stories from the period during which the review board was created.
- Many citizen review boards maintain a blog on their website as a way of pushing out timely information and seeking comment from residents. Does your local citizen review board maintain a blog? If so, what topics do the recent posts cover?

Now that you have described the mission and functions of the board, please address the following:

- What improvements, if any, would you make to the website so that it is more easily navigable for users?
- Does the website suggest anything about the relationship the board has with the police department it oversees? If so, please describe?
- How robust does the citizen review board appear to be? From reading the materials on the website, do you have confidence that your police citizen review board is an effective tool of police accountability?

Bibliography

"12 Crucial Law Enforcement Policies." Accessed October 14, 2021. https://www.powerdms.com/policy-learning-center/12-crucial-law-enforcement-policies.

18 U.S. Code §242 (n.d.).

"18 U.S. Code § 242—Deprivation of Rights Under Color of Law | U.S. Code | US Law | LII / Legal Information Institute." Accessed November 12, 2021. https://www.law.cornell.edu/uscode/text/18/242.

42 U.S.C. §1983 (n.d.).

"About—Civilian Complaint Review Board (CCRB)." Accessed September 8, 2021. https://www1.nyc.gov/site/ccrb/about/about.page.

"ACLU Seeks Federal Probe of Taylor Police for Use of Force, Bias." Accessed October 14, 2021. https://www.freep.com/story/news/local/michigan/wayne/2021/10/07/aclu-seeks-federal-investigation-taylor-police/6040161001/.

Alpert, Geoffrey P., and Kyle McLean. "Where Is the Goal Line? A Critical Look at Police Body-Worn Camera Programs." *Criminology and Public Policy* 17, no. 3 (2018): 679–688. https://doi.org/10.1111/1745-9133.12374.

Anderson, Rick. "Game of Drones: How LAPD Quietly Acquired the Spy Birds Shunned by Seattle." *LA Weekly*, 2014. https://www.laweekly.com/game-of-drones-how-lapd-quietly-acquired-the-spy-birds-shunned-by-seattle/.

Atherley, Loren T., and Matthew J Hickman. "Officer Decertification and the National Decertification Index." *Police Quarterly* 16, no. 4 (2013): 420–437.

"Bailey v. City of Philadelphia, Court of Appeals, 3rd Circuit (2010).

Balko, Radley. *Rise of the Warrior Cop: The Militarization of America's Police Forces*. PublicAffairs, 2021.

Banton, Michael. *The Policeman in the Community*. New York: Basic Books, 1964. https://books.google.com/books/about/The_Policeman_in_the_Community.html?id=F0NMwQEACAAJ.

Berry, Joshua. "The DOD Law of War Manual Returns Hollow Point Bullets to Armed Conflict." Just Security, August 4, 2015. https://www.justsecurity.org/25200/dod-law-war-manual-returns-hollow-point-bullets-armed-conflict/.

"Body-Worn Camera Laws Database." National Conference of State Legislators (NCSL), 2021. https://www.ncsl.org/research/civil-and-criminal-justice/body-worn-cameras-interactive-graphic.aspx.

Brooks, Rosa, and Christy Lopez. "Policing in a Time of Pandemic: Recommendations for Law Enforcement." Covid-19 Rapid Response Impact Initiative | White Paper 7. Cambridge, MA, April 10, 2020.

Brown, Gregory R. "The Blue Line on Thin Ice: Police Use of Force Modifications in the Era of Cameraphones and YouTube." *The British Journal of Criminology* 56, no. 2 (2016): 293–312.

Brown v. Illinois, 422 U.S. 590 (1975).

Brown v. Mississippi, 297 U.S. 278 (1936). https://scholar.google.com/scholar_case?case=3444593443250044452&hl=en&as_sdt=6&as_vis=1&oi=scholarr.

Bureau of Justice Assistance. "Body Worn Camera Toolkit: Body-Worn Camera Frequently Asked Questions." Washington, DC, 2015. https://bja.ojp.gov/sites/g/files/xyckuh186/files/media/document/BWC_FAQs.pdf.

Campbell, Alec, Richard A. Berk, and James J. Fyfe. "Deployment of Violence: The Los Angeles Police Department's Use of Dogs." *Evaluation Review* 22, no. 4 (1992): 535–561.

Cheh, Mary. "Are Lawsuits an Answer to Police Brutality?" In *Police Violence: Understanding and Controlling the Police Abuse of Force*, edited by William Geller and Hans Toch, 247–272. New Haven, CT: Yale University Press, 1996.

Cheung, Helier. "George Floyd Death: Why US Protests Are So Powerful This Time." BBC News, June 8, 2020. https://www.bbc.com/news/world-us-canada-52969905.

Chirambwi, Kudakwashe. "Militarizing Police in Complex Public Emergencies." *Peace Review* 28, no. 2 (2016): 171–177.

Collins v. City of Milwaukee, Case No. 17-CV-234-JPS (E.D. Wis. Jun. 14, 2017).

Commission on Accreditation for Law Enforcement Agencies. "CALEA Law Enforcement Manual." 2019. http://www.slcpd.com/ass3ts/uploads/2019/11/CALEA-Law-Enforcement-Manual-v-6.5-all-standards.pdf.

Dai, Mengyan, Wu He, Xin Tian, Ashley Giraldi, and Feng Gu. "Working With Communities on Social Media Varieties in the Use of Facebook and Twitter by Local Police." *Online Information Review* 41, no. 6 (2017): 782–796. https://doi.org/10.1108/OIR-01-2016-0002.

Davis, Oliver. "Theorizing the Advent of Weaponized Drones as Techniques of Domestic Paramilitary Policing." *Security Dialogue* 50, no. 4 (2019): 344–360.

Dickerson v. United States, 530 U.S. 428, 120 S. Ct. 2326, 147 L. Ed. 2d 405 (2000). https://scholar.google.com/scholar_case?case=12360733536043994298&q=dickerson+v.+united+states+530+u.s.+428&hl=en&as_sdt=6,47&as_vis=1.

Eaglin, Jessica M. "To 'Defund' the Police." 73 *Stanford Law Review Online* 120 (2021).

Ericson, Richard V. "Rules in Policing: Five Perspectives." *Theoretical Criminology* 11, no. 3 (2007): 367–401.

Fallik, Seth Wyatt, Ross Deuchar, and Vaughn J Crichlow. "Body-Worn Cameras in the Post-Ferguson Era: An Exploration of Law Enforcement Perspectives." *Journal of Police and Criminal Psychology* 35, no. 3 (2020): 263–273. https://doi.org/10.1007/s11896-018-9300-2.

Fan, Mary D. "Body Cameras, Big Data, and Police Accountability." *Law & Social Inquiry* 43, no. 4 (2018): 1236–1256. https://doi.org/10.1111/LSI.12354.

Faull, Andrew. "State Abuses Could Match the Threat of COVID-19 Itself." Institute for Security Studies, 2020. Accessed April 14, 2020. https://issafrica.org/iss-today/state-abuses-could-match-the-threat-of-covid-19-itself.

Floyd v. City of New York, 959 F. Supp. 2d 668 - Dist. Court, SD New York (2013).

"Four Former Minneapolis Police Officers Indicted on Federal Civil Rights Charges for Death of George Floyd; Derek Chauvin Also Charged in Separate Indictment for Violating Civil Rights of a Juvenile." Justice News: U.S. Department of Justice, Office of Public Affairs, May 7, 2021. https://www.justice.gov/opa/pr/four-former-minneapolis-police-officers-indicted-federal-civil-rights-charges-death-george.

Fyfe, James J. "Police Use of Deadly Force: Research and Reform." *Justice Quarterly* 5 (1988): 165–205. https://doi.org/10.1080/07418828800089691.

Graham v. Connor, 490 U.S. 386 (1989).

Harmon, Rachel. "Legal Remedies for Police Misconduct." In *Academy for Justice, a Report on Scholarship and Criminal Justice Reform*, edited by Erik Luna, 27–50. Academy for Justice, 2017. https://scholar.google.com/scholar_case?case=8826656230568767300&q=brown+v.+illinois&hl=en&as_sdt=6,39&as_vis=1.

Helmreich, Robert L., and Ashleigh C. Merritt. "Safety and Error Management: The Role of Crew Resource Management." In *Aviation Resource Management*, 107–119. New York: Routledge, 2017.

Herbert, Steve. "The Normative Ordering of Police Territoriality: Making and Marking Space With the Los Angeles Police Department." *Annals of the Association of American Geographers* 86, no. 3 (1996): 567–582. https://doi.org/10.1111/j.1467-8306.1996.tb01767.x.

History.com Editors. "LAPD Officers Beat Rodney King on Camera." History, A&E Television Networks, 2021. https://www.history.com/this-day-in-history/police-brutality-caught-on-video.

"International Reaction to George Floyd Killing | Black Lives Matter News." Al Jazeera, June 2, 2020. https://www.aljazeera.com/news/2020/6/2/international-reaction-to-george-floyd-killing.

Kane, Robert J. "Compromised Police Legitimacy as a Predictor of Violent Crime in Structurally Disadvantaged Communities." *Criminology* 43, no. 2 (2005): 469–497. https://doi.org/10.1111/j.0011-1348.2005.00014.x.

Kane, Robert J., and Michael D. White. *Jammed Up: Bad Cops, Police Misconduct, and the New York City Police Department*. New York: NYU Press, 2013. https://nyupress.org/9780814748411/jammed-up/.

Kaplan, Caren, and Andrea Miller. "Drones as 'Atmospheric Policing': From US Border Enforcement to the LAPD." *Public Culture* 31, no. 3 (2019): 419–445. https://doi.org/10.1215/08992363-7532679.

Laufs, Julian, and Zoha Waseem. "Policing in Pandemics: A Systematic Review and Best Practices for Police Response to COVID-19." *International Journal of Disaster Risk Reduction* 51 (2020): 101812. https://doi.org/10.1016/J.IJDRR.2020.101812.

Maguire, Edward. *Organizational Structure in American Police Agencies: Context, Complexity, and Control*. Albany: State University of New York, 2003.

Mapp v. Ohio, 367 U.S. 643 (1961).

Mazerolle, Lorraine, Emma Antrobus, Sarah Bennett, and Tom R. Tyler. "Shaping Citizen Perceptions of Police Legitimacy: A Randomized Field Trial of Procedural Justice." *Criminology* 51, no. 1 (2013): 33–63. https://doi.org/10.1111/j.1745-9125.2012.00289.x.

McCoy, Candice. "How Civil Rights Lawsuits Improve American Policing." In *Holding Police Accountable*, edited by Candice McCoy, 111–160. Washington, DC: Urban Institute Press, 2009.

"Minneapolis Police Department Policy and Procedure Manual, Volume Five—Code of Conduct and Use of Force." 2021. https://www.minneapolismn.gov/media/-www-content-assets/documents/MPD-Policy-and-Procedure-Manual.pdf.

Miranda v. Arizona, 384 U.S. 436 (1966).

Monell et al. v. Department of Social Services of the City of New York et al., 436 U.S. 658 (1978).

N.Y. Penal Law §§125.10, 35.30. (n.d.).

O'Brien, Anne-Marie, and Robert J Kane. "Policing as a Social Determinant of Health: The Impact of Drug Enforcement on Prenatal Care Utilization in Urban Communities." *Medical Research Archives* 6, no. 2 (2018): 1–14.

"Operations Over People General Overview." Accessed October 16, 2021. https://www.faa.gov/uas/commercial_operators/operations_over_people/.

Oregon v. Mathiason, 429 U.S. 492 (1977).

Palmer, Chris. "Philadelphia Police Department to Fire 13 Officers Over Offensive Facebook Posts." *The Philadelphia Inquirer*, July 18, 2019. https://www.inquirer.com/news/philadelphia-police-officer-firings-facebook-posts-database-20190718.html.

Palmer, Chris, Stacey Burling, Nathaniel Lash, and Julie Shaw. "Group Catalogs Racist, Intolerant Facebook Posts by Hundreds of Philly Police Officers."

The Philadelphia Inquirer, June 1, 2019. https://www.inquirer.com/news/philadelphia/police-philadelphia-facebook-comments-racist-20190601.html.

Pereira, Ivan. "3 Former Officers Charged in George Floyd's Death Make 1st Court Appearance." ABC News, June 4, 2020. https://abcnews.go.com/US/officers-charged-floyds-death-make-1st-court-appearance/story?id=71066710.

Perez, Douglas W. *Common Sense About Police Review*. Philadelphia: Temple University Press, 1994.

"Police Face a 'Crisis of Trust' with Black Motorists. One State's Surprising Policy May Help." Accessed October 14, 2021. https://www.nbcnews.com/news/us-news/traffic-stops-are-flashpoint-policing-america-reformers-are-winning-big-n1280594.

President's Task Force on 21st Century Policing. "Final Report of the President's Task Force on 21st Century Policing." Washington, DC, 2015.

"Probe Spurred by Elijah McClain's Death Finds Aurora Police 'Racially Biased' | TheHill." Accessed October 14, 2021. https://thehill.com/homenews/state-watch/572475-probe-spurred-by-elijah-mcclains-death-finds-aurora-police-racially.

"Protests Around the World as George Floyd Death Draws International Sympathy and Scorn Today." CBS News/AP, June 1, 2020. https://www.cbsnews.com/news/protests-around-the-world-george-floyd-death-international-sympathy-and-scorn-today-2020-06-01/.

Reisig, Michael D., and Camille Lloyd. "Procedural Justice, Police Legitimacy, and Helping the Police Fight Crime." *Police Quarterly* 12, no. 1 (2009): 42–62. https://doi.org/10.1177/1098611108327311.

Sabel, Charles F., and William H. Simon. "The Duty of Responsible Administration and the Problem of Police Accountability." *Yale Journal on Regulation* 33 (2016): 165–212.

Salter, Michael. "Toys for the Boys? Drones, Pleasure and Popular Culture in the Militarisation of Policing." *Critical Criminology* 22 (2013): 163–177. https://doi.org/10.1007/s10612-013-9213-4.

Screws v. United States, 325 U.S. 91 (1945).

Sisti, Dominic, Cyndi Rickards, and Arthur Caplan. "Cops Must Roll up Their Sleeves to Protect Themselves and the Public." *Chicago Sun Times*, October 20, 2021. https://chicago.suntimes.com/2021/10/20/22736454/cops-must-roll-up-sleeves-protect-themselves-public.

Skolnick, Jerome, and James J. Fyfe. *Above the Law: Police and the Excessive Use of Force*. New York: Free Press, 1993.

Skolnick, Jerome H., and Candace McCoy. "Police Accountability and the Media." *American Bar Foundation Research Journal* 9, no. 3 (1984): 521–557. http://www.jstor.org/stable/828317.

State of Minnesota v. Derek M. Chauvin, 27 CR 20 (4th Dist. Minn 2021).

Tahir, Madiha. "Louder Than Bombs." *The New Inquiry* 16 (2012): 100–110.

Tennessee v. Garner, 471 U.S. 1 (1985).

Torres v. Madrid, 592 U.S. (2021).

Trinkner, Rick, Jonathan Jackson, and Tom R. Tyler. "Bounded Authority: Expanding 'Appropriate' Police Behavior Beyond Procedural Justice." *Law and Human Behavior* 42, no. 3 (2018): 280–293. https://doi.org/10.1037/lhb0000285.

Tyler, Tom R., Jeffrey Fagan, and Amanda Geller. "Street Stops and Police Legitimacy: Teachable Moments in Young Urban Men's Legal Socialization." *Journal of Empirical Legal Studies* 11, no. 4 (2014): 751–785. https://doi.org/10.1111/jels.12055.

Walker, Samuel. "'Not Dead Yet': The National Police Crisis, a New Conversation About Policing, and the Prospects for Accountability-Related Police Reform." *University of Illinois Law Review* 2018, no. 5 (2018): 1777–1841.

Walker, Samuel. *Police Accountability: The Role of Citizen Oversight*. Belmont, CA: Wadsworth, 2001.

Walker, Samuel, and Carol Archbold. *The New World of Police Accountability*. 3rd ed. Beverly Hills, CA: Sage, 2020.

Wall, Tyler. "Unmanning the Police Manhunt: Vertical Security as Pacification." *Socialist Studies/Études Socialistes*, 2013.

Wash. Rev. Code §9A.16.040. (n.d.).

Wasserman, Robert, and Mark H Moore. "Values in Policing." *Perspectives on Policing*. A Publication of the National Institute of Justice, the U.S. Department of Justice, and Kennedy School of Government, Harvard University, November 1988.

Weeks v. United States, 232 US 383 (1914).

"Weeks v. United States." Oyez. Accessed November 9, 2021. https://www.oyez.org/Cases/1900-1940/232us383.

White, Michael D., Natalie Todak, and Janne E. Gaub. "Examining Body-Worn Camera Integration and Acceptance Among Police Officers, Citizens, and External Stakeholders." *Criminology & Public Policy* 17, no. 3 (2018): 649–677. https://doi.org/10.1111/1745-9133.12376.

Wooditch, Alese, Craig D. Uchida, Shellie E. Solomon, Lauren Revier, Christine Connor, Mariel Shutinya, John McCluskey, and Marc L. Swatt. "Perceptions of Body-Worn Cameras: Findings From a Panel Survey of Two LAPD Divisions." *American Journal of Criminal Justice* 2020 45, no. 3 (2020): 426–453. https://doi.org/10.1007/S12103-020-09517-5.

CHAPTER 11

From Records to Data to Prediction

The Big Data Revolution in Policing

Historically, we called them records: the bits of information police officers collected on individuals in the form of field contact (or interrogation) cards, written warnings, citations, and reports. These were paper records stored in various locations, such as the officer's own notebook, that often found their way into a binder or file cabinet someplace in the police department. They were disparate, usually independent, observations that placed people who had been contacted by the police at certain places at certain times. It was often the job of detectives during a criminal investigation to scour these paper forms for leads that might help link a suspect to a person, a place, or an event.

In the early 1990s, for example, when the author of this book was an undergraduate criminal justice student, he worked for a district attorney's office as an investigative intern. Part of his training for that position was to get certified by the county to issue parking citations. When the intern went into the field (which usually involved traveling to the Department of Motor Vehicles to obtain the driving records of suspects), he was encouraged to write as many parking tickets as possible along his route. This was not a revenue-generating activity

Podcast Episode: "A Visit Inside a Police Department's Record Management System"

Scan the QR code or enter the short URL shown below into a browser window to listen to this chapter's podcast. https://bit.ly/3s8SlmN

as some might expect. Rather, the parking citations served as an official point of contact that placed a potential suspect's vehicle at a given place at a specific time and date. When a burglary or other crime occurred somewhere within the jurisdiction, detectives would often start their investigations by going to the parking citation "database" (i.e., a physical binder that held copies of all citations) to see if a parking ticket had been issued to a vehicle near the crime location at a proximate date and time. If so, the cited vehicle became the starting point of the investigation.

These days, although citations are still important as points of contact, the process of placing people at specific locations on specific dates and times has been made more efficient with license plate readers, police body-worn cameras, closed-circuit TV, and other physical contacts between police officers and members of the public. How do these pipelines of data work, and where do police departments store the information they collect? In other words, how do police departments turn these seemingly random bits of information into "big data"? Answering that question allows us to move into an examination of one of the more controversial aspects of big data usage: predictive policing, or using historical data to predict where crimes will occur in the short run, and in some cases, who might commit them. This chapter examines how police departments collect, store, and use information to investigate and anticipate the where and who of criminal behaviors.

By the end of this chapter, readers should be able to answer the following questions:

1. What is a police department records management system (RMS)?
2. How do crime analysts use data drawn from RMSs and other sources to "visualize" crime patterns and make connections among possible criminal offenders?
3. How did preventive patrol evolve into so-called hot-spot and smart policing?
4. What were the catalysts of police departments moving from traditional preventive patrol to hot-spot policing and predictive policing?
5. How do predictive policing algorithms use "training" and "test" data to "learn" how to predict crime in real-world policing environments?
6. How do potential biases become built into predictive policing algorithms through the incorporation of unbalanced data and other sources?

Records Management Systems: The Hub of the Virtual Police Department

What we used to call records, we now call data: digitized pieces of information stored in police department records management systems (RMSs), or as we described in Chapter 2, the "virtual" police department. A police department's RMS is a server that stores all the documents and other information created by agency personnel. According to the Law Enforcement

Information Technology Standards Council (LEITSC), a national organization established in 2002 by the National Institute of Justice and Bureau of Justice Assistance to create standards for police department data management:

> RMS is an agency-wide system that provides for the storage, retrieval, retention, manipulation, archiving, and viewing of information, records, documents, or files pertaining to law enforcement operations.[1]

Police officers and other agency employees flood their RMS servers with data that come in from field interviews (e.g., stop-and-frisk contacts), crime and arrest reports, accident reports, firearms permits, licenses, booking sheets, mug shots, fingerprints, and yes, parking tickets. Even members of the public contribute to the data collected and stored in the RMS through their calls for service (CFS). When a person calls the police (or 911 more generally), the conversation they have with the dispatcher is reduced to a digital form that includes the location of the caller, a description of the event about which they are calling (e.g., burglary, robbery, suspicious person, "man with a gun"), and the nature of the police response. The recording of the call is usually stored in the computer-aided dispatch (CAD) system, and the digitized description of the incident usually transfers from the CAD to the RMS.

A key component of the RMS is that it "covers the entire lifespan of records development."[2] This means that a record—such as a missing persons report—can be initiated by a police officer in the field and can then be added to or updated by other personnel as more information about the missing person comes into the agency. This goes for virtually all documents or records created by and stored in the RMS. Moreover, the RMS includes the software that creates the forms, including all the data fields, which means that as information is added to forms, it is automatically captured as usable information.

RMSs are more than just a storage device, however. The RMS is usually constructed as a large relational database that allows police officers, crime analysts, and other authorized personnel to perform queries based on names, aliases, CFS, street intersections and addresses, vehicles, property, and other data points to efficiently retrieve information that might help solve a crime, generate some intelligence, serve as evidence in court, or at least produce a lead. In addition to providing access to agency-owned records and documents, the RMS should also connect to important external databases, such as the state Department of Motor Vehicles, the National Crime Information Center, and others.[3]

Whereas a police officer or detective sitting at a terminal—or from a laptop computer in a patrol car—can retrieve information about specific

---

[1] Penn, Pennix, and Coulson, *Records Management Handbook,* x.
[2] Penn, Pennix, and Coulson, x.
[3] Penn, Pennix, and Coulson, x.

people, property, and incidents, crime and intelligence analysts can use networking and geospatial software to generate "big-picture" patterns showing connections. For example, analysts can conduct a "link analysis" that creates a tree diagram visualizing connections among people based on cell phone call records, social media posts, emails, and registered vehicles, among other pieces of information. Figure 11.1 represents a basic hypothetical link analysis tree created by a hypothetical crime analyst hoping to connect four criminal suspects to each other.

To conduct the link analysis, the crime analyst used data from the police department's RMS, city-owned closed-circuit TV feeds, and data from the state Department of Motor Vehicles. The analyst used Suspect A's car as the common connection to the other three suspects. The crime analyst found through an examination of closed-circuit TV footage that Suspect B was caught on video driving Suspect A's car. The crime analyst was also able to determine through searching the citation and field contact databases that Suspect C had been stopped and ticketed while driving the vehicle, and Suspect D was stopped and issued a written warning while driving Suspect A's car. The value of link analysis is that it allows crime and intelligence analysts to harness the vast quantities of data police departments collect—or have access to—in an attempt to draw connections among people, property, places, and events. It is important to note that the current example represents an elementary case study of what is possible with link analysis. Such analyses often use many more objects of connection (e.g., registered vehicles, call detail records, social media accounts, schools, etc.) to connect dozens of people (or more) for the purposes of solving crimes and learning how future crimes might be in the planning.

Crime and intelligence analysts also use data from the RMS to examine spatial crime patterns and make recommendations about resource deployments. For example, a crime analyst employed by the San Francisco Police

Figure 11.1 ▶

Basic Link Analysis Diagram for Hypothetical Criminal Investigation

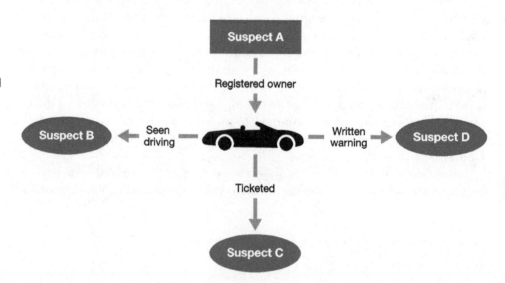

Department might notice that a particular police district is experiencing an increased number of recent drug arrests. When plotted on a map, the drug arrests might appear to be randomly distributed, but when submitted to a hot-spot analysis, the drug arrests show the locations of significant clustering. Figure 11.2 shows the results of such an analysis, in this case conducted in the Mission Police District of San Francisco using drug arrests for the previous three months.

The maps in Figure 11.2 show the Mission District within the context of the broader city, as well as the street-level drug arrest hot-spot results. As the hot-spot map indicates, the drug arrests over the prior three months appear to be randomly located in three of the four general quadrant areas of the Mission District. Looks can be deceiving, though, because a mapping surface is only two-dimensional and obscures the possibility that some arrests could have been made at the same XY coordinates. This would effectively place a number of points on top of each other, which a two-dimensional mapping surface will not show. The astute crime analyst therefore conducts a hot-spot analysis, which identifies clusters of drug arrests. In a nutshell, hot-spot analysis identifies small-scale areas—in this case, 600-by-600-foot grids—where points (i.e., drug arrests) land closer to each other than random chance alone would predict. These point clusters appear as red and orange hot-spot grids on the map. The hot-spot analysis shown in Figure 11.2 identified 18 hot spot locations at the 99 percent confidence interval, indicating highly significant clustering of drug arrests in these locations.

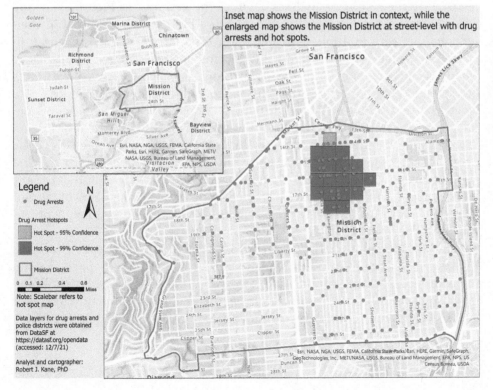

◀ **Figure 11.2**

Analysis of Drug Arrest Hot Spots in the Mission Police District of San Francisco: September 8, 2021 to December 7, 2021

The crime analyst can show the commander of the Mission District the results of the hot-spot analysis, providing actionable information to make some decisions. The first thing the commander might do is address these three questions:

1. Did the hot spots emerge because officers in that part of the district are being too aggressive with their arrests? If so, the commander can work with them to bring their numbers down to "normal" levels.
2. Has something about the land use in that area changed, which is bringing more drug dealers to the area? For example, did one or more buildings become abandoned, or did a halfway house open, which might encourage street-level drug dealing? If so, the commander might work with representatives from the city to decrease the "risky" land use.
3. Does the emergence of drug arrest hot spots foreshadow possible increases in violence, given the turf wars that sometimes result from increased drug dealing?

If the commander rules out Question 1, then she might convene her team of officers and supervisors to develop a violence-prevention plan that can hopefully decrease the potential for violence, despite the increased drug activity.

Modern crime analysis—or what crime science scholar Eric Piza has called "modern policing"[4]—is largely made possible when crime analysts have access to an RMS that receives data in virtually real time, as well as the tools to work with those data. This allows crime and intelligence analysts to visualize the results of analyses, such as those shown in Figures 11.1 and 11.2. Police officers in the United States are increasingly deployed in their jurisdictions with multiple data collection instruments at their disposal: license plate readers, dashboard cameras, body-worn cameras, ticket books, accident report and field interrogation "forms" (although, increasingly, forms are screen-based). It is becoming useful to think of police officers as data collection lenses that permeate virtually every part of a policing jurisdiction; one of their primary uses these days is to feed the RMS with information that crime and intelligence analysts can use to connect people to people, people to places, and people to events. But lest we forget, we call them data, and increasingly, we call them big data; but really, they are people. Virtually every point of contact police officers make and convert to a piece of datum[5] involves a person. And for the most part, those are persons of color. More on this in the next section.

At this moment, society finds itself in the midst of the big data revolution in policing. In the past, police detected crimes when they happened upon them in a patrol car. Indeed, such was the promise of scientific-era policing: Cover the streets with officers in marked cars to randomly scour their beats, and the police department would give the impression that its officers

---

[4] Piza and Baughman, *Modern Policing Using ArcGIS Pro.*
[5] It is important to remember that *data* are plural and *datum* is singular.

were everywhere. It is an idea that seems old fashioned by today's standards. Today, a camera at an intersection maintains eyes on the street 24 hours a day, capturing images that detectives and crime and intelligence analysts can review from the comfort of a computer terminal to try to place someone at that intersection.

With police departments expanding their crime analysis capacities, using police officers in part as data collection lenses, and with private companies selling consumer data to police agencies,[6] the era of data-driven policing is well under way. How can police departments fully exploit the data they collect? Yes, they can conduct real-time crime analysis, create hot-spot maps showing crime concentrations, and use data to inform the deployment of policing resources. As policing moves through the new millennium, though, collecting and using data for operational purposes, it has become clear that real-time data are no longer good enough. Some police departments have pushed the envelope by moving from explaining crime patterns to trying to predict them. This prediction movement that started in the mid-2000s has snowballed into a new type of policing—one based on algorithms, artificial intelligence, and machine learning. It has been made possible by sophisticated RMSs.

Since 2009, when the National Institute of Justice (NIJ)—the research division of the U.S. Department of Justice—held its first symposium on what was then the emerging concept of predictive policing, many police departments around the United States have moved to adopt the strategy. In 2009 the Los Angeles Police Department was one of just six U.S. police agencies to have been awarded an NIJ grant to implement and test the efficacy of predictive policing.[7] Known as the "LAPD Experiment," predictive policing in Los Angeles was implemented to aid in the department's counterterrorism efforts, reduce robbery, and help the department conduct social network analyses.[8] How does predictive policing work? Can it really reduce crime? What are the potential social costs of the strategy?

Transitioning to Predictive Policing

Starting in the 1930s and accelerating through the 1950s, police departments deployed marked police cars to engage in preventive patrol—a strategy heralded by O. W. Wilson, who was by 1950 perhaps the most visible police administrator in the United States.[9] As discussed in Chapter 2, the strategy of "preventive patrol" led uniformed police officers to be deployed mostly in cars to designated beat areas so they could quickly respond to calls for service and—importantly—give an impression that the police were

---

[6] Ferguson, *Rise of Big Data Policing: Surveillance, Race, and the Future of Law Enforcement.*
[7] National Institute of Justice, "Predictive Policing Symposiums," 3.
[8] National Institute of Justice, 3.
[9] Bopp, "OW Wilson and the Search for a Police Profession."

everywhere.[10] As Wilson noted in his classic textbook on police administration, "Patrol is an indispensable service that plays a leading role in (attempting) . . . to eliminate opportunity for (criminal) misconduct."[11] What seemed like a common-sense strategy to reduce crime—using the police to randomly patrol their beat areas and then respond to calls for service—was challenged by research conducted in Kansas City in the 1970s.

In 1974, a group of scholars published the results of a study showing that preventive patrol had little to no effect on most crimes, citizen fear of crime, or satisfaction with police services.[12] The findings of that Kansas City Preventive Patrol Experiment suddenly cast doubt on the very idea of how uniformed policing was conducted in the United States. Indeed, some of the doubt created by the findings in Kansas City might have become part of the catalyst for the development and testing of new or alternative policing strategies, such as foot patrol experiments,[13] and early discussions of, and experiments with, problem-oriented policing.[14] But if randomized patrols could not prevent crime, then what would?

In 1989, scholar Lawrence Sherman and his colleagues published a study they conducted on a strategy called "hot-spot" policing.[15] Their findings showed that in the city of Minneapolis over a one-year period, 50 percent of all police calls for service were concentrated in just 3 percent of all addresses or intersections in the city. This finding led Sherman and colleagues to argue that, rather than police patrolling randomly in beats, as had been the paradigm for at least 40 years, the police should focus their crime-fighting deployments on identified hot spots of crime. Breaking up hot spots, they argued, would have a much greater impact on overall crime rates than having officers simply drive around in their beats waiting to be called. Since Sherman and colleagues published the results of their Minneapolis hot-spot study, a vast body of hot-spot policing research has been conducted, generally showing that police presence in hot-spot locations can effectively reduce crime, at least in the short term.[16]

---

[10] Bopp.

[11] Wilson, *Police Administration*.

[12] Kelling et al., "The Kansas City Preventive Patrol Experiment: A Summary Report."

[13] The Police Foundation, "The Newark Foot Patrol Experiment."

[14] Eck and Spelman, *Problem-Solving: Problem-Oriented Policing in Newport News*; Goldstein, "Improving Policing: A Problem-Oriented Approach."

[15] Sherman, Gartin, and Buerger, "Hot Spots of Predatory Crime: Routine Activities and the Criminology of Place."

[16] Braga, Papachristos, and Hureau, "Hot Spots Policing Effects on Crime"; Sherman and Weisburd, "General Deterrent Effects of Police Patrol in Crime 'HOT SPOTS': A Randomized, Controlled Trial"; Rinehart Kochel and Weisburd, "The Impact of Hot Spots Policing on Collective Efficacy: Findings from a Randomized Field Trial"; Ariel, Weinborn, and Sherman, "'Soft' Policing at Hot Spots—Do Police Community Support Officers Work? A Randomized Controlled Trial"; Telep, Mitchell, and Weisburd, "How Much Time Should the Police Spend at Crime Hot Spots? Answers from a Police Agency Directed Randomized Field Trial in Sacramento, California"; Taylor, Koper, and Woods, "A Randomized Controlled Trial of Different Policing Strategies at Hot Spots of Violent Crime"; Braga and Bond, "Policing Crime and Disorder Hot Spots: A Randomized Controlled Trial"; Weisburd and White, "Hot Spots of Crime Are Not Just Hot Spots of Crime: Examining Health Outcomes at Street Segments"; Ariel, Sherman, and Newton, "Testing Hot-Spots Police Patrols against No-Treatment Controls: Temporal and Spatial Deterrence Effects in the London Underground Experiment"; Koper, "Just Enough Police Presence: Reducing Crime and Disorderly Behavior by Optimizing Patrol Time in Crime Hot Spots."

Hot-spot policing soon evolved into "smart" policing, where teams of researchers partnered with police departments to identify hot spots of certain types of crimes and then deploy officers to those locations in an effort to "break up" the hot spots.[17] The idea was to improve the crime-fighting performance of police departments by having some patrol teams focus their presence on identified hot spots for specific crimes. In some cities, such as Glendale, Arizona, police officers addressed hot spots of convenience store crimes.[18] In Boston, the police used problem-oriented policing strategies to try to reduce violent crime in identified hot spots.[19] Smart policing, however, still relied on historic or nearly real-time crime data in an effort to create the hot spots on a map and develop an action plan to address them. It was not until smart policing became "intelligence-led" policing that scholars and crime analysts could combine their efforts to try to predict where future crime would occur based on current and historical observations.[20]

Implementing Predictive Policing

In 2013 a report published by the Rand Corporation—a major research think tank—examined the state of the science of the emerging predictive policing strategy, provided examples of how it had been implemented across several cities, and described the ways in which prediction might allow police departments to prevent crime.[21] By 2015 at least two software platforms had become well established and helped move predictive policing into mainstream police operations. Based on machine learning algorithms, the new software promised the ability to predict future crime based on historic crime data. For many U.S. police departments, prediction was the key to crime prevention. Since then, many U.S. police departments have partnered with the software firms to practice this new strategy.[22]

The Rand report offers a concise definition of predictive policing:

> Predictive policing is the application of analytical techniques—particularly quantitative techniques—to identify likely targets for police intervention and prevent crime or solve past crimes by making statistical predictions.[23]

---

[17] Braga and Schnell, "Evaluation of Place-Based Policing Strategies: Lessons Learned from the Smart Policing Initiative in Boston"; Coldren, Huntoon, and Medaris, "Introducing Smart Policing: Foundations, Principles, and Practice"; White and Katz, "Policing Convenience Store Crime: Lessons from the Glendale, Arizona Smart Policing Initiative"; Ratcliffe et al., *Smart Policing Initiative Final Report*.

[18] White and Katz, "Policing Convenience Store Crime: Lessons from the Glendale, Arizona Smart Policing Initiative."

[19] Braga and Schnell, "Evaluation of Place-Based Policing Strategies: Lessons Learned from the Smart Policing Initiative in Boston."

[20] Ratcliffe, *Intelligence-Led Policing*.

[21] Perry et al., *Predictive Policing: The Role of Crime Forecasting in Law Enforcement Operations*.

[22] Degeling and Berendt, "What Is Wrong About Robocops as Consultants? A Technology-Centric Critique of Predictive Policing," 348.

[23] Perry et al., *Predictive Policing: The Role of Crime Forecasting in Law Enforcement Operations*, 1.

In the United States, police agencies apply predictive policing software for two general purposes: (1) to predict where future crimes will occur in the near term, and (2) to predict who might commit future crimes in the near term.[24] The former is place-based, whereas the latter is offender-based, although they often work in tandem because potential offenders are often connected to specific communities. It is also the case, however, that most police departments engaged in predictive policing have not focused on predicting who will offend, as such predictions tend to draw scrutiny and criticism from privacy and civil rights groups.[25] To make their place-based predictions, the software programs employ algorithms that use historical crime and other data to create "risk" assessments for certain crimes (e.g., residential burglary) at certain places. The predictive algorithms are largely based on two different perspectives of crime: near repeat theory,[26] and Risk Terrain Modeling (RTM).[27]

■ **Near repeat theory:** This approach to predictive policing draws conceptually from the field of seismology, assuming that—like earthquakes and their aftershocks—certain types of crimes are likely to be committed in a serial pattern (e.g., one after the other) in roughly the same location over a short period of time.[28] Near repeat algorithms use the occurrences of recent crimes in small-scale locations (e.g., 500-by-500-foot grids in a city) to predict similar crimes in the short term (e.g., within 14 days of the previous event), either in the same grid or in adjoining grids. Near repeat analyses are best at predicting residential burglaries because of the serial nature of burglaries.[29] Recently, near repeat analysis has been used to predict shooting locations in Philadelphia, although with limited success.[30]

■ **Risk Terrain Modeling (RTM):** This approach to predictive policing uses recent crimes in its predictive algorithm but also incorporates a great deal of additional data to create a "risk terrain" across a jurisdiction. The additional data sources often include weather patterns, zoning designations, land use (e.g., number of liquor stores or schools in a grid), housing density, and demographic information.[31] As with near repeat analysis, RTM lays grids over a jurisdiction and assigns risk values for crime in each grid based on factors presumed to cause crime.[32]

---

[24] Degeling and Berendt, "What Is Wrong About Robocops as Consultants? A Technology-Centric Critique of Predictive Policing," 347.
[25] Degeling and Berendt, 348.
[26] Ratcliffe and Rengert, "Near-Repeat Patterns in Philadelphia Shootings."
[27] Caplan, Kennedy, and Miller, "Risk Terrain Modeling: Brokering Criminological Theory and GIS Methods for Crime Forecasting."
[28] Mohler and Short, "Geographic Profiling from Kinetic Models of Criminal Behavior."
[29] Degeling and Berendt, "What Is Wrong About Robocops as Consultants? A Technology-Centric Critique of Predictive Policing," 349.
[30] Ratcliffe et al., "The Philadelphia Predictive Policing Experiment."
[31] Kennedy et al., "Vulnerability and Exposure to Crime: Applying Risk Terrain Modeling to the Study of Assault in Chicago."
[32] Caplan, Kennedy, and Miller, "Risk Terrain Modeling: Brokering Criminological Theory and GIS Methods for Crime Forecasting."

Whether the predictive policing software uses an algorithm based on near repeat theory or RTM (or a combination of the two), the functional outcome is the same: The software identifies several grids across a larger geography and designates them as likely locations for a crime within the next several days. Once the predictions are made, the police department has at least three options for how it can use the crime predictions:

1. It can simply alert officers who work the beats in which the predictions are made that the likelihood of a specific type of crime being committed there is high. As such, the officers should be on heightened alert for suspicious people and conditions.
2. It can deploy additional marked patrol cars to the areas identified as high risk over the coming week or 14 days with the primary job of preventing the predicted crime.
3. It might send unmarked cars and plainclothes officers into the crime-predicted grids to try to gather intelligence about who might be planning the crime, and when and where it might be committed.

The following hypothetical case study of predictive policing uses public data and geographic information system (GIS) software to visualize a potential predictive policing application in action.

A Case Study in Predictive Policing

Let us imagine that a police commander in the 22nd Police District of Philadelphia decides to conduct a predictive policing analysis of residential burglaries throughout the district. Let us also imagine that the Philadelphia Police Department uses CrimeStop, a fictitious predictive policing software platform that relies on the same assumptions as actual predictive policing programs in use today by many U.S. police departments.[33] As a predictive policing platform, CrimeStop uses an algorithm that incorporates a combination of near repeat and RTM assumptions, meaning that it uses recent crime occurrences and their locations as primary predictors of near-term crime, but it also uses other "risky" elements of the local geography, such as:

■ Historic crimes.
■ Crimes deemed near repeats (i.e., occur within 14 days of each other in a small-scale area).
■ Sociodemographic indicators of the local area (e.g., household income, percentage of households receiving public assistance income, median household size, etc.).
■ Proximity to nearest police stations.

---

[33] Ratcliffe et al., "The Philadelphia Predictive Policing Experiment."

- Proximity to other indicators of "risky" land use, such as bars, liquor stores, parks, hospitals, and so on.
- Traffic patterns.
- Weather.
- Cyclical events (e.g., sporting events, concerts, outdoor markets, etc.).

CrimeStop not only includes these sources of data, but it weights them differently based on their presumed importance as factors that can predict crime in a given jurisdiction. As such, near repeat crimes are weighted more heavily than historic crimes because they are considered predictive of near-term crimes.

In carrying out its analysis, CrimeStop lays a grid matrix, known as a *fishnet*, over the analysis geography, in this case Philadelphia's 22nd Police District. In the real world, a fishnet is made of a mesh material that allows water to escape while trapping fish. If a fishnet could be rolled out flat over a geographic region, it would look like a woven series of grids, resembling the digital fishnet created by CrimeStop. By default, CrimeStop creates individual grids, or cells, that measure 500-by-500-feet (2,500 square feet), which in Philadelphia represents just over one square city block.[34] These grids are known as activity grids. The program then sums all the data elements listed above for each grid, weighting the near repeat crimes most heavily. It then creates prediction scores for each grid until it identifies up to three grids that are most likely to experience a crime within the next several days. For present purposes, let us say the commander specifies a five-day prediction window. The likely crime grids are known as *mission grids*. Figure 11.3 is a visual representation of the predictive policing process.

The maps in Figure 11.3 show the 22nd District within the context of the entire city, as well as a street-level map of the 22nd District. Note that all residential burglaries that occurred in the district within the past three months are also plotted on the map. CrimeStop will weight those recent burglaries more heavily in terms of their crime prediction potential than burglaries committed farther back in time. Notice that the software imposed "activity" grids over the district. These grids measure 500-by-500-feet in length and width and contain all the data that will be used for the predictive analysis.

When the analysis concludes, the program identifies a small subset of grids that will become the mission grids. Indicated in green on the map, the mission grids are the locations assigned the highest risk values for near-term residential burglaries—that is, grids in which burglaries should occur within the next five days. To select those three grids as the mission grids, the software might have detected that, all other things being equal, a short series of recent burglaries in those grids were strong predictors of near-term burglaries in those same grids.

---

[34] Groff and McCord, "The Role of Neighborhood Parks as Crime Generators."

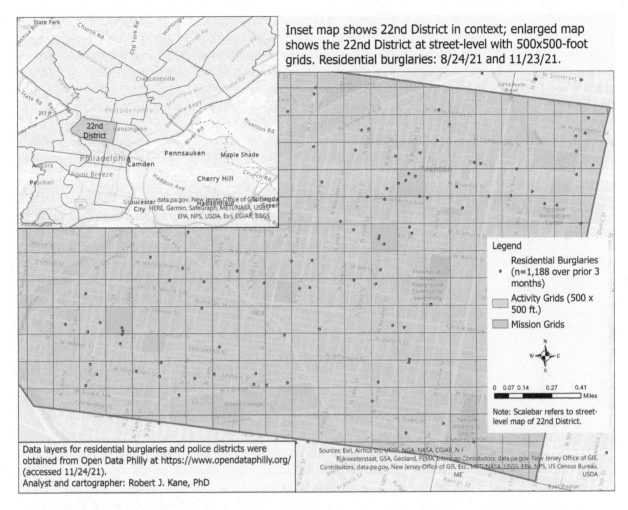

Inset map shows 22nd District in context; enlarged map shows the 22nd District at street-level with 500x500-foot grids. Residential burglaries: 8/24/21 and 11/23/21.

Legend

• Residential Burglaries (n=1,188 over prior 3 months)

Activity Grids (500 x 500 ft.)

Mission Grids

0 0.07 0.14   0.27   0.41
Miles

Note: Scalebar refers to street-level map of 22nd District.

Data layers for residential burglaries and police districts were obtained from Open Data Philly at https://www.opendataphilly.org/ (accessed 11/24/21).
Analyst and cartographer: Robert J. Kane, PhD

Sources: Esri, Airbus DS, USGS, NGA, NASA, CGIAR, N F Rijkswaterstaat, GSA, Geoland, FEMA, Intermap Contributors, data.pa.gov, New Jersey Office of GIS, Contributors, data.pa.gov, New Jersey Office of GIS, Esc, METI/NASA, USGS, EPA, NPS, US Census Bureau, ME   USDA

▲ **Figure 11.3**

Hypothetical Visualization of a Predictive Policing Application in Philadelphia

Referring back to the previous discussion, the police commander has at least three options for translating the information contained in Figure 11.3 into action:

1. Alert existing patrol teams of possible impending burglary attempts in those three areas and direct them to pay special attention to the mission grids over the next five days.
2. Send designated patrol teams into the mission grids to aggressively patrol those areas (similar to saturation patrolling).
3. Send unmarked cars with plainclothes officers into the mission grids to try to learn where the burglaries will occur and who plans to commit them, and then initiate surveillance of the areas with the idea of catching the burglars in the act.

The problem is, if no new burglaries or attempted burglaries occur in the mission grids during the subsequent five days, the police commander will have no idea if the predictions were correct in the first place, or if the extra police presence devoted to the mission grids actually prevented the crimes. Such is the conundrum of predictive policing: Deploying extra police to prevent a crime that was predicted to have occurred cannot, by itself, confirm the reliability of predictive policing if the crime did not happen. Indeed, this is the paradox of crime prevention in general: How do we know our efforts to prevent crime worked if the crime did not occur?

To a considerable extent, the confidence placed in predictive policing resides in the presumed quality of the predictions. If police administrators are pretty sure the software accurately predicted the likely locations of future crime, and they send extra police officers into those mission grids to try to disrupt that crime, then when the crimes do not occur, they can conclude it was because of their policing efforts to stop the crime. Just how accurate are the prediction algorithms, though, and how do we know if they really predict? To answer those questions, we need to examine the process of creating the mission areas as visualized in Figure 11.3. The following discussion draws on several technical and academic sources to provide a broad overview of the technical aspects of predictive policing.[35]

Specifications and Assumptions of Predictive Policing

Regardless of the type of software platform used, predictive policing is developed using an artificial intelligence (AI) algorithm, which creates predictions based on "training" data and "test" data,[36] a process that is collectively known as machine learning. To train the AI algorithm, an analyst feeds vast amounts of historic data, including the locations of previous crimes, into a statistical model that attempts to predict where crimes have occurred in the past. During the training process, the AI runs in excess of 100 predictive models that produce decision trees showing different pathways toward accurately predicting the "likely locations" of crimes (i.e., mission grids in Figure 11.3).[37] After each model estimation, the algorithm compares its predicted location to the actual location of the historic crime and then makes adjustments in how it uses and weights the different factors before rerunning the predictive model. After many iterations, and once the AI algorithm has "learned" which factors most reliably predict the locations of crimes within the grids and how to weight them, the analyst moves on to the testing phase.

---

[35] Harris, "Product Feature: Predictive Policing Helps Law Enforcement 'See Around the Corners'"; Caplan, Kennedy, and Miller, "Risk Terrain Modeling: Brokering Criminological Theory and GIS Methods for Crime Forecasting"; Perry et al., *Predictive Policing: The Role of Crime Forecasting in Law Enforcement Operations*; Ratcliffe and Rengert, "Near-Repeat Patterns in Philadelphia Shootings"; National Institute of Justice, "Predictive Policing Symposiums"; Azavea, "Hunchlab: Under the Hood."
[36] Degeling and Berendt, "What Is Wrong About Robocops as Consultants? A Technology-Centric Critique of Predictive Policing," 351.
[37] Ratcliffe et al., "The Philadelphia Predictive Policing Experiment," 21.

Using test data (which are also historical), the AI applies what it learned during the initial training phase to predict likely locations of crime based on the factors and weights it identified as important during the training phase. Although the testing data are also historic, they are considered an approximation of real-world data because the AI has moved from learning to predicting. As such, during the test period, analysts are able to determine how accurately the AI algorithm predicts likely crime locations because they still know where the historic crimes occurred, even if the algorithm does not. Research and simulation have shown that predictive policing AI algorithms can accurately predict likely locations for crime more than 90 percent of the time they are run on testing data.[38]

To return to our hypothetical example of predictive policing in Philadelphia's 22nd Police District, the district commander would be justified in presuming the accuracy of the AI, at least in the testing data. Moving predictive policing from the world that exists inside a computer program to the real world in which police actually operate is a big leap, though. Indeed, some applications of predictive policing have shown that when moving into the real world of police operations, the prediction accuracies can drop to between 25 and 35 percent.[39] Some of the difficulty of accurately predicting crime in the physical environment can be based on the distances between recent crimes and how they are labeled near repeats. Some of the difficulty has to do with specifying the size of the activity and mission grids, as smaller grids reduce the accuracy of the predictions. Some of the inaccuracy has to do with the assumption of "statistical regularity" of the data that inform the predictions.[40] That is, the prediction algorithms must assume that the factors that predicted historic crimes will be the same factors that predict future crimes. If something about the social ecology of place changes in a given jurisdiction—or if something historic (e.g., a pandemic) has changed between using testing data and deploying the AI into the real world—then the prediction accuracy will be compromised.

Still, some analysts minimize the importance of how accurately the AI predicts likely locations of crime. They argue that even though an algorithm might falsely predict a likely location for a crime, those false positives can be "offset" by the relatively few "true positives" (i.e., correct predictions) because of the potential net crime reduction.[41] That is, although a police department might incur some financial cost by deploying teams of officers to areas falsely identified as likely locations for crime, the jurisdiction as a

[38] Degeling and Berendt, "What Is Wrong About Robocops as Consultants? A Technology-Centric Critique of Predictive Policing"; Shapiro, "Predictive Policing for Reform? Indeterminacy and Intervention in Big Data Policing."
[39] Mohler and Short, "Geographic Profiling from Kinetic Models of Criminal Behavior"; Hunt, Hollywood, and Saunders, *Evaluation of the Shreveport Predictive Policing Experiment.*
[40] Degeling and Berendt, "What Is Wrong About Robocops as Consultants? A Technology-Centric Critique of Predictive Policing."
[41] Drawve, "A Metric Comparison of Predictive Hot Spot Techniques and RTM," 389.

whole could enjoy a net social benefit in terms of crime reduction if the re-deployed officers prevent one or more crimes that were predicted to occur in a mission grid. It is the same logic health care teams sometimes use to weigh the costs and benefits of administering a treatment that might or might not work: It can't hurt, and it might help.

Does such logic really hold true for predictive policing? Is it really the case that moving officers from place to place under the assumption that a specific type of crime is about to be committed in those places does not hurt? Suppose the redeployed officers, in their attempts to root out the pre-sumed crime, start aggressively conducting stop-and-frisk activities with any-one who looks like they might be planning to commit a crime? Although the Supreme Court has ruled that high-crime locations can form some basis for reasonable suspicion,[42] the Court has not yet ruled on whether the predicted "likelihood" of a near-term crime might also serve as a basis for reasonable suspicion. Moreover, to which extent might the biases that are potentially built into prediction policing algorithms perpetuate unequal police treatment of certain groups of people residing in certain communities? The presumed benefits of predictive policing aside, the strategy has come, so far, with sev-eral considerable social costs.

Data Don't Speak for Themselves and Other Criticisms of Predictive Policing

If the only cost of predictive policing was financial, due to the redeploy-ment of officers into areas based on false predictions, then criticisms of the strategy would focus less on equity and more on economics. But as several academic studies[43] and media reports[44] have suggested, the costs of predic-tive policing should be measured more in terms of its social, rather than its monetary, price tag.

Perhaps the most common criticism of predictive policing is the consis-tent finding that its algorithms perpetuate racial biases in policing because they tend to identify Black and Brown communities—and individuals—as likely objects of near-term crime. As some scholars have noted, this overiden-tification of communities and individuals of color has much to do with the

---

[42] Illinois v. Wardlow, 528 U.S. 119 (2000).
[43] Degeling and Berendt, "What Is Wrong About Robocops as Consultants? A Technology-Centric Cri-tique of Predictive Policing"; Saunders, Hunt, and Hollywood, "Predictions Put Into Practice: A Quasi-Experimental Evaluation of Chicago's Predictive Policing Pilot"; Perry et al., *Predictive Policing: The Role of Crime Forecasting in Law Enforcement Operations*; Shapiro, "Predictive Policing for Reform? Indeterminacy and Intervention in Big Data Policing"; Ratcliffe et al., "The Philadelphia Predictive Po-licing Experiment."
[44] Rodrigo, "Police Technology Under Scrutiny Following Chicago Shooting"; Gladstone, "Biased Algo-rithms, Biased World"; LA Times Editorial Board, "The Problem with LAPD's Predictive Policing"; Con-treras, "Technology, Policing and Racial Bias"; Hvistendahl, "How the LAPD and Palantir Use Data to Justify Racist Policing."

use of "unbalanced" training and testing data.[45] To counter that imbalance, training and testing data for creating the algorithm should include as much variety as possible among the factors used for prediction; otherwise, the algorithm risks overidentifying people or places that are overly represented in the data as likely crime objects.

For example, imagine that a police department wishes to predict the locations of new illicit drug markets so it can send police officers to those likely locations to preempt the emergence of the markets. To create the predictions, analysts would likely use locations of previous drug markets and drug arrests, along with many community demographic factors, to train and test the AI algorithm. If the police department focused most or all of its enforcement efforts on open-air drug markets located in communities of color in the past—to the exclusion of high schools located in mostly White communities where students have been known to illegally sell prescription drugs—then the algorithm will ignore the White communities in favor of the communities of color as likely locations for the emerging drug markets. Why? Because it was in the Black and Brown communities where the police made all their previous arrests, and those previous arrests will help feed the near repeat analysis to predict the locations of future drug markets. This is one factor that creates unbalanced training and testing data sets: not having enough White offenders or White communities to create reliable predictions.

It is difficult to overstate the problem of using unbalanced data for training and testing AI algorithms. Predictive policing models that rely extensively on historic police practices to inform the AI will use those prior policing activities to help identify "likely" crime locations. If the historic data are biased, so, too, will be the predictions made from them. That is only part of the problem with using unbalanced data sets, however. The next problem is much more human: Police commanders who rely on predictive policing algorithms to identify likely locations of future crime can, when challenged to defend their deployments, argue that police personnel did not decide where to redeploy police officers; the "computer" did. Such a justification—"The data speak for themselves!"—is one of the major pitfalls of predictive policing because it can allow biases to perpetuate through the process of training, testing, and deploying the AI in real-world environments without police personnel taking responsibility for potentially perpetuating biased policing practices.

Another potential problem with predictive policing is how police officers might behave in communities that have been identified as likely crime locations. As scholar Matthias Leese noted in an article on the costs and benefits of predictive policing:

> Patrol officers when carrying out their tasks on the basis of (predictive policing) . . . show a tendency to be more suspicious as compared to randomized

---

[45] Degeling and Berendt, "What Is Wrong About Robocops as Consultants? A Technology-Centric Critique of Predictive Policing," 351.

patrols. In neighborhoods where there is an allegedly higher risk for certain types of crime, surveillance and control activities are therefore likely to be intensified.[46]

Leese's point is particularly salient when considering that in real-world policing environments, predictive policing predictions have been shown to be just about 35 percent accurate.[47] Thus, if predictive policing algorithms incorrectly identify likely crime locations virtually two-thirds of the time, then officers who employ aggressive enforcement tactics (e.g., conducting many stop-and-frisks) on the bases of those false predictions might be bringing elevated coercion into communities they police for no good reason. Such elevated levels of coercion could intensify any potential underlying conflict that might have already existed between the police and local community members.[48]

A final critique of predictive policing is not one that gets much attention in mainstream discussions, likely because few commentators outside the scholarly arena have considered it. What happens when predictive policing algorithms use data for training and testing that were later found to be illegally obtained? Should police departments that have engaged in so-called dirty policing be allowed to use information found to be illegal or illegally obtained as factors that help build predictive policing algorithms?[49]

Recall our discussion of stop-and-frisk in Chapter 9, and in particular our case study of stop-and-frisk as a crime control strategy in Philadelphia. As noted in that chapter, the Philadelphia Police Department was sued in 2009 and ultimately agreed in a settlement arrangement to reform its practices in ways that would reduce its racial disparities in stop-and-frisk and decrease the number of illegal stops and frisks.[50] As an ACLU study found in 2018, though, over at least a six-month period in that year, 30 percent of "frisks" conducted on pedestrians were illegal; they violated the Warrant Clause of the Fourth Amendment.[51] That means that under the Exclusionary Rule, any weapons or contraband recovered on the basis of those illegal frisks should have been excluded from any subsequent criminal proceedings.

Philadelphia also practices predictive policing; as with other police departments, it likely incorporates historic stop-and-frisk data (particularly

---

[46] Leese, "Predictive Policing: Proceed, but With Care," 3–4.

[47] Mohler and Short, "Geographic Profiling from Kinetic Models of Criminal Behavior"; Hunt, Hollywood, and Saunders, *Evaluation of the Shreveport Predictive Policing Experiment.*

[48] Kane, "Compromised Police Legitimacy as a Predictor of Violent Crime in Structurally Disadvantaged Communities"; Kurbin and Weitzer, "Retaliatory Homicide: Concentrated Disadvantage and Neighbourhood Culture."

[49] For a worthwhile and expanded discussion of this issue, the interested reader should see Richardson, Schultz, and Crawford, "Dirty Data, Bad Predictions: How Civil Rights Violations Impact Police Data, Predictive Policing Systems, and Justice."

[50] Consent Decree, Bailey v. City of Philadelphia et al. (C.A. No. 10-5952, E.D. Penn, June 21, 2011). Available as Document No. 16, Case 2:10-Cv-05952-SD at https://Aclupa.Org/Sites/Default/Files/Field_documents/Bailey_consent_decree_6-21-11_.pdf.

[51] ACLU Pennsylvania, "After Seven Years, Report Shows Philadelphia Police Continue to Illegally Stop and Frisk Pedestrians."

those that resulted in arrest) for training and testing its predictive policing algorithm. Unless police personnel were vigilant about going back into the department's historic stop-and-frisk database to remove the arrests that were made on the basis of illegal frisks (which would have amounted to 30 percent of all frisks in just six months of 2018 alone), it meant the department would have used illegally obtained evidence to help build its predictive policing AI algorithm. The question is simple: Should the fruits of illegal policing be allowed to inform a police department's predictive policing AI? Excluding arrests based on illegally obtained evidence would potentially undercount the numbers of weapons and contraband on the street at a given time, perhaps decreasing the specificity of the AI algorithm. Should a police department be allowed to use potentially important information about weapons and contraband that officers obtained illegally? If so, what becomes of systems of accountability designed to protect communities against abusive or illegal policing? To date, these remain open questions.

Some Concluding Observations

Since the broad integration of RMSs into police operations, most U.S. police departments have developed the capacity to collect and process vast amounts of information. Much of this information is collected by police officers during their encounters with members of the public through crime and victim reports, accident reports, field interrogations (i.e., *Terry* stops), traffic stops, use-of-force reports, and others. However, police departments also collect and maintain information about their own personnel in the form of deployments, assignments, citizen complaints, and other disciplinary actions. It therefore makes sense that, armed with this information, police departments have acquired the tools necessary to analyze the data they collect to tell the story of crime in their local jurisdictions.

What happens, though, when the information they use to tell that story comes from biased police practices? When police officers (or departments more generally), for example, fail to enforce prescription drug laws vigorously in White high schools, and rather focus their drug enforcement efforts on the more public drug trafficking markets located in mostly Black and Brown communities, what part of the crime story is being left untold? How about when police departments use stop-and-frisk against Black and Brown men in mostly White communities or business districts because they look "out of place"? It is for these reasons that police departments should be compelled to share more of the data they collect with the public, and that data sharing should become part of a system of police accountability as described in Chapter 10.

In the past 10 years, many police departments across the United States have placed much of their crime data on open access web portals that members of the public can freely access. Sometimes, police departments even place their arrest, stop-and-frisk, and CFS data on open access portals, which allows members of the public, advocacy groups, and researchers to scrutinize the information for potential patterns of biased policing. Making so much of their data open to the public represents a significant step forward for police departments, given that most agencies historically regarded such information as proprietary and made it very difficult for members of the public to acquire them.[52]

Still, even though police departments routinely release data they have collected via encounters with the people they police, they still often fail to release data on their own officers—data that would help the public hold the police accountable. For example, most police departments do not regularly release information on rates, types, or locations of citizen complaints against police; they do not routinely release data on use-of-force encounters; and they do not routinely release data that would show whether police officers who transferred from other police agencies had records of many citizen complaints. Although police departments have improved their data sharing behaviors in the past decade, they remain reluctant to share information that would allow the public to evaluate the general quality of individual police officers employed in their local jurisdictions. Again, referring back to Chapter 10, a vigorous system of police accountability should include data sharing with the public on certain personnel issues. After all, the public consents to being policed; the public funds police services through taxes; and ultimately, the public pays the civil damages that result from lawsuits against the police department.

Moreover, it makes sense that as police departments have increased their capacities to collect and harness large quantities of information, they would ultimately move from simply describing crime patterns to trying to predict them. Indeed, predictive policing is the digital embodiment of the coercion paradigm: Its users assume that crime fighting is the primary purpose of the police, and that deploying greater enforcement resources to a "likely crime area" will disrupt predicted criminal activity. If deploying greater enforcement resources into specified areas to prevent crime came with only a financial cost, then the conversation about its social utility would be different. As described in this chapter, though, predictive policing has been fraught with racial bias, in part due to the unbalanced training and testing data used to generate the predictions. Yet, short of banning predictive policing, as Santa Cruz, California, did in 2020,[53] the strategy is likely to remain an important component of U.S. policing.

Because predictive policing is likely here to stay—at least in the near term—its use should be constantly monitored and evaluated by groups external to the police department. Again, such monitoring speaks to a vigorous system of police accountability that requires the police department to share its data and decision tree models with stakeholders who would likely be

[52] Kane, "Collect and Release Data on Coercive Police Actions."
[53] Sturgill, "Santa Cruz Becomes the First U.S. City to Ban Predictive Policing."

affected by predictive policing strategies. Ultimately, society might come to determine that predictive policing is too biased, too unreliable, and too easily used as a justification for ramping up the number of coercive encounters police officers initiate with the public in certain communities. Until such time, though, it remains society's responsibility to ensure that predictive policing is practiced with as much transparency as possible to identify and correct potential biases in how the strategy is applied.

To a great extent, police departments' collection and use of data represents the fulcrum that balances the systems of police accountability with a recruitment paradigm designed to bring in the most qualified police officers. It is therefore fitting that this chapter on police and big data falls between the chapters on police accountability and police recruitment. We have reached the point in this book where it is time to acknowledge that policing wields great power in our society—power that extends beyond pedestrian stops and use of force. It is the power of information that is used to determine where, and on whom, to focus their enforcement efforts. This power implicates the need for a strong system of police accountability so that when police power is misused, it can be corrected; and it also implicates the need to hire and retain police officers capable of seeing that the mission of police extends beyond mere crime fighting. In part, that is what the next chapter is all about: creating a new recruitment paradigm that will help move policing beyond coercion.

Questions for Review and Reflection

Question 1. RMS: The Hub of the Virtual Police Department

Records management systems store all data created by the police department, including information about who was stopped, who was arrested, who was cited, and where and when these events took place. The RMS can potentially include massive amounts of information on thousands, hundreds of thousands, and even millions of individuals who are somehow "captured" by a data collection lens of a police department, whether that lens is a traffic camera, a police officer's field interrogation card, a police body-worn camera, or a police officer's arrest or crime incident report.

■ What are the social and justice implications of allowing police departments to collect vast quantities of information about everyone they contact, whether the people are victims or offenders of crimes?

☐ Should people be allowed to view the information police departments keep on them, much like consumers are allowed to view their credit reports?

☐ Should police departments be required to actively share—perhaps on an annual basis—the extent of the information they have on any given individuals?

☐ What are some additional social and justice implications of allowing police departments to collect and retain data on members of the public?

- Given that the chapter refers to the RMS as the "virtual police department," should this so-called virtual department have a separate police chief whose job is to manage all the information collected and stored in the RMS?
  - □ If so, how would you envision the separation of powers between the chief of the physical police department and the chief of the virtual police department?
  - □ Would these be two separate agencies whose chiefs would report to the mayor or other local government executive?
- Do police departments have a duty to destroy or otherwise delete the information they have collected on individuals after a certain amount of time?
  - □ If so, what would be a reasonable amount of time?
  - □ Should there be different data destruction schedules for different categories of people on whom police departments have data? For example, should police departments be allowed to keep data on offenders longer than they do on victims?
  - □ If you do not believe that police departments should be required to maintain data destruction time frames, does this mean people do not have the "right to be forgotten," as is the law in the European Union?

Question 2. The Use and Potential Misuse of Predictive Policing

Predictive policing is a crime prevention strategy some police departments use to assign risk scores to small-scale geographic locations (usually 500-by-500-foot grids) in an effort to predict crime over a 7-to-14-day period. Predictive policing uses a combination of near repeats analysis and Risk Terrain Modeling to create risk scores using historical crime data, as well as many other sources of local land use and demographic information.

- Given the low accuracies of predictive policing algorithms, should police departments be allowed to base an entire crime analysis strategy around predictive policing? If so, why? If not, why not?
- What does it mean when critics argue that much of the training and testing data sets used to create predictive policing algorithms are "unbalanced"? What is meant by the term "unbalanced"?
  - □ What are the implications of police departments using unbalanced data sets to train their AI algorithms on predictive policing? How might such unbalanced data sets contribute to racially biased policing practices?
  - □ How might police departments address the issue of unbalanced data sets for training and testing the predictive police AI algorithms?
  - □ Do data really "speak for themselves" when it comes to predictive policing?
- In what ways might predictive policing lead to more aggressive behaviors among police officers who work in communities that have been assigned high-risk predictive policing scores (suggesting a crime is predicted to occur very soon)?
  - □ Should police officers be allowed to know when their beats have been assigned high-risk values by the predictive policing algorithms? Why or why not?
  - □ If a police beat has been assigned a high-risk value by the predictive policing AI, should police departments deploy outside officers to try to detect the predicted crime? If so, how might those officers treat members of the community?

Question 3. The Moral Implications of Prediction

As noted in the chapter, predictive policing software uses large quantities of historic crime and arrest data to "feed" its AI and create risk predictions for crime in the near term within small-scale territories. As further noted, the prediction reliabilities for crime tend to be low, and if the historical crime and arrest data show any racial biases, then those biases will likely show up in the crime-risk values.

- Given all we know about the social costs of predictive policing, is it even moral for police departments to use the strategy? Please make a moral argument to either justify the use of predictive policing or condemn its usage in U.S. police departments.

Exercise

Exercise **Developing a System of Accountability with Predictive Policing**

Assume you are a member of your county board of supervisors and that you have an interest in police integrity and reform. The local police chief comes before the board and announces his intentions to implement predictive policing in his department. You and the other members of the board of supervisors approve the chief's request to implement predictive policing, but you also decide to create an oversight committee called the County Independent Predictive Policing Auditor (CIPPA) that will monitor the practices of predictive policing in the county. The idea is to ensure that predictive policing is practiced in the most ethical and race-neutral ways possible.

Your assignment for this exercise is to write a proposal that creates the CIPPA using the following template:

- Describe the general philosophy, role, and mission of the CIPPA.
- What authority will the CIPPA have to fulfill its role?
  - Will it have the authority to see any and all data used by the predictive policing software platform?
  - Will it have access to all data in the RMS?
  - Will it have the authority to shut down or control certain aspects of predictive policing, or will it simply have the authority to report to the county board of supervisors on predictive policing practices?
- What policies will the CIPPA create to ensure that predictive policing is conducted ethically? For example, will it develop policies that control the following:
  - The types of data that can be used (or not used) for the training and testing of the predictive policing AI algorithm?
  - Whether people who were ultimately not convicted of the crimes for which they were arrested must be removed from the historical data sets used to train and test the predictive policing AI algorithm?
  - The use of balanced data sets for training and testing the AI?
  - Whether officers are told that they are working in beats that have been assigned high-risk values by the predictive policing program?
- What kinds of authority will the CIPPA be given to ensure it can enforce the policies it creates?
  - Will the CIPPA have the authority to compel the chief of police to make changes to the predictive policing algorithm and practices based on findings made by CIPPA analysts?
  - Will the CIPPA have only auditing authority, which means the most it can do is submit reports and complaints to the county board of supervisors regarding the predictive policing practices?

- What will be the administrative structure of the CIPPA?
  □ Will the CIPPA have a single director, or will it be governed by a steering committee?
  □ How many different units or divisions will the CIPPA contain, and what will they do?
  □ Will CIPPA employ different analysts with responsibilities for monitoring different aspects of predictive policing and the police data that feed the AI?
  □ Will the CIPPA have a community relations or outreach division that will consult with the community on issues related to predictive policing? If so, how will the CIPPA work with the community to help monitor predictive policing activities?

- How frequently and in what format will the CIPPA create reports resulting from its audits of predictive policing?

To complete this exercise, you should conduct web research to learn about the primary ethical and operational issues associated with predictive policing. Lots of organizations, such as the Brennan Center for Justice, have written reports on the ethics and challenges of predictive policing. Many news outlets have published stories about the use and misuse of predictive policing, which you might also consult. Finally, you should consider visiting the websites of one or more police citizen review boards to borrow from them some of the structural and administrative features you might use to develop your CIPPA.

Bibliography

ACLU Pennsylvania. "After Seven Years, Report Shows Philadelphia Police Continue to Illegally Stop and Frisk Pedestrians." 2018. https://www.aclupa.org/en/press-releases/after-seven-years-report-shows-philadelphia-police-continue-illegally-stop-and-frisk.

Ariel, Barak, Lawrence W. Sherman, and Mark Newton. "Testing Hot-Spots Police Patrols Against No-Treatment Controls: Temporal and Spatial Deterrence Effects in the London Underground Experiment." *Criminology*, August (2019): 101–128. https://doi.org/10.1111/1745-9125.12231.

Ariel, Barak, Cristobal Weinborn, and Lawrence W. Sherman. "'Soft' Policing at Hot Spots—Do Police Community Support Officers Work? A Randomized Controlled Trial." *Journal of Experimental Criminology* 12, no. 3 (2016). https://doi.org/10.1007/s11292-016-9260-4.

Azavea. "Hunchlab: Under the Hood." Azavea, 2015. https://cdn.azavea.com/pdfs/hunchlab/HunchLab-Under-the-Hood.pdf.

Bopp, W. J. "OW Wilson and the Search for a Police Profession." Washington, DC, 1977. https://www.ncjrs.gov/App/Publications/abstract.aspx?ID=47846.

Braga, Anthony A., and Brenda J. Bond. "Policing Crime and Disorder Hot Spots: A Randomized Controlled Trial." *Criminology* 46, no. 3 (2008): 577–607. https://doi.org/10.1111/j.1745-9125.2008.00124.x.

Braga, Anthony, Andrew Papachristos, and David Hureau. "Hot Spots Policing Effects on Crime." *Campbell Systematic Reviews* 8, no. 1 (2012): 1–96. https://doi.org/10.4073/csr.2012.8.

Braga, Anthony A., and Cory Schnell. "Evaluation of Place-Based Policing Strategies: Lessons Learned From the Smart Policing Initiative in Boston." *Police Quarterly* 16 (2013): 339–357.

Caplan, Joel M., Leslie W. Kennedy, and Joel Miller. "Risk Terrain Modeling: Brokering Criminological Theory and GIS Methods for Crime Forecasting." *Justice Quarterly* 28, no. 2 (2011): 360–381. https://heinonline.org/HOL/Page?handle=hein.journals/jquart28&id=372&div=22&collection=journals.

Coldren, James R., Jr., Alissa Huntoon, and Michael Medaris. "Introducing Smart Policing: Foundations, Principles, and Practice." *Police Quarterly* 16, no. 3 (2013): 275–286.

Consent Decree, Bailey v. City of Philadelphia et al. (C.A. No. 10-5952, E.D. Penn, June 21, 2011). Available as Document No. 16, Case 2:10-Cv-05952-SD at https://Aclupa.Org/Sites/Default/Files/Field_documents/Bailey_consent_decree_6-21-11_.pdf.

Contreras, Russell. "Technology, Policing and Racial Bias." Axios, October 16, 2021. https://www.axios.com/technology-policing-and-racial-bias-bb0de2a2-0bce-4d40-a327-7a478bb16cb8.html.

Degeling, Martin, and Bettina Berendt. "What Is Wrong About Robocops as Consultants? A Technology-Centric Critique of Predictive Policing." *AI and Society* 33, no. 3 (2018): 347–356. https://doi.org/10.1007/s00146-017-0730-7.

Drawve, Grant. "A Metric Comparison of Predictive Hot Spot Techniques and RTM." *Justice Quarterly* 33, no. 3 (2016): 369–397. https://doi.org/10.1080/07418825.2014.904393.

Eck, John E., and William Spelman. *Problem-Solving: Problem-Oriented Policing in Newport News*. Washington, DC: Police Executive Research Forum, 1987.

Ferguson, Andrew G. *Rise of Big Data Policing: Surveillance, Race, and the Future of Law Enforcement*. New York: NYU Press, 2017.

Gladstone, Brooke. "Biased Algorithms, Biased World." On the Media | WNYC Studios, November 22, 2019. https://www.wnycstudios.org/podcasts/otm/episodes/biased-algorithms-biased-world-on-the-media.

Goldstein, Herman. "Improving Policing: A Problem-Oriented Approach." *Crime & Delinquency* 25, no. 2 (1979): 236–258. https://doi.org/10.1177/001112877902500207.

Groff, Elizabeth, and Eric S. McCord. "The Role of Neighborhood Parks as Crime Generators." *Security Journal* 25, no. 1 (2012): 1–24. https://doi.org/10.1057/sj.2011.1.

Harris, Scott. "Product Feature: Predictive Policing Helps Law Enforcement 'See Around the Corners.'" *The Police Chief*, October 2014. https://www.policechiefmagazine.org/product-feature-predictive-policing-helps-law-enforcement-see-around-the-corners/.

Hunt, Priscillia, John S. Hollywood, and Jessica M. Saunders. *Evaluation of the Shreveport Predictive Policing Experiment*. Santa Monica, CA: Rand Corporation, 2014. https://www.ojp.gov/ncjrs/virtual-library/abstracts/evaluation-shreveport-predictive-policing-experiment.

Hvistendahl, Mara. "How the LAPD and Palantir Use Data to Justify Racist Policing." *The Intercept*, January 30, 2021. https://theintercept.com/2021/01/30/lapd-palantir-data-driven-policing/.

Illinois v. Wardlow, 528 U.S. 119 (2000).

Kane, Robert J. "Collect and Release Data on Coercive Police Actions." *Criminology & Public Policy* 6, no. 4 (2007): 773–780. https://doi.org/10.1111/j.1745-9133.2007.00485.x.

Kane, Robert J. "Compromised Police Legitimacy as a Predictor of Violent Crime in Structurally Disadvantaged Communities." *Criminology* 43, no. 2 (2005): 469–497. https://doi.org/10.1111/j.0011-1348.2005.00014.x.

Kelling, George L., Tony Pate, Duane Dieckman, and Charles E. Brown. "The Kansas City Preventive Patrol Experiment: A Summary Report." Washington, DC: The Police Foundation, 1974.

Kennedy, Leslie W., Joel M. Caplan, Eric L. Piza, and Henri Buccine-Schraeder. "Vulnerability and Exposure to Crime: Applying Risk Terrain Modeling to the Study of Assault in Chicago." *Applied Spatial Analysis and Policy* 9, no. 4 (2016): 529–548. https://doi.org/10.1007/s12061-015-9165-z.

Koper, C. S. "Just Enough Police Presence: Reducing Crime and Disorderly Behavior by Optimizing Patrol Time in Crime Hot Spots." *Justice Quarterly* 12, no. 4 (1995): 649–672. https://doi.org/10.1080/07418829500096231.

Kurbin, C. E., and R. Weitzer. "Retaliatory Homicide: Concentrated Disadvantage and Neighbourhood Culture." *Social Problems* 50, no. 2 (2003): 157–180. https://doi.org/10.1525/sp.2003.50.2.157.

LA Times Editorial Board. "The Problem With LAPD's Predictive Policing." *Los Angeles Times*, March 16, 2019. https://www.latimes.com/opinion/editorials/la-ed-lapd-predictive-policing-20190316-story.html.

Leese, Matthias. "Predictive Policing: Proceed, but With Care." *Policy Perspectives* 8, December (2020): 1–4.

Mohler, George O., and Martin B. Short. "Geographic Profiling From Kinetic Models of Criminal Behavior." *SIAM Journal on Applied Mathematics* 72, no. 1 (2012): 163–180.

National Institute of Justice. "Predictive Policing Symposiums." Washington, DC: U.S. Department of Justice, Office of Justice Programs, 2009. https://www.ojp.gov/pdffiles1/nij/242222and248891.pdf.

Penn, Ira A., Gail B. Pennix, and Jim Coulson. *Records Management Handbook*. New York: Routledge, 2016.

Perry, Walter L., Brian McInnis, Carter C. Price, Susan Smith, and John S. Hollywood. *Predictive Policing: The Role of Crime Forecasting in Law Enforcement Operations*. Santa Monica, CA: Rand Corporation, 2013. https://doi.org/10.7249/RR233.

Piza, Eric, and Jonas H. Baughman. *Modern Policing Using ArcGIS Pro*. Redlands, CA: Esri Press, 2021.

The Police Foundation. "The Newark Foot Patrol Experiment." Washington, DC: Police Foundation, 1981.

Ratcliffe, Jerry H. *Intelligence-Led Policing*. 2nd ed. New York: Routledge, 2016.

Ratcliffe, Jerry, Elizabeth Groff, Cory Haberman, and Evan Sorg. *Smart Policing Initiative Final Report*. Philadelphia, PA: Temple University, 2012.

Ratcliffe, Jerry H., and George F. Rengert. "Near-Repeat Patterns in Philadelphia Shootings." *Security Journal* 21, no. 1 (2008): 58–76. https://doi.org/10.1057/PALGRAVE.SJ.8350068.

Ratcliffe, Jerry H., Ralph B. Taylor, Amber Perenzin Askey, Kevin Thomas, John Grasso, Kevin J. Bethel, Ryan Fisher, and Josh Koehnlein. "The Philadelphia Predictive Policing Experiment." *Journal of Experimental Criminology* 17 (2020): 15–41. https://doi.org/10.1007/s11292-019-09400-2.

Richardson, Rashida, Jason M. Schultz, and Kate Crawford. "Dirty Data, Bad Predictions: How Civil Rights Violations Impact Police Data, Predictive Policing Systems, and Justice." *New York University Law Review* 94, no. 2 (2019): 192–233. https://papers.ssrn.com/sol3/papers.cfm?abstract_id=3333423#.

Rinehart Kochel, Tammy, and David Weisburd. "The Impact of Hot Spots Policing on Collective Efficacy: Findings From a Randomized Field Trial." *Justice Quarterly* 36, no. 5 (2019): 900–928. https://doi.org/10.1080/07418825.2018.1465579.

Rodrigo, Chris Mills. "Police Technology Under Scrutiny Following Chicago Shooting." *The Hill*, April 21, 2021. https://thehill.com/homenews/state-watch/549612-police-technology-under-scrutiny-following-chicago-shooting.

Saunders, Jessica, Priscillia Hunt, and John S. Hollywood. "Predictions Put Into Practice: A Quasi-Experimental Evaluation of Chicago's Predictive Policing Pilot." *Journal of Experimental Criminology* 12, no. 3 (2016): 347–371. https://doi.org/10.1007/s11292-016-9272-0.

Shapiro, Aaron. "Predictive Policing for Reform? Indeterminacy and Intervention in Big Data Policing." *Surveillance & Society* 17, no. 3–4 (2019). https://doi.org/10.24908/ss.v17i3/4.10410.

Sherman, Lawrence W., Patrick R. Gartin, and Michael E. Buerger. "Hot Spots of Predatory Crime: Routine Activities and the Criminology of Place." *Criminology* 27, no. 1 (1989): 27–56. https://doi.org/10.1111/j.1745-9125.1989.tb00862.x.

Sherman, Lawrence W., and David Weisburd. "General Deterrent Effects of Police Patrol in Crime 'HOT SPOTS': A Randomized, Controlled Trial." *Justice Quarterly* 12, no. 4 (1995): 625–648. https://doi.org/10.1080/07418829500096221.

Sturgill, Kristi. "Santa Cruz Becomes the First U.S. City to Ban Predictive Policing." *Los Angeles Times*, June 26, 2020. https://www.latimes.com/california/story/2020-06-26/santa-cruz-becomes-first-u-s-city-to-ban-predictive-policing.

Taylor, Bruce, Christopher S. Koper, and Daniel J. Woods. "A Randomized Controlled Trial of Different Policing Strategies at Hot Spots of Violent Crime." *Journal of Experimental Criminology* 7, no. 2 (2011): 149–181. https://doi.org/10.1007/s11292-010-9120-6.

Telep, Cody W., Renée J. Mitchell, and David Weisburd. "How Much Time Should the Police Spend at Crime Hot Spots? Answers from a Police Agency Directed Randomized Field Trial in Sacramento, California." *Justice Quarterly* 31, no. 5 (2014): 905–933. https://doi.org/10.1080/07418825.2012.710645.

Weisburd, David, and Clair White. "Hot Spots of Crime Are Not Just Hot Spots of Crime: Examining Health Outcomes at Street Segments." *Journal of Contemporary Criminal Justice* 35, no. 2 (2019): 142–160. https://doi.org/10.1177/1043986219832132.

White, Michael D., and Charles M. Katz. "Policing Convenience Store Crime: Lessons from the Glendale, Arizona Smart Policing Initiative." *Police Quarterly* 16, no. 3 (2013): 305–322.

Wilson, O. W. *Police Administration*. 2nd ed. New York: McGraw-Hill, 1963.

PART III

Creating the New Idea of Police

CHAPTER 12

"They Just Want to Hire Themselves!"

Examining Police Officer Selection in the United States

As a co-op institution, Drexel University builds professional experiences into its undergraduate curriculum for most majors. During designated terms, students leave the university for six months to work in professional settings related to their fields of study. One such student, a senior undergraduate studying criminology and justice studies—the department in which the author of this book serves as professor and department head—sought to work his co-op as a crime analyst intern at a large suburban police department. Although not a sworn police officer position, the crime analyst position still requires job candidates to successfully meet most of the same pre-employment screening requirements as police officer candidates. The student's interview process did not go well. When he returned to Drexel's criminology department to debrief, he was indignant, recounting that, despite his extensive training in the tools of crime analysis (e.g., GIS, cell phone records analysis, and network analysis), the interviewers at the police department treated him as an unworthy applicant.

Podcast Episode: "The Quest to Create a Screening-in Police Recruitment Process"

Scan the QR code or enter the short URL shown below into a browser window to listen to this chapter's podcast.
https://bit.ly/3s8SlmN

At first, he said, his interactions with the detective sergeant and crime analysts conducting the interview had been positive, focusing mostly on his technical skills and the knowledge of crime theories he used to inform his answers. But then they moved into a discussion about the types of data the police department used for predictive policing purposes. This led the student to caution his interviewers that because arrest and stop-and-frisk data often contained so few White suspects, the data sets were often racially and ethnically "unbalanced," leading the predictive algorithms to overidentify people of color as high-crime-risk individuals. The student's comment was apparently not taken well: From that point forward, the interviewers became almost hostile toward him for questioning their predictive policing strategies.

Toward the end of the interview, the student suggested that it could be important for the police department to integrate measures of neighborhood health with its local crime data to help determine the best ways to deploy police officers into communities. The student reasoned that police officers had a unique opportunity to create safe places in parks or community centers to help improve the health behaviors of residents in certain neighborhoods. At that point, according to the student, the sergeant running the interview testily reminded the student that police officers were deployed into communities for law enforcement, not social work, and they weren't interested in working as "nurses." When the student finished recounting the story, he looked at the professor and exclaimed, "Doc! These cops! They just want to hire themselves!"

This chapter examines the typical processes that most U.S. police departments use to screen applicants for the purposes of determining who would make successful police officers. Readers will come to understand that, even though the Drexel student above had applied for a position as a crime analyst and not a police officer, his observation about police department administrators wanting to hire "themselves" rings true. This chapter will explain that by police administrators hiring "themselves," they perpetuate policing's emphasis on selecting candidates who maintain strong law enforcement orientations. By the end of this chapter readers should be able to answer the following questions:

1. What are the primary selection techniques in use today by most U.S. police departments, sheriff's departments, and state police agencies to screen applicants for sworn positions (i.e., police officers and sheriff's deputies)?
2. How is the background investigation typically used during the pre-employment hiring process?
3. What do we know about the relationship between police academy performance and successful policing beyond the academy?
4. In what ways has the use of psychological test batteries as a selection technique led to an identifiable "police personality"? What are the characteristics of that personality?

5. How does the conventional police personality evolve over time into the working personality of police? How does this evolution differentially affect police officers of color?

6. What are the differences between the traditional screening-out method used by police departments and the screening-in strategy proposed in this chapter?

7. In what ways might the police occupation benefit by shifting its pre-employment screening practices from selecting "warriors" to selecting "guardians"?

The Police Officer Selection Process

The first thing to understand about police officer selection is that all states in the United States manage their own selection processes, create their own selection criteria, and even decide the order in which the different components of the process are administered. Tribal police departments, such as for the Navajo Nation,[1] and the federal government, such as the U.S. Capitol Police[2] and the U.S. Supreme Court Police,[3] also set their own standards for hiring police officers. In most states and the federal government, the governing body that sets the standards for their police officers is called the Commission on Peace Officers Standards and Training (POST). For example, the Los Angeles Police Department initiates its hiring process with an online application and an online multiple-choice exam,[4] whereas the Mobile, Alabama, Police Department begins its process with the physical agility test, administering the written exam in person somewhat later in the sequence.[5] Although all cities within a state must adhere to their state's POST requirements, they are allowed some latitude in determining the order of steps in the application process. Still, and despite some differences, the selection process for police officers remains reasonably consistent across cities and states in the United States. The following is a discussion of the major components of the police officer selection process using the State of California Peace Officers Standards and Training process as the model, given that it provides an exhaustive set of steps.[6]

The Application

It would seem obvious that the application process comes first because without the application, how would a police department know to start the

---

1 "Home | Navajo Police Department."
2 "Becoming a USCP Police Officer | United States Capitol Police."
3 "Jobs — The Supreme Court Police."
4 Los Angeles Police Department, "Join LAPD: LAPD Hiring Process."
5 Mobile Police Department, "The Application Process."
6 CA.Gov | Commission on Peace Officer Standards and Training, "Peace Officer Candidate Selection Process."

application process with any given individual? As a gateway to the hiring process, though, the application is more than just an administrative initiator; it is the first formal step taken by people who believe they would be a good fit for policing and who want to pursue it as a career. Admittedly, people enter policing with many different intentions, but the application itself serves as the official declaration of an intent to enter the police occupation. The question is this: How do police departments convey the message about who would seem like a good fit for the job? This is where the application and recruitment process become linked, as will be discussed in greater detail below.

Written Exam

If the application is accepted (which usually involves the police department running a cursory criminal history check on the person who submitted the application), the next step in the process is often the written exam. There are at least 20 identified entry-level police officer selection exams,[7] which are often generically referred to collectively as the entry-level POST exam. The POST exam is usually administered in the format of a multiple-choice test and will often contain one or more short essay questions. The entry-level POST exam is usually designed to assess an applicant's ability to successfully complete the academic components of the training academy. During the academy, for example, police recruits are trained to write reports that must stand up in court—and in particular, that must withstand cross-examination by an opposing attorney. The typical entry-level POST exam for police officers is designed to assess a candidate's writing and reasoning skills at a level that can predict success in creating such reports while cadets are going through the academy.

Physical Ability Test

Although not every state (including California) requires a physical ability test (also called a physical agility test), most police departments do require some assessment of applicant fitness during the selection process. This can come in the form of a physical exam that also includes body mass index measurements.[8] As with the written exam, physical ability tests are designed to assess an applicant's ability to successfully complete the physical fitness requirements of police academy training. Typical physical ability tests during the selection process might include jogging a mile under a certain time, completing a certain number of pull-ups, or running a certain number of sprints while wearing a simulated utility belt.

---

[7] "Most Common Police Officer Selection Tests | Police Test Prep."
[8] "Calculate Your BMI — Standard BMI Calculator."

Oral Interview

For many applicants, the oral interview is the most consequential component of the police officer selection process.[9] It usually represents the first time the applicant actively interacts with members of the police department's hiring committee. The committee poses a series of questions to the candidate designed to assess their personal and professional experiences, problem-solving and communication skills, interest and motivation for pursuing a career in policing, interpersonal skills, and community engagement.[10] Despite some research showing that the oral interview does not distinguish capable from noncapable police candidates,[11] it remains a crucial element of the police officer selection process. Oral interviews are used again during the police promotional process (e.g., when officers apply for promotion within their departments).[12]

Background Investigation

Candidates who successfully complete the oral interview will be subjected to a comprehensive background investigation designed to identify aspects of the candidate's background that might disqualify them from becoming a police officer. At this stage in the process, candidates are often assigned a background investigator who will be the candidate's primary point of contact throughout the remainder of the pre-employment selection process. The background investigator usually provides the candidate with a document known as the Personal History Statement (PHS), designed to collect an exhaustive compilation of the candidate's background and history. After completing the PHS, the candidate returns it to the background investigator, who then sets out (often with a small team) to verify all the information in the document. Investigators usually visit the candidate's close family members, as well as present and former significant others. They visit current and prior employers, current and past roommates, and any other people identified as significant in the candidate's life. Depending on the age of the candidate, investigators might visit prior high school teachers or college professors.

In addition to wanting to learn about a candidate's present and prior relationships, the background investigators are also interested in learning about any prior (or current) drug use, whether prescription or illegal drugs. They will also conduct an extensive investigation of the candidate's potential criminal history: police contacts (via stop-and-frisk), arrests, and convictions. Investigators will also endeavor to learn as much as possible about the candidate's financial history. Writing from a place of personal experience

---

[9] This statement comes via more than 30 years of associating with countless police officers and police applicants, and an overall knowledge of the policing occupation.

[10] CA.Gov | Commission on Peace Officer Standards and Training, "Peace Officer Candidate Selection Process."

[11] Doerner, "The Utility of the Oral Interview Board in Selecting Police Academy Admissions."

[12] "How to Answer Police Officer Oral Board Interview Questions."

with the police selection process, the author of this book believes there is very little about a candidate's personal history that background investigators will not learn. Any errors or omissions made by the candidate during the background investigation subject the candidate to disqualification from the selection process.

Finally, once the background check is concluded, many police agencies require their applicants to submit to a detection of deception examination, such as a polygraph or voice stress analysis. The most common is the polygraph exam, during which the examiner asks the candidate to verify all the information contained in the personal history statement.

Medical and Psychological Evaluations

At some point during the selection process, but often at the end, many police departments require applicants to submit to both a medical and a psychological evaluation. The medical evaluation generally consists of a comprehensive physical exam, designed to identify any health conditions that might disqualify a person from becoming a police officer. The psychological exam can be administered as an oral exam, a written exam, or a combination of the two. Psychological exams, whether written or oral (or a combination), generally require applicants to complete a supplementary personal history statement that focuses on mental health and personality issues. It is not uncommon for police departments to administer standardized personality assessments, such as the Minnesota Multiphasic Personality Inventory (MMPI), the California Personality Inventory (CPI), and the Inwald Personality Inventory (IPI), in an effort to learn about potential personality disorders, any prejudices the candidate might harbor toward different groups of people, or other risk factors, such as impulse control problems and poor judgment.[13]

Police applicants who successfully navigate the screening process and pass their background investigations are usually added to a department's rank-ordered list of eligible people to hire. These hiring lists are usually good for one year. By the end of the pre-employment screening process, some applicants will have already completed (or will be in the process of completing) their police academy training, in which case they will have paid out of pocket for the training as a way of increasing their chances of being hired by the department to which they have applied. Other applicants will have applied to police agencies that operate their own training academies or send their recruits to a regional academy, in which case, they will be hired by a department and then paid to attend the academy. In total, the hiring process in U.S. police departments can take up to one year, or even longer in some cases. Indeed, at least since 2013, some researchers and policymakers have argued for the need to streamline the police officer hiring process, citing instances

---

[13] Lough and von Treuer, "A Critical Review of Psychological Instruments Used in Police Officer Selection."

where police departments have lost highly qualified candidates because it takes so long to successfully complete the prehiring process.[14]

A Summary of Police Selection Techniques

It is instructive at this point to present data on the screening techniques that U.S. police departments currently use to determine police officer eligibility. For this, we turn to the same 2016 Law Enforcement Management and Administrative Statistics (LEMAS) data that we examined in Chapter 6. Recall that the LEMAS survey, conducted by the Bureau of Justice Statistics, represents the most comprehensive national survey of local, county, and state police agencies in the United States.[15] The LEMAS survey has been periodically administered to a large national sample of police agencies since 1987, with the most recent administration occurring in 2016. Table 12.1 summarizes the police officer screening techniques as reported by the police departments that completed the 2016 LEMAS survey.

Table 12.1 summarizes police selection techniques across types of police agencies included in the LEMAS survey, delineated by local, county, or regional police; sheriff's departments; and state police agencies. As the data in Table 12.1 show, over half of all local police departments and sheriff's departments require a written aptitude exam as part of the prehiring screening, and 87 percent of all primary state police agencies require them. The majority of all police agencies require a physical fitness or agility test, and virtually all of them require a personal interview. Moreover, virtually all agencies in the LEMAS data require a background (or personal history) check of applicants. Almost all agencies conduct criminal history and driving checks as part of those background investigations. Most agencies conduct a credit check, as well. Interestingly, there was considerable variability in the use of polygraph exams as a selection tool. Whereas 78 percent of primary state police departments report using polygraph exams, only 39 percent of local police and sheriff's departments use them.

Increasingly, over the past decade, anecdotal experience has indicated that police departments have been increasingly looking into applicants' social media presence as part of the police officer selection process. Applicants might be asked to sit with their background investigator and instructed to pull up all their social media feeds for review. Some departments even reportedly print hard copies of applicants' social media feeds. The data in Table 12.1 confirm some of these anecdotal reports, which were usually made by students who had applied for police officer or crime analyst positions prior to their university graduation. At least as recently as 2016, when the most current LEMAS survey was conducted, 79.4 percent of all local, county,

---

[14] Morison, "Hiring for the 21st Century Law Enforcement Officer: Challenges, Opportunities, and Strategies for Success."
[15] "Law Enforcement Management and Administrative Statistics (LEMAS) | Bureau of Justice Statistics."

Table 12.1. Police Officer Screening Techniques Among Types of U.S. Police Agencies

Screening Technique	Local, County, or Regional Police Department (*n* = 2,135)	Sheriff's Department (*n* = 600)	Primary State or Highway Patrol Department (*n* = 49)
Written aptitude test	1,246 (58.8%)	341 (57.3%)	40 (87.0%)
Physical agility or fitness test	1,508 (71%)	420 (70.4%)	46 (100.0%)
Personal/oral interview	2,127 (99.8%)	599 (99.8%)	46 (100.0%)
Background/personal history	2,116 (99.3%)	597 (99.5%)	46 (100.0%)
■ Criminal record	2,126 (99.8%)	596 (99.5%)	46 (100.0%)
■ Driving record	2,112 (99.2%)	596 (99.5%)	46 (100.0%)
■ Credit history	1,448 (68.8%)	364 (61.2%)	44 (95.7%)
■ Social media	1,679 (79.4%)	452 (76%)	41 (89.1%)
■ Polygraph exam	819 (39.1%)	233 (39.2%)	36 (78.3%)
Psychological inventory	1,648 (77.8%)	434 (73.1%)	44 (95.7%)
Psychological interview	1,652 (78.1%)	407 (68.4%)	43 (93.5%)
Drug test	1,929 (90.9%)	541 (90.5%)	44 (95.7%)
Medical exam	1,960 (92.4%)	547 (91.3%)	45 (97.8%)
Mediation and conflict management skills	539 (25.5%)	141 (23.9%)	7 (15.2%)
Understanding diverse cultural populations	627 (29.6%)	157 (26.5%)	8 (17.4%)
Problem-solving ability assessment	835 (39.6%)	232 (39.2%)	29 (63.0%)

Note: Data from United States Department of Justice, Office of Justice Programs, Bureau of Justice Statistics. Law Enforcement Management and Administrative Statistics (LEMAS), 2016. Inter-university Consortium for Political and Social Research, 2020-08-20. https://doi.org/10.3886/ICPSR37323.v1.

and regional police departments conduct reviews of applicants' social media feeds during the prehiring process; 76.0 percent of sheriff's departments review social media feeds; and fully 89.1 percent of primary state and highway patrol agencies conduct them.

For the most part, police agencies participating in the 2016 LEMAS survey used a generous combination of the most traditional prehiring screening techniques, from written exams and physical fitness tests to background investigations and psychological exams. And to be clear, all these techniques are designed to screen out people deemed unqualified or unfit to become police officers.[16] When it comes to written tests, physical fitness exams, and even oral interviews, it is all about minimum scores to qualify the candidate to move to the next phase of the selection process. The criminal history, credit and driving records checks, and reviews of social media feeds are designed to identify applicants with problems in such personal histories and to screen them out based on those problems.

One of the more interesting findings in Table 12.1 is the identification of screening techniques that most police agencies do not use. For example, just 25.5 and 23.9 percent of police and sheriff's departments, respectively, screen for mediation or conflict resolution skills; and only 15.2 percent of primary state police and highway patrol departments do so. Moreover, 29.6 and 26.5 percent of local police and sheriff's departments, respectively, screen for applicants' understanding of diverse cultural populations, and just 17.4 percent of primary state police and highway patrol agencies do so. Finally, somewhat larger percentages of police agencies screen for problem-solving abilities: 39.6 and 39.2 percent of all local police and sheriff's departments, respectively, do so, and 63.0 percent of primary state police and highway patrol agencies do. Still, in the aggregate (i.e., pooling all police department types together), 40 percent (i.e., less than half) of all agencies included in the LEMAS survey reported that they screened for problem-solving abilities.

Why is this important? Because screening out for certain characteristics or personal history is much different than screening in for applicants' understanding of the importance of cultural diversity, applicants' abilities to mediate or engage in conflict resolution, and applicants' abilities to solve problems. Research, for example, has suggested that police departments can protect themselves and the public against officer misconduct if they exclude people with serious criminal histories, recent problematic contacts with the criminal justice system, and problematic employment histories (e.g., being disciplined or terminated from prior jobs).[17] Screening out for problematic personal histories designed to limit bad policing is not the same as screening in for traits or personal perspectives that might lead to good policing, though. We examine this issue of screening out vs. screening in in greater detail below. In the meantime, it is prudent to consider what the traditional police officer selection process has yielded in terms of predicting success in policing.

---

[16] Metchik, "An Analysis of the 'Screening Out' Model of Police Officer Selection."
[17] Kane and White, *Jammed Up: Bad Cops, Police Misconduct, and the New York City Police Department.*

Some Results of the Screening-Out Model

Among policing scholars, policymakers, and police command staff, two questions are often asked about police pre-employment screening:

1. Do the screening techniques used by police departments predict successful policing or successful police academy performance?[18]
2. Do the prehiring screening techniques select candidates with a certain personality profile, such as the so-called authoritarian personality?[19]

In terms of answering the first question, a primary difficulty resides in the fact that few people can actually define "successful" policing.[20] For some, successful policing is evidenced by officers not getting into trouble for misconduct. For others, successful policing is rising through the ranks of the police department. Perhaps successful policing is a combination of those things; perhaps it is neither. From a more macro-level perspective, successful policing can occur when police officers demonstrably improve the life chances of people they encounter in the communities they serve.[21] Again, this is something to be discussed in more detail in Chapter 13. In the meantime, a few studies have taken up the question of whether the typical police officer prehiring process predicts successful academy performance, and if so, to what extent that academy performance predicts successful policing.

In 2008, policing scholar Michael White published a study that examined the extent to which "good" police officers might be identified early, based on their police academy performance. White noted that identifying predictors of "good" policing was difficult, given the "unclear mandate" society has given police.[22] Still, as White argued, throughout the early 2000s, police academies across the country began revising their curricula to ground academy training in more realistic simulations of street-level policing. As such, by the time he conducted his study in a "large metropolitan police department,"[23] that department had created a training curriculum that came close to approximating several types of police field encounters. Thus, from White's perspective, if certain academy experiences could reasonably simulate certain police field experiences, then perhaps the factors that predicted successful academy performance during those simulations could also predict successful police officer performance in actual field encounters.

In his study of 1,556 police recruits who were part of the same academy class, White generally found that recruit reading level was the single best

---

[18] Henson et al., "Do Good Recruits Make Good Cops? Problems Predicting and Measuring Academy and Street-Level Success."
[19] Balch, "The Police Personality: Fact or Fiction?"; Adlam, "The Police Personality: Psychological Consequences of Being a Police Officer."
[20] e.g., Skolnick and Fyfe, *Above the Law: Police and the Excessive Use of Force.*
[21] Fyfe, "'Good' Policing."
[22] White, "Identifying Good Cops Early: Predicting Recruit Performance in the Academy," 29.
[23] White, 34.

predictor of academy performance, including the simulated field encounters. Indeed, even though other recruit characteristics were also significant predictors of academy performance—for example, being male, White, and young—White's findings showed that recruits who were male, White, and young also had the highest reading scores compared to other groups coming into the academy. Thus, taken in the aggregate, reading level—as an indirect measure of academic readiness—was the most important personal characteristic that predicted academy performance. But does this finding really generalize to predicting good, or successful, policing?

In a replication and extension of White's 2008 findings, scholar Billy Henson and colleagues examined academy class performance of police recruits in a Midwestern city, as well as their subsequent performance as police officers.[24] As with White's study, Henson and colleagues' findings indicated that incoming academic preparedness—as measured by recruits' scores on the civil service exam—and being White significantly predicted successful academy performance. Henson and colleagues noted that race was likely an indirect measure of recruit "socioeconomic status,"[25] which could explain why White recruits achieved higher academy class scores than recruits from other racial and ethnic groups.

Unlike White, in his 2008 study, however, Henson and colleagues found that male recruits performed no better or worse in the academy than female recruits, but that male recruits did achieve higher scores on both their first- and second-year job performance evaluations as police officers. Henson and colleagues offered the following possible explanation for their gender findings:

> Despite the increase in the number of female officers over time, policing remains a male-dominated profession. Moreover, while there is no evidence to substantiate this assertion, it appears that the evaluation process may be biased against women. Alternatively, female officers may be better adept at handling disputes without invoking their arrest powers. Since performance evaluations are often based on producing numbers (i.e., tickets issued, people arrested), female officers may be assigned lower evaluation scores due to their reliance on other strategies than arrest to resolve disputes.[26]

Although Henson and colleagues could offer no data to support their speculations about gender, they were correct in noting that policing remains a highly male-dominated field: As of 2013 (the last year for which data are available), just 12.2 percent of all full-time police officers in the United States identified as female, and this percentage was markedly lower in departments serving midsize and small population jurisdictions.[27] Indeed, in departments

---

[24] Henson et al., "Do Good Recruits Make Good Cops? Problems Predicting and Measuring Academy and Street-Level Success."
[25] Henson et al., 13.
[26] Henson et al., 20.
[27] Reaves, "Local Police Departments, 2013: Personnel, Policies, and Practices," 4.

serving jurisdictions of between 50,000 and 99,000 people, 9.7 percent of sworn officers identified as female, and that number shrank to 6.1 percent in police agencies serving populations of fewer than 2,500 residents.[28]

Why is this gender imbalance so important in policing? Because in organizations—and other settings—that contain a dominant group (i.e., a group that represents a large majority of the organization's members), the norms, the rules, and productivity expectations tend to be set by that dominant group;[29] frequently, that dominant group takes action to reward itself and its members for performing tasks it has deemed desirable to the organization, often at the expense of the nondominant groups.[30] In policing, this can mean that, because most of the policies and expectations around productivity are created by a mostly male group, the productivity standards might disadvantage female officers in ways that Henson and colleagues suggested in their passage quoted above.

Interestingly, in the studies of both White and Henson and colleagues, reading level emerged as the strongest characteristic—and literally, one of the few direct characteristics—to significantly predict successful police academy performance and (in Henson et al.'s case) first- and second-year job performance as police officers. One might therefore conclude that police departments should strive to recruit officers with a college education, but as a collective occupation, it does not. Whereas more than of 23 percent of all police officers work for an agency that requires a two-year college degree at entry, only 10 percent of all local police departments require at least a two-year degree at entry.[31] Only 1 percent of all police agencies require a four-year degree at entry.[32] Thus, even though reading levels—or more broadly, academic readiness—predicted both police academy and police officer success (at least, for the latter, during the first two years of service), the police institution has not capitalized on this finding by increasing the entry-level requirements for the occupation.

Turning to the question of whether the traditional police selection process screens for a certain personality profile, the research in this area is nuanced. Historically, police departments have used various psychological batteries and interviews (as described above) primarily to identify candidates whose personalities likely would not lend themselves to police work.[33] Psychological tests continue to screen out applicants whose scores suggest an inability to function in high-stress working environments; as well as those with negative attitudes toward ethnic minorities, women, and people of different sexual orientations; and those with personality disorders, poor

---

[28] Reaves, 4.

[29] Fu et al., "Evolution of In-Group Favoritism."

[30] Perry et al., "Barriers to Multiculturalism: Ingroup Favoritism and Outgroup Hostility Are Independently Associated With Policy Opposition"; Grimm, Utikal, and Valmasoni, "In-Group Favoritism and Discrimination Among Multiple Out-Groups."

[31] Reaves, "Local Police Departments, 2013: Personnel, Policies, and Practices."

[32] Reaves, 7.

[33] Lough and von Treuer, "A Critical Review of Psychological Instruments Used in Police Officer Selection."

decision-making, and impulse control problems.[34] Although it is difficult to make the case that people with personality disorders, intolerance toward different cultural groups, and impulse control problems would make good police officers, these tests are designed to exclude people who likely would be bad law enforcers. The tests do virtually nothing, however, to identify candidates who could make excellent police officers across a broader set of occupational domains, such as problem-solving skills and the desire to work with community organizations, characteristics that would lend themselves well to community policing.[35]

In fact, as policing scholar Eric Metchik noted, screening out undesirable candidates "has traditionally been favored by police administrative personnel because of its emphasis on improving the public's evaluation of officers as effective crime fighters."[36] The entire application process in most police departments—including the psychological screening—is designed to exclude those who do not possess a law enforcement mentality. As Metchik further noted, "Specifically, it has been felt that officers with poor stress tolerance, prejudicial attitudes, or impaired judgment, thought processes, or interpersonal skills are at a distinct disadvantage in terms of the aggressive yet controlled activities required to apprehend and safely manage criminal suspects."[37]

Again, it is difficult to argue that police candidates with personality disorders and problems with intolerance should be screened into policing, but it is also the case that by screening out strictly for a presumed lack of law enforcement competence likely excludes many candidates who would excel in other aspects of policing—an important point given that research has consistently shown that most of what police officers do on a daily basis has little do with law enforcement.[38] Indeed, the mismatch between what police officers expect to be doing on the job (i.e., crime fighting) and what they actually spend most of their time doing (i.e., "service" over law enforcement) has been associated with officers' intentions to leave the occupation.[39]

Researchers have noted that the "police personality" appears to evolve over time. Undesirable job candidates are screened out as a result of pre-employment psychological batteries, yielding academy recruits who have "basically the same personality constructs going into the force—in essence,

---

[34] Metchik, "An Analysis of the 'Screening Out' Model of Police Officer Selection"; Twersky-Glasner, "Police Personality: What Is It and Why Are They Like That?"

[35] Henson et al., "Do Good Recruits Make Good Cops? Problems Predicting and Measuring Academy and Street-Level Success."

[36] Metchik, "An Analysis of the 'Screening Out' Model of Police Officer Selection," 79.

[37] Metchik, 80.

[38] Huey and Ricciardelli, "'This Isn't What I Signed up for': When Police Officer Role Expectations Conflict With the Realities of General Duty Police Work in Remote Communities"; Greene and Klockars, "What Police Do"; Kane, "Policing in Public Housing: Using Calls for Service to Examine Incident-Based Workload in the Philadelphia Housing Authority."

[39] Glissmeyer, Bishop, and Fass, "Role Conflict, Role Ambiguity and Intention to Quit the Organization: The Case of Law Enforcement Officers."

a baseline."[40] This baseline personality, which often distinguishes successful applicants from unsuccessful applicants, generally includes the traits of assertiveness, self-assurance, aspirations for higher social status, masculinity, above-average intelligence, and the ability to perceive social situations.[41] As early as 1977, psychology scholar Robert Balch referred to this collection of traits as a "conventional" personality.[42] That is, as a distinct occupational group, police recruits are characterized by a conventional personality. Once on the job, however, that personality begins to change.

Policing scholar Larry Gould conducted one of the few identified longitudinal studies of police recruits, measuring their personality characteristics at different points from the time they entered the police academy to when they reached 42 months on the job. Gould found that during the 42-month study period, the police officers participating in the research experienced significant and substantial increases in paranoia, anger, cynicism, depression, dominance, and hostility.[43] Thus, what started as a baseline personality of conventionality ultimately evolved into something that resembled Jerome Skolnick's "working personality" of police, which develops in police officers as a result of the subcultural elements of danger, authority, and isolation (recall Chapter 5). Indeed, as Gould noted, "the policing environment tends to have a negative effect on police officers."[44]

Gould's study was striking for showing how the evolving personality traits differentially affected officers by race and gender. For example, White male officers experienced a 27 percent increase in paranoia over the 42-month study period, which was far greater than the increases experienced by White females and Black males. Black female officers, however, experienced a 52 percent increase in paranoia over the study period. Moreover, White male and female officers experienced 13.6 and 10.0 percent increases, respectively, in anger levels over the study period, whereas Black males and females experienced increases of 48 and 53 percent, respectively, suggesting that the police work environment evoked frustration among Black officers at much higher rates than White officers. Finally, Black male and female officers became substantially more cynical, depressed, and hostile over time than did White male and female officers, again suggesting the high toll that policing takes on officers of color.

In the end, what begins with a screening process that weeds out applicants with personality disorders, a lack of tolerance for stress, social awkwardness, and poor judgment results in a collective group of police recruits who possess largely the same personality profile characterized by assertiveness, self-assurance, a desire for social mobility, and relatively high functional intelligence. Over time, the police working environment appears to

---

[40] Twersky-Glasner, "Police Personality: What Is It and Why Are They Like That?," 65.
[41] Twersky-Glasner; Hogan and Kurtines, "Personological Correlates of Police Effectiveness."
[42] Balch, "The Police Personality: Fact or Fiction," 25.
[43] Gould, "A Longitudinal Approach to the Study of the Police Personality: Race/Gender Differences," 49.
[44] Gould, 48.

transform this conventional personality into a "working" personality characterized by suspicion, cynicism, and "prejudice and distrust of the unusual."[45] Notably, the police work environment takes a disproportionately negative toll on Black male and female officers.

A primary problem with the screening-out paradigm is that it focuses on selecting recruits with a law enforcement mentality and excluding people with personality traits deemed problematic to the job of policing. Focusing on such a narrow conceptualization of the police role likely prohibits several groups of otherwise high-quality applicants from being hired as police officers. Thus, the screening-out process as practiced by generations of police departments has created a self-perpetuating cycle of police pre-employment screening wherein some number of successful police recruits—who are selected based largely on their law enforcement mentality—ultimately rise through the ranks of their respective police organizations, and then reach positions where they are conducting the hiring, looking for candidates with whom they can identify. As police scholar Twersky-Glasner noted, "Persons who can demonstrate characteristics and traits like those already on the force stand a greater chance of being hired."[46] In other words, and as the savvy undergraduate student identified at the start of this chapter put it, "They just want to hire themselves!"

There is a growing sense among researchers and policymakers that the traditional screening-out process has led to a "warrior" mentality among police officers that can help explain, for example, the rise of police paramilitarism,[47] and perhaps even several specific incidents of deadly force, such as the shooting of Michael Brown in Ferguson and the killing of George Floyd in Minneapolis. Additionally, the so-called warrior mentality might also explain how the police in Ferguson responded so quickly with military-like deployments when public demonstrations began in the wake of the shooting of Michael Brown.[48] Although screening out for criminal histories, personality disorders, and prejudices against ethnic and other cultural groups is probably a good thing for policing, failing to screen in for traits such as problem-solving, respect (not just tolerance) for different cultural groups, and mediation or conflict resolution abilities likely limits the collective worldview of the police occupation. As the President's Task Force on 21st Century Policing argued, it is time for police in the United States to move beyond hiring "warriors" and begin hiring "guardians."[49]

---

[45] Twersky-Glasner, "Police Personality: What Is It and Why Are They Like That?," 64.

[46] Twersky-Glasner, 65.

[47] Balko, *Rise of the Warrior Cop: The Militarization of America's Police Forces*; Kappeler and Kraska, "Normalising Police Militarisation, Living in Denial"; Balko, "Overkill: The Rise of Paramilitary Police Raids in America"; Kraska, "Militarization and Policing—Its Relevance to 21st Century Police."

[48] Taub, "What Was THAT? A Guide to the Military Gear Being Used Against Civilians in Ferguson"; Curry and Martinez, "Ferguson Police's Show of Force Highlights Militarization of America's Cops"; Patrick and Currier, "Ferguson Highlights Police Use of Military Gear and Tactics"; "Ferguson Unrest: From Shooting to Nationwide Protests."

[49] President's Task Force on 21st Century Policing, "Final Report of the President's Task Force on 21st Century Policing," 11.

Hiring "Guardians," Not "Warriors"

In Book 8 of *The Republic*, in his dialogue with Socrates, Plato wrote, "In a republic that honors the core of democracy—the greatest amount of power is given to those called guardians. Only those with the most impeccable character are chosen to bear the responsibility of protecting the democracy."[50] This quotation was also integrated into the Final Report of the President's Task Force on 21st Century Policing, submitted to then-President Obama in 2015. The Task Force was created as a result of both the shooting of Michael Brown in Ferguson and the rapidly deployed paramilitary response of the Ferguson and St. Louis County Police Departments when demonstrations began.[51] In that report the Task Force identified the need for U.S. police departments to move beyond hiring "warriors" and begin hiring "guardians." Part of the inspiration for this recommendation appears to have come from an article that Task Force member Sue Rahr published a year before the President's Task Force was created. In that article, Rahr, who was at the time serving as executive director for the Washington State Criminal Justice Training Commission, noted:

> In 2012, we began asking the question, "Why are we training police officers like soldiers?" Although police officers wear uniforms and carry weapons, the similarity ends there. The missions and rules of engagement are completely different. The soldier's mission is that of a warrior: to conquer. The rules of engagement are decided before the battle. The police officer's mission is that of a guardian: to protect. The rules of engagement evolve as the incident unfolds. Soldiers must follow orders. Police officers must make independent decisions. Soldiers come into communities as an outside, occupying force. Guardians are members of the community, protecting from within.[52]

Rahr's comments embody the spirit of this book's new idea of police and the protection of life mandate it proposes. The points she made could be easily applied to the case study of Jazmine Headley from Chapter 4, where this book introduced the new idea of police.

Recall from Chapter 4 Jazmine Headley's encounter with four officers from the New York City Police Department. Ms. Headley was the young mother who entered the SNAP office in Brooklyn with her one-year-old son, hoping to renew her benefits. Unable to find a chair in the waiting area, she sat on the floor to wait for her turn to be called. A security guard approached and asked her to leave because she was (he claimed) causing a disturbance by sitting on the floor. When she refused to leave, the security guard called the police. Four NYPD officers arrived, asked her first to leave, and then—when she attempted to explain her situation—ordered her to surrender her son

---

[50] Plato, *The Republic*, 236.
[51] President's Task Force on 21st Century Policing, "Final Report of the President's Task Force on 21st Century Policing," III.
[52] Rahr, "Transforming the Culture of Policing from Warriors to Guardians in Washington State," 3-4.

to them.[53] Ms. Headley refused to give up her son, which led the officers to escalate the encounter, drawing and threatening the use of a Taser and ultimately tackling her and ripping her son from her arms. She was then arrested for trespassing and endangering a child, although all charges were dropped very soon after she was booked.

Using Rahr's quoted passage above as a framework to help distinguish between warriors and guardians, the NYPD officers, acting as warriors, treated Ms. Headley as though they were occupiers—that is, like she was an enemy who needed to be "conquered," rather than as a member of their community who needed protection. Rahr also noted that whereas it is the job of soldiers to follow orders that were given before a campaign, it is the role of police to change their responses (or "rules of engagement") as events during an encounter evolve. In the case of Ms. Headley, the four NYPD officers never changed their engagement with her, despite the new information they were taking in during their encounter with her. They treated her as a warrior would treat an enemy: as a threat. Bringing this point back to the President's Task Force, their final report recommends that police departments select applicants as police officers for their guardianship mentality rather than a warrior mentality.

But how to get there? Given the discussion in this chapter about how the law enforcement mentality of the police is maintained and perpetuated through a selection cycle that favors "hiring themselves," it would seem that some form of intervention would be necessary to break that cycle. The President's Task Force made an additional observation in its final report that is relevant to this issue. In the report, the authors noted that to move beyond the cycle of simply screening out for warriors to screening in for guardians, police departments must link the selection process to the recruitment processes.[54]

This point takes us back to the application process identified earlier in the chapter, wherein people formally declare their intentions to become a police officer. The question is this: Who makes such a declaration? Currently, when police departments post police officer job openings, they frequently issue open calls for applicants. In some jurisdictions, departments do little more than simply list the jobs on the local human resources website; in other places, the police might do some local advertising to encourage people to apply. In either case, the point is to generate as many applications for the openings as possible so that the department has enough people to screen out. As a result, police departments largely defer to public ideas of the police role, passively waiting for people who think they know what policing is about to file their applications.

In this way, recruitment is largely separate from the application process. Historically, police departments have been able to generate great interest in

[53] Southall, "'Appalling' Video Shows the Police Yanking 1-Year-Old from His Mother's Arms."
[54] President's Task Force on 21st Century Policing, "Final Report of the President's Task Force on 21st Century Policing," 17.

their police officer positions without active recruitment efforts. Indeed, the author's own lived experience confirms that, historically, on many occasions at the start of the written exam for police department applicants, the proctors of the exam (who are often police officers) have been known to say something like, "Our department currently hires about 1 in 100 applicants. Look around the room right now. Which one of you will be hired?" Although there is no way to systematically verify the accuracy of the "1 in 100" assertion, its sentiment suggests that police departments have not had to actively recruit to generate job applicants.

There is evidence that things are changing in policing with respect to recruitment and hiring, however. In a National Public Radio interview in June 2021, Chuck Wexler, executive director of the Police Executive Research Forum (PERF)—among the most highly respected nonprofit policing research organizations in the United States—noted that police departments nationally have been experiencing large numbers of retirements and resignations and have had a hard time generating applications for open police officer positions.[55] Other news and research outlets have reported the same thing, attributing the difficulty in recruiting and keeping police officers to increased violent crime, national protests against police use of force, and more recently, the pandemic.[56] As Wexler noted in his NPR interview, "We are in unchartered territory right now. . . . Policing is being challenged in ways I have never seen."[57]

It would seem that at a time when police departments appear to be experiencing difficulties in attracting people to the job, departments could begin to link the recruitment process to the application process. They could create media campaigns designed to reach people they have historically excluded or at least overlooked. If warriors—or people who bring a specific law enforcement orientation to the application process—are applying in smaller numbers than before, then the time might be right for police departments to rebrand themselves to actively recruit guardians. As part of that process, they might begin to screen in for the three characteristics identified in Table 12.1 that most departments have thus far ignored: mediation and conflict management skills, understanding of diverse cultural populations, and problem-solving abilities.

Some Concluding Observations

Policing is a street-level occupation. It is messy; it is unpredictable; and it requires sound decision-making and discretion by those who practice it. As noted in Chapter 5 in the discussion of the policing subculture, policing is

---

[55] Westervelt, "Cops Are Leaving Their Departments in Droves and Few Want to Take Their Place: NPR."
[56] Police Executive Research Forum, "The Workforce Crisis, and What Police Agencies Are Doing About It"; Mellen, "Unprecedented Challenges in Hiring, Retaining Police Recruits."
[57] Westervelt, "Cops Are Leaving Their Departments in Droves and Few Want to Take Their Place: NPR."

both sacred and profane: Police officers see many people during their first moments of life, their final moments of life, and at many hallowed moments in between. Officers work in dangerous settings that are largely invisible to most members of society. They regularly come into contact with people who have committed almost unthinkable acts of cruelty. To meet the challenges and responsibilities of the job, the police institution needs to bring people into the occupation who possess the emotional and integral dexterity to perform under some very high-stress circumstances.

A recruitment process designed around the concept of screening out applicants primarily to preserve a collective law enforcement mentality fails to respect and even comprehend the complexities of the job. Policing will always need to employ some type of screening-out method to exclude people who are not suitable for the occupation. This is true for one simple fact: Many people call the police on the worst day of their lives. When they make that decision to call, they deserve a police officer who will bring the authority and expertise to take over where the person who called is unable to function. That person deserves an officer who does not have a personality disorder, does not hold prejudicial attitudes toward women and ethnic minorities, and will not look for opportunities to steal valuables while presumably offering to help. Thus, screening out should remain part of the prehiring selection process—to protect the occupation and the community from people not worthy of the public trust—but it should not *be* the paradigm. Screening in should be the paradigm, where police departments actively seek to attract people from a variety of backgrounds who would bring a variety of perspectives to the job.

Questions for Review and Reflection

Question 1. Reexamining the Police Screening-Out Process

For generations, police departments in the United States have relied on a consistent model of selecting police officers, which typically includes a written test, physical ability test, oral interview, background investigation, medical and psychological exam, and frequently a deception detector (e.g., polygraph) exam.

- What has been the overall result of this police officer selection paradigm? Who has it excluded? Who has it favored?

- Of all the selection techniques identified in Table 12.1, which do you think are the most reliable in selecting "good" police officers? Which do you think are the least reliable?

- Should a police officer applicant's social media feeds be subject to scrutiny during the application process? Should police departments be allowed to exclude people with "problematic" social media posts in their recent history or distant past? If so, should they be subject to exclusion for the people they follow or are "friends" with online? What of First Amendment rights?

Question 2. Predicting Successful Academy and Police Officer Performance

As noted in the chapter, research on who makes a good police recruit has shown that high reading scores (or academic readiness) seem to be the best collective predictor of police academy success, and even policing success during the first two years of service. That same research, however, also finds that younger White males have achieved the highest reading scores in academy classes that have been studied, which can explain why they achieve outstanding police academy performance.

- To what extent might the findings related to reading level, race, and gender represent a selection bias that exists in the real world and that permeates policing?
- To what extent might the reading level findings be used to exclude—or perhaps devalue—academy recruits of color and those who identify as female?
- If reading levels are indeed related to socioeconomic status, as Henson and colleagues speculated in their study of police academy performance, how can police academies (and police departments by extension) ensure that recruits of color are not systematically discriminated against based on the communities they grew up in?

Question 3. Bringing in the Guardians

The President's Task Force on 21st Century Policing recommended that police departments transition from screening out for candidates with "warrior" mentalities to screening in for candidates with "guardian" mentalities.

- How can police departments change their hiring practices so that recruitment and selection are linked in ways that can help bring guardians to the applicant pools?
- Moving beyond the labels, what do you think are the traits—or characteristics—that make up "warrior" and "guardian" mentalities? Are there any overlaps between warrior and guardian traits?
- To what extent should policing still seek to hire some warriors while also trying to hire guardians? Is there still a role for warriors in U.S. policing?

Exercises

Exercise 1. Reordering the Selection Criteria for Police Officer Candidates

Table 12.1 shows the typical selection criteria U.S. police departments reported using at the last LEMAS survey administration in 2016. Although departments did not rank-order the importance of certain selection criteria over others, we can—to some extent—infer the importance police departments have placed on the selection criteria based on the percentages of departments that used them. In this exercise, you will rank-order the selection criteria that appear in Table 12.1, indicating which criteria you believe are the most important and which are the least important when selecting police recruits. Your goal is to create a set of rank-ordered selection criteria that you believe would identify candidates who would make good police officers. To complete the exercise, take the following steps.

- Create a definition of the "good" police officer. This definition will guide the process by which you create a rank-ordered list of selection criteria. Your definition of a good police officer should be about a single paragraph in length.

- Re-create Table 12.1 as a spreadsheet or a table within a word processing document, entering the selection criteria in the order in which you believe they should be weighted by police departments when considering applicants for the job of police officer. In the cells next to each selection criterion, indicate why you ranked the criterion where you did in the list.

- As part of your re-creation of Table 12.1, you should feel free to give one or more selection criteria a "zero," which indicates that you would not use it at all as part of the police officer selection process. For any selection criterion you exclude from the process, list it in the table and describe why you believe it is unimportant. When doing so, keep in mind that certain criteria (e.g., criminal history, poor employment history, etc.) have been shown to predict bad policing (i.e., police misconduct). So, if you exclude them, be sure to explain why.

- You should also feel free to add an additional set of criteria you believe would be important to include as part of the selection process but that do not currently appear in Table 12.1. If you do this, explain why.

- After you complete the task, write a brief summary that explains your thought process for ranking the selection criteria as you did, for excluding any techniques that appear in Table 12.1, and for including new techniques that currently do not appear in Table 12.1.

Exercise 2. From Screening Out to Screening In: Reimaging the Traditional Police Officer Selection Process

As noted in the chapter, generations of policing have relied on a process of screening out candidates deemed unworthy of the police officer's job, which has resulted in a psychologically homogenous police occupational group. The President's Task Force on 21st Century Policing recommended that U.S. police departments move beyond the screening-out model that has created an occupational group of warriors in favor of a screening-in model that should attract guardians to the applicant pools. For this exercise, reimagine the traditional police selection model by creating a new model designed to screen in for guardians, or applicants who would make good police officers. In creating this new model, consider the following.

- As you begin the reimagining process, write a paragraph that defines good policing and the characteristics that good police officers should possess. This will be your guide as you develop the recruitment and selection criteria.

- Will you keep any of the current steps in the police officer selection process, such as the written exam, physical ability test, oral interview, psychological testing, and personal history investigation? If so, which parts? If not, what will you replace the current process with?

- Will you keep any or all of the selection techniques that currently appear in Table 12.1? If so, which ones?

- How will you link the recruitment process to the application process to generate pools of applicants who will fit your ideas of good policing and good police officers?

- As part of your new recruitment plan, how will you reach out to communities that have been traditionally excluded from, or ignored by, police departments?

- Conduct some online research to identify potential models for your reimagined police recruitment and screening-in hiring process. You might identify police departments currently engaged in community outreach and other screening-in techniques from which your new plan can borrow. Remember that it is not necessary to "reinvent the wheel." If you identify one or more police agencies already engaging in some of the screening-in techniques you value, feel free to adopt them as part of yours.

Bibliography

Adlam, K. Robert. "The Police Personality: Psychological Consequences of Being a Police Officer." *Journal of Police Science & Administration* 10, no. 3 (1982): 344–347.

Balch, Robert W. "The Police Personality: Fact or Fiction?" *The Journal of Criminal Law, Criminology, and Police Science* 63, no. 1 (1972): 106–119.

Balch, Robert W. "The Police Personality: Fact or Fiction." In *The Dysfunctional Alliance: Emotion and Reason in Justice Administration*, edited by D. B. Kennedy, 10–25. Cincinnati, OH: Anderson, 1977.

Balko, Radley. "Overkill: The Rise of Paramilitary Police Raids in America." Washington, DC, 2006. http://www.ncjrs.gov/App/publications/abstract.aspx?ID=238405.

Balko, Radley. *Rise of the Warrior Cop: The Militarization of America's Police Forces.* PublicAffairs, 2021.

"Becoming a USCP Police Officer | United States Capitol Police." Accessed February 4, 2022. https://www.uscp.gov/becoming-uscp-police-officer.

CA.Gov | Commission on Peace Officer Standards and Training. "Peace Officer Candidate Selection Process." Accessed February 2, 2022. https://post.ca.gov/peace-officer-candidate-selection-process.

"Calculate Your BMI - Standard BMI Calculator." Accessed February 4, 2022. https://www.nhlbi.nih.gov/health/educational/lose_wt/BMI/bmicalc.htm.

Curry, Colleen, and Luis Martinez. "Ferguson Police's Show of Force Highlights Militarization of America's Cops." ABC News, 2014. https://abcnews.go.com/US/ferguson-police-small-army-thousands-police-departments/story?id=24977299.

Doerner, William G. "The Utility of the Oral Interview Board in Selecting Police Academy Admissions." *Policing: An International Journal of Police Strategies & Management* 20, no. 4 (1997): 777–785. https://doi.org/10.1108/13639519710368143.

"Ferguson Unrest: From Shooting to Nationwide Protests." BBC News, 2015. http://www.bbc.com/news/world-us-canada-30193354.

Fu, Feng, Corina E. Tarnita, Nicholas A. Christakis, Long Wang, David G. Rand, and Martin A. Nowak. "Evolution of In-Group Favoritism." *Scientific Reports* 2 (2012): 1–6. https://doi.org/10.1038/srep00460.

Fyfe, James J. "'Good' Policing." In *The Socio-Economics of Crime and Justice*, edited by Brian Forst, 269–299. New York: Routledge/Taylor and Francis, 1993. https://books.google.com/books?hl=en&lr=&id=IOlmDAAAQBAJ&oi=fnd&pg=PA269&dq=fyfe+good+policing&ots=wFKazkphOs&sig=-NhnXfmpUgxCYY6MNq8ck3w3aC0#v=onepage&q=fyfe good policing&f=false.

Glissmeyer, Michael, James W. Bishop, and R. David Fass. "Role Conflict, Role Ambiguity and Intention to Quit the Organization: The Case of Law Enforcement Officers." In *Decision Sciences Institute Annual Conference, 38th Southwest*, 458–469, 2007.

Gould, Larry A. "A Longitudinal Approach to the Study of the Police Personality: Race/Gender Differences." *Journal of Police and Criminal Psychology* 15, no. 2 (2000): 41–51. https://doi.org/10.1007/BF02802664.

Greene, Jack R., and Carl B. Klockars. "What Police Do." In *Thinking About Police: Contemporary Readings*, 2nd ed., edited by Carl B. Klockars and Stephen D. Mastrofski, 273–284. New York: McGraw-Hill, 1991.

Grimm, Veronika, Verena Utikal, and Lorenzo Valmasoni. "In-Group Favoritism and Discrimination Among Multiple Out-Groups." IWQW Discussion Papers, No. 05/2015, Friedrich-Alexander-Universität Erlangen-Nürnberg, Institut Für Wirtschaftspolitik Und Quantitative Wirtschaftsforschung (IWQW), Nürnberg, 2015.

Henson, Billy, Bradford W. Reyns, Charles F. Klahm, IV, and James Frank. "Do Good Recruits Make Good Cops? Problems Predicting and Measuring Academy and Street-Level Success." *Police Quarterly* 13, no. 1 (2010): 5–26. https://doi.org/10.1177/1098611109357320.

Hogan, Robert, and William Kurtines. "Personological Correlates of Police Effectiveness." *The Journal of Psychology* 91, no. 2 (1975): 289–295.

"Home | Navajo Police Department." Accessed February 4, 2022. https://www.npd.navajo-nsn.gov/.

"How to Answer Police Officer Oral Board Interview Questions." Accessed February 4, 2022. https://www.police1.com/police-jobs-and-careers/articles/the-toughest-oral-board-questions-and-how-to-answer-them-2zMbXEYByHLVbnt3/.

Huey, Laura, and Rose Ricciardelli. "'This Isn't What I Signed up for': When Police Officer Role Expectations Conflict With the Realities of General Duty Police Work in Remote Communities." *International Journal of Police Science and Management* 17, no. 3 (2015): 194–203. https://doi.org/10.1177/1461355715603590.

"Jobs — The Supreme Court Police." Accessed February 4, 2022. https://www.supremecourt.gov/jobs/police/police.aspx.

Kane, Robert J. "Policing in Public Housing: Using Calls for Service to Examine Incident-Based Workload in the Philadelphia Housing Authority." *Policing* 21, no. 4 (1998): 618–631. https://doi.org/10.1108/13639519810241656.

Kane, Robert J., and Michael D. White. *Jammed Up: Bad Cops, Police Misconduct, and the New York City Police De-*

partment. New York: NYU Press, 2013. https://nyupress .org/9780814748411/jammed-up/.

Kappeler, Victor E., and Peter B. Kraska. "Normalising Police Militarisation, Living in Denial." *Policing and Society* 25, no. 3 (2015): 268–275. https://doi.org/10 .1080/10439463.2013.864655.

Kraska, P. B. "Militarization and Policing—Its Relevance to 21st Century Police." *Policing* 1, no. 4 (2007): 501– 513. https://doi.org/10.1093/police/pam065.

"Law Enforcement Management and Administrative Statistics (LEMAS) | Bureau of Justice Statistics." Accessed February 6, 2022. https://bjs.ojp.gov/data-collection /law-enforcement-management-and-administrative -statistics-lemas.

Los Angeles Police Department. "Join LAPD: LAPD Hiring Process." Accessed February 2, 2022. https:// www.joinlapd.com/there-are-seven-steps-application- process.

Lough, Jonathan, and Kathryn von Treuer. "A Critical Review of Psychological Instruments Used in Police Officer Selection." *Policing* 36, no. 4 (2013): 737–751. https://doi.org/10.1108/PIJPSM-11-2012-0104.

Mellen, Greg. "Unprecedented Challenges in Hiring, Retaining Police Recruits." Police1, 2021. https://www .police1.com/police-recruiting/articles/why-law -enforcement-is-facing-unprecedented-challenges-in -hiring-and-keeping-recruits-pFiTKCXrne6ccNfB/.

Metchik, Eric. "An Analysis of the 'Screening Out' Model of Police Officer Selection." *Police Quarterly* 2, no. 1 (1999): 79–95. https://doi.org/10.1177/109861119900200104.

Mobile Police Department. "The Application Process." Accessed June 2, 2022. https://www.mobilepd.org /application-process/.

Morison, Kevin P. "Hiring for the 21st Century Law Enforcement Officer: Challenges, Opportunities, and Strategies for Success." Washington, DC, 2017.

"Most Common Police Officer Selection Tests | Police Test Prep." Accessed February 4, 2022. https://www .policetest.info/most-common.

Patrick, Robert, and Joel Currier. "Ferguson Highlights Police Use of Military Gear and Tactics." *St. Louis Dispatch*, August 15, 2014. https://www.stltoday.com /news/local/metro/ferguson-highlights-police-use-of -military-gear-and-tactics/article_69176ce4-f888- 58ff-b33a-64924d2beb6d.html.

Perry, Ryan, Naomi Priest, Yin Paradies, Fiona Barlow, and Chris Sibley. "Barriers to Multiculturalism: Ingroup Favoritism and Outgroup Hostility Are Independently Associated With Policy Opposition." 2017. https://doi.org/10.31219/osf.io/nk334.

Plato. *The Republic.* Edited by Richard W. Sterling and William C. Scott. New York: W.W. Norton, 1996.

Police Executive Research Forum. "The Workforce Crisis, and What Police Agencies Are Doing About It." PERF, Washington, DC, 2019.

President's Task Force on 21st Century Policing. "Final Report of the President's Task Force on 21st Century Policing." Washington, DC, 2015.

Rahr, Sue. "Transforming the Culture of Policing From Warriors to Guardians in Washington State." *International Association of Directors of Law Enforcement Standards and Training Newsletter* 25, no. 4 (2014): 3–4.

Reaves, Brian. "Local Police Departments, 2013: Personnel, Policies, and Practices." Bureau of Justice Statistics. Washington, DC, 2015.

Skolnick, Jerome, and James J. Fyfe. *Above the Law: Police and the Excessive Use of Force.* New York: Free Press, 1993.

Southall, Ashley. "'Appalling' Video Shows the Police Yanking 1-Year-Old from His Mother's Arms." *The New York Times*, December 9, 2018. https://www.nytimes .com/2018/12/09/nyregion/nypd-jazmine-headley -baby-video.html.

Taub, Amanda. "What Was THAT? A Guide to the Military Gear Being Used Against Civilians in Ferguson." Vox, 2014. https://www.vox.com/2014/8/18/6003377 /ferguson-military-gear.

Twersky-Glasner, Aviva. "Police Personality: What Is It and Why Are They Like That?" *Journal of Police and Criminal Psychology* 20, no. 1 (2005): 56–67. https:// doi.org/10.1007/BF02806707.

Westervelt, Eric. "Cops Are Leaving Their Departments in Droves and Few Want to Take Their Place: NPR." Accessed February 18, 2022. https://www.npr .org/2021/06/24/1009578809/cops-say-low-morale -and-department-scrutiny-are-driving-them-away -from-the-job.

White, Michael D. "Identifying Good Cops Early: Predicting Recruit Performance in the Academy." *Police Quarterly* 11, no. 1 (2008): 27–49.

CHAPTER 13

Integrating the New Idea of Policing into U.S. Police Departments

As noted in the first chapter, this book is intended as both an introduction to police in the United States and an examination of police and society. It was meant to describe the police in full enough detail to give readers a solid foundational knowledge of police and policing in the United States. It was also intended to explain the police by contextualizing their descriptions in historical, organizational, subcultural, and sociological terms. With that explanation came some critique of the police institution, in particular the identified coercion paradigm that, at least since the escalation of the war on drugs in the 1980s and 1990s, continues to drive most contemporary police strategies.[1] Finally, the book was designed to introduce a new way of thinking about the police and their role by proposing a protection of life mandate designed to minimize the emphasis that police and society place on coercion as a primary police function. Viewing the police role, as this book has argued, through a protection of life rather than a strict law enforcement lens can help distinguish a future version of policing from aspects of the institution's past that have produced harmful outcomes for certain individuals and groups.

---

[1] Fernandes and Crutchfield, "Race, Crime, and Criminal Justice: Fifty Years Since the Challenge of Crime in a Free Society"; Jones, "Terry v. Ohio: Its Failure, Immoral Progeny, and Racial Profiling"; Beckett, "The Uses and Abuses of Police Discretion: Toward Harm Reduction Policing"; Rahr and Rice, "From Warriors to Guardians: Recommitting American Police Culture to Democratic Ideals."

Podcast Episode: "Creating Police Universities in the United States: A Way to Professionalize the Occupation?"

Scan the QR code or enter the short URL shown below into a browser window to listen to this chapter's podcast.
https://bit.ly/3s8SlmN

The protection of life—or the author's assertion of a *new* idea of police—is not about reform so much as it is about redefining the police mandate and the mentality that officers bring to their encounters with the public. From a theoretical standpoint, the book has argued that policing must move beyond the philosophical grounding of Max Weber, who defined the state as an entity that owned a monopoly on the legitimate use of violence, to the one proposed by Emile Durkheim that envisioned the state as an entity that calls citizens to moral action by working to achieve its own moral ends. This chapter elaborates on that previous discussion to help the reader understand how policing might adopt the protection of life as its primary mandate. Flowing from that discussion is the assertion that any attempt to change the police mandate must start with changing the recruitment and officer selection paradigm so that policing screens in desirable applicants rather than screening out those deemed unsuitable for the job as it is currently understood.

As a case study in how the protection of life might be integrated into current police tactics and strategies, the chapter briefly revisits stop-and-frisk, which was referred to in Chapter 9 as the "pinnacle" of police coercion. In many U.S. cities, stop-and-frisk has been used as a presumed method for police departments to take guns off the street and reduce overall violent crime through aggressively stopping and frisking of people in targeted neighborhoods.[2] The reality is that, although the stop-and-frisk strategy has been shown to achieve minor crime reductions specifically in crime hot spots,[3] it generally results in the discovery of few weapons (or other contraband) being found and relatively small numbers of arrests made. Yet stops *and* frisks are ubiquitous in cities, highly invasive, and have often been disproportionately aimed at people and communities of color.[4] Thus, as this chapter argues, to the extent that the recruitment paradigm can change, then a new conversation about the role of stop-and-frisk—and other police strategies—might be

---

[2] Goode, "Philadelphia Defends Policy on Frisking, With Limits"; Weisburd et al., "Do Stop, Question, and Frisk Practices Deter Crime?: Evidence at Microunits of Space and Time"; Greene, "Zero Tolerance: A Case Study of Police Policies and Practices in New York City."

[3] Weisburd et al., "Do Stop, Question, and Frisk Practices Deter Crime?: Evidence at Microunits of Space and Time."

[4] Vito, Higgins, and Vito, "Police Stop and Frisk and the Impact of Race: A Focal Concerns Theory Approach"; Meares, "Programming Errors: Understanding the Constitutionality of Stop-and-Frisk as a Program, Not an Incident"; Fradella and White, "Reforming Stop-and-Frisk"; White and Fradella, *STOP AND FRISK: The Use and Abuse of a Controversial Policing Tactic*; Harris, "Across the Hudson: Taking the Stop and Frisk Debate Beyond New York City"; ACLU Pennsylvania, "After Seven Years, Report Shows Philadelphia Police Continue to Illegally Stop and Frisk Pedestrians"; Meares, "The Law and Social Science of Stop and Frisk"; Huq, "The Consequences of Disparate Policing: Evaluating Stop and Frisk as a Modality of Urban Policing."

initiated that results in more police *service* and less police *coercion* in some of the most vulnerable communities in the United States.

By the end of this chapter, readers should be able to answer the following questions:

1. How might society create a definition of police informed by the philosophies of Emile Durkheim?
2. How might the "difference principle" help reduce groupthink and protect against occupational misconduct in policing?
3. To what extent might stop-and-frisk evolve from a crime control strategy to a public health initiative?
4. In what ways might both the police and society benefit from normalizing a new idea of police?

Weber vs. Durkheim

A great deal of this book has relied on the substance of Carl Klockars's 1985 book, *The Idea of Police,* as its starting point for introducing a new idea of police. Recall that Klockars rooted his idea of police in a means-based definition, arguing that the police should be defined as nothing more and nothing less than an institution whose members maintain the general right to use coercive force within the boundaries of the state.[5] Klockars argued that, given the myriad role expectations of police, it becomes impossible to define them in terms of what they do because definitions of what they do—and are expected to do—tend to vary across the different publics with which they interact. As such, Klockars argued that ends-based definitions of police (e.g., defining them as crime fighters, law enforcers, public servants, or people who keep us safe) often reveal more about the person giving the definition than about the police institution itself. People who define the police as crime fighters, for example, might expect police officers to arrest every person they catch committing a criminal offense. However, as we learned in Chapter 3, police officers frequently choose not to arrest certain people for certain offenses, even when they have the probable cause to do so.

A means-based definition, Klockars argued, applies to all police at all times and should be based on the tool society gives the police to accomplish their mission rather than on what society expects them to do with that tool. Some police officers do fight crime and enforce the law, but not all officers perform these activities all the time; yet, they are still police officers. Some officers engage in profit-motivated misconduct, which seems the antithesis to fighting crime and enforcing the law. But even they are still police officers, and they gain access to our daily lives precisely because they are police officers, even if they use that access as an opportunity to steal property, traffic

---

[5] Los Angeles Police Department, "Join LAPD: LAPD Hiring Process."

in guns and drugs, or engage in excessive force. Why? Because society has given them the general right to use coercive force. This is why we call them, and this is what Klockars meant when he argued for a means-based understanding of the police.

Klockars grounded his definition, or idea, of police in Egon Bittner's theory of police, which also argued that the police exist precisely because they possess the general right to use coercive force.[6] In this sense, Bittner also defined police based on the means society gives them to accomplish their mission, even though that mission is not always made clear.[7] Although Bittner never actually acknowledged this in his writings,[8] his conceptualization of the police is an almost perfect analogue to Max Weber's conceptualization of the state—that is, an entity that owns a monopoly on violence.[9] Indeed, both Klockars and Bittner defined the police in almost the exact way that Max Weber defined the state: based on the single tool that sets them apart from all other institutions.

In this book, we have appealed to Weber's conceptualization of the state on several occasions—and in particular, Chapter 4—largely arguing that if society is to reimagine the police, it must do so from a different starting point than that used by Weber to conceptualize the state. It similarly must move beyond the way Bittner and Klockars conceptualized the police. Let us first clarify how the Weberian perspective has influenced the mentality of the police institution since Weber did most of his writing.

It is likely the case that most police administrators do not think about how Max Weber's political philosophy might be driving their decisions to develop crime control strategies. Similarly, it is likely that most members of the public do not view police actions—such as a car stop—through the lens of Weberian politics. Indeed, many people have never even heard of Max Weber, despite living in a society where Weberian political thought has become a most useful framework for understanding the police. Weber's influence on policing is much more subtle—and yet, far more pervasive—than most people likely consider. Society tends to think of the police in terms of social control. Since the conception of modern policing, their mission has been to control. They control people, places, events, situations, protesters, demonstrations, crime scenes, accident scenes, traffic, and crowds. Of course, they also control who becomes a police officer, and even who is eligible to apply for the job.

Chapter 1 of this book argued that policing is driven by a coercion paradigm. Coercion is simply another way to operationalize control. Hotspot policing is a method police use to control crime in small-scale, high-crime locations;[10] stop-and-frisk is a method police use to control crime by

---

[6] Bittner, *The Functions of Police in Modern Society.*
[7] White, "Identifying Good Cops Early: Predicting Recruit Performance in the Academy."
[8] Brodeur, "An Encounter With Egon Bittner."
[9] Weber, *From Max Weber: Essays in Sociology.*
[10] Ariel, Sherman, and Newton, "Testing Hot-Spots Police Patrols Against No-Treatment Controls: Temporal and Spatial Deterrence Effects in the London Underground Experiment."

controlling who is allowed to traverse public space without interruption.[11] The concept of control—and the threat of violence that always lurks in the background—is the driver of virtually all policing strategies and tactics. That control is made possible by the general right to use coercive force, which represents a shorthand for Weberian political philosophy.

And this is okay. It is perfectly legitimate to associate the police with control. After all, their ability to control—that is, the general right to use coercive force—is why society maintains a police institution at all. It seems less okay to think of the police exclusively in terms of the general right to use coercive force, though. This is where society and the police have gotten it wrong. Since the beginning, society has given the police an inconsistent mandate and has allowed them (the police) to develop their coercive capacities beyond public purview. Perhaps it is only through advances in audiovisual technology that society has begun to see global images of police paramilitarism and abuses of force.[12] If the post-Ferguson and post–George Floyd protests are any indication, it would appear that society has begun to understand how much it has gotten it wrong with respect to allowing the police to emphasize its crime-fighting role and quietly develop its paramilitary capabilities.

This is where Durkheim comes in. Recall in Chapter 4 our discussion of Emile Durkheim, who did most of his writing during the mid- to late nineteenth century. Durkheim conceptualized the state in much more optimistic terms than did Weber, arguing that the state should serve as society's moral example. To summarize briefly, Durkheim observed that industrialization was causing a disruption to the social ties that connected people to their communities and local kinship groups.[13] As such, the state had the responsibility to bound the citizenry together through its own moral actions. As part of its moral obligations, the state should recognize that some criminality will always exist and that the social norms that define deviant or criminal behavior tend to change over time[14] (e.g., readers might consider the recent social evolution of the acceptance of marijuana and the movement to decriminalize its use across many states). As a result, although a state should sanction crime, it should do so with restraint and without treating offenders as if they are somehow morally defective. Indeed, as Durkheim argued, if state responses to crime are overly oppressive, then such responses can undermine the very social solidarity that Durkheim argued the state could promote among the citizenry.

In his discussions of how the industrial revolution ruptured society's social norms and created anomie—a collective sense of normlessness in society,

---

[11] Fagan et al., "Stops and Stares: Street Stops, Surveillance, and Race in the New Policing."
[12] Taub, "What Was THAT? A Guide to the Military Gear Being Used Against Civilians in Ferguson"; Patrick and Currier, "Ferguson Highlights Police Use of Military Gear and Tactics"; Sanfiorenzo, "How the Rodney King Beating Became the First Viral Video."
[13] Varga, "Social Morals, the Sacred and State Regulation in Durkheim's Sociology."
[14] Durkheim, *Durkheim: The Division of Labour in Society.*

which has been linked to increased suicides[15] and crime[16]—Durkheim could have been writing about the United States in 2022. As the U.S. Census Bureau recently found, the United States is a country in transition: Just since 2010, it has become significantly more ethnically and racially diverse[17] and considerably more foreign born. A recent Pew Research Center study showed that as of 2018, 13.7 percent of the U.S. population was foreign born, a figure that has quadrupled since the 1960s.[18] Contemporary U.S. society is experiencing great social fluidity in much the same way that the United States and Europe did during the industrial revolution when Durkheim was writing. Add to that fluidity a global pandemic, which research is already showing to have created anomie in U.S. society,[19] and we are potentially left with a similar sense of collective normlessness that existed during the economically turbulent times of nineteenth-century Western Europe and the United States.

Using Durkheim's conception of the state as a framework helps us reimagine how the police institution can move beyond Weber for its theoretical rationale to become an institution that links rather than divides, as described in Chapter 5, under a revised version of the thin blue line. Indeed, and as discussed in Chapter 2, such a reimagining is not a call for police reform so much as a conceptual push to rethink policing as an institution that has the obligation to try to achieve a moral end. That moral end is the protection of life. This is the new idea of police that this book proposes.

This new idea does not mean that policing should abandon its collective mandate to reduce or prevent crime; it simply recognizes that it is time for policing to evolve beyond control as both its means and its mandate. It is time to recognize that, as noted in Chapter 4, although coercion will always represent the threat behind the badge, the badge must come to symbolize something bigger than the threat of coercion. Getting there requires both society and the police to reframe how they view the institution. It is time to integrate Weber and Durkheim to create a version of the police that maximizes the good they can accomplish while minimizing the harm they might produce. To get there, several key aspects of the police institution must be addressed, and this starts with recruitment.

Police Recruitment: Valuing Differences

Chapter 12 examined the recruitment and screening processes that most police departments around the country use to hire police officers. As noted in

[15] Kushner and Sterk, "The Limits of Social Capital: Durkheim, Suicide, and Social Cohesion"; Durkheim, *Suicide: A Study in Sociology*.
[16] Baumer and Gustafson, "Social Organization and Instrumental Crime: Assessing the Empirical Validity of Classic and Contemporary Anomie Theories."
[17] Jensen et al., "2020 U.S. Population More Racially and Ethnically Diverse Than Measured in 2010."
[18] "Immigrants in America: Key Charts and Facts | Pew Research Center."
[19] Wesenberg, "COVID-19 and the Rise of the Conspiracy: Examination of COVID Related Conspiracies Using Durkheimian Concepts"; Knowles, "The Impact of COVID-19 on Youth Offending"; Gould, "Anomic America."

that chapter, the police officer selection process historically has been designed to screen out applicants deemed unsuitable for the job.[20] This screening-out process has generally yielded a homogenous workforce in terms of personality characteristics. Indeed, several studies have found that recruits who enter the police academy typically possess the personality traits of assertiveness, self-assurance, aspirations for higher social status, masculinity, above-average intelligence, and the ability to perceive social situations.[21] Balch referred to this collection of traits as a "conventional" personality,[22] which has become the baseline personality of the police occupation.

From the perspective of the new idea of police, there are at least two fundamental problems with policing's focus on screening out for homogeneity: First, groups that lack racial, ethnic, gender, and worldview diversity tend also to lack "thought diversity."[23] Thought diversity is key to organizational problem-solving because it values different perspectives and creates "opportunities for innovation" during the problem-solving process.[24] An absence of thought diversity in human groups can lead to groupthink, which Fernandez and Baker described as:

> when one or two people or personality styles dominate a group's culture so completely that there is no room for those with other styles, perspectives, needs, or beliefs to get their ideas on the table. This can take the form of people hiring only those who think as they do, or of the dominant thinkers badgering others into accepting their ideas.[25]

Fernandez and Baker went on to note that, "In groupthink, conformity reigns supreme," which discourages group members from speaking up or speaking out when they identify a different way of doing things. Taken collectively, the dynamic of groupthink may be created in part by the historic process of police departments wanting to "hire themselves," as discussed in Chapter 12.

Moreover, groupthink could lead to the subcultural element of conformity that not only encourages loyalty, but also creates intense in-group solidarity among police officers.[26] Groupthink might help explain, for example, why at least three police officers stood by as Derek Chauvin violated the policy of his own police department by placing George Floyd in a neck restraint, and then watched as Chauvin slowly killed a defenseless and noncombative Mr. Floyd. Traditional police culture is not kind to police officers who violate

---

[20] Metchik, "An Analysis of the 'Screening Out' Model of Police Officer Selection."
[21] Twersky-Glasner, "Police Personality: What Is It and Why Are They Like That?"; Hogan and Kurtines, "Personological Correlates of Police Effectiveness"; Gould, "A Longitudinal Approach to the Study of the Police Personality: Race/Gender Differences."
[22] Balch, "The Police Personality: Fact or Fiction," 25.
[23] Fernandez, "Creating Thought Diversity: The Antidote to Group Think," 670.
[24] Fernandez, 670.
[25] Fernandez, 670.
[26] Bagshaw, "Is Diversity Divisive? A Positive Training Approach."

the conventions of conformity,[27] which are likely rooted in groupthink and at least partly linked to the ways in which the police institution screens applicants for homogeneity.

A second problem with the screening-out process for selecting police officers is that groups with little thought diversity do not solve problems nearly as well as groups characterized by racial, ethnic, gender, and worldview diversity.[28] Moreover, diverse groups solve problems even better than the single most expert individual in a group.[29] Thus, if we think of crime as a problem to be solved, then the research on group problem-solving suggests that a police occupation made up of individuals who possess largely the same baseline personality and worldview likely will not develop particularly effective solutions to solve crime.

As a way to illustrate how diverse groups might outperform homogeneous groups, we will construct a hypothetical scenario below. We will not use real people, nor will we use actual data. The scenario just serves to highlight the points made above.

Let us suppose we assemble two groups of adults and ask them to develop a solution to reduce violent crime in U.S. cities. This is a timely topic, given the violent crime increases in cities since the start of the COVID-19 pandemic.[30] Let us assume the membership composition for both groups is as follows:

- Group 1 membership: Five active police officers.
- Group 2 membership: One police officer, one school teacher, one registered nurse, one letter carrier (postal worker), and one formerly incarcerated adult.

When we pose the question, "How can we reduce violent crime in U.S. cities?," what kinds of crime solutions might we expect from these two groups? Based on the research described above, we can imagine that Group 1's solution will be heavily rooted in elements of coercion and control, given that its membership includes only police officers. Here are the hypothetical solutions Group 1 might offer:

- More stops-and-frisks to take guns and other contraband off the street.
- More special units operations (e.g., corner sweeps, increased prosecutions, etc.) to deter crime in public spaces.
- Identify crime hot spots and deploy officers to those areas to break up the hot spots through arrests.
- Greater use of predictive policing as a presumed method for interrupting crime in identified high-risk areas before it occurs.

---

[27] Silver et al., "Traditional Police Culture, Use of Force, and Procedural Justice: Investigating Individual, Organizational, and Contextual Factors."

[28] Hong and Page, "Groups of Diverse Problem Solvers Can Outperform Groups of High-Ability Problem Solvers"; Larson, "Deep Diversity and Strong Synergy: Modeling the Impact of Variability in Members' Problem-Solving Strategies on Group Problem-Solving Performance."

[29] Page, Scott. "The Difference: How the Power of Diversity Creates Better Groups, Firms, Schools, and Society." Princeton, NJ: Princeton University Press, 2007.

[30] Fuller and Arango, "Police Pin a Rise in Murders on an Unusual Suspect: Covid."

From Group 2, we might anticipate more varied solutions to the crime problem, given the diversity of group membership. Indeed, members of Group 2 might identify solutions that initially might not even seem relevant to crime, but that—when considered collectively—form a multifaceted approach to addressing the crime problem:

- Using schools as a more comprehensive institution for children of crime-prone ages by offering meals, homework assistance, and cocurricular programming through early evening hours.
- Treating violence as a public health issue by ensuring that local residents have greater access to healthy foods, working with police to offer safe spaces for outdoor exercise, and offering high-quality primary health care in mobile clinics.
- Working with neighborhoods to increase supervision activities among local adults, take greater responsibility for neighborhood children, and try to reduce conflict on the street block.
- Identify crime hot spots and deploy officers to those areas to break up the hot spots through arrests.

As this hypothetical scenario suggests, whereas all solutions proposed by Group 1 (the police officer group) are rooted in traditional crime control strategies—some of which might indeed produce short-term crime reductions[31]—those identified by Group 2 are much more varied and presumed to target the crime problem at different points along the criminological continuum. That is, whereas the solutions offered by Group 1 addressed the crime problem at its point of commission (i.e., where and when the crimes were being committed), the solutions offered by Group 2 addressed the crime problem primarily along its points of origin—attempting to head off the crime before it was committed. These different solutions represent the differences between so-called upstream and downstream approaches to crime prevention and reduction.

Downstream problem-solving responds to crime where it occurs at the street level, emphasizing enforcement tactics and strategies, such as vigorous arrest operations, designed to reduce future crime through a combination of deterrence (i.e., discouraging people from committing crimes out of fear of being arrested) and incapacitation (i.e., taking people off the streets through arrest, rendering them unable to commit future crimes).[32] Such approaches are rooted in enforcement and control, or more simply, the coercion paradigm. Although some enforcement options are justified and probably even necessary to immediately address safety concerns in neighborhoods, too much enforcement tends to backfire: Overly aggressive law enforcement, particularly in vulnerable communities, has been shown to cause increases

---

[31] *e.g.*, Braga and Weisburd, *Policing Problem Places: Crime Hot Spots and Effective Prevention.*
[32] Kane, "On the Limits of Social Control: Structural Deterrence and the Policing of 'Suppressible' Crimes."

in violent crime because local residents often cease their cooperation with the police out of frustration and loss of police legitimacy.[33] That is, downstream approaches to crime control carry significant limitations.

Upstream problem-solving responds to crime before it has the opportunity to occur. Note that for Group 2, three of the four proposed solutions had nothing to do with policing or the criminal justice system more generally and seemed to spring from the varied expertise and presumed life experiences of group members. Proposing, for example, to lengthen the school day and offer meals and cocurricular activities for students decreases the amount of idle time that children would otherwise have. Such an approach—keeping children occupied by constructive activities at school—can decrease the opportunities for neighborhood conflict to develop that are often linked to crime—particularly, violent crime. Moreover, although Group 2 did incorporate a police response as part of the crime-reduction solution, it appears at the bottom of the list. This was intentional: Placing greater emphasis on upstream solutions to solve the problem makes downstream solutions less central to the overall mix of proposed solutions.

Finally, going back to the research on the importance of thought diversity within groups, we can expect that even the most expert police officer, in terms of tactics and strategies, in Group 1 likely would not perform as well as the composite membership of Group 2 in terms of identifying effective solutions to the violent crime problem because that officer would likely apply just a single tool toward solving the problem.[34] This happens because experts often view a problem through their expert lens, which does not include the perspectives of those outside their professional discipline. In policing, the expert lens is coercion.

As previously noted, the above scenario was purely hypothetical and made a few assumptions about the police officers in Group 1. First, it assumed that they did not bring any thought diversity to the problem, and that they were a singular product of the police recruitment paradigm that values homogeneity over diversity (at least in terms of worldview). In the group dynamics research literature, thought diversity is more technically referred to as "cognitive diversity" and relates to the differences among individuals in terms of worldviews, intellectual perspectives, and life experiences.[35] Cognitive diversity is essential to group problem-solving because it leads to "tool diversity," which is the idea that people with different perspectives bring different solutions—or tools—to bear on the problem at hand. In policing, that problem might be how to handle an uncooperative suspect, how to address recent convenience store crimes, when to conduct a stop-and-frisk, how to

---

[33] Kurbin and Weitzer, "Retaliatory Homicide: Concentrated Disadvantage and Neighbourhood Culture"; Kane, "Compromised Police Legitimacy as a Predictor of Violent Crime in Structurally Disadvantaged Communities."

[34] Larson, "Deep Diversity and Strong Synergy: Modeling the Impact of Variability in Members' Problem-Solving Strategies on Group Problem-Solving Performance."

[35] Mohammed and Ringseis, "Cognitive Diversity and Consensus in Group Decision Making: The Role of Inputs, Processes, and Outcomes," 311–314.

disperse a crowd of people who have gathered at the scene of an accident, and how to communicate with people experiencing a mental health crisis. Taken collectively, cognitive diversity and tool diversity make up the "difference" concept in group dynamics—a demonstrated recipe for effective group-level problem-solving.[36]

Applying the "Difference" to Policing

According to group dynamics scholar Scott Page, the difference concept assumes that, in terms of problem-solving capacities, highly diverse groups outperform homogeneous groups because of the cognitive diversity among group members.[37] As noted, this diversity of perspectives means that members bring diverse tools—or solutions—to the problem-solving process. The key, according to Page, is to assemble groups with members who possess a shared identification of the problem and the group's mission, while maximizing group members' nonoverlapping cognitive perspectives. Such an approach to group creation ensures that the group members possess a shared sense of purpose while maintaining enough cognitive diversity to bring a varied set of tools to the mission.

Returning to applying a hypothetical example to policing, Figure 13.1 illustrates how the difference concept can be applied to policing.

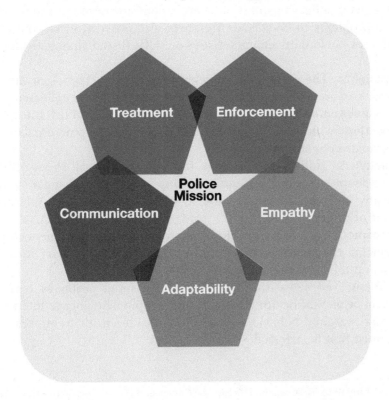

◀ **Figure 13.1**

Illustration of the Difference Concept as It Relates to Policing

---

[36] Page, *The Difference: How the Power of Diversity Creates Better Groups, Firms, Schools, and Societies.*
[37] Page.

Figure 13.1 shows the overlap and divergence of five different personality characteristics or skills that different groups of police officers working in a police organization might possess: treatment, enforcement, empathy, adaptability, and communication. Notice that some of these characteristics share some overlap with others, but they are mostly distinct from one another. This distinctness, or nonoverlap, represents cognitive diversity and shows that not all police officers in the department think alike.

The engulfing gray region in Figure 13.1 represents the common understanding of the police mission that all officers share. Whereas the five characteristics or skills show little overlap—again, suggesting high levels of cognitive diversity—the gray area represents what researchers call "cognitive consensus"[38]—that is, the shared sense of purpose that exists within the organization or group. Cognitive consensus is important in groups and organizations because it helps ensure that group members define the mission and the problems that need solving in much the same way as each other.[39] Figure 13.1 shows that although members of the group possess some shared characteristics, they are also largely independent of one another. It is in these areas of nonoverlap that different sets of individuals bring cognitive diversity to the group or occupation while still sharing a common sense of purpose, or cognitive consensus.

Again, relating Figure 13.1 to a policing exercise indicates that the members of a given police organization share a common sense of the police mission and problems to be solved. Members also possess, in varying degrees, five different personality characteristics or skills (listed alphabetically):

- **Adaptability:** The capacity to quickly modify one's tactics or attitudinal approach to an evolving situation as new information is collected.
- **Communication:** A skill set that allows a person to establish interpersonal connections with other people in ways that might help de-escalate potentially violent encounters.
- **Empathy:** An ability to put oneself in the metaphorical shoes of less fortunate people or people genuinely having a hard time living a lawful life. Empathy also applies to the ways in which officers might interact with victims of crime.
- **Enforcement:** The mindset that law enforcement is a primary component of policing that requires officers to enforce the law and try to maintain order in public and private spaces.
- **Treatment:** The sense that crime and its related problems represent a physical or mental health issue and that people who engage in criminality or other marginal behaviors should be considered for treatment, even if they must first be arrested.

---

[38] Mohammed and Ringseis, "Cognitive Diversity and Consensus in Group Decision Making: The Role of Inputs, Processes, and Outcomes," 314–316.
[39] Page, "Where Diversity Comes From and Why It Matters?"; Mohammed and Ringseis, "Cognitive Diversity and Consensus in Group Decision Making: The Role of Inputs, Processes, and Outcomes."

The first thing to remember for this exercise is that all the hypothetical people represented in Figure 13.1 are police officers. They have been trained in law, tactics, and strategies of policing and share a common understanding of what it means to be a police officer and the problems that need solving. Next, the five personality characteristics or skills represented in Figure 13.1 are the dominant characteristics of the officers working in the organization. Some officers share some of those characteristics with other officers, but large numbers of officers share few if any of those five characteristics with others. From the difference perspective, Figure 13.1 represents a useful blend of cognitive consensus and cognitive diversity and would likely facilitate effective problem-solving among police officers.

For example, suppose a group of six officers was dispatched to a street corner where it was alleged that several teenage boys were dealing illegal drugs. As the officers arrived, several people scattered, but the officers were able to detain three apparent teenagers. The teenagers became hostile toward officers and refused to answer most questions. A crowd began to form, which is common in urban areas when a police action takes place; and the people in the crowd began to criticize the police for "bullying" three local kids. Here is a problem that needs to be solved.

If all officers shared the single enforcement personality characteristic to the exclusion of the other characteristics shown in Figure 13.1, then they might order the crowd to disperse under threat of arresting those who do not leave, and then take the uncooperative kids to the ground to get them into handcuffs. That action would likely escalate the conflict with the people in the crowd, which would require officers to stand their ground while continuing to take the kids into custody and order the crowd to disperse. Ultimately, the officers would have to muscle their way through the incident, likely making several arrests and potentially having to use moderate to significant amounts of physical force to "solve" the problem.

What if the group of officers possessed some combination of the five characteristics shown in Figure 13.1? It is true that officers would need to secure the scene, detain the teenage suspects, and perhaps even frisk them for potential weapons (enforcement), but they could also allow for a certain degree of verbal resistance and hostility while calmly talking to and treating the boys with the respect they deserve (empathy and treatment). As the crowd formed and people began criticizing the officers, one or two officers could have appealed to the sensibilities of these local residents by saying something like, "We're not here to unnecessarily jam anyone up. But we need to know who these boys are. Does anyone know them, or know who takes care of them? We could really use your help" (communication and adaptability). In the end, the officers might have to arrest the kids, but at least they can do so while treading as lightly as possible on the dignity of the community, and without escalating a conflict to the point that required them to make multiple arrests and use physical force.

Applying the "Difference" to Police Officer Selection

Integrating the difference concept into police recruitment will require police departments to largely flip the screening-out paradigm that excludes candidates viewed as unsuitable for policing to a screening-in paradigm that actively recruits applicants with diverse intellectual perspectives, worldviews, gender identification, and racial and ethnic identification. As part of a new recruitment process that would hopefully include new messaging about the role of police—that is, integrating the new idea into police department mission statements—departments would need to link the recruitment process to the application process to ensure that they attract candidates with broad perspectives. This means redefining the police mission to extend beyond law enforcement and crime control so that a more diverse set of people would apply for the job in the first place, which could happen with the proper public messaging.

Health researchers and organizations have successfully used radio, television, and billboards as media to promote public service announcements (PSAs) encouraging healthy behaviors. Such PSAs have been particularly effective for smoking cessation campaigns, reaching people with depressive symptomology, and promoting health behaviors more generally.[40] Some research has even found that fictional story lines—such as on popular television shows—promoting healthy behaviors can have a positive effect on their viewing audiences.[41] The research on health-related PSAs might be generalizable to policing if police departments initiate campaigns to change the way the public should view the police. Hollywood could help by creating television dramas that show police as more than crime fighters and law enforcers.

There remain two caveats to creating a screening-in police selection process. First, given that policing is an office of public trust, even a new recruitment paradigm will need to impose some exclusionary conditions that prohibit people with certain personal histories from entering the occupation. As discussed in Chapter 12, for example, research has shown that police departments can limit officer misconduct if they exclude people with serious criminal histories, recent problematic contacts with the criminal justice system, and problematic employment histories (e.g., being disciplined or terminated from prior jobs). They can similarly reduce overall levels of organizational misconduct by imposing such restrictions on potential job applicants.[42] In this way, police departments would still screen out to limit bad policing while screening in to encourage good policing.

---

[40] Snyder, "Health Communication Campaigns and Their Impact on Behavior"; Lienemann and Siegel, "Increasing Help-Seeking Outcomes Among People With Elevated Depressive Symptomatology With Public Service Announcements: An Examination of Functional Matching and Message Sidedness"; Calfano and Green, "Assessing the Efficacy of Radio Public Service Announcements: Results from Three Field Experiments."

[41] Bavin and Owens, "Complementary Public Service Announcements as a Strategy for Enhancing the Impact of Health-Promoting Messages in Fictional Television Programs."

[42] White and Kane, "Pathways to Career-Ending Police Misconduct"; Kane and White, *Jammed Up: Bad Cops, Police Misconduct, and the New York City Police Department.*

The second caveat to a new screening-in process is more structural. Despite scholarship arguing for the value that screening in could bring to policing,[43] and despite recent calls by policymakers and high-profile police executives to reduce the emphasis on screening out in favor of screening in,[44] policing as currently practiced might not be ready to embrace a new model of recruitment that values bringing in candidates with nontraditional views of the police mission. It just takes a few progressive police chiefs or commissioners around the country to allow researchers to help develop and evaluate even just limited applications of a screening-in recruitment process. Once evidence can be generated showing the value of screening in to policing, the institution itself could adopt the new paradigm, although this would likely take a full generation of policing to accomplish.

Still, a screening-in recruitment and officer selection paradigm that values cognitive diversity among applicants who become recruits, in conjunction with a reimaging of the police role, could create a version of U.S. policing that harnesses the good that the institution can accomplish while minimizing the harm it otherwise might produce. In large measure, many of the operational issues identified in this book as problematic, such as an overreliance on predictive policing and aggressive stop-and-frisk programs, could be minimized as new generations of police officers see a mission that is broader than crime control and law enforcement, which can change the collective mentality of the institution.

Reforming Stop-and-Frisk

Let us start from a place that acknowledges the importance of stop-and-frisk as a police field tactic. As Chief Justice Earl Warren noted in his majority opinion in *Terry v. Ohio*, the state maintains an interest in preventing criminal behavior, which means allowing police officers to conduct brief investigatory stops of individuals in the public domain based on reasonable suspicion of potential criminal behavior.[45] Moreover, once the police initiate the investigatory stop, the officers have an interest in protecting their own safety by ensuring the person(s) they stopped do not possess dangerous weapons. If, during the investigatory stop, officers believe the detainee(s) might be armed, then they (the officers) have the right to conduct a pat-down search of the suspects' outer clothing to detect any possible weapons. In this way, stop-and-frisk is considered a "one-off"[46] intrusion based strictly on reasonable suspicion and the need to preserve officer safety.

---

[43] Lough and von Treuer, "A Critical Review of Psychological Instruments Used in Police Officer Selection"; Fradella and White, "Reforming Stop-and-Frisk"; Metchik, "An Analysis of the 'Screening Out' Model of Police Officer Selection"; Grant and Grant, "Officer Selection and the Prevention of Abuse of Force."
[44] President's Task Force on 21st Century Policing, "Final Report of the President's Task Force on 21st Century Policing."
[45] Terry v. Ohio, 392 U.S. 1 (1968).
[46] Meares, "Programming Errors: Understanding the Constitutionality of Stop-and-Frisk as a Program, Not an Incident," 163.

As Chapter 9 showed, though, the police have moved well beyond the use of stop-and-frisk as a field tactic by making it a crime control strategy.[47] Throughout the 2000s, as noted in Chapter 9, many studies have shown the racially disparate impacts of stop-and-frisk, a strategy that has been primarily focused on individuals and communities of color.[48] Civil rights groups during the first decade of the twenty-first century filed several federal lawsuits against big-city police departments alleging that stop-and-frisk violated the Equal Protection Clause of the Fourteenth Amendment by creating patterns and practices that disproportionately placed individuals of color at risk of being stopped and frisked.[49] Still, although several lawsuits have led to federal oversight of local police departments,[50] no identified court has ruled the stop-and-frisk crime control strategy illegal, per se.

As a crime control strategy—and as driven by policing's coercion paradigm—stop-and-frisk represents the veritable definition of a downstream approach to crime reduction. It occurs at the presumed time and place of criminal activity, it relies almost exclusively on police officers' authority to detain individuals in public places, and it is highly invasive. Yet, as a crime control strategy, it brings questionable value to communities. Indeed, referring back to Table 9.1 and the case study of stop-and-frisk in Philadelphia, the Philadelphia Police Department in 2021 conducted 13,349 pedestrian stops across the city, finding weapons or other contraband in just 13 percent of those stops. As a crime control strategy, stop-and-frisk appears highly inefficient at best. What if stop-and-frisk was driven by a different policing paradigm that could allow it to become something more of an upstream approach to crime control by emphasizing the protection of life and overall community well-being? What might that look like?

To answer that question requires a fuller examination of the factors leading to stops in the first place. Although it is common to regard pedestrian stops as fully discretionary (i.e., made based on the officer's judgment), many stops could be considered nondiscretionary. They occur because (1) the officer recognizes a person in a community who has an outstanding arrest warrant, (2) a citizen directs an officer to stop someone they saw allegedly commit a crime, or (3) police officers witness some form of criminal activity that leads them to make the stop. Such stops may be considered

[47] Meares.

[48] Vito, Higgins, and Vito, "Police Stop and Frisk and the Impact of Race: A Focal Concerns Theory Approach"; White and Fradella, STOP AND FRISK: The Use and Abuse of a Controversial Policing Tactic; Harris, "Across the Hudson: Taking the Stop and Frisk Debate Beyond New York City"; ACLU Pennsylvania, "After Seven Years, Report Shows Philadelphia Police Continue to Illegally Stop and Frisk Pedestrians"; Huq, "The Consequences of Disparate Policing: Evaluating Stop and Frisk as a Modality of Urban Policing"; Gelman, Fagan, and Kiss, "An Analysis of the New York City Police Department's 'Stop-and- Frisk' Policy in the Context of Claims of Racial Bias"; Fagan et al., "Stops and Stares: Street Stops, Surveillance, and Race in the New Policing"; Fagan and Davies, "Street Stops and Broken Windows: Terry, Race and Disorder in New York City."

[49] E.g., Floyd v. City of New York, 959 F. Supp. 2d 668 - Dist. Court, SD New York (2013); Bailey v. City of Philadelphia, Court of Appeals, 3rd Circuit (2010).

[50] Consent Decree, Bailey v. City of Philadelphia et al. (C.A. No. 10-5952, E.D. Penn, June 21, 2011). Available as Document No. 16, Case 2:10-Cv-05952-SD at https://Aclupa.Org/Sites/Default/Files/Field _documents/Bailey_consent_decree_6-21-11_.pdf.

nondiscretionary because the officers who make them are directed by external instruments, such as local residents and arrest warrants. Such nondiscretionary stops would be expected to result in relatively high arrest rates because the officers made the stops based on a high presumption of guilt (a requirement for probable cause arrests).

Discretionary stops, or what some police departments often call "mere encounter" stops, are those made by officers when they contact people they deem suspicious or who are seen committing quality-of-life crimes in communities, such as playing loud music, drinking alcoholic beverages in public, or blocking sidewalks for social gatherings. Mere encounter stops are highly discretionary on the part of officers, and they typically result in low rates of contraband recovery and arrests.[51]

It is in the area of mere encounter stops that the protection of life mandate can likely achieve its greatest impact on stop-and-frisk. The traditional stop-and-frisk strategy relies on coercion and control for its operational legitimacy, but a new strategy we might call SAFE stops could be created that draws on policing's cognitive diversity (assuming policing evolves to a screening-in selection process) to redefine the nature of police-citizen interactions, particularly in vulnerable communities. SAFE stops could be guided by the following principles:

- **Service:** Recognizing that the primary goals of a police officer are to provide service to communities and to approach everyone as if they are a client.
- **Assessment:** Bringing more than just a law enforcement mentality into communities by assessing the needs of everyone who lives there. Through assessment, police can decide how best to use their coercive authority to improve life for the residents of vulnerable communities.
- **Foster:** Interacting with members of the public in ways that demonstrate respect for communities and the people who live there—including the people involved in criminal activity. Fostering respect means that community members will trust officers and cooperate with them when needed.
- **Enforcement:** Using their authority when necessary to respond to crime, make arrests, and even use force when the circumstances demand it.

Officers guided by the SAFE stop philosophy could decide not to stop every person in a community for committing some form of quality-of-life violation or who is seen as suspicious. In deciding whether to make a mere encounter stop, officers could ask themselves—and each other—what service to the community such a stop would serve, and how much conflict a stop-and-frisk would generate relative to the police legitimacy that not making the

---

[51] Among local jurisdictions that make their stop-and-frisk data publicly available, none of them distinguishes between mere encounter and other types of stops, making it impossible to calculate precise contraband hit rates and arrest rates for the various types of pedestrian stops. Information on mere encounter stops comes from the author's experience working with police departments on research or stop-and-frisk litigation. Data from those activities are not public.

stop could preserve. Moreover, by reducing the number of mere encounter stops in communities, police workgroups could find themselves with more time to focus their efforts on other activities, such as working with local residents to create safe spaces to engage in outdoor exercise. They could coordinate with local health care systems to bring mobile health clinics into the community to ensure that local residents are keeping up with health and wellness care. These activities can be considered upstream approaches to crime control because contributing to the health and wellness of communities can reduce crime, as children remain in school, adults remain employed, and everyone feels a greater sense of hope in their communities.[52]

Among all public employees—even more than teachers—police officers are deployed across all areas of public space. They see people in crisis, but they also meet many people during their regular duties who are not in crisis. Many people want information that police officers can provide, and others want assistance with non-crime-related issues.[53] SAFE stops provide a way for a new generation of policing to reorder the importance it places on enforcement and control during police-citizen encounters; and, again, it would give officers the time they need to become more fully integrated into communities. Indeed, whereas the stop-and-frisk strategy of the twentieth and early twenty-first centuries operationalized the "thin blue line" of policing as a line that divides, the SAFE stop approach can become a policing strategy that envisions the thin blue line as one that connects—a philosophy fully consistent with the way Durkheim viewed the role of the state during turbulent and uncertain times.

Some Concluding Observations

Transitioning policing from the coercion paradigm to a new idea that values the protection of life over mere law enforcement could allow the police to maximize the good they bring to society while minimizing the harm some of their activities have been shown to produce. The United States is made up of many vulnerable communities, whether in highly urbanized areas characterized by high crime, racial segregation, and systemic economic resource deprivation, or small rural locations characterized by poverty, few healthy career options, and devastation by the opioid epidemic. The police have a role to fulfill in all these places. Indeed, whereas many groups have called for "defunding" the police since the homicide of George Floyd, this book argues for expanding the mission of police at a time when U.S. society is

---

[52] Fitzpatrick and LaGory, *Unhealthy Cities: Poverty, Race, and Place in America*; Fitzpatrick and LaGory, *Unhealthy Places: The Ecology of Risk in the Urban Landscape*; Kane, "The Ecology of Unhealthy Places: Violence, Birthweight, and the Importance of Territoriality in Structurally Disadvantaged Communities."
[53] Kane, "Policing in Public Housing: Using Calls for Service to Examine Incident-Based Workload in the Philadelphia Housing Authority"; Greene and Klockars, "What Police Do"; Huey and Ricciardelli, "'This Isn't What I Signed up for': When Police Officer Role Expectations Conflict With the Realities of General Duty Police Work in Remote Communities."

experiencing great social transition and the enduring crippling effects of a global pandemic. No other public institution besides the police is organized and deployed in every community in the United States to keep eyes on the streets and make regular contact with everyday people. So, why should most interactions between the police and the public be characterized by coercion and control when policing can offer so much more than that?

A new police selection process that screens officers into the job based on racial, ethnic, gender, and worldview diversity can help policing redefine the nature of the police mission, the types of problems to be solved, and the tools officers can use to solve them. Community policing was once seen as the institutional alternative to the coercion paradigm, which sought to apply upstream solutions to crime by engaging in creative ways with local community residents and institutions. However, community policing practice was not supported by a change in the police selection paradigm: Police departments continued to "hire themselves," ensuring that the coercion mandate of traditional policing would remain intact. Along the way, police departments held true to the notion that the thin blue line of policing was there to help separate the "good" people from the "criminals," and society allowed this myth to perpetuate.

Policing is a thin blue line. In fact, it's many thin blue lines that connect people to services, to institutions outside the criminal justice system, to local ministries, and to other people who can help in a crisis. Many police officers in the United States already practice a protection of life mandate. They treat people with the respect they deserve; they do not see every interaction with a member of the public as an opportunity to exert control over them; they do not force conflict with people who do not immediately comply with verbal commands. The trick is to systematize these actions so they become part of expected policing practice rather than an exception to the rule. When the United States calls the police, it deserves officers who will bring more than their definition. It deserves officers who can become more than their definition. And to get there requires the police and society to move beyond the original idea of police to a *New* idea that fosters a mandate based on the protection of life.

Questions for Review and Reflection

Question 1. Reconciling the Original Idea and the New Idea of Police

As argued in this chapter, U.S. policing has been driven by a coercion paradigm that emphasizes crime fighting, law enforcement, and control. The chapter also argued for a new mandate of police that would emphasize the protection of life over law enforcement.

- Are crime fighting and law enforcement compatible with a protection of life mandate?
- Does the protection of life mean that policing will no longer be the crime-fighting institution in the United States?
- Could the protection of life bring out the best in policing while minimizing the harm it sometimes causes? If yes, how? If no, why not?
- How is a protection of life mandate different from the current police mandate? To answer that question requires you to first define the current police mandate.
- If the new idea of police as represented in this book is rooted in a protection of life mandate, what would be your version of a new idea of police? Something similar, or something far different?

Question 2. Durkheim vs. Weber to Bring a Better Understanding to the Police

As with Chapter 4, this chapter made an appeal to the political philosophies of Max Weber and Emile Durkheim to help readers learn the differences between two approaches to defining the state.

- In what ways were the references to Weber and Durkheim helpful for illustrating the differences between how we might reconceptualize our definition and role of the police?
- In what ways were the appeals to Durkheim and Weber not helpful? What leads you to draw your conclusions?
- Does Durkheimian political philosophy help society understand how the state—and by extension, the police—might come to represent a moral authority that leads by its own moral actions? Can the police really become an institution that promotes moral cohesion in society?
- Is policing really guided by a Weberian political philosophy? If so, how? If not, why? Can

a political philosophy really drive policing when most people have never even heard of Weber?
- How do we take the best of Weber and Durkheim to create a new idea of police, even if that new idea is not a protection of life mandate?

Question 3. Applying the Difference Concept to Police Officer Selection

This chapter has argued that the best prospects society has for reimaging the police role is to change the police officer selection paradigm in a way that screens in desirable candidates instead of screening out those deemed unsuitable for policing. Moreover, any screening-in process should value job candidates with nonoverlapping intellectual perspectives and worldviews.

- What is the difference concept and how might it be applied to police officer selection?
- Can the police institution strive for too much diversity in terms of worldviews and perspectives among recruits and officers? If so, provide some examples.
- How can police departments ensure the police officers achieve cognitive consensus while also valuing cognitive diversity? Where's the sweet spot?
- What values and expertise should police departments screen in for? Explain and justify your answer.
- Are law enforcement and crime control values still important to policing even if the screening-in process minimizes their importance? Explain the rationale that drives your answer.
- How can police departments get the message out that they are interested in hiring new "types" of officers?

Bibliography

ACLU Pennsylvania. "After Seven Years, Report Shows Philadelphia Police Continue to Illegally Stop and Frisk Pedestrians." 2018. https://www.aclupa.org/en /press-releases/after-seven-years-report-shows -philadelphia-police-continue-illegally-stop-and-frisk.

Ariel, Barak, Lawrence W. Sherman, and Mark Newton. "Testing Hot-Spots Police Patrols Against No-Treatment Controls: Temporal and Spatial Deterrence Effects in the London Underground Experiment." *Criminology*, August (2019): 101–128. https://doi.org/10.1111 /1745-9125.12231.

Bagshaw, Mike. "Is Diversity Divisive? A Positive Training Approach." *Industrial and Commercial Training* 36, no. 4 (2004): 153–157.

Bailey v. City of Philadelphia, Court of Appeals, 3rd Circuit (2010).

Balch, Robert W. "The Police Personality: Fact or Fiction." In *The Dysfunctional Alliance: Emotion and Reason in Justice Administration*, edited by D. B. Kennedy, 10–25. Cincinnati, OH: Anderson, 1977.

Baumer, Eric P., and Regan Gustafson. "Social Organization and Instrumental Crime: Assessing the Empirical Validity of Classic and Contemporary Anomie Theories." *Criminology* 45, no. 3 (2007): 617–663. https:// doi.org/10.1111/j.1745-9125.2007.00090.x.

Bavin, Lynda M., and R. Glynn Owens. "Complementary Public Service Announcements as a Strategy for Enhancing the Impact of Health-Promoting Messages in Fictional Television Programs." *Health Communication* 33, no. 5 (2018): 544–552.

Beckett, Katherine. "The Uses and Abuses of Police Discretion: Toward Harm Reduction Policing." *Harvard Law and Policy Review* 10 (2016): 77.

Bittner, Egon. *The Functions of Police in Modern Society*. Chevy Chase, MD: National Institute of Mental Health, 1970. https://www.google.com/books/edition /The_Functions_of_the_Police_in_Modern_So /rQcXAAAAIAAJ?hl=en&gbpv=1&printsec=frontcover.

Braga, Anthony A., and David L. Weisburd. *Policing Problem Places: Crime Hot Spots and Effective Prevention*. New York: Oxford University Press, 2010. https://doi .org/10.1093/acprof:oso/9780195341966.001.0001.

Brodeur, Jean Paul. "An Encounter with Egon Bittner." *Crime, Law and Social Change* 48, no. 3–5 (2007): 105–132. https://doi.org/10.1007/s10611-007-9084-2.

Calfano, Brian Robert, and Donald P. Green. "Assessing the Efficacy of Radio Public Service Announcements: Results From Three Field Experiments." *Electronic News* 13, no. 3 (2019): 134–151.

Consent Decree, Bailey v. City of Philadelphia et al. (C.A. No. 10-5952, E.D. Penn, June 21, 2011). Available as Document No. 16, Case 2:10-Cv-05952-SD at https:// Aclupa.Org/Sites/Default/Files/Field_documents /Bailey_consent_decree_6-21-11_.pdf.

Durkheim, Emile. *Durkheim: The Division of Labour in Society*, 2nd ed., edited by Steven Lukes. London: Palgrave Macmillan, n.d.

Durkheim, Emile. *Suicide: A Study in Sociology*. New York: Routledge, 2005.

Fagan, Jeffrey, Anthony Braga, Rod Brunson, and April Pattavina. "Stops and Stares: Street Stops, Surveillance, and Race in the New Policing." *Fordham Urban Law Journal* 43, no. 3 (2016): 539.

Fagan, Jeffrey, and Garth Davies. "Street Stops and Broken Windows: Terry, Race and Disorder in New York City." *SSRN*, 2001. https://doi.org/10.2139/ssrn.257813.

Fernandes, April D., and Robert D. Crutchfield. "Race, Crime, and Criminal Justice: Fifty Years Since the Challenge of Crime in a Free Society." *Criminology and Public Policy* 17, no. 2 (2018): 397–417. https:// doi.org/10.1111/1745-9133.12361.

Fernandez, Claudia Plaisted. "Creating Thought Diversity: The Antidote to Group Think." *Journal of Public Health Management and Practice* 13, no. 6 (2007): 670–671.

Fitzpatrick, Kevin, and Mark LaGory. *Unhealthy Cities: Poverty, Race, and Place in America*. New York: Routledge, 2013.

Fitzpatrick, Kevin, and Mark LaGory. *Unhealthy Places: The Ecology of Risk in the Urban Landscape*. New York: Routledge, 2002.

Floyd v. City of New York, 959 F. Supp. 2d 668 - Dist. Court, SD New York (2013).

Fradella, Henry F., and Michael D. White. "Reforming Stop-and-Frisk." *Criminology, Criminal Justice, Law & Society* 18, no. 3 (2017): 45–65.

Fuller, Thomas, and Tim Arango. "Police Pin a Rise in Murders on an Unusual Suspect: Covid." *New York Times*, November 15, 2021. https://www.nytimes.com /2020/10/29/us/coronavirus-murders.html.

Gelman, Andrew, Jeffrey Fagan, and Alex Kiss. "An Analysis of the New York City Police Department's 'Stop-and-Frisk' Policy in the Context of Claims of Racial Bias." *Journal of the American Statistical Association* 102, no. 479 (2007): 813–823. https://doi .org/10.1198/016214506000001040.

Goode, Erica. "Philadelphia Defends Policy on Frisking, With Limits." *New York Times*, July 12, 2012. https://www.nytimes.com/2012/07/12/us/stop-and -frisk-controls-praised-in-philadelphia.html.

Gould, Henry Alexander. "Anomic America." PhD dissertation, Dartmouth College, 2021.

Gould, Larry A. "A Longitudinal Approach to the Study of the Police Personality: Race/Gender Differences." *Journal of Police and Criminal Psychology* 15, no. 2 (2000): 41–51. https://doi.org/10.1007/BF02802664.

Grant, J. D., and J. Grant. "Officer Selection and the Prevention of Abuse of Force." In *And Justice for All: Understanding and Controlling Police Abuse of Force*, edited by William Geller and Hans Toch, 151–162. Washington, DC: Police Executive Research Forum, 1995.

Greene, Jack R., and Carl B. Klockars. "What Police Do." In *Thinking About Police: Contemporary Readings*, 2nd ed., edited by Carl B. Klockars and Stephen D. Mastrofski, New York: McGraw-Hill, 1991.

Greene, Judith A. "Zero Tolerance: A Case Study of Police Policies and Practices in New York City." *Crime & Delinquency* 45, no. 2 (1999): 171–187.

Harris, David A. "Across the Hudson: Taking the Stop and Frisk Debate Beyond New York City." *New York University Journal of Legislation and Public Policy* 16, no. 853 (2013): 1–24.

Hogan, Robert, and William Kurtines. "Personological Correlates of Police Effectiveness." *Journal of Psychology* 91, no. 2 (1975): 289–295.

Hong, Lu, and Scott E. Page. "Groups of Diverse Problem Solvers Can Outperform Groups of High-Ability Problem Solvers." *Proceedings of the National Academy of Sciences* 101, no. 46 (2004): 16385–16389.

Huey, Laura, and Rose Ricciardelli. "'This Isn't What I Signed up for': When Police Officer Role Expectations Conflict With the Realities of General Duty Police Work in Remote Communities." *International Journal of Police Science and Management* 17, no. 3 (2015): 194–203. https://doi.org/10.1177/1461355715603590.

Huq, Aziz Z. "The Consequences of Disparate Policing: Evaluating Stop and Frisk as a Modality of Urban Policing." *Minnesota Law Review* 101, no. 6 (2017): 2397–2480.

"Immigrants in America: Key Charts and Facts | Pew Research Center." Accessed March 1, 2022. https://www.pewresearch.org/hispanic/2020/08/20/facts-on-u-s-immigrants/.

Jensen, Eric, Nicholas Jones, Mean Rabe, Beverly Pratt, Lauren Medina, Kimberly Orozco, and Lindsay Spell. "2020 U.S. Population More Racially and Ethnically Diverse Than Measured in 2010." U.S. Census Bureau, August 12, 2021. https://www.census.gov/library/stories/2021/08/2020-united-states-population-more-racially-ethnically-diverse-than-2010.html.

Jones, Russell L. "Terry v. Ohio: Its Failure, Immoral Progeny, and Racial Pofiling." *Idaho Law Review* 54, no. 2 (2018): 511–542.

Kane, Robert J. "Compromised Police Legitimacy as a Predictor of Violent Crime in Structurally Dis-advantaged Communities." *Criminology* 43, no. 2 (2005): 469–497. https://doi.org/10.1111/j.0011-1348.2005.00014.x.

Kane, Robert J. "The Ecology of Unhealthy Places: Violence, Birthweight, and the Importance of Territoriality in Structurally Disadvantaged Communities." *Social Science and Medicine* 73, no. 11 (2011): 1585–1592. https://doi.org/10.1016/j.socscimed.2011.08.035.

Kane, Robert J. "On the Limits of Social Control: Structural Deterrence and the Policing of 'Suppressible' Crimes." *Justice Quarterly* 23, no. 2 (2006): 186–213. https://doi.org/10.1080/07418820600688768.

Kane, Robert J. "Policing in Public Housing: Using Calls for Service to Examine Incident-Based Workload in the Philadelphia Housing Authority." *Policing* 21, no. 4 (1998): 618–631. https://doi.org/10.1108/13639519810241656.

Kane, Robert J., and Michael D. White. *Jammed Up: Bad Cops, Police Misconduct, and the New York City Police Department*. New York: NYU Press, 2013. https://nyupress.org/9780814748411/jammed-up/.

Knowles, Leanne, Jade. "The impact of COVID-19 on youth offending." PhD dissertation, University of Hull, 2021.

Kurbin, C. E., and R. Weitzer. "Retaliatory Homicide: Concentrated Disadvantage and Neighbourhood Culture." *Social Problems* 50, no. 2 (2003): 157–180. https://doi.org/10.1525/sp.2003.50.2.157.

Kushner, Howard I., and Claire E. Sterk. "The Limits of Social Capital: Durkheim, Suicide, and Social Cohesion." *American Journal of Public Health* 95, no. 7 (2005): 1139–1143.

Larson, James R., Jr. "Deep Diversity and Strong Synergy: Modeling the Impact of Variability in Members' Problem-Solving Strategies on Group Problem-Solving Performance." *Small Group Research* 38, no. 3 (2007): 413–436.

Lienemann, Brianna A., and Jason T. Siegel. "Increasing Help-Seeking Outcomes Among People With Elevated Depressive Symptomatology With Public Service Announcements: An Examination of Functional Matching and Message Sidedness." *Journal of Health Communication* 23, no. 1 (2018): 28–39.

Los Angeles Police Department. "Join LAPD: LAPD Hiring Process." Accessed February 2, 2022. https://www.joinlapd.com/there-are-seven-steps-application-process.

Lough, Jonathan, and Kathryn von Treuer. "A Critical Review of Psychological Instruments Used in Police Officer Selection." *Policing* 36, no. 4 (2013): 737–751. https://doi.org/10.1108/PIJPSM-11-2012-0104.

Meares, Tracey L. "The Law and Social Science of Stop and Frisk." *Annual Review of Law and Social Science* 10, no. 1 (2014): 335–352. https://doi.org/10.1146/annurev-lawsocsci-102612-134043.

Meares, Tracey L. "Programming Errors: Understanding the Constitutionality of Stop-and-Frisk as a Program, Not an Incident." *University of Chicago Law Review* 82, no. 1 (2015): 159–179. https://doi.org/10.2139/ssrn.2524930.

Metchik, Eric. "An Analysis of the 'Screening Out' Model of Police Officer Selection." *Police Quarterly* 2, no. 1 (1999): 79–95. https://doi.org/10.1177/109861119900200104.

Mohammed, Susan, and Erika Ringseis. "Cognitive Diversity and Consensus in Group Decision Making: The Role of Inputs, Processes, and Outcomes." *Organizational Behavior and Human Decision Processes* 85, no. 2 (2001): 310–335. https://doi.org/10.1006/obhd.2000.2943.

Page, Scott E. *The Difference: How the Power of Diversity Creates Better Groups, Firms, Schools, and Societies.* Princeton, NJ: Princeton University Press, 2007.

Page, Scott E. "Where Diversity Comes From and Why It Matters." *European Journal of Social Psychology* 44, no. 4 (2014): 267–279.

Patrick, Robert, and Joel Currier. "Ferguson Highlights Police Use of Military Gear and Tactics." *St. Louis Dispatch*, August 15, 2014. https://www.stltoday.com/news/local/metro/ferguson-highlights-police-use-of-military-gear-and-tactics/article_69176ce4-f888-58ff-b33a-64924d2beb6d.html.

President's Task Force on 21st Century Policing. "Final Report of the President's Task Force on 21st Century Policing." Washington, DC, 2015.

Rahr, Sue, and Stephen K. Rice. "From Warriors to Guardians: Recommitting American Police Culture to Democratic Ideals." *New Perspectives in Policing.* Washington, DC, National Institute of Justice, 2015.

Sanfiorenzo, Dimas. "How the Rodney King Beating Became the First Viral Video." Okayplayer, September 2021. https://www.okayplayer.com/news/rodney-king-beating-viral.html.

Silver, Jasmine R., Sean Patrick Roche, Thomas J. Bilach, and Stephanie Bontrager Ryon. "Traditional Police Culture, Use of Force, and Procedural Justice: Investigating Individual, Organizational, and Contextual Factors." *Justice Quarterly* 34, no. 7 (2017): 1272–1309. https://doi.org/10.1080/07418825.2017.1381756.

Snyder, Leslie B. "Health Communication Campaigns and Their Impact on Behavior." *Journal of Nutrition Education and Behavior* 39, no. 2 (2007): S32–S40.

Taub, Amanda. "What Was THAT? A Guide to the Military Gear Being Used Against Civilians in Ferguson." Vox, 2014. https://www.vox.com/2014/8/18/6003377/ferguson-military-gear.

Terry v. Ohio, 392 U.S. 1 (1968).

Twersky-Glasner, Aviva. "Police Personality: What Is It and Why Are They Like That?" *Journal of Police and Criminal Psychology* 20, no. 1 (2005): 56–67. https://doi.org/10.1007/BF02806707.

Varga, Ivan. "Social Morals, the Sacred and State Regulation in Durkheim's Sociology." *Social Compass* 53, no. 4 (2006). https://doi.org/10.1177/0037768606070408.

Vito, Anthony, George Higgins, and Gennaro Vito. "Police Stop and Frisk and the Impact of Race: A Focal Concerns Theory Approach." *Social Sciences* 10, no. 6 (2021): 230. https://doi.org/10.3390/socsci10060230.

Weber, Max. *From Max Weber: Essays in Sociology.* Edited by H. H. Gerth and C. Wright Mills. London: Routledge, 1991. https://www.amazon.com/Max-Weber-Essays-Sociology-dp-0343212765/dp/0343212765/ref=mt_other?_encoding=UTF8&me=&qid=.

Weisburd, David, Alese Wooditch, Sarit Weisburd, and Sue Ming Yang. "Do Stop, Question, and Frisk Practices Deter Crime?: Evidence at Microunits of Space and Time." *Criminology and Public Policy* 15, no. 1 (2016): 31–56. https://doi.org/10.1111/1745-9133.12172.

Wesenberg, Madison. "COVID-19 and the Rise of the Conspiracy: Examination of COVID Related Conspiracies Using Durkheimian Concepts." *Crossing Borders: Student Reflections on Global Social Issues* 3, no. 1 (2021). https://doi.org/10.31542/cb.v3i1.2248.

White, Michael D. "Identifying Good Cops Early: Predicting Recruit Performance in the Academy." *Police Quarterly* 11, no. 1 (2008): 27–49.

White, Michael D., and Henry F. Fradella. *STOP AND FRISK: The Use and Abuse of a Controversial Policing Tactic.* New York: NYU Press, 2019. https://nyupress.org/books/9781479857814/.

White, Michael D., and Robert J. Kane. "Pathways to Career-Ending Police Misconduct." *Criminal Justice and Behavior* 40, no. 11 (2013): 1301–1325. https://doi.org/10.1177/0093854813486269.

"5 Responses to a Sovereign Citizen at a Traffic Stop." Accessed July 13, 2021. https://www.police1.com/patrol-issues/articles/5-responses-to-a-sovereign-citizen-at-a-traffic-stop-FZ4ruThuMxTHVgEO/.

"12 Crucial Law Enforcement Policies." Accessed October 14, 2021. https://www.powerdms.com/policy-learning-center/12-crucial-law-enforcement-policies.

18 U.S. Code §242 (n.d.).

"18 U.S. Code § 242—Deprivation of Rights Under Color of Law | U.S. Code | US Law | LII / Legal Information Institute." Accessed November 12, 2021. https://www.law.cornell.edu/uscode/text/18/242.

42 U.S.C. §1983 (n.d.).

"About—Civilian Complaint Review Board (CCRB)." Accessed September 8, 2021. https://www1.nyc.gov/site/ccrb/about/about.page.

"About Us | CALEA® | The Commission on Accreditation for Law Enforcement Agencies, Inc." Accessed June 4, 2021. https://www.calea.org/about-us.

"ACLU-PA and Civil Rights Firm File Class Action Lawsuit Against Philadelphia Police Department for Racial Profiling | ACLU Pennsylvania." 2010. https://live-aclu-pennsylvania.pantheonsite.io/en/press-releases/aclu-pa-and-civil-rights-firm-file-class-action-lawsuit-against-philadelphia-police.

ACLU Pennsylvania. "After Seven Years, Report Shows Philadelphia Police Continue to Illegally Stop and Frisk Pedestrians." 2018. https://www.aclupa.org/en/press-releases/after-seven-years-report-shows-philadelphia-police-continue-illegally-stop-and-frisk.

"ACLU Seeks Federal Probe of Taylor Police for Use of Force, Bias." Accessed October 14, 2021. https://www.freep.com/story/news/local/michigan/wayne/2021/10/07/aclu-seeks-federal-investigation-taylor-police/6040161001/.

"Adam-12 (TV Series 1968–1975) - IMDb." Accessed February 18, 2021. https://www.imdb.com/title/tt0062539/?ref_=fn_al_tt_1.

Adams v. Williams, 407 U.S. 143 (1972).

Adlam, K. Robert. "The Police Personality: Psychological Consequences of Being a Police Officer." *Journal of Police Science & Administration* 10, no. 3 (1982): 344–347.

Agar, Michael, and Heather Schacht Reisinger. "A Heroin Epidemic at the Intersection of Histories: The 1960s Epidemic Among African Americans in Baltimore." *Medical Anthropology* 21, no. 2 (2002): 115–156. https://doi.org/10.1080/01459740212904.

Alpert, Geoffrey P., and Roger G. Dunham. *Understanding Police Use of Force: Officers, Suspects, and Reciprocity.* Cambridge, UK: Cambridge University Press, 2004.

Alpert, Geoffrey P., and Kyle McLean. "Where Is the Goal Line? A Critical Look at Police Body-Worn Camera Programs." *Criminology and Public Policy* 17, no. 3 (2018): 679–688. https://doi.org/10.1111/1745-9133.12374.

American Bar Foundation. *The Administration of Criminal Justice in the United States: Pilot Project Report.* Vol. 5. Chicago: American Bar Foundation, 1958. https://www.google.com/books/edition/The_Administration_of_Criminal_Justice_i/_cQ_AAAAIAAJ?hl=en.

Anderson, James, and Lee Kennett. *The Gun in America: The Origins of a National Dilemma.* Westport, CT: Praeger, 1975.

Anderson, Rick. "Game of Drones: How LAPD Quietly Acquired the Spy Birds Shunned by Seattle." *LA Weekly,* 2014. https://www.laweekly.com/game-of-drones-how-lapd-quietly-acquired-the-spy-birds-shunned-by-seattle/.

Andres, Scottie. "Derek Chauvin: What We Know About the Former Officer Charged in George Floyd's Death." CNN, June 1, 2020. https://www.cnn.com/2020/06/01/us/derek-chauvin-what-we-know-trnd/index.html.

Ariel, Barak, Lawrence W. Sherman, and Mark Newton. "Testing Hot-Spots Police Patrols Against No-Treatment Controls: Temporal and Spatial Deterrence Effects in the London Underground Experiment." *Criminology,* August (2019): 101–128. https://doi.org/10.1111/1745-9125.12231.

Ariel, Barak, Cristobal Weinborn, and Lawrence W. Sherman. "'Soft' Policing at Hot Spots—Do Police Community Support Officers Work? A Randomized Controlled Trial." *Journal of Experimental Criminology* 12, no. 3 (2016). https://doi.org/10.1007/s11292-016-9260-4.

Ashforth, Blake E., and Glen E. Kreiner. "'How Can You Do It?' Dirty Work and the Challenge of Constructing a Positive Identity." *The Academy of Management Review* 24, no. 3 (1999): 413–434.

Atherley, Loren T., and Matthew J. Hickman. "Officer Decertification and the National Decertification Index." *Police Quarterly* 16, no. 4 (2013): 420–437.

Avakame, Edem F., and James J. Fyfe. "Differential Police Treatment of Male-on-Female Spousal Violence: Additional Evidence on the Leniency Thesis." *Violence Against Women* 7, no. 1 (2001): 22–45. https://doi.org/10.1177/10778010122182280.

Azavea. "Hunchlab: Under the Hood." Azavea, 2015. https://cdn.azavea.com/pdfs/hunchlab/HunchLab-Under-the-Hood.pdf.

Bagshaw, Mike. "Is Diversity Divisive? A Positive Training Approach." *Industrial and Commercial Training* 36, no. 4 (2004): 153–157.

Bailey v. City of Philadelphia, Court of Appeals, 3rd Circuit (2010).

Balch, Robert W. "The Police Personality: Fact or Fiction?" *Journal of Criminal Law, Criminology, and Police Science* 63, no. 1 (1972): 106–119.

Balch, Robert W. "The Police Personality: Fact or Fiction." In *The Dysfunctional Alliance: Emotion and Reason in Justice Administration*, edited by D. B. Kennedy, 10–25. Cincinnati, OH: Anderson, 1977.

Balko, Radley. "Overkill: The Rise of Paramilitary Police Raids in America." Washington, DC, 2006. http://www.ncjrs.gov/App/publications/abstract.aspx?ID=238405.

Balko, Radley. *Rise of the Warrior Cop: The Militarization of America's Police Forces.* PublicAffairs, 2021.

Banks, Duren, Joshua Hendrix, Matthew Hickman, and Tracey Kyckelhahn. "National Sources of Law Enforcement Employment Data." Washington, DC, 2016.

Banton, Michael. *The Policeman in the Community.* New York: Basic Books, 1964. https://books.google.com/books/about/The_Policeman_in_the_Community.html?id=F0NMwQEACAAJ.

Baumer, Eric P., and Regan Gustafson. "Social Organization and Instrumental Crime: Assessing the Empirical Validity of Classic and Contemporary Anomie Theories." *Criminology* 45, no. 3 (2007): 617–663. https://doi.org/10.1111/j.1745-9125.2007.00090.x.

Bavin, Lynda M., and R. Glynn Owens. "Complementary Public Service Announcements as a Strategy for Enhancing the Impact of Health-Promoting Messages in Fictional Television Programs." *Health Communication* 33, no. 5 (2018): 544–552.

Beckett, Katherine. "The Uses and Abuses of Police Discretion: Toward Harm Reduction Policing." *Harvard Law and Policy Review* 10 (2016): 77.

"Becoming a USCP Police Officer | United States Capitol Police." Accessed February 4, 2022. https://www.uscp.gov/becoming-uscp-police-officer.

Bennett, Richard R. "Calling for Service: Mobilization of the Police Across Sociocultural Environments." *Police Practice and Research* 5, no. 1 (2004): 25–41. https://doi.org/10.1080/1561426042000191314.

Berry, Joshua. "The DOD Law of War Manual Returns Hollow Point Bullets to Armed Conflict." Just Security, August 4, 2015. https://www.justsecurity.org/25200/dod-law-war-manual-returns-hollow-point-bullets-armed-conflict/.

Betz, Joseph. "Police Violence." In *Moral Issues in Police Work*, edited by F. A. Elliston and M. Feldberg, 177–196. Totowa, NJ: Rowman and Allanheld, 1988.

Binder, Arnold, and Peter Scharf. "The Violent Police-Citizen Encounter." *The Annals of the American Academy of Political and Social Science* 452 (1980): 111–121.

Bittner, Egon. "Florence Nightingale in Pursuit of Willie Sutton: A Theory of the Police." In *The Potential for Reform of Criminal Justice*, edited by Herbert Jacob, 352. London: Sage, 1974.

Bittner, Egon. *The Functions of Police in Modern Society.* Chevy Chase, MD: National Institute of Mental Health, 1970. https://www.google.com/books/edition/The_Functions_of_the_Police_in_Modern_So/rQcXAAAAIAAJ?hl=en&gbpv=1&printsec=frontcover.

"Body-Worn Camera Laws Database." National Conference of State Legislators (NCSL), 2021. https://www.ncsl.org/research/civil-and-criminal-justice/body-worn-cameras-interactive-graphic.aspx.

Bopp, W. J. "OW Wilson and the Search for a Police Profession." Washington, DC, 1977. https://www.ncjrs.gov/App/Publications/abstract.aspx?ID=47846.

Braga, Anthony A., and Brenda J. Bond. "Policing Crime and Disorder Hot Spots: A Randomized Controlled Trial." *Criminology* 46, no. 3 (2008): 577–607. https://doi.org/10.1111/j.1745-9125.2008.00124.x.

Braga, Anthony A., Andrew V. Papachristos, and David M. Hureau. "The Effects of Hot Spots Policing on Crime: An Updated Systematic Review and Meta-Analysis." *Justice Quarterly* 31, no. 4 (2014): 633–663. https://doi.org/10.1080/07418825.2012.673632.

Braga, Anthony, Andrew Papachristos, and David Hureau. "Hot Spots Policing Effects on Crime." *Campbell Systematic Reviews* 8, no. 1 (2012): 1–96. https://doi.org/10.4073/csr.2012.8.

Braga, Anthony A., and Cory Schnell. "Evaluation of Place-Based Policing Strategies: Lessons Learned from the Smart Policing Initiative in Boston." *Police Quarterly* 16 (2013): 339–357.

Braga, Anthony A., and David L. Weisburd. *Policing Problem Places: Crime Hot Spots and Effective Prevention*, 2010. https://doi.org/10.1093/acprof:oso/9780195341966.001.0001.

Brodeur, Jean Paul. "An Encounter With Egon Bittner." *Crime, Law and Social Change* 48, no. 3–5 (2007): 105–132. https://doi.org/10.1007/s10611-007-9084-2.

Bronfenbrenner, Urie. *The Ecology of Human Development: Experiments by Nature and Design.* Cambridge, MA: Harvard University Press, 1979.

Brooks, Connor. "Federal Law Enforcement Officers, 2016—Statistical Tables." Washington, DC, 2019. https://www.bjs.gov/content/pub/pdf/fleo16st.pdf.

Brooks, Rosa, and Christy Lopez. "Policing in a Time of Pandemic: Recommendations for Law Enforcement." Covid-19 Rapid Response Impact Initiative | White Paper 7. Cambridge, MA, April 10, 2020.

Brown, Gregory R. "The Blue Line on Thin Ice: Police Use of Force Modifications in the Era of Cameraphones and YouTube." *The British Journal of Criminology* 56, no. 2 (2016): 293–312.

Brown, L. P. "Community Policing: A Partnership With Promise." *The Police Chief* 59 (1992): 45–47.

Brown, Robert A. "Policing in American History." *Du Bois Review* 16, no. 1 (2019): 189–195. https://doi.org/10.1017/S1742058X19000171.

Brown v. Illinois, 422 U.S. 590 (1975).

Brown v. Mississippi, 297 U.S. 278 (1936).

Bureau of Justice Assistance. "Body Worn Camera Toolkit: Body-Worn Camera Frequently Asked Questions." Washington, DC, 2015. https://bja.ojp.gov/sites/g/files/xyckuh186/files/media/document/BWC_FAQs.pdf.

CA.Gov | Commission on Peace Officer Standards and Training. "Peace Officer Candidate Selection Process." Accessed February 2, 2022. https://post.ca.gov/peace-officer-candidate-selection-process.

"Calculate Your BMI - Standard BMI Calculator." Accessed February 4, 2022. https://www.nhlbi.nih.gov/health/educational/lose_wt/BMI/bmicalc.htm.

Calfano, Brian Robert, and Donald P. Green. "Assessing the Efficacy of Radio Public Service Announcements: Results from Three Field Experiments." *Electronic News* 13, no. 3 (2019): 134–151.

Campbell, Alec, Richard A. Berk, and James J. Fyfe. "Deployment of Violence: The Los Angeles Police Department's Use of Dogs." *Evaluation Review* 22, no. 4 (1992): 535–561.

Caplan, Joel M., Leslie W. Kennedy, and Joel Miller. "Risk Terrain Modeling: Brokering Criminological Theory and GIS Methods for Crime Forecasting." *Justice Quarterly* 28, no. 2 (2011): 360–381. https://heinonline.org/HOL/Page?handle=hein.journals/jquart28&id=372&div=22&collection=journals.

Carr, Patrick J., Laura Napolitano, and Jessica Keating. "We Never Call the Cops and Here Is Why: A Qualitative Examination of Legal Cynicism in Three Philadelphia Neighborhoods." *Criminology* 45, no. 2 (2007): 1–36. http://users.soc.umn.edu/~uggen/Carr_CRIM_07.pdf.

Carroll, Leo, and M. Lilliana Gonzalez. "Out of Place: Racial Stereotypes and the Ecology of Frisks and Searches Following Traffic Stops." *Journal of Research in Crime and Delinquency* 51, no. 5 (2014): 559–584. https://doi.org/10.1177/0022427814523788.

Cashmore, E., and E. McLaughlin, eds. *Out of Order? Policing Black People.* London: Routledge/Taylor and Francis, 1991.

"Charles Haid - IMDb." Accessed July 22, 2020. https://www.imdb.com/name/nm0354024/?ref_=ttfc_fc_cl_t9.

Cheh, Mary. "Are Lawsuits an Answer to Police Brutality?" In *Police Violence: Understanding and Controlling the Police Abuse of Force*, edited by William Geller and Hans Toch, 247–272. New Haven, CT: Yale University Press, 1996.

Cheung, Helier. "George Floyd Death: Why US Protests Are So Powerful This Time." *BBC News*, June 8, 2020. https://www.bbc.com/news/world-us-canada-52969905.

Chimel v. California, 395 U.S. 752 (1969).

Chirambwi, Kudakwashe. "Militarizing Police in Complex Public Emergencies." *Peace Review* 28, no. 2 (2016): 171–177.

City of New Orleans. "NOPD - Consent Decree - City of New Orleans." 2019. https://nola.gov/nopd/nopd-consent-decree/.

Cohen, Deborah A., Thomas A. Farley, and Karen Mason. "Why Is Poverty Unhealthy? Social and Physical Mediators." *Social Science and Medicine* 57, no. 9 (2003): 1631–1641. https://doi.org/10.1016/S0277-9536(03)00015-7.

Cohen, Lawrence E., and Marcus Felson. "Social Change and Crime Rate Trends: A Routine Activity Approach." *American Sociological Review* 44, no. 4 (1979): 588–608.

Coldren, James R., Jr., Alissa Huntoon, and Michael Medaris. "Introducing Smart Policing: Foundations, Principles, and Practice." *Police Quarterly* 16, no. 3 (2013): 275–286.

Collins, Patricia, Jack R. Greene, Robert J. Kane, Robert Stokes, and Alexis Piquero. *Implementing Community Policing in Public Housing: Philadelphia's 11th Street Corridor Program.* Washington, DC: U.S. Department of Justice, 1999.

Collins v. City of Milwaukee, Case No. 17-CV-234-JPS (E.D. Wis. Jun. 14, 2017).

Commission on Accreditation for Law Enforcement Agencies. "CALEA Law Enforcement Manual." 2019. http://www.slcpd.com/ass3ts/uploads/2019/11/CALEA-Law-Enforcement-Manual-v-6.5-all-standards.pdf.

Commission on Peace Officer Standards and Training. "Basic Course Unit Guide: Weaponless Defense." Sacramento, CA, 1990. https://www.ncjrs.gov/pdffiles1/Digitization/133229NCJRS.pdf.

Consent Decree, Bailey v. City of Philadelphia et al. (C.A. No. 10-5952, E.D. Penn, June 21, 2011). Available as Document No. 16, Case 2:10-Cv-05952-SD at https://Aclupa.Org/Sites/Default/Files/Field_documents/Bailey_consent_decree_6-21-11_.pdf.

Conti, Norman. "A Visigoth System: Shame, Honor, and Police Socialization." *Journal of Contemporary*

Ethnography 38, no. 3 (2009): 409–432. https://doi.org/10.1177/0891241608330092.

Contreras, Russell. "Technology, Policing and Racial Bias." Axios, October 16, 2021. https://www.axios.com/technology-policing-and-racial-bias-bb0de2a2-0bce-4d40-a327-7a478bb16cb8.html.

Cooper, Alexia, and Erica Smith. "Homicide Trends in the United States, 1980–2008." *Patterns & Trends.* Vol. 17. Washington, DC, 2011. https://doi.org/10.2307/2061058.

COPS Office. "Advancing Public Safety through Community Policing: The First 25 Years of the COPS Office." Washington, DC, 2021.

"COPS Office." Accessed March 11, 2021. https://cops.usdoj.gov/.

Cordner, Gary, and Elizabeth Perkins Biebel. "Problem-Oriented Policing in Practice." *Criminology and Public Policy* 4, no. 2 (2005): 155–180. https://doi.org/10.1111/j.1745-9133.2005.00013.x.

Corsaro, Nicholas, James Frank, and Murat Ozer. "Perceptions of Police Practice, Cynicism of Police Performance, and Persistent Neighborhood Violence: An Intersecting Relationship." *Journal of Criminal Justice* 43, no. 1 (2015): 1–11. https://doi.org/10.1016/j.jcrimjus.2014.10.003.

Crank, John P. *Understanding Police Culture.* 2nd ed. New York: Routledge, 2015. https://books.google.com/books?hl=en&lr=&id=wRugBAAAQBAJ&oi=fnd&pg=PP1&dq=police+culture&ots=qScQCOmu2N&sig=sHK8RZ_xKg1TOO235D7i9D3S73k#v=onepage&q=police culture&f=false.

Cumming, Elaine, Ian Cumming, and Laura Edell. "Policeman as Philosopher, Guide and Friend." *Social Problems* 12 (1965): 276–286.

Curry, Colleen, and Luis Martinez. "Ferguson Police's Show of Force Highlights Militarization of America's Cops." ABC News, 2014. https://abcnews.go.com/US/ferguson-police-small-army-thousands-police-departments/story?id=24977299.

Dai, Mengyan, Wu He, Xin Tian, Ashley Giraldi, and Feng Gu. "Working With Communities on Social Media Varieties in the Use of Facebook and Twitter by Local Police." *Online Information Review* 41, no. 6 (2017): 782–796. https://doi.org/10.1108/OIR-01-2016-0002.

Davis, Kenneth Culp. *Discretionary Justice: A Preliminary Inquiry.* Baton Rouge: Louisiana State University Press, 1969. https://www.amazon.com/Discretionary-Justice-Kenneth-Culp-Davis/dp/0313225036.

Davis, Oliver. "Theorizing the Advent of Weaponized Drones as Techniques of Domestic Paramilitary Policing." *Security Dialogue* 50, no. 4 (2019): 344–360.

Degeling, Martin, and Bettina Berendt. "What Is Wrong About Robocops as Consultants? A Technology-Centric Critique of Predictive Policing." *AI and Society* 33, no. 3 (2018): 347–356. https://doi.org/10.1007/s00146-017-0730-7.

del Carmen, Rolando V. "Terry v. Ohio." In *Criminal Procedure and the Supreme Court: A Guide to the Major Decisions on Search and Seizure, Privacy, and Individual Rights,* edited by Rolando V. del Carmen and Craig Hemmens, 57–74. Lanham, MD: Rowman and Littlefield, 2010.

Delehanty, Casey, Jack Mewhirter, Ryan Welch, and Jason Wilks. "Militarization and Police Violence: The Case of the 1033 Program." *Research and Politics* 4, no. 2 (2017): 1–7. https://doi.org/10.1177/2053168017712885.

de Lint, Willem. "Autonomy, Regulation and the Police Beat." *Social and Legal Studies* 9, no. 1 (2000): 55–83. https://doi.org/10.1177/096466390000900104.

de Lint, Willem, Sirpa Virta, and John Edward Deukmedjian. "The Simulation of Crime Control." *American Behavioral Scientist* 50, no. 12 (2007): 1631–1647. https://doi.org/10.1177/0002764207302472.

"Deprivation of Rights Under Color of Law." Accessed July 8, 2021. https://www.justice.gov/crt/deprivation-rights-under-color-law.

Dickerson v. United States, 530 U.S. 428, 120 S. Ct. 2326, 147 L. Ed. 2d 405 (2000).

Do, D. Phuong, Brian Karl Finch, Ricardo Basurto-Davila, Chloe Bird, Jose Escarce, and Nicole Lurie. "Does Place Explain Racial Health Disparities? Quantifying the Contribution of Residential Context to the Black/White Health Gap in the United States." *Social Science and Medicine* 67, no. 8 (2008): 1258–1268. https://doi.org/10.1016/j.socscimed.2008.06.018.

Doerner, William G. "The Utility of the Oral Interview Board in Selecting Police Academy Admissions." *Policing: An International Journal of Police Strategies & Management* 20, no. 4 (1997): 777–785. https://doi.org/10.1108/13639519710368143.

Donovan, Kathleen M., and Charles F. Klahm. "The Role of Entertainment Media in Perceptions of Police Use of Force." *Criminal Justice and Behavior* 42, no. 12 (2015): 1261–1281. https://doi.org/10.1177/0093854815604180.

Dowler, K. "Police Dramas on Television." *Oxford Research Encyclopedia of Criminology,* 2016. https://oxfordre.com/criminology/view/10.1093/acrefore/9780190264079.001.0001/acrefore-9780190264079-e-175.

"Dragnet 1967 (TV Series 1967–1970) - IMDb." Accessed February 18, 2021. https://www.imdb.com/title/tt0061248/?ref_=fn_al_tt_2.

Drawve, Grant. "A Metric Comparison of Predictive Hot Spot Techniques and RTM." *Justice Quarterly* 33, no. 3 (2016): 369–397. https://doi.org/10.1080/07418825.2014.904393.

Drawve, Grant, Shaun A. Thomas, and Jeffery T. Walker. "Bringing the Physical Environment Back Into Neighborhood Research: The Utility of RTM for Developing an Aggregate Neighborhood Risk of Crime Measure." *Journal of Criminal Justice* 44 (2016): 21–29. https://doi.org/10.1016/j.jcrimjus.2015.12.002.

Drug Enforcement Administration. "History: 1985–1990," n.d. https://www.dea.gov/sites/default/files/2018-07/1985-1990 p 58-67custom2.pdf.

Dulaney, Marvin W. *Black Police in America*. Bloomington: Indiana University Press, 1996.

Dunlap, C. J., Jr. "The Police-Ization of the Military." *Journal of Political & Military Sociology* 27, no. 2 (1999): 217.

Durkheim, Emile. *Durkheim: The Division of Labour in Society*, edited by Steven Lukes. 2nd ed. London: Palgrave Macmillan, n.d.

Durkheim, Emile. *Rules of Sociological Method*, edited by Steven Lukes. New York: Free Press, n.d.

Durkheim, Emile. *Suicide: A Study in Sociology*. New York: Routledge, 2005.

Eaglin, Jessica M. "To 'Defund' the Police." 73 *Stanford Law Review Online* 120 (2021).

Eck, John E., and William Spelman. *Problem-Solving: Problem-Oriented Policing in Newport News*. Washington, DC: Police Executive Research Forum, 1987.

Ekins, Emily. "Policing in America: Understanding Public Attitudes Toward the Police. Results from a National Survey." December 7, 2016. https://www.cato.org/survey-reports/policing-america.

Engel, Robin S., Robert E. Worden, Nicholas Corsaro, Hannah D. McManus, Danielle Reynolds, Hannah Cochran, Gabrielle T. Isaza, and Jennifer Calnon Cherkauskas. *The Power to Arrest*. New York: Springer International, 2019. https://doi.org/10.1007/978-3-030-17054-7.

Ericson, Richard V. "Rules in Policing: Five Perspectives." *Theoretical Criminology* 11, no. 3 (2007): 367–401.

Evans, Richard J. *Rethinking German History: Nineteenth-Century Germany and the Origins of the Third Reich*. London: Routledge, 1987. https://www.amazon.com/Rethinking-German-History-Routledge-Revivals-dp-1138842842/dp/1138842842/ref=mt_other?_encoding=UTF8&me=&qid=1602348156.

Fagan, Jeffrey, Anthony Braga, Rod Brunson, and April Pattavina. "Stops and Stares: Street Stops, Surveillance, and Race in the New Policing." *Fordham Urban Law Journal* 43, no. 3 (2016): 539.

Fagan, Jeffrey, and Garth Davies. "Street Stops and Broken Windows: Terry, Race and Disorder in New York City." *Fordham Urban Law Journal* 28 (2000): 457–504. https://doi.org/10.2139/ssrn.257813.

Fallik, Seth Wyatt, Ross Deuchar, and Vaughn J. Crichlow. "Body-Worn Cameras in the Post-Ferguson Era: An Exploration of Law Enforcement Perspectives." *Journal of Police and Criminal Psychology* 35, no. 3 (2020): 263–273. https://doi.org/10.1007/s11896-018-9300-2.

Fan, Mary D. "Body Cameras, Big Data, and Police Accountability." *Law & Social Inquiry* 43, no. 4 (2018): 1236–1256. https://doi.org/10.1111/LSI.12354.

Farrell, Graham. "Crime Concentration Theory." *Crime Prevention and Community Safety* 17, no. 4 (2015): 233–248. https://doi.org/10.1057/cpcs.2015.17.

Faull, Andrew. "State Abuses Could Match the Threat of COVID-19 Itself." Institute for Security Studies, 2020. Accessed April 14, 2020. https://issafrica.org/iss-today/state-abuses-could-match-the-threat-of-covid-19-itself.

Fayard, Anne-Laure, Ileana Stigliani, and Beth A. Bechky. "How Nascent Occupations Construct a Mandate: The Case of Service Designers' Ethos." *Administrative Science Quarterly* 62, no. 2 (2017): 270–303. https://doi.org/10.1177/0001839216665805.

"FBI Releases 2019 Participation Data for the National Use-of-Force Data Collection." 2020. https://www.fbi.gov/news/pressrel/press-releases/fbi-releases-2019-participation-data-for-the-national-use-of-force-data-collection.

Federal Bureau of Investigation. "2018 Crime in the United States - Police Employee Data." Accessed August 4, 2020. https://ucr.fbi.gov/crime-in-the-u.s/2018/crime-in-the-u.s.-2018/topic-pages/police-employee-data.

Federal Bureau of Investigation. "National Use-of-Force Data Collection." Accessed June 11, 2021. https://www.fbi.gov/services/cjis/ucr/use-of-force.

"Federal Bureau of Investigation Crime Data Explorer—Use-of-Force." Accessed June 11, 2021. https://crime-data-explorer.app.cloud.gov/pages/le/uof.

"Felony | Wex | US Law | LII / Legal Information Institute." Accessed October 1, 2020. https://www.law.cornell.edu/wex/felony.

Ferguson, Andrew G. *Rise of Big Data Policing: Surveillance, Race, and the Future of Law Enforcement*. New York: NYU Press, 2017.

"Ferguson Unrest: From Shooting to Nationwide Protests." BBC News, 2015. http://www.bbc.com/news/world-us-canada-30193354.

Fernandes, April D., and Robert D. Crutchfield. "Race, Crime, and Criminal Justice: Fifty Years Since the Challenge of Crime in a Free Society." *Criminology and Public Policy* 17, no. 2 (2018): 397–417. https://doi.org/10.1111/1745-9133.12361.

Fernandez, Claudia Plaisted. "Creating Thought Diversity: The Antidote to Group Think." *Journal of Public Health Management and Practice* 13, no. 6 (2007): 670–671.

Fitzpatrick, Kevin, and Mark LaGory. *Unhealthy Cities: Poverty, Race, and Place in America*. New York: Routledge, 2013.

Fitzpatrick, Kevin, and Mark LaGory. *Unhealthy Places: The Ecology of Risk in the Urban Landscape*. New York: Routledge, 2002.

Florida v. Royer, 460 U.S. 491 (1983).

Floyd v. City of New York, 959 F. Supp. 2d 668 - Dist. Court, SD New York (2013).

"Four Former Minneapolis Police Officers Indicted on Federal Civil Rights Charges for Death of George Floyd; Derek Chauvin Also Charged in Separate Indictment for Violating Civil Rights of a Juvenile." Justice News: U.S. Department of Justice, Office of Public Affairs, May 7, 2021. https://www.justice.gov /opa/pr/four-former-minneapolis-police-officers -indicted-federal-civil-rights-charges-death-george.

Fradella, Henry F., and Michael D. White. "Reforming Stop-and-Frisk." *Criminology, Criminal Justice, Law & Society* 18, no. 3 (2017): 45–65.

Fu, Feng, Corina E. Tarnita, Nicholas A. Christakis, Long Wang, David G. Rand, and Martin A. Nowak. "Evolution of In-Group Favoritism." *Scientific Reports* 2 (2012): 1–6. https://doi.org/10.1038/srep00460.

Fuller, Thomas, and Tim Arango. "Police Pin a Rise in Murders on an Unusual Suspect: Covid." *New York Times*, November 15, 2021. https://www.nytimes.com /2020/10/29/us/coronavirus-murders.html.

Furman v. Georgia, 408 U.S. 238 (1972).

Fyfe, James J. "Administrative Interventions on Police Shooting Discretion: An Empirical Examination." *Journal of Criminal Justice* 7, no. 4 (1979): 303–323. https://www.sciencedirect.com/science/article/pii /0047235279900655.

Fyfe, James J. "Blind Justice: Police Shootings in Memphis." *Journal of Criminal Law and Criminology* 73, no. 2 (1982): 707–722. https://doi .org/10.2307/1143112.

Fyfe, James J. "'Good' Policing." In *The Socio-Economics of Crime and Justice*, edited by Brian Forst, 269–299. New York: Routledge/Taylor and Francis, 1993. https://books.google.com/books?hl=en&lr=&id =IOlmDAAAQBAJ&oi=fnd&pg=PA269&dq=fyfe +good+policing&ots=wFKazkphOs&sig= -NhnXfmpUgxCYY6MNq8ck3w3aC0#v=onepage&q =fyfe good policing&f=false.

Fyfe, James J. "Police Use of Deadly Force: Research and Reform." *Justice Quarterly* 5 (1988): 165–205. https:// doi.org/10.1080/07418828800089691.

Fyfe, James J. "Training to Reduce Police-Civilian Violence." In *Police Violence: Understanding and Controlling the Police Abuse of Force*, edited by William Geller and Hans Toch, 165–179. New Haven, CT: Yale University Press, 1996.

Fyfe, James J., David A Klinger, and Jeanne M Flavin. "Male-on-Female Spousal Violence." *Criminology* 35, no. 3 (1997): 455–473.

Garner, Joel H., Matthew J. Hickman, Ronald W. Malega, and Christopher D. Maxwell. "Progress Toward National Estimates of Police Use of Force." *PLOS ONE* 13, no. 2 (2018): e0192932. https://doi.org/10.1371 /journal.pone.0192932.

Gelman, Andrew, Jeffrey Fagan, and Alex Kiss. "An Analysis of the New York City Police Department's 'Stop-and- Frisk' Policy in the Context of Claims of Racial Bias." *Journal of the American Statistical Association* 102, no. 479 (2007): 813–823. https://doi .org/10.1198/016214506000001040.

Gladstone, Brooke. "Biased Algorithms, Biased World." On the Media | WNYC Studios, November 22, 2019. https://www.wnycstudios.org/podcasts/otm/episodes /biased-algorithms-biased-world-on-the-media.

Glasner, Philip, and Michael Leitner. "Evaluating the Impact the Weekday Has on Near-Repeat Victimization: A Spatio-Temporal Analysis of Street Robberies in the City of Vienna, Austria." *ISPRS International Journal of Geo-Information* 6, no. 1 (2016): 3. https:// doi.org/10.3390/ijgi6010003.

Glissmeyer, Michael, James W. Bishop, and R. David Fass. "Role Conflict, Role Ambiguity and Intention to Quit the Organization: The Case of Law Enforcement Officers." In *Decision Sciences Institute Annual Conference, 38th Southwest*, 458–469, 2007.

Goffman, Erving. *The Presentation of Self in Everyday Life*. New York: Doubleday, 1956.

Goffman, Erving. *Stigma: Notes on the Management of Spoiled Identity*. New York: Simon & Schuster, 1963.

Goldkamp, John. "Minorities as Victims of Police Shootings: Interpretations of Racial Disproportionality and Police Use of Deadly Force." *Justice System Journal* 2, no. 2 (1976): 169–183.

Goldstein, Herman. "Improving Policing: A Problem-Oriented Approach." *Crime & Delinquency* 25, no. 2 (1979): 236–258. https://doi.org/10.1177/001112877902500207.

Goldstein, Herman. "Toward Community-Oriented Policing: Potential, Basic Requirements, and Threshold Questions." *Crime & Delinquency* 33, no. 1 (1987): 6–30. https://doi.org/10.1177/0011128787033001002.

Goode, Erica. "Philadelphia Defends Policy on Frisking, With Limits." *New York Times*, July 12, 2012. https://www.nytimes.com/2012/07/12/us/stop-and -frisk-controls-praised-in-philadelphia.html.

Gottfredson, Michael R., and Don M. Gottfredson. *Decision Making in Criminal Justice: Toward the Rational Exercise of Discretion*. New York: Springer, 1988. https://doi.org/10.1007/978-1-4757-9954-5_1.

Gould, Henry Alexander. "Anomic America." Dartmouth College, 2021.

Gould, Larry A. "A Longitudinal Approach to the Study of the Police Personality: Race/Gender Differences." *Journal of Police and Criminal Psychology* 15, no. 2 (2000): 41–51. https://doi.org/10.1007/BF02802664.

Graham v. Connor, 490 U.S. 386 (1989).

Grant, J. D., and J. Grant. "Officer Selection and the Prevention of Abuse of Force." In *And Justice for All: Understanding and Controlling Police Abuse of Force*, edited by William Geller and Hans Toch, 151–162. Washington, DC: Police Executive Research Forum, 1995.

Gravitte v. North Carolina DMV (2002).

Graybill, Andrew R. *Policing the Great Plains: Rangers, Mounties, and the North American Frontier, 1875–1910*. Lincoln: University of Nebraska Press, 2007.

Greenberg, Kenneth S., ed. *Nat Turner: A Slave Rebellion in History and Memory*. New York: Oxford University Press, 2003. https://books.google.com/books?hl=en&lr=&id=FoAeDQAAQBAJ&oi=fnd&pg=PR7&dq=nat+turner+rebellion&ots=T0TIjlenN5&sig=5a0QSQPYWCa54hv1a72GU8hgXYU#v=onepage&q=nat turner rebellion&f=false.

Greene, Evarts B., and Virginia D. Harrington. *American Population Before the Federal Census of 1790*. Baltimore: Genealogical Publishing, 1997. https://www.amazon.com/American-Population-Before-Federal-Census/dp/0806313773.

Greene, Jack R. "Community Policing in America: Changing the Nature, Structure, and Function of the Police." In *Policies, Processes, and Decisions of the Criminal Justice System*, edited by Julie Horney, John Martin, Doris L. MacKenzie, Ruth Peterson, and Dennis Rosenbaum (Crim Just 2000: V.3.), 299–370. Washington, DC: National Institute of Justice, 2000. https://books.google.com/books?id=npJYG7kS-3AC&printsec=frontcover#v=onepage&q&f=false.

Greene, Jack R., and Carl B. Klockars. "What Police Do." In *Thinking About Police: Contemporary Readings*, edited by Carl B. Klockars and Stephen D. Mastrofski, 2nd ed. New York: McGraw-Hill, 1991.

Greene, Jack R., and Stephen D. Mastrofski. *Community Policing: Rhetoric or Reality*. Santa Barbara, CA: Praeger, 1988. https://www.google.com/books/edition/Community_Policing/7ZraAAAAMAAJ?hl=en.

Greene, Judith A. "Zero Tolerance: A Case Study of Police Policies and Practices in New York City." *Crime and Delinquency* 45, no. 2 (1999): 171–187. https://doi.org/10.1177/0011128799045002001.

Gregg v. Georgia, 428 U.S. 153 (1976).

Grimm, Veronika, Verena Utikal, and Lorenzo Valmasoni. "In-Group Favoritism and Discrimination Among Multiple Out-Groups." IWQW Discussion Papers, No. 05/2015, Friedrich-Alexander-Universität Erlangen-Nürnberg, Institut Für Wirtschaftspolitik Und Quantitative Wirtschaftsforschung (IWQW), Nürnberg, 2015.

Groff, Elizabeth, and Eric S. McCord. "The Role of Neighborhood Parks as Crime Generators." *Security Journal* 25, no. 1 (2012): 1–24. https://doi.org/10.1057/sj.2011.1.

Grogger, Jeffrey. "The Effect of Arrests on the Employment and Earnings of Young Men." *Quarterly Journal of Economics* 110, no. 1 (1995): 51–71. https://doi.org/10.2307/2118510.

Hall, Richard H., Norman J. Johnson, and J. Eugene Haas. "Organizational Size, Complexity, and Formalization." *American Sociological Review* 32, no. 6 (1967): 903–912.

Hallak, Maram, Kathryn Quina, and Charles Collyer. "Preventing Violence in Schools." In *Violence in Schools: Cross-National and Cross-Cultural Perspectives*, edited by Florence Denmark, Herbert H. Krauss, Robert W. Wesner, Elizabeth Midlarsky, and Uwe P. Gielen, 275–292. New York: Springer, 2005. https://doi.org/10.1007/0-387-28811-2_14.

Harcourt, Bernard E. "Reflecting on the Subject: A Critique of the Social Influence Conception of Deterrence, the Broken Windows Theory, and Order-Maintenance Policing New York Style." *Michigan Law Review* 97, no. 2 (1998): 291–389. https://doi.org/10.2307/1290289.

Harkavy, Robert E. "National Humiliation in International Politics." *International Politics* 37 (2000): 345–368.

Harmon, Rachel. "Legal Remedies for Police Misconduct." In *Academy for Justice, a Report on Scholarship and Criminal Justice Reform*, edited by Erik Luna, 27–50. Academy for Justice, 2017. https://scholar.google.com/scholar_case?case=8826656230568767300&q=brown+v.+illinois&hl=en&as_sdt=6,39&as_vis=1.

Harris, David A. "Across the Hudson: Taking the Stop and Frisk Debate Beyond New York City." *New York University Journal of Legislation and Public Policy* 16, no. 853 (2013): 1–24.

Harris, David A. "'Driving While Black' and All Other Traffic Offenses: The Supreme Court and Pretextual Traffic Stops." *Journal of Criminal Law & Criminology* 87, no. 2 (1997): 544–582. http://www.autolife.umd.umich.edu/Race/R_Casestudy/R_Casestudy1.htm.

Harris, David A. *Profiles in Injustice: Why Police Profiling Cannot Work*. New York: The New Press, 2002.

Harris, Scott. "Product Feature: Predictive Policing Helps Law Enforcement 'See Around the Corners.'" *The Police Chief*, October 2014. https://www.policechiefmagazine.org/product-feature-predictive-policing-helps-law-enforcement-see-around-the-corners/.

Helmreich, Robert L., and Ashleigh C. Merritt. "Safety and Error Management: The Role of Crew Resource Management." In *Aviation Resource Management*, 107–119. New York: Routledge, 2017.

Henson, Billy, Bradford W. Reyns, Charles F. Klahm, IV, and James Frank. "Do Good Recruits Make Good Cops? Problems Predicting and Measuring Academy and Street-Level Success." *Police Quarterly* 13, no. 1 (2010): 5–26. https://doi.org/10.1177/1098611109357320.

Herbert, Steve. "The Normative Ordering of Police Territoriality: Making and Marking Space With the Los Angeles Police Department." *Annals of the Association of American Geographers* 68, no. 3 (1996): 567–582. https://doi.org/10.1111/j.1467-8306.1996.tb01767.x.

Herbert, Steve. "Police Subculture Reconsidered." *Criminology* 36, no. 2 (1998): 343–370. https://doi.org/10.1111/j.1745-9125.1998.tb01251.x.

Herbert, Steve. *Policing Space: Territoriality and the Los Angeles Police Department.* Minneapolis: University of Minnesota Press, 1996. https://www.upress.umn.edu /book-division/books/policing-space.

Heritage, John. "Revisiting Authority in Patient–Physician Interaction." In *Diagnosis as Cultural Practice*, edited by Monica Heller and Richard J. Watts, 83–102. New York: Mouton de Gruyter, 2005.

Hill, Evan, Ainara Tiefenthaler, Christiaan Triebert, Drew Jordan, Haley Willis, and Robin Stein. "How George Floyd Was Killed in Police Custody." *New York Times*, May 31, 2020. https://www.nytimes.com/2020/05/31 /us/george-floyd-investigation.html.

"Hill Street Blues - Emmy Awards, Nominations and Wins | Television Academy." Accessed August 3, 2020. https://www.emmys.com/shows/hill-street-blues.

Hine, Kelly A., Louise E. Porter, Nina J. Westera, and Geoffrey P. Alpert. "Too Much or Too Little? Individual and Situational Predictors of Police Force Relative to Suspect Resistance." *Policing and Society* 28, no. 5 (2018): 587–604. https://doi.org/10.1080/10439463.2 016.1232257.

Hinkle, Joshua C., David Weisburd, Cody W. Telep, and Kevin Petersen. "Problem-Oriented Policing for Reducing Crime and Disorder: An Updated Systematic Review and Meta-Analysis." *Campbell Systematic Reviews* 16, no. 2 (2020). https://doi.org/10.1002/cl2.1089.

History.com Editors. "LAPD Officers Beat Rodney King on Camera." History, A&E Television Networks, 2021. https://www.history.com/this-day-in-history/police-brutality-caught-on-video.

Hodgkinson, Sarah, and Nick Tilley. "Policing Anti-Social Behaviour: Constraints, Dilemmas and Opportunities." *Howard Journal of Criminal Justice* 46, no. 4 (2007): 385–400. https://doi.org/10.1111/j.1468 -2311.2007.00484.x.

Hogan, Robert, and William Kurtines. "Personological Correlates of Police Effectiveness." *Journal of Psychology* 91, no. 2 (1975): 289–295.

"Home | Navajo Police Department." Accessed February 4, 2022. https://www.npd.navajo-nsn.gov/.

Hong, Lu, and Scott E. Page. "Groups of Diverse Problem Solvers Can Outperform Groups of High-Ability Problem Solvers." *Proceedings of the National Academy of Sciences* 101, no. 46 (2004): 16385–16389.

"How Municipal WiFi Works | HowStuffWorks." Accessed August 7, 2020. https://computer.howstuffworks.com /municipal-wifi.htm.

"How to Answer Police Officer Oral Board Interview Questions." Accessed February 4, 2022. https://www .police1.com/police-jobs-and-careers/articles/the -toughest-oral-board-questions-and-how-to-answer -them-2zMbXEYByHLVbnt3/.

Howell, K. Babe. "Broken Lives From Broken Windows: The Hidden Costs of Aggressive Order-Maintenance Policing." *NYU Review of Law & Social Change* 33 (2009): 271–329.

Huey, Laura, and Rose Ricciardelli. "'This Isn't What I Signed up for': When Police Officer Role Expectations Conflict With the Realities of General Duty Police Work in Remote Communities." *International Journal of Police Science and Management* 17, no. 3 (2015): 194–203. https://doi.org/10.1177/1461355715603590.

Hughes, E. C. "Work and the Self." In *Social Psychology at the Crossroads*, edited by J. H. Rohrer and M. Sherif, 313–323. New York: Harper and Brothers, 1951.

Hunt, Priscillia, John S. Hollywood, and Jessica M. Saunders. *Evaluation of the Shreveport Predictive Policing Experiment.* Santa Monica, CA: Rand Corporation, 2014. https:// www.ojp.gov/ncjrs/virtual-library/abstracts/evaluation -shreveport-predictive-policing-experiment.

Huq, Aziz Z. "The Consequences of Disparate Policing: Evaluating Stop and Frisk as a Modality of Urban Policing." *Minnesota Law Review* 101, no. 6 (2017): 2397–2480.

Hvistendahl, Mara. "How the LAPD and Palantir Use Data to Justify Racist Policing." *The Intercept*, January 30, 2021. https://theintercept.com/2021/01/30/lapd-palantir -data-driven-policing/.

Iannone, Nathan, Marvin D. Iannone, and Jeff Bernstein. *Supervision of Police Personnel.* 9th ed. New York: Pearson, 2019.

"Iconic TV Series Catchphrases - IMDb." Accessed June 16, 2020. https://www.imdb.com/list/ls094232413/?ref_=nm_rls_1.

Illinois v. Wardlow, 528 U.S. 119 (2000).

"Immigrants in America: Key Charts and Facts | Pew Research Center." Accessed March 1, 2022. https://www .pewresearch.org/hispanic/2020/08/20/facts-on-u-s -immigrants/.

"International Reaction to George Floyd Killing | Black Lives Matter News." Al Jazeera, June 2, 2020. https:// www.aljazeera.com/news/2020/6/2/international-reac-tion-to-george-floyd-killing.

Jensen, Eric, Nicholas Jones, Mean Rabe, Beverly Pratt, Lauren Medina, Kimberly Orozco, and Lindsay Spell. "2020 U.S. Population More Racially and Ethnically Diverse Than Measured in 2010." U.S. Census Bureau, August 12, 2021. https://www.census.gov /library/stories/2021/08/2020-united-states-population -more-racially-ethnically-diverse-than-2010.html.

"Jobs - The Supreme Court Police." Accessed February 4, 2022. https://www.supremecourt.gov/jobs/police/police.aspx.

"John Locke on the Idea That 'Wherever Law Ends, Tyranny Begins' (1689) | Online Library of Liberty." Accessed March 19, 2021. https://oll.libertyfund.org /quote/john-locke-on-the-idea-that-wherever-law-ends -tyranny-begins-1689.

Johnson, Lallen T., and Robert J. Kane. "Deserts of Disadvantage: The Diffuse Effects of Structural Disadvantage on Violence in Urban Communities." *Crime and Delinquency* 64, no. 2 (2018): 143–165. https://doi.org/10.1177/0011128716682228.

Jones, Russell L. "Terry v. Ohio: Its Failure, Immoral Progeny, and Racial Profiling." *Idaho Law Review* 54, no. 2 (2018): 511–542.

Kane, Robert J. "Abolish Police? No, But Change Recruitment." *Philadelphia Inquirer*, June 8, 2020. https://www.inquirer.com/opinion/commentary/abolish-police-reform-recruitment-george-floyd-20200608.html.

Kane, Robert J. "Collect and Release Data on Coercive Police Actions." *Criminology & Public Policy* 6, no. 4 (2007): 773–780. https://doi.org/10.1111/j.1745-9133.2007.00485.x.

Kane, Robert J. "Compromised Police Legitimacy as a Predictor of Violent Crime in Structurally Disadvantaged Communities." *Criminology* 43, no. 2 (2005): 469–497. https://doi.org/10.1111/j.0011-1348.2005.00014.x.

Kane, Robert J. "The Ecology of Unhealthy Places: Violence, Birthweight, and the Importance of Territoriality in Structurally Disadvantaged Communities." *Social Science and Medicine* 73, no. 11 (2011): 1585–1592. https://doi.org/10.1016/j.socscimed.2011.08.035.

Kane, Robert J. "On the Limits of Social Control: Structural Deterrence and the Policing of 'Suppressible' Crimes." *Justice Quarterly* 23, no. 2 (2006): 186–213. https://doi.org/10.1080/07418820600688768.

Kane, Robert J. "Patterns of Arrest in Domestic Violence Encounters: Identifying a Police Decision-Making Model." *Journal of Criminal Justice* 27, no. 1 (1999): 65–79. https://doi.org/10.1016/S0047-2352(98)00037-3.

Kane, Robert J. "Policing in Public Housing: Using Calls for Service to Examine Incident-Based Workload in the Philadelphia Housing Authority." *Policing* 21, no. 4 (1998): 618–631. https://doi.org/10.1108/13639519810241656.

Kane, Robert J. "Responding to Restraining Orders in Domestic Violence Incidents: Identifying the Custody-Threshold Thesis." *Criminal Justice and Behavior* 27, no. 3 (2000): 561–580.

Kane, Robert J. "The Social Ecology of Police Misconduct." *Criminology* 40, no. 4 (2002): 867–896. https://doi.org/10.1111/j.1745-9125.2002.tb00976.x.

Kane, Robert J. "What Current Police Reform Efforts Lack: A Call to Federalize." *The Hill*, July 17, 2020. https://thehill.com/opinion/criminal-justice/507847-what-current-police-reform-efforts-lack-a-call-to-federalize.

Kane, Robert J., and Shea W. Cronin. "Maintaining Order Under the Rule of Law: Occupational Templates and the Police Use of Force." *Journal of Crime and Justice* 34, no. 3 (2011): 163–177. https://doi.org/10.1080/0735648X.2011.609732.

Kane, Robert J., Joseph L. Gustafson, and Christopher Bruell. "Racial Encroachment and the Formal Control of Space: Minority Group-Threat and Misdemeanor Arrests in Urban Communities." *Justice Quarterly* 30, no. 6 (2013): 957–982. https://doi.org/10.1080/07418825.2011.636376.

Kane, Robert J., and Michael D. White. *Jammed Up: Bad Cops, Police Misconduct, and the New York City Police Department*. New York: NYU Press, 2013. https://nyupress.org/9780814748411/jammed-up/.

Kansas City Police Department, Missouri. "Police Response Time Analysis, 1975." Kansas City, MO: Kansas City Police Department, 2006. https://doi.org/10.3886/ICPSR07760.v1.

Kaplan, Caren, and Andrea Miller. "Drones as 'Atmospheric Policing': From US Border Enforcement to the LAPD." *Public Culture* 31, no. 3 (2019): 419–445. https://doi.org/10.1215/08992363-7532679.

Kappeler, Victor E., and Peter B. Kraska. "Normalising Police Militarisation, Living in Denial." *Policing and Society* 25, no. 3 (2015): 268–275. https://doi.org/10.1080/10439463.2013.864655.

Kappeler, Victor E., Richard D. Sluder, and Geoffrey P. Alpert. "Breeding Deviant Conformity: The Ideology and Culture of Police." In *Critical Issues in Policing: Contemporary Readings*, edited by Roger G. Dunham, Geoffrey P. Alpert, and Kyle D. McLean, 8th ed., 187–213. Long Grove, IL: Waveland Press, 2020.

Karsch, Mitchell W. "Excessive Force and the Fourth Amendment: When Does Seizure End?" *Fordham Law Review* 58, no. 4 (1990): 823–841. https://ir.lawnet.fordham.edu/flr/vol58/iss4/10.

Kasarda, John D. "The Structural Implications of Social System Size : A Three-Level Analysis." *American Sociological Review* 39, no. 1 (1974): 19–28.

Kelling, George L. "Police and Communities: The Quiet Revolution." *Perspectives on Policing*, no. 1. Washington, DC: National Institute of Justice, 1988.

Kelling, George L., Tony Pate, Duane Dieckman, and Charles E. Brown. "The Kansas City Preventive Patrol Experiment: A Summary Report." Washington, DC, 1974.

Kennedy, David M. *Deterrence and Crime Prevention: Reconsidering the Prospect of Sanction*. New York: Routledge, 2012.

Kennedy, Leslie W., Joel M. Caplan, Eric L. Piza, and Henri Buccine-Schraeder. "Vulnerability and Exposure to Crime: Applying Risk Terrain Modeling to the Study of Assault in Chicago." *Applied Spatial Analysis and Policy* 9, no. 4 (2016): 529–548. https://doi.org/10.1007/s12061-015-9165-z.

Kerr, Peter. "Opium Dens for the Crack Era." *New York Times*, May 18, 1986.

King, Daniel, and John A. Conley. "The 1967 President's Crime Commission Report: Its Impact 25 Years Later." *The Police Journal: Theory, Practice and Principles* 67, no. 3 (1994): 269–274.

King, Laura, Kurtis Lee, and Jaweed Kaleem. "George Floyd's Death and the National Conversation: Pain, Anger and Hope." *Los Angeles Times*, June 5, 2020. https://www.latimes.com/world-nation/story/2020-06-05/george-floyds-death-sparks-voices-on-americas-deep-pain-and-searing-rage.

Kirk, David S., and Robert J. Sampson. "Juvenile Arrest and Collateral Educational Damage in the Transition to Adulthood." *Sociology of Education* 86, no. 1 (2013): 36–62. https://doi.org/10.1177/0038040712448862.

Klinger, David A. "Demeanor or Crime? Why 'Hostile' Citizens Are More Likely to Be Arrested" *Criminology* 32, no. 3 (1994): 475–493.

Klinger, David A. "Negotiating Order in Patrol Work: An Ecological Theory of Police Response to Deviance." *Criminology* 35, no. 2 (1997): 277–306. https://doi.org/10.1111/j.1745-9125.1997.tb00877.x.

Klinger, David, Richard Rosenfeld, Daniel Isom, and Michael Deckard. "Race, Crime, and the Micro-Ecology of Deadly Force." *Criminology and Public Policy* 15, no. 1 (2016): 193–222. https://doi.org/10.1111/1745-9133.12174.

Klockars, Carl B. *The Idea of Police*. Thousand Oaks, CA: Sage, 1985.

Knowles, Leanne Jade. "The Impact of COVID-19 on Youth Offending." University of Hull, 2021.

Koper, C. S. "Just Enough Police Presence: Reducing Crime and Disorderly Behavior by Optimizing Patrol Time in Crime Hot Spots." *Justice Quarterly* 12, no. 4 (1995): 649–672. https://doi.org/10.1080/07418829500096231.

Kovera, Margaret Bull. "Racial Disparities in the Criminal Justice System: Prevalence, Causes, and a Search for Solutions." *Journal of Social Issues* 75, no. 4 (2019): 1139–1164. https://doi.org/10.1111/josi.12355.

Kraska, P. B. "Militarization and Policing—Its Relevance to 21st Century Police." *Policing* 1, no. 4 (2007): 501–513. https://doi.org/10.1093/police/pam065.

Kraska, Peter B., and Victor E. Kappeler. "Militarizing American Police: The Rise and Normalization of Paramilitary Units." *Social Problems* 44, no. 1 (1997): 1–18. https://doi.org/10.2307/3096870.

Kriesburg, L. "Centralization and Differentiation in International Non-Governmental Organizations." *Sociology and Social Research* 61, no. 1 (1976): 1–23.

Kurbin, C. E., and R. Weitzer. "Retaliatory Homicide: Concentrated Disadvantage and Neighbourhood Culture." *Social Problems* 50, no. 2 (2003): 157–180. https://doi.org/10.1525/sp.2003.50.2.157.

Kushner, Howard I., and Claire E. Sterk. "The Limits of Social Capital: Durkheim, Suicide, and Social Cohesion." *American Journal of Public Health* 95, no. 7 (2005): 1139–1143.

Lane, Roger. "Urban Police and Crime in Nineteenth-Century America." *Crime and Justice* 15 (1992): 1–50. https://doi.org/10.1086/449192.

Langworthy, Robert H., and Lawrence F. Travis. *Policing in America: A Balance in Forces*. Upper Saddle River, NJ: Prentice Hall, 1999.

"The Largest Police Departments in the US - WorldAtlas." Accessed August 28, 2020. https://www.worldatlas.com/articles/the-largest-police-departments-in-the-us.html.

Larson, James R., Jr. "Deep Diversity and Strong Synergy: Modeling the Impact of Variability in Members' Problem-Solving Strategies on Group Problem-Solving Performance." *Small Group Research* 38, no. 3 (2007): 413–436.

The LA Times Editorial Board. "The Problem With LAPD's Predictive Policing." *Los Angeles Times*, March 16, 2019. https://www.latimes.com/opinion/editorials/la-ed-lapd-predictive-policing-20190316-story.html.

Laufs, Julian, and Zoha Waseem. "Policing in Pandemics: A Systematic Review and Best Practices for Police Response to COVID-19." *International Journal of Disaster Risk Reduction* 51 (2020): 101812. https://doi.org/10.1016/J.IJDRR.2020.101812.

La Vigne, Nancy, Jocelyn Fontaine, and Anamika Dwivedi. "How Do People in High-Crime, Low-Income Communities View the Police?" Washington, DC, 2017.

"Law Enforcement Management and Administrative Statistics (LEMAS) | Bureau of Justice Statistics." Accessed February 6, 2022. https://bjs.ojp.gov/data-collection/law-enforcement-management-and-administrative-statistics-lemas.

Leese, Matthias. "Predictive Policing: Proceed, but With Care." *Policy Perspectives* 8, December (2020): 1–4.

Lehning, James, R. *To Be a Citizen: The Political Culture of the Early French Third Republic*. Ithaca, NY: Cornell University Press, 2001.

Lentz, Susan A., and Robert H. Chaires. "The Invention of Peel's Principles: A Study of Policing 'Textbook' History." *Journal of Criminal Justice* 35, no. 1 (2007): 69–79. https://doi.org/10.1016/j.jcrimjus.2006.11.016.

Lienemann, Brianna A., and Jason T. Siegel. "Increasing Help-Seeking Outcomes Among People With Elevated Depressive Symptomatology With Public Service Announcements: An Examination of Functional Matching and Message Sidedness." *Journal of Health Communication* 23, no. 1 (2018): 28–39.

Lilley, David, and Sameer Hinduja. "Organizational Values and Police Officer Evaluation: A Content Comparison Between Traditional and Community Policing Agencies." *Police Quarterly* 9, no. 4 (2006): 486–513. https://doi.org/10.1177/1098611105281628.

Lipsky, M. *Street-Level Bureaucracy: Dilemmas of the Individuals in Public Services.* New York: Russell Sage Foundation, 1980.

Little, Craig B., and Christopher P. Sheffield. "Frontiers and Criminal Justice: English Private Prosecution Societies and American Vigilantism in the Eighteenth and Nineteenth Centuries." *American Sociological Review* 48, no. 6 (1983): 796. https://doi.org/10.2307/2095326.

Logan, Wayne A. "An Exception Swallows a Rule: Police Authority to Search Incident to Arrest." *Yale Law & Policy Review* 19, no. 2 (2001): 381–441.

Los Angeles County Sheriff's Department. "About Us." Accessed December 29, 2021. https://www.lasd.org/about_us.html.

Los Angeles Police Department. "Join LAPD: LAPD Hiring Process." Accessed February 2, 2022. https://www.join-lapd.com/there-are-seven-steps-application-process.

Lough, Jonathan, and Kathryn von Treuer. "A Critical Review of Psychological Instruments Used in Police Officer Selection." *Policing* 36, no. 4 (2013): 737–751. https://doi.org/10.1108/PIJPSM-11-2012-0104.

Lum, Cynthia. "The Influence of Places on Police Decision Pathways: From Call for Service to Arrest." *Justice Quarterly* 28, no. 4 (2011): 631–665. https://doi.org/10.1080/07418825.2010.526130.

Lum, Cynthia, and Daniel S. Nagin. "Reinventing American Policing." *Crime and Justice* 46, no. 1 (2017): 339–393. https://doi.org/10.1086/688462.

Lundman, Richard J., and Robert L. Kaufman. "Driving While Black: Effects of Race, Ethnicity, and Gender on Citizen Self-Reports of Traffic Stops and Police Actions." *Criminology* 41, no. 1 (2003): 195–220. https://doi.org/10.1111/j.1745-9125.2003.tb00986.x.

Madhani, Aamer. "Federal Judge Approves Consent Decree for Chicago Police Department." *USA Today*, January 21, 2019. https://www.usatoday.com/story/news/nation/2019/01/31/chicago-police-department-consent-decree-reforms-attorney-general-lisa-madigan/2734415002/.

Maguire, Edward. *Organizational Structure in American Police Agencies: Context, Complexity, and Control.* Albany: State University of New York, 2003.

Manly, Laura. "Being Careful Out There? Hardly." *New York Times*, May 1, 2014. https://www.emmys.com/shows/hill-street-blues.

Manning, Peter K. "The Police: Mandate, Strategies, and Appearances." In *Policing: A View From the Street*, edited by Peter K. Manning and John Van Maanen. Santa Monica, CA: Goodyear, 1978.

Manning, Peter K. "The Police: Mandates, Strategies, and Appearances." In *Policing: Key Readings*, edited by Tim Newburn, 191–214. New York: Routledge, 2005.

Manning, Peter K. *The Technology of Policing: Crime Mapping, Information Technology, and the Rationality of Crime Control.* New York: NYU Press, 2008. https://nyupress.org/9780814761366/the-technology-of-policing/.

Mapp v. Ohio, 367 U.S. 643 (1961).

Marier, Christopher J., and Richard K. Moule. "Feeling Blue: Officer Perceptions of Public Antipathy Predict Police Occupational Norms." *American Journal of Criminal Justice* 44, no. 5 (2019): 836–857. https://doi.org/10.1007/s12103-018-9459-1.

Mastrofski, Stephen D. "Community Policing: A Skeptical View." In *Police Innovations: Contrasting Perspectives*, edited by David L. Weisburd and Anthony A. Braga, 2nd ed., 45–68. New York: Cambridge University Press, 2019. https://www.google.com/books/edition/Police_Innovation/Z7OQDwAAQBAJ?hl=en&gbpv=1&dq=community+policing:+a+skeptical+view&pg=PA45&printsec=frontcover.

Mastrofski, Stephen D. "Controlling Street-Level Police Discretion." *Annals of the American Academy of Political and Social Science* 593 (2004): 100–118. https://doi.org/10.1177/0002716203262584.

Mastrofski, Stephen D., and James J. Willis. "Police Organization Continuity and Change: Into the Twenty-First Century." *Crime and Justice* 39, no. 1 (2010): 55–144. https://doi.org/10.1086/653046.

Mastrofski, S. D., J. J. Willis, and T. R. Kochel. "The Challenges of Implementing Community Policing in the United States." *Policing* 1, no. 2 (2007): 223–234. https://doi.org/10.1093/police/pam026.

"May 2018 National Occupational Employment and Wage Estimates." U.S. Bureau of Labor Statistics, Occupational Employment Statistics, 2018. https://www.bls.gov/oes/current/oes_nat.htm#33-0000.

Maynes, Mary Jo. *Taking the Hard Road: Life Course in French and German Workers' Autobiographies in the Era of Industrialization.* Chapel Hill: University of North Carolina Press, 1995.

Mazerolle, Lorraine, Emma Antrobus, Sarah Bennett, and Tom R. Tyler. "Shaping Citizen Perceptions of Police Legitimacy: A Randomized Field Trial of Procedural Justice." *Criminology* 51, no. 1 (2013): 33–63. https://doi.org/10.1111/j.1745-9125.2012.00289.x.

Mazerolle, Lorraine G., Justin Ready, Bill Terrill, and Frank Gajewski. *Problem-Oriented Policing in Public Housing: Final Report of the Jersey City Project.* Washington, DC: U.S. Department of Justice, 1999.

McCartney, Steve, and Rick Parent. *Ethics in Law Enforcement.* Victoria, BC, Canada: BCcampus, 2015.

McCleskey v. Kemp, 481 U.S. 279 (1987).

McCoy, Candice. "How Civil Rights Lawsuits Improve American Policing." In *Holding Police Accountable*, edited by Candice McCoy, 111–160. Washington, DC: Urban Institute Press, 2009.

Meares, Tracey L. "The Law and Social Science of Stop and Frisk." *Annual Review of Law and Social Science* 10, no. 1 (2014): 335–352. https://doi.org/10.1146/annurev-lawsocsci-102612-134043.

Meares, Tracey L. "Programming Errors: Understanding the Constitutionality of Stop-and-Frisk as a Program, Not an Incident." *University of Chicago Law Review* 82, no. 1 (2015): 159–179. https://doi.org/10.2139/ssrn.2524930.

Meehan, Albert J., and Michael C. Ponder. "Race and Place: The Ecology of Racial Profiling African American Motorists." *Justice Quarterly* 19, no. 3 (2002): 399–430. https://doi.org/10.1080/07418820200095291.

Mellen, Greg. "Unprecedented Challenges in Hiring, Retaining Police Recruits." Police1, 2021. https://www.police1.com/police-recruiting/articles/why-law-enforcement-is-facing-unprecedented-challenges-in-hiring-and-keeping-recruits-pFiTKCXrne6ccNfB/.

Metchik, Eric. "An Analysis of the 'Screening Out' Model of Police Officer Selection." *Police Quarterly* 2, no. 1 (1999): 79–95. https://doi.org/10.1177/109861119900200104.

"Metropolitan Police - UK Parliament." Accessed August 25, 2020. https://www.parliament.uk/about/living-heritage/transformingsociety/laworder/policeprisons/overview/metropolitanpolice/.

"Metropolitan Police Department, District of Columbia." The Officer Down Memorial Page. Accessed August 28, 2020. https://www.odmp.org/agency/2463-metropolitan-police-department-district-of-columbia.

Mettler, Katie, and Antonia Noori Farzen. "Jazmine Headley Case: Charges Dropped Against Mother Whose Baby Was Torn Away by NYPD in Viral Video." *The Washington Post*, December 12, 2018. https://www.washingtonpost.com/nation/2018/12/11/prosecutors-drop-charges-against-new-york-mother-whose-baby-was-yanked-away-by-police/.

"Michael Conrad - IMDb." Accessed June 16, 2020. https://www.imdb.com/name/nm0175700/.

"Michael Warren - IMDb." Accessed July 22, 2020. https://www.imdb.com/name/nm0912966/?ref_=tt_ov_st_sm.

Mignon, Sylvia I., and William M. Holmes. "Police Response to Mandatory Arrest Laws." *Crime & Delinquency* 41, no. 4 (1995): 430–442. https://doi.org/10.1177/0011128795041004004.

Miller, Wilbur R. *Cops and Bobbies: Police Authority in New York and London, 1830–1870*. Chicago: University of Chicago Press, 1976.

"Minneapolis Police Department Policy and Procedure Manual, Volume Five—Code of Conduct and Use of Force." 2021. https://www.minneapolismn.gov/media/-www-content-assets/documents/MPD-Policy-and-Procedure-Manual.pdf.

Minnesota v. Dickerson, 508 U.S. 366 (1993).

Miranda v. Arizona, 384 U.S. 436 (1966).

"Misdemeanor | Wex | US Law | LII / Legal Information Institute." Accessed October 1, 2020. https://www.law.cornell.edu/wex/misdemeanor.

Mobile Police Department. "The Application Process." Accessed June 2, 2022. https://www.mobilepd.org/application-process/.

Mohammed, Susan, and Erika Ringseis. "Cognitive Diversity and Consensus in Group Decision Making: The Role of Inputs, Processes, and Outcomes." *Organizational Behavior and Human Decision Processes* 85, no. 2 (2001): 310–335. https://doi.org/10.1006/obhd.2000.2943.

Mohler, George O., and Martin B. Short. "Geographic Profiling From Kinetic Models of Criminal Behavior." *SIAM Journal on Applied Mathematics* 72, no. 1 (2012): 163–180.

Monell et al. v. Department of Social Services of the City of New York et al., 436 U.S. 658 (1978).

Monkkonen, Eric H. "History of Urban Police." *Crime and Justice* 15 (1992): 547–580. https://doi.org/10.20595/jjbf.19.0_3.

Monkkonen, Eric H. *Police in Urban America: 1860–1920*. New York: Cambridge University Press, 1981.

Montgomery, David. "The Shuttle and the Cross: Weavers and Artisans in the Kensington Riots of 1844." *Journal of Social History* 5, no. 4 (1972): 411–446. https://doi.org/10.1353/jsh/5.4.411.

Morison, Kevin P. "Hiring for the 21st Century Law Enforcement Officer: Challenges, Opportunities, and Strategies for Success." Washington, DC, 2017.

Morrison, Ken. *Marx, Durkheim, Weber: Formations of Modern Social Thought*. Thousand Oaks, CA: Sage, 1995.

Morrow, Weston J., Samuel G. Vickovic, Lisa M. Dario, and John A. Shjarback. "Examining a Ferguson Effect on College Students' Motivation to Become Police Officers." *Journal of Criminal Justice Education* 30, no. 4 (2019): 585–605. https://doi.org/10.1080/10511253.2019.1619793.

"Most Common Police Officer Selection Tests | Police Test Prep." Accessed February 4, 2022. https://www.policetest.info/most-common.

Muir, William Ker. *Police: Streetcorner Politicians*. University of Chicago Press, 1977.

National Institute of Justice. "Predictive Policing Symposiums." Washington, DC: U.S. Department of Justice, Office of Justice Programs, 2009. https://www.ojp.gov/pdffiles1/nij/242222and248891.pdf.

Nickels, Ernest L. "A Note on the Status of Discretion in Police Research." 2007. https://doi.org/10.1016/j.jcrimjus.2007.07.009.

Novak, Kenneth J., and Mitchell B. Chamlin. "Racial Threat, Suspicion, and Police Behavior: The Impact of Race and Place in Traffic Enforcement." *Crime and Delinquency* 58, no. 2 (2012): 275–300. https://doi.org/10.1177/0011128708322943.

N.Y. Penal Law §§125.10, 35.30. (n.d.).

O'Brien, Anne-Marie, and Robert J. Kane. "Policing as a Social Determinant of Health: The Impact of Drug Enforcement on Prenatal Care Utilization in Urban Communities." *Medical Research Archives* 6, no. 2 (2018): 1–14.

"Operations Over People General Overview." Accessed October 16, 2021. https://www.faa.gov/uas/commercial_operators/operations_over_people/.

Oppel, Richard A., Derrick Bryson Taylor, and Nicholas Bogel-Burroughs. "Breonna Taylor's Case and Death: What We Know." *New York Times*, October 2, 2020. https://www.nytimes.com/article/breonna-taylor-police.html.

Oppenlander, Nan. "Coping or Copping Out: Police Service Delivery in Domestic Disputes." *Criminology* 20, no. 3/4 (1982): 449–465. http://10.0.4.87/j.1745-9125.1982.tb00471.x%0Ahttps://libproxy.wlu.ca/login?url=http://search.ebscohost.com/login.aspx?direct=true&AuthType=ip,cookie,url,uid&db=i3h&AN=16731779&site=ehost-live.

Oregon v. Mathiason, 429 U.S. 492 (1977).

Osborne, Randall. "Observations on Police Cynicism: Some Preliminary Findings." *North American Journal of Psychology* 16, no. 3 (2014): 607.

"Overview | NYPD Monitor." Accessed April 2, 2021. http://nypdmonitor.org/overview/.

Oxford English Dictionary. Oxford, UK: Oxford University Press, 2000.

Page, Scott E. *The Difference: How the Power of Diversity Creates Better Groups, Firms, Schools, and Societies*. Princeton, NJ: Princeton University Press, 2007.

Page, Scott E. "Where Diversity Comes From and Why It Matters?" *European Journal of Social Psychology* 44, no. 4 (2014): 267–279.

Palmer, Chris. "Philadelphia Police Department to Fire 13 Officers Over Offensive Facebook Posts." *Philadelphia Inquirer*, July 18, 2019. https://www.inquirer.com/news/philadelphia-police-officer-firings-facebook-posts-database-20190718.html.

Palmer, Chris, Stacey Burling, Nathaniel Lash, and Julie Shaw. "Group Catalogs Racist, Intolerant Facebook Posts by Hundreds of Philly Police Officers." *Philadelphia Inquirer*, June 1, 2019. https://www.inquirer.com/news/philadelphia-police-philadelphia-facebook-comments-racist-20190601.html.

Palmer, Stanley H. *Police and Protest in England and Ireland: 1780–1850*. New York: Cambridge University Press, 1988.

Patrick, Robert, and Joel Currier. "Ferguson Highlights Police Use of Military Gear and Tactics." *St. Louis Dispatch*, August 15, 2014. https://www.stltoday.com/news/local/metro/ferguson-highlights-police-use-of-military-gear-and-tactics/article_69176ce4-f888-58ff-b33a-64924d2beb6d.html.

Penn, Ira A., Gail B. Pennix, and Jim Coulson. *Records Management Handbook*. New York: Routledge, 2016.

Pereira, Ivan. "3 Former Officers Charged in George Floyd's Death Make 1st Court Appearance." ABC News, June 4, 2020. https://abcnews.go.com/US/officers-charged-floyds-death-make-1st-court-appearance/story?id=71066710.

Perez, Douglas W. *Common Sense About Police Review*. Philadelphia: Temple University Press, 1994.

Perry, Ryan, Naomi Priest, Yin Paradies, Fiona Barlow, and Chris Sibley. "Barriers to Multiculturalism: Ingroup Favoritism and Outgroup Hostility Are Independently Associated With Policy Opposition." 2017. https://doi.org/10.31219/osf.io/nk334.

Perry, Walter L., Brian McInnis, Carter C. Price, Susan Smith, and John S. Hollywood. *Predictive Policing: The Role of Crime Forecasting in Law Enforcement Operations*. Santa Monica, CA: Rand Corporation, 2013. https://doi.org/10.7249/RR233.

Peterson, Ruth, Lauren Krivo, and Mark Harris. "Disadvantage and Neighborhood Violent Crime: Do Local Institutions Matter?" *Journal of Research in Crime and Delinquency* 37, no. 1 (2000): 31–63. https://doi.org/10.1177/0022427800037001002.

Pinizzotto, A. J., E. F. Davis, S. B. Bohrer, and B. J. Infanti. "Law Enforcement Restraint in the Use of Deadly Force Within the Context of 'the Deadly Mix.'" *International Journal of Police Science & Management* 14, no. 4 (2012): 285–298. https://doi.org/10.1350/ijps.2012.14.4.289.

Piquero, Alex, and Alfred Blumstein. "Does Incapacitation Reduce Crime?" *Journal of Quantitative Criminology* 23 (2007): 267–285.

Piza, Eric, and Jonas H. Baughman. *Modern Policing Using ArcGIS Pro*. Redlands, CA: Esri Press, 2021.

Plato. *The Republic*. Edited by Richard W. Sterling and William C. Scott. New York: W.W. Norton, 1996.

Police Executive Research Forum. "The Workforce Crisis, and What Police Agencies Are Doing About It." PERF, Washington, DC, 2019.

"Police Face a 'Crisis of Trust' With Black Motorists. One State's Surprising Policy May Help." Accessed October 14, 2021. https://www.nbcnews.com/news/us-news/traffic-stops-are-flashpoint-policing-america-reformers-are-winning-big-n1280594.

The Police Foundation. "The Newark Foot Patrol Experiment." Washington, DC, 1981.

"Police Officer License and Certifications." Accessed September 10, 2020. https://www.policeofficer.education/police-officer-license-certifications/.

Pollack, Hannah. "Doctors, Military Officers, Firefighters, and Scientists Seen as Among America's Most

Prestigious Occupations," September 10, 2014. https://theharrispoll.com/when-shown-a-list-of-occupations-and-asked-how-much-prestige-each-job-possesses-doctors-top-the-harris-polls-list-with-88-of-u-s-adults-considering-it-to-have-either-a-great-deal-of-prestige-45-2/.

President's Commission on Law Enforcement and the Administration of Justice. "The Challenge of Crime in a Free Society." Washington, DC, 1967. https://doi.org/10.3138/cjcor.9.4.347.

President's Task Force on 21st Century Policing. "Final Report of the President's Task Force on 21st Century Policing." Washington, DC, 2015.

"Probe Spurred by Elijah McClain's Death Finds Aurora Police 'Racially Biased' | TheHill." Accessed October 14, 2021. https://thehill.com/homenews/state-watch/572475-probe-spurred-by-elijah-mcclains-death-finds-aurora-police-racially.

"Protests Around the World as George Floyd Death Draws International Sympathy and Scorn Today." CBS News/AP, June 1, 2020. https://www.cbsnews.com/news/protests-around-the-world-george-floyd-death-international-sympathy-and-scorn-today-2020-06-01/.

Pugh, D. S., D. J. Hickson, C. R. Hinings, and C. Turner. "Dimensions of Organizational Commitment." *Administrative Science Quarterly* 13, no. 1 (1968): 65–105.

Radil, Steven M., Raymond J. Dezzani, and Lanny D. McAden. "Geographies of U.S. Police Militarization and the Role of the 1033 Program." *Professional Geographer* 69, no. 2 (2017): 203–213. https://doi.org/10.1080/00330124.2016.1212666.

Rahr, Sue. "Transforming the Culture of Policing From Warriors to Guardians in Washington State." *International Association of Directors of Law Enforcement Standards and Training Newsletter* 25, no. 4 (2014): 3–4.

Rahr, Sue, and Stephen K. Rice. "From Warriors to Guardians: Recommitting American Police Culture to Democratic Ideals." *New Perspectives in Policing.* National Institute of Justice, 2015.

Ratcliffe, Jerry H. *Intelligence-Led Policing.* 2nd ed. New York: Routledge, 2016.

Ratcliffe, Jerry, Elizabeth Groff, Cory Haberman, and Evan Sorg. *Smart Policing Initiative Final Report.* Philadelphia, PA: Temple University, 2012.

Ratcliffe, Jerry H., and George F. Rengert. "Near-Repeat Patterns in Philadelphia Shootings." *Security Journal* 21, no. 1 (2008): 58–76. https://doi.org/10.1057/PALGRAVE.SJ.8350068.

Ratcliffe, Jerry H., Ralph B. Taylor, Amber Perenzin Askey, Kevin Thomas, John Grasso, Kevin J. Bethel, Ryan Fisher, and Josh Koehnlein. "The Philadelphia Predictive Policing Experiment." *Journal of Experimental Criminology* 17 (2020): 15–41. https://doi.org/10.1007/s11292-019-09400-2.

Reaves, Brian. "Local Police Departments, 2013: Personnel, Policies, and Practices." Bureau of Justice Statistics. Washington, DC, 2015.

Reichel, Philip L. "Southern Slave Patrols as a Transitional Police Type." *American Journal of Police* 7, no. 2 (1988): 51–77.

Reiner, Robert. "Revisiting the Classics: Three Seminal Founders of the Study of Policing: Michael Banton, Jerome Skolnick and Egon Bittner." *Policing and Society* 25, no. 3 (2015): 308–327. https://doi.org/10.1080/10439463.2015.1013753.

Reisig, Michael D., and Camille Lloyd. "Procedural Justice, Police Legitimacy, and Helping the Police Fight Crime." *Police Quarterly* 12, no. 1 (2009): 42–62. https://doi.org/10.1177/1098611108327311.

Reiss, Albert J. *The Police and the Public.* New Haven, CT: Yale University Press, 1971. https://books.google.com/books?hl=en&lr=&id=2ErEylE6PUgC&oi=fnd&pg=PP12&dq=thin+blue+line+in+policing&ots=tHzLJnkdw1&sig=Ammri4L13o3NuhL4cEFKueSMMGA#v=snippet&q=blue line&f=false.

Reiss, Albert J. "Policing a City's Central District, The Oakland Story." Washington, DC, 1985. https://play.google.com/books/reader?id=kpHaAAAAMAAJ&hl=en&pg=GBS.PP1.

Renauer, Brian C. "Neighborhood Variation in Police Stops and Searches: A Test of Consensus and Conflict Perspectives." *Police Quarterly* 15, no. 3 (2012): 219–240. https://doi.org/10.1177/1098611112447746.

Reuss-Ianni, Elizabeth. *Two Cultures of Policing: Street Cops and Management Cops.* New Brunswick, NJ: Transaction Publishers, 1983.

Richardson, Rashida, Jason M. Schultz, and Kate Crawford. "Dirty Data, Bad Predictions: How Civil Rights Violations Impact Police Data, Predictive Policing Systems, and Justice." *New York University Law Review* 94, no. 2 (2019): 192–233. https://papers.ssrn.com/sol3/papers.cfm?abstract_id=3333423#.

Rinehart Kochel, Tammy, and David Weisburd. "The Impact of Hot Spots Policing on Collective Efficacy: Findings From a Randomized Field Trial." *Justice Quarterly* 36, no. 5 (2019): 900–928. https://doi.org/10.1080/07418825.2018.1465579.

Ristroph, Alice. "The Thin Blue Line From Crime to Punishment." *Journal of Criminal Law and Criminology* 108, no. 2 (2018): 305–334.

Robb, Graham. *Victor Hugo: A Biography.* New York: W.W. Norton, 1997.

Robbins, S. P. *Organization Theory: Structure, Design, and Application.* 2nd ed. Englewood Cliffs, NJ: Prentice Hall, 1987.

Rodrigo, Chris Mills. "Police Technology Under Scrutiny Following Chicago Shooting." The Hill, April 21, 2021. https://thehill.com/homenews/state-watch/549612 -police-technology-under-scrutiny-following-chicago -shooting.

Roe, Kathleen M., Meredith Minkler, Frances Saunders, and Gregg E. Thomson. "Health of Grandmothers Raising Children of the Crack Cocaine Epidemic." *Medical Care* 34, no. 11 (1996): 1072–1084.

Rosenbaum, Dennis P., Amie M. Schuck, Sandra K. Costello, Darnell F. Hawkins, and Marianne K. Ring. "Attitudes Toward the Police: The Effects of Direct and Vicarious Experience." *Police Quarterly* 8, no. 3 (2005): 343–365. https://doi.org/10.1177/1098611104271085.

Rosenfeld, Richard, Robert Fornango, and Andres F. Rengifo. "The Impact of Order-Maintenance Policing on New York City Homicide and Robbery Rates: 1988–2001." *Criminology* 45, no. 2 (2007): 355–384. https://doi.org/10.1111/j.1745-9125.2007.00081.x.

Ross, Cody T., Bruce Winterhalder, and Richard McElreath. "Racial Disparities in Police Use of Deadly Force Against Unarmed Individuals Persist After Appropriately Benchmarking Shooting Data on Violent Crime Rates." *Social Psychological and Personality Science* 12, no. 3 (2020): 323–332. https://doi.org/10.1177/1948550620916071.

Roundtree, Pamela Wilcox, and Kenneth C. Land. "Burglary Victimization, Perceptions of Crime Risk, and Routine Activities: A Multilevel Analysis Across Seattle Neighborhoods and Census Tracts." *Journal of Research in Crime and Delinquency* 33, no. 2 (1996): 147–180. https://doi.org/10.1177/0022427896033002001.

Rubinstein, Jonathan. *City Police*. New York: Farrar, Straus and Giroux, 1973.

Sabel, Charles F., and William H. Simon. "The Duty of Responsible Administration and the Problem of Police Accountability." *Yale Journal on Regulation* 33 (2016): 165–212.

Salter, Michael. "Toys for the Boys? Drones, Pleasure and Popular Culture in the Militarisation of Policing." *Critical Criminology* 22 (2013): 163–177. https://doi.org/10.1007/s10612-013-9213-4.

Sampson, R. J., S. W. Raudenbush, and F. Earls. "Neighborhoods and Violent Crime: A Multilevel Study of Collective Efficacy." *Science* 277, no. 5328 (1997): 918. https://doi.org/10.1126/science.277.5328.918.

Sampson, Robert J., and Dawn Jeglum Bartusch. "Legal Cynicism and (Subcultural?) Tolerance of Deviance: The Neighborhood Context of Racial Differences." *Law & Society Review* 32, no. 4 (1998): 777–804. https://doi.org/10.2307/827739.

San Diego Police Department. "Evaluating the Analysis and Response Components of Problem Solving in Community Policing." San Diego, CA, 1998.

Sanfiorenzo, Dimas. "How the Rodney King Beating Became the First Viral Video." Okayplayer, September 2021. https://www.okayplayer.com/news/rodney -king-beating-viral.html.

Santos, Rachel Boba. *Crime Analysis With Crime Mapping*. 4th ed. Thousand Oaks, CA: Sage, 2017.

"The SARA Model | ASU Center for Problem-Oriented Policing." Accessed March 8, 2021. https://popcenter .asu.edu/content/sara-model-0.

Saunders, Jessica, Priscillia Hunt, and John S. Hollywood. "Predictions Put Into Practice: A Quasi-Experimental Evaluation of Chicago's Predictive Policing Pilot." *Journal of Experimental Criminology* 12, no. 3 (2016): 347–371. https://doi.org/10.1007/s11292-016-9272-0.

Schempf, Ashley, Donna Strobino, and Patricia O'Campo. "Neighborhood Effects on Birthweight: An Exploration of Psychosocial and Behavioral Pathways in Baltimore, 1995–1996." *Social Science and Medicine* 68, no. 1 (2009): 100–110. https://doi.org/10.1016 /j.socscimed.2008.10.006.

Schifano, Fabrizio, and John Corkery. "Cocaine/Crack Cocaine Consumption, Treatment Demand, Seizures, Related Offences, Prices, Average Purity Levels and Deaths in the UK (1990–2004)." *Journal of Psychopharmacology* 22, no. 1 (2008): 1–10.

Scott, Michael. *Problem-Oriented Policing: Reflections on the First 20 Years*. Washington, DC: U.S. Department of Justice, Office of Community Oriented Policing Services, 2000.

Scott, Richard W. *Organizations: Rational, Natural, and Open Systems*. 5th ed. Upper Saddle River, NJ: Prentice Hall, 2002. https://www.amazon.com/W-Richard -Scott-dp-013016559X/dp/013016559X/ref=mt _other?_encoding=UTF8&me=&qid=.

Screws v. United States, 325 U.S. 91 (1945).

"Seattle Police Department - Settlement Agreement History." Accessed July 8, 2020. https://www.seattle.gov /police/about-us/professional-standards-bureau /settlement-agreement-history.

Shalin, Dmitri. "Pragmatism and Social Interactionism." *American Sociological Review* 51, no. 1 (1986): 9–29.

Shapiro, Aaron. "Predictive Policing for Reform? Indeterminacy and Intervention in Big Data Policing." *Surveillance & Society* 17, no. 3–4 (2019). https://doi .org/10.24908/ss.v17i3/4.10410.

Shenon, Philip. "24 Task Forces Sought by Meese to Fight Crack." *New York Times*, October 3, 1986.

Sherman, Lawrence W. "Policing Domestic Violence 1967–2017." *Criminology and Public Policy* 17, no. 2 (2018): 453–465. https://doi.org/10.1111/1745-9133.12365.

Sherman, Lawrence W., and Richard A. Berk. "The Specific Deterrent Effects of Arrest for Domestic Assault." *American Sociological Review* 49, no. 2 (1984): 261–272. https://doi.org/10.2307/2095575.

Sherman, Lawrence W., Patrick R. Gartin, and Michael E. Buerger. "Hot Spots of Predatory Crime: Routine Activities and the Criminology of Place." *Criminology* 27, no. 1 (1989): 27–56. https://doi.org/10.1111/j.1745-9125.1989.tb00862.x.

Sherman, Lawrence W., and Dennis P. Rogan. "Effects of Gun Seizures on Gun Violence: 'Hot Spots' Patrol in Kansas City." *Justice Quarterly* 12, no. 4 (1995): 673–693. https://doi.org/10.1080/07418829500096241.

Sherman, Lawrence W., and David Weisburd. "General Deterrent Effects of Police Patrol in Crime 'HOT SPOTS': A Randomized, Controlled Trial." *Justice Quarterly* 12, no. 4 (1995): 625–648. https://doi.org/10.1080/07418829500096221.

Silver, Jasmine R., Sean Patrick Roche, Thomas J. Bilach, and Stephanie Bontrager Ryon. "Traditional Police Culture, Use of Force, and Procedural Justice: Investigating Individual, Organizational, and Contextual Factors." *Justice Quarterly* 34, no. 7 (2017): 1272–1309. https://doi.org/10.1080/07418825.2017.1381756.

Simon, John. "The Fleeing Felon Rule." *Saint Louis University Law Journal* 30, no. 4 (1986): 1259–1278.

Sisti, Dominic, Cyndi Rickards, and Arthur Caplan. "Cops Must Roll up Their Sleeves to Protect Themselves and the Public." *Chicago Sun Times*, October 20, 2021. https://chicago.suntimes.com/2021/10/20/22736454/cops-must-roll-up-sleeves-protect-themselves-public.

"Six Days in July—Coverage of the 1967 Detroit Riots - YouTube." Accessed February 18, 2021. https://www.youtube.com/watch?v=xH-x7uGSDZM.

Skogan, Wesley G. *Disorder and Decline: Crime and the Spiral of Decay in American Neighborhoods*. Berkeley: University of California Press, 1992.

Skogan, Wesley G., and Susan M. Hartnett. *Community Policing, Chicago Style*. New York: Oxford University Press, 1997.

Skogan, Wes, and Susan Hartnett. "Community Policing in Chicago." In *Policing: Key Readings*, edited by Tim Newburn, 428–441. New York: Routledge, 2005.

Skolnick, Jerome. *Justice Without Trial: Law Enforcement in Democratic Society*. New York: Wiley, 1966. https://doi.org/10.2307/2574920.

Skolnick, Jerome. *Justice Without Trial: Law Enforcement in Democratic Society*. 4th ed. New Orleans, LA: Quid Pro Books, 2011.

Skolnick, Jerome. "A Sketch of the Policeman's Working Personality." In *Race, Ethnicity, and Policing: New and Essential Readings*, edited by Stephen Rice and Michael White, 15–31. New York: NYU Press, 2010.

Skolnick, Jerome, and James J. Fyfe. *Above the Law: Police and the Excessive Use of Force*. New York: Free Press, 1993.

Skolnick, Jerome H., and Candace McCoy. "Police Accountability and the Media." *American Bar Foundation Research Journal* 9, no. 3 (1984): 521–557. http://www.jstor.org/stable/828317.

Snyder, Leslie B. "Health Communication Campaigns and Their Impact on Behavior." *Journal of Nutrition Education and Behavior* 39, no. 2 (2007): S32–S40.

Southall, Ashley. "'Appalling' Video Shows the Police Yanking 1-Year-Old From His Mother's Arms." *New York Times*, December 9, 2018. https://www.nytimes.com/2018/12/09/nyregion/nypd-jazmine-headley-baby-video.html.

"Sovereign Citizens Movement | Southern Poverty Law Center." Accessed July 9, 2021. https://www.splcenter.org/fighting-hate/extremist-files/ideology/sovereign-citizens-movement.

St. George, Donna. "Ousted From School." *The Washington Post*, May 8, 2011. https://www.washingtonpost.com/local/education/ousted-from-school/2011/05/31/AGElfXMH_story.html.

State of Minnesota v. Derek M. Chauvin, 27 CR 20 (4th Dist. Minn. 2021).

Stewart, Nikita. "$625,000 Settlement for Woman Whose Child Was Torn From Her Arms." *New York Times*, December 13, 2019. https://www.nytimes.com/2019/12/13/nyregion/jazmine-headley-video-settlement.html.

Stewart, Nikita. "Jazmine Headley, Whose Child Was Torn From Her Arms at a City Office, Gets a Public Apology." *New York Times*, February 4, 2019. https://www.nytimes.com/2019/02/04/nyregion/jazmine-headley-nypd-arrest.html.

Straus, Murray A., and Richard J. Gelles. "Societal Change and Change in Family Violence from 1975 to 1985 as Revealed by Two National Surveys." *Journal of Marriage and Family* 48, no. 3 (1986): 113–132. https://doi.org/10.4324/9781315126401.

Strecher, Victor. "People Who Don't Even Know You." In *The Police and Society: Touchtone Readings*, edited by Victor Kappeler and Brian P. Schaefer, 4th ed., 241–257. Long Grove, IL: Waveland Press, 2019.

Stretesky, Paul B., Amie M. Schuckt, and Michael J. Hogan. "Space Matters: An Analysis of Poverty, Poverty Clustering, and Violent Crime." *Justice Quarterly* 21, no. 4 (2004): 817–841. https://doi.org/10.1080/07418820400096001.

Stucky, Thomas D., and John R. Ottensmann. "Land Use and Violent Crime." *Criminology* 47, no. 4 (2009): 1223–1264. https://doi.org/10.1111/j.1745-9125.2009.00174.x.

Sturgill, Kristi. "Santa Cruz Becomes the First U.S. City to Ban Predictive Policing." *Los Angeles Times*, June 26, 2020. https://www.latimes.com/california/story/2020-06-26/santa-cruz-becomes-first-u-s-city-to-ban-predictive-policing.

Tahir, Madiha. "Louder Than Bombs." *The New Inquiry* 16 (2012): 100–110.

Taub, Amanda. "What Was THAT? A Guide to the Military Gear Being Used Against Civilians in Ferguson." Vox, 2014. https://www.vox.com/2014/8/18/6003377/ferguson-military-gear.

Taylor, Bruce, Christopher S. Koper, and Daniel J. Woods. "A Randomized Controlled Trial of Different Policing Strategies at Hot Spots of Violent Crime." *Journal of Experimental Criminology* 7, no. 2 (2011): 149–181. https://doi.org/10.1007/s11292-010-9120-6.

Taylor, Ralph B. "The Incivilities Thesis: Theory, Measurement, and Policy." In *Measuring What Matters: Proceedings From the Policing Research Institute Meetings*, edited by Robert H. Langley, 65–88. Washington, DC: National Institute of Justice, 1999.

Telep, Cody W., Renée J. Mitchell, and David Weisburd. "How Much Should the Police Spend at Crime Hot Spots? Answers From a Police Agency Directed Randomized Field Trial in Sacramento, California." *Justice Quarterly* 31, no. 5 (2014): 905–933. https://doi.org/10.1080/07418825.2012.710645.

Telep, Cody W., and David Weisburd. "What Is Known About the Effectiveness of Police Practices in Reducing Crime and Disorder?" *Police Quarterly* 15, no. 4 (2012): 331–357. https://doi.org/10.1177/1098611112447611.

Tennessee v. Garner, 471 U.S. 1 (1985).

Terpstra, Jan. "Two Theories on the Police—The Relevance of Max Weber and Emile Durkheim to the Study of the Police." *International Journal of Law, Crime and Justice* 39, no. 1 (2011): 1–11. https://doi.org/10.1016/j.ijlcj.2011.01.009.

Terrill, William. "Police Use of Force: A Transactional Approach." *Justice Quarterly* 22, no. 1 (2005): 107–138. https://doi.org/10.1080/0741882042000333663.

Terrill, William, and Michael D. Reisig. "Neighborhood Context and Police Use of Force." *Journal of Research in Crime and Delinquency* 40, no. 3 (2003): 291–321. https://doi.org/10.1177/0022427803253800.

Terry v. Ohio, 392 U.S. 1 (1968).

"This Week in Universal News: The March on the Pentagon, 1967—The Unwritten Record." Accessed February 18, 2021. https://unwritten-record.blogs.archives.gov/2014/10/20/this-week-in-universal-news-the-march-on-the-pentagon-1967/.

Thompson, Sara K., and Rosemary Gartner. "The Spatial Distribution and Social Context of Homicide in Toronto's Neighborhoods." *Journal of Research in Crime and Delinquency* 51, no. 1 (2014): 88–118. https://doi.org/10.1177/0022427813487352.

"Today in History - September 9." Library of Congress, Washington, DC. Accessed August 25, 2020. https://www.loc.gov/item/today-in-history/september-09/.

Torres v. Madrid, 592 U.S. (2021).

Trinkner, Rick, Jonathan Jackson, and Tom R. Tyler. "Bounded Authority: Expanding 'Appropriate' Police Behavior Beyond Procedural Justice." *Law and Human Behavior* 42, no. 3 (2018): 280–293. https://doi.org/10.1037/lhb0000285.

Trojanowicz, Robert, and Davide Carter. "Philosophy and Role of Community Policing." Washington, DC, 1988.

Turney, K., and K. Harknett. "Neighborhood Disadvantage, Residential Stability, and Perceptions of Instrumental Support Among New Mothers." *Journal of Family Issues* 31, no. 4 (2010): 499–524. https://doi.org/10.1177/0192513X09347992.

Twersky-Glasner, Aviva. "Police Personality: What Is It and Why Are They Like That?" *Journal of Police and Criminal Psychology* 20, no. 1 (2005): 56–67. https://doi.org/10.1007/BF02806707.

Tyler, Tom R., Jeffrey Fagan, and Amanda Geller. "Street Stops and Police Legitimacy: Teachable Moments in Young Urban Men's Legal Socialization." *Journal of Empirical Legal Studies* 11, no. 4 (2014): 751–785. https://doi.org/10.1111/jels.12055.

Tyler, Tom R., Jonathan Jackson, and Avital Mentovich. "The Consequences of Being an Object of Suspicion: Potential Pitfalls of Proactive Police Contact." *Journal of Empirical Legal Studies* 12, no. 4 (2015): 602–636. https://doi.org/10.1111/jels.12086.

Uggen, Christopher, Mike Vuolo, Sarah Lageson, Ebony Ruhland, and K. Hilary Whitham. "The Edge of Stigma: An Experimental Audit of the Effects of Low-Level Criminal Records on Employment." *Criminology* 52, no. 4 (2014): 627–654. https://doi.org/10.1111/1745-9125.12051.

Ullman, Harlan, James P. Wade, and L. A. Edney. *Shock and Awe: Achieving Rapid Dominance*. Washington, DC: Center for Advanced Concepts and Technology, National Defense University, 1996. https://www.google.com/books/edition/_/bNfTAQAACAAJ?hl=en&sa=X&ved=2ahUKEwjMjqfYrffqAhXsknIEHS4qB3cQre8FMBF6BAgOEAc.

U.S. Department of Justice. "Local Police Departments: Policies and Procedures, 2016." Bureau of Justice Statistics. Washington, DC, 2020. http://www.ojp.usdoj.gov.

U.S. Department of Justice. "Justice Department Releases Report on Civil Rights Division's Pattern and Practice Police Reform Work." 2017. https://www.justice.gov/opa/pr/justice-department-releases-report-civil-rights-division-s-pattern-and-practice-police-reform.

U.S. Department of Justice. "U.S. v. City of Los Angeles - Consent Decree – Introduction." 2015. https://www.justice.gov/crt/us-v-city-los-angeles-consent-decree-introduction.

U.S. Department of Justice, Office of Justice Programs, Bureau of Justice Statistics. "Law Enforcement Management and Administrative Statistics (LEMAS), 2016. ICPSR37323-V1." Ann Arbor, MI: Inter-university

Consortium for Political and Social Research [producer and distributor], 2020.

"The Use-of-Force Continuum | National Institute of Justice." Accessed May 18, 2021. https://nij.ojp.gov/topics/articles/use-force-continuum#citation--0.

Van Maanen, John. "The Asshole." In *Policing: A View From the Street*, edited by Peter K. Manning and John Van Maanen, 221–238. Santa Monica, CA: Goodyear, 1978.

Varga, Ivan. "Social Morals, the Sacred and State Regulation in Durkheim's Sociology." *Social Compass* 53, no. 4 (2006). https://doi.org/10.1177/0037768606070408.

Vélez, María B. "The Role of Public Social Control in Urban Neighborhoods: A Multilevel Analysis of Victimization Risk." *Criminology* 39 (2001): 837–864. https://doi.org/10.1111/j.1745-9125.2001.tb00942.x.

Vito, Anthony, George Higgins, and Gennaro Vito. "Police Stop and Frisk and the Impact of Race: A Focal Concerns Theory Approach." *Social Sciences* 10, no. 6 (2021): 230. https://doi.org/10.3390/socsci10060230.

Walker, Sam. *Popular Justice*. New York: Oxford University Press, 1980.

Walker, Samuel. "'Not Dead Yet': The National Police Crisis, a New Conversation About Policing, and the Prospects for Accountability-Related Police Reform." *University of Illinois Law Review* 2018, no. 5 (2018): 1777–1841.

Walker, Samuel. *Police Accountability: The Role of Citizen Oversight*. Belmont, CA: Wadsworth, 2001.

Walker, Samuel. *Sense and Nonsense About Crime and Drugs: A Policy Guide*. 8th ed. Stamford, CT: Cengage Learning, 2015.

Walker, Samuel. *Taming the System: The Control of Discretion in Criminal Justice, 1950–1990*, 2011. https://doi.org/10.1093/acprof:oso/9780195078206.001.0001.

Walker, Samuel, and Carol Archbold. *The New World of Police Accountability*. 3rd ed. Beverly Hills, CA: Sage, 2020.

Wall, Tyler. "Unmanning the Police Manhunt: Vertical Security as Pacification." *Socialist Studies/Études Socialistes*, 2013.

Wash. Rev. Code §9A.16.040.

Wasserman, Robert, and Mark H. Moore. "Values in Policing." *Perspectives on Policing*. A Publication of the National Institute of Justice, the U.S. Department of Justice, and Kennedy School of Government, Harvard University, November 1988.

Watkins, Beverly Xaviera, and Mindy Thompson Fullilove. "The Crack Epidemic and the Failure of Epidemic Response." *Temple Political & Civil Rights Law Review* 10 (2001): 371–386.

Weber, Max. *From Max Weber: Essays in Sociology*. Edited by H. H. Gerth and C. Wright Mills. London: Routledge, 1991. https://www.amazon.com/Max-Weber-Essays-Sociology-dp-0343212765/dp/0343212765/ref=mt_other?_encoding=UTF8&me=&qid=.

Websdale, Neil. *Understanding Domestic Homicide*. Boston: Northeastern University Press, 1999.

Weeks v. United States, 232 U.S. 383 (1914).

"Weeks v. United States." Oyez. Accessed November 9, 2021. https://www.oyez.org/Cases/1900-1940/232us383.

Weisburd, David, and Shai Amram. "The Law of Concentrations of Crime at Place: The Case of Tel Aviv-Jaffa." *Police Practice and Research* 15, no. 2 (2014): 101–114.

Weisburd, David, and Clair White. "Hot Spots of Crime Are Not Just Hot Spots of Crime: Examining Health Outcomes at Street Segments." *Journal of Contemporary Criminal Justice* 35, no. 2 (2019): 142–160. https://doi.org/10.1177/1043986219832132.

Weisburd, David, Alese Wooditch, Sarit Weisburd, and Sue Ming Yang. "Do Stop, Question, and Frisk Practices Deter Crime? Evidence at Microunits of Space and Time." *Criminology and Public Policy* 15, no. 1 (2016): 31–56. https://doi.org/10.1111/1745-9133.12172.

Wesenberg, Madison. "COVID-19 and the Rise of the Conspiracy: Examination of COVID Related Conspiracies Using Durkheimian Concepts." *Crossing Borders: Student Reflections on Global Social Issues* 3, no. 1 (2021).

Westervelt, Eric. "Cops Are Leaving Their Departments in Droves and Few Want to Take Their Place: NPR." Accessed February 18, 2022. https://www.npr.org/2021/06/24/1009578809/cops-say-low-morale-and-department-scrutiny-are-driving-them-away-from-the-job.

White, Michael D. "Identifying Good Cops Early: Predicting Recruit Performance in the Academy." *Police Quarterly* 11, no. 1 (2008): 27–49.

White, Michael D. "Transactional Encounters, Crisis-Driven Reform, and the Potential for a National Police Deadly Force Database." *Criminology and Public Policy* 15, no. 1 (2016): 223–235. https://doi.org/10.1111/1745-9133.12180.

White, Michael D., and Henry F. Fradella. *STOP AND FRISK: The Use and Abuse of a Controversial Policing Tactic*. New York: NYU Press, 2019. https://nyupress.org/books/9781479857814/.

White, Michael D., and Robert J. Kane. "Pathways to Career-Ending Police Misconduct." *Criminal Justice and Behavior* 40, no. 11 (2013): 1301–1325. https://doi.org/10.1177/0093854813486269.

White, Michael D., and Charles M. Katz. "Policing Convenience Store Crime: Lessons from the Glendale, Arizona Smart Policing Initiative." *Police Quarterly* 16, no. 3 (2013): 305–322.

White, Michael D., Justin T. Ready, Robert J. Kane, Carl T. Yamashiro, Sharon Goldsworthy, and Darya Bonds

Mcclain. "Examining Cognitive Functioning Following TASER Exposure: A Randomized Controlled Trial." *Applied Cognitive Psychology* 29, no. 4 (2015): 600–607. https://doi.org/10.1002/acp.3128.

White, Michael D., Natalie Todak, and Janne E. Gaub. "Examining Body-Worn Camera Integration and Acceptance Among Police Officers, Citizens, and External Stakeholders." *Criminology & Public Policy* 17, no. 3 (2018): 649–677. https://doi.org/10.1111/1745-9133.12376.

Whren v. United States, 517 U.S. 806 (1996).

Wickersham, George W. "National Commission on Law Observance and Enforcement: Report." Washington, DC, 1931.

Wilson, James Q., and Barbara Boland. "The Effect of the Police on Crime." *Law & Society Review* 12, no. 3 (1978): 367–390.

Wilson, O. W. *Police Administration*. New York: McGraw-Hill Education, 1950. https://www.amazon.com/Police-Administration-W-Wilson/dp/0070707243.

Wilson, O. W. *Police Administration*. 2nd ed. New York: McGraw-Hill, 1963.

Wolf, Ross, Charlie Mesloh, Mark Henych, and L. Frank Thompson. "Police Use of Force and the Cumulative Force Factor." *Policing* 32, no. 4 (2009): 739–757. https://doi.org/10.1108/13639510911000795.

Wooditch, Alese, Craig D. Uchida, Shellie E. Solomon, Lauren Revier, Christine Connor, Mariel Shutinya, John McCluskey, and Marc L. Swatt. "Perceptions of Body-Worn Cameras: Findings from a Panel Survey of Two LAPD Divisions." *American Journal of Criminal Justice* 45, no. 3 (2020): 426–453. https://doi.org/10.1007/S12103-020-09517-5.